# Java™ 2 Bible

# Java™ 2 Bible

**Aaron E. Walsh, Justin Couch, Daniel H. Steinberg**

IDG Books Worldwide, Inc.
An International Data Group Company

Foster City, CA ✦ Chicago, IL ✦ Indianapolis, IN ✦ New York, NY

**Java™ 2 Bible**

Published by
**IDG Books Worldwide, Inc.**
An International Data Group Company
919 E. Hillsdale Blvd., Suite 400
Foster City, CA 94404
www.idgbooks.com (IDG Books Worldwide Web site)

ISBN: 0-7645-4632-5

Printed in the United States of America

10 9 8 7 6 5 4 3 2 1

1B/SV/QY/QQ/FC

Distributed in the United States by IDG Books Worldwide, Inc.

Distributed by CDG Books Canada Inc. for Canada; by Transworld Publishers Limited in the United Kingdom; by IDG Norge Books for Norway; by IDG Sweden Books for Sweden; by IDG Books Australia Publishing Corporation Pty. Ltd. for Australia and New Zealand; by TransQuest Publishers Pte Ltd. for Singapore, Malaysia, Thailand, Indonesia, and Hong Kong; by Gotop Information Inc. for Taiwan; by ICG Muse, Inc. for Japan; by Intersoft for South Africa; by Eyrolles for France; by International Thomson Publishing for Germany, Austria and Switzerland; by Distribuidora Cuspide for Argentina; by LR International for Brazil; by Galileo Libros for Chile; by Ediciones ZETA S.C.R. Ltda. for Peru; by WS Computer Publishing Corporation, Inc., for the Philippines; by Contemporanea de Ediciones for Venezuela; by Express Computer Distributors for the Caribbean and West Indies; by Micronesia Media Distributor, Inc. for Micronesia; by Chips Computadoras S.A. de C.V. for Mexico; by Editorial Norma de Panama S.A. for Panama; by American Bookshops for Finland.

For general information on IDG Books Worldwide's books in the U.S., please call our Consumer Customer Service department at 800-762-2974. For reseller information, including discounts and premium sales, please call our Reseller Customer Service department at 800-434-3422.

For information on where to purchase IDG Books Worldwide's books outside the U.S., please contact our International Sales department at 317-596-5530 or fax 317-596-5692.

For consumer information on foreign language translations, please contact our Customer Service department at 800-434-3422, fax 317-596-5692, or e-mail rights@idgbooks.com.

For information on licensing foreign or domestic rights, please phone +1-650-655-3109.

For sales inquiries and special prices for bulk quantities, please contact our Sales department at 650-655-3200 or write to the address above.

For information on using IDG Books Worldwide's books in the classroom or for ordering examination copies, please contact our Educational Sales department at 800-434-2086 or fax 317-596-5499.

For press review copies, author interviews, or other publicity information, please contact our Public Relations department at 650-655-3000 or fax 650-655-3299.

For authorization to photocopy items for corporate, personal, or educational use, please contact Copyright Clearance Center, 222 Rosewood Drive, Danvers, MA 01923, or fax 978-750-4470.

**Library of Congress Cataloging-in-Publication Data**
Walsh, Aaron E.
    Java 2 bible / Aaron Walsh, Justin Couch, Daniel Steinberg.
        p.  cm.
    ISBN 0-7645-4632-5 (alk. paper)
    1. Java (Computer program language)  I. Couch, Justin.  II. Steinberg, Daniel, 1959-  III. Title.
QA76.73.J38  W3575    2000
005.2'762--dc21                                00-058173

 is a registered trademark or trademark under exclusive license to IDG Book Worldwide, Inc. from International Data Group, Inc. in the United States and/or other countries.

 is a registered trademark of IDG Books Worldwide, Inc.

 is a registered trademark of IDG Books Worldwide, Inc.

# ABOUT IDG BOOKS WORLDWIDE

Welcome to the world of IDG Books Worldwide.

IDG Books Worldwide, Inc., is a subsidiary of International Data Group, the world's largest publisher of computer-related information and the leading global provider of information services on information technology. IDG was founded more than 30 years ago by Patrick J. McGovern and now employs more than 9,000 people worldwide. IDG publishes more than 290 computer publications in over 75 countries. More than 90 million people read one or more IDG publications each month.

Launched in 1990, IDG Books Worldwide is today the #1 publisher of best-selling computer books in the United States. We are proud to have received eight awards from the Computer Press Association in recognition of editorial excellence and three from Computer Currents' First Annual Readers' Choice Awards. Our best-selling *...For Dummies*® series has more than 50 million copies in print with translations in 31 languages. IDG Books Worldwide, through a joint venture with IDG's Hi-Tech Beijing, became the first U.S. publisher to publish a computer book in the People's Republic of China. In record time, IDG Books Worldwide has become the first choice for millions of readers around the world who want to learn how to better manage their businesses.

Our mission is simple: Every one of our books is designed to bring extra value and skill-building instructions to the reader. Our books are written by experts who understand and care about our readers. The knowledge base of our editorial staff comes from years of experience in publishing, education, and journalism — experience we use to produce books to carry us into the new millennium. In short, we care about books, so we attract the best people. We devote special attention to details such as audience, interior design, use of icons, and illustrations. And because we use an efficient process of authoring, editing, and desktop publishing our books electronically, we can spend more time ensuring superior content and less time on the technicalities of making books.

You can count on our commitment to deliver high-quality books at competitive prices on topics you want to read about. At IDG Books Worldwide, we continue in the IDG tradition of delivering quality for more than 30 years. You'll find no better book on a subject than one from IDG Books Worldwide.

John Kilcullen
Chairman and CEO
IDG Books Worldwide, Inc.

*Eighth Annual
Computer Press
Awards ≥1992*

*Ninth Annual
Computer Press
Awards ≥1993*

*Tenth Annual
Computer Press
Awards ≥1994*

*Eleventh Annual
Computer Press
Awards ≥1995*

# Credits

**Acquisitions Editors**
John Osborn
Greg Croy

**Project Editors**
Andy Marinkovich
Michael Koch
Matt Lusher

**Technical Editor**
David Williams

**Copy Editors**
Mildred Sanchez
Chrisa Hotchkiss

**Project Coordinators**
Louigene Santos
Danette Nurse
Marcos Vergara

**Graphics and Production Specialists**
Bob Bihlmayer
Jan Contestable
Darren Cutlip
Michael Lewis
Ramses Ramirez

**Quality Control Technician**
Dina F Quan

**Book Designer**
Drew R. Moore

**Illustrator**
Rashell Smith
Gabriele McCann

**Proofreading and Indexing**
York Production Services

**Cover Design**
Evan Deerfield

# About the Authors

**Aaron E. Walsh** is chairman of Mantis Development Corporation, a Boston-based software development firm specializing in advanced media and network technologies. Aaron is an international best-selling technology author and he has written *Java™ For Dummies* (IDG Books Worldwide), the original *Java™ Bible* (IDG Books Worldwide), and *Foundations of Java™ Programming for the World Wide Web* (IDG Books Worldwide). He has been building state-of-the-art software for over two decades, and was an early convert to the Java programming language back in the good old days when it was originally known as Oak. Today, Aaron teaches Java programming and Internet software development and Web application development at Boston College, consults for high technology companies, and conducts related workshops and lectures at industry conferences. Aaron has been granted United States Patents #5,867,161 and #6,067,086, for a modern graphical user interface for local and Internet information reference and retrieval that is embodied in the **Living Desktop™** application, the Java source code for which is available at JavaBible.com (http://www.javabible.com/) especially for Java Bible readers.

**Justin Couch** is a software architect specializing in distributed systems and virtual reality. Justin is an author of and contributor to many books on both VRML and Java ranging from beginner to highly advanced topics. Well known in the 3D graphics community through the early VRML specification writing and Java 3D development, he currently maintains the Java 3D FAQ and the Java 3D community site j3d.org (http://www.j3d.org/). Furthermore, he has been involved in much behind-the-scenes development of various Java APIs and he is the author/reviewer of a number of ISO specifications. Justin has a large range of Open Source software libraries available from his site for download available at http://www.vlc.com.au/

**Daniel H. Steinberg** is a trainer, consultant, and author for Java-related technologies. He is a regular contributor to *JavaWorld Magazine* and is the editor of *JavaWorld Magazine*'s monthly CodeMasters Challenge. He also contributes to IBM's developerWorks' Java Zone. Daniel is a member of both the Mathematics and Computer Science Departments at Oberlin College. He, his wife, two daughters, and dog live in Cleveland, Ohio. Daniel works with area and national organizations to promote mathematics education. Mostly, he likes to hang out with his family.

*To my family, with love. — Aaron Walsh*

*To my sister, Jill, who started me writing about Java and continues to support and encourage me in this enterprise. — Daniel Steinberg*

# Preface

**W**elcome to *Java™ 2 Bible*, a book designed to teach programmers how to develop dynamic, distributed Web content and desktop applications using Java. Although experience with C or C++ is helpful, it's not required; this book teaches you how to create and deploy dynamic software products using the most exciting programming language ever!

Unlike many programming books that get placed on the bottom shelf of your bookcase, this one is different: *Java™ 2 Bible* is designed to be both a guide and a reference for the most important aspects of the technology. As you learn the ropes of Java, you'll appreciate the attention given in each chapter, teaching you the ins and outs of the language and the issues you'll face along the way. Once you're comfortable programming in Java, this book takes on an entirely different appeal.

As an introduction to the massive Java 2 platform, *Java™ 2 Bible* is packed with information necessary to refine your programming skills. Specifically, you'll find it rich with source code examples, essential application programming interface (API) tables, hints, tips, and warnings that are meant for the experienced Java programmer. As a result, you'll find yourself turning to this book long after it has helped you become a master Java developer.

 Visit JavaBible.com (http://www.javabible.com/) to get your hands on the complete source code listings in this book, errata, Java 1.0 and 1.1 chapters from the original Java Bible, links to programming tools and articles, and much more!

## What You'll Need

The only tools you'll need to become an experienced Java programmer is this book and a computer capable of running the Java Software Development Kit (Java SDK). Appendix A, "Installing and Configuring the SDK," shows you how to obtain online the most current Java SDK, free of charge, and how to install it so that you'll have all the tools you'll need to write, compile, test, and debug all levels of Java programs.

We've also created a special Web site especially for you, the Java 2 Bible reader. Simply fire up your Web browser and visit the official JavaBible.com site (http://www.javabible.com/) to get source code listings found in this book, updates to the text, errata, and links to scores of Java 2 resources including in-depth articles, cutting-edge development tools, source code, and much more.

# Use It or Lose It: How to Use This Book

The only way to learn a programming language is to use it! And that's exactly what this book is designed to do: Get you up and running with Java. Although the text itself is meant to be read, the examples in it are meant to be used.

Of course, as you get more experienced with Java, you'll outgrow the introductory programs provided in the text. That's why the listings become more complicated the deeper you get into it, and why such a wide range of real, working applets and applications (and their source code) have been provided on the JavaBible.com Web site (`http://www.javabible.com/`). Think of this book and JavaBible.com as inseparable, and use them both.

Feel free to jump around from part to part or chapter to chapter as you see fit. If you've already dabbled in the Java language and know how to write and compile programs, there's absolutely no need to learn it all over again. Instead, you might want to take a peek at the tables, tips, warnings, and other reference materials provided for the experienced programmer.

As you read this book, you'll notice we flip-flop between the UNIX and Windows styles when it comes to entering commands on the command line (see "Command-line entries" below) or discussing the SDK tools. Because Java is a cross-platform technology, we attempt to give equal play to both platforms. Because the majority of the book was written on a Windows system; however, you'll notice that the text and examples tend to favor that platform.

Whether you're a Windows user or a UNIX user, however, you should realize that any platform-specific material presented in the text must be adapted to the particular machine you are using. Once you are comfortable doing so, the material discussed in this book will be easily applied to the platform you use. We don't use Macintosh computers for Java development, for example, although the programs in the book should run on any properly equipped Mac (one on which a Java 2 SDK or equivalent development environment has been installed).

## The Many Versions of Java

Like every hot technology, Java is constantly evolving. The *Java™ 2 Bible* that you hold in your hands teaches you how to develop state-of-the-art software programs for the Java 2 platform in general, using the Java 2 SDK version 1.3 in particular. (Java 2 SDK version 1.3 was the latest and greatest version of Java to hit the Web as this book went to press.) The predecessor to this book, the original Java Bible, covered Java versions 1.0, 1.1, and a good deal of Java 2 version 1.2.

Today, however, with Java 2 strongly entrenched in the development community, we've decided to focus entirely on the most current version of Java and leave previous versions for the JavaBible.com site. In other words, use the book you're now holding to learn Java 2, and visit JavaBible.com to get your hands on a ton of text and code related to Java 1.0 and Java 1.1. Between the two resources, you'll be so full of Java that you'll be bulging at the seams!

Following is an overview of what you can expect from this book. It is arranged into parts that are named to give you the sense that you're stepping into the driver's seat of a new car — a bright, shiny, and powerful new car known as Java that will take you as far as you want to go in the programming world.

**Part I, Starting the Engine: Introducing Java**, is the foundation for the entire book. This part introduces the Java 2 platform, which includes the Java programming language and related concepts. You gain an understanding of how the Java programming language was developed and why Java has become all the rage with Internet developers. You are introduced to object-oriented programming concepts and design methodologies. After that introduction, you learn how to build your own Java applications and Web-based applets.

This part also introduces you to a few of the tools that comprise Sun's Java Development Toolkit (SDK) — the tools you use to create your own Java programs. (Appendix A, "Installing and Configuring the SDK", provides a summary of the SDK tools that you'll use throughout the remainder of this book.)

**Part II, Getting Up to Speed: Nuts and Bolts of Java**, introduces the brass tacks of the Java programming language. Beginning with the basic concepts of tokens, types, and values, these chapters explore the nooks and crannies of the Java language. Here you are introduced to the nuts and bolts of Java programming, such as defining and using variables, controlling program flow, creating your own classes, and handling exceptions. Several fundamental Java 2 packages and classes — including strings and arrays — are reviewed in detail as well. In addition, you learn how to create reusable and robust Java programs by taking advantage of key object-oriented programming techniques such as inheritance, composition, and polymorphism.

**Part III, Accelerating into the Curve: Core Class Libraries**, tells you all about Java 2's most important core class libraries, including collections, utilities, and data structures. Here you'll also learn how to handle input and output, which is followed by a detailed discussion of multithreaded programming with Java 2. Finally, Part III teaches you how to tap into Java's powerful network capabilities, after which you'll learn how to integrate Java with databases by way of the Java Database Connectivity (JDBC) Application Programming Interface.

**Part IV, Looking out the Windshield: User Interaction**, shows you how to create functional user interfaces with the Abstract Windowing Toolkit (AWT), Java Foundation Classes (JFC), and Swing GUI facilities. This part shows you how to add graphics, fonts, windows, and user-interface controls — such as buttons, list boxes, combo boxes, menus, and sliders — to your own Java applications. In addition, Part IV shows you how to trap and respond to events, such as mouse movement and keyboard activity.

**Part V, Parking It: Deploying Applets and Applications**, teaches you how to deploy your applets and applications for the world to see. Why keep a work of beauty to yourself, after all?

# Conventions Used in this Book

As you go through this book, you'll find a few unique elements in nearly every chapter, such as source code listings and special icons that grab your attention. These are conventions established to help make the text easy to read and consistent from start to finish, each of which is explained below.

## Source code

Any time you encounter source code, it will be in a special font; this applies to code listings as well as code fragments. This way, it's easy to identify code throughout the book. Whether in a fragment or a numbered listing, code in the text appears in the following style:

```java
import java.net.*;
public class GetAddresses {
    public static void main(String[] argv) {
        InetAddress ia;
        try {
            ia = InetAddress.getLocalHost();
            System.out.println("Local host: " + ia);
            ia = InetAddress.getByName(null);
            System.out.println("Null host: " + ia);
            ia = InetAddress.getByName("www.idgbooks.com");
            System.out.println("IDG host: " + ia);
        } catch(UnknownHostException e) {
            System.out.println(e);
        }
    }
}
```

Code elements that appear in the running text — such as the names of objects, classes, variables, methods, and the like — are also shown in the code font (for example, the `JComponent` class or the `toCharArray()` method), as are the file and folder names and Web URLs.

## Command-line entries

Any time a command-line entry appears in the book, it will reside on its own line and in the code style to distinguish it from the rest of the text. Although the majority of command-line examples are in the Microsoft Windows MS-DOS prompt format, many are in the UNIX format. In most cases, the precise format doesn't matter because you're able to use the command for your particular platform as long as you follow the format conventions for it. Many times, command-line entries are generic enough to be used as-is, regardless of the platform you're running; therefore, the command-line prompt is identified with a greater-than symbol (>), as in the following example:

```
> javac myprogram.java
```

If you are unfamiliar with the Windows MS-DOS prompt, through which Java commands are issues, visit JavaBible.com for help.

## Icons

A number of special icons appear throughout the book to call your attention to topics of special relevance and interest.

The Note icon is used to bring your attention to things you might otherwise be tempted to highlight with a fluorescent marker.

The Tip icon is used to point out a tip or technique that will save you time, effort, money, or all three!

The Caution icon is used to alert you to potential problems that might wreak havoc on your Java programs. Throughout the text, this icon pinpoints bugs, errors, oversights, gaffes, and anything else that may disrupt your Java programs.

The Cross Reference icon refers you to other sections and chapters in the book, as well as to the book's Web site (http://www.javabible.com/), and other Web sites that contain additional coverage of the topic being discussed. Often these sites are provided to give you information that can't be squeezed into this book, such as articles, API documentation, source code, or other resources that we hope you'll find valuable in your quest to become a Java expert.

# Acknowledgments

**A** book of this size takes a tremendous amount of effort to produce, and often an army of talented writers and developers to make it a reality. I would like to extend special thanks to John Osborn for spearheading the original *Java™ Bible* and the updated *Java™ 2 Bible*, as well as my coauthors, Justin Couch and Daniel Steinberg, for their outstanding work and dedication to this book. I would also like to thank Piroz Mohseni for writing the JDBC material found in this book, and John Fronckowiak for his substantial work on the original Java Bible. In addition, I would like to say a personal thank you to the many people at IDG Books Worldwide who made this book possible, especially Greg Croy, Michael Koch, Andy Marinkovich, and Matt Lusher. Finally, I would like to thank David Williams, who, as technical editor of this book, ensured that our writing and code was technically ready for publication.

—*Aaron E. Walsh*

What made this project fun was the community of people that helped create it. Justin and Aaron were full of great ideas, timely advice, and allowed me to benefit from their experience. I'd like to echo Justin's thanks to Piroz, John, Andy, Matt, and David. Thanks to John Osborn for bringing me to this project and to Chrisa Hotchkiss for helping me to say what I meant. Nothing would have been possible without the support and help of Kimmy the wonderwife. Thanks also to my parents and my in-laws for doing double duty watching my daughters Maggie Rose and Elena. Finally, I don't know how to thank Michael Koch enough. In addition to his work as editor, he helped keep me on schedule and provided invaluable suggestions.

—*Daniel H. Steinberg*

# Contents at a Glance

# Contents

· · · · · · · · · · · · · · · · · · · · · · · · · · · · · · · · · · · · · · · · ·

## Chapter 7: About Variables, Methods, Expressions, and Controlling Flow . . . . . . . . . . . . . . . . . . . . . . 195

## Chapter 8: Creating and Using Arrays and Strings . . . . . . . . . . 227

## Chapter 9: Classes, Interfaces, and Packages . . . . . . . . . . . . . . 271

## Chapter 10: Inheritance, Composition, and Polymorphism . . . . . 303

## Chapter 11: Exceptions and Error Handling . . . . . . . . . . . . . . 323

# Part III: Accelerating in the Curve: Core Class Libraries 341

## Part IV: Looking out the Windshield: User Interaction 553

### Chapter 17: Abstract Windowing Toolkit (AWT) Overview . . . . . . 555

## Chapter 24: Swing Odds and Ends . . . . . . . . . . . . . . . . . . 755

# Part V: Parking it: Deploying Applets and Applications 775

## Chapter 25: Deploying Applets and Applications . . . . . . . . . . 777

# Starting the Engine: Introducing Java

✦ ✦ ✦ ✦

✦ ✦ ✦ ✦

# An Overview of Java

**W**hat is Java? This entire book is devoted to answering that question while teaching you how to use the Java technology. Java is arguably the most important advance in programming technology of the past decade; it promises a whole new programming paradigm of portability and robust object-oriented capabilities. By the time you finish this book, you will have learned how to develop distributed Web-based programs, known as Java applets, as well as standalone desktop applications using the very latest Java technology: Java 2 Platform, implementation version 1.3. Or, more simply, Java 2 version 1.3.

To understand exactly what the terms "Java 2" and "version 1.3" means it's helpful to consider how Java came to be in the first place. In other words, it's time for a quick trip down memory lane.

## A Brief History of Java

Sun Microsystems developed the Java programming language in 1991 as part of a research project that sought to create software for consumer electronic devices such as television sets, television set-top boxes, and VCRs. Java's primary goal at that time was to be small, fast, efficient, and easily portable to a wide range of hardware devices. Pursuing that goal has made Java the general-purpose programming language it is today.

Sun used Java in several projects, but it really was behind the scenes and out of public view until the release of the HotJava browser in 1994. Sun wrote HotJava quickly to demonstrate the prowess of Java as a language for the Internet and to show the complexity of possible applications that could be developed. Although it was no barn-burner in the commercial Web browser marketplace, HotJava (itself written in Java) proved that dynamic and interactive Web pages could be created with Java. Specifically, HotJava kicked off the early craze for Java applets (little Java programs that could be woven directly into Web pages).

Netscape Navigator 2 (for Windows) was the first commercial browser to support Java 1.0, which was quickly followed by Internet Explorer. When Java hit the Web, it hit big time. Other than the Web itself, no technology at the time received as much media attention and hype as Java. It promised, after all, to bring the Web to life in ways that previously weren't possible. And it also promised to give us completely cross-platform applications because Java developers could write a single program that was deployable across a wide range of computer platforms (Windows, Macintosh, Solaris, and more).

The first Java Development Toolkits (JDKs, later renamed Software Development Toolkit, or SDK) were released to the public around the same time Java applets were making a big splash on the Web in the mid 1990s. Version 1.0 of the JDK included tools for developing applets and applications for Sun Solaris 2.3, Windows NT, Windows 95, and Macintosh systems. Shortly after the first JDK release and the integration of Java into Netscape Navigator, Java took the world by storm — and it hasn't stopped making news since!

Over time, Java has evolved considerably from it's rather humble beginnings as a cross-platform environment that you could use to create simple applets and rudi-mentary standalone applications. Today it has matured into a full-blown computing "platform" in its own right, a platform that Sun initially trumpeted would topple the dominant Microsoft Windows platform.

Although Java hasn't succeeded in displacing Windows, it has become the de facto standard for Internet software development currently in use by over 2 million devel-opers around the world. Interestingly, the current trend in Java development has shifted from the client side of the Web where it began, to the server-side (such as application and transaction servers running behind many commercial Web sites) and desktop applications. Applets, which first sparked the Java revolution years ago, have become less important lately because of the steady rise in popularity of alternate client-side Web technologies such as JavaScript, Flash and Shockwave.

After a major 1.1 version update to Java a few years after the debut of Java 1.0, Java really began to hit its stride as a sophisticated software development environment. With Java 1.1 the computing community was buzzing with the possibility of a truly substantial Java platform that could deliver on earlier Java hype, one that might indeed be a Windows killer. Although that wasn't the case with Java 1.1, the next major upgrade to Java was enough to finally give Windows a run for its money as far as many developers were concerned. With Java 1.2, Sun ushered in the era of the *Java platform*.

In late 1998, Sun unveiled Java 1.2, around which the company orchestrated a major marketing campaign for what it called the "Java 2 Platform," or, more simply, Java 2. Java 2 was effectively a branding effort by Sun to indicate that the technology was finally ready for prime time (previously the concept of a Java platform had no number associated with it). At the time of this writing, Java 1.3 is the most current *version* of Java available for the Java 2 Platform.

Unfortunately, Java 2 is merely a catchall brand name for the Java platform that has yet to be reflected in the actual implementation *versions* of Java. A Java implementation, as you'll learn shortly, is really the meat and potatoes that developers rely on to create and run their Java programs. Sun's sudden, and unexpected, introduction of Java 1.2 as the first implementation of a Java 2 Platform caused great confusion among developers who were merely expecting a 1.3 revision to Java in late 1998, and still confuses developers to this very day.

Technically speaking, Java 1.3 is the latest and greatest version of the Java implementation for the Java 2 Platform; it's what we'll be using throughout this book. More specifically, we'll be creating programs using the Java 2 Platform Standard Edition, a mouthful of words more commonly called J2SE. J2SE gives us everything we need to create powerful Java 2 applets and applications for today's desktop computers (see Appendix A to learn how to install J2SE if you haven't already done so).

Meanwhile, Sun's Java 2 Platform Enterprise Edition (J2EE) is available for mission-critical, enterprise-class applications, while the Java 2 Platform Micro Edition (J2ME) is designed specifically for use with consumer devices such cellular phones, television set-top boxes, and personal digital assistants (PDAs). For our needs, J2EE is too much, and J2ME is too little, while J2SE is just right. If Goldylocks were a software developer, J2SE would be the piping hot bowl of porridge that she ate before taking a snooze in papa Bear's high-backed programming chair!

Eventually, Java implementation version numbers will catch up to the Java 2 Platform brand name, which promises to bring even more confusion to an already confusing situation. What, after all, would "Java 2 version 2" really mean to anyone not aware of the fact that there is a difference between the "Java 2" platform brand name and a specific implementation version?

**Tip**     To learn more about the general term Java platform, fire up your browser and visit http://java.sun.com/nav/whatis/. To learn about the specific Java 2 Platform, visit http://java.sun.com/java2/. Alternately, you can jump directly to the J2SE site visit http://java.sun.com/j2se/ to learn more about the specific version of Java we'll be using throughout this book.

# Introducing the Java Environment

If you're new to programming, this will be a whole new world for you; if you're already a developer but don't know Java, you'll most likely be convinced to switch to Java as a primary programming language. But before you toss your old development environment out the window, perhaps an introduction to Java is in order. After all, Java is a rich and complex new technology, with many facets that work together to get the job done.

Following is a brief overview of Java's main features. You'll find more detailed information on these topics in subsequent chapters of this book.

## The Java language

The Java language is an object-oriented programming language developed and promoted by Sun Microsystems. Although its roots are in C++, it is a completely new software development language. Unlike C++, it is entirely object-oriented and designed expressly with distributed, platform-independent environments in mind. The Java language is designed to create executable content, such as applets, applications, and handlers. In fact, Sun's HotJava Web browser, the world's first Java-savvy browser, is an application written entirely in the Java language.

## Java class libraries (a.k.a. Java API)

Every Java-enabled system comes with a standard suite of libraries that contain prebuilt object templates, or *classes*, that developers can use to construct their own programs. With Java 2, several thousand classes are actually provided, giving you a bevy of premade code templates that you can use as is or customize (extend) for your own purposes. Standard Java class libraries are available for practically every conceivable need you might have, including windowing, graphical user interface construction, input/output, networking, and many more. (See Appendix A for a description of each Java 2 class library, or *package* as they're known in Java lingo.) Java's extensive class libraries are sometimes called the Java application programming interface (API), because they define the standard Java interfaces that developers have at their disposal when creating programs of their own.

## The Java runtime environment

Once you have written a program in the Java language, it's up to the runtime environment to execute the code. The Java runtime environment, also called the Java architecture, is made up of the Java language and the Java Virtual Machine (JVM), which together provide the means to execute Java code. The Java runtime environment is portable and platform-neutral; it is the basis of Java's distributed computing capabilities, and it is available for most popular personal computing platforms.

Currently, the Java runtime environment is available to end users through Web browsers such as Sun's HotJava browser, Netscape Communications Corp.'s Netscape Navigator browser, and Microsoft's Internet Explorer. Java-savvy Web browsers such as these let people experience a very specific form of Java, the Java applet, which you'll learn more about later in this chapter.

Although using Java-savvy Web browsers is the most common way in which people experience the Java technology, it's by no means the only way. Standalone runtime environments are also available, allowing end users to run full-blown desktop applications that aren't embedded in Web pages like Java applets are.

The most current form of Java, Java 2, comes with a very powerful Java runtime environment that you'll use throughout the remainder of this book to develop and test your own Java applications. Using Sun's free Java 2 Software Development Toolkit (SDK), you'll have all the Java tools you'll need to write, debug, and deploy all forms of Java programs.

## The Java Virtual Machine

The Java Virtual Machine is a well-defined specification that you must follow when writing Java code. All Java code is compiled for use on this nonexistent machine, which is actually a set of specifications for how the code should be generated during the program compilation process. Writing code that runs under the Java Virtual Machine helps ensure platform independence. To guarantee true platform independence, though, your application must include no code native to a particular platform, and it must depend on no native methods of that or any other platform. Truly platform-independent code that is entirely Java can be certified by Sun as "100 Percent Pure Java," as defined by Sun at http://java.sun.com/100percent/.

You really won't deal directly with the Virtual Machine when writing Java programs unless, of course, you're porting it to a new platform. But even that's unlikely because at the time of writing, the Virtual Machine has already been ported to a number of platforms, including Sun Solaris, Windows 2000, Windows NT, Windows 98, Windows 95, Windows 3.1, and Apple Macintosh, BeOS, OpenVMS, FreeBSD, IRIX, NEXTStep, OS/390, OS/400, RiscOS, VxWorks, SunOS, AIX, BSDI, Digital Unix, HP 3000, Linux, NetBSD, OpenBSD, OSF/1, SCO, UnixWare, AmigaOS, DG/US, EPOC 16, HP-UX, MachTen, NetWare, OS/2, Reliant Unix, Solaris, and UXP/DS. The Microsoft Windows and Sun Solaris Java Virtual Machine are directly provided by Sun.

Many Java-enabled browsers, such as Netscape Communicator and Internet Explorer, provide their own Java Virtual Machine implementations. This point is important for developers, since the Java Virtual Machine supported in your favorite Web browser probably does not include support for the latest Java features. It took Netscape almost six months after the release of Java version 1.1 to include its complete support in Netscape Communicator, and due to legal wrangling, Internet Explorer's Java Virtual Machine still doesn't support all of the Java 1.1 features. As of this writing, neither Navigator nor Explorer support Java 2, forcing developers to use the Java plug-in technology described in Chapter 25 to deploy Web-based applets that are based on this version of Java.

## Java tools

Sun's SDK comes with a bevy of tools, giving developers everything they need to develop Java programs. Among the tools provided with the Java 2 SDK are a compiler, an interpreter, a documentation generator, and a debugger, as well as a large suite of premade software libraries that you'll use to create your very own Java programs. In addition, the SDK comes with a convenient Applet Viewer tool that allows you to run Java applets outside of a Java-savvy Web browser. (Browsers such as HotJava, Netscape Navigator, and Internet Explorer are very resource-intensive and can slow down the development process. Applet Viewer, on the other hand, is small, fast, and efficient, making it ideal for early-stage applet testing.)

## Java applets

*Java applets* are small programs that are woven directly into Web pages, and so require a browser that understands Java (meaning a browser that has a Java run-time environment built into it) in order to run. They are pieces of executable Java code that are typically embedded in HTML documents using the <APPLET> tag. (Java 2 applets must be woven into Web pages using the <OBJECT> and <EMBED> tags, as you'll learn in Chapter 25, "Deploying Applets and Applications.") When a Java-capable browser accesses such a page, it automatically downloads the executable code pointed to by the special tag. When the code arrives, the Java runtime environment executes it within the browser.

Applets are different from applications because they can not run on their own; they must instead be executed within a Java-savvy browser or using a special tool such as Applet Viewer.

## Java applications

Standalone software applications written in the Java language are known as *Java applications*. They can be executed on the desktop, outside of a typical Java-enabled environment (such as a Java-savvy Web browser or Applet Viewer). Sun's HotJava browser, for example, is actually a standalone Java application that you can run on your desktop computer as you would any other program. Although Java applets initially received all the attention because they can inject otherwise lifeless Web pages with interactive content, Java applications have gained in popularity over the years.

## Other Java programs

Although applets and applications are the most common forms of Java programs, which is why they're the focus of this book, other types of Java programs can be created as well, including JavaBeans, servlets, and handlers.

*JavaBeans* are Java software components that may be visually assembled by non-programmers using a visual builder tool. Unlike Java classes that must be assembled into functional programs by a software developer such as yourself, JavaBeans are designed specifically to be visually manipulated through a visual interface similar to that of Visual Basic and other visual program assembly tools. Such tools allow non-programmers to "wire together" JavaBeans software components on a visual level, freeing them from the code-level integration we're used to as programmers.

*Servlets* can be thought of as server-side applets, or special purpose programs that execute on the Web server instead of the end user's browser, like applets do. Java servlets are an alternative to the popular Common Gateway Interface (CGI) scripts that are typically written in PERL. As such, servlets can be controlled through script commands embedded in client-side Web pages in a manner similar to that of Microsoft's Active Server Pages (ASP).

*Handlers* are special pieces of Java code that process incoming information and convert it into an object that a Java environment can use. Although handlers are typically used only in Sun's HotJava browser, they illustrate how Java can be used to dynamically extend the capabilities of Web browsers and other programs that are routinely confronted with new and unknown types of information. In essence, handlers provide the HotJava browser with a mechanism for dynamically learning how to deal with incoming data.

Java supports two types of handlers: protocol handlers and content handlers. *Protocol handlers* extend HotJava's knowledge of (you guessed it) protocols. If the browser comes across a protocol it doesn't understand, it can dynamically learn the protocol by simply downloading and executing the associated protocol handler, assuming one exists. *Content handlers*, on the other hand, extend HotJava's knowledge of (surprise, surprise) content, such as images, sounds, and other forms of Web-based information.

# Defining Java

Now that you know more about Java, it's time to go beyond the concepts and get to know the entire Java environment — the Java language, runtime environment, and tools — on a deeper level. And what better way to start than with the technology at the center of it all?

The Java technology consists of three entities:

✦ The language itself

✦ A runtime environment

✦ A set of tools

At the core of everything is the programming language formerly known as Oak, which was eventually renamed Java for legal reasons. (A different technology also named Oak existed before Sun's Oak language came along.) Without the language itself (now known simply as Java), the runtime environment and tools would have no purpose. And so it only makes sense that more often than not, when people speak casually of Java, they are usually referring to the programming language.

But what makes the language so revolutionary? Haven't we been introduced to a number of programming-language "revolutions" over the years, each of which failed in one way or another to measure up to the hype surrounding them? In the software-development industry, we're accustomed to new languages that promise to change the way we program, revolutionize software development, make our jobs easier, and advance the state of the art. So why get in a tizzy about Java? What's so great about it that we should believe the hype and bother to learn a new programming paradigm at the expense of time and money?

These are all valid questions, many of which will be answered in this book, while others will be answered only in the years to come. For now, Java is still relatively new. Yes, Java has been publicly available since 1995, but it's only now matured to the point that it can actually live up to the hype that surrounded the technology when it first busted onto the scene over half a decade ago. For years, the computer industry has been buzzing about the potential of Java, and with Java 2, the technology is ready to deliver on its early promises. So what's all the buzz about? What makes Java special? To find out, we can start with the rousing marketing message that came directly from Sun when Java 1.0 was first introduced to the world in the summer of 1995:

> Java: A simple, object-oriented, distributed, interpreted, robust, secure, architecture-neutral, portable, high-performance, multithreaded, and dynamic language.

That's quite a mouthful of buzzwords, especially considering that just about every one of them is a goal in the forefront of modern software development. Rather than simply accepting this definition and moving on, let's see how the Java language actually embodies these qualities.

## Simple

Programming isn't simple, no matter how you look at it. Even the most rudimentary programming languages such as BASIC are far too complex for the average computer user to whip up a functional software product. No, the general public will never think Java is simple and you probably won't, either. The 11 buzzwords that Sun used to describe the Java language are enough to send tingles of fear up and down a nonprogrammer's spine, and they can also be daunting to novice programmers. But what about those of us who develop software for a living or hack around with code from time to time just to keep ourselves amused?

Well, to experienced developers, the Java language indeed appears simple when compared to many other serious programming languages. Java is not overly simple, mind you, but simple enough to get going without having to spend time learning a completely new language. For starters, Java is designed to be as close to C and C++ as possible, to ensure that today's massive base of C and C++ programmers can migrate easily to the new language. Because Java has its roots in C/C++, anyone already familiar with these languages will get up to speed with Java in no time.

C programmers, however, will need a little more time to get into the Java frame of mind compared to C++ developers. Java is an object-oriented language that closely resembles C++, while C is a procedural language that is similar to Java mainly in terms of syntax. As a result, C programmers must first learn to think in terms of objects, while C++ programmers are already in an object-oriented frame of mind.

Not only that, but procedural programmers altogether unfamiliar with C syntax (do we have any Pascalites in the room?) will have to come up to speed with both object-oriented programming and the syntax of the Java language.

Although C++ programmers have an advantage right off the bat, C programmers need only familiarize themselves with the object-oriented approach to software development before plunging right in. And everyone else? Well, it's a bit more work than learning a new syntax.

Luckily, Java is easier to learn than C++ because the Java language designers intentionally removed much of the difficulty that programmers encountered with C++. Indeed, Java was built to be easier to learn and use than C++; as a result, it does give up some of the power found in C++. However, the C++ features that Java omits are not used as often as one might think and often they lead to overly complex programs that are difficult to maintain.

Specifically, pointers, operator overloading, multiple inheritance, and extensive automatic coercion have been omitted from Java (although method overloading is supported). If you are a C++ programmer, you may be clutching your chest and breathing quick, shallow gasps of air at this very moment. But until you regain control of your lungs and vocal cords, you'd be hard-pressed to figure out whether it's from joy or shock.

You can't please everyone all the time, and Java doesn't try to. By eliminating what it believed to be the worst of C++ — for better or worse — the Java team stripped away much of the complexity of the language. Score one for simplicity.

While reducing complexity, the Java team introduced automatic garbage collection to further simplify the language. Although this makes the internal Java system more complex overall, it takes the burden of memory management off the programmer. Not only is Java software easier to write, thanks to the fact that memory management comes "for free," but bugs related to memory are dramatically reduced. Score two for simplicity.

## Object-oriented

If Java is at all complex, it is because the language is entirely object-oriented. To the uninitiated, object-orientated programming (OOP) can be a frightening concept. But to those who are comfortable with thinking in terms of objects, it is pure bliss. If you haven't already given object-oriented software development a shot, or if you have abandoned earlier efforts to learn this new way of programming out of sheer frustration, now is the time to take up the challenge. You won't be sorry.

The premise of object-oriented programming is simple: every programming task is considered in terms of objects and their relationships to one another. Generally speaking, an *object* is a self-contained body of executable code; objects contain both data and the routines that manipulate that data. In contrast, procedural languages such as C, typically deal with data and routines separately; data is passed into a routine, where it is manipulated and returned to the caller.

Objects, on the other hand, are similar in nature to the biological cells that our bodies are made of. Like cells, objects have information inside of them on which they can act. Objects are self-contained, and so can operate on their own, or they can be combined together to create more sophisticated structures. Similarly, every cell in our body is a unique, self-contained entity that does something special yet can be combined with other cells to create more sophisticated structures such as tissue. Tissue, in turn, can be combined with other tissues to form complete organs, and organs can be combined to form entire systems such as our respiratory or digestive system.

In essence, objects follow the same principle as cells; objects are self-contained entities that can be combined with other objects to create ever more sophisticated structures that ultimately culminate into entire programs. Although the details of object-oriented programming in Java are covered in the chapters that follow, objects also exhibit a special quality worth mentioning now: *inheritance*. New objects can be created, or *derived*, from existing objects. The new object inherits the capabilities of its parent, yet can be customized as needed. Inheritance gives object-oriented languages such as Java a wonderful mechanism for reusing code, meaning you can get more done in less time.

> **Note**
>
> In object-oriented terminology, a "class" is complied source code that acts as a template from which "objects" spring to life. As a programmer, you will write Java code to create classes that are brought to life as objects when your program is run. In the spirit of this conversation, Java classes could be compared to the DNA structure of a cell, while objects would be an actual living cell. Java classes can also be compared to the architectural blueprints of a house, while an object would be the house built from such plans. Although this is an extremely simplified view of the relationship between classes and objects, it will suffice for now. For specific details, turn to Chapter 2.

To help make the value of object-oriented programming more concrete, consider the task of writing a program in terms of building a sculpture out of Legos. Procedural programming languages force you to hand-craft every single Lego brick from scratch, requiring an inordinate amount of time and effort on the programmer's part. Each brick requires considerable attention to how it looks, feels, and fits into the larger work.

Object-oriented programming puts the focus on the larger work itself, on what the final sculpture should be. Rather than creating a hand-crafted brick for each part of the whole, the object-oriented approach relies on a generic form of a Lego brick, from which all other such bricks are derived. You save the time and effort of hand-crafting individual bricks; you simply use the generic brick as a template and build on that. (See Figure 1-1.) The template gives you all the basic properties, and you customize it to fit your needs. The result is a dramatic increase in productivity and reusability.

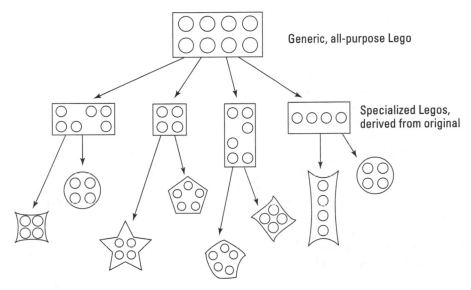

Generic, all-purpose Lego

Specialized Legos, derived from original

Highly specialized Legos, derived from specialized ones

**Figure 1-1:** Deriving specialized objects from generic objects

For instance, if you derived a special-purpose brick from the generic brick as you worked on (say) the hands of a sculpture, you'd only need to tweak each piece of Lego a bit more to get it to look like a finger. Heck, they all look and act about the same; they just need a little bit of customizing here and there. Why fashion a different type of brick for each of the ten fingers? Simply customize your basic template to look like a finger, and then derive the rest of the fingers from that. You could then derive the toes of your sculpture from the fingers you've created. (They're just stubby little fingers anyway.) No sense crafting those little fellas from scratch, no sir.

When all is said and done, you've put more attention and work into the sculpture as a whole than into the individual bricks. And the biggest benefit? The next time you need to create a Lego sculpture — even though it may differ in form and function from your previous one — the bulk of the real work is already done. You simply derive the new sculpture from your existing one, tweaking it here and there to customize it as needed. Sure, this is a simplified view of object-oriented programming, but the basic approach is the essence of working with objects.

In the object-oriented world, you focus primarily on the design of your bricks (objects) and on the operations that go along with it (methods). If you have done a good enough job of defining the basic, all-purpose piece of Lego (and have not been all thumbs about it, to stretch this analogy even further), you can then derive a wide variety of special-purpose pieces of Lego from it.

The object-oriented functions of Java are essentially those of C++. Although current C++ programmers will feel right at home, those without object-oriented experience will need to spend a little time getting comfortable with this terminology and its associated concepts. To help jump-start the process, we'll explore object-oriented programming in more detail in Chapter 2.

Note   Although C is not an object-oriented language, it forms the basis for C++. Because Java is rooted in C++, Java code will look very familiar to C programmers, as far as the syntax of the language is concerned.

## Distributed

Java is built with network communications in mind; sophisticated network capabilities are an inherent part of the Java technology. Java has a comprehensive library of network objects that deal with protocols such as the Transmission Control Protocol/Internet Protocol (TCP/IP), the Hypertext Transfer Protocol (HTTP), and the File Transfer Protocol (FTP). As a result, Java programs can open and access resources residing on the Internet with the same ease that you would normally expect when accessing a local file system.

This is another dramatic advantage over C and C++. You don't have to worry about implementing the details of networks yourself; Java comes with everything needed for truly distributed computing. A good example of this is the HotJava browser which, thanks to the Java language, understands how to access and handle objects over the World Wide Web. Most other programming languages require you to either write these networking layers yourself or purchase a library of networked code for this purpose; Java provides these capabilities from the start.

## Interpreted

The Java language is interpreted. In other words, an interpreter must be available for each hardware architecture and operating system on which you want to run Java applications. Traditionally, interpreted programs are not converted into machine code, as compiled programs are. Instead, they remain in a human-readable form, which an interpreter executes line by line.

Software developers often cringe at the thought of using interpreted language for "serious" programming projects. Interpreted languages are notorious for being slow in comparison to their compiled brethren and often draw heat for that reason alone.

Through the innovative use of its virtual machine (VM), however, Java overcomes many of the speed issues that bog down other interpreted languages. Java code actually goes through a compile process that outputs what is known as Java bytecode. Java bytecode is machine-independent, conforming to the Java Virtual Machine's specifications, and you can run it on any system that supports the Java environment. This code is at an intermediate stage, not fully compiled, but close enough to actual machine code that the interpretation process takes much less time than it would otherwise.

To further reduce the overhead of interpretation, Java implements multithreading (which permits programs to juggle several tasks at once as you'll later learn) and handles interpretation efficiently in the background. Compiling Java code to an intermediate stage — and then interpreting it in the background through threads — results in much faster interpretation and gives Java a significant speed boost over traditional interpreted languages.

**Note** The Java Virtual Machine (JVM) is not really a machine at all! It's a set of specifications that define how Java bytecode is to be handled on a given computer system. Java programs can execute on any computer that has a Java Virtual Machine present.

## Robust

Reliability is extremely important to software developers, especially professionals whose reputations and careers are on the line for the products they create. It behooves us, therefore, to create robust programs that are likely to succeed under unknown or adverse conditions. Although this goal may sound obvious, many languages (C in particular) are a long way from providing developers with the tools needed for developing robust programs.

The C language, for example, is very relaxed in terms of type checking, resulting in programming errors that fall through the cracks, only to surface later — and often at the most inopportune moments. C++ is a much more strongly typed language, but because it is rooted in the C language, it fails to catch a number of bugs during compile time. Not so with Java.

Java requires declarations, ensuring that the data types passed to a routine are exactly the data types the routine requires. Furthermore, Java doesn't allow automatic casting of data types, as C and C++ do; the programmer must explicitly write casts. By forcing the programmer to do so, Java drastically reduces the likelihood that slippery logic errors will be introduced into your code.

The most significant difference between Java and C/C++ is the use of a pointer model that prohibits overwriting memory and corrupting data. Instead of pointer arithmetic, Java supports true arrays on which subscript (boundary) checking is enforced. Since a programmer can't mistakenly overwrite data or access an array element out of bounds, the language eliminates the possibility of these common bugs. The result is a very robust development system that frees the programmer from such concerns.

**Note** Java, unlike C/C++, eliminates entirely the support for true pointers.

# Secure

Any time network access happens, security concerns become a big issue. Security has always been a worry, even on the local level before networks became so popular. Now that executable content is available, imagine the Trojan horses that might hide the most horrible viruses and interlopers come to invade our privacy. After all, what better way to get into a user's computer system than through the front door? Because applets are automatically downloaded and executed, they'd never know what hit 'em, right?

Not so. The Java team designed Java for networked and distributed environments from the onset, and it addressed the issue of security from the very beginning. Security is a critical part of the Java environment. Java allows you to create virus-free, tamper-free systems, thanks to the number of security checks it performs before a piece of code can be executed.

First of all, pointers and memory allocation are removed during compile time. By blocking memory allocation and memory access until runtime, Java prevents programmers from assuming memory locations in advance and "jumping" into memory.

Second, the interpreter verifies all bytecodes before they are executed, as shown in Figure 1-2. If the code isn't valid Java code, it won't execute. Deviant code is blocked before it can become a problem. Potentially dangerous activities such as as illegal access to memory space, violation of access privileges, illegal class access, and illegal data conversions are not permitted. As a result, a potential virus has no way of gaining access to data structures, objects, or memory locations.

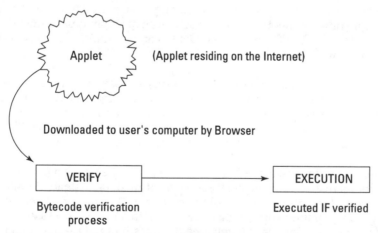

**Figure 1-2:** Java's interpreter verifies all bytecode.

And finally, all Java applets operate inside a "sandbox" security model: they are treated as untrusted code executing in a trusted environment. This means that all applets downloaded from the Web are restricted in what they can do once they reach your machine. Even after passing the bytecode-verification process, applets are prohibited from accessing files on your computer unless you specifically give the applet permission to do so. Nor can they make network connections outside of the Web server they came from without permission. This prevents applets from accessing Web resources other than those available on the site from which they were downloaded, unless the user grants the applet such capabilities. As an added security measure, applets are prohibited from executing any code (such as external code libraries and applications) that cannot be verified in the same way that an applet itself is, as illustrated in Figure 1-3.

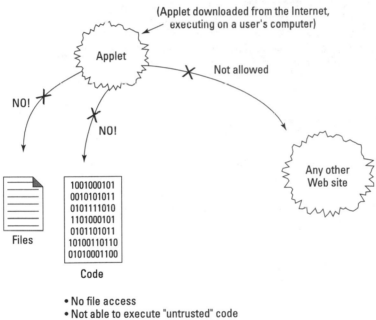

**Figure 1-3:** Applet security restrictions

However, we all know that every security measure employed by Java is nothing more than a juicy enticement to the world of virus authors and thrill-seeking hackers. Although in theory, Java shouldn't be possible to infiltrate, in truth, no software system is impenetrable, including Java. In the rare instances where Java security holes have been found, Sun's Java team has immediately sealed them. Such is the cat-and-mouse game of security in our modern world. Compared to other programming languages, however, Java is much more secure and, as a result, has become the de-facto language for creating network-aware programs.

## Levels of Trust

Java 1.0.x applets were forced to live and die entirely inside the sandbox security model, meaning they had no way of reaching out beyond the narrow scope of capabilities imposed by that version of the technology. Java 1.1 later introduced an "all-or-nothing" security model, which meant that users could grant such applets complete access to system and network resources. Unfortunately, the all-or-nothing security model introduced with Java 1.1 meant that an applet would gain full-blown access to all resources even if it needed only one specific type of access. With Java 1.1, there was no way for the user to specify that an applet could read files only off the local system; for example, granting a Java 1.1 applet any form of access privilege gives it full access to local and network resources regardless of which capabilities it actually needs.

Java 2 finally introduced the notion of "levels of trust" (or "fine-grained" security), a security model in which an applet can be granted specific capabilities based on what it needs to do. An applet that needs to read a file that resides on the user's computer, for example, can be granted only that privilege and no more. Visit Sun's Java security Web page (`http://java.sun.com/security/`) to learn more details about Java security.

## Architecture-neutral

Because Sun designed Java to support distributed applications over computer networks, you can use it with a variety of CPU and operating-system architectures. To achieve this design goal, a Java compiler produces architecture-neutral object files, or Java bytecode, from the Java source code you write. Assuming that the Java runtime environment exists on the client-system end, the resulting bytecode executes regardless of platform.

This architecture works not only for networks, but also for standard software distribution. With Java you can create a single executable that can be run on any computer that has the Java runtime environment, as shown in Figure 1-4.

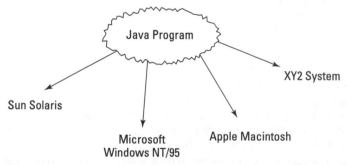

**Figure 1-4:** Java is architecture-neutral (platform-independent).

## The Java Runtime Environment

The Java runtime environment is actually an interpreter that converts architecture-neutral Java bytecode files into native machine code that can be executed. A Java runtime environment is typically installed on end-user systems when the user installs a Java-savvy Web browser such as Netscape Navigator or Internet Explorer. Although this is the most popular way to get a Java runtime environment up and running, it's only useful for running Java applets embedded in Web pages. To run full-blown Java applications, you must install a Java runtime environment that operates independent of Web browsers. This is easy enough, since Sun's Java SDK—and most Java development tools, for that matter—come with a standalone Java runtime environment.

Because Java runtime environments are merely Java bytecode interpreters that conform to the JVM, vendors are free to produce their own. (People often use the terms *Java runtime environment* and *Java Virtual Machine* interchangeably because the Java runtime environment is an implementation based on the JVM specification.) In fact, it's only a matter of time before all major operating system vendors build Java runtime environments directly into the operating system. (Microsoft and Apple already bundle earlier versions of Java into their operating systems, although not Java 2.) When they do, users won't have to bother installing a runtime environment themselves; Java will be supported at the operating-system level!

Such platform independence is possible thanks to a compiler that generates byte-code instructions that are completely independent of any specific computer architecture. As a result, Java programs can be executed on any computer since the bytecodes they are composed of may be dynamically translated into native machine code by any Java runtime environment.

## Portable

Assuming the Java runtime environment is present on a given computer, Java byte-code will execute properly. Thanks to its architecture-neutral capabilities, the Java system is highly portable.

One part of the portability equation is Java's representation of data types. C and C++, although touted as being highly portable, are hampered by being implementation-dependent. That is, the size of primitive data types and the arithmetic performed on them, changes from system to system. An `int` (integer data type) on one system isn't necessarily the same size as an `int` on another, for example. As a result, ease of portability suffers.

In Java, however, primitive data-type sizes and the behavior of arithmetic on these types are explicitly specified. For example, `int` is always a signed 32-bit integer value, and `float` is always a 32-bit floating-point number conforming to the

Institute of Electrical and Electronics Engineers' IEEE 754 specifications. When you use primitive data types in Java, their representation and arithmetic behavior are consistent from system to system.

The Java class libraries include portable interfaces for each platform on which the runtime environment is available. For example, an abstract `Window` class and implementations of it are available for Sun Solaris, Windows, and MacOS. When using such graphics interfaces, Java automatically loads the appropriate platform-specific graphical user interface item that corresponds to a window for the current machine.

Finally, the entire Java system itself is portable, as it features a clean portability boundary that is well documented by Sun. The Java system can therefore be ported to just about any computing environment, the most popular of which are already available (Windows, Macintosh, Solaris, and many others).

## High-performance

Java performance is impressive for an interpreted language, mostly because of the development of just-in-time (JIT) compilers that optimize the bytecodes on the fly. According to Sun, Java programs execute at speeds "nearly indistinguishable" from native C/C++ programs.

Although interpreting bytecodes is faster than interpreting raw programming languages, since they are already in an intermediate stage, the Java architecture is also designed to reduce overhead during runtime. Additionally, threads are incorporated into the language, which further enhances the overall perceived speed of Java executables.

**Note**     Although Java's performance is impressive when compared to other interpreted languages, developers in the past have voiced concern that it was too slow to use in cases where raw speed is a factor. Some accounts have Java programs running anywhere from 10 to 30 times slower than their C/C++ counterparts. While the debate over whether the original version of Java was fast enough for mission-critical applications, Sun dramatically improved the overall speed of Java with the release of Java 2. In addition, Sun has recently released the HotSpot technology as part of the latest Java 1.3 implementation, which further narrows the performance gap between Java and native code (see the related HotSpot Virtual Machine sidebar).

In addition, several leading software tool vendors, such as IBM, Symantec, Microsoft, and Metrowerks, have developed JIT compilers that convert Java applet bytecode into optimized native machine code on the fly, as it is downloaded over the Web and immediately before execution. As a result of JIT compilers, browser vendors have greatly increased the speed of Java applet execution in their products. The past few releases of both Netscape Navigator and Microsoft's Internet Explorer have taken advantage of JIT compiler technology, making non-JIT Java-savvy browsers look slow by comparison.

## HotSpot Virtual Machine

Several months after Sun released Java 2 in December of 1998, a new and extremely fast virtual machine called the Java HotSpot Virtual Machine was also released. Sun's HotSpot VM gets its name from the fourth-generation bytecode interpreter technology JavaSoft acquired when it purchased Animorphic Systems several years ago. HotSpot VM achieves faster speeds by enabling the VM to identify areas (hot spots) in bytecode that can be highly optimized when converted into machine code. In addition, HotSpot also looks for repetitive method calls that can be dynamically integrated into the application and inlined for faster execution. Although HotSpot is relatively new, it promises to deliver Java applications that execute at speeds similar to native C and C++ applications. Starting with Java 1.3, the HotSpot VM comes as part of the standard Java implementation. Specifically, Sun's HotSpot Client Virtual Machine is a replacement for previous Java 2 virtual machines and JIT compilers that improves applet and application runtime performance. To learn more about HotSpot visit http://java.sun.com/j2se/1.3/docs/guide/performance/hotspot.html.

## Multithreaded

*Multithreading* is a major feature of Java, giving executables the ability to maintain several threads of execution at one time. Not to be confused with multitasking—the capability of an operating system to run more than one program at once—multithreading permits *programs* to juggle several tasks at once.

For instance, in a nonthreaded environment, only one line of execution exists for programs. Typically, an event loop is used to keep track of the particular task at hand. This loop identifies which task is to be executed (such as refreshing the contents of a window, tracking user input, or printing a document), and passes it off to the appropriate routine(s). Once the task is handled, another can begin. Because only one task at a time can be handled, the system must wait until the current task has been completed before handling a new one.

Although programming languages such as C and C++ allow the developer to implement multithreading, it takes a considerable amount of effort compared to Java, which implements threading synchronization directly. Based on C.A.R. Hoare's widely used monitor and condition-variable paradigm, Java supports multithreading in a clean and robust implementation.

So what can you do with threads? Just about anything, really; you can assign each line of execution to a thread and synchronize that thread with other threads as needed. They can dramatically improve interaction with users, handling multiple requests at once. With threads, real-time response times are possible.

A good example of threads in action is the garbage collection feature of the Java language. This facility is a low-priority thread that runs in the background as other tasks are executing. It monitors objects and all references to them, disposing of them when they are no longer in use. Because a thread running in the background controls this process, other threads go on undisturbed.

Another powerful example of multithreading would be a program that supports simultaneous input, output, and user interaction, such as taking real-time audio input from a microphone while synchronizing it with a video image being played on the screen. In this case, such a system could match incoming audio to the lips of computer-generated characters in real time. Such a computer karaoke program would take all the difficulty out of singing in sync with a video image, always the most embarrassing part of the party piece. (On second thought, is there any part karaoke that isn't embarrassing?)

Okay, this is pretty demanding. Although it's unlikely that you could developsuch a program using Java today, future versions of the technology may be fast enough to keep up. Nonetheless, it's a valid example of threads handling different parts of a program.

For the power of multithreading to be fully realized, however, the systems on which Java code is executed must also support threads. Because true preemptive multitasking and multithreading are at the foundation of all modern operating system developments, in the near future, most platforms will be up to par. For the time being, Java's multithreading capabilities are limited by the underlying architectures of the systems on which it executes.

## Dynamic

Fundamentally, distributed computing environments must be dynamic. Java was designed to adapt in a constantly evolving environment. It is capable of incorporating new functionality, regardless of where that functionality comes from — the local computer system, local and wide area networks, and the Internet are all potential contributors.

In object-oriented C++ environments, as in most programming environments, developers don't write every line of code themselves. Instead, they rely on a wide array of class libraries to extend the functionality of their programs. If a developer needs to add support for a particular feature, such as the ability to play moving videos, he or she simply links in new class libraries that can handle the job.

Sometimes, these libraries are distributed in ways the developer can't control, such as with an operating system or windowing environment. In such cases, updates to libraries might reach the customer before a developer has the chance to recompile the program using them. When a customer is running an old version of the developer's product, and it attempts to dynamically link in an updated library such as this, there is the potential for real problems. Since the program hasn't been recompiled to handle the updated class library, it will likely break.

If the developer had the ability to simply recompile the program with the updated library, and then get it into customers' hands in time, everything would be fine. In this regard, the object-oriented goal of C++ falls short of the mark.

Contrast these limitations of C++ with Java, which is capable of dynamically linking in new class libraries, methods, and instance variables at runtime, without fear of breaking the system. Java can also determine the type and capabilities of a class at runtime through a query, making it possible to either dynamically link in new classes or abort the mission altogether depending on the results of such queries. These abilities give Java programs a level of flexibility during execution not possible with most other programming languages.

# Java in a Nutshell

It's clear that the Java language is an extremely sophisticated and powerful new entry into the world of programming. It's also clear that the language is a perfect fit for the World Wide Web. But what's not so clear is where Java will be in a year or two.

Yes, it started off with tremendous momentum. The Web world is all wound up over Java's potential, and for good reason. Just the first few Java applets to hit the Web were impressive enough, beyond anything the Web had to offer by itself, and reams of even more impressive work have surfaced, and continue to do so, since the language moved from release to release. The fact that Java itself was used to create the HotJava browser proves that the language is capable of more than applets; it can also be used for full-blown applications.

But will it survive and become the next great programming language? Will it ever equal or overthrow C++ in terms of industry acceptance? Although this remains to be seen, Java 2 is clearly positioned to continue the technology's steady rise. For starters, it is based on technology that the next generation of software programs will require. Like it or not, we're moving into a networked world where distributed computing will become the norm. Today there is every indication that Java 2 is well on its way to becoming the de-facto standard for server-side application development. (A lot of commercial Web sites are built atop sever-side Java applications, and almost every serious Web server supports server-side Java as well.)

Java has everything it takes to make the transition from desktop to network-based computing a smooth one. It was built specifically for that, and it's clearly up to the task. However, the professional software development industry is slow to change and Java might not have had such a brilliant chance were it not easily learned by C++ programmers and had it not maintained compatibility with both C and C++.

The ability to use C and C++ within Java is very important. C++ succeeded where Objective C did not because C++ was backward compatible with the volumes of C code that programmers had spent years developing. Companies have a lot of time and effort represented in old code, not to mention money, and so it's to Java's benefit that it can coexist with legacy C/C++ source code.

# Java Versus C/C++

Java was developed to address the inadequacies of C++; perhaps now is the best time to take a look at the differences between Java and the C/C++ languages.First, remember that Java is closer to C++ than to C. It's a fully object-oriented language, while C is not. C++ maintained a backward compatibility with C, and in doing so, sacrificed the possibility of becoming a full-fledged object-oriented language.

Sure, C++ is more than capable in terms of object-oriented development, there's no denying that. Many people believe that C++ is the be-all-and-end-all of programming languages and they staunchly defend its position in the object-oriented programming world. But there are just as many, if not more, people who feel it falls short of being a true object-oriented language. In fact, that's exactly what prompted the development of Java; C++ just didn't cut it for Sun developers creating a next-generation consumer electronics platform. As a result, Java was born.

While the years-old debate over C++ and its viability as an OOP language rages, which I'm not eager to get into here, let's take a look at what Java does differently than C/C++.

## Data types

Java omits three key data types that C/C++ supports: pointers, unions, and structs (short for structure). Let's take a closer look at each.

### Pointers

Conventional wisdom insists that C and C++ programmers must become proficient in the use of pointers if they are to master these languages. Although pointers are no problem once you've spent the time learning how to use them and become comfortable with the nuances of their implementation, beginners often struggle greatly with them. Despite these difficulties, mastering the use of pointers made it possible for C/C++ programmers to directly access memory locations and infiltrate the innards of data structures.

Significantly, Java does away with pointers entirely, passing all arrays and objects by reference without the use of the pointer type at all. As a result, memory locations can't be infiltrated as they could (and often are) with C/C++. The lack of a pointer type makes it impossible for a program to accidentally, or intentionally, overwrite data at a location in memory. This makes for a much more secure and bug-free development experience, because the whole pointer-management process is eliminated.

### Unions and structs

Both union and struct data types are omitted from the Java language, immediately raising the question, "How can this be good?"

Although these types do not exist, the Java language provides similar functionality within the framework of an object. For example, a typical C/C++ struct needed to define the various fields of a book record used in an inventory control program might look something like this:

```
struct Book {
  char title[TITLESIZE];      // book name
  int pubCode;                // code to identify publisher
  char authLast[NAMESIZE];    // author's last name)
  long isbnCode;              // ISBN book code
  int quantity;               // number of books in stock
  double msrp;   // manufacturer's suggested retail price
  double (*calc_price)(double, double); // purchase price

};
```

Aside from the fact that this is a simple example, whereas lots of additional information might be included in a real implementation, the above structure is very typical of those found in many C/C++ implementations. (C++ developers will be quick to recognize that a struct in that language is actually implemented as a special case of a class.) The last line, in particular, is worth looking at:

```
double (*calc_price)(double, double);
```

This line of code is actually a pointer to a function. When the structure for a book is allocated and initialized, the programmer must supply one of these, as defined in the struct declaration. In our example, the `calc_price` function takes two doubles as arguments and returns a double that is the computed sale price of the book. Such a `calc_price` function might look like this:

```
double calc_price (double msrp, double discount) {
 /* calculate and return price based on discount percentage: */
return (msrp - (msrp*discount));
};
```

Here we have a struct that lays out the various fields to be used and a function that is used to calculate the sale prices, based on whatever the current discount percentage is. When a book record is allocated and initialized, the function pointer goes along with it:

```
main(){
struct Book JavaBible = {
 "Java 2 Bible", // title
 3435,            // publisher code
 "Walsh, Couch, Steinberg",   // author's last name
 4367758,         // ISBN code
 100,             // number in stock
 49.95,           // msrp
 calc_price       // pointer to a function
 };
}
```

Now, suppose the book was being sold at a discount of 15 percent. In C, the following line of code would perform the calculation and output the sale price:

```
printf("price = %f\n", JavaBible.calc_price (JavaBible.mspr,
    0.15));
```

This is all well and good, but what happens in Java, where structs don't exist?

In Java, classes (the code template from which objects are created) perform all the functionality of unions and structs, making those data types obsolete. In addition, classes in Java allow the programmer to write cleaner code that combines the *data* (the variables that describe the structure of the book) and *methods* (the routines that operate on the data; `calc_price`, in this case) in one unit, while providing a mechanism for keeping certain information private.

For instance, many fields of the book record shouldn't be available to routines other than those that have an absolute need to modify their content. With C, any field in the `Book` structure can be easily accessed and changed. This might seem like a good idea at first, but in reality, only certain pieces of code should have access to this private information. This is exactly what Java provides, as shown in Listing 1-1.

## Listing 1-1: **The Book class definition**

```
class Book {
  private String title;
  private int pubCode;
  private String authLast;
  private long isbnCode;
  private int quantity;
  private double msrp;

  double calc_price (double discount) {
   return (msrp - (msrp*discount));

   /* notice that this function is part of the
      class definition itself, and is not an
      external function, as with C */
  }

  // The "constructor" used to create and initialize an object
  // from this Book class follows:

  Book (String a_title, int a_code, String a_auth,
        long a_isbn, int a_quant, double a_msrp) {
    title = a_title;
    pubCode = a_code;
    authLast = a_auth;
    isbnCode = a_isbn;
```

```
        quantity = a_quant;
        msrp = a_msrp;
    }
}
```

What we have here is the same basic concept of a structure and the `calc_price` function, yet all bundled up into a single object. The `Book` class, the code template from which an object can be created when executed, not only describes all the data but also the routine `calc_price` previously residing outside the structure. Here, the routine is part of the object, an inherent part of the class. As such, it references the data element `msrp` directly to perform the calculation.

## Classes and methods

In Java, as with other OOP languages, we have declared what is known as a class (`Book`) and the method (`calc_price`) that goes along with it. You can think of a class as a template for creating objects, where an object is a variable created from a given class. Classes can include both data, known as instance variables, and the routines that operate on that data, known as methods. In the `Book` class example we've been working with, both data and methods are included in the declaration.

A number of standard instance variables (`title`, `pubCode`, `authLast`, `isbnCode`, `quantity`) have been declared, all of which are specified as being `private`. Since every variable in the `Book` class is private, objects other than those created from the original `Book` class cannot access them. This prevents the `Book` class variables from being accessed or modified without proper cause; it keeps this data safe and private, available only to those methods that should have access to it.

We've also included a second method that has the same name as the class itself (`Book`). Methods having the same name as the class they are part of are known as *constructors*, and they are invoked when a new object is created from that class. When put into action, a new `Book` object is instantiated from the class we created:

```
class MyClass {
    public static void main(String args[]) {
        Book bible = new Book("Java 2 Bible", 3435,
                              "Walsh, Couch, Steinberg",
                              4367758, 100, 49.95);
        System.out.println("Price = " + bible.calc_price(0.15));
    }
}
```

What we have with Java is functionally equivalent to what we had with structs and a separate `calc_price` routine, yet it's all within one easy-to-use chunk of code — the `Book` class!

Additionally, we've been able to create code that prevents unauthorized use of instance variables. This is easily seen in our example, as we can calculate the price of a book without having to access `msrp` directly. The `calc_price` method has access to the private `msrp` instance variable and performs the calculation for us without our having to reference this data directly. We simply feed the `calc_price` method a discount percentage and it does the rest.

No matter how many different `Book` objects are instantiated, we need to pass a discount amount only to the `calc_price` method for each. We don't have to bother accessing this value directly and are freed of the responsibility of keeping track of variables such as these. We let the object take care of itself, as it should.

## Operators

As you'll see in Chapter 7, Java supports almost all operators found in C, and the Java operators have the same precedence and associativity as their C counterparts. In addition, Java introduces several new operators:

+

>>>

& and |

instanceof

+

Although + may appear to be the arithmetic addition operator, when applied to strings, it is actually a concatenation operator. As you'll learn in Chapter 8, Java strings are objects that may be joined together (concatenated) with the + operator.

**Note**    Although it might appear that having two operators of the same name implies operator overloading, Java doesn't support overloading of operators as C++ does. The arithmetic + and string concatenation + operators are two completely different operators, each operating on its own data types.

### >>>

In Java, the >>> operator performs a right shift with sign extension. All integer values in Java are signed values. As a result, Java introduces a >>> operator that performs a right shift while treating the value on which it is operating as an unsigned value: bits are shifted right with zero sign extension.

### & and |

Although the & and | operators perform bitwise operations when applied to integral values (& performs a bitwise AND, | performs a bitwise OR), it's another story when these operators are applied to Boolean values. Unlike C/C++, where Boolean values may be treated as integral values, Java Booleans are actually objects that resolve to true or false. As a result, when these two operators are applied to Boolean values, logical operations are performed (& performs a logical AND, | performs a logical OR).

Java's logical & and | operators always evaluate both operands. They don't "short-circuit" when the result is known after evaluating only the left operand (as their C/C++ counterparts do). In cases where you want a short-circuit logical evaluation, use the && and || operators.

 **Note** Since pointers are not implemented in Java, the & (dereference) operator from C/C++ isn't supported. For that matter, neither is the * (reference) operator.

### instanceof

Java's instanceof operator is used to determine if an object was created from a specific class. (Objects and classes are explained in Chapter 2.)

 **Note** Although the instanceof operator may conjure up fond memories of a similar-sounding operator found in C/C++, Java doesn't support sizeof. You'll also note that, unlike C/C++, Java doesn't support the comma operator to combine two expressions into one, except in a very limited fashion in the conditional portion of for loops, as discussed in Chapter 7.

## Command-line arguments

*Command-line arguments* are those arguments sent to an application program when it is invoked from, you guessed it, the command line. For instance, when you are at the DOS prompt in a DOS environment, you execute a program by typing the name of the program (where > is the command line prompt):

```
> crunch
```

In this example, the program named crunch would be executed. We've simply typed the program name at the command prompt and pressed Enter. The program, if available, is executed. Let's say, for illustrative purposes, that crunch takes two files and compresses them into a single file. How do we specify which files to compress and the name of the file that would result? Since we didn't provide command-line arguments, crunch might prompt us for the names of each when it is executed:

```
> crunch
    First File to crunch: fileone
    Second File to crunch: filetwo
    Compress and save as: mycrunch
```

This is fairly straightforward, since crunch prompted us for the name of each file to compress and the name of the file to save the compressed files into. Here, we'd expect the file mycrunch to contain our crunched files, when all is said and done.

But what if we didn't want to bother with these prompts and knew right from the beginning which files to compress? If crunch supported command-line arguments, we could supply these names at the same time as we execute the program:

```
> crunch fileone filetwo mycrunch
```

Upon executing, crunch would see that the file names had been specified as command-line arguments and bypass further prompting altogether. The result would be the same as if we had manually entered the names at each prompt, although the use of command-line arguments makes the process a little faster, since we don't have to bother typing these three file names upon executing.

Some programs expect all user input to come directly from the command line at execution time and don't bother to prompt you for information if it has been omitted from the command line. These programs simply return an error message, if even that, to let you know they were unable to complete the job successfully.

So how does a program such as crunch get these command-line arguments and make use of them? In C/C++, the operating system passes them directly to the program through the use of argument variables:

argc    A numeric value that specifies the total number of arguments appearing on the command line

argv    A pointer to an array of strings containing the arguments

In C/C++, the operating system passes the entire command line as arguments to the program, including the name of the program itself. In our example, then, the first argument in the argv parameter would be crunch. But Java is a little different; in Java, only one parameter is passed to the executable:

args    An array of strings that contain the arguments

The args parameter is simply an array containing the command-line arguments. Rather than bothering with two parameters, as C/C++ does, Java only needs this one.

But how does the Java program know how many parameters are included, since only an array is passed, without the benefit of an argc parameter? It's simple: arrays in Java include a length variable that can be used to extract the number of arguments in the array itself, eliminating the need for an argc parameter:

```
args.length  /* retrieve the number of elements
                stored in the "args" array */
```

Another difference between Java and C/C++ command-line arguments is seen in the content of the argument array. Where the C/C++ argv parameter contains the name of the program itself, such as crunch, Java's args parameter contains only the command-line arguments (such as fileone, filetwo, and mycrunch, in our crunch example). In Java, the name of the application being invoked is the same as the name of the initial class executed where the main method is defined. (It is possible for several classes to contain a main method.) As a result, Java already knows the name of the program being executed and doesn't need to be told this explicitly, as it does with C/C++. The Java runtime environment just passes along the command-line arguments, and that's enough. (See Chapter 8 for more details.)

## Strings

In C/C++, strings are really nothing more than a null-terminated (/n) array of characters. But in Java, they are first-class objects. Actually, two classes exist for strings, String and StringBuffer (both of which are discussed in Chapter 8). Java strings offer four main advantages over C/C++ strings:

✦ Consistency: As objects, the manner in which strings are obtained and their elements accessed is consistent across all strings and all systems.

✦ Predictability: Java strings function predictably every time, thanks to well-defined programming interfaces for both the String and StringBuffer classes.

✦ Reliability: String and StringBuffer classes perform extensive testing for boundary conditions at runtime, catching errors before they become a real problem.

✦ Localization of text: Strings consist of Unicode characters, which makes localization of text transparent.

Java strings are covered in more detail in Chapter 8, but for now, it's worth noting that strings have always caused difficulty for C/C++ programmers. Because strings are such an important part of any programming language, Java makes it possible to use them to their fullest extent without the difficulties often encountered with C/C++.

**Note** The Java String class is used to represent strings that will not change. StringBuffer, on the other hand, is specifically for strings that will change during the course of program execution.

## Comments

Java supports both C and C++ style comments, in addition to an altogether new comment syntax. Here's a brief example of the three types of comments you can use in Java:

```
int i; /* this is the ANSI-C style comment */
int i; // this is the C++ style, limited to one line
int i; /** And here's a completely new comment syntax! Notice
that this comment begins with a slash and two asterisk
characters and can span many lines, just as with ANSI-C
comments. But what's the difference, besides the extra
asterisk at the beginning of this comment? */
```

Although Java supports both C and C++ comments, it also introduces a special type of comment that does just what any comment does. It tells the compiler (or interpreter) to ignore everything inside the comment, since it's there only to help people make sense of the code.

Besides functioning as a regular comment, this new comment serves a special purpose — automatic documentation generation. That's right — documentation generated automatically from comments. This documentation is created as a series of HTML files that not only help document your programs, but also show the hierarchy of your code in relation to the larger system of Java classes! (See Figure 1-5.) And since it's in the HTML format, you can navigate through this documentation just as you would any other Web page. All thanks to an odd-looking comment.

This special type of comment, formally known as a *documentation comment* (or "doc comment"), is often found at the beginning of class and method definitions to assist in the creation of code documentation. In addition, doc comments can be applied to variables.

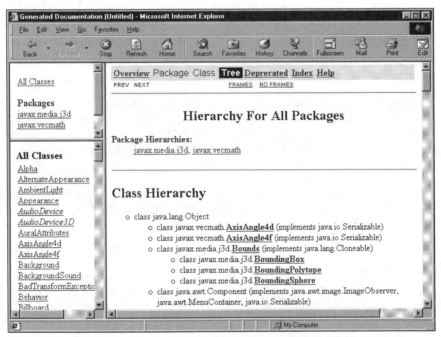

**Figure 1-5:** Documentation automatically generated from a documentation comment, showing this class in relation to others in the system

With doc comments, you use /** to indicate that what comes between it and the closing */ should be treated as documentation when encountered by the javadoc tool. (javadoc is one of the many tools that come with Sun's Java SDK) You can embed special documentation tags (doc tags), which begin with the @ character, within doc comments to further extend the automatic document generation performed by javadoc:

```
/**
 * A bogus class definition whose only purpose is to show
 * the format of doc comments and doc tags in action:
 * @version    1.0 August 2000
 * @author     Aaron E. Walsh
 */
class BogusClass {
...
}
```

When run through the javadoc tool, the previous comment would generate documentation with an associated version and author entries. Doc comments and doc tags can be a great help when you're documenting software developed with Java. For details on using doc comments, point your browser to:

```
http://java.sun.com/products/jdk/javadoc/writingdoccomments.html
```

## Odds 'n ends

Although we've discussed the most obvious areas where Java differs from C and C++, there are a few other points you'll want to be aware of when making the transition to Java:

✦ Through a mechanism known as *varargs*, C and C++ provide for a variable number of arguments to be passed to a function. This is not supported with Java; arguments in Java are passed into a single string array (args) whose length variable can be used to determine the number of elements it contains (args.length).

✦ Although goto is a reserved word in Java, it is not implemented or supported.

✦ Boolean data types are true literals in Java, not a representation of the integers 0 and 1, as they are in C and C++. Java Boolean data types, therefore, cannot be typecast into integers. (A Java type "wrapper" must be used instead, as explained in Chapter 8.)

✦ #define and #include (preprocessor mechanisms) are not available in Java, although they are available in C and C++.

✦ Java does not provide enumerated primitive types.

These odds and ends, and those detailed previously, sum up the differences between the Java and the C/C++ languages. However, there are a number of areas where Java and these languages are similar.

To make the transition from either C or C++ relatively easy, Java maintains a lot of the look and feel of those languages. For instance, the style of Java programs (such as the use of whitespace, comments, and grouping of code) is much the same as in C and C++. Just as with C/C++, whitespace and comments (with the exception of doc comments) are ignored by Java altogether and are used only to make code more readable to human beings. For instance, the example Book class we created earlier could just have easily been written without whitespace and comments:

```
class Book {String title;int pubCode;String authLast;long
isbnCode;int quantity;private double msrp;double calc_price
(double discount) {return (msrp-(msrp*discount));} Book(String
a_title, int a_code, String a_auth, long a_isbn, int a_quant,
double a_msrp){title=a_title;pubCode=a_code;authLast=
a_auth;isbnCode = a_isbn; quantity=a_quant; msrp=a_msrp;}}
```

Although this makes for ugly reading to you and me, Java doesn't care. For that matter, neither does C or C++. White space and comments simply make the code more understandable and prettier to look at for our sake.

Another point you'll notice immediately about Java, which it shares with C/C++, is case sensitivity. Case matters, so you have to pay special attention to exactly how you mix and match upper- and lowercase letters in class, method, and variable names. For instance, the variable myJavaThing is not the same as MyJavaThing.

And while we're on the subject, it's worth noting that classes are typically capitalized, but variables, methods, and objects are not. This is merely a convention of Java (one also seen in C++), so you can in fact do whatever you want when it comes to capitalization. However, in the interest of code readability and maintenance, it's better to stick to the conventional way of doing things.

C/C++ programmers will also find comfort in the way Java code is arranged. As with C/C++, you usually indent statements to reflect their hierarchy within a block of code, and you balance curly braces ({ }) to show the nesting of functions.

With Java, you make your code more readable by using curly braces to separate blocks of code and semicolons to separate statements. These conventions should be familiar to C/C++ programmers.

These factors, taken together, make the Java language enough like C++ in both syntax and the implementation of object-oriented devices (such as classes, methods, objects, and inheritance) that C++ programmers will have little problem leaping feet first into it.

C programmers, on the other hand, must first become comfortable with the entire object-oriented approach to software development—which is discussed in detail in Chapter 2.

# Summary

Sun's Java technology consists of the Java language, a runtime environment, and a suite of software development tools that you'll use to create programs throughout the remainder of this book. The Java language is simple, object-oriented, distributed, interpreted, robust, secure, architecture-neutral, portable, multithreaded, dynamic, and capable of high performance. The runtime environment is a combination of a Virtual Machine specification and an extensive collection of premade libraries (the Java class libraries, also known as the Java API) that together can run Java programs.

✦ Java-savvy browsers are the most common form of runtime environment, although they are capable of running only Java applets (special-purpose Java programs that are woven into Web pages). To run Java applications (standalone Java programs that run on the desktop, independent of the Web), a different type of runtime environment is needed, such as the runtime provided for free in Sun's Java 2 SDK.

✦ The Java language is similar to C and C++ in many ways, yet it is an entirely object-oriented language, whereas C and C++ are not. C++ is close, but not entirely object-oriented in the way Java is. C, on the other hand, is a procedural programming language that has a similar syntax to Java, although it is not object-oriented in the least. Similar to other object-oriented languages, Java classes are source code templates that define objects. Objects, in turn, can be considered the "live" bundles of code that contain both data and routines that operate on that data.

✦    ✦    ✦

# Object-Oriented Programming and Terminology

**B**ecause Java is an object-oriented programming (OOP) language, it only makes sense for us to take time to find out what that means. If you are a programmer already experienced with object-oriented concepts and terminology, you may choose to skim this chapter and refresh your memory, or skip it altogether, depending on your comfort level with the topic. Or, you may want to devote some serious time to the following material. This chapter provides the keys to fully unlocking Java's potential, for, without a solid understanding of object-oriented programming, making sense of this new language is next to impossible.

If you are new to object-oriented programming, you may become overwhelmed by the end of this chapter. Hyperventilation is understandable, if not expected, because so many of the concepts found in the object-oriented world run counter to the way you're normally taught to program. If you're new to OOP, I'd suggest taking a moment to search the Web for Java-related information, such as is available at Sun's Java site (http://java.sun.com/), IDG's Java World (http://www.javaworld.com), or Gamelan (http://www.gamelan.com), followed by a quick trip to your local library or bookstore. By all means, proceed with this book, but while you're at it, take the time to learn more about object-oriented programming. This type of programming is a very different approach to software development than most of us have experienced before. You've probably spent a great amount of time learning procedural programming languages such as Pascal and C, which are not object-oriented, and that makes it extremely difficult to think of software development from this new perspective.

Despite the fact that object-oriented programming is over 30 years old, originating with the Simula67 language introduced in 1967 and later popularized by the SmallTalk language, the term *object-oriented programming* has been misused and misunderstood since it was first coined, and it continues to be a source of confusion even today.

Several schools of thought exist regarding what OOP is and what constitutes a "real" object-oriented programming language — these are the result of programmers trying to make sense of and establish a standard way of defining the term. In fact, in professional software engineering circles, the term *object-oriented programming* represents only one portion of a much larger software development process. In this sense, OOP refers to the actual implementation in code that comes after the processes of *object-oriented analysis* (OOA) and *object-oriented design* (OOD) have been completed.

Although object-oriented concepts and terminology aren't very difficult to learn on a superficial level, it takes time for the principles to sink in, to settle, to become a natural part of our thinking. Because of this, some observers claim that learning the object-oriented approach is overly difficult and not worth the effort. Such thinking is a shame, because the potential benefits are tremendous. Anything worth learning usually takes a bit of effort, and OOP is no exception.

But fear not — I won't attempt to turn you into a master of the art of object-oriented programming, nor will I introduce highly technical concepts and terminology here. And I only briefly discuss OOP as a part of object-oriented analysis and object-oriented design; a number of books dedicate themselves entirely to these subjects. Instead, I attempt to give you a clear understanding of OOP as it relates to the task at hand — learning Java. As you'll soon see, the rewards are great and the effort is relatively small, once you understand the basic concepts we're about to explore.

# What Can You Expect from This Chapter?

How are objects created? How are messages sent? How does encapsulation work? These are some of the questions this chapter answers. Objects, messages, and encapsulation are just a few of the terms covered here. As we proceed from term to term, concept to concept, I'll try to maintain a vein of continuity — a theme of learning:

1. After talking about objects, I'll plunge directly into *abstraction*, a way of thinking that's crucial to our ability to properly define objects.

2. Abstraction is followed by a look at the state and behavior of an object, known in Java terminology as *data* and *methods*.

3. After exploring the internal workings of objects, I take a closer look at *encapsulation*, the interface each object has and the messages objects send to each other.

4. Next, I'll ease into *modularity*, which lets us change the internal data of an object using a black-box approach, and *classification*, which lets us define the external properties of objects.

5. Finally, I'll take a look at *inheritance* — a powerful OOP capability that lets you use existing objects to construct new ones.

Keep in mind that the concepts we'll cover are not unique to Java; they are fundamental to the practice of object-oriented software development. However, although the concepts are the same, the actual terms vary among languages. For instance, in Java the behavior of an object is implemented using *methods*, while C++ calls them *member functions*.

Because this book focuses on Java, I present all object-oriented terms and concepts to you as they are formally known in the Java language. And because I suspect that the majority of people reading this have had experience with C and/or C++, I will point out similarities between Java's object-oriented implementation and those languages as much as possible.

# Object-Oriented Terminology

Superficially, *object-oriented* means nothing more than looking at the world in terms of objects. In life, we are surrounded by objects: clothes, dishes, appliances, pets, cars, bikes, computers, friends, neighbors, and so on (see Figure 2-1).

**Figure 2-1:** In life, we are surrounded by objects.

Each of these objects has traits that we use to identify them. For instance, my cat is a black shorthair with a white crest on his chest. Harley can further be identified by his green eyes and the extra two toes he has on each paw. (That's right, seven toes per paw — it looks a little funny but doesn't seem to bother him.)

Harley is also incessantly hungry, no matter how often I feed the little fellow. The fact that he's hungry helps identify him. When a friend drops by for lunch, it's not uncommon for me to say, "Keep your eyes on your sandwich or the hungry one will get to it." By saying "the hungry one," I've identified Harley as opposed to Bennett, the other cat likely to be rubbing up against my guest's leg.

While I'm at it, allow me to identify the Bennett object also. Bennett is the yin to Harley's yang: she's pure white, has blue eyes, and the softest fur I've ever known a cat to have. She's sweet and gentle, whereas Harley's a holy terror. Bennett prefers to snuggle up and sleep on my chest while the hungry one holds the rest of the house hostage in search of food.

Interesting, perhaps, but what do my cats have to do with object-oriented programming?

What I've done is identify two objects according to what they look like and how they act. How about another rousing example?

I live in a city, so two more objects I deal with every day are the subway train and/or the taxicab I take to work. The subway train object is underground, about 200 feet long, and holds about 100 people in each of its many sections. It is slow, noisy, and not very comfortable, but it is relatively inexpensive to ride to work. A taxicab, on the other hand, is about 12 feet long, runs above ground on four wheels, holds only me and the driver, and is fast, quiet, and comfortable by comparison. Unfortunately, the cost of a taxi ride to the office is about ten times that of the train.

Fascinating, huh? Well, not really, but the point is that I'm able to easily identify objects by their traits. In object-oriented programming, the object is essential. It is the focus of the entire process and the cause for much confusion among procedural programmers. Procedural programmers are accustomed to writing *procedures* (also known as functions or routines) that act upon, or manipulate, data. They do not think in terms of objects because they don't need to. But in object-oriented programming, the object is at the heart of everything.

Object-oriented programmers look at the world in terms of objects. They see how objects look, how they act, and how they interact with other objects. When developing software, they create entities in code known as *objects*. These code objects contain traits, just as their real-world counterparts do.

As with real-life objects, programming objects contain details that list their characteristics. The object Harley, for instance, could contain the following details:

✦ Has short, black hair

✦ Has white crest on his chest

✦ Has green eyes

✦ Has four legs

✦ Has seven toes per paw

✦ Is always hungry

✦ Eats Whiskas Seaside Supper

✦ Sleeps on the bed

✦ Jumps from couch to table

✦ Scratches the curtains . . .

Clearly, this list could go on forever—the number of his whiskers, his length, shape, medical history, and so on. What we have to do is *abstract* the data we think will be relevant.

Just as the preceding list enables us to identify the object Harley, software objects contain details that define how they appear, what knowledge they contain, and how they behave. The purpose of software objects is to combine data (regarding appearance and knowledge) and behavior into a nifty package, just as objects in the real world do.

Software objects have special names for these traits: *state* and *behavior*. We will consider this distinction in a moment, but let's first turn to the need for abstraction.

## Abstraction

"Everything essential and nothing more" is about the cleanest definition of *abstraction* I can think of. Consider Harley. His essential functions are eating, sleeping, and creating chaos; everything else is merely a detail that gets those functions done.

Humans are great at abstraction; as Figure 2-2 illustrates, it's something we do naturally. When I hop in the driver's seat of my car, I don't think about the power train, axle, tires, radiator, engine, fan belt, and all the other things that make it possible for me to drive. Heck no, I think about the essential function of the car—to get me from A to B—as I whip down the back streets and open roads of Boston.

Not having to consider the finer details of my car's inner workings enables me to concentrate on the tasks at hand — driving and keeping my eyes peeled for traffic cops. Abstraction enables me to focus on the essential and ignore the nonessential. It frees me to think of the bigger picture.

**Figure 2-2:** Abstraction is part of human nature.

When creating software objects, we must apply this principle of abstraction. We must consider what the essence of each object is and not think at all about the details of implementation or other elements that distract from the process.

Even though we do it in the course of our everyday lives, abstraction can be difficult to do consciously if we're accustomed to thinking in terms of procedural programming. But without abstraction, our objects will be stuffed full of data and behavior that doesn't really belong there. Ideally, during the process of abstraction, we don't even consider implementation. We focus on the objects involved in solving a problem and their relation to one another long before the details of coding become important. Indeed, software objects enable us to model problems more closely, because problems are made up of either real or conceptual objects.

To define an object, we must first identify the essential functions of the object and then select only the data relevant to those functions. In Harley's case, he has three distinct functions: eating, sleeping, and creating mayhem. Accordingly, I can abstract details essential to those functions and reject the rest:

✦ Is always hungry

✦ Eats Whiskas Seaside Supper

✦ Sleeps on the bed

✦ Jumps from couch to table

✦ Scratches the curtains

Through the process of abstraction, we can easily identify objects by their most essential traits, as illustrated in Figure 2-3.

• Always hungry
• Eats Whiskas Seaside Supper
• Sleeps on the bed
• Jumps from couch to table
• Scratches the curtains

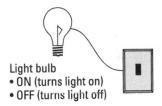

Light bulb
• ON (turns light on)
• OFF (turns light off)

• Holds about 100 people
• Noisy
• Uncomfortable
• Slow
• Inexpensive

• Comfortable
• Holds few people
• Fast
• Expensive

**Figure 2-3:** Identifying objects by their traits

# Combining state and behavior

A key concept of object-oriented programming is the capability to represent both data and the functions that operate on that data in one software bundle known as an object. By placing all data and the functions that operate on it inside a bundle of code, we create something unique. The data and functions that make up a software object are known as state and behavior.

Looking at the essential details of Harley, for example, both state and behavior emerge. But it's not just Harley we need to consider; every object contains state and behavior:

✦ State is what the object knows or looks like. In the case of a cat object, the state is its fur color and texture, eye color, breed, personality, and so on.

✦ Behavior, on the other hand, is how the object acts. Meowing, scratching, rubbing, begging for food, and the like are examples of behavior.

Although an object's state and behavior change over time, together they form the identity of that object, as you can see in Figure 2-4.

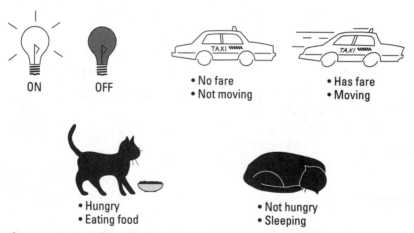

ON          OFF          • No fare          • Has fare
                         • Not moving       • Moving

• Hungry          • Not hungry
• Eating food     • Sleeping

**Figure 2-4:** Together, an object's state and behavior identify it.

Objects contain only state and behavior that are appropriate for them. For instance, a cat object doesn't have any need to understand how much to charge for every mile it travels, although this is an essential capability of every taxicab object. The cat object contains only those characteristics that apply to a cat, while the taxicab object contains only those that apply to a taxicab. They are *self-contained*.

Figure 2-5 shows a generic way to illustrate objects. This representation is intentionally amorphous — a blob of information containing state on the inside surrounded by behavior. Although a number of techniques are possible for illustrating objects, I chose this one because it is clean, simple, and easy to understand. The idea is that state is hidden from the outside world, something only the object itself can change. An object's behavior, in fact, is the only mechanism that can alter that object's state. In this sense, state is protected.

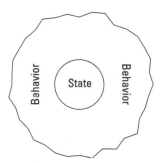

**Figure 2-5:** State is hidden from the rest of the world; only the behavior of the object can change it.

For instance, if Harley is hungry, only when he eats will the feeling of hunger subside. Yes, his ability to get food depends on other factors too, but in the final analysis, it's his behavior that changes his state. If he doesn't eat, he'll stay hungry. If he eats, the state of hunger is transformed into a state of comfort. From an OOP perspective, only Harley can change his state.

## Data and methods

In Java, an object's state consists of *data* (such as constants and variables), while behavior is implemented as functions called *methods* (see Figure 2-6). The combination of data and methods together maintains state and behavior. The idea of data and methods is nothing new, although you're probably accustomed to using the term *procedure*, *function*, or *routine* rather than the term *method*.

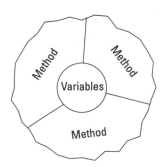

**Figure 2-6:** An object consists of data and methods.

The only new concept here is the terminology and how data and methods are combined together into a single, self-contained bundle of live code known as an object. I use the term *live* to distinguish objects from the source code templates known as classes from which they are created, as you'll learn later.

Procedural programmers are used to writing functions that sit out in the open, to be called upon whenever needed; whereas, object-oriented programmers embed those functions inside objects. Say, for example, that you were to write a procedural program in any language that modeled the behavior of Harley. After you got over the shock of being asked to write a program simulating my cat, you'd probably start by spending a few moments thinking about him.

You know he has fur and that it's of a specific color. You also know he has four legs, each having a paw with seven toes. (Some of you may think this is the mark of the devil, and after living with this little monster for the past few years, so do I — but that's another story.)

After thinking about it for a while, you'd realize that only some of the possible data really apply to the simulation. Variables such as `hungry`, `thirsty`, `awake`, `asleep`, and the like are more closely related to Harley's behavior than are the purely physical ones. You might write them down on a piece of paper or type them into your computer.

In fact, you'd probably start coding right off the bat, perhaps beginning with the global variables that apply to Harley. Maybe you'd combine them into a data structure for the sake of convenience, maybe not. You'd then consider the conditions or events in Harley's life that affect this data. For instance, when he's hungry, he eats. After he eats, he becomes sleepy and eventually finds a warm spot to snooze while his food digests. Upon waking, he has a burst of energy and burns up the food by running around the house, leaping from chair to couch to kitchen table like a lunatic — at which point he becomes hungry again. Come to think of it, that's *all* Harley ever does. . . .

In a procedural world, you would write a bunch of functions (the equivalent of object methods) that could be called from anywhere as needed, including `Eat()`, `Sleep()`, and `GoCrazy()`, each capable of altering the global data or data passed in when called. In effect, you would be creating each procedure in Harley's life that applies to this simulation. In the end, you would have a bunch of data (global variables, local variables, data structures, or a combination of each) and a bunch of functions. You'd also have an event loop of some sort that runs continually, calling functions such as `Eat()` as specific events are encountered or when conditions such as `Hungry=TRUE` trigger such actions.

In an object-oriented approach, you spend much less time writing code and a whole lot more time defining the objects themselves. You think about Harley in terms of an object, attempting to model your code after him as closely as possible. In this sense, he isn't a collection of data and routines residing in different files. As Figure 2-7 demonstrates, you create an object containing all data and methods having to do with him.

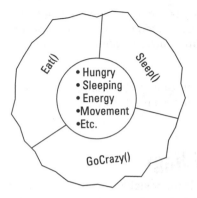

**Figure 2-7:** We define the object's data and methods.

OOP is therefore unlike procedural programming, where data can be accessed and modified by any function. Instead, data residing inside an object is surrounded by the methods of that object, protected from direct manipulation (a feature known as encapsulation, as you'll learn in the next section).

To manipulate the data of an object, you must send it a *message* requesting that the object invoke, or run, one of its own methods. In Java, methods consist of three parts:

✦ The name of the object to receive the message

✦ The name of the method to execute

✦ Optional parameters required by the method

In the case of my troublesome feline, the name of the object is

```
Harley
```

the name of the method to execute is

```
eat
```

and the parameter required by the method is

```
catfood
```

Taken all together, Harley's method would be invoked as follows:

```
Harley.eat(catfood);
```

The preceding line of code illustrates the use of *dot notation*, and it is similar to how a C programmer would access an element in a data structure. A period, or *dot*, is used to separate the object name (appearing to the left of the dot) from the method and any parameters it may require (which together comprise the message being sent to the object). Here, when the object Harley receives the message `eat catfood`, his `eat` method is invoked with `catfood` as a parameter. In Java, as with other object-oriented languages, dot notation is the standard mechanism for executing methods inside objects.

As mentioned previously, only the methods of an object can change that object's data. This powerful concept is called encapsulation, and it is central to object-oriented programming.

## Encapsulation (information hiding)

The idea of hiding data inside an object, making it unavailable to anything but that object's methods, is known as *encapsulation* (also called *information hiding*). Encapsulation extends to the implementation of methods themselves, meaning that the details of an object's inner workings are never available to anything but the object itself.

Encapsulation is very powerful because it permits objects to operate completely independently of each other as discrete, self-contained bundles of data and code. The only way to access information in an object is through its methods; these form an *interface* (see the next section) that remains consistent to the world outside of the object.

But encapsulation doesn't apply only to data; it also pertains to the implementation details of the methods themselves, without concern for other objects (and frequently comes into play as such routines are optimized, updated to fix bugs, or rewritten altogether). Because objects have an interface through which they communicate, the underlying data and implementation details are hidden and protected. Thanks to encapsulation, both data and implementation can change without breaking the system. In fact, entire objects can be replaced with new objects, assuming the interface of each new object is the same as that of the object it replaces.

Encapsulation prevents objects from becoming dependent on each other's inner details, which is desirable because otherwise small changes in an object might cause tremendous damage to a program if such changes were to break the interface replied on by other parts of the system. Bug fixes, code optimization, and entire code rewrites are possible because encapsulation allows such alterations to take place without disrupting communication between the object being updated and other objects in a system.

Think of encapsulation in terms of your computer. When you upgrade the hard disk, RAM, or the CPU, you don't have to worry about how upgrading affects your ability to interact with your system. Sure, it will have more storage capacity, be able to run more programs at the same time, and be faster; that's why you upgraded. But you don't depend on the internals of your computer to interact with it. You can swap these out as needed without disturbing other parts of the system and causing your computer to come to a grinding halt. This is the power of encapsulation; the internal details of objects are hidden so that their underlying implementation can change without breaking the system.

Encapsulation makes it possible for you to treat objects like discrete "black boxes." Each object serves a specific purpose, and you don't have to be concerned about internal implementation. Conceptually, information goes in one end of a black box and comes out the other. We don't know or care what's going on inside; we only know what we can put into the box and what it will give back, as illustrated in Figure 2-8.

**Figure 2-8:** Encapsulation enables objects to be treated like discrete black boxes.

We can string together any number of black boxes, each performing a specific task, to build as large and complex a system as we need. And, thanks to encapsulation, we can even tinker with the internals of any black box without crashing the works. Better yet, we can replace whole black boxes with better black boxes as they are developed. The entire system is modular, much like the internals of the computer itself (see Figure 2-9).

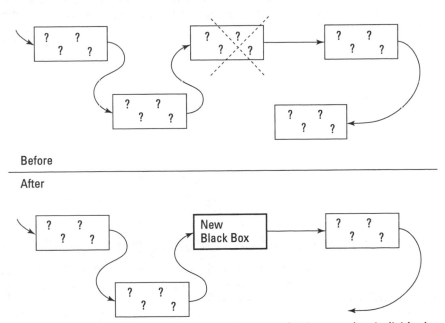

**Figure 2-9:** Encapsulation enables us to change and string together individual objects with a great deal of freedom.

# Interfaces

Software objects are complex on the inside, just as their real-world counterparts are. On the outside, however, software objects are uncomplicated. They provide a simple interface, or means of access, to their data and behavior, through which other objects can interact with them. Think for a moment of a television set. Inside, it's a mess of electrical components: a picture tube, one or more speakers, and all kinds of stuff I have no idea how to deal with. But thanks to my remote control, I don't need to know anything about the complex innards to enjoy using it.

My remote control is the interface to my television, enabling me to communicate with it. I can turn it off or on, change channels, turn the volume up or down, and even adjust the picture's horizontal and vertical holds, tint, and hue (fancy remote, huh?). With the remote control, which is itself an object (for which the buttons are the interface), I am able to get functionality from my television without messing around with the guts of the system.

Objects interact with each other through similar interfaces all the time. One object produces a response in reaction to the messages it gets from another object. This is just like my cat. Opening a can of cat food and putting it in front of Harley's face triggers specific behavior. Objects send messages to each other, setting off behavior, as shown in Figure 2-10. Using dot notation, as explained in the "Data and methods" section earlier in this chapter, a good deal of the Java code you write involves sending messages to objects.

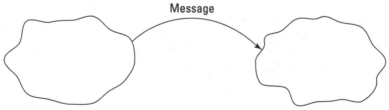

**Figure 2-10:** Objects trigger behavior between each other by sending messages.

# Messages: objects communicating with objects

With a software program full of objects, each able to access and modify only its own data through its own methods, how does anything ever get done? After all, it does begin to sound as if we have a bunch of well-defined entities that are very lonely in the world, capable of interacting only with themselves. A highly introspective, if not entirely isolated, group of software objects, yes?

No. Objects aren't ships lost at sea, out of radio contact. They have the ability to send messages to one another, thereby triggering the execution of methods inside each other, as Figure 2-11 demonstrates.

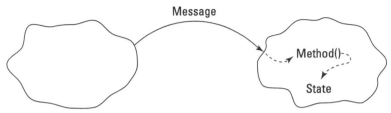

**Figure 2-11:** A message sent from one object to another triggers a method inside the target object.

Think of a microwave oven. In and of itself, your microwave doesn't do much but sit there waiting to be called into action. When you want to heat up some food, you put the food inside and close the door. You then send the microwave a message, such as "Heat for two minutes at full power," by pressing the appropriate buttons on the front. Because you're using the interface provided with the microwave—the buttons on the front—your message is understood and carried out. In OOP lingo, you are one object sending another object a message through that object's well-defined interface.

You must send messages in accordance with the interface of an object or your message won't be understood. For instance, you might try using your television's remote control on the microwave and send the message "Change to Channel 25 and turn up the volume," but you'll wait an awfully long time before "The X Files" appears!

In object-oriented programming, objects are constantly communicating with each other through a complex web of messages, as illustrated in Figure 2-12. Not only are the messages sent by objects able to trigger the execution of methods inside other objects, but they can also contain parameters that those methods require.

Following our television analogy, sending the message "Change station to Channel 25" to the television object might look something like this in Java code:

```
Television.changeStation(25);
```

The television object, Television, receives the message changeStation with the number 25 as a parameter. The period, or dot, separating the object and message is intentional. In most object-oriented languages, as with Java, the object receiving the message is on the left and the message is on the right. The dot sits between the object and the message, with no spaces, and in effect, says, "Send the message on my right to the object on my left."

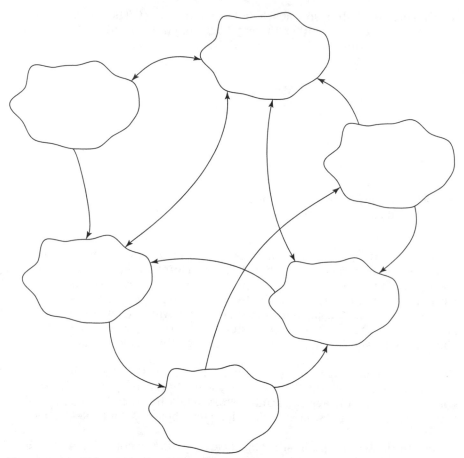

**Figure 2-12:** Objects weave a complex web of messages to communicate with each other.

In our example, keep in mind that messages contain the name of the method to execute. When the object `Television` receives a message such as the one illustrated, it looks inside itself for a method named `changeStation`. If such a method exists, it is executed, with a value of 25 as the parameter.

The beautiful thing about messages is that they are generic, in the sense that any object can send a message to any other object, even if they exist in different programs or on entirely different computer systems. Objects existing on the Internet halfway around the world can send and receive messages to or from any other objects over the Internet. This is the capability that makes distributed objects possible, and you will see it more and more as software programs begin to "live" on networks.

# Modularity

We have seen that objects are self-contained bundles of live code that encapsulate both data and methods and that they can send messages to each other through interfaces. Because data and behavior are neatly packaged inside objects, and because the only way to access data is through the interface defined by the methods, you can change the internal workings of an object without breaking the rest of the system. The result is a major benefit to the software developer: *modularity*.

Modularity is based on discrete programming objects, which you can change without affecting the system as a whole, and it is greatly enhanced by encapsulation. You develop and maintain each object's source code independently of other objects, and the only way to access and change information inside an object is through methods. This represents true code modularity.

Not only can you change the implementation details of an object without affecting any other part of the system, but you can replace or rewrite entire objects from the ground up as long as the interface doesn't change or inheritance isn't abused in the method. (See "Inheritance" later in this chapter.)

Think of it in terms of electrical wiring. Each wire in an electrical system is connected to the others in a predefined way: it has an interface. These interfaces differ (wall sockets, adapters, surge protectors, and so on), but each piece of wiring has one. Additionally, each wire is designed to fit perfectly within the context of the system as a whole. It is created with a special purpose in mind, reflected in its length, material, and type of interface.

When a wire breaks or begins to corrode and to perish, an electrician comes to the rescue. He or she locates the piece of the system causing the problem and replaces it with another; no muss, no fuss. Assuming our electrician has the wire needed, it's replaced then and there. One wire is removed and another put in its place. Because the interface for the wires is consistent, the process is simple and painless.

Our electrician doesn't have to worry about creating a wire from scratch; he or she can rely on one having been created specifically for the job. This is the beauty of modularity, be it in electrical wiring or software development: You can yank out one part and put in another without bringing down the whole system (see Figure 2-13).

# Classification

*Classification*, grouping items according to how they look and act, is another key concept in object-oriented programming. In the real world, everything is classified. We categorize what we know about into classes to help us better understand and remember what their general properties are. Cadillacs are in the automobile class, ferns are in the Filicales class, trout are in the Salmonidae class, and we are in the Homo sapiens class.

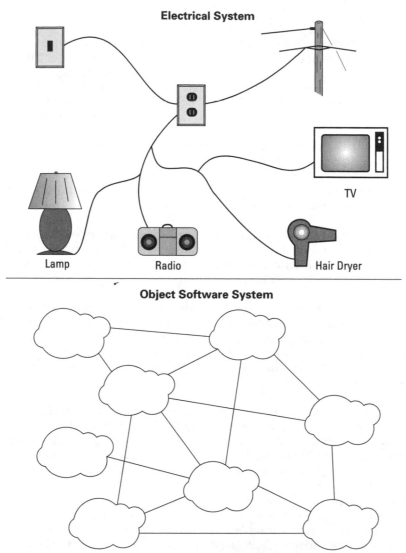

**Figure 2-13:** An object-oriented software system is as modular as an electrical system in a house.

In object-oriented programming we classify those items that we know about as well. Specifically, we classify objects. We group them into classes according to their characteristics. Classes and objects go hand in hand and are so similar that programmers often use the two terms interchangeably. You'll find a distinct difference between them, however.

*Classes* are the blueprints, the source-code templates from which *objects* are created. You can see this in Figure 2-14. These blueprints contain all of the programming code describing state and behavior, meaning classes define all the data and methods an object will possess.

**Generic Class Template**

```
class Name {
   ...Variables...
   ...
   ...
   Method() {
   ...Variables...
   }
   Method() {
   ...Variables...
   }
   Method() {
   ...Variables...
   }
   }
```

**Figure 2-14:** Classes are the code templates from which objects are created.

**Generic Object**

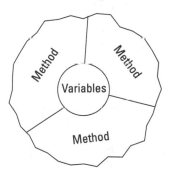

When we think of objects, we tend to think of conceptual entities that contain both state and behavior and are able to communicate by way of messages. Objects don't magically appear, however. We must, in fact, create the class that acts as the code template for our objects. We can also use any of the classes provided by Java, for which the code has already been written — all we have to do is use it.

**Note**  Java ships with a very large library of prebuilt classes (formally known as the Java class library) that are organized into *packages*, as described in later chapters. Using the Java class library, you can instantly add sophisticated features to your programs (such as networking, graphical user interfaces, sound, and animation) without much effort. All you have to do is *import* into your own program the package(s) containing the class(es) that you want to use and then create objects from those classes. Although this may sound complicated, it's really a snap, as you'll see in the following chapters.

Whether you create your own objects or rely on those provided by the Java system, it's important to know that an object cannot exist without a class that first defines the data, methods, and interfaces that the object will have. And so, to work with an object you must first have a class that defines what the object will be. Each and every object is created, or *instantiated*, from a class.

It might help to think of objects and classes in terms of C structs and variables derived from those structs. A *struct* (short for structure) defines a group of data types, from which a programmer can create any number of variables (memory permitting, of course). For example, the following C struct defines a basic Point structure:

```
struct Point {
  int h; /* horizontal coordinate */
  int v; /* vertical coordinate */
};
```

This struct could be regarded as a class; it's the template from which new Point variables are created:

```
Point myPt, yourPt, ourPt; /* just making my Points! */
```

In this example, we've created three different variables (myPt, yourPt, and ourPt), all having the same internal structure (two integer variables, h and v) defined by the Point struct. We have, in essence, created objects from a template. This is exactly the purpose that classes serve; they are templates from which objects are created.

Classes, however, don't just define data types. They also define methods, giving the object its behavior and an interface through which that object communicates with other objects. In Java, a class definition has the following form:

```
class Name {
 . . . instance variables . . .
 . . . method declarations . . .
 }
```

Although you can declare your methods first and the instance variables last when programming in Java, it's good coding practice to follow the preceding example. The Java keyword class begins the definition for a class. You provide the class with a name (such as Point). The data and methods of the class are enclosed in the curly braces ({}) that begin and end the class definition block.

**Note** To write Java code that is in compliance with Sun's recommended naming conventions, your Java class names should always begin with an uppercase letter (Point, Button, Window, and so on), even when the class name contains two or more words (PixelPoint, ImageButton, and WindowWasher, for example). Variables and method names, however, should always begin with a lowercase letter. (Final, or constant, data members should be named using all uppercase characters, in contrast.) For more details, see Part II, "Getting Up to Speed: Nuts and Bolts of Java."

Let's take a look at the structure of Point, this time written as a Java class. The variables representing horizontal and vertical would be the same, but we might also want to include a method for setting these variables and one each for retrieving the value of these variables as illustrated in Listing 2-1.

---

### Listing 2-1: **Point.java**

```
class Point {
    private int h; /* horizontal coordinate */
    private int v; /* vertical coordinate */

    public void setPoint (int newH, int newV) {
        h = newH;
        v = newV;
    }
    public int getH() {
        return (h);
    }
    public int getV() {
        return (v);
    }
}
```

---

Now, this certainly has a lot more meat than the C struct we created, and for good reason. The Point class contains three methods: setPoint() to set the horizontal and vertical integer variables; getH() to retrieve the horizontal variable; and getV() to retrieve the vertical variable. Fair enough, but what's going on with the keywords private and public?

**Note** Java classes are typically stored in plain text files that have the same name as the class itself in addition to the *.java* file extension. The Point class defined here, for example, would be stored in a text file named Point.java that must first be compiled before it can actually be used to create objects of this type. The Java compiler will create a bytecode class file named Point.class based on the contents of the Point.java source code file, which is what you'll use to create live Point objects. (Objects are created from classes.) Because this chapter is concerned with the general concept of OOP rather than the specific mechanics of Java, I'll forego the discussion of compiling and running Java programs for the time being. See Chapter 4 to learn how to create, compile, and run your Java programs.

### Private Versus Public

Remember that objects have the capability to encapsulate, or hide, their data. No need exists for other objects to access the variables of a `Point` object directly; thus, they are both declared as `private` when we create our class. The only way to set or retrieve this data is through a `Point` object's `public` methods, which any other object can do by simply sending a message. This leads me to the issue of *instantiation*; the act of creating an object from a class.

 **Note**    Java provides four levels of access control: public, protected, private, and unspecified (which indicates package level access). Each of these is discussed in Chapter 4 and Chapter 9.

### Instantiation

Until we create an object from our new class, nothing is really going on. Before we can work with an object, we must instantiate one. (You can think of instantiation as simply a fancy way of saying "create.") Typically, the following format is used to instantiate objects from a Java class:

```
ClassName variableName = new ClassConstructor( );
```

The name of the class comes first, followed by the name of the variable that will receive a reference (similar to a pointer) to the object reference that will be created. This, in essence, tells the Java runtime system that you wish to stuff an object reference of a specific type into a variable. Next, the equal (=) sign is used to assign the object reference to the variable. Finally, the new keyword appears, followed by what's known as a class *constructor* that will do the dirty work of creating and initialize the object.

Because a constructor is actually a special-purpose method contained inside the class, a pair of parenthesis ( ) come after the constructor name. Constructors, as the following chapters explain, always have the same name as the class itself, and they may or may not have parameters. Finally, the entire line of code is terminated with a semicolon (;).

Following is an example of this form of instantiation in action:

```
Point myPt = new Point();
```

The preceding line of code would appear in any Java program that wishes to create a `Point` object from the `Point` class created earlier. Note, however, that this line of code does *not* appear inside the `Point` class. (The `Point` class has no reason to instantiate itself!) For the purposes of this discussion, you can assume that the `Point` class code that you saw earlier was typed into a Java source code file named `Point.java`. The `Point.java` file was then compiled to create a Java class file named `Point.class`, which is the class file called into action when the previous line of code is executed. (That is, the `Point` object is created from the `Point` class stored in the compiled bytecode `Point.class` file.)

With this in mind, take another look at the previous line of code and see if you can determine what it does. As you may have deduced, it creates a Point object from the Point class we created earlier. The Point object is a live bundle of code residing in memory, a reference to which is stored in the variable named myPt; in other words, this line of code creates a Point object *instance* that can be accessed through the myPt variable.

The new operator followed by Point() creates an object of type Point in memory, to which the myPt variable now refers; this is the part of the instantiation process that actually creates and initializes the object (giving value to it at the beginning of its lifetime). The myPt variable is said to be a reference data type because it refers to an object in memory. Specifically, the myPt variable is of type Point, because Point is the type of object that this variable references.

**Note**  In Java there are two fundamental data types: reference and primitive data types. Reference data types refer to objects. (You can think of a reference to an object as being a pointer to an object, although Java doesn't actually support pointers in the way that C or C++ does.) Reference data types are sometimes called composite data types because they can be composed of primitive values as well as references to other objects. Primitive data types, on the other hand, are simple or basic data types that cannot be decomposed into subsidiary values, and include integers (byte, short, int, long), real numbers (float, double), characters (char), and Boolean types (true/false). The Point object, for example, is composed of two primitive integer values. In this example, the myPt variable is considered a reference data type because it will contain a reference (internal pointer) to a Point object after this line of code executes. Through the myPt variable, you can then access the primitive integer data that the object it refers to contains. To learn more about data types, see Chapter 6.

Now, let's suppose we want to do something with the object that we've just created. How about setting the horizontal and vertical coordinates, and then, just for fun, we can retrieve and copy them into local variables. Once we have a reference to the object in memory, which is exactly what we have in the myPt variable, we can do just that:

```
myPt.setPoint(145,124);      /* set the h and v variables */

int theHorizontal = myPt.getH(); /* get myPt h value, and
                                     assign to a variable */

int theVertical = myPt.getV();   /* get myPt v value, and
                                     assign to a variable */
```

In the previous three lines of code, we've used the myPt variable to set and then retrieve variables stored in the Point object that this variable references. First, we invoke the object's setPoint() method. The setPoint() method takes two integer parameters that are used to set the object's internal h and v variables. Here we set the `Point` instance's h and v variables to 145 and 124, respectively. (Review the `Point` class code to see how this method works.) After these `Point` object variables have been set, we then use our `myPt` reference to extract each one individually and assign their contents to new integer variables (`theHorizontal` and `theVertical`).

So, what we have done in this set of examples should be pretty clear by now:

1. We created a class named `Point`, which had instance variables h and v and three methods: one to set the variables; the other two to retrieve them.

2. We then instantiated an object of class `Point`, to which a reference is stored in the `myPt` variable.

3. Through our object reference variable `myPt`, we've set the instance variables contained in the object it points to and then retrieved each and assigned it to a local variable. (The `theHorizontal` variable was set to 145, while the `theVertical` variable was set to 124.)

Although this is a relatively simple example of creating and using a class in Java, it should help to put the concepts of objects and classes into the proper perspective. Later in this book, you'll create much more substantial classes, from which sophisticated objects will be brought to life. And thanks to another powerful OOP concept, inheritance, you'll be able to draw life from existing classes. If this sounds like a trailer for the movie *Dawn of the Living Dead*, read on.

## Inheritance

It's time we sink our teeth into the real meat on the bones of OOP: *inheritance*. Inheritance is arguably the most powerful feature of any object-oriented language, as it allows you to reuse code as never before.

When we speak of classes and classification, we mean items that can be grouped together in accordance with specific traits. Harley is a member of the Felis class, you and I are members of the Homo sapiens class, and so on. But what's the real advantage to classification in software programming?

Inheritance, my Homo sapien friend.

A class defines the general, all-purpose state and behavior (data and methods) for all objects that will be derived from that class. For example, suppose I create a class called `TimePiece`. `TimePiece` is an abstraction of the concept of keeping track of time. In it, I have a variable called time (surprise, surprise). I also have two methods, one to set the time (`setTime`) and one to display it (`displayTime`). These are set out in Figure 2-15.

```
class TimePiece {
  int time;

public void setTime (int NewTime) {
  time = NewTime;
}
public void displayTime() {
  System.out.println (time);
}
}
```

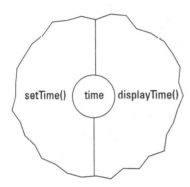

**Figure 2-15:** The class TimePiece, showing its data and methods

This is all well and good, but what's important to understand is that all objects we create using `TimePiece` will have a `time` variable and both the `setTime()` and `displayTime()` methods. This means we can create a bunch of different `TimePiece` objects, such as a wristwatch, alarm clock, or grandfather clock, and each inherits the traits of the `TimePiece` class. This also means we don't have to write new methods for each type of clock we create, as shown in Figure 2-16.

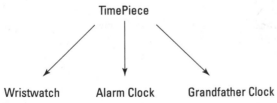

**Figure 2-16:** All objects instantiated from the class TimePiece inherit its data and methods.

Suppose that we recognize the need for an alarm as well. We could add an alarm method directly to the TimePiece class and each new object created using TimePiece would then come with an alarm. Or, we could simply use TimePiece as the basis for an entirely new class, which we'll call TimeAlarmPiece.

In other words, you can create a *subclass* of the TimePiece class. This would make TimePiece the *superclass* (parent class) from which the subclass TimeAlarmPiece inherits data and methods. In a sense, TimeAlarmPiece becomes a child of TimePiece.

While this new class automatically inherits the data and methods of TimePiece, we can add entirely new data members and methods to it as we wish. Thanks to inheritance, we can create an entirely new subclass of TimePiece that has all the traits of its superclass, plus whatever capabilities we add. You can see the relationship between subclass and superclass in Figure 2-17.

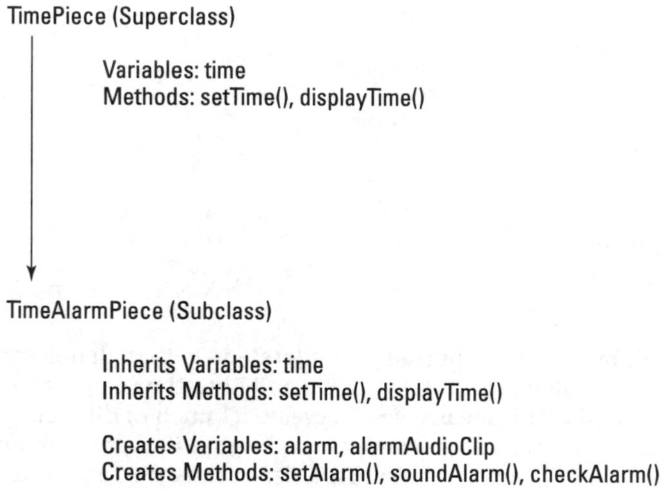

TimePiece (Superclass)

> Variables: time
> Methods: setTime(), displayTime()

TimeAlarmPiece (Subclass)

> Inherits Variables: time
> Inherits Methods: setTime(), displayTime()
>
> Creates Variables: alarm, alarmAudioClip
> Creates Methods: setAlarm(), soundAlarm(), checkAlarm()

**Figure 2-17:** Creating a subclass makes TimePiece a superclass.

In Java, you use the extends keyword to create a subclass from an existing class. The extends keyword implies that your new class will inherit capabilities from its superclass and also extend, or enhance, these capabilities as needed. To create a subclass of TimePiece called TimeAlarmPiece, for example, you follow this basic template:

```
class TimeAlarmPiece extends TimePiece {
   ...instance variables specific to this new class...
   ...method declarations specific to this new class...
}
```

The `TimeAlarmPiece` class created in this example is a subclass of the existing `TimePiece` class, meaning `TimeAlarmPiece` inherits the data and methods contained in `TimePiece`. The new `TimeAlarmPiece` class, however, isn't merely a copy of TimePiece; `TimeAlarmPiece` can contain its own data and methods as well. You might, for example, add to `TimeAlarmPiece` new variables and methods necessary to build an alarm capability into this class, in which case, `TimeAlarmPiece` truly would extend the functionality of `TimePiece`.

> **Note**
>
> Java supports two special keywords, *this* and *super*, which allow a class to distinguish between its own data members and methods and those of its superclass. A subclass, for example, can use the *super* keyword to invoke a method of its superclass (`super.setTime()`, for example) or access a variable contained in the superclass, while it could use the *this* keyword when dealing with its own methods and variables of the same name (`this.setTime()`, for instance) or omit the *this* keyword altogether in such cases. To learn more about *this* and *super*, refer to Chapter 9.

## Reusable code

This capability to reuse existing code to create new objects is a profound feature of OOP; the only new code we have to write is that needed for the alarm. The `TimePiece` code comes for free; we're reusing it (through inheritance) to create an entirely new class that understands alarms.

The result is a dramatic increase in proficiency; the new class is up and running in a fraction of the time it would take to write a new one from scratch that has the same capabilities. And, to further dramatize the power of inheritance, we can use the new `TimeAlarmPiece` class to create any number of objects that require both time and an alarm. Any object instantiated from the `TimeAlarmPiece` class automatically knows how to deal with both time and alarms.

To add even more drama to the concept of inheritance, we'll take it one step further and extend the `TimeAlarmPiece` class to create an entirely new class capable of dealing with time, alarms, and mathematical calculations. That's right, we can create a subclass of the `TimeAlarmPiece` subclass and get all the time and alarm traits for free. We need only add code to handle calculations, and *voilà*, we have a class from which we can create a wristwatch that tells the time, sets and sounds an alarm, and calculates the excessive cost of our electricity bill.

The following Java code snippets, for example, show the basic class body structures for three different class files: `TimePiece`, `TimeAlarmPiece`, and `WristWatch`:

```
class TimePiece {
    ...instance variables specific to this new class...
    ...method declarations specific to this new class...
}
```

```
class TimeAlarmPiece extends TimePiece {
   ...instance variables specific to this new class...
   ...method declarations specific to this new class...
}

class WristWatch extends TimeAlarmPiece {
   ...instance variables specific to this new class...
   ...method declarations specific to this new class...
}
```

The TimePiece class is the topmost superclass, from which TimeAlarmPiece is derived. (Thus, TimeAlarmPiece is said to be a direct descendant of TimePiece.) TimeAlarmPiece has its own data and methods that give this class added functionality that TimePiece doesn't have (such as the alarm capability).

The WristWatch class then extends TimeAlarmPiece, giving WristWatch all the capabilities of TimeAlarmPiece. This means that WristWatch has really inherited capabilities from two classes: directly from TimeAlarmPiece and indirectly from TimePiece. The class hierarchy, or inheritance tree, for these three classes can therefore be represented as follows:

```
TimePiece
   |
   |--- TimeAlarmPiece
          |
          |--- WristWatch
```

## Class Hierarchy/Inheritance Tree

As a class is extended through subclassing, the resulting objects become more and more specialized.

A *class hierarchy*, or *inheritance tree*, refers to the family of classes that result from the act of subclassing. At the top level, the class is generic; it becomes more specialized as it goes down. A class hierarchy often resembles the roots of a tree, with offshoots at many levels, as shown in Figure 2-18.

 **Caution**    Because object-oriented programming lends itself so beautifully to the concept of inheritance, your custom class libraries can quickly grow out of control if you create subclasses without considerable thought. Without foresight and proper design considerations, object-oriented systems can run rampant, like multiplying bacteria in a warm petri dish. Therefore, the practice of object-oriented analysis (OOA) and object-oriented design (OOD) have become as important to serious software development as object-oriented programming itself.

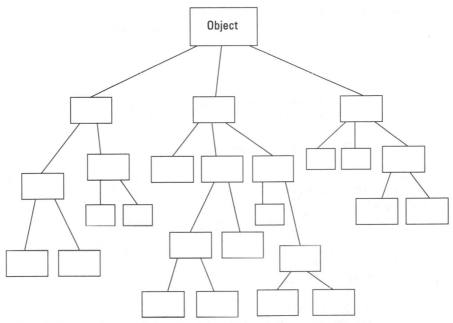

**Figure 2-18:** A class hierarchy of ten resembles the roots of a tree.

# Object-Oriented Analysis and Design

*"In OOA, we seek to model the world by identifying the classes and objects that form the vocabulary of the problem domain; and in OOD, we invent the abstractions and mechanisms that provide the behavior that this model requires." — Grady Booch*

It is very easy to become entangled in object-oriented programming because of the technology's flexible nature. Therefore, professional software engineers such as Grady Booch, Ivar Jacobson, and James Rumbaugh are attempting to establish a standard way of applying object-oriented techniques to software development.

**Note**    Booch, Jacobson, and Rumbaugh are known as the "three amigos" responsible for creating the Unified Modeling Language (UML). UML is the synthesis of several different approaches to software modeling, and it provides a standard language and notation that developers can use for OOA/OOD. To learn more about UML, visit http://www.rational.com/uml/.

Object-oriented analysis (OOA) and object-oriented design (OOD) ensure that object-oriented programming is done with foresight and in the best way possible for each problem we attempt to resolve. Programming comes only after a thorough analysis of the problem and the careful design of a solution.

One aspect of OOA/OOD is having a *notation method*. A notation method provides a way for us to map out a program on paper, whiteboard, or other media before committing it to code. It serves much the same purpose as flowcharts do for procedural programming—it gives us a visual idea of how everything works without the need for actual code.

Once we have decided how we want to subdivide our classes and objects (data, methods, and interfaces), a notation method lets us represent them and their often complex relationships with other objects. The Booch Method created by Grady Booch is one of many popular notation methods.

I won't assert that you need to adopt object-oriented analysis and object-oriented design methodologies in order to learn OOP. That's simply not the case. In fact, you can begin programming in Java without even learning much about object-oriented programming in advance if you really want to. But in reality, you're much better off learning about object-oriented analysis and object-oriented design while learning the language. You may find them of no use to you at this point, or you may find them exceptionally helpful. It depends on what you want to do with Java and how you plan to use the language.

Either way, it's worth checking out as you get deeper into Java programming. The fastest and cheapest way to learn more about object-oriented analysis and design is to fire up your Web browser and head to a search engine such as Yahoo (`http://www.yahoo.com`) or Alta Vista (`http://www.altavista.com/`). You can perform searches using the acronyms OOA and OOD, or you can search for the full terms object-oriented analysis and object-oriented design.

# Summary

Object-oriented programming is the foundation of the Java programming language. You need to understand the concepts of OOP before you jump into Java.

✦ OOP is based on a few key concepts: abstraction, state and behavior (data and methods), and encapsulation (information hiding).

✦ Objects are self-contained, modular bundles of code that contain both state (data) and behavior (methods).

✦ Classes are the templates, or blueprints, from which "live" objects are instantiated (created).

✦ Objects are self-contained and communicate with the outside world through a well-defined interface.

✦ Inheritance is one of the most powerful features of object-oriented programming because it enables you to reuse your code.

✦ A class hierarchy, or inheritance tree, graphically depicts class/superclass relationships.

✦ Object-oriented programming is just the tip of the iceberg — object-oriented analysis and object-oriented design techniques help you create and manage your object-oriented development projects.

✦     ✦     ✦

# Java Design Basics

**B**efore diving in and writing your first Java applet or
application, it's important to consider the design of
Java programs in general. By "design," I mean not only the
overall design — how it looks, what it does, how it interacts
with the user, and so forth — but also the internal organization of the source code needed to create the program in the
first place.

Although discussing design concepts before covering the
language may seem akin to putting the cart before the horse,
in truth, it's not as off-the-wall as you might think. Since many
programmers are likely to be up and running with Java in
no time, there's no telling whether they'll bother to read the
various chapters in this book before cranking out functional
applets and applications for the world to see and use.

So, I'm discussing design issues here rather than at the end
of the book, with the hope that if you take the time to skim
this chapter before reading on, much of it will sink in and
stick with you along the way. If you're whipping out programs
within 24 hours of picking up this book, as many experienced
C and C++ programmers will be doing, be sure to consider the
design guidelines presented here, even if you don't need to
read every chapter that follows.

And, aside from the practical issue of catching you before
you surf off into the sunset with Java and browser in tow,
there's another reason for discussing design basics here:
Because I won't discuss implementation details at all, I can
paint an overall portrait — in broad strokes — of the general
techniques and practices that you'll learn by reading the rest
of this book.

In the coming chapters, you'll read in detail about the various
features of the Java language and learn how to create your

own standalone applications and executable Web content. By covering each major topic in a separate chapter, I hope to get right to the meat (artichoke heart, if you're a vegetarian) of each feature. I've laid out the book in a linear fashion, proceeding from topic to topic as you might encounter them were you to explore the language on your own with little more than a vague idea of what it held in store.

If you didn't get an overview in this chapter first, a significant and unreasonable burden would land squarely on your shoulders: to understand each of the basic design issues before releasing an applet or application upon our global village, you'd have to read the entire book from front to back!

To ease this burden, this chapter gives you a sneak peek at topics and issues well in advance of actually exploring them. You'll gain a better understanding of what Java programs can and cannot do, what they should and shouldn't do, and what you can expect as challenges to your programming prowess. By taking the time here and now to consider general design issues, you might save your forehead the pain of being beaten against the keyboard out of frustration later on.

# Sketching Program Objects and a User Interface

Today, with midnight hacking in vogue, sleepless nights at the keyboard an honorable living, and cutting every conceivable corner to get products to market on schedule being the mantra of many software companies, taking time to put ideas on paper may seem a bit old-fashioned. But no matter how you slice it, sketching out your programs in advance will save you a great deal of time in the long run. (See Figure 3-1.)

And I'm not talking flowcharts here. I am merely suggesting that the time you take to step away from the keyboard and place your ideas on that flat white stuff you had consigned to the garbage can of history will more than pay for itself when it comes to implementation. If you're an experienced programmer, chances are you already follow a design process for projects before even beginning to code. And if you're new to programming, it's a good habit to get into.

Since Java is an object-oriented programming (OOP) language, your programs will consist of objects that interact with each other. As you learned in Chapter 2, "Object-Oriented Programming with Java," objects can be easily represented on paper as "amorphous blobs that do something."

By taking the time to work out the "blobs" and how they interact with one another on paper, you'll save yourself a good deal of wasted implementation effort. Much like the master artist who sketches renditions of a masterpiece before—and even during its creation — you'll have an opportunity to refine your programs on an abstract level before committing to a single line of code.

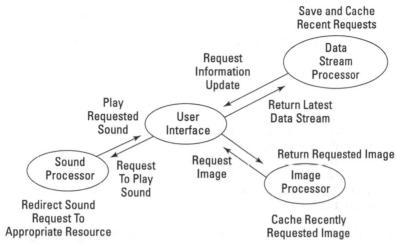

**Figure 3-1:** Taking the time to sketch out the design of your program and the relationships of its objects can save time down the road.

Once you begin to code, you're essentially strapping yourself into a straitjacket; your initial attempt may not turn out to be the best solution after all, and it might even strangle your good intentions in the end. Without sketching the program in advance, you'll barrel ahead and almost certainly make a mess of the code, since you won't give adequate time to considering the various classes you'll be coding and the objects they give birth to. Certainly, the most simple of programs won't be an issue, but try and implement larger applets or applications off the cuff, and you'll find yourself looking at a mighty unattractive spaghetti dinner of code, when all is said and done.

Aside from sketching your program objects and their relationship with each other, it's also crucial to put on paper the user interface (UI) your program will require. Notice I didn't say graphical user interface (GUI), which tends to be limited to windowing elements (buttons, scrollbars, windows, dialog boxes, and the like). Instead, I'm referring to the interface at large: precisely what will the user experience when he or she encounters your program?

This is all-encompassing and not limited to windowing elements. Everything a person will see, hear, or do when using your program is part of the UI. And yes, I do mean hear. Since applets and applications can play sound with as little as one line of code, you must consider what audio yours will support (if any) and how that fits in with the rest of the program.

Again, there's no need to whip out a slide rule and sweat out the exact details. You need only sketch the UI your applet (or application) will support to get a better idea of how it will look and sound to those who use it. Rather than waste time coding elements that you might later reorganize or omit altogether, you should work through the UI of your program before committing to a single line of code.

As a general rule, I prefer to sketch the UI before anything else is done. Typically, I let an idea for a program rattle around for a while, thinking through the details of what it should look like and how it should act. Once I've roughed it out in my head for a few days or longer, I then begin to sketch out the user interface.

Invariably, I discover user interface elements that I've left out or want to drop that I would never have noticed in a purely mental design. If you go straight to code relying only on loosely organized thoughts, you will likely start in the wrong direction and waste a great deal of time. Instead, it pays to take the UI ideas you're considering out of your mind and place them on paper. Once there, you can tweak, massage, and rework them as much as necessary, since this is an iterative process (and one that you might spend a lot of time with if you're anything like me).

Once I'm satisfied with the UI, I sketch out the various objects the program needs. This may take several attempts or be a quick and surprisingly easy process. Whatever the case, before I begin so much as a line of code, I know a great deal about what my program will ultimately look like and what code I have to write to get it there.

Contrast this approach with diving into code head-first like a manic surfer on the beach at Maui who can't wait to get into the water (which, I admit, I sometimes do when overcome with excitement for a particular project). Despite my best efforts and the most honest intentions, I'm almost never satisfied with programs I develop in this manner, and I often spend a great deal of time trying to fix avoidable design mistakes that I made early on. The code may look and act as it's supposed to on the surface, but under the covers is another matter altogether.

Any program that you create without taking the time to think the overall design and user interface through will be much less elegant, and even downright ugly, when compared to its well-considered counterparts. Worse still, such hastily developed programs are typically inflexible and much more difficult to maintain than they should be. Except in cases where the program is a prototype or "one-off" effort (made for a special purpose that won't require an upgrade and won't find itself in the hands of customers), you'll eventually need to rewrite most, if not all, of the code to bring it up to snuff.

Unless you're writing such disposable programs, do yourself a tremendous favor and spend the necessary up-front time placing your ideas on paper and working through the overall design of your projects before committing to code. You won't be sorry.

Many experienced Java developers report that the language makes them two to four times more productive than C or C++. This means developers can produce Java programs much, much faster than with other languages. Smart developers ensure that Java saves them time up front by properly designing their programs long before they actually code. Any savings in development time that Java might afford you can easily be lost fixing poorly conceived programs down the road.

# Giving the User Control

When designing your programs, it's a good idea to remember that every person who encounters them will have a different opinion about what is and isn't cool. Although a thumping background soundtrack and spinning disco balls on a Web page, for example, may seem like the ultimate multimedia experience to you, not everyone will agree. Likewise, fancy splash screens and animated buttons aren't exactly what some users expect of their desktop application.

Whenever you choose to add nifty features such as looping soundtracks (audio that plays continuously by starting over when the end is reached), loud sounds, and animation, you need to give users a way to turn off the ones they don't like. For example, the user might turn off an animation by clicking it, stop a looping sound-track by clicking a button, or mute all audio sources at once by clicking another button (or by pressing a specific key as described in the section "Single Button").

Exactly how you give the user control is your business. Sometimes buttons aren't possible, and so you might consider a less obvious interface element, such as a check box or simply a mouse click. However you do it, give users a choice and let them know how to control the various elements of your program. After all, Web surfers aren't likely to come back if they're annoyed by your creative use of Java, nor are customers likely to purchase a desktop application that is more distracting than it is useful.

## Mouse control

There are two aspects to consider with regard to the mouse control: single- or double-clicks, and single or multiple buttons.

### Single-Clicks

For most programs, the mouse is the primary control mechanism. You can easily determine if it has been clicked, released, moved, or even been clicked and dragged without first being released. In contrast, early versions of Java couldn't easily determine if a double-click had occurred.

The original version of Java didn't support double-clicking, so programmers had to write their own code to calculate the time between each click and determine if such an event has occurred. With Java 2, however, finding out if a user double-clicked an item isn't such a big deal. However, when it comes to applets, supporting double-clicks is generally a bad idea.

The Web is, by design, a single-click navigation system. Not only will use of double-clicking confuse the Web user, but it breaks with the tradition of the Web. The vast majority of Java applets rely on single mouse clicks alone, and so should yours unless you have a good reason to do otherwise.

As a result, you should design your applet around single-clicks, and unless it's absolutely necessary, eliminate double-clicks altogether. Desktop applications, on the other hand, have always supported double-clicks, so you shouldn't feel obligated to use single-clicks in your Java applications.

### Single Button

Java originally supported only a one-button mouse. Since Java 1.1, however, Java has supported up to three mouse buttons, enabling more sophisticated mouse control. This might sound like a good feature to add to your Java programs, but you'll find it's not always a good idea.

If you design your programs to understand and respond to specific mouse buttons, you'll be cutting a large population of users out of the loop (Windows, Macintosh, and UNIX systems each have a different number of mouse buttons.) This is fine if you are creating a program for users of a specific computer system, but why limit your audience?

Instead, use the keyboard to modify a mouse click. For example, when the mouse is clicked and no keys are pressed, treat it as a standard mouse event. When the mouse is clicked and the Shift key is pressed, treat it as you would a special mouse button. Of course, you're not limited to the Shift key when it comes to modifying mouse clicks, but there are a few cross-platform considerations that you should be aware of when incorporating keyboard control into your program.

## Keyboard control

Because writing Java programs that require a multibutton mouse will needlessly limit your audience, you may rely on the keyboard to signal special user input. In this way, you can react to different combinations of keyboard and mouse down events.

When using the keyboard to modify a mouse click, it's a good idea to limit the keys you support to the Shift and Ctrl keys. These are available on almost every personal computer, and they are used by standard software programs to modify mouse clicks. The concept of Shift-clicking or Ctrl-clicking is familiar to the majority of personal computer users, and these keyboard-mouse combinations can make your program easier to use.

Avoid obtuse keyboard modifiers, and only use those that might help the user remember what key to press when clicking the mouse. Suppose, for example, that you write a video game that uses the mouse to control a submarine. Clicking the mouse alone might launch a torpedo, while clicking the mouse while holding down the P key might activate the periscope.

## Applets: stop when stopped!

When a Web page is accessed with a Java-savvy browser, all applets embedded in that page are told to start. At this point, applets load the sounds and graphics they need (if any) and do their stuff.

When the Web page is left, either by the user navigating to another page or the browser being quit altogether, all applets embedded in the page are told to stop. It is here that you'll bring your applet activity to a screeching halt. However, this process isn't handled for you automatically.

The programmer is responsible for stopping any sounds that are currently playing, bringing animation to a standstill and halting all threads in the applet. Rarely, if ever, does an applet have a good reason to continue along its merry way when the page it is embedded in has been exited. By ceasing all activity upon receiving the stop message, your applets become well-behaved and courteous inhabitants of the Web pages in which they are embedded.

## Flexible applets

If you've looked at the HTML code in which many applets are embedded, you may have noticed the word PARAM used inside the <APPLET> tag. The PARAM attribute lets applets receive data through HTML code, which allows Web page authors to configure applets for their specific needs without actually dealing with Java code (that's our job!).

Applets that use parameters are much more flexible than those that don't. Instead of creating several slightly different versions of the same applet, you can use the PARAM attribute to customize a single applet. By responding to parameters embedded in the HTML code, an applet can behave uniquely in different pages.

Java applications don't support user-configurable parameters in the way that applets do. This is because applications aren't woven into Web pages as applets are. Instead, Java applications are run on the command line (by issuing a command at the DOS prompt, for example), and, as a result, support command-line attributes. Command-line attributes are, essentially, the equivalent of applet parameters.

# Bandwidth Considerations

Because Java makes creating Web pages with sophisticated animation and sounds a snap, those new to the language often tend to lose themselves in the excitement of applets. In addition, applications are easily networked, thanks to Java's built-in networking packages. As a result, it's quite easy to create desktop applications that can reach out and grab files off the Web or exchange files over the network.

Iceberg-sized images and audio clips abound on the high seas of the Web. And while this may be just fine for the developer who has access to the Web via a T1 line or cable connection, the equivalent of an ocean liner, the rest of the world isn't so fortunate; creaky wooden rafts and pontoon boats are the norm.

Since bandwidth is a major issue with the majority of users, you must consider the lowest common denominator. Although you might try to convince yourself that 56 Kbps is the norm, with ISDN, DSL, and cable modem access not far behind, many folks today surf the Web at speeds of 28.8 Kbps or less. Sure, the technophiles are working with all the latest gadgets, but the masses . . . well, that's a completely different story. To offer your applets to everyone without penalizing those with slower access, takes extra effort and means you should assume the average access speed is no higher than 28.8 Kbps, with a large percentage of folks on the Web still dog-paddling along at 14.4 Kbps and even 9600 bps!

## Battling bandwidth bottlenecks

Although applets themselves are quite small and come across the wire in no time, the graphics and audio files they often use are tremendous by comparison. And while applications are generally much larger by comparison, they too must grapple with the size of media files in our networked world. To prevent serious bottlenecks when downloading such files over the network, there are several techniques that you can use to decrease transmission time.

### Converting Sound Files

Java originally only supported Sun's AU format for sound files (audio files that end with the .au extension), which uses μLaw (pronounced mu-law) encoding. If you intend to use sound files that can be heard by the largest audience, therefore, you'll have to convert your existing audio files to this 8-bit, 8 kHz, single-channel (mono) format. This will ensure that your audio clips can be played by every Java runtime out there.

Java 2, however, supports many other sound file formats. Although you can use a variety of sound formats with Java 2, you may find that the original AU format is the best in terms of bang-for-the-buck because of the compression that this format offers.

Although the AU format creates files that are smaller in size than other formats, the sound quality isn't the best. As a result, you may find yourself fiddling with various sound editing functions in an attempt to eliminate the hiss you'll hear when converting higher-quality sounds to this format. Whether you use the original AU format or one of the many formats supported by Java 2, keep in mind that there are a number of techniques you can employ to ensure the high quality sound at lowest disk file sizes.

 **Tip** Sun users can create sounds in the AU format using the Audiotool application. Windows users can use the GoldWave utility to create and export sounds in AU and other popular formats, including several of those supported by Java 1.3 (http://www.goldwave.com/).

To reduce the size of sound files as much as possible, you'll want to keep only the absolutely essential portions of it around. Cut out any preceding or trailing silence, although you may be tempted to keep it.

Since cutting out every second of preceding and trailing silences tends to make sounds begin and end abruptly, many programmers figure keeping a second or two of dead space on either end of the sound clip is worth the extra download time. However, you can achieve the same results by applying a fade-in effect to the beginning of the sound and a fade-out effect at the end. These two effects give nice, smooth transitions instead of abrupt starts and stops. Not only is the sound more professional and appealing, but you'll trim off a bit of the download time in the process.

## Opting for Sound Loops

Sound is such an effective way to grab attention and add impact to a program that many first-timers overuse it. Rather than playing a large number of audio clips, consider whether looping would be a reasonable alternative. When you loop a sound file, it will repeat itself continuously until you tell it to stop.

## Java 1.3 Sound Support

Whereas the original version of Java supported only Sun's AU (.au) format for applet sounds (with no sound support for applications at all!), Java 2 version 1.3 offers a much more sophisticated Sound API. As a result, rich sound capabilities are available to both Java applets and applications. Through the Sound API Java programs can play, capture, and audio and MIDI (Musical Instrument Digital Interface) data. AIFF, AU, WAV, MIDI Type 0 and Type 1, and Rich Music Format (RMF) are supported. Mono and stereo sounds stored in 8- and 16-bit format are supported, with sample rates ranging from 8 kHz to 48 kHz. In addition, up to 64 total channels of digital audio and synthesized MIDI sounds can be mixed in Java's all-software mixing process. For details, visit the Java 1.3 sound guide (http://java.sun.com/j2se/1.3/docs/guide/sound/) or Sun's home of the Sound API (http://java.sun.com/products/java-media/sound/).

The result can be quite powerful, especially if the sound clip you loop is subtle. Instead of bombarding the user with sound after sound, sucking up valuable network bandwidth in the process in the case of applets, consider this option: You'll be happy to know that you can play any number of sounds at once, meaning you don't have to stop a sound loop to play another sound clip. All sounds you play at the same time will be mixed together, allowing for a rich audio production with minimal effort on your part.

# Using images and colors

Java supports the use of Graphics Interchange Format (GIF) and Joint Photographic Experts Group (JPEG) images, meaning that it gives you a nice and easy mechanism for retrieving these images from the Web and displaying them in your programs. Java also supports a 32-bit color model (8 bits each for red, green, and blue color components, and 8 bits for alpha transparency), which allows the programmer to define and use more than 16 million different colors for use in drawing primitive graphics (lines, rectangles, ovals, polygons, and so forth) and fonts.

Although the use of color applied to primitive graphics doesn't negatively affect bandwidth, images do. Since the JPEG format is supported, you can use 24-bit color images within your programs. With GIF, you're currently limited to a palette of 256 colors. This is a limitation of the GIF file format, not Java, although 24-bit GIF files will soon be possible through an enhancement of this popular type of graphic.

### Image Palette Reduction

Regardless of which format you use, graphic images suck up disk space and bandwidth. To reduce the amount of time it takes an image to travel across the wire or the amount of storage it consumes, you must cut down the amount of data used to represent it. Luckily, the most popular graphics programs on the market (Adobe Photoshop, CorelDraw!, Fractal Design Painter, and others such as the Paint Shop Pro shareware program) allow us to cut file sizes by reducing the amount of colors used to display an image.

Rather than using a full palette of 256 colors, you may find that only a small number are necessary to represent the image. By removing unused colors from the palette, you conserve storage space and decrease download times. And you can further reduce the palette by forcing colors close to one another to map to a certain value. For example, rather than having 16 different shades of gray in an image, you might reduce the palette to support only three shades. This technique applies to all colors, meaning you can reduce the entire palette of an image to significantly reduce its size.

Certainly, there is a tradeoff between the quality of the image and overall storage size. However, you (or the graphic artist at your company) can typically reduce the palette considerably without adversely affecting the image quality. (See Figures 3-2 and 3-3.)

**Figure 3-2:** Reducing the palette of colors can significantly reduce the storage size of an image. This image icontains several hundred colors and requires 200KB of disk space.

**Figure 3-3:** After palette reduction, this image contains only 40 colors and takes up less than 100KB of disk space. Can you tell the difference?

## GIF versus JPEG

When using images, you'll eventually need to decide on a format to support. Java supports both GIF and JPEG formats, but there are a number of factors that may make one preferable over the other. Start by taking a look at the GIF format.

You'll find several benefits with GIF images. For starters, the GIF format is highly efficient and has built-in compression that produces relatively small file sizes for images that lend themselves to this format. In addition, GIF images support transparency and interlacing, which can greatly enhance the visual appeal of your applet. GIF is also particularly adept at representing text and flat-colored artwork (such as cartoons and illustrations).

JPEG images, on the other hand, can contain more than 256 colors, and they can be compressed to a higher degree than GIF when a large number of colors are involved. The JPEG format currently doesn't support transparency or interlacing. JPEG, however, is excellent at representing photographic-quality images (something GIF is notoriously poor at).

### Transparency

Transparency allows the graphic artist to specify any color in an image as transparent. When the image is rendered on the screen, this color isn't shown. Instead, whatever is underneath it shows through (typically the background color, although other images may be drawn underneath, as well).

Without transparency, images are displayed using all colors in the palette, including the background color of the image. As a result, they may appear quite unattractive under certain circumstances — unless the color of these portions matches exactly the underlying background. (See Figure 3-4.) Therefore, the GIF format is the only choice for images that must have a see-through portion.

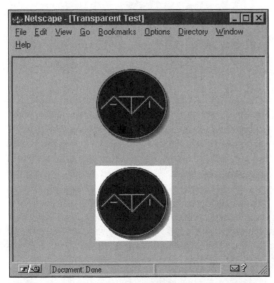

**Figure 3-4:** Transparency allows you to specify a color in an image as see-through.

### Interlacing

Interlacing, another feature supported by the GIF format, allows images to be incrementally drawn on the screen as they come across the wire. Rather than appearing only after the entire image is transmitted, interlaced images appear on the screen a little at a time as they are transmitted over the network.

The effect is similar to watching a Polaroid photograph develop before your eyes; you have an idea of what the image is before it is completely downloaded, and you see it materialize on the page over time. If you give users something to watch as the image becomes clearer, they aren't as likely to abort the process and go elsewhere. Instead, many will stick around and watch these images as they gradually appear.

## GIF and JPEG: The Bottom Line

Since the GIF format supports both transparency and interlacing, in addition to being the default format for Web graphics, you'll more often than not find it a better choice for your applets than JPEG.

However, GIF images are currently limited to 256 (8-bit) colors. The JPEG format, on the other hand, supports over 16 million (24-bit) different colors. In cases where you absolutely must have more than 256 colors in an image, you'll have to use the JPEG format.

JPEG images are compressed using a *lossy* compression algorithm, a technique in which information is discarded, or lost, during compression, allowing you to specify a tradeoff between image quality and storage size. When you use high levels of compression, these images lose information (hence, the term lossy). Future versions of the JPEG format may include support for transparency and interlacing, although at the moment, neither are available.

A new version of the JPEG format, called JPEG Progressive Download (fondly known as Progressive JPEG), is similar in nature to an interlaced GIF. As these images come across the wire, they are displayed incrementally. At first they look blurry, but they become sharper and more defined as the image data is downloaded, until finally the entire image is clearly visible. Unfortunately, this new JPEG format is not yet supported by Java. However, future versions of Java are expected to support it.

Although you might think the choice of formats is clear — use GIF in most situations and turn to JPEG only when you need more than 256 colors — you ought to consider that some early releases of Java for Windows dither ALL graphics to 256 colors before displaying them! This is because supporting more than 256 colors on Windows-based machines proved too time consuming for the first release of Java. So, even if you use JPEG images, their beauty will be lost on Windows users who have an outdated version of Java.

If you can do it, you're better off using GIF images. Since most users won't be able to see the difference anyway, there's no sense wasting disk space or bandwidth with high-resolution JPEG images, unless you have no choice.

In general, you should keep the total amount of material that has to download for each Web page (text, graphics, sound files, and so on) under 250K. If you have a lot of graphics and are above 250K in total Web page material, you should consider using the JPEG format, simply to gain the highest degree of compression possible. Since images with more than 100 colors tend to compress more efficiently in the JPEG format than they do with GIF, first target images with the most colors for JPEG compression.

If you still have too much data to download, consider reducing the overall amount of material on the page. You can also reduce the dimensions of the images, cropping out excess material altogether. And, of course, you can always use the JPEG format with the highest degree of compression for all your images. Just be aware that you'll lose both the transparency and interlacing features available with the GIF format.

Finally, there is the user's equipment to consider. Many computer users can't see more than 256 colors on their screen anyway. In fact, a large number of systems connected to the Web can't even display that many. For some, the upper limit is 16 colors or less!

Although I wouldn't spend a great deal of time attempting to accommodate systems at the lowest end, I highly recommend that you assume the majority of users can see only up to 256. So the choice between JPEG and GIF becomes even easier.

**Tip**     You can bundle together class files, images, sounds, and any other files your program uses into a single compressed Java Archive (JAR). JAR files are similar to ZIP compressed files, although they are especially for Java. See Chapter 25, "Deploying Applets and Applications" to learn how to compress and bundle your program files in this format.

# User System Considerations

In addition to considering bandwidth, you must also consider the variety of systems your programs will run on once they become available to a global population. Just as most users lack ultrafast connections to the Web, they're often surfing with systems that are remarkably less powerful than those we use to develop applets and applications. As a result, you must develop your Java programs to run on a wide variety of systems, from entry-level boxes to silicon-heavy hot rods.

In addition to raw computing horsepower, you must also consider the wide range of video displays on which your programs will be viewed. In short, you must design your applets and applications to run on just about every system out there, or risk alienating those whose systems aren't up to your personal standards. This means eliminating excessive processing and media consumption and streamlining your programs in ways that you might not consider necessary based on your own computer setup.

To do this, you have to think in terms of absolute efficiency from the get-go, cutting out every unnecessary bit and byte of code and media (sounds and images) possible, and testing the results as you go along on a variety of low-end computer systems.

## Using built-in colors

When using colors for rendering primitive graphics (such as lines, rectangles, ovals, and polygons), stick to the predefined colors supplied by Java. Although you can define your own colors, with over 16 million options, it's a bad idea to assume the user will ever see them. Because many users have only 256 colors on their systems, and some only 16, any custom color that you define will usually be converted to the closest match or dithered down to accommodate less capable monitors. Your efforts will be lost on all but those who happen to use systems like yours. To be safe, use the built-in colors and only define others when absolutely necessary.

### Color Matching

To complicate matters, you can't guarantee that an image or color will be consistent across multiple platforms. Colors on a Windows machine won't necessarily look the same as those on a Sun machine, and they will look different once again on a Macintosh. As more platforms become Java-savvy, the disparity will grow.

To combat this problem, stick to minimal palettes and built-in colors. Don't spend too much time trying to get an image or color just right until you've had a chance to view it on a variety of platforms. The time you spend tweaking an image or color may well be wasted, since few users will have exactly the same system and display setup as you.

Instead, go for attractive and clean images. Avoid subtle hue shifts, fine lines in special colors, custom palettes, and the like. Before you spend too much time refining an image or creating custom colors for your primitives, take a look at it from a different perspective: put what you have on the Web, and view it with as many different systems and browsers as possible. If you don't have access to a particular platform, ask a friend who does to give his or her opinion. The earlier in the development process you do this, the better off you'll be.

### Animation

The most eye-catching feat an applet or application can do is animate images and graphics. When items move around the screen, you can't help but look at them. Unfortunately, you must also be aware of the diversity of systems on which your animations will be run.

Animation takes horsepower, and if you've spent time honing an animation to look ideal on your system, you can guarantee it won't appear that way to everyone else. What happens when an animation created on a high-end workstation is run on an entry-level personal computer? Digital road kill, that's what.

In such cases, the animation may be considerably slower than you'd expect. As a result, it loses its appeal to those with less capable systems; low-end users won't find it nearly as fascinating or slick as those using high-performance systems.

Interestingly enough, the exact opposite can happen when an animation is developed specifically for low-end systems. The developer might have spent considerable time and effort making the animation as fast as possible on a low-end development system, but when it's executed on a much faster machine, it runs the risk of being so fast that it can't be appreciated — or even seen!

To reduce the risk on both fronts, you must assume that your programs will be run on a wide range of systems. Some will be blazing fast, perhaps souped up with multiple processors, while others will be painfully slow by comparison.

Don't despair! There's no need to throw yourself over the nearest cliff. Just hang on for a few more minutes; as you'll soon see, there are a few optimization techniques you can use to create animations that execute smoothly in all cases.

### Frame rate support

First, always assume your programs will run on machines that are considerably faster than yours. Although you may have a top-of-the-line system today, tomorrow it will be old news. In particular, if you are to prepare for tomorrow's fastest machines, you need to exercise control over how fast the individual frames in an animation are drawn. Although you might think that no delay between frames is ideal, nothing could be further from the truth.

With no delay between frames, the animation will run at breakneck speed. It might seem perfect on your machine, but on faster computers it may become a blur roughly equivalent to a shooting star seen through the windshield of a moving car on a foggy night. Inserting a delay between each frame, however, gives your eyes a moment to actually see the various stages of animation; you effectively apply the breaks a wee bit between frames, giving your feeble eyeballs just enough time to focus on the current frame before advancing to the next one in the series.

Unfortunately, a problem arises when you control the frame rate with only faster systems in mind. Suppose, for example, that you've inserted a half-second delay between every frame in an animation. This is fine when running on fast machines, preventing blur, but when run on low-end systems, it could be a tremendous detriment to the animation.

The problem is that on slower machines, the frame rate is already slow enough for the frames to be painfully visible, so why add another half-second delay? In practice, you might need to eliminate the artificial delay altogether to compensate for this.

Rather than inserting a delay between every frame, you need only ensure that a specific amount of time has passed between the previous frame and the one about to be drawn. If the machine is incredibly fast, you'll want to delay the process a bit, but if the machine is incredibly slow, you'll want to draw the next frame as quickly as possible.

Although this may sound like a lot of work, you'll be happy to know that it's pretty easy to do. You simply enter a loop that does nothing but check to see if it's time to draw, and exit the loop when enough time has passed between the last frame being drawn and the current one. Following is *pseudocode* (not the real McCoy, merely a rough idea having no direct relationship to a specific programming language) for just such a timing device, which would take place just before each frame is drawn:

```
while (timepassed < framerate) {
   update timepassed variable
     ... do nothing else but loop while waiting ...
}
... draw the current frame ...
timepassed = 0; // reset timer
```

**Tip**    Java 1.3 includes a Timer class (java.util.Timer) and a TimerTask class (java.util.TimerTask) that are especially useful for animation and other time sensitive tasks.

### Reduce overhead

The technique of controlling frame rate should only be coupled with a serious effort to reduce any overhead that might occur within your animations. The easiest way to do this when animating a series of images is to reduce the storage size of each image, as discussed in "Bandwidth Considerations" earlier in this chapter.

If the images in an animation are massive in size, low-end machines will barely be able to keep up with it. Likewise, low-end machines might not be up to the task if the calculations required to derive the next frame in a computer-generated animation (in other words, not animating a series of images, but generating each frame on the fly) require a great degree of computational power. Although high-end systems won't have a problem keeping up with each frame of the animation, and may even require an artificial delay between each, many low-end systems will be left in the dust.

To allow low-end machines in on the fun, it's a good idea to streamline all parts of your animations. When animating images, you can reduce the storage size of each one by reducing the color palettes, as described earlier, and by restricting the overall dimensions of each image. When generating animation frames on the fly, you should give considerable attention to making the frame generation algorithm as tight and efficient as possible. And in both cases, you should use threads to prevent processing bottlenecks from monopolizing the central processing unit (CPU).

**Note**    Threads are a powerful, complex feature of many modern operating systems, and Java allows us to tap into them with relative ease. Threads give us the capability to run many different tasks concurrently, without forcing us to keep track of the state of each task. (That is, we can set up threaded objects that run independent of our main program, without our having to write terribly complicated code to manage everything that's going on.) For details on using threads in your Java programs, see Chapter 14, "Threads."

To further reduce overhead, you can decrease the download time of individual images used in an applet animation by placing all of them in one image file. If you do this, the user downloads a single *animation strip file*, which is a single image file that contains all of the images instead of a number of separate images (each of which would require a separate HTTP network connection otherwise). The images in an animation strip file are transmitted across the wire more efficiently and without the overhead of multiple connections. To use this method, you draw the appropriate portion of the animation strip on the screen rather than drawing a number of different images one after another. And instead of loading each individual image into memory, the single file is loaded into memory.

## Processing bottlenecks

Depending on what your programs do, they may or may not suck up a considerable amount of system resources. For those that are computationally intensive or manage a large number of images, it's important to reduce potential bottlenecks. Any time one task blocks others, such as when your program uses input/output (I/O) streams or performs complex computations, you should consider implementing the task in its own thread.

Threads are dealt with fully in Chapter 14, "Threads," but suffice it to say here that they allow multiple tasks to occur at once when multiple central processing units are available, or are so interwoven with one another that they appear to be happening at the same time even on systems that have only one processor. And, since a time-consuming task running in a thread can yield to other threads, you can eliminate processing bottlenecks; each task gets a crack at the CPU without requiring the current task to be completed in entirety.

At times when your program is immersed in a particularly time-consuming activity (such as retrieving large chunks of data from a file, or performing complex calculations), it's a good idea to let the user know what's going on. If too much time passes before the applet or application somehow informs the user that events are going along as planned, they may assume that the program isn't working properly or simply become impatient and abandon your Web page or quit the program altogether.

There are a number of ways to indicate to the user that your program is involved in a time-consuming task. You can display a message, such as "Processing . . . Please Wait," either in the program itself or, in the case of applets, on the status bar portion of the browser. (If you want to display a message in the status bar, however, keep in mind that not every browser on the market may have one, and, for those that do, remember that users are free to hide them from view entirely!)

A more subtle approach is to change some aspect of the program to visually indicate that activity is taking place. A small animation showing sand pouring through an hourglass might be appropriate, or perhaps a blinking "WORKING" image would do the trick. You might even consider a subtle sound loop or play a sound clip of a voice saying, "Please wait." Whichever way you do it, it's a good idea to let users know they'll have to be patient.

If the process is particularly long, you should consider altering the message occasionally. If the same message appears for a long period of time, users might think the system has frozen or is not working properly. If the message alternates, the frame rate changes, or the rate of an animation alters as time passes, they'll be less likely to think something is wrong and abandon ship.

## Choosing fonts

When using fonts to display text, you'll need to be careful about which ones you choose. Since you can't be sure which fonts are installed on the various machines on which your applet will be executed, it's important to determine if a font you want to use is available to all systems before attempting to use it. If you try to use a font that isn't installed on everyone's computer, a font substitution will take place that might ruin the visual effect you had planned.

It's simple, and recommended, to find out which fonts are installed. To do so, you use the `getFontList( )` method of the `Toolkit` class. However, you don't have to bother if you're using the widely installed Dialog, Helvetica, Times Roman, Courier, and Symbol fonts; these fonts are available on practically every Java-savvy computer system.

# File Access and Network Considerations

The majority of applets you create will require external data stored in a file (such as images, audio clips, and so on), which must be located on the Web. Because of the security restrictions imposed by current browser implementations, applets fetched from the Net can't access local files, so any files an applet accesses must be stored on the same Web server that the applet itself resides on.

## Retrieving files

Save yourself the frustration of trying to access local files, or files located anywhere but on the server where the applet itself resides, as it would be an exercise in futility. Since applets simply aren't allowed to touch files residing anywhere outside of the server on which they themselves come from, it's hopeless to even try to access files on the user's machine or other Web servers.

Although Java 2 supports fine-grained levels of security that allow applets both local and remote file access, most uses will veto such activity (applets have to get permission from the user to perform these operations), and so you're better off designing your applets to retrieve files from their own server. However, the same isn't true for Uniform Resource Locator (URL) connections. Your applets can open any valid URL and have the browser automatically load the page. (See Chapter 5, "Stepping Through Code," for details on the showDocument() method)

These restrictions on Java applets do not apply to Java applications. Applications can access files on the user's local system, or from anywhere on the Web (assuming, of course, that they can make a connection to the Web server on which such files are located). As a general courtesy, however, it's a good idea to let the user know when such activity is taking place (by displaying an animated icon that conveys network activity, for example).

## Testing locally, releasing globally

Although your applets can't load files located on the user's own computer without their express permission, or on a server other than the one they come from, you can do the majority of development and testing on your local system.

Rather than going through the process of uploading each revision of your applet to the Web and testing it from afar, you can write and test your applets locally, assuming the data files they require are also local. If an applet's directory layout on your local computer system is the same as the one on the server the applet will be uploaded onto, and if all of the files the applet requires are present and in the same relative directories, you can greatly streamline the development process.

In this case, you can write and test applets locally and merely upload them to the server when you are ready to test them in a networked environment. Of course, you'll want to test them extensively after you've placed them on the Web. However, developing and testing locally can still save you a great deal of time.

# Other Considerations

There are a number of other design issues to consider when developing Java programs. For starters, you must assume that your applets (and possibly applications) will be accessed by a global community. As a result, the end user's language and computing platform are out of your control.

## Images — a universal language

Since not everyone in the world speaks your language (except, perhaps, the language of love—but that's another story altogether), try to minimize the amount of text you use. If possible, use images and icons to convey meaning rather than words.

In many cases, of course, text is required and you'll have no choice. But when you do have a choice, opt for images rather than words.

You should also consider the concept your images convey. Even though images are often more easily understood than words, just because you're using them doesn't mean the concept they convey is universal. In cases where your applet must be understood by a diverse audience, it's a good idea to have the graphic artist creating the artwork used in your applet to consult with a multilingual specialist or agency beforehand.

 **Caution**   Avoid language and images that could be construed as racist, sexist, or culturally insensitive. What may be appropriate to you, might be offensive to others. In cases where you are developing applications for a specific market place, you should consider using Java's internationalization packages to localize your program for a specific language.

## Layout managers

Because Java programs can be run on a variety of platforms, it can be a bit difficult to ensure that your graphical elements will always appear in the proper positions on the screen. If you attempt to explicitly position elements (buttons, scrollbars, pop-up menus, drawing and painting areas, for example) at exact locations on the screen, you're flirting with disaster. The system of coordinates on your computer won't map exactly to others, so your neat and tidy layout may become an ugly mess (or even impossible to use) on other platforms.

To overcome this difficulty, Java uses layout managers, which are dealt with in detail in Chapter 20, "Layout Managers and More Components." With layout managers, you don't place elements on the screen using explicit coordinates. Instead, the order in which you add them, and the layout manager associated with such elements, dictates where they'll be placed. When your program's graphical user interface is displayed, the layout manager positions the elements in their proper places, regardless of which platform the applet or application is executed on. Furthermore, when the user resizes your program, the layout manager takes care of repositioning each element accordingly. By using Java's layout managers, you can ensure that your program's graphical user interface will look and act as it should across a wide array of platforms.

## Interapplet communications

In many cases, a single applet won't be appropriate for your needs. For example, you might require applet activity in one part of a Web page to be coordinated with activity in another part of the page. You might also need to have standard Web content appear between the two different areas, preventing you from creating one big applet that spans the entire page.

Rather than creating one giant applet, it may be easier and more appropriate to create two. Since applets in a Web page can send each other messages, they can effectively "talk" to each other. In fact, you can have any number of applets in a Web page, all communicating with one another. (See Chapter 5, "Stepping Through Code.")

## Dual-purpose programs

At times, you'll develop Java programs that will be deployed both in applet and application form. There may be differences between the two, but portions may be exactly the same. When this is the case, you don't have to develop both programs separately. Instead, you can write one body of code that can be executed as both an applet and an application, as illustrated in Chapter 25, "Deploying Applets and Applications." Doing so saves the time and effort of managing two different versions of essentially the same program, and it ensures that consistency and code integrity exists between the two.

# Managing Source Code

When it comes time to implement your applet, you'll have to carefully consider the code you will write in addition to the design issues discussed earlier in this chapter. Although much of the time and effort you spend will go into the overall design of the applet and the objects that will make it possible, eventually you'll have to get down to the nitty-gritty and write the actual source code. When programming in Java, there are number of common Java development practices that you can follow to make the process go as smoothly as possible.

## Only one class to a source file

As you learned in Chapter 2, "Object-Oriented Programming with Java," objects are created using code templates known as classes. When creating a large number of classes, you should consider placing each in its own source code file.

By separating classes into their own source files, the concept of programming in terms of objects is strongly reinforced. Classes in separate files can interact with others only in a well-defined manner, meaning you won't be tempted to take shortcuts that might compromise the integrity of your code.

When you compile an applet or application whose classes exist in multiple source files, each is automatically compiled in turn. You don't have to worry about compiling every source file on your own, making the separation that much easier.

For many smaller programs, however, saving each class in a separate source code file may be more hassle than it's worth. When you are beginning to program in Java, as with any language, it helps to start out with small programs and work your way to more complex ones as your understanding grows.

When you place more than one class in the same source file, be sure to remember that each class should be written as its own island and have no knowledge of the innards of other classes. Even if classes aren't physically separate, their implementation should be independent from that of others. Later, when your programs become more complex, you may choose to separate classes into their own files.

Keep in mind as you set forth on your Java programming adventure, that each source code file can contain only one public class. If you attempt to place more than one public class inside a single source code file, the Java compiler will refuse to compile the file!

**Tip**    Although it is possible to access an object's public variables directly from another object, you should instead use methods to set and retrieve variables. In addition, you should consider making your own variables private to prevent such direct access. By making a variable private, you force other objects to interact with it only through methods, reinforcing the modularity and encapsulation of your code. Methods used to get or set variables are known as *accessor methods*, and typically begin with "get" and "set" (for example, `getPoint()` and `setPoint()` ). To learn more about accessor methods see, Chapter 6, "Tokens, Types, and Values."

## Document, document, document

As with most programming languages, it's highly recommended that you document your programs as they are written, using code comments. Document? Comments?! Yep. But before you jam that index finger down your throat in an attempt to clear your now queasy stomach, hear me out.

Although many programmers tend to gloss over source code documentation or avoid it altogether, it's an important part of the process. So important, in fact, that Java provides a special comment that is used to generate documentation files in HTML format — complete with hyperlinks — directly from source code. By making the process of documentation so easy, Java encourages even the most hasty programmers to properly comment their code.

Thanks to Java's special document comments, or doc comments — which look almost exactly like the standard C comments (with the exception of an added asterisk) — creating code documentation is a cinch. In addition to making your source code easier to understand when it comes time to enhance or maintain the work you've done, you can use doc comments to produce lovely HTML documentation that you would otherwise have had to create by hand. (See Chapter 5, "Stepping Though Code" for details.)

Thanks to doc comments, a single effort on your part (and a simple one at that) produces two extremely useful forms of code documentation. You can't beat that, can you?

# Choosing variable names

When you're using variables, it's important to choose clear and understandable names for them. Just as with source-level documentation using comments, some programmers tend to choose terse, if not entirely cryptic, variable names.

Reading and maintaining such code is more difficult than it should be, and it can be especially frustrating and time consuming for people other than the original programmer. Even in cases where you'll be the only one to see the code, it's smart to use descriptive variable names. As time passes, you'll find reading the code a pleasure because it remains readily understandable.

In Java, variable names can be any length, so you're not restricted in how many characters you can use. Employ as many as you feel necessary to ensure that the names make sense.

Of course, some variables don't merit distinguished names. Take, for example, variables used to control the iteration of loops and other control-flow structures. Typically, single-character names (such as i or x) are just fine, since experienced programmers recognize such variables as being specific to the loop. In these cases, using a descriptive variable name (such as `loopCounter` or `iterationCount`) buys little, if any, value and may even make the code more difficult to read by cluttering an otherwise clean implementation.

Since different types of variables serve different purposes in your programs, be sure to follow the recommended naming conventions when it comes to actually giving your variables identifying names. Chapter 6, "Java Syntax: Tokens, Types, and Values," describes the conventions for identifiers (names given to variables, classes, and methods).

# Altering variables

In Java, there is no such real concept of a "global" variable. Instead, objects contain variables, which other objects may or may not be able to alter directly depending on how access to the variable is specified. (You specify access using access specifiers, which are known formally as field modifiers. Access specifiers are discussed in detail in Chapter 9.)

As a general rule, however, objects should assume no knowledge whatsoever of the details of other objects in a program. This means that an object shouldn't be able to directly access another object's variables, regardless of how access to such variables is specified. Instead, the object should politely request through a method call that the other object access its own variables and return the result or modify the value it holds.

For example, if object A wants to retrieve a variable inside object B, it should ask B for the variable. Likewise, if object A wants to change the value of a variable in object B, it should ask object B to alter its own variable. This way, your objects won't have intimate knowledge of one another, and you can easily replace or update one without affecting the others. You accomplish such behavior by using accessor methods, which are nothing more than methods used to retrieve and/or alter the value of an object's variable. Thanks to accessor methods, the objects in your Java programs are much more modular in nature, letting you easily update or alter them in the future without worrying about "breaking" hard-coded dependencies among objects. You'll learn more about accessor methods in Chapter 7.

## Avoiding native code

Although Java allows programmers to use non-Java, or native, source code (such as C code), you should always rewrite the code in standard Java if possible.

To make a clean transition to Java, you shouldn't try to use your existing non-Java source code unless absolutely necessary. Instead, you should take the time to rewrite that code in Java to avoid potentially compromising the object-oriented nature of your programs.

Aside from the fact that it's good practice to use pure Java code in your programs, only C may be integrated at this time (unless you use the Java Native Interface—JNI). So you shouldn't even consider using code in other languages. If, however, you rely on existing C code that simply can't be rewritten in Java, you can integrate this native code into your Java programs. If you do so, however, be forewarned—you'll likely spend the majority of your bug-fixing time inside the native code you introduce into your programs! And, you'll certainly lose the advantage of platform independence.

## Peeking under the covers

One of the best ways to learn how to program in Java is to look at the work of others. In addition to getting your hands on source code from sites such as JavaWorld (http://www.javaworld.com/) and Gamelan (http://www.gamelan.com/), you should spend some time looking at the source code provided with Java itself. The SDK, which provides all the tools you'll need to write your own Java programs, gives us a great deal of code to examine.

Along with the SDK's own applets, thousands of lines of Java code are used to implement the prebuilt standard Java class libraries you'll use to write your own programs. In particular, the SDK class source files provide an excellent insight into the Java language. They illustrate every aspect of the Java language and are documented with source code comments. Don't be afraid to peek under the covers; you'll see how the Java team at Sun writes Java code, and learn a great deal in the process.

**Tip**    Source code for the Java class library is bundled into a compressed Java Archive named `src.jar`, which is located in the main Java folder created when you installed the SDK. JAR files are actually compressed in the ZIP format, meaning you can change the file extension of the file from .*jar* to .*zip* and then uncompress it with a standard ZIP utility (such as WinZip, available on the Web at `http://www.winzip.com/`). Alternately, you can decompress `src.jar` using Java's own jar tool, as described in Chapter 25, " Deploying Applets and Applications."

## Getting organized with packages

Once you've written a fair amount of Java code, you'll be faced with the challenge of managing it. You'll eventually want to reuse classes you've written and organize your growing base of code for future reuse.

In Java you can easily organize classes into packages (discussed in Chapter 9, "Classes, Interfaces, and Packages"). You can think of packages as collections of classes that allow you to efficiently organize and reuse existing Java code.

The Java system comes with a number of packages all ready for you to use. These packages contain a large number of prebuilt classes written by the Java team at Sun, many of which you'll use in your own programs. (See Appendix A, "Installing and Configuring the SDK" for a list of these packages.)

# Summary

Before diving in and writing your first Java applet, it's important to first consider the design of applets. Remember that "design" means not only the overall design — how it looks, what it does, how it interacts with the user, and so forth — but also the internal organization of the source code needed to create the applet in the first place.

✦ Remember that every person who encounters your program will have a different opinion as to what is and isn't cool; keep animation and sound effects to a minimum unless they're an integral part of your program (such as a video game).

✦ Assume that the average user connects to the Web using dialup modems no faster than 28.8 Kbps. Iceberg-sized images and audio clips abound on the high seas of the Web. And while this may be just fine for the developer who has access to the network via a T1 line, DSL or cable connection, the equivalent of an ocean liner, the rest of the world isn't so fortunate; creaky wooden rafts and pontoon boats are the norm. To conserve bandwidth, consider compressing your program files into an easily managed Java Archive.

✦ Along with bandwidth concerns, you must consider the variety of systems on which your programs will run, especially applets because they are available to a global population. Just as most users lack ultrafast connections to the Web, they're often surfing with systems that are remarkably less powerful than those we use to develop applets. As a result, you must design applets to run on a wide variety of systems, from entry-level boxes to silicon-heavy hot rods.

✦ The majority of programs you create will require external data stored in a file (such as images, audio clips, and so on), which are often located on the Web. Because of the security restrictions imposed by current browser implementations, applets fetched from the Net can't access local files, so any files an applet accesses must be stored on the same Web server on which the applet itself resides.

✦ When designing your Java programs, you should have only one class to a source code file; add as much documentation as possible; use understandable variable names; provide methods to manipulate object variables; and avoid using any native code.

✦ ✦ ✦

# HelloWorld Application and Applet

**I**n this chapter, we take a closer look at the difference between Java applications and Java applets by writing the infamous HelloWorld program. Here, you examine the source code for both the application and applet version of HelloWorld as you get to know the structure and purpose of both types of Java programs. You also execute each to better understand how they differ from a runtime standpoint.

## Application Versus Applet

The two fundamental forms of Java programs are the application and the applet. We refer to Java programs that are capable of being executed outside the context of a Web browser as *applications*. The primary difference between applications and applets is their purpose.

Java applications are just like the traditional desktop applications we're familiar with, although they require the presence of the Java runtime environment to be executed, as do applets. Unlike applets, however, Java applications aren't meant to exist on the Internet and to be executed as World Wide Web content. They are, instead, full-blown applications that exist and are executed on users' local computer systems, just as traditional applications (such as your word processor, graphics application, or spreadsheet).

Java *applets*, on the other hand, are designed to live on the network and to be executed as part of a Web page. That's why they're referred to as *executable content*; although they are imbedded in Web pages, just as standard content is, they are really little software programs and can be executed as such.

### Java Web Start

At the time this book went to press, Sun introduced a new "Java Web Start" API that promises to radically simplify the way in which Java and Java programs are installed on end user systems. Java Web Start allows you to create a "one click" Web page installer for your Java programs. In other words, end users can seamlessly install Java on their computer along with all of your program's custom classes by merely clicking on a Web page hyperlink. For details on this exciting new Java technology visit the Java Web Start home page at `http://java.sun.com/products/javawebstart/`

Applets require a Java-savvy browser such as Netscape Navigator (version 2 or later) or Microsoft's Internet Explorer (version 3 or later) because they must be downloaded from the network and, in essence, be given to the browsers' built-in Java runtime environment to be executed.

**Note**    Applets that take advantage of the new features of Java 2 (such as Swing graphical user interfaces discussed in Part IV of this book) require the Java plug-in to run because the runtime environment of today's Web browsers hasn't yet been updated to understand these new capabilities. Sun's Java plug-in allows applets to be executed by Sun's standalone Java 2 Java Runtime Environment (JRE), bypassing the browser's default runtime environment. (See Chapter 25, "Deploying Applets and Applications," for details.)

Because of their different purposes, applications and applets are structured differently, both in terms of their code and in how they are ultimately executed. To examine these differences, we'll walk step-by-step through the process of creating a HelloWorld application and applet.

HelloWorld is a simple program, with little practical purpose other than to illustrate the structure and syntax of real Java code and the process of compiling and executing such code. When executed, the program does nothing more than output Hello World! to the screen. Because the application version is a little less complex in terms of code and execution than the applet version, let's start with that.

## HelloWorld Application

Before we get into the nitty-gritty, be aware that Java programs, both applications and applets, are executed by a Java runtime environment. As a result, they are not considered standalone native programs because they require the presence of a Java environment that can interpret and execute the bytecode of which they consist.

In creating the HelloWorld application, we shall go through the following steps:

1. Set up a directory (folder) structure to store our code, including a master directory and subdirectories (subfolders).

2. Enter and save the source code using a standard text editor (such as Notepad).

3. Compile the source code using SDK's Java compiler tool (javac).

4. Execute the compiled application using the SDK's Java launcher tool (java), which passes the bytecode file created during the compilation process to a Java interpreter that can actually run the program and output the results to the computer screen.

**Tip**    If you're new to DOS, refer to Appendix A, "Installing and Configuring the SDK," to learn the essential commands you'll need for this and future chapters. (See the section entitled "The DOS Prompt Tango.") The rest of this book, this chapter included, assumes that you've read Appendix A (specifically the discussions about DOS and the SDK Java tools).

## Application directory structure

Before you begin writing a Java program, it's a good idea to set up a directory (folder) structure to store your code. In most instances, you'll create a new directory for each program, so I recommend a master directory in which all these subdirectories will reside. The location and name you choose for your master directory is up to you. I chose to create a master directory called code on the root level of my C hard drive (c:\code) for the sake of convenience.

Inside my master code directory, I created a subdirectory called Hello, in which the source code and compiled classes for my HelloWorld program are kept, as you can see in Figure 4-1. For the following example, let's assume that you have also created a Hello directory inside your master directory.

```
MS-DOS Prompt

C:\Java\aewcode>dir
 Volume in drive C is Server C
 Volume Serial Number is 347F-46BB

 Directory of C:\Java\aewcode

01/26/98  12:10p       <DIR>          .
01/26/98  12:10p       <DIR>          ..
01/26/98  12:10p       <DIR>          Hello
               3 File(s)              0 bytes
                          3,805,422,080 bytes free

C:\Java\aewcode>
```

**Figure 4-1:** Creating a hierarchy of directories for your HelloWorld program

How you create a directory depends entirely on the platform you use. Windows users can create directories in the Windows environment using their mouse (by selecting the File ⇨ New ⇨ Folder menu item while in Windows Explorer), or by issuing the mkdir command at the DOS prompt. Sun users can also use the mkdir command. Macintosh users, however, don't have a command line at which to enter such commands. They must select the New Folder item (using their mouse or the keyboard equivalent for this item) located under the File menu while inside the Finder.

## Entering and saving the source

Using a text editor such as Notepad or SimpleText, enter the following source code and save it as a plain ASCII text file named HelloWorldApp.java inside your Hello directory. Don't forget to include the .java extension, or the compiler won't be able to see it!

```
class HelloWorld {
  public static void main (String args[]) {
    System.out.println("Hello World!");
  }
}
```

Alternately, you can place each opening curly brace ({) on its own line if you prefer:

```
class HelloWorld
{
  public static void main (String args[])
  {
    System.out.println("Hello World!");
  }
}
```

It really doesn't matter how you organize your code blocks, as coding style is largely a matter of personal taste (unless you must follow strict coding conventions for an organization, which vary widely from organization to organization). You'll see both techniques in this book and the Java programs that you encounter on the Web. In fact, to conserve space yet distinguish between class and method code blocks we often place the opening curly brace of classes on a new line, but place them on the same line as methods:

```
class HelloWorld
{
  public static void main (String args[]){
    System.out.println("Hello World!");
  }
}
```

Did you notice that the name of the class, HelloWorld, isn't exactly the same as the name of the file in which it is saved? This is because we didn't specify the class as being a *public* class. If we had, the name of the source code file would have to be the same as the public class it contains. If this were the case, the source code file would be named HelloWorld.java to reflect the public `HelloWorld` class it defines. However, because our class isn't public, the file name can be anything we like. For details on public classes, see the section "Introducing Access Modifiers" in this chapter or refer to Chapter 9, "Classes, Interfaces and Packages."

## Declaring a new class

Before actually compiling the program, we'll walk through each line of code to get a better feel for the Java language—beginning with the first line:

```
class HelloWorld {
```

This line declares a new class, `HelloWorld`, the body of which begins following the opening curly brace (`{`). The closing brace (`}`) on the last line of our source code signifies the end of the class definition, which is the blueprint from which `HelloWorld` objects will be instantiated. Together, the opening and closing braces (`{ }`) form a *code block*, inside of which the source code that defines this class will appear (that is, one or more lines of Java code can appear between the opening and closing braces).

**Note**    A class declaration is also known as a *class signature*, and gives the class a formal name (HelloWorld, in this example), defines its accessibility to other Java classes, and also specifies the parent class from which it inherits state (data) and behavior (methods). Together, these characteristics form a unique sequence of characters for every class (the *signature*). In this example, both the access modifier and parent class are omitted from the class signature for the sake of simplicity. As a result, the default accessibility rules apply to this class, and it is automatically considered a direct descendant of the top-level `Object` class, from which all other Java classes are ultimately derived. (`Object` is a generic class found at the very top of the Java class hierarchy.)

Keep in mind that Java is an object-oriented language, where the fundamental building blocks are objects. In fact, everything in Java is an object; the language doesn't support global functions or global variables. This means that everything emanates from an object template, formally known as a class. What we are doing here is creating a class, the blueprint for an object. The class includes all the code for state (data) and behavior (methods), although in this example, we only have methods and no explicitly declared data.

All classes are derived, or are *subclassed*, from existing classes. In the case of our `HelloWorld` class, we do not explicitly specify which class it is a subclass of. When no *superclass* (a parent class from which a child subclass is derived) is specified, the default is assumed to be class `Object`. Although we could have explicitly specified that `HelloWorld` is a subclass of `Object`, as shown in the class signature below, there's no need to do so:

```
class HelloWorld extends Object {
```

In this example, we use the keyword `extends` to specify `HelloWorld` as a subclass of `Object`, although our original implementation performs the same function by default. When we later rewrite HelloWorld as an applet, we'll actually subclass the `Applet` class. In this case, we must explicitly extend the `Applet` class, as you'll see later. Let's move on with our application for now.

## Declaring a new method

The second line declares the `main()` method, which takes a string parameter that will contain any command-line arguments provided when the application is executed. Let's take a look at the implementation of the first line of code, or *method signature*, for the `main()` method:

```
public static void main (String args[]) {
```

Just as with C and C++, a `main()` function must be included in a Java application; without it, the interpreter would have no idea where to begin executing. (In Java, functions or routines are called methods.) And just as with C/C++, Java applications can be executed with command-line arguments. The arguments for Java are passed to the program through the string parameter, `args[]`.

> **Note**    This line declares a new method, `main( )`, the body of which begins following the opening curly brace ({) and ends with the closing brace (}) found immediately before the closing brace of the class definition itself. Inside method code blocks such as this are the lines of Java code that define how the method will behave when run. The method code block is said to be *nested* inside the class code block, as it resides inside (or nests in) the opening and closing braces of the class.

Although you must include the `string args[]` parameter in your `main()` method signature, you are under no obligation to use it. We ignore the `args[]` parameter in this example because we have no need to use command-line arguments in this extremely simple program. While command-line arguments are covered in more detail in Chapter 8, "Creating and Using Arrays and Strings" it's worth noting here that the `args[]` parameter is itself an object. It's an object of type `String`, a class defined to handle storage of character strings (whereas the `StringBuffer` class supports manipulation of strings). However, we do nothing with the `args[]` object in `HelloWorld`, so let's press on and take a closer look at the `main()` method itself.

Of most interest are the keywords preceding `main()`, specifically `public`, `static`, and `void`. As with C/C++, `void` simply means this method does not return any data. If it did, the data type it returned would be written in place of it. Straightforward enough, but what about the keywords `public` and `static`?

## Introducing access modifiers

The keyword `public` is an access modifier. It specifies that the `main()` method can be called by any object. This means the `main()` method is openly available to other objects and is not in any way restricted.

Java supports four access modifiers (`public`, `private`, `protected`, and "unspecified" or blank) that can be applied to both methods and data, giving the programmer control over method and variable accessibility to other objects.

Access modifiers are used to control the visibility (accessibility) of data and methods as seen by other objects in a program. By applying one of the three access modifier keywords (`public`, `private`, or `protected`) to classes, data, or methods, you can control the capability of other objects to use them. To apply an access modifier, include the appropriate keyword when declaring the data, class, or method:

```
private int   miles;  // private integer variable
public void main (String args[]) { } // public main() method
protected class HelloWorld { } // protected HelloWorld class
```

Although access control is discussed in more detail in Chapter 6, "Tokens, Types and Values," and Chapter 9, "Classes, Interfaces and Packages," you should always consider to what extent the data, classes, and methods in your programs will be accessible to other parts of your program. With this in mind, consider the various levels of control provided through access modifiers (specifically how they open up or restrict access to classes, data, and methods to subclasses and classes found in other packages).

 **Note**    Packages are used to organize Java classes, and they are described in detail in Chapter 9, "Classes, Interfaces, and Packages."

## public

Methods and data specified as `public` are accessible to any class, regardless of the package to which the class belongs. Classes can also be specified as `public`, making them available to other classes in other packages. In fact, Java requires that every applet be declared as `public`. However, only one `public` class is permitted in a source file. When a class is declared as being `public`, it must reside in a source code file of the same name (for example, a `public` `HelloWorld` class must be stored in a source code file named HelloWorld.java).

## private

Data and methods specified as `private` are accessible only from inside their own class and aren't available to methods in any other class (including subclasses). Unlike the public access modifier, `private` cannot be applied to classes. As a general rule you should always create `private` data members (variables, counters, etc.) and only provide access to them via methods (in other words, create highly encapsulated classes whose internal data structures aren't directly accessible).

Because very early versions of Java supported `private` classes, some of the older source code you may encounter on the Web might actually specify classes as `private`. Attempting to compile such code using the current release of the Java compiler, however, will result in an error. To remedy the problem, simply remove the `private` keyword wherever it is applied to classes.

## protected

Data and methods specified as `protected` are accessible only from inside their class or subclasses of their class. (Subclasses can even override `protected` methods and data.) As such, the `protected` specifier is preferred to `private` in cases where you want subclasses to have access to data and methods, but require tighter access restrictions than the `public` specifier provides. The `protected` modifier can't, however, be applied to classes (only class members, such as data and methods).

**Caution**   Use the `protected` access modifier with caution when applying it to your data members. Because subclasses can access and alter `protected` data members of your class you run the risk of unwittingly painting yourself into a corner (you can't change the name or data types of your own `protected` data members without fear that you'll "break" subclasses that access them directly!). A better approach is to declare your data members as `private` and provide a `protected` method through which subclasses can access that data (as a general rule of thumb it's always best to create highly encapsulated classes whose internal data elements aren't directly accessible).

## <blank> (unspecified)

If you don't specify an access modifier for methods and data, Java treats them as "friendly" members, having limited public accessibility. Such methods and data are accessible to other classes in the same package, but not to classes in other packages. If you don't explicitly specify a class access modifier, by default, it will be available only to classes within the package in which it is declared. (See Chapter 9, "Classes, Interfaces, and Packages.") This is also known as *package-level access.*

**Note**   Classes that aren't declared as being in a specific package are considered to be in a "default" package. As a result, if you don't place your class in a package it will go into a default package that is common to all classes that have no specific package defined (all of which have access to your unspecified methods and data). See Chapter 9, "Classes, Interfaces and Packages" to learn more about packages.

## static

Technically speaking, `static` is not an access modifier, although I include it here because it's important to understand the role this modifier plays as you step through the source code in this chapter. The keyword `static` specifies the `main()` method as a *static* method (more commonly known as a class method). Just like with access modifiers, the `static` modifier can be applied to both data and methods. When applied, `static` indicates that the method or variable can be accessed without first requiring that an object of the class they are part of be instantiated. (See the sidebar "Class Versus Instance.") If the keyword `static` is not explicitly applied to a method or variable, it is automatically considered to be an instance method or variable.

## Accessing an Object's Data and Methods

The final line in our HelloWorld program is the one that does all the work, at least as far as displaying the words "Hello World!" are concerned.

```
System.out.println("Hello World!");
```

What we've done is send the string "Hello World!" to the System class for output (in this case, standard output [STDOUT], typically the terminal or monitor). Because all data and methods in the System class are static, we don't need to instantiate an object of this class prior to referencing data and methods, as we have done. (Again, see the sidebar, "Class Versus Instance.") But what's going on with the two dots?

Periods, or dots, are used to access an object's data and methods. The syntax, described earlier in Chapter 2, "Object-Oriented Programming with Java," is known as *dot notation*, and it's similar to how you'd access struct (structure) elements in C and C++. Suppose you wanted to directly access the horizontal variable of the Point class we talked about earlier in Chapter 2. Although in that example, we declared both the horizontal and vertical data as private, if we had declared them public, the following would have done the trick:

```
int x = myPoint.h; // access and assign myPoint's h
                   // variable to x
```

# Compiling the source code

You're now ready to compile the source code, assuming you have typed it in and saved it as a plain ASCII text file with the name HelloWorldApp.java. Going on that assumption, and also that the directory in which you've saved the source file is named Hello (where Hello> is the command prompt), you would now run the Java compiler (javac):

```
Hello> javac HelloWorldApp.java
```

Assuming your file didn't contain typing errors, it should compile just fine. If not, the compiler will spit out a line or more showing you where the error was found. (See Figure 4-2.)

If this is the case, open your file and compare it carefully to the following source code:

```
class HelloWorld {
  public static void main (String args[]) {
    System.out.println("Hello World!");
  }
}
```

Be sure all the curly brackets ({}) for both the class and method are included, and check your spelling. Fix any problems, save the file, and try again. When the contents of your text file exactly match the HelloWorld source code shown here, you should have no problem compiling.

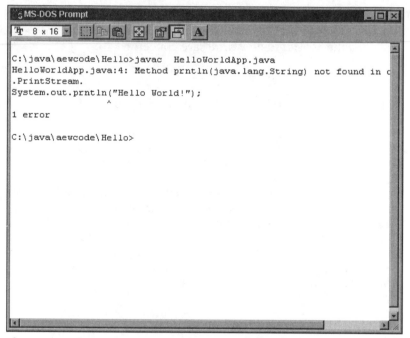

```
C:\java\aewcode\Hello>javac  HelloWorldApp.java
HelloWorldApp.java:4: Method println(java.lang.String) not found in c
.PrintStream.
System.out.prntln("Hello World!");
                 ^
1 error

C:\java\aewcode\Hello>
```

**Figure 4-2:** If your file contains errors, the compiler will spit out a line or more showing you where they were found.

**Tip**

Java is case sensitive! As far as Java is concerned, the string "Hello" is very different from "hello," "HELLO," or any other case variation. When typing in the code samples from this and other chapters, you must take great care to use the proper case. (The same is true for Java file names — don't forget to use the proper mixture of upper- and lowercase in your source code file names or you won't be able to compile them.)

You'll know the compiler is successful when no error messages are reported. Assuming you're in the Hello directory, where your source file is also located, the following is typical of a successful compilation (where Hello> is the prompt):

```
Hello> javac HelloWorldApp.java
Hello>
```

Because no errors were reported here, the compiler was able to convert the class defined in the source file into a corresponding binary bytecode file called HelloWorld.class. For every class the compiler comes across in a source file, it creates a bytecode file of the same name. Check to see if a bytecode file was indeed created. (Type the DIR command in DOS, or open the Hello folder with your mouse.) Your Hello directory should now contain two files: HelloWorldApp.java and HelloWorld.class.

Once you have successfully compiled the source code, which results in a binary bytecode file being generated in the same directory, it's time to run the program.

## Class Versus Instance

In Java, data and methods can be either class or instance members of the class in which they are declared, as indicated by the presence or absence of the `static` modifier. For example, the `main()` method of `HelloWorld` is a `static` method, which makes this method a class member. If the keyword `static` were not part of the method signature, such as in the following example, `main()` would instead be considered an instance method of the class `HelloWorld`:

```
public void main (String args [])
```

Static methods and data are associated with the class rather than with an instance of the class and are also known as *class data* or *class methods*. This is a fitting name because each class variable and class method occurs once per class; instance methods and data occur once per instance of a class. The difference between class and instance members is significant, especially when it comes to data.

By occurring only once per instance of a class, class members are shared by *all* objects created from a class. That is, all objects created from a given class share the class data and class methods defined in that class. Instance data and instance methods, on the other hand, are created anew each time an object is created—each object gets it own unique copy, which is entirely independent of those of other objects.

Class members can therefore be considered global to a class, even though true global variables aren't supported in Java. When an object changes the value of a class variable, all objects instantiated from that same class see the result. Because of this, class data is often used to share data intended to be common to all objects created from a particular class. Instance members, on the other hand, are unique to an object. (Instance variables, for example, can be modified independently of those used by another object, every object contains its own copy.)

To refer to instance methods and data, an object must first be instantiated from that class, after which it can access the methods and data through the instance. With static methods and data, however, there is no need to instantiate an object before referring to these class members. They can instead be accessed directly through the class by referring to the formal class name (as opposed to an object instance).

The use of a `static` method is seen in HelloWorld, as we call upon the `System` class to output a string of characters without first instantiating an object of that class:

```
System.out.println("Hello World!");
```

`System.out` refers to the `out` variable in the `System` class. We didn't instantiate an object from the `System` class, yet we are able to directly refer to the `static` `out` variable using

the class name ("System"). Because the `System` class declares `out` as a `static` variable, we can access it directly without the need for instantiation as the line of code here illustrates. If `out` were not declared as a `static` variable, we would have to first instantiate an object from the `System` class and then use that object to get to the variable.

*Continued*

*(continued)*

When the `System` class is loaded into an application, the Java interpreter automatically creates `out` and all other static data in that class. Because `out` is created automatically, the instance method `println()` it contains can be invoked, as we have done (The `println()` method is an instance method of `out`.) Java enables the programmer to cascade together (combine) references to static and instance methods and data, as we have done here (which accounts for the two dots in this particular line of code; the first dot accesses the `out` variable, while the second dot accesses the `println()` method of that variable).

In the `System` class, discussed in detail in Chapter 8, "Creating and Using Arrays and Strings," one of the members is `out`. The `out` member is itself an object, of which `println()` is a method. So, what we've done in the last line of HelloWorld code is access the `System` class's `out` variable, executing its `println()` method, passing our "Hello World!" string as a parameter.

## Executing the application

When you execute a Java application, you're executing bytecode. Therefore, you must pass the bytecode file created during the compilation process to the Java launcher (java):

```
Hello> java HelloWorld
```

Notice that we do *not* include the .class extension! The interpreter assumes you passed it just the file name of the class, not the file name and extension, for which it will automatically assume the extension is .class. If you give the launcher the .class extension, it will look for a file named HelloWorld.class.class and come up empty-handed. If you make this mistake, or do it intentionally just for kicks, an error message such as the following will be generated:

```
"Can't find class HelloWorld/class"
```

Also, notice that we have provided the interpreter with exactly the same upper- and lowercase formatting of the class name. This is no mistake, because Java is case sensitive. As far as Java is concerned, `HelloWorld` is not the same as a `helloworld`, `helloWorld`, or any other variation. Sure, you and I might recognize them as the same, but Java sees each as different. Be sure to provide the launcher with the precisely formatted name of the bytecode file, which should also be an exact replica of the compiled `HelloWorld` class.

Assuming that you enter the class name exactly, the bytecode file will be loaded by the interpreter and the `main()` method will be executed. When the line of code containing `System.out.println()` is reached, "Hello World!" is sent to the standard output device (STDOUT in C/C++), which is the computer screen by default, as shown in Figure 4-3.

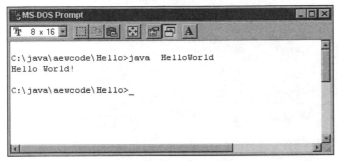

**Figure 4-3:** If you have successfully executed the bytecode, "Hello World!" is output.

Congratulations! You've just written, compiled, and executed your first Java application. Sure, it's no Microsoft killer, but that'll come in time. In the meantime, let's take a look at our HelloWorld program written and executed as an applet.

# HelloWorld Applet

Remember, while an application is executed using the Java interpreter and without any need whatsoever for a Java-savvy browser, applets are executed from within a Java-savvy browser.

Because of this, applets are a little more complicated to get up and running than applications. Not much, mind you, but a little. For starters, you have to create an HTML file (a Web page) that references the applet. And you also have to add a few more lines of code to your source file to let the Java compiler and runtime system know that these programs are applets and not applications. But once you get the hang of it, you'll find that these are really easy steps. Let's start by taking a look at the directory structure for our HelloWorld applet.

## Applet directory structure

Just as with an application, you'll need to create a directory to hold the source code file, compiled bytecode file, and HTML file for your applet. For this project, I created a HelloApplet directory right alongside the Hello directory created for the application version. Now, directories for both the applet and application version reside in my master code directory, as can be seen in Figure 4-4. Of course, the directory structure you choose is completely up to you.

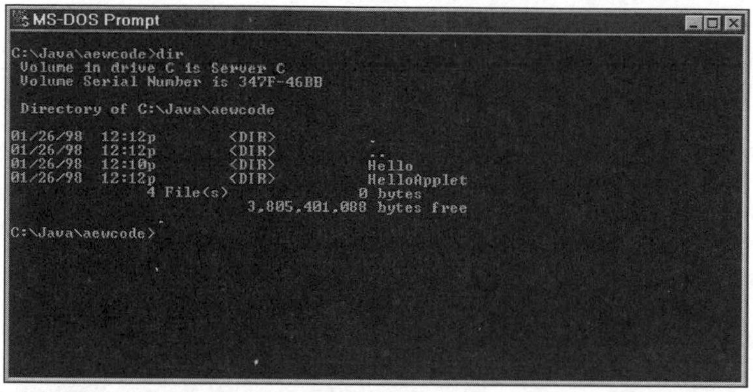

**Figure 4-4:** Directories for both the applet and application version of HelloWorld should now reside in your master directory.

## Entering and saving the source

As you did with the application version of this program, you'll need to type the following source code and save it as a text file in your HelloApplet directory. Because the class we are defining here is called `HelloWorldApplet`, you should name the source code file HelloWorldApplet.java. And, just as before, be sure to include the .java extension when naming the file:

```
import java.applet.*;
import java.awt.Graphics;

public class HelloWorldApplet extends Applet {
  public void init() {
    resize(200,150);
  }
  public void paint(Graphics g) {
    g.drawString("Hello World!",50,100);
  }
}
```

Once you have entered this code, it must be saved in a plain ASCII text file named HelloWorldApplet.java. If the class you are defining in an applet does not have the same name as the text file in which you save it, the compiler spits out an error message. This is because the class for our applet is defined as being `public`, meaning the source code file in which it resides must have the same name.

Suppose, for example, you entered the previous code exactly as shown but saved the file as HelloWorldStuff.java instead. The compiler would abort the mission and give you the following error message:

```
"Public class HelloWorldApplet must be defined in a file called
HelloWorldApplet.java"
```

However, if you enter the code exactly as shown and save it in an ASCII text file named HelloWorldApplet.java, you'll be all set. At this point, the applet is ready to be compiled. But before we do that, let's take a look at the new code our applet requires.

## Import

Right off the bat, our applet uses two lines of code not seen in the application version:

```
import java.applet.*;
import java.awt.Graphics;
```

These are very similar to the #include feature found in C/C++. Here, we are importing classes into our applet, methods of which our applet will use. The classes are from two different packages, or organized collections of classes, that come with Java: the applet package and the Abstract Windowing Toolkit (AWT). For more information on packages, see Chapter 9, "Classes, Interfaces and Packages;" for more information on the AWT, see Part IV, "Looking out the Windshield: User Interaction."

Take another look at the first line of import code:

```
import java.applet.*;
```

This import statement tells the compiler to give our applet access to every class in the java.applet package. This is done with the asterisk (*) character, or wildcard, which essentially means "everything at this package level." (You can think of packages in terms of directories, or folders, where periods separate directory names. The contents of this particular package would be written using standard DOS directory notation as java\applet\*.*.) Contrast this with the second line of code:

```
import java.awt.Graphics;
```

This line imports *only* the Graphics class from the AWT package. Here, the class we want to use in our applet — Graphics — is explicitly stated. Together, these two lines will provide our applet with minimal functionality that every applet requires, as you'll soon see. The java.applet package contains the classes that allow an applet to run inside a Web page, while the java.awt.Graphics class allows the applet to draw and paint on the screen, as described in the next section.

**Note**    I've intentionally used two different package import techniques here, wildcard and explicit, to give you an idea of how to use each. Since I need access to only one class in each package for my simple applet, I would normally have imported each class explicitly (`java.applet.Applet` and `java.awt.Graphics`). In cases where I need access to more than one class in a package, however, I prefer to use the wildcard approach. It's important to note that importing classes and entire package contents into your programs only gives you *access* to these files; they're not actually bundled into your compiled code as you might expect. The Java classes that your program uses are loaded dynamically at runtime; they don't actually become part of your program's bytecode. Thus, there is no penalty for importing an entire package using the wildcard technique.

## Class Declaration

Unlike the application, the class declaration for our applet is much more involved:

```
public class HelloWorldApplet extends Applet {
```

We specify the `HelloWorldApplet` class as being `public,` an access modifier indicating that this class is available to all other objects regardless of the packages of which they may be a part. We also explicitly state that this applet subclasses another. By extending the class `Applet` found in the `java.applet` package, the `HelloWorldApplet` class inherits the data and behavior in `Applet`. Because it is a subclass of the `Applet` class, `HelloWorldApplet` can be considered a more specialized version of `Applet`.

We could alternately have omitted the `import java.applet` statement entirely and simply referenced the precise `Applet` class name as follows:

```
public class HelloWorldApplet extends java.applet.Applet {
```

In this example, the `import` statement isn't needed because the compiler knows exactly which class we're talking about as a result of our preceding the class name `Applet` with the name of the package in which it is found (`java.applet`). Either approach is acceptable, as Chapter 9, "Classes, Interfaces, and Packages," explains, and the end result is the same in both cases: our `HelloWorldApplet` class inherits both state (data) and behavior (methods) from the `Applet` class found in the `java.applet` package.

Contrast this with the HelloWorld application we created earlier, which does not explicitly extend an existing class. By not specifying a particular class, `HelloWorld` became, by default, a subclass of `Object`. In the case of our applet, however, we need to inherit the properties of the `java.applet.Applet` class. All applets must extend this class, so this code is essential here and in any other applet you'll create. The inheritance tree—also known as a class hierarchy—for `HelloWorldApplet` is shown in Figure 4-5.

**Note**   Applet **can also extend** JApplet, **which is a** Swing **class that is itself a subclass of** java.applet.Applet. **Because** JApplet **is a** Swing **class, it's not yet widely supported by Web browsers, so it requires the use of the Java plug-in. See Part IV, "Look and Feel: User Interaction and User Interfaces," to learn more about Swing, and Chapter 25, "Deploying Applets and Applications," for Java plug-in details.**

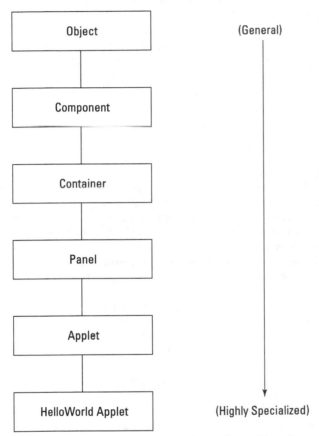

**Figure 4-5:** The inheritance tree for HelloWorldApplet

## Method Declaration/Overriding

At a minimum, most applets will declare two methods: init() and paint(). These methods are defined by the superclasses of all applets, including our HelloWorldApplet subclass. Specifically, init() is defined by the Applet class, while paint() is defined by the Container class (and originally defined in the

Component **class, of which** Container **is a descendant). Because these methods already exist within the inheritance tree of** HelloWorldApplet, **our class is said to** *override* **both** init() **and** paint().

By declaring a method in our class with the same name as one in a superclass, we replace, or override, the superclass's method with our own. Hence, we override the init() and paint() methods with our own specialized version of these methods. Let's take a closer look at each.

The first method we override, init(), takes no parameters, returns nothing, and is declared public. In fact, the only thing we do here is instruct the applet to resize itself to 200 pixels wide and 150 pixels high. The method used to do this, resize(), is part of the Applet class. Because we have imported Applet, we can invoke its methods:

```
public void init() {
   resize(200,150);
}
```

When our applet is executed and the resize() method call is encountered, the run-time environment will look inside the HelloWorldApplet class for the corresponding method definition (one having the same name and parameter types — two integer values, in this case). Since such a method does not exist in the HelloWorldApplet class, the runtime will then look for it in the Applet superclass. If resize() is found inside Applet, it will be executed. If not, the runtime will then look inside the superclass of the Applet class, meaning it will search for a resize() method in the Panel class.

The search will continue in this way all the way up the class hierarchy, until the top-level Object class is reached. If the method isn't found in Object, the runtime will generate an error. (In practice, such an error is first caught by the compiler, which will report that it can't find the given method during the compilation process.) The Applet class actually contains a matching resize() method; however, the runtime has no need to hunt up the hierarchy in this particular case. It will find and execute the resize() method defined by Applet.

**Note** Most Web browsers ignore the resize() method and instead rely on the **HEIGHT** and **WIDTH** attributes of the <APPLET> tag (described later) for sizing purposes. The Applet Viewer tool, however, respects the resize() method and will resize the applet accordingly.

After overriding init(), which is defined in the Applet class, we then override paint(), **which is a method defined in the** Container **class that gives applets the ability to draw and paint on the screen. Similar to** init(), **the** paint() **method is** public **and returns nothing. It does, however, take one parameter: a** Graphics **object. When called,** paint() **is passed an object of class** Graphics. **It uses this object, invoking the** drawString() **method contained in it, to draw our "Hello World!" string in the browser window at the location 50,100 (x,y).**

Unlike the `System.out.println()` code used in our application to output to `STDOUT`, applets use `paint()` to output to the browser window:

```
public void paint(Graphics g) {
    g.drawString("Hello World!",50,100);
}
```

The methods we've overridden are quite simple, as you can see, having only one line of executable code each. And thanks to Java's automatic garbage collection, we don't have to worry about disposing of memory or objects; we simply enter the code and let the Java runtime environment take care of these memory-management issues.

> Both `init()` and `paint()` are invoked automatically when an applet is first loaded into an applet environment (that is, the Applet Viewer tool or a Web browser). The `init()` method is called only once, however, as it is used for initialization purposes (such as setting variables, or resizing the applet as we've done here). The `paint()` method, on the other hand, is automatically called every time the applet area needs to be redrawn (such as when the Web page it is embedded inside of is resized, or a window is moved over the applet area). These and other applet methods that you will learn about later are called automatically by the Java runtime environment; you don't have to invoke them yourself. (See Chapter 5, "Stepping Through Code," for details.)

## Compiling your new applet

Java applets are compiled exactly as their application counterparts. If you've typed the code precisely as shown and saved it in a file named HelloWorldApplet.java, you should have no problem compiling your new applet. Enter the following at the command line (where HelloApplet> is the prompt indicating that you're inside the directory containing the source file):

```
HelloApplet> javac HelloWorldApplet.java
```

If the compiler is successful, a binary bytecode file named HelloWorldApplet.class will be created in the same directory as your source file. If not, double-check your source code against the previous listing and try again.

## Executing the applet (Part I)

Unlike applications, Java applets cannot be executed directly with the Java launcher. If you try, the launcher will tell you it can't find the `main()` method required for all applications. That's no surprise because we never declared `main()`

in our applet. As a result, the launcher will tell you that it can't find that method by throwing an "*exception*" (similar to a fit, as you'll learn in the chapters that follow):

```
HelloApplet> java HelloWorldApplet
Exception in thread "main" java.lang.NoSuchMethodError: main
```

To execute an applet, we must first create an HTML file that explicitly references it, using the `<APPLET>` tag, and then open that file with the Applet Viewer tool or a Java-savvy browser. Luckily, this is fairly easy.

## Creating an HTML file

Using the same text editor as you did to create your source code files, create a new file and enter the following:

```
<HTML>
<HEAD>
<TITLE> Hello World Applet Test </TITLE>
</HEAD>
<BODY>
Here is our applet:
<APPLET CODE="HelloWorldApplet.class" WIDTH=200 HEIGHT=150>
</APPLET>
</BODY>
</HTML>
```

When you're done, save this as a plain ASCII text file with the name TestApplet.html in the same directory as your new source and bytecode files. You can choose any name you want, but I'll use this name when referring to the HTML file.

All the HTML code you see here is standard, plain, vanilla stuff, except the following line:

```
<APPLET CODE="HelloWorldApplet.class" WIDTH=200 HEIGHT=150>
```

This is the line of HTML that tells a Java-savvy browser about our applet. The byte-code file is listed in quotes because it's the compiled code that the browser will load and execute. Notice that the entire class name and the .class extension is required. If .class is omitted, the applet may not be found (depending on how the browser you're using deals with `<APPLET>` tags). To be safe, and ensure that every Java-savvy browser out there can find your applet, be sure to include the .class extension. Also, the class name must match that generated by the compiler exactly. (See the section called "Considering HTML Case Sensitivity" later in this chapter.)

Because our applet is being executed locally, and because it exists in the same directory as the HTML file, there is no need to specify anything more than the name of the applet class file along with an initial width and height setting. However, if our applet was in a different directory than the HTML file, we would need to provide additional information (specifically the CODEBASE attribute discussed in the next chapter and Chapter 8, "Creating and Using Arrays and Strings").

**Tip**      An applet's initial width and height are determined by the <APPLET> tag WIDTH and HEIGHT attributes that you use when weaving your applet into a Web page. However, when the resize() method is encountered, some applet environments (such as the Applet Viewer tool) will dynamically resize the applet accordingly. Most Web browsers, however, simply ignore the resize() method and rely strictly on the <APPLET> tag for sizing purposes. You should therefore never rely on resize() when it comes to setting the size of your applets that are destined to live inside of Web pages, and you can omit this method entirely if desired.

## Using the WIDTH and HEIGHT attributes

These two attributes of the <APPLET> tag, both of which are required, instruct the browser to create a display canvas of these dimensions when first loading the applet. The canvas is where your applet will be displayed in the browser, and it can often be controlled from within the applet itself using the resize() method.

For our purposes, the WIDTH and HEIGHT attributes are the same as those used in our applet's resize() method, called in init(). We could have two different sets of values, although the resize() method is called after the HTML file is parsed, effectively overriding the dimensions provided in HTML. By supplying the same dimensions in HTML as we have in our source code, the canvas remains the same size when the applet is loaded by the browser as when it was actually executed.

## Considering HTML case sensitivity

Except for the class name, which must be written exactly and in the same case format as the bytecode file generated by the compiler, the <APPLET> tag is not case sensitive. That means you can write everything in this tag in upper-, lower-, or even mixed case. I've used uppercase for readability, although you should feel free to do as you wish.

For instance, either of the following three lines of HTML code would be fine:

```
<APPLET CODE="HelloWorldApplet.class" WIDTH=200 HEIGHT=150>
<applet code="HelloWorldApplet.class" width=200 height=150>
<Applet Code="HelloWorldApplet.class" Width=200 Height=150>
```

## Executing the applet (Part II)

Because an applet must be executed through a Java-savvy browser or similar environment, such as the Applet Viewer tool, we need only load our HTML file with one to see the results. However, it may not be terribly convenient to repeatedly launch a full-blown browser (or run it continuously) during the course of development. Therefore, I recommend using Applet Viewer when initially testing your applets.

In practice, Applet Viewer is just as effective, yet executes faster and uses much less memory. To execute your program with this program, simply provide it with your HTML file:

```
HelloApplet> appletviewer TestApplet.html
```

Notice that the entire file name is included, even the .html extension. This is because Applet Viewer expects the entire file name and will generate an error message if it can't locate the file you give it. However, if everything is in order, it will create a window and execute HelloWorldApplet in it. This is demonstrated in Figure 4-6.

**Figure 4-6:** If everything is in order, Applet Viewer will create a window and execute HelloWorldApplet.

Although Applet Viewer will execute any applets it finds in an HTML file, it won't display anything else. If you want to see the page as it will look to the world when placed on the Web (with text, graphics, hyperlinks, and anything else that's part of the page but isn't generated by an applet), you need to use a Java-savvy browser such as Netscape's or Microsoft's latest beauties.

## Living on the Web

Of course, in reality, your applets will be on a World Wide Web server waiting to be executed when visitors load your pages with a Java-savvy browser. In this case, the HTML file you create may specify the URLs of remote applets it expects to execute (See the CODEBASE discussion in the following chapter and Chapter 8, "Creating and Using Arrays and Strings.")

## JAR Files

Just as you can use a glass jar to store your tomatoes and peaches, you can use Java Archive (JAR) files to store your Java files. JAR files store Java packages, classes, and resources (such as images and sound files) in a compressed form. Because it takes time to download information over the Internet, if you can cram more information into less space your applets will load faster. When adding applets to your HTML files, the `<ARCHIVE>` attribute of the `<APPLET>` tag is used to specify a JAR file. Chapter 25, "Deploying Applets and Applications," reviews the process of weaving JAR files into Web pages"" and creating your own JAR files.

In the next chapter, we'll expand on the HelloWorld applet, adding sound and graphics. This new version of HelloWorld will exist on the Web, so we'll also update our source code to better handle life in cyberspace.

## Onward and upward

Although the HelloWorld application and applet aren't much to look at, they have helped you better understand the Java language and development environment. In fact, you've actually created two platform-independent programs, one of which — the applet — is capable of living on the Web. Not bad, considering it only took a handful of code.

In the next chapter we'll build on this to get a better understanding of how to create more sophisticated Java programs. We'll also upload the final applet to the Web, accessing it from there instead of from the hard disk. So, it's onward and upward with HelloWorld, but it's goodbye for now.

# Summary

Although the HelloWorld application and applet aren't much to look at, implementing them has given you a valuable skill: You can now create, compile, and run the two most popular forms of Java. In fact, you have created two platform-independent programs, one of which (the applet) is capable of living on the Web. Not bad, especially when you consider that it only took a handful of code.

Along the way we covered the following ground:

✦ Creating a new Java program from scratch using a plain text editor such as NotePad or SimpleText, with which you type Java code into a text file and save it as a file having the .java extension (such as HelloWorld.java)

✦ Compiling Java programs using the Java compiler (javac), which converts Java source code files into bytecode class files (i.e., HelloWorld.class).

✦ Executing Java applications using the Java launcher (java), a command line tool provided with the SDK.

✦ Using the HTML <APPLET> tag to weave a Java applet on a Web page, which can then be viewed with any Applet-savvy program (such as the SDK appletviewer program or a modern Web browser).

✦    ✦    ✦

# Stepping Through Code

**H**aving completed the simplistic HelloWorld applet and
application examples, it's time to improve on the work
we've started. In this chapter, we'll add an image and sound-
track to the HelloWorld applet. In doing so, we'll see how
classes are extended (subclassed) in Java, and learn more
about the mechanics of Java programming. Let's first consider
a question you'll ask yourself often when using Java: enhance
or extend?

## To Enhance or Extend?

When you develop software in any object-oriented programming (OOP) language, you'll often ask yourself whether the
task or program at hand should enhance existing classes or
extend them to create more specialized subclasses. In many
programs, you'll often do both.

To enhance an existing class means to add new data items
(such as variables or constants) or methods to that class.
To extend a class means you create a subclass that will contain new data or methods while the superclass itself remains
untouched. That is, you add your data and/or methods to the
subclass (perhaps even overriding methods in the superclass)
to get the state and behavior you want, without changing a
line of code in the superclass.

Whether to enhance or extend an existing class depends a
great deal on what it is you want to do. To make this decision,
you need to have a clear understanding of the class itself.
You need to ask yourself two basic questions:

1. Does the class have the essential data and behavior
   you need, and would it be easy to add to it?

2. Does the new functionality you want to add apply to
   all instances of the class, or just some?

If the functionality you want to add applies to the entire class (in other words, all instances require such functionality) and is easy to fit in with the class's existing data and behavior, then it's a good candidate for enhancing. If it lacks much of the data or functionality you require, or the new functionality only applies to *some* of the instances of the class, you're probably better off creating a custom subclass to contain your new functionality than you are modifying the original class.

Be very cautious when attempting to enhance an existing class. What you are actually doing is rewriting it. Therefore, you must take great care not to alter the public interface it currently supports for interacting with other objects, lest you "break" the class. If you change how it interacts with other objects, either by substantially changing its publicly accessible data and/or methods, the integrity of the class will be compromised and any programs or classes relying on it will suffer.

Tip    When you create your own classes, as you'll do later in this chapter, be certain to take advantage of Java's encapsulation capabilities by forcing all variable access to take place through methods. By making your class variables private, other classes (and even subclasses of your class) have no direct access to them except through the methods that you create. As a result, you'll eliminate the ability of other classes to become dependent on the internal structure of your class; in the future, you'll be able to enhance your custom class as long as you don't rename or change the parameters of existing methods (specifically the order, number, or data type of parameters).

While the decision to enhance or extend is made on a case-by-case basis, you'd do well to consider extending a class whenever possible. This, after all, is one of the key reasons OOP is so powerful. You don't have to go in and rewrite functions and data structures every time you need new functionality. In other words, you don't have to modify the source code and risk breaking the public interface on which other programs rely. Instead, you can simply create a subclass, inheriting all the data and behavior of the superclass, and add any specialized data and behavior that you need. In this case, you don't need access to the source code at all; as long as you know where the class file is, you're in business. In other words, enhancing requires access to the source code of the class that you wish to customize, while extending requires only the class. (You don't need the source code of a class to extend it!)

We can accomplish our task—adding sound and graphics to the HelloWorld applet and application created in the previous chapter—by either enhancing or extending these existing classes. Because the existing HelloWorld applet and application classes are so simplistic, however, there's really no good reason to extend them except as an exercise in learning more about inheritance and how it works. And

## Java Class Library Source Code

In many cases, you'll find that the existing classes supplied with Java (the class libraries) aren't enough for your programming needs. You can't, practically speaking, enhance the Java classes that are part of the Java runtime environment (that is, the class library that is installed along with the Java Runtime Environment (JRE), Software Development Kit (SDK), or a Java-enabled browser, for instance) because these are an integral part of the Java platform and doing so would only customize *your* particular Java setup — you'd have to somehow convince users to install your custom version of these classes over their standard installation, a dicey prospect at best.

A better alternative, should you actually need to enhance a core Java class, is to get your hands on the class library source code that ships with the SDK. (See Appendix A to find out where these files are located.) These source files are provided to you independent of the runtime classes, meaning you can customize them as needed and simply distribute the results along with your applet or application. The preferred route, of course, is to simply extend those premade classes that are part of the Java class library, as you'll do in this chapter. (In this case, you don't need access to the source code at all because you can extend a compiled class file without regard for its source code.)

Finally, you can always create your own custom classes from scratch by extending the top-level `Object` class (a general-purpose class from which all Java classes ultimately descend) when you can't find a premade class in the Java class library that makes sense to extend for your purposes.

that's exactly what we'll do, starting with the `HelloWorldApplet` class. This will help us become more comfortable with the concept of extending a superclass to inherit its state and behavior.

## Extending the HelloWorldApplet class

Because we're going to extend the class, we need to create a new ASCII text file for the source code in Listing 5-1, which will then be compiled and executed. Create a new file using whatever text editor you prefer, enter the source code, and then save it in the same directory as the `HelloWorldApplet` class.

This code isn't very complex, by any stretch of the imagination, and it's not very flexible, as you'll soon see. We'll add some meat to this bare-boned media applet in a moment, but for now, this is all you need to digest the concept of extending an existing class.

**Listing 5-1: MediaHelloWorld extends HelloWorldApplet**

```java
import java.applet.*;
import java.awt.*;

/**
 * Listing 5-1, Java 2 Bible (http://www.JavaBible.com/)
 *
 * MediaHelloWorld.java, an extension of HelloWorldApplet.
 *
 * This class displays "Hello World!" by invoking the paint()
 * method of its HelloWorldApplet superclass. It also extends
 * HelloWorldApplet, adding code that lets this new applet display
 * an image on screen and play a looping background audio track.
 *
 * @author Aaron E. Walsh
 * @version 1.0, 25 August 2000
 */
public class MediaHelloWorld extends HelloWorldApplet
{
  private Image      myImage;
  private AudioClip  myAudio;

  /**
   * Initialize applet via the init() "life cycle" method.
   */
  public void init()
  {
    super.init(); // let superclass init first (resize applet)

    myImage = getImage(getCodeBase(), "images/world.gif");
    myAudio = getAudioClip(getCodeBase(), "audio/hello.au");
  }


  /**
   * Draw image, then invoke the paint() methods of the
   * HelloWorldApplet superclass to draw "Hello World!"
   * text on the screen.
   */
  public void paint(Graphics g)
  {
    g.drawImage(myImage, 0, 0, this);
    super.paint(g); // draw text via superclass
  }
```

```
/**
 * Play audio when applet's start() "life cycle" method
 * is invoked. Loop audio track indefinitely.
 */
public void start()
{
  myAudio.loop();
}

/**
 * Stop playing audio when applet's stop() "life cycle"
 * method is invoked so that sound doesn't continue to
 * play when applet's Web page is no longer active!
 */
public void stop()
{
  myAudio.stop();
}
}
```

Name your new file MediaHelloWorld.java, and be sure to include the .java extension or the compiler won't be able to find it, as the previous chapter explains. It's also particularly important that you place this file inside the same directory as the original HelloWorld class file or source file.

Because MediaHelloWorld extends our HelloWorld applet class, the javac compiler must be able to access the HelloWorldApplet class to successfully compile MediaHelloWorld. This is why it's a good idea to place your MediaHello World.java source code file in the same directory as the HelloWorldApplet class. However, as long as it's in the class path (specified using the CLASSPATH compiler option as described in Appendix A), any applet you create can extend HelloWorldApplet.

At this point, you should also create two new directories (folders) inside the same directory as your source code: audio and images. The audio directory will contain the sound file, and images will hold the GIF file used in this example. To make life easier, you can simply download a compressed archive containing these directories and files from JavaBible.com (http://www.javabible.com/), the official support Web site established for this book. (From this site you can get all the source code for the Java 2 Bible you are now reading, as well as the text and source for the original Java Bible.)

## Sound File Formats

Java versions prior to the Java 2 platform (a.k.a. Java 1.2) only support Sun's AU audio format, the file format in which the "hello.au" sound file appearing throughout this chapter is stored. If you're using an earlier version of Java or wish to have your applets accessible to the broadest range of Web users, you have to save sound files as 8-bit, 8KHz, with only one channel, as we've done with hello.au. To convert existing sound files to the AU format, use the audio tool application if you're a Sun workstation user, or the shareware program GoldWave (http://www.goldwave.com/) if you're a Windows user. Macintosh users, on the other hand, can use the SoundMachine shareware program (http://www.java-bible.com/go/soundmachine).

Java 2 includes a number of audio enhancements, including a new sound engine and support for audio in applications as well as applets. Java applications couldn't play sound previously. The "Java Sound" engine now supports the AIFF, AU, and WAV audio file formats. It also supports these MIDI-based song file formats: TYPE 0 MIDI, TYPE 1 MIDI, and RMF. Java sound can render 8-bit or 16-bit audio data in mono or stereo, with sample rates from 8KHz to 48KHz.

If you enter the source code exactly as shown in Listing 5-1 or download it from the Java Bible Web site (http://www.javabible.com/), it should compile without a hitch, assuming it resides in the same directory as the HelloWorldApplet class file (HelloWorldApplet.class) or source file (HelloWorldApplet. java). To compile your new file, type the following at the command line:

```
javac MediaHelloWorld.java
```

When the Java compiler is run on your new source file, it will look for HelloWorldApplet.class, because that class is the one that is extended. If the compiler can't locate HelloWorldApplet.class, it will look for the HelloWorldApplet.java source file and compile it if available. If successful, the compiler will create a new class named MediaHelloWorld.class.

If the compiler insists that it can't find the HelloWorldApplet class, be sure that it (or the HelloWorldApplet.java source code file) is inside the same directory as your new MediaHelloWorld.java file. If it's not, or if it isn't in the CLASSPATH at all, the compiler won't be able to find it.

If both HelloWorldApplet.class and its source, HelloWorldApplet.java, are missing, the compiler will tell you so:

```
MediaHelloWorld.java:15: Superclass HelloWorldApplet of class
MediaHelloWorld not found.
public class MediaHelloWorld extends HelloWorldApplet {
                                     ^
1 error
```

A class, such as HelloWorldApplet.class, will be accessible to your Java programs if it resides in the same directory as the program itself (or the program source code that you intend to compile, such as MediaHelloWorld, in this example). Classes are also available to your programs if they reside in the directory specified by the Java CLASSPATH setting (see Appendix A, "Installing and Configuring the SDK" ), or when located in the Java extensions directory described in Appendix D.

**Tip**    You can use the asterisk (*) character as a wildcard in place of an actual file name when compiling with the javac tool, which tells the compiler to compile every .java source code file in the current directory: javac *.java

## Creating the HTML file

Before we examine MediaHelloWorld in great detail, you may want to run the program and tinker with the code. To do so, you'll have to create a new HTML Web page file and weave the MediaHelloWorld applet into it as you did with HelloWorld Applet in the previous chapter. Simply create a plain ASCII text file with the following contents, and save it inside the directory in which your compiled MediaHello World class resides. (Give it whatever name you'd like, and don't forget to include an .htm or .html file extension.):

```
<HTML>
<HEAD>
<TITLE> MediaHelloWorld Applet Test </TITLE>
</HEAD>
<BODY>
Here is our MediaHelloWorld applet:
<APPLET CODE="MediaHelloWorld.class" HEIGHT=150 WIDTH=200>
</APPLET>
</BODY>
</HTML>
```

Once you've woven the MediaHelloWorld applet into a Web page, it's time to actually test the results. You should develop and test your applets using Applet Viewer initially, moving on to a Java-savvy Web browser when you've worked out all the kinks. Applet Viewer is fast, takes up less memory, and doesn't cache applets as a Web browser might. As a result, you can guarantee that Applet Viewer will load your applet class fresh every time it is executed.

After you've entered the previous HTML code into your text editor and saved it as a plain text file having either the .htm or .html file extension, you're then ready to execute the applet embedded therein. For the purpose of this section, let's assume that you've named the HTML file test.html. If you use this name, you simply enter the following command line to execute the applet using the Applet Viewer program. (See Figure 5-1.):

```
appletviewer test.html
```

**Caution**

If you use a Web browser that happens to cache files by default, as most browsers do, you'll have to flush the cache or quit the browser and start anew each time you want to execute a freshly compiled class. In fact, many programmers who use Web browsers exclusively when it comes time to test their applets can't understand why their little bundles of joy don't work as expected, even after substantial changes to the source code. Most of the time it's because their particular Java-savvy browser is running an old, cached version of their applet instead of the freshly compiled one, which leads to a great deal of frustration, to say the least!

Navigator and Internet Explorer are notorious for loading outdated, cached applets even after the applet has been updated. Play it safe and make sure that your applets run as expected in Applet Viewer *before* you try to load them in a Web browser. When testing in a Web browser, you should take the time to restart you browser whenever you make changes to the applet so that you can be certain that the browser isn't loading an outdated version.

This, of course, assumes that the HTML file is located locally. You can also use Applet Viewer to execute applets on the Web by providing a URL that points to the HTML document, instead of its name. The following index.html file, for example, resides on the Web, so a standard URL is passed to Applet Viewer in this case:

```
appletviewer http://www.LivingDesktop.com/index.html
```

Running Applet Viewer with Web-based applets as we've done here is a technique that will come in particularly handy when you want to test pages after you've placed them on the Internet, as described in Chapter 25. If you're anxious to get on the Web, feel free to jump ahead. You can always return to the following code dissection after the joy of launching your first Web-based applet has subsided.

**Figure 5-1:** MediaHelloWorld, residing locally, as executed by Applet Viewer

# Stepping Through the Code

In this section, we'll step through the source code shown in Listing 5-1 to give you a better idea of what each new variable and method does. In the process, you'll get a better feel for how subclasses communicate with their superclass through use of the super keyword, and how an implicit this keyword is used to differentiate between methods and variables of a subclass that have the same name as those in the superclass. You'll also see that this particular example is lacking a great deal in terms of good coding style, which we'll soon resolve.

## Importing classes

To begin with, let's take a look at the classes our new program imports:

```
import java.applet.*;
import java.awt.*;
```

These two lines of code are very similar to those found in HelloWorldApplet.java. Because we're creating an applet, we need to import the base Applet class which is found in the java.applet package. This is accomplished with the first import statement, which every applet must include. (Or alternately, you can import the specific class that you want to use, which in this case is java.applet.Applet.) As you learned in the previous chapter, classes (and entire packages as seen here) can be imported into your program so that you can use them. (Refer to Chapter 4 to learn more about importing classes and packages.)

The second import statement, however, is slightly different from its HelloWorldApplet.java counterpart. Here, we instruct the compiler to import classes in the Abstract Windowing Toolkit (AWT) package, not just the Graphics class imported in HelloWorldApplet. Because this applet requires additional classes found in the AWT, specifically those that deal with the Image class, let's import all classes in the java.awt package rather than specify each class in this package that we'd like to use.

With these two lines of code, all of the classes our applet relies on are available to the program. If we had required additional classes, we could have imported them in precisely the same way as we imported the java.applet and java.awt packages.

## Fundamental Applet Methods

Every Java applet inherits four key methods from the java.applet.Applet class: init(), start(), stop(), and destroy(). These methods (see Table 5-1) give applets the ability to respond to major events, such as when a Web page containing the applet is first loaded by the viewer, is reloaded, or is left by the user, and these methods together constitute the life cycle methods common to every applet.

In addition, every applet inherits a `paint()` method, through which it can paint information (such as text, lines, images, and so forth) to the applet's onscreen area ("canvas"), as well as an `update()` method responsible for "clearing" the applet's canvas in between each call to `paint()` (see Table 5-2). Because these six methods are so closely tied to the birth, life, and death of every applet, they are the fundamental methods that every Java programmer should be familiar with.

Tip    The API tables appearing in this book cover only a small portion of the material found in the massive Java 2 Platform, version 1.3 documentation suite. In particular, these tables include what we think are the essential classes and methods you'll need while reading the *Java 2 Bible*. They're just the beginning, however. Sun's *Java 2 SDK Documentation* practically busts at the seams with release notes, Java platform API specifications, feature guides, tool documentation, and demos for the Java 2 SDK, Standard Edition (J2SE). You can browse Sun's complete J2SE Documentation Version 1.3.0 documentation online, or only the 1.3 API portion of it (classes and methods). Alternately, you download all 23 whopping megabytes of the documentation suite to your own computer for offline reference:

**Online all documentation:** `http://java.sun.com/j2se/1.3/docs/`

**Online API documentation:** `http://java.sun.com/j2se/1.3/docs/api/`

**Download:** `http://java.sun.com/j2se/1.3/docs.html`

## Import Versus #include

Although Java's `import` mechanism is similar to the `#include` directive used in C/C++, there is an important and fundamental difference between the two. Java's `import` statement merely gives your own classes access to other classes, such as those in the class libraries provided with every standard Java implementation (`java.applet.Applet`, for example, which is found in the `java.applet` library) or custom classes given to you by (or purchased from) other programmers. By importing a class, you essentially tell the compiler where it is and that you plan to use it; at runtime, any class that you use is dynamically located and loaded by Java's "class loader" mechanism. If it can be loaded, the class is then dynamically linked into your program. This allows every Java class to remain entirely separate from the classes they use; Java will pull in referenced classes on demand as they are actually needed. (This goes hand in hand with a Java feature known as *late binding*, whereby method calls are bound at runtime instead of compile time.)

As a result, your classes stay lean and mean; no extra code is added to your program when you import a class. This is in sharp contrast to the C/C++ `#include` mechanism, which links in the code you reference at compile time. This increases the overall size of the program and also makes it difficult to maintain or update because making a change to one part of a C or C++ program typically requires a recompile of the entire program (including any `#include` code). After recompiling, the resulting executable must then be redistributed to the end user, whereas Java classes can be updated and replaced independently of one another.

## Table 5-1
## Applet "Life Cycle" Methods

| Method | Description |
|---|---|
| `public void init()` | Override this method to initialize the applet each time it's loaded or reloaded. At the very least, this is where most applets initialize variables used throughout their program or load parameters from the HTML file in which they are embedded. |
| `public void start()` | Override this method to begin actual applet execution, like when the page containing the applet is loaded or reloaded by the user. The user can trigger this method multiple times by navigating between pages (by pressing the browser Forward and Back buttons, for example, forcing the page containing your applet to be loaded more than once). |
| `public void stop()` | Override this method to terminate applet execution when the user leaves the Web page containing the applet or quits the browser. This method, like `start()`, can be invoked multiple times in response to user browsing activity. |
| `public void destroy()` | Override this method if you need to do a final cleanup in preparation for final unloading (such as when the user closes the window containing your Web page or quits the Web browser altogether, meaning your page will be unloaded for good). |

## Table 5-2
## Applet Painting Methods

| Method | Description |
|---|---|
| `public void paint (Graphics g)` | Override this method if you wish to display text, graphics, or images on the applet canvas. This method is called by the AWT every time the applet's visual appearance needs to be refreshed (in other words, when the applet first becomes visible to the user, when it's scrolled off the screen and then back on, when the page it's in is reloaded, or when the applet itself requests to be repainted using the `repaint()` method). Before `paint()` is called, the `update()` method is first invoked. |

*Continued*

| Table 5-2 *(continued)* | |
| --- | --- |
| **Method** | **Description** |
| `public void update (Graphics g)` | The `paint()` method is invoked by `update()`, which is responsible for clearing the applet's onscreen display before `paint()` is actually called. Because the applet area is cleared before every call to `paint()`, applets that do a lot of painting often suffer from annoying flicker due to the clearing process. Override `update()` and call `paint()` directly, without bothering to clear the applet area, if you wish to reduce flicker. (See Part IV for more information.) |

The environment in which your applet is run (known as the *applet context*, which is typically a Web browser or Applet Viewer) is responsible for calling each of the four life-cycle methods. When the Web page containing your applet is first loaded into a Web browser, for example, it's the Web browser that calls the `init()` method of your applet. This gives you a little time to do any initialization your program requires before the applet is actually displayed on the screen.

After `init()`, the browser then calls `start()`, which is also called every time the page is reloaded or revisited. The `start()` method is the place where most applets start an animation thread, for example, or begin playing a background sound track as we do later in this chapter.

**Note**

The environment in which an applet is run is formerly known as the *applet context*. The term applet context is nothing more than a quick and easy way to say "the context in which an applet is executed," as the following section describes in detail.

Each time the Web page containing your applet is exited, the browser calls your applet's `stop()` method, allowing you to cease any activity before the new page is loaded. When `stop()` is called, you should stop any graphics animation that may be taking place, for example, as well as any sounds that are currently playing. If the user revisits your page, the `start()` method will be called, allowing you to pick up where you left off when `stop()` was invoked.

When the Web page containing your applet becomes unreachable, the browser will call your applet's `destroy()` method. When the user closes the Web browser window containing your applet, for example, or quits the Web browser altogether, the end has come for good, so `destroy()` will be called to let you release any resources that may have been allocated (open files, for example, or event listeners, as you'll see later in Part III and IV of this book).

Although the applet context is responsible for invoking the appropriate life-cycle methods of an applet, the Java windowing system is responsible for calling update() when needed, which in turn calls the paint() method. Every applet, after all, is ultimately a Java Component object that knows how to paint on itself. Remember that the java.applet.Applet class is actually a highly specialized component since Applet is a direct descendant of Panel, which in turn extends Container, which itself extends Component. As such, the Java AWT is responsible for handling a wide variety of applet windowing events (such as painting, mouse clicks, keyboard events, and so forth), including the update() and paint() calls.

**Tip**  The JApplet class is a more recent alternative to the venerable Applet class that has been around since Java 1.0. Unfortunately, many browsers do not yet support JApplet since it's a Java 2 technology. (Remember that Java 2 has yet to find its way into the majority of user's Web browsers.) JApplet extends Applet, ultimately making JApplet even more highly specialized than Applet (javax.swing.JApplet adds support for the Java Foundation Classes (JFC) and Swing component architecture). For most applets, the Applet class is more than adequate, and it also has the benefit of being supported by all Java-savvy browsers. Therefore, we use Applet as the base class for most applets in this book, although you can just as easily extend the JApplet class should you wish to create applets that have more sophisticated user interfaces by using JFC or Swing. To learn more about JApplet, JFC, and Swing, see Part IV of this book.

**Note**  The distinction between those methods for which the applet context is responsible and those the AWT handles isn't terribly critical when you're first writing applets, so it may be convenient to think that the applet context calls all of the fundamental methods described here. When you start writing Java applications, however, the distinction becomes very important because applications don't run inside a Web browser, Applet Viewer, or any other form of applet context that manages the program's life-cycle methods. As a result, applications don't have init(), start(), stop(), or destroy() methods; you must handle such things yourself, as you will learn in Part IV of this book.

Although you're under no obligation to override any of these methods, the chances are pretty good that you'll end up overriding most, if not all of them, to create fully functional applets. Nearly every applet has a use for these methods. If your applet has no use for one of these methods, however, simply ignore it (that is, don't bother to override it, in which case your applet's parent java.applet.Applet class method of the same name will be called). The destroy() method, for example, is only necessary if you've allocated resources that need to be freed when the applet page is no longer reachable by the browser, so you'll use this method least of all. Similarly, you only need to override the update() method if you'd like to skip the canvas-clearing process that takes place by default before paint() is called.

Following is the basic structure of an applet, including these six methods:

```
public class AnyApplet extends java.applet.Applet {
   . . .
   public void init() { . . . }
   public void start() { . . . }
   public void stop() { . . . }
   public void paint(Graphics g) { . . . }
   public void update(Graphics g) { paint(g); }
   public void destroy() { . . . }
   . . .
}
```

As stated earlier, not every applet is obligated to override all six methods. The most simple applets, such as our original HelloWorld applet, need only implement init() and possibly paint(). However, most applets are more complex. Those that change their visual appearance, play sounds, or interact with the user, for example, will likely override start() and stop() as well.

Such is the case with the MediaHelloWorld applet detailed in this chapter. A sound clip is played continuously once start() is executed and it stops playing when stop() is called. You'll notice, however, that we don't bother to override destroy(), as we do everything necessary to clean up in our stop() method, which is called before destroy(). Applets that must release resources they access upon executing, however, can rely on destroy() as a final step in bringing their applet to a successful close.

In addition to the basic applet functionality our program requires, the Applet class also provides the AudioClip interface we'll use to load and play a sound track.

## Applet Context

Java applets are peculiar beasts. Not only are they Java classes, but they have the unique ability to live inside of Web pages. Unlike applications that are executed on the desktop, applets are executed inside a Web browser or a specialized tool such as Applet Viewer. As the name suggests, the applet context is simply the environment, or context, in which an applet is running at any given moment.

Most end users will execute applets only within the context of a Web browser such as Netscape Navigator or Internet Explorer, while software developers such as you will also run applets in the context of Applet Viewer. Different applet contexts offer the applet different options at runtime; applets can communicate with the applet context and invoke special methods that the context may or may not support. Nearly every applet context can load images and sounds for the applet, for example.

To do so, the applet simply calls the corresponding method (see Table 5-3). But not all applet contexts are equal, meaning you can't expect Applet Viewer to support all of the same features as a full blown Web browser.

Web browsers allow applets to load Web pages on demand. (An applet might use the Web browser to display Web pages to the user while it runs, for example, or simply redirect the user to an entirely new page when it has finished executing.) Applet Viewer, on the other hand, doesn't care at all about Web pages, just the applet imbedded in them. As a result, Applet Viewer ignores the showDocument() methods that let you load a Web page via an applet (see Table 5-4).

To take advantage of applet-context features such as these, the applet must have some way of gaining access to the applet context in which it is running. This is made possible by way of a call to getAppletContext(), as the following snippet of code illustrates:

```
getAppletContext().showStatus("Applet loading...please wait!");
```

In this example, the applet context is called upon to display a string of text in its status area. (Web browsers and Applet Viewer have a small status area where the applet can display messages by calling the showStatus() method, as shown here.) The call to getAppletContext() returns a reference to an AppletContext interface object, through which any of the methods seen in Table 5-4 may be invoked. Here the showStatus() method is invoked on the applet context, which displays the string "Applet loading. . . please wait!" in the status are.

Likewise, most Java-enabled Web browsers support interapplet communications in cases where more than one applet is embedded into the same Web page. If you want to have your applets "talk" to each other, the <APPLET> tags in your HTML file must be configured with a NAME attribute, as the following illustrates:

```
<APPLET CODE="Player.class" HEIGHT=400 WIDTH=400 NAME="Sound">
```

Any other applet woven into the same Web page can then get a reference to the applet named "Sound" (which is actually a reference to an instance of the Player class; the NAME attribute does not have to be the same as the class provided in the CODE attribute). To get a reference to the named applet, any applet in the same page simply invokes the AppletContext's getApplet() method. Through this reference, the public data and methods of the named applet can be accessed. For example:

```
Applet noisy = getAppletContext().getApplet("Sound");
noisy.startLooping(); // invoke public method
```

## Table 5-3
## Applet Audio and Image Methods

| Method | Description |
|---|---|
| `public Image getImage (URL url)` | Gets an image pointed to by the URL parameter, which must be an absolute URL. This method always returns immediately, regardless of whether the image exists; only when the applet tries to draw the image on the screen is the image data actually loaded. While the image is being loaded, it will be incrementally painted on the screen. |
| `public Image getImage (URL url, String name)` | Gets an image. The base location of the image is pointed to by the absolute URL parameter, while the `String` parameter specifies a location relative to the URL. (See previous `getImage()` method for loading details.) |
| `public AudioClip getAudioClip(URL url)` | Gets an audio clip pointed to by the URL parameter, which must be an absolute URL. This method always returns immediately, regardless of whether the audio clip exists; only when the applet tries to play the audio clip is the audio data actually loaded. |
| `public AudioClip getAudioClip(URL url, String name)` | Gets an audio clip. The base location of the clip is pointed to by the absolute URL parameter, while the `String` parameter specifies a location relative to the URL. (See previous `getAudioClip()` method for loading details.) |
| `public static final AudioClip newAudioClip (URL url)` | Gets an audio clip pointed to by the URL parameter, which must be an absolute URL. This method is declared as static, meaning it can be called directly through the `Applet` class without the need for an actual object reference. As a result, this method can be used by applications that wish to load an audio clip as follows: `Applet.newAudioClip(...);` |
| `public void play (URL url)` | Plays the audio clip pointed to by the absolute URL. URL. Nothing happens if the audio clip can't be found or loaded. |
| `public void loop()` | Plays audio clip repeatedly. |
| `public void play()` | Plays audio clip once. |
| `public void stop()` | Stops playing audio clip. |

## Table 5-4
## AppletContext Methods

| Method | Signature | Description |
| --- | --- | --- |
| getApplet | `public Applet getApplet (String name)` | Gets the named applet in the Web document, where "name" is a string that corresponds to the HTML `<APPLET>` tag NAME attribute. |
| getApplets | `public Enumeration getApplets()` | Returns an enumeration of all applets in the Web page. |
| showDocument | `public void showDocument (URL url)` | Loads the specified Web page, replacing the currently viewed Web page. This method may be ignored by some applet contexts such as Applet Viewer). |
| showDocument | `public void showDocument (URL url, String target)` | Loads the specified Web page as directed by the target argument. Target may be:<br><br>`"_self"` to show the page in the window and frame that contain the applet.<br><br>`"_parent"` to show the page in the applet's parent frame.<br><br>`"_top"` to show the page in the top-level frame of the applet's window.<br><br>`"_blank"` to show the page in a new, unnamed top-level window. |

## Documentation comments

Following the `import` command is a special comment, created to help developers generate HTML documentation for their programs:

```
/**
 * Listing 5-1, Java 2 Bible (http://www.JavaBible.com/)
 *
 * MediaHelloWorld.java, an extension of HelloWorldApplet.
 *
 * This class displays "Hello World!" by invoking the paint()
 * method of its HelloWorldApplet superclass. It also extends
```

```
* HelloWorldApplet, adding code that lets this new applet display
* an image onscreen and play a looping background audio track.
*
* @author Aaron E. Walsh
* @version 1.0, 25 August 2000
*/
```

This comment looks and acts in a similar way to the standard C comment, although an extra asterisk (*) is added to the first line of code (/**) and special author and version variables are included using the @ character.

Inside a document comment, the @ character (known as a Java documentation *tag*) specifies special variables that are used when generating documentation with the javadoc tool. In this example, the applet author and version number have been specified.

You can place document comments before any class or method declaration to serve as standard human-readable comments ignored by the compiler. In addition, you can use comments to help automate the document-creation process and take some of this burden from the programmer.

The javadoc tool is executed at the command line in much the same way as the javac compiler that you've been using all along. All you have to do is supply the full name of the Java source code file, including the .java file extension, following the javadoc tool as follows:

```
javadoc MediaHelloWorld.java
```

When this command line is executed, the javadoc tool will scan through the MediaHelloWorld source code file looking for documentation comments, from which it will create HTML documentation files. By default, the HTML files generated by javadoc are stored in the same folder as the Java source code file, although you can supply command-line parameters to the tool specifying an alternate directory if you'd like. (See Appendix A to learn about the options available when running this and other SDK tools.)

**Tip**    Type javadoc at the command line and press Enter (or Return) on your keyboard to see a listing of the command-line options this tool supports, or refer to Appendix A or B for a summary of these options. To learn more about javadoc, see Appendix A and B, or visit http://java.sun.com/products/jdk/javadoc/

The documentation that the javadoc tool generates is quite extensive, even when run on a simple source code file such as our MediaHelloWorld applet. Javadoc creates a file named index.html, which is your main entry point into the documentation. Upon opening index.html, you'll find a wealth of information about MediaHelloWorld, starting with the inheritance tree (class hierarchy) of the class, followed by summary and detail listings of variables and methods declared by the class as well as those it inherits. In addition, the default documentation contains an alphabetical listing of class methods, package information, a list of deprecated (outdated) classes and/or methods used by the class, and other useful information for Java programmers.

The default documentation produced by javadoc does not, however, include author and version information. Because javadoc ignores the @author and @version documentation tags by default, you'll have to include command-line parameters as follows to produce HTML documentation with such information:

```
javadoc MediaHelloWorld.java -author -version
```

Upon seeing the command line -author and -version options, javadoc will produce HTML documentation based on information you supply as @author and @version tags. The MediaHelloWorld class summary, for example, now appears in the index.html documentation file as:

```
public class MediaHelloWorld
extends HelloWorldApplet

Listing 5-1, Java 2 Bible (http://www.JavaBible.com/)
MediaHelloWorld.java, an extension of HelloWorldApplet. This
class displays "Hello World!" by invoking the paint() method of
its HelloWorldApplet superclass. It also extends
HelloWorldApplet, adding code that lets this new applet display
an image onscreen and play a looping background audio track.

Version:
1.0, 25 August 2000
Author:
Aaron E. Walsh
See Also:
Serialized Form
```

Although extensive code documentation is extremely important in many cases where your source code will be maintained by other developers or you yourself down the road, often it may be overkill. If you believe that too many cooks spoil the broth, you might also find that too many docs spoil the code. Source code documentation is supposed to make your code easier to understand and maintain, and be relatively friendly to those who may not be familiar with it. Too much documentation, however, can do just the opposite for some programmers. Many professional software developers actually believe that properly written code is self-documenting and that extra documentation actually clutters the source.

Consider, for example, the following version of Listing 5-1 written without source code comments. You'll also notice that the opening brace ("{") of each code block has been moved onto the same line as the method signature itself, a coding style that many Java developers use to further conserve space. In addition, the extra carriage returns found in the init() method have been removed because it might be considered wasted *white space* (a term used to describe nontext characters, such as spaces, tabs, and carriage returns).

Although the following listing is functionally the same as the one found in Listing 5-1, it's much more compact. Many experienced Java developers may actually prefer to read code like this because it's crisp and clean and without excessive and potentially distracting comments and white space. As you become more experienced reading Java source code, you'll probably feel the same way. Therefore, and also because we aim to make the best use of the space available on each page of this book, you'll find that most of our code listings have minimal comments and conservative use of white space. In addition, we sometimes place the opening brace on the same line as the class or method signature, as seen in this code:

```java
import java.applet.*;
import java.awt.*;

public class MediaHelloWorld extends HelloWorldApplet {
  private Image       myImage;
  private AudioClip   myAudio;

  public void init() {
    super.init();
    myImage = getImage(getCodeBase(), "images/world.gif");
    myAudio = getAudioClip(getCodeBase(), "audio/hello.au");
  }

  public void paint(Graphics g) {
    g.drawImage(myImage, 0, 0, this);
    super.paint(g);
  }

  public void start() {
    myAudio.loop();
  }

  public void stop() {
    myAudio.stop();
  }
}
```

## Class declaration

The MediaHelloWorld class declaration follows the documentation comment. Unlike our original HelloWorld applet, which extended the Applet class, MediaHelloWorld actually extends the HelloWorldApplet class:

```java
public class MediaHelloWorld extends HelloWorldApplet {..}
```

By extending the HelloWorldApplet class, MediaHelloWorld inherits all data and behavior in that class. Although there isn't much to inherit—only the capability to output "Hello World!"—you'll soon see how powerful this ability to subclass an existing class is. And because we've inherited all the traits of HelloWorldApplet, we automatically get the functionality found in class Applet (in other words, we inherit from the entire inheritance tree).

As with all applets, the MediaHelloWorld class is declared as public using the public access modifier, meaning this class can be called from any other class in any other package. (See the previous chapter for an overview of access modifiers.) Although it's unlikely that you'd actually want to call MediaHelloWorld into action from another class, as it's merely a simple applet, you'll soon create other classes that are more useful when combined in other programs.

**Note**

> Because the MediaHelloWorld class is declared as being public, it must reside in a file of the same name with exactly the same spelling (MediaHelloWorld.java). All public classes must be stored in a file of the same name, which in turn means that only one public class can be defined inside a single source code file. A source code file can, however, contain any number of nonpublic class definitions (such as private, or default-level classes). It's generally good programming practice, however, to place each class in its own source code file.

As you may recall from the previous chapter, the Applet class itself has a parent class called Panel, which in turn descends from other classes that are part of Java's built-in class library. The class hierarchy, or inheritance tree, of MediaHello World, is therefore one level deeper than that of the HelloWorldApplet class, at the top of which sits the Object class as follows:

```
java.lang.Object
     |
     +--java.awt.Component
            |
            +--java.awt.Container
                   |
                   +--java.awt.Panel
                          |
                          +--java.applet.Applet
                                 |
                                 +--HelloWorldApplet
                                        |
                                        +--MediaHelloWorld
```

Because HelloWorldApplet is the immediate superclass of MediaHelloWorld, we use the super keyword to "reach up and into" HelloWorldApplet from within MediaHelloWorld. If you take a close look at the MediaHelloWorld init() and paint() method, you'll see the super keyword in action; MediaHelloWorld calls super.init() and super.paint() to invoke these methods of its parent class, as described in the "Methods" section later in this chapter.

As you learned in the previous chapter, every class that you create is actually a subclass of some other class, even if you don't specifically say so. Consider, for example, the following class declaration:

```
class Fish {
  ...
}
```

Because we haven't explicitly extended a specific class, as we've done with Media HelloWorld, the Fish class is automatically assumed to be a subclass of the top-level Object class. As far as Java is concerned, we could just as well have declared the Fish class as follows:

```
class Fish extends Object {
  ...
}
```

In both Fish class declarations, the top-level class we're extending is Object, the master class from which all other classes ultimately descend, although the first declaration doesn't explicitly say so. Whether a class is a direct subclass of Object, as Fish is, or a subclass of some other class, every Java class is *ultimately* a descendant of Object. The MediaHelloWorld applet, for example, can trace its roots to the Object class (as you can see from the class hierarchy described earlier), meaning it has inherited capabilities from Object just as the Fish class has (a few of which are listed in Table 5-5).

The Object class is part of the java.lang package, which is the only package that is automatically available to your own classes automatically. As a result, you don't have to bother importing the java.lang package; every class it contains, including Object, is available to every Java class. The java.lang package contains classes that are fundamental to the Java programming language, such as those used to implement basic math functions, numbers, packages, objects, strings, threads, and more. Because the Object class is so general in design, it can be used as a container in which other types of objects can be stored. For example, the following variable declarations are valid because every specific object instance can ultimately be considered to have come from the Object class:

```
Object myFish = new Fish();
Object myString = "Hello World";
Object myDate = new Date();
```

Keep in mind, however, that Object is useful only as a container for other objects. If you'd like to invoke specific class methods on an instance contained in an Object, for example, you must actually perform a cast to tell Java which type of class the generic object should be treated as:

```
(Fish)myFish.swim();
(String)myString.endsWith(".java");
(Date)myDate.getTime();
```

Table 5-5
**Essential Object Methods**

| Method | Description |
|---|---|
| `public boolean equals(Object obj)` | Indicates whether one object reference is "equal to" another, meaning the two objects point to the same place in memory. If the objects are equal, `true` is returned. If not, `false` is returned. Because `equals()`, as defined by the `Object` class, can only be used to determine whether two object references are equal, not the contents of those objects, subclasses often override this method to provide a more meaningful comparison. |
| `public String toString()` | Returns a `String` representation of the object. Subclasses typically override `toString()` to return information that is unique to the class. This method is called automatically whenever an object is concatenated with a string. For example: `System.out.println(`"Look at what I have caught:" + myFishInstance`);` |
| `protected void finalize() throws Throwable` | An object's `finalize()` method is called by Java's automatic garbage collector when it determines that there are no more references to the object (that is, when the object is no longer needed). Subclasses typically override `finalize()` to dispose of system resources or to perform other cleanup before being garbage collected. An object's `finalize()` method is conceptually equivalent to an applet's `dispose` method. (Applets have a special `dispose` method, so `finalize()` isn't necessary for applets.) |

# Variables

Immediately following the `MediaHelloWorld` class declaration, two private instance variables are declared:

```
private Image  myImage;
private AudioClip  myAudio;
```

Instance variables, as you may recall from the previous chapter, are available to every instance of a class (each object created by a class), whereas class variables are shared by every instance. Class variables can be easily identified in Java code by the presence of the *static* modifier preceding the variable data type, as the following example illustrates:

```
private static Image myImage;
private static AudioClip myAudio;
```

Because the `MediaHelloWorld` class is an applet, however, it is very unlikely to be used by any other class. (You simply weave it into a Web page because that's what applets are for.) As a result, it doesn't really make much difference whether or not we declare our variables as being class or instance variables—no instances of `MediaHelloWorld` are going to be created by other classes, so there is no need to bother considering how they'll be accessed by other classes. The same goes for the `private` access modifier; we really don't have to worry about hiding these variables from other classes, but we do so because it's good programming practice to create fully encapsulated classes in this way.

Although these variables could have been declared anywhere inside the body of our class, as long as they're not inside a method (which would restrict their access to that method, making them *local* variables instead of instance variables), we've placed both variables immediately after the class signature for easy reading.

You've probably already figured out that these are the two variables that will actually hold our graphic and sound data: `myImage` stores a reference to the image data, while `myAudio` is used to store a reference to the audio clip. The `myImage` variable is declared as being an `Image` data type, and `myAudio` is declared to be of the `AudioClip` data type. A variable's data type, as you may have deduced, regulates the type of information that can be stuffed into that variable. If, for example, we declared each to be of the `int` data type, only integer values could be stored in `myImage` and `myAudio`. (See Part II of this book to learn about data types and variables in detail.)

Variables are declared in Java as in the following format:

**MODIFIERS    DATA_TYPE    NAME       [INITIAL VALUE; OPTIONAL]**

The `myImage` and `myAudio` variables are both considered *reference* data types, as each variable will be used to contain a reference to an object; `myImage` will contain a reference to an `Image` object, and `myAudio` will contain a reference to an `AudioClip` object. Later, we'll add a few primitive variables to `MediaHelloWorld`, which will be used to hold integer values.

Note    Java supports two main data types: reference and primitive data types. Reference data types refer to objects in memory, so it's convenient to think of a reference variable as being a pointer to an object even though Java doesn't actually support pointers in the way that C or C++ does. In contrast, primitive data types are simple or basic data types by comparison, and include numbers (`byte`, `short`, `int`, `long`, `float`, and `double`) characters (`char`), and `boolean` types that can hold `true` and `false` values). For details, see Chapter 6 and 7.

Because we haven't given either of our instance variables an initial value, Java will do so for us. Java does not, however, provide default initial values for local variables declared in a method, constructor, or static blocks of code; the compiler will force you to provide an initial value yourself.

As you can see from Table 5-6, reference data types are initialized to null by default when no initial value is supplied. (The null Java keyword is used to indicate that no valid object reference exists.) Although reference data types are initialized to null by default, we could have done the same ourselves with the following declarations:

```
private Image  myImage = null;
private AudioClip  myAudio = null;
```

### Table 5-6
### Default Initial Values

| Data Type | Default Initial Value |
|---|---|
| boolean | false |
| char | '\u0000' |
| byte, short, int, long | 0 |
| float | +0.0f |
| double | +0.0 |
| reference | null |

Java is a strongly typed language, meaning that every single variable that you declare must have a name and data type. The Image data type we've declared for myImage is defined in the java.awt package class (Image is defined by the java.awt.Image class, to be precise), which is available to MediaHelloWorld because we've imported that package. We wouldn't have been able to declare myImage as being an Image data type if that package or class wasn't imported into the program because the complier wouldn't know which class we were talking about otherwise. The AudioClip class, on the other hand, is part of the java.applet package, which we've also imported.

**Note**    Although you must import the package containing the class (or interface) that you'll use for a data type, or the exact class (or interface) itself, you don't have to do the same when it comes to primitive data types. (Later in this chapter, you'll learn more about interfaces.) Primitive data types are available to your programs by default, so there is no package or class to import when declaring primitive variables.

We've declared the myImage and myAudio variables as being private using the private access modifier, as there is no need to allow other classes direct access to these variables. In fact, you should never define a variable that's available directly to other classes (such as a public variable) if you want to create a fully encapsulated class; instead, your variables should only be available through methods.

Suppose, for example, that myImage and myAudio were declared as being public:

```
public Image  myImage;
public AudioClip  myAudio;
```

In this case, any class that creates an instance of MediaHelloWorld can access these variables directly. Consider the following theoretical snippet of code, assuming it appears in a class other than MediaHelloWorld:

```
MediaHelloWorld myRef = new MediaHelloWorld();
myRef.myAudio.loop(); // directly access the audio variable
```

Although this example is purely hypothetical, because it is hard to imagine why a class would bother to instantiate a MediaHelloWorld object in the first place, the issue of direct variable access is very real. In the previous example, a class has made itself dependent on the internal structure of MediaHelloWorld by directly accessing the myAudio variable. Although this would be fine if MediaHelloWorld were guaranteed to stay as is forever, meaning direct variable reference would never be disrupted, to assume such long-term stability in the classes you use is one step away from insanity.

Down the road, we might decide to enhance MediaHelloWorld to use an array of audio clips instead of just one, or we might simply decided to rename the myAudio variable for some reason that strikes our fancy. If we made such changes to MediaHelloWorld, any classes that directly access the myAudio variable of our original MediaHelloWorld class will "break" with the newly updated class. To avoid this potential calamity, we need only declare myAudio as being private, and also create a method that gives classes access to it.

The public start() method seen in Listing 5-1, for example, gives all other classes the ability to play the audio clip contained in MediaHelloWorld without directly accessing the variable itself. Following is the "right way" for a class to expose its functionality (using public or protected methods instead of direct data member access):

```
MediaHelloWorld myRef = new MediaHelloWorld();
myRef.start(); // start the applet to play the sound clip
```

## Methods

Of the six key methods described earlier in the "Fundamental Applet Methods" section, our MediaHelloWorld program overrides four: init(), paint(), start(), and stop(). Let's take a close look at the function of each of these methods.

## The init() Method

MediaWorldApplet overrides four methods, beginning with init(), which you'll almost always override in your own applets. The purpose of init(), as the name implies, is to initialize your applet when it is first loaded into a Web page or other applet context (such as Applet Viewer). Following is the init() method defined by the MediaWorldApplet class:

```
public void init() {
    super.init();
    myImage=getImage(getCodeBase(), "images/world.gif");
    myAudio=getAudioClip(getCodeBase(), "audio/hello.au");
}
```

However, this init() method is quite different than the one we created for our original HelloWorld applet from which MediaHelloWorld is derived. In HelloWorld Apple, we simply resized the applet canvas in which our "Hello World!" string was to be drawn. Here, things are quite different. Although MediaHelloWorld does, in fact, resize the applet canvas, it does so by invoking the init() method in its superclass:

```
super.init();
```

By executing the init() method of MediaWorldApplet's superclass, as this line of code does, HelloWorldApplet's init() is called! Sure, the only thing it does is resize the applet canvas, but the point is that we were able to execute the init() method of the superclass without having to duplicate code. It's not a drastic savings in code in this example, but it could be tremendous in others.

**Caution**

Although Sun's Applet Viewer supports the resizing of the applet canvas, there's no guarantee that every Java-savvy Web browser will do the same. As a result, you shouldn't rely on resize() working correctly when it's called. However, every <APPLET> tag is required to include both a HEIGHT and WIDTH attribute. Every Java-savvy browser will use the values supplied through these attributes to automatically set the size of an applet's canvas when it is first executed.

It doesn't matter how much or how little code we're saving in this example — it could be millions of lines or just one — the end result is that our new applet doesn't have to duplicate effort. We inherit the variables and methods we've already created in HelloWorldApplet, and we can access them from our new class, thanks to the super keyword. As you can see in the paint() method, we don't even have to bother rewriting the code that outputs "Hello World!"

The next two lines in init() retrieve the image and audio data and assign appropriate object references to them. Actually, the data isn't loaded at this time; only when an image is drawn, or a sound file played, does the download take place. After all, why load the data if it never gets used?

## The this and super Keywords

Java provides two special keywords, this and super to give you convenient access to the current object and its superclass. The this keyword is a reference to the current object, while a reference to its superclass is available using super. You can use these keywords, discussed in detail in Part II of this book, anywhere in the body of a class.

You can also use this to invoke the current object's constructor (a special method used to initialize an object), although typically, you don't use it to invoke methods because the method name alone will do the trick:

```
this(parameterList); // invoke current object's constructor
this.methodName(); // functional equivalent to methodName();
```

Meanwhile, super is typically used to invoke a method or constructor in the superclass:

```
super.methodName();  // invoke superclass method
super(parameterList); // invoke superclass constructor
```

### Getting to Base with getCodeBase()

The two methods getImage() and getAudioClip() are courtesy of classes imported into our program. They both rely on another method, getCodeBase(), also made possible thanks to the imported Applet class.

Many applets, such as MediaHelloWorld, use external data (such as graphic images and audio files) that may be stored outside of the directory in which the applet resides, so there must be a way to tell the applet where these files are. This is quite easy, thanks to two methods implemented in the Applet class: getCodeBase() and getDocumentBase(). Both methods return a URL object, which is used to tell the applet where the external data files reside, as Table 5-7 explains.

These methods are extremely useful because they enable your applet to locate files relative to itself or to the HTML document in which it is embedded. They work in both local and networked environments, so it doesn't matter if your applet is executed from your hard disk or the World Wide Web. Thanks to getCodeBase() and getDocumentBase(), your applet will be able to find the files it needs regardless of where it is executed, assuming these files are located relative to the class when using getCodeBase(), or to the HTML document when using getDocumentBase().

In Chapter 25, you'll upload the compiled MediaWorldApplet class and associated audio and image files to your Web server. And because we use getCodeBase() to reference these files, Java will be able to locate them as easily as when the applet is executed locally.

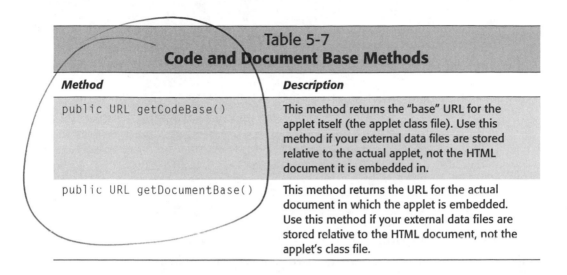

Table 5-7
**Code and Document Base Methods**

| Method | Description |
|---|---|
| `public URL getCodeBase()` | This method returns the "base" URL for the applet itself (the applet class file). Use this method if your external data files are stored relative to the actual applet, not the HTML document it is embedded in. |
| `public URL getDocumentBase()` | This method returns the URL for the actual document in which the applet is embedded. Use this method if your external data files are stored relative to the HTML document, not the applet's class file. |

### The <APPLET> Tag and CODEBASE

So far, you've created applets that are stored in the same directory as the HTML Web page in which they're embedded. The <APPLET> tag that you use to weave applets into Web pages, however, supports an attribute called CODEBASE that you can use to separate your applet class files from the HTML pages in which they executed.

You can actually reuse your applet class files in many different Web pages by merely supplying an absolute or relative URL to the <APPLET> tag CODEBASE attribute, as the following snippet of HTML code illustrates:

```
<HTML>
<HEAD>
<TITLE> MediaHelloWorld Absolute CODEBASE Test </TITLE>
</HEAD>
<BODY>
Here is our MediaHelloWorld applet:
<APPLET CODEBASE="http://www.javabible.com/anywhere/xyz/"
  CODE=MediaHelloWorld.class HEIGHT=150 WIDTH=200>
</APPLET>
</BODY>
</HTML>
```

In this example, the browser will load MediaHelloWorld.class from `http://www.javabible.com/anywhere/xyz/`, meaning the applet class and HTML file reside in separate folders. The CODEBASE attribute also accepts relative URLs, allowing you to place your applet class files in a directory that is relative to the HTML file, as the following example illustrates:

```
<HTML>
<HEAD>
<TITLE> MediaHelloWorld Relative CODEBASE Test </TITLE>
</HEAD>
<BODY>
Here is our MediaHelloWorld applet:
<APPLET CODEBASE="classes/hellostuff/"
  CODE=MediaHelloWorld.class HEIGHT=150 WIDTH=200>
</APPLET>
</BODY>
</HTML>
```

## The paint() Method

After overriding `init()`, we then override the `paint()` method:

```
public void paint(Graphics g) {
   g.drawImage(myImage, 0, 0, this);
   super.paint(g);
}
```

This implementation uses `drawImage()` to draw the graphic at the specified horizontal and vertical position on the applet canvas, which is 0,0 in this case (a point that specifies the upper-lefthand corner of the applet canvas). Although we've hardcoded the integer values 0,0 into `MediaHelloWorld`'s `drawImage()` method for now, later we'll change the point at which the image is drawn using a custom `Point` class that stores x,y coordinate values. For now, however, you should pay particular interest to the `drawImage()` parameter `this`, which is a reference to the current object (in other words, `this` is a reference to the `MediaHelloWorld` object as explained earlier in the sidebar "The `this` and `super` Keywords").

The `drawImage()` method, described in more detail in Part IV, takes as its last argument an `ImageObserver` object. Image observers are responsible for keeping track of images as they are loaded, a process that can take a long time when loading over a network. However, because applets themselves can act as `ImageObserver` objects, you don't have to instantiate them yourself in most cases.

Instead, you can pass a reference to the applet using the keyword `this`. Because `this` refers to the current object, which is the applet itself, you can get by without bothering to instantiate an `ImageObserver` object.

After drawing the image, we call the `paint()` method of our superclass with the line:

```
super.paint(g);
```

This outputs "Hello World!" to the applet canvas, just as it did in class HelloWorld Applet, where it was declared. Because "Hello World!" is output after we draw the image, it appears over the image itself (assuming the image is large enough to over-lap with the text). If you wanted the image to be drawn over the text, you could simply reverse the order of these two lines.

### The start() and stop() Methods

Although the init() and paint() methods should be familiar to you by now, the remaining code overrides methods that our original HelloWorldApplet did not. The start() and stop() methods are used to begin and end our audio sound-track, which is referenced by myAudio after init() is called.

When the applet is begun, start() is called. It is here that we execute the loop() method declared in the AudioClip interface. (See Table 5-3.) When the applet is terminated (this occurs when the user unloads the Web page in which the applet is embedded), stop() is invoked. It is here that we execute the stop() method for AudioClip, which interrupts the looping sound track:

```java
public void start() {
  myAudio.loop();
}

public void stop() {
  myAudio.stop();
}
```

These two methods are commonly overridden by applets because they provide a mechanism for applets to begin and end their activities in response to the user load-ing and unloading the Web page in which the applet is embedded. For more informa-tion on start() and stop() and the three additional methods often overridden by applets, see the "Fundamental Applet Methods" section earlier in this chapter.

# Creating New Classes

After reading the previous chapter, and stepping through the above source code examples step-by-step, you're more than ready to create your very own classes. Throughout the rest of this book, you'll spend the bulk of your time creating cus-tom classes that use various classes from the core Java class libraries.

To jump start this process, we've created a few simple classes here that you can begin experimenting with immediately. Each source code listing is thoroughly docu-mented with Java documents and code comments, and so you should be able to walk step-by-step through each and figure out what they do without much difficulty.

If you have a problem creating, compiling, or running any of these applets, simply backtrack to the material presented in the previous sections or even the previous chapter to refresh your memory about the required steps.

Each Java class listing appears in the order that you should create it. Begin with Listing 5-2, followed by 5-3, 5-4, 5-5, and so forth until you've created and compiled each class. Following the Java source code listings you will find sample applet classes and HTML pages that allow you to use these custom classes (see Listing 5-7 and Listing 5-8).

Alternately, you can create your own HTML pages. Remember, however, that if a class doesn't extend `Applet` it can't be woven directly into a Web page, and if it doesn't include a `main()` method it can't be executed as an application; such classes are designed to be used within the context of an applet or application as they have no means to be executed by themselves.

**Tip**

These examples take advantage of several `Graphics` object methods, in addition to other core Java class libraries. If you would like to learn more about a particular piece of code in these listings, try looking up the class or method name in the index of this book, and then turn to the page where it is discussed in detail. Alternately, you can plunge right in and see for yourself what these classes and methods do. (Visit JavaBible.com to download these examples and all other complete source listings found in this book).

## Listing 5-2: **The Custom Point class**

```
/**
 * Listing 5-1, Java 2 Bible <http://www.JavaBible.com/>
 *
 * Point.java
 * A simple "Point" class used to store x and y integer values,
 * typically used to store coordinates for drawing on a 2D
 * plane (x,y).
 *
 *
 * @author Aaron E. Walsh
 * @version 1.0, 25 August 2000
 */
class Point
{
  private int x, y;  // private instance variables

  // ---------------------------------------------
  // Constructors create and initialize "live"
  // objects from their class file. This Point
  // class has two constructors: a default (no
```

```
// argument) constructor, and a constructor
// that accepts two integer values used to
// initialize the x,y variables.
//
// NOTE: Constructors are really nothing more
// than special purpose methods, although they
// return no value (not even void!) and always
// have the exact same name as the class itself.
// A class can have an unlimited number of
// constructors as long as the arguments are
// unique for each (either in number or type).
// You can't, for example, create two different
// constructors that each take exactly two int
// arguments.
// ----------------------------------------------

Point () {
  this.x = 0;  // default x coordinate is 0
  this.y = 0;  // default y coordinate is 0
}

Point (int x, int y) {
  this.x = x;
  this.y = y;
}

// ----------------------------------------------
// Accessor ("getter") methods are used to get
// data from an object. This Point class has
// two accessor methods: getX() and getY()
// ----------------------------------------------

int getX() {
  return x;
}

int getY() {
  return y;
}

// ----------------------------------------------
// Mutator ("setter") methods are used to change
// the state of an object, typically by altering
// variable data. This Point class has three
// mutator methods: setX(), setY(), and setXY()
// ----------------------------------------------
void setX(int newX) {
  x = newX;
}
```

*Continued*

## Listing 5-2 *(continued)*

```java
void setY(int newY) {
  y = newY;
}

void setXY(int newX, int newY) {
  x = newX;
  y = newY;
}


}
```

## Listing 5-3: **MediaHelloWorld uses Point**

```java
import java.applet.*;
import java.awt.*;

/**
 * Listing 5-3, Java 2 Bible <http://www.JavaBible.com/>
 *
 * This version uses a custom Point object to store
 * coordinates used to draw the image onscreen.
 *
 * @author Aaron E. Walsh
 * @version 1.0, 25 August 2000
 */
public class MediaHelloWorld extends HelloWorldApplet
{
  private Image       myImage;
  private AudioClip   myAudio;
  private Point       myPoint;   // for x,y coordinates

  /**
   * Initialize applet via the init() lifecyle method.
   * Don't call superclass init() this time to prevent
   * resizing of applet when run in appletviewer.
   */
  public void init()
  {
    myImage = getImage(getCodeBase(), "images/world.gif");
    myAudio = getAudioClip(getCodeBase(), "audio/hello.au");

    myPoint = new Point(125, 100); // construct Point object
  }

  /**
```

```
 * Draw image, then invoke the paint() methods of the
 * HelloWorldApplet superclass to draw "Hello World!"
 * text on the screen.
 */
public void paint(Graphics g)
{
  // use the Point object to place image on screen:
  g.drawImage(myImage, myPoint.getX(), myPoint.getY(), this);

  super.paint(g); // draw text via superclass
}

/**
 * Play audio when applet's start() life cycle method
 * is invoked. Loop audio track indefinitely.
 */
public void start()
{
  myAudio.loop();
}

/**
 * Stop playing audio when applet's stop() lifecycle
 * method is invoked so that sound doesn't continue to
 * play when applet's Web page is no longer active!
 */
public void stop()
{
  myAudio.stop();
}
}
```

## Listing 5-4: **Pixel extends Point**

```
import java.awt.Color;

/**
 * Listing 5-4, Java 2 Bible <http://www.JavaBible.com/>
 *
 * Pixel.java
 * Extends the Point class to add color to the basic
 * x,y capabilities of Point.
 *
 * @author Aaron E. Walsh
 * @version 1.0, 25 August 2000
 */
public class Pixel extends Point
```

*Continued*

Listing 5-4 *(continued)*

```
{
  private Color c;


  /**
   * Default constructor sets color to white.
   * Default constructor of Point superclass
   * is automatically invoked since we don't
   * explicitly do so, which sets the x,y
   * values for this Pixel to defaults (0,0).
   */
  public Pixel ( ) {
    setColor(Color.white); // default to white
  }


  /**
   * This constructor accepts x,y integers and a color.
   */
  public Pixel (int x, int y, Color c) {
    super(x,y);  // invoke Point superclass constructor
    setColor(c); // set the color of this Pixel object
  }


  /**
   * Sets the color of this Pixel object.
   */
  public void setColor (Color newColor) {
    c = newColor;
  }

  /**
   * Gets the color of this Pixel object.
   */
  public Color getColor () {
    return c;
  }

}
```

Figure 5-2 shows the following code listing running in Applet Viewer.

**Figure 5-2:** The PixelPaint applet seen running in Applet Viewer

## Listing 5-5: **PixelPaint applet for all browsers**

```java
import java.applet.*;
import java.awt.*;

/**
 * Listing 5-5, Java 2 Bible <http://www.JavaBible.com/>
 *
 * PixelPaint.java
 * This applet uses a Pixel object (which is an extension
 * of Point) to store x,y and color data used in the paint()
 * method to draw tiny colored rectangles on the screen.
 *
```

*Continued*

**Listing 5-5** *(continued)*

```
 * Notice that we don't need to deal with the start() or
 * stop() "life cycle" methods in this applet, as we no
 * longer start/stop an audio clip. This applet simply
 * draws colored pixels on the screen.
 *
 * Be sure to increase the HEIGHT and WIDTH attributes of
 * your HTML page's <APPLET> tag; otherwise, some drawing
 * will be offscreen (beyond the applet dimensions).
 *
 * Figure 5-2 shows this applet running in Applet Viewer.
 *
 * @author Aaron E. Walsh
 * @version 1.0, 25 August 2000
 */
public class PixelPaint extends Applet
{
  private Pixel pix;  // store color pixel data

  public void init()
  {
    super.init(); // let Applet superclass paint itself first

    pix = new Pixel(); // construct default Pixel object
  }


  public void paint(Graphics g)
  {
    super.paint(g);

    // first, let's create a small blue rectangle without
    // the help of our Pixel object (hard-code values):

    g.setColor(Color.blue);     // set drawing color
    g.drawRect(10, 10, 1, 1); // draw tiny 1x1 rectangle


    // Next we'll use the Pixel object to draw a variety
    // of colored rectangles onscreen. Note that this
    // first one will be difficult to see because the
    // default color of our pixel is white (close to default
    // applet background color), but we'll draw it anyway
    // just for fun:

    g.setColor(pix.getColor());
    g.drawRect(pix.getX(), pix.getY(), 1, 1);

    // Now let's put the Pixel mutator and accessors to work
    // and really get some mileage out of the object, starting
    // with a red pixel:
```

```java
pix.setXY(100,30);          // change x,y pixel data
pix.setColor(Color.red);    // and the pixel color
g.setColor(pix.getColor());
g.drawRect(pix.getX(), pix.getY(), 1, 1);

// now a yellow pixel:
pix.setXY(315,100);
pix.setColor(Color.yellow);
g.setColor(pix.getColor());
g.drawRect(pix.getX(), pix.getY(), 1, 1);

// now a green pixel:
pix.setXY(222,73);
pix.setColor(Color.green);
g.setColor(pix.getColor());
g.drawRect(pix.getX(), pix.getY(), 1, 1);

// To automate things, we can use a for loop (let's
// create a few hundred randomly positioned magenta
// pixels). Notice that this is grossly inefficient,
// as we're setting randomly generated x and y values
// in our Pixel object only to immediately retrieve
// them. We do it only to illustrate the use of the
// setX() and setY() methods inherited from Point.
// You'll also notice that the int randomX and randomY
// variables are created each time through the loop,
// although you would normally declare these ints
// before getting into the loop: there's no reason to
// declare these int data types anew with every loop
// iteration, although we do so here to show that data
// type declaration and initialization can take place
// in the same statement. We also print them out for
// testing and debugging purposes. Normally, you'd skip
// the new int declaration entirely and simply place
// the randomization code directly into Pixel's setX()
// and setY() methods like so:
//
//
//pix.setX((int)Math.round(getSize().width*Math.random()));
// pix.setY((int)Math.round(getSize().height * Math.random()));
//

  g.setColor(Color.magenta); // set the draw color first

  for (int i=0; i<200; i++) {

   // The java.lang package is automatically available to all Java
```

*Continued*

**Listing 5-5** *(continued)*

```
        // classes, so we don't have to explicitly import that
        // package or
        // the specific java.lang.Math class in order to use Math:

        int randomX - (int)Math.round(getSize().width *
Math.random());
        int randomY = (int)Math.round(getSize().height *
Math.random());

        pix.setX(randomX);
        pix.setY(randomY);

        g.drawRect(pix.getX(), pix.getY(), 1, 1);

        // print data to standard output for validation and debugging:
        System.out.println("Loop Iteration Counter #:" + i);
        System.out.println("Random x,y: " + randomX + "," +
randomY);
        System.out.println("Pixel x,y: " + pix.getX() + "," +
pix.getY());
        System.out.println();
    }

    // DONE! Notice that the Pixel object color is still green,
    // however, since we set the draw color directly (not via Pixel),
    // so our pix variable still references a red-colored Pixel
    // object.
    //
    // Also notice that the getSize() method defined in Component is
    // only available in Java 1.1 and higher, meaning this
    // applet will
    // NOT RUN in Java 1.0 browsers! To support Java 1.0
    // browsers, you
    // can replace getSize() with the now outdated size() method like
    // so (they both report back the size of a component, which
    // Applet
    // ultimately is):
    //
    // int randomX = (int)Math.round(size().width * Math.random());
    // int randomY = (int)Math.round(size().height * Math.random());
    }
}
```

**Note** The following examples require the Java 2 Plugin, which is discussed in detail in Chapter 25, "Deploying Applets and Applications." You can dive into these examples now, or wait until you've had a chance to become more familiar with the Java Plugin described in that chapter. In addition, you'll have to know how to convert your HTML files into a format that the Java Plugin can handle (which is also covered in Chapter 25).

The Java Plugin is installed along with Java 2 automatically, and can be configured using the Java Plugin 1.3 Control Panel shown in Figure 5-3.

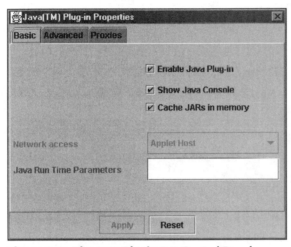

**Figure 5-3:** The Java Plugin 1.3 Control Panel

## Listing 5-6: **PixelPaint Applet for Java 2 only**

```java
import java.applet.*;
import java.awt.*;
import javax.swing.JApplet;


/**
 * Listing 5-6, Java 2 Bible <http://www.JavaBible.com/>
 *
 * PixelPaint.java
 * For Java 2 enabled Web browsers.
 * Sun's Java Plugin (shown in Figure 5-3) is
```

*Continued*

## Listing 5-6 *(continued)*

```
 * required since most browsers can't run this
 * Java 2 applet today (see Part V for details).
 *
 * Other than extending JApplet instead of Applet, this
 * Java 2 version of PixelPaint is exactly the same as
 * the original version created for all browsers. (See
 * Listing 5-5 for original, heavily commented code).
 *
 * @author Aaron E. Walsh
 * @version 1.0, 25 August 2000
 */
public class PixelPaint extends JApplet
{
  private Pixel pix;

  public void init()
  {
    super.init();
    pix = new Pixel();
  }


  public void paint(Graphics g)
  {
    super.paint(g);

    // first, let's create a small blue rectangle without
    // the help of our Pixel object (hard-code values):

    g.setColor(Color.blue);
    g.drawRect(10, 10, 1, 1);


    // Next we'll use the Pixel object to draw a variety
    // of colored rectangles onscreen.

    g.setColor(pix.getColor());
    g.drawRect(pix.getX(), pix.getY(), 1, 1);

    // Now let's put the Pixel mutator and accessors to work:

    pix.setXY(100,30);
    pix.setColor(Color.red);
    g.setColor(pix.getColor());
    g.drawRect(pix.getX(), pix.getY(), 1, 1);
```

```
    // now a yellow pixel:
    pix.setXY(315,100);
    pix.setColor(Color.yellow);
    g.setColor(pix.getColor());
    g.drawRect(pix.getX(), pix.getY(), 1, 1);

    // now a green pixel:
    pix.setXY(222,73);
    pix.setColor(Color.green);
    g.setColor(pix.getColor());
    g.drawRect(pix.getX(), pix.getY(), 1, 1);


    // To automate things, we can use a for loop:

    g.setColor(Color.magenta);

    for (int i=0; i<200; i++) {
        int randomX = (int)Math.round(getSize().width *
Math.random());
        int randomY = (int)Math.round(getSize().height *
Math.random());

        pix.setX(randomX);
        pix.setY(randomY);

        g.drawRect(pix.getX(), pix.getY(), 1, 1);

        // print data to standard output for validation and debugging:
        System.out.println("Loop Iteration Counter #:" + i);
        System.out.println("Random x,y: " + randomX + "," +
randomY);
        System.out.println("Pixel x,y: " + pix.getX() + "," +
pix.getY());
        System.out.println();
    }
  }
}
```

---

**Note**

Following are the HTML source code files for the PixelPaint applets. You can create your own as well (visit JavaBible.com to download these and all other complete source listings in this book).

### Listing 5-7: **TestPixelPaint.html for all Java-aware Web browsers**

```
<HTML>
<HEAD>
<TITLE> PixelPaint Applet Test </TITLE>
</HEAD>
<BODY>
<APPLET CODE="PixelPaint.class" HEIGHT=500 WIDTH=500>
</APPLET>
</BODY>
</HTML>
```

The Java Plugin 1.3 HTML converter, shown in Figure 5-4, must be used in cases where you create Java 2 applets because the `<APPLET>` tag must be converted into a corresponding `<OBJECT>` tag for Internet Explorer and an `<EMBED>` tag for Netscape Navigator.

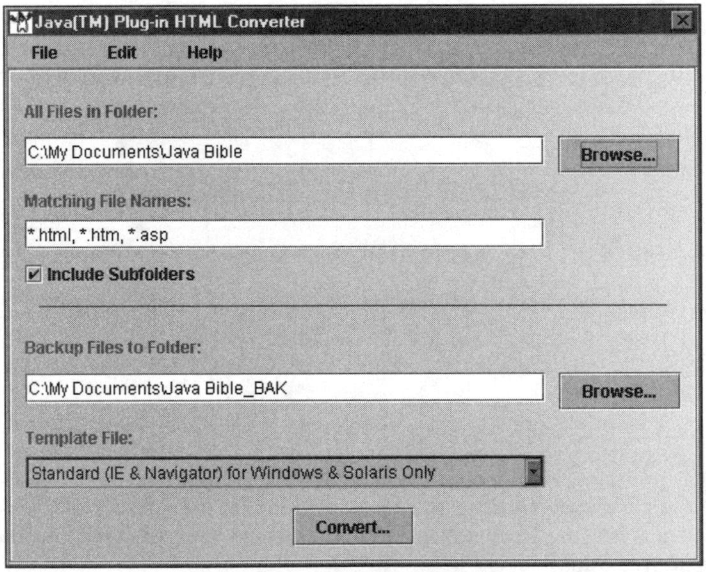

**Figure 5-4:** The Java Plugin 1.3 HTML converter

The Java Plugin will automatically download and install if necessary (see Figure 5-5), and it typically installs on Windows systems at C:\Program Files\JavaSoft\JRE\1.3\ along with the JRE, consuming nearly 5MB of hard disk space in total.

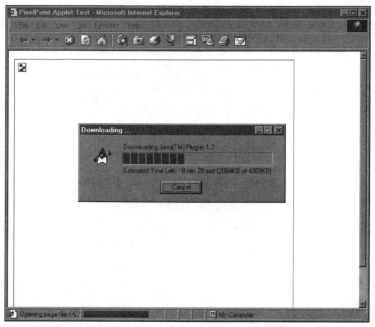

**Figure 5-5:** Downloading the Java Plugin

## Listing 5-8: **TestPixelPaint.html for Java Plugin version 1.3 (see Figures 5-4 and 5-5)**

```
<HTML>
<HEAD>
<TITLE> PixelPaint Applet Test </TITLE>
</HEAD>
<BODY>
<!--"CONVERTED_APPLET"-->
<!-- CONVERTER VERSION 1.3 -->
<OBJECT classid="clsid:8AD9C840-044E-11D1-B3E9-00805F499D93"
WIDTH = 500 HEIGHT = 500
codebase="http://java.sun.com/products/plugin/1.3/jinstall-13-
win32.cab#Version=1,3,0,0">
<PARAM NAME = CODE VALUE = "PixelPaint.class" >

<PARAM NAME="type" VALUE="application/x-java-
applet;version=1.3">
<PARAM NAME="scriptable" VALUE="false">
<COMMENT>
```

*Continued*

---

**Listing 5-8** *(continued)*

```
<EMBED type="application/x-java-applet;version=1.3"  CODE =
"PixelPaint.class" WIDTH = 500 HEIGHT = 500  scriptable=
false pluginspage="http://java.sun.com/products/plugin/1.3/
plugin-install.html"><NOEMBED></COMMENT>

</NOEMBED></EMBED>
</OBJECT>

<!--
<APPLET CODE = "PixelPaint.class" WIDTH = 500 HEIGHT = 500>

</APPLET>
-->
<!--"END_CONVERTED_APPLET"-->

</BODY>
</HTML>
```

---

# Summary

It is very simple to add images and soundtracks to Java applets. Once you've considered whether your applet should be enhanced or extended, it's merely a matter of implementing the code that will do the work. Between the `java.applet.Applet` class and the `java.applet.AppletContext` and `java.applet.AudioClip` interfaces, you'll have access to all the objects and methods needed to load and use images and audio clips, open new Web pages, and implement interapplet communications.

Compiling the code is easy — just as you saw in the previous chapter — and so is creating an HTML Web page in which your applet will live. When creating Java 2-only applets, however, you'll have to convert your Web pages to run in conjunction with the Java Plugin. (Because no browsers today directly support Java 2, you must redirect applets written specifically for Java 2 to run on a standalone Java 2 JRE.) Fortunately, the freely available Java Plugin HTML converter makes this job a cinch (see Chapter 25 for details).

Whereas very simple applets may require you to write only one class file (the one you create by extending Applet, or, in the case of Java 2-only applets, the `JApplet` class), in most cases, you'll create your own custom classes to further enhance the capabilities of your program. In both cases, you'll typically compose your classes from many of the core classes that come with Java.

✦ Every class, even applet classes, are ultimately a descendant of Java's top-level Object class. As such, every class inherits the methods defined by Object.

✦ All applets inherit four "life cycle" methods from the java.applet.Applet class that they extend: init(), start(), stop(), and destroy(). These methods are called by the applet context, which is typically a Web browser or Applet Viewer.

✦ In addition to the life cycle methods, every applet also inherits the paint() and update() methods, both of which are managed by the AWT. These methods are used to draw in the applet canvas.

✦ The java.applet.Applet class also defines methods for retrieving images and sounds, such as getImage() and gctAudioClip(). Images are drawn on the screen by calling the drawImage() method defined in the Graphics class, an instance of which is passed to the paint() method whenever paint() is invoked. Audio clips, on the other hand, are played by invoking either the play() or loop() method of the AudioClip class. To stop an audio clip that is playing, simply send it the stop() method.

✦ Applets that extend the javax.swing.JApplet class (instead of the typical java.applet.Applet class) can take advantage of JFC and Swing GUI com ponents. Unfortunately, JFC and Swing are part of Java 2 so they aren't sup- ported by all browsers. In this case, the Java Plugin must be used to redirect the applet to run on an appropriate Java 2 JRE instead of the browser's built- in JRE. Fortunately, the Java Plugin HTML Converter utility can automate the otherwise tedious task of converting your <APPLET> tags to corresponding <OBJECT> and <EMBED> tags.

✦ ✦ ✦

# Getting up to Speed: The Nuts and Bolts of Java

# Java Syntax: Tokens, Types, and Values

In Part I, you've seen that you write an object-oriented program by creating classes. These classes serve as templates for making objects. An object consists of two things (change things to "basic components"): what it knows and what it does. The "what it knows" part comprises the data that it stores and the other objects that it knows about. The data are called variables, attributes, fields, or properties. The "what it does" part refers to its methods for changing and interacting with what it knows. For the most part, the "what it knows" part is nobody's business except the object itself.

To you, the programmer, an object-oriented program consists of objects that interact with each other. As you write your program, you concentrate on figuring out which objects need to send which messages to other objects. If you are writing a graphical user interface (GUI) program, then you make sure the program can respond to mouse clicks or movement, the buttons being pressed, and text being typed. You are following the action and making sure that your objects do everything the user needs to accomplish. Formally, this method of design begins with what are called *use cases*.

You might create objects called Dad, Mom, Esmerelda, and Car. If Esmerelda wishes to use the Car, she may send a message to Dad. Dad is an object who knows that he better check with the Mom object. The Mom object might then give permission to the Dad object to give Esmerelda a way to access the Car object (in other words, a handle to the car). But a computer isn't a dad, mom, child, or car. It doesn't have these real objects hidden inside anywhere. These objects, methods, and variables help *us* to understand our model better, but that isn't the way the computer views the world that you have created.

The compiler translates the code that you write using a text editor to a format that the Java Virtual Machine (JVM) can understand. For the most part, the input to a Java program is made up of ASCII characters. Java actually uses an extension to ASCII called *Unicode* (which contains the ASCII characters as the first 128 characters). You can find out more at `http://www.unicode.org`.

The compiler first translates the input file to a stream in Unicode that consists of input characters and line terminators. It discards comments and white spaces and breaks the remaining text into pieces that it understands called *tokens*. It then uses its rules of grammar to interpret what is meant by these tokens.

In this chapter, we will follow the same path as the compiler. We'll begin with a discussion of comments and white spaces followed by a look at tokens. After the section on tokens, there's a section on types and values. You'll need this material later when you encounter examples of variables, methods, and classes. Rather than present each piece when it is needed, you'll find all of it here so that you can refer back when you need it. In other words, there's no reason to read this chapter from start to finish — just skim it so you know what's here. To make this a more useful reference later, some of the examples use features that have not yet been covered.

**Tip**    For even more information, check out Sun's official document: the Java Language Specification by James Gosling, Bill Joy, and Guy Steele. The material in this chapter is distilled from this document. If you'd like to further explore Java syntax, you can download the Java Language Specification from Sun's Web site at `http://java.sun.com/docs/books/jls/index.html`.

# The Elements the Compiler Ignores

Now this is silly. We are beginning our discussion of the syntax you have to use when programming in Java by examining elements that the compiler ignores and the Virtual Machine never sees. When you compile your program, the compiler starts by removing comments and unnecessary white space: blank spaces, horizontal tabs, form feeds, and line terminators.

The inexperienced programmer might ask, "If the compiler is going to throw all of my comments and tabs and pretty formatting away, why bother?" Well commented, easy-to-read code will save you time and money. Unfortunately, these good habits are often not rewarded by "penny wise, pound foolish" managers.

Picture this: A C++ programmer, let's call him John, writes at least one comment every few lines. John also takes time to carefully add to the documentation while coding. It's only a question of time until his boss starts complaining. The boss says he's paying John to program — and that means writing lines of code. John spends a lot of time thinking about a problem and designing his solution before he writes a line of code. He writes the comments and the documentation as he creates the program and then tests the program after he is done. Often, John has fewer lines of code than the boss expects; on the other hand, he always has more lines of working code than anyone else. When John is done with a program, it's always easy for other programmers to take his code and modify it or add functionality. The other programmers don't always understand what makes it so easy for them to join the project. They seldom maintain the level of comments and documentation. They are too busy meeting output quotas based on volume of code produced.

## Comments

As you are writing a program, you know what each part does and why you did it this way. Take time to include comments now while all of this is in your head. Later, when you or someone else has to go back and alter your code, it will be clear why you wrote a certain line of code, for example:

```
return s+=3;
```

Otherwise, you'll wonder what s is and why you added 3 to it before returning.

There are three kinds of comments used in Java: traditional comments, single-line comments, and documentation comments. We could have written the HelloWorld application with comments in any of the following ways:

```
/* HelloWorld.java
This file contains our first sample program. You may remember
it from Chapter 5 previous chapter. */

/** The class HelloWorld contains no methods or variables. It
has only a main method that prints "Hello World" in the console
window */

class HelloWorld
{
  public static void main (String args[])
  {
    System.out.println("Hello World!"); //the print statement
  }
}
```

### Traditional Comments

This is the comment you knew and loved in both C and C++. The format is the following:

```
/* text to be ignored on one
   or more lines */
```

Here, all of the text between /* and */ is ignored. Notice that this means that line terminators are also ignored, so this type of comment can occupy one or more lines. Don't nest traditional comments. For example, if you put one inside another, as in this example:

```
/* comment 1 starts /* comment 2 starts inside 1 */ oops */
```

the second /* is ignored because it is between the first /* and the first */. So you end up with a comment followed by the characters oops */.

## Single-Line Comments

A single-line comment is the familiar style introduced in C++. The format is the following:

```
//text to be ignored
```

All of the text from the // to the end of the line is ignored. Some editors automatically produce new lines when you enter too much text. This means that you may end up with an error like this:

```
//text to be ignored is so wordy that at the end of the line
another line is begun which is no longer being ignored.
```

Here, the second line is not counted as part of the comment. You can certainly use the traditional comment style to produce the single-line comment. When making a quick note about the code in that line, the single-line comment is quite handy.

## Documentation Comments

The traditional and single-line comments are great for providing comments for you or someone else who is reading through your code. Java provides a new comment that can be used to generate documentation in HTML using the *javadoc* tool. Here is a sample format for the documentation comment:

```
/** Here is the beginning of a documentation comment. This text
will be ignored by the compiler but can be used by the
"javadoc" tool to generate HTML code. Notice that these
comments can be on one or more lines. */
```

All of the text from the /** to the */ is ignored by the compiler. In the HelloWorld example, the documentation comment about the HelloWorld class comes directly before the class is declared. In general, you should put a documentation comment right in front of your declaration of a class, interface, constructor, method, or field. Sun recommends that your document comments begin with a brief sentence that completely summarizes the entity it belongs to.

To produce the documentation using these comments, you would type

```
javadoc filename.java
```

at the command prompt. To generate documentation for the entire package, you can replace `filename` with the wildcard (*) character. The `javadoc` tool will produce documentation that includes the class names and members (the methods and variables) along with the documentation for the *public* and *protected* members. We haven't yet discussed scope, but Java has keywords to indicate who has access to what. If you want to generate comments for *private* and friendly members, you generate them by typing

```
javadoc -private filename.java
```

at the command prompt. There are also several tags that allow you to add different features to your documentation. For example, you can hyperlink to other documentation using the `@see` tag. There are also tags that indicate the author and version as well as those that can describe parameters taken and returned by a method. Tags are also included to indicate that a feature has been deprecated or that a method throws an exception. These tags are `@author`, `@version`, `@param`, `@return`, `@deprecated`, and `@exception`.

## White space and coding style

The proper use of white space will make your code much more readable and understandable. Hey wait — isn't that what comments do? Comments are used to remind you of what your intention was with a piece of code or what this method does or what you plan to use that variable for. Indenting helps you see the structure of a class. You can visually tell where a method begins and ends. If you will be looping through some procedure until some condition is met, the white space will help you see the big picture.

So what is white space? It is either a space, a horizontal tab, a form feed, or a line terminator. Here a line terminator is either a newline, a return, or a return followed by a newline. For you ASCII fans, these white-space elements are one of the following ASCII characters: SP, HT, FF, LF, CR, or CR followed by LF.

You'll have to make lots of choices when deciding on a coding style. You should decide on conventions for naming various methods and variables. You should also have consistent rules for how you display elements on the page. As with most decisions, consistency is more important than your actual choice. Take another look at the `HelloWorld` code:

```
class HelloWorld {
  public static void main (String args[]) {
    System.out.println("Hello World!"); //the print statement
  }
}
```

Notice that it is immediately clear where the `main ()` method ends. The closing bracket (}) is directly under the p in `public`. Similarly, the closing bracket (}) that is directly under the c in `class` closes out the description of the `HelloWorld` class.

Some people would argue about the opening brackets, however. Some people prefer them to be on the same line as what they are opening and others would rather see the following code:

```
class HelloWorld
{
  public static void main (String args[])
  {
    System.out.println("Hello World!"); //the print statement
  }
}
```

Which style you choose probably doesn't really matter. What matters is that the look is uniform.

# Tokens

After discarding the white space and comments, the compiler then translates your code into the discrete elements called *tokens*. The tokens used in Java are as follows:

- ✦ Keywords
- ✦ Identifiers
- ✦ Literals
- ✦ Separators
- ✦ Operators

Once your source code has been translated into tokens, the compiler can check that the grammar rules of the Java language have been followed. It's kind of like when a sentence that you are reading just doesn't sound right. In the back of your head, you may hear your English teacher telling you not to end your sentence in a preposition. In other words, the teacher has ignored what you were saying while translating the pieces into parts of speech. Once the teacher accepts that you have used a legitimate construction, then he or she will listen to what you are saying (or make you diagram the sentence).

## Keywords

You will be making up names for classes, methods, variables, and other components that you will be creating while programming. Suppose you create a new device that extends a car's life by four years. You don't want to call that device a toaster oven. People already have a fixed idea by what is meant by a toaster oven and they won't get a clear idea of your product if you give it a name like that.

Keywords are words for which the compiler already has a set meaning. If you are using a clever editor or integrated development environment (IDE), it will color the keywords as you type them to visually indicate that these are special words that Java already knows about. A nice side effect of this feature is that you know immediately if you have a typo in a keyword name because it won't appear with the special colors. Of course, you can program in Java with a simple text editor and the `javac` compiler provided by Sun.

Table 6-1 contains the reserved keywords for the 1.2 release of the Java SDK (the first release of Java 2). In addition, the words `false`, `true`, and `null` are reserved words that *aren't* keywords. They are literals, and we'll look at them in a minute. You can't use any of these reserved words to name your classes, methods, or variables. Rather than go through the 47 keywords and describe what each one does here, let's wait until we get to the relevant section. To be complete, it turns out that Java doesn't have a set meaning for all of the keywords; `const` and `goto` are reserved as keywords even though they aren't used yet.

| Table 6-1 Java Keywords | | | | | |
| --- | --- | --- | --- | --- | --- |
| abstract | boolean | break | byte | case | catch |
| char | class | const | continue | default | do |
| double | else | extends | final | finally | float |
| for | goto | if | implements | import | instanceof |
| int | interface | long | native | new | package |
| private | protected | public | return | short | static |
| super | switch | synchronized | this | throw | throws |
| transient | try | void | volatile | while | |

# Identifiers

An *identifier* is the name of a class, method, or variable. You can create your name using a sequence made up of any of the letters, numbers of symbols on your keyboard (the ASCII characters), or Unicode characters.

## Legal Identifiers

Identifiers can be any length and must begin with a Java letter. You cannot use any of the reserved words (the keywords or the words `false`, `true`, and `null`) for an identifier.

How do you know when you are using a Java letter and when you are using a Java digit? Java letters are the letters a–z and A–Z together with the underscore character (_) and the Dollar symbol ($). You can check out the Unicode Web site for lists of which sequences correspond to letters and which ones correspond to digits in other alphabet and number systems.

When are two identifiers the same? As you go through the two identifiers in order, their Unicode characters must be the same all the way through. This means that Java is case sensitive, so `snowflake` and `snowFlake` are not the same. This also means that if you use the same letter in two different alphabets, the identifiers won't be the same even though they may appear to be identical. The Unicode characters for the same letter in different alphabets is different.

## Naming Conventions

By this point in your life, you know that even though something is technically legal, you shouldn't necessarily do it. For example, you wouldn't want to name a variable `_$__$_`. If you have the need to rebel against some sort of authority, choose another avenue to express your independence. The idea is to make your code readable, sensible, and to avoid possible name conflicts.

For example, if you have an object that represents a lamp, it might contain a variable indicating whether it is on or off. Jumping ahead of ourselves, we would make this variable a Boolean so that it could be only either `true` or `false`. So call the variable `isOn`. Someone reading the code would immediately get the idea that when `isOn` is `true`, you mean to convey that the light is on, and when `isOn` is `false`, you mean to convey that the light is off. Names for such variables are usually lowercase except for the first letter of each word after the first. So the lamp object could contain `lightSwitch`, `bulb`, and `pleatedLightShade`.

Sun suggests that class names should be nouns or noun phrases with the beginning of each word being capitalized. You might see class names such as `Discussion Group`, `School`, or `SchoolBusDriver`. Analogously, method names should be verbs or verb phrases in lowercase letters except for the first letter of every word after the first. As you will see, we will use methods such as `getIsOn()` to find out whether the `isOn` variable is currently `true` or `false` and the `setIsOn(false)` or `setIsOn(true)` methods to set the value of the `isOn` variable. Often, constant names are descriptive terms using all uppercase letters with _ between words. Examples could be `MAX_VELOCITY`, `PI`, or `SPEED_OF_LIGHT`. Some variables are used only within a small part of the program. For example, you might have a variable that is used for a calculation within a method, is a counter for a loop, or is a parameter being used as an argument in a method. It is less important that you choose a long descriptive name because the variable or parameter is only being used locally. Feel free to use a short descriptive name in all lowercase letters.

# Literals

Soon you will be dealing with many different types of variables. Consider these examples:

```
int purchaseNumber = 7;
boolean isOn = true;
String phrase = "This is a string";
```

As you will see, the first word in each of the two lines indicates which type of variable we are talking about. So `purchaseNumber` is an integer that Java calls an `int`. You've seen that `purchaseNumber`, `isOn`, and `phrase` are identifiers. In this case, they are the names of the variables. Each of these variables is being given a value. The source code that represents the value given to a primitive type, String type, or null type is called a *literal*. In this case, 7, `true`, and This is a string are literals.

This is the part of learning Java that may seem a bit frustrating. Every new concept refers to other new concepts. We haven't gotten to types yet, but they're used in the definition of literals. The problem is that no matter where we start, to learn the language efficiently, we will have to do a little of this. The main idea here is that in Java, there are integers and floating-point numbers. There are also Booleans, characters, and strings. These are the primitive types and are handled a bit differently by Java than the types you create yourself. Here are the various types of literals.

## Numbers

Java has two types of *numeric literals*: integer literals and floating-point literals. Integers are the numbers . . . . -3, -2, -1, 0, 1, 2, 3, . . . while floating-point numbers have a decimal representation 3.4, -902.88374, or 3.1415926.

### Integer literals

You can express an *integer literal* in basically three ways: decimal (base 10), hexadecimal (base 16), or octal (base 8). An integer literal is of type `int` unless it ends with an ASCII letter *L*, in which case it is of type `long`. The difference between these two types is that there is more range available when using `long`. For `int`, the range is from $2^{31}$ to $2^{31}-1$ (from -2,147,483,648 to 2,147,483,647). For `long`, the range is from $2^{63}$ to $2^{63}-1$ (from -9,223,372,036,854,775,808 to 9,223,372,036,854,775,807).

*Decimal literals* are either positive or zero. A decimal number consists of either a single digit from 0 to 9 or a digit from 1 to 9 followed by one or more digits from 0 to 9. Decimal literals could include 127, 0, or 67992L. Decimal literals are between 0 and 2147483647 if they are of type `int` and between 0 and 9223372036854775807L for type `float`.

*Hexadecimal literals* represent integers that are positive, negative, or 0. They consist of a leading 0x or 0X (zero and an upper- or lowercase x) followed by one or more hexadecimal digits. The hexadecimal digits are 0, 1, 2, 3, 4, 5, 6, 7, 8, 9, a, b, c, d, e, f. Here, *a* is the hexadecimal digit equivalent to the decimal 10, *b* is the hexadecimal digit equivalent to the decimal 11, . . . , and *f* is the hexadecimal digit equivalent to 15. You can also use the uppercase letters A through E to represent the numbers 10 through 15. You could write the decimal 47 in hexadecimal as 0x2f. This would be 2*16 + 15. Hexadecimals can be of type long. Hexadecimal literals are between 0x80000000 and 0x7fffffff for type int and between 0x8000000000000000L and 0x7fffffffffffffffL for type float.

*Octal literals* can represent integers that are positive, negative, or 0. They consist of a leading 0 (zero) followed by zero, one, or more digits between 0 and 7. For example, the number 47 written in octal would be 057. Octals can also be of type long. Octal literals are between 020000000000 and 017777777777 for type int and between 01000000000000000000000L and 0777777777777777777777L for type long.

### Floating-point literals

*Floating-point literals* are numbers that use either a decimal point, scientific notation, or both in their representation. A floating-point literal is composed of five parts:

✦ A whole-number part

✦ A decimal point (the standard period character ".")

✦ A fractional part

✦ An exponent

✦ A type suffix

Really, to be a floating-point literal, you need only two conditions: at least one digit that is either part of the whole number part or the fractional part; either a decimal point or an exponent.

The exponent is either the letter *e* or *E* followed by a signed integer. So 3.1e2 is another way of writing 310. We could also write 0.031 or 3.1E-2.

The suffix is one of the following: f, F, d, or D. The suffix indicates whether the floating-point literal is to be considered of type double or type float. Without a suffix, a floating-point literal is treated as a double. A finite, nonzero float literal is between 1.40239846e-45f and 3.40282347e+38f, and a finite nonzero double literal is between 4.94065645841246544e-324 and 1.79769313486231570e+308. The float and double classes each contain constants POSITIVE_INFINITY and NEGATIVE_ INFINITY as well as a Not-a-Number (NaN) constant NaN.

## Boolean Literals

As you've seen, the `boolean` type is like a switch than can have only two positions: on and off. A *boolean literal* is either `true` or `false`. That's it—there are no other possible values. Notice that unlike C and C++, the boolean literals in Java don't have integer values. Although this means that your code will be more readable and easy to follow, it also means that C and C++ programmers might not be able to use some of their favorite shortcuts.

## Character Literals

A *character literal* in Java represents exactly one character. It can be expressed as either of the following:

✦ A single character such as `a`, `A`, `b`, or `B`

✦ An escape sequence enclosed in single quotes such as `'\t'`, `'\u0009'`, or `'\b'`

Here are character literal escape codes together with the special characters that they represent:

| | |
|---|---|
| \b | backspace (BS) |
| \t | horizontal tab (HT) |
| \n | linefeed (LF) |
| \f | form feed (FF) |
| \r | carriage return (CR) |
| \" | double quote (") |
| \' | single quote (') |
| \\ | backslash (\) |

Don't use the Unicode escapes unless you need to and you know what you are doing. Remember that they are processed in a first pass by the compiler. If you can use one of the these escape codes, please do so.

## String Literals

A *string literal* is made up of any number of characters enclosed in double quotes. This also includes the string literal `""`, which contains no characters and is called the *empty string*. A string literal can include any of the characters described in character literals. One warning is that you don't want to include a line terminator between the opening and closing double quotes. For example, the string literal

```
"I'm a little programmer     //don't do this
short and stout"
```

will produce a compile-time error. If you have a long string and need to break it up, use the + to act as a concatenation operator. In other words, you would write the following:

```
"I'm a little programmer " + //do this if your string is long
"short and stout"
```

This example still won't understand that it should be displayed on two lines. To generate a new line, you could write it with an escape sequence:

```
"I'm a little programmer '\n' short and stout"
```

## Separators

Let's look back at the HelloWorld code once again. ( Who would have thought that there was so much to it?):

```
class HelloWorld
{
  public static void main (String args[])
  {
    System.out.println("Hello World!"); //the print statement
  }
}
```

Notice that the curly braces ({ and }) help you and the compiler organize what makes up the body of the main method and the body of the class HelloWorld. The main method takes inputs and the round braces (( and )) indicate where the argument list begins and ends. Inside of this argument list is an array, so we see the characters [ and ]. Each statement ends with a semicolon (;). Somewhere within something called System is something called out, which has a method called println. The period (.) is a way of linking together this path from where we are to the println method. Finally, suppose we had a method add:

```
add(x,y){...}
```

This method takes two arguments x and y, which are separated by a comma (,).

These nine characters are the separators in Java. They are used to organize your code into pieces that the compiler understands and to help you make sure that the compiler is interpreting the operations as you intend them to be. The following is the complete list of separators:

```
{ } ( ) [ ] ; , .
```

## Operators

*Operators* are characters or combinations of characters that are used to perform calculations and comparisons, and to manipulate data. Table 6-2 lists the 37 tokens that are the Java operators. In the next chapter, we'll look in more detail at these operators. You'll see what they do and what the rules are for precedence and associativity.

| Table 6-2 Java Operators | | | | | | | | | |
|---|---|---|---|---|---|---|---|---|---|
| = | > | < | ! | ~ | ? | : | == | <= | >= |
| != | && | \|\| | ++ | -- | + | - | * | / | & |
| \| | ^ | % | << | >> | >>> | += | -= | *= | /= |
| &= | \|= | ^= | %= | <<= | >>= | >>>= | | | |

# Types and Values

According to Bill Joy, one of his goals for Java is that more errors will be caught while the programmer is still thinking about and understanding that piece of code. Throughout this part of the book, we will encounter features built into the language to support this aim. One of these checks is that Java is a strongly typed language. It's as if you make a promise when you use a variable or return an expression that it will be of a certain type. This allows the compiler to check to see if what is being delivered matches what was promised.

As you begin to write programs in the next chapter, you'll see types everywhere. For every variable, you will have to declare its type—it's a variable's way of saying "this is how I need to be treated." For methods, you will declare the types of its arguments and of its resulting value—it's a method's way of saying "this is the input I expect and the order in which I expect it, and here's what I'll be sending back to you." In fact, you will have types for every parameter in constructors and exception handlers as well. Not only does this help the compiler check that everything is okay, but it makes your code more readable. You can look and see that you are setting a variable that holds integers to the result of a method that returns a boolean and know that something is wrong.

Java has two basic types: primitive types and reference types. You saw examples of *primitive types* during the discussion of literals. These are the boolean and numeric types. The *reference types* are class types, interface types, and array types. An additional reference type is the `null` type. One way to view the differences between these two types is to look at the corresponding data values that can be stored in variables. A variable of a reference type holds either a null reference or a reference to either an instance of the specified class, to a class that implements the specified interface, or to an array of objects of the specified type. By contrast, a variable of a primitive type actually holds a value of that type.

# Primitive types and values

One feature of primitive types is that they are defined so that their representation and behavior is the same in the various implementations of Java on all platforms. Another feature is that once you have declared a variable of a certain primitive type, it will only hold values of that type. You can change the value of what that variable stores but only to another value of the same type. Primitive types are either *numeric types* or the `boolean` type.

## The Boolean Type

### The boolean type and values

We've already spent some time with the `boolean` type. As you learned in the discussion of `boolean` literals, a `boolean` type represents a logical quantity with the two possible values: `true` and `false`.

### Boolean operators

You can compare two booleans using the relational operations `==` and `!=` to test for equals and not equals. For example, say you have `boolean` variables b and c. Then b==c is true if both variables are true or if both variables are false.

You can apply the logical-complement operator (`!`) to a `boolean` variable or expression to change it from `true` to `false` or from `false` to `true`. You can also build compound expressions using these logical operators: logical and (`&`), logical or (`|`), and logical exclusive or (`^`). For example,

```
(expression1) & (expression2)
```

is `true` only when each of the expressions are true. You can also use the conditional-and (`&&`) and conditional-or (`||`) operators. These operators stop evaluating when they can return a value. For example, consider

```
(expression1) && (expression2)
```

As soon as either expression evaluates to `false`, we could stop checking the other because the compound expression will be false.

The conditional operator (`? :`) evaluates the `boolean` and returns the value before the colon (`:`) if the `boolean` is `true` and the value after the colon if the `boolean` is `false`. An example is provided in the next paragraph.

C programmers have gotten used to treating `boolean`s as integers with 0 as false and 1 or, for some, any nonzero value being true. The fact that you can't cast a `boolean` to an integer or vice versa should tell you that this behavior is not encouraged. You can convert an integer x to a `boolean` by using the `boolean` != operator. Note that x  != 0 will return true if x is different from 0 and will return `true` if x is zero. You can convert a `boolean` b to an integer using the conditional operator. The expression b?1:0 will return 1 if b is `true` and 0 if b is `false`.

You can compare two `boolean`s using the standard less than (<), greater than (>), less than or equal to (<=), and greater than or equal (>=) to operators. You can also combine assignment with the &, |, and ^ operators to get &=, |=, and ^=. For example, a&=b is the same as a = a & b.

A final boolean operator is the string concatenation operator +. If you have a `String` followed by + followed by a `boolean` value, the operator converts the `boolean` to a `String` and then attaches it to the end of the other `String`.

You'll use booleans for control flow in your program. Maybe you'll want to execute one method if a statement is `true` and another if it is `false`, or maybe you'll want to repeat an operation until a statement is `true`. You'll see these in future chapters when the `if`, `for`, `while`, and `do` statements are covered.

## Numeric Types

Just as in the discussion of literals, numeric types are either *integral types* or *floating-point types*. Hey wait a minute — this takes care of numbers and `boolean` is also taken care of. What about characters? The `char` type is an integral type whose values are 16-bit unsigned integers representing Unicode characters. The other integral types differ in their size, but they are all signed two's-complement integers. (This is the way they represent negative numbers.) These integral types are `byte`, `short`, `int`, and `long`, which hold 8-, 16-, 32-, and 64-bit integers, respectively. The floating-point types are `float` and `double`, which are IEEE 754 floating-point numbers and 32- and 64-bit integers, respectively. For more details on the IEEE 754 specification, see the "IEEE Standard for Binary Floating-Point Arithmetic," ANSI/IEEE Std. 754-1985.

## Numeric Values

Table 6-3 shows the legal range for each numeric type and the default value for a variable of that type. Each range given is inclusive. In other words, the legal values include the boundary values given. You can cast from any numeric type to any other numeric type.

For floating-point values, you'll notice that there are positive and negative infinities and zeros. There is also a value NaN. It is sometimes useful to test whether a number actually is a finite number before performing an operation. You could do this by checking that it is not negative infinity, not positive infinity, and not NaN.

Finite nonzero values of float and double are of the form . The *s* is the sign of the number and is either +1 or -1. The *m* is a positive integer. For float, *m* is less than and for double, *m* is less than . For float, *e* is an integer between -149 and 104; for double, *e* is an integer between -1075 and 970.

| Table 6-3 Legal Value Ranges and Default Values for Primitive Types | | |
|---|---|---|
| **Type** | **Default Value** | **Legal Range** |
| byte | 0 | -128 to 127 |
| short | 0 | -32768 to 32767 |
| int | 0 | -2147483648 to 2147483647 |
| long | 0L | -9223372036854775808 to 9223372036854775807 |
| char | '\u0000' | '\u0000' to '\uffff' |
| float | 0.0f | NaN, negative infinity, negative finite values, negative zero, positive zero, positive finite values, and positive infinity |
| double | 0.0d | NaN, negative infinity, negative finite values, negative zero, positive zero, positive finite values, and positive infinity |
| boolean | false | true and false |

## Numeric Operations

Numeric operators can be used to compare two operands or to perform an operation on one or two numeric values. This section should be familiar to those with programming experience.

### Comparison operators

Comparison operators compare two numeric values and decide whether the statement is true or false. In other words, a comparison operator always results in a value of type boolean. For example, the statement 5<3 has the value false. The comparison operators are ==, !=, <, <=, >, and >=.

### Numerical operators

Numerical operators take one or more numerical values and the result of the operation is again a numerical value. (The next chapter is more specific about what types the operators take and return.)

Operators tend to be called unary or binary depending on how many inputs they take. Consider the two examples -3 and 7-3. In the first example, the minus sign (-)

only takes the number 3 as its input and returns the opposite of 3, namely -3 (like that's been cleared up now. . .). In the second example, the minus sign (-) takes both the number 7 and the number 3 as its inputs and returns the difference between the two values.

So saying, Java includes the following unary operators for every numerical value: unary plus and minus (+ and -), the absolute value operator (abs()), and the prefix and postfix increment and decrement operators (++ and --).

The binary numerical operators are the additive operators (+ and -) and the multiplicative operators, including the remainder operator (*, /, and %). The expression

```
51 % 15
```

has the value 6 since 51/15 leaves a remainder of 6. When the operands are integral type, division by zero results in an arithmetic exception being thrown. This includes the case in which you are using the remainder operator with a zero as the right-hand operand.

The operators +=, -=, *=, /=, and %= are combinations of the indicated arithmetic operation and assignment. For example

```
a+=7
```

is equivalent to the more readable expression

```
a=a+7
```

Each has the same meaning. The first seems to represent the instructions "increase the value of variable a by 7 and store it in a." The second seems to say "replace the value stored in the variable a with the value stored in the variable a plus 7."

If the result of an integer operation overflows (that is, it is beyond the legal range of the result type), it will be reduced by modulo arithmetic. It is important, therefore, to ensure that your variables are capable of storing the range of values that might be returned when assigning the result of operations to variables.

There are a few slight differences between integer and floating-point operations. For example, when the unary increment (++) or decrement (–) operators are used with a floating-point operand, the value of 1.0 is added to the operand. (When applied to integers, the value of 1 is added.)

Another difference occurs with the modulo (%) operator. When applied to integers (such as 10%4), the remainder of the division operation, 10/4, is returned as an integer (2). When the modulo operator is applied to a floating-point number, the remainder of the division operation is returned as a floating-point value.

Floating-point operations will never generate an `ArithmeticException` error, however, as explained in the previous chapter. Instead, the value NaN, is used to represent the result of operations that don't return a number.

The presence of a NaN can produce unexpected results when dealing with floating-point data types. Since NaN is unordered, the result of a <, <=, >, >=, or == comparison between a NaN and another value is always false. In fact, == always produces false when both operands are NaN. On the other hand, the result of a != comparison with a NaN is always true, even if both operands are NaN.

Java also defines the conditional operator (? :). This is technically a ternary operator, as it takes three pieces of information as inputs. Its behavior is the same as in the case of the conditional operator described for `boolean`s.

As previously mentioned, the *cast* operator allows you to convert from any numerical value to any other numerical value. When you cast a floating-point value to an integral value, Java uses the *round toward zero* rule. This amounts to just lopping off the information to the right of the decimal point. So `(int) 3.14159` would be 3 and `(int)(-3.14159)` would be `-3`.

Finally, there is the string concatenation operator (+). If you have a binary addition where the first operand is a `String` and the second operand is a numerical value, the number will be converted to a `String` representation (so it will look the same from our point of view), and the two strings will then be concatenated.

For integral types, there are a few additional operators. There is the unary bitwise complement operator (~). There are also the signed and unsigned shift operators (<<, >>, and >>>) as well as the integer bitwise operators (&, |, and ^).

The numerical operators will result in a value of type `int` or `long` if your operands are both integral types. In fact, any integer operator other than the shift operator that is applied to a `long` and an `int` will treat the operands as `long`s and return a `long`. For example, if you add a `long` and an `int`, the `int` is first widened into a `long`, the two are added, and the result will be a `long`. Similarly, if one of the operands is an integral type and the other is a `float`, the integral type will be widened to a `float`, the operation will be carried out using the 32-bit floating-point arithmetic, and the result of the operation will be a `float`. Finally, if one of the operands is a `double` and the other is a `float` or an integral type, the nondouble will be widened, the operation will be carried out using the 64-bit floating-point arithmetic, and the result of the operation will be a `double`.

## Reference types and values

A variable is just a storage location. The type associated with the variable tells it how big this storage location needs to be. If the variable is a primitive type, then the value of the variable is stored at this location. If the variable is a reference type, then the variable stores a pointer to the object (if the reference type is `class` or `interface`) or array and not the object or array itself. This is handy. Some objects are pretty big. You wouldn't want the overhead of passing them around. This way, you are just passing the reference to the object around. This can be a bit confusing because, as you will see, it means that dealing with objects and `arrays` is very different from dealing with primitive types.

## Creating Objects and Reference Variables

Let's return to the lamp example from the section on naming conventions. In Java, you should think of a class as a template. So a Lamp class would contain all of the variables and methods that a specific lamp would need, but the Lamp class is not itself a lamp. One or more of the methods that a Lamp class contains (although possibly not explicitly) is called a *constructor*. It is used for creating or instantiating an object from the class definition. In other words, we would create an actual instance of a Lamp class using the `new` keyword.

```
new Lamp(); // instantiates Lamp object by calling constructor
```

Note that the constructor has the same name as the class. It may take zero or more arguments. You need to write a different constructor for each sequence of arguments you might want to pass in. The number and type of arguments (in order) that you enter when you want to create a new instance of a class must exactly match the arguments in one of the constructors you have written.

We might create a new lamp and pass in information on whether it is initially turned on or off. We could send that information using the following code:

```
new Lamp(true);//Lamp is created with isOn=true
```

You could also have created a new lamp and passed in information on how many light bulbs it contains:

```
new Lamp(3);//Lamp is created with 3 lightbulbs
```

You could even send it both pieces of information at once:

```
new Lamp(true,3);//Lamp is created with 3 lightbulbs turned on
```

This is an example where type is very important in Java. How does it know which constructor to use? The second and third constructors both take one argument but one is an `int` and one is a `boolean`.

So now we have created four lamps but we have no way of accessing them. It's as if we're sitting on the couch watching television and can't find the remote control. We're not going to walk the 10 feet to change the channel. We've lost our connection to the television. In our example, we haven't yet created the remote controls. We do this by declaring a variable with a reference type and set it equal to the new lamp. So we will first announce that we are creating a variable that will hold a reference to a `Lamp` with this code:

```
Lamp myLamp;
```

And then we will create a new `Lamp` that is on and assign `myLamp` to point to it:

```
myLamp = new Lamp(true);
```

So we can declare a reference variable and not initialize it. We could have declared and initialized it in one line by writing the following:

```
Lamp myLamp = new Lamp();
```

## Accessing Methods and Variables

Continuing with our `Lamp` example, let's say that the `Lamp` class contains the `boolean` variable `isOn` and the `int` variable `numberOfBulbs`. As we discussed before, we might also like to have the `getIsOn()` method, which tells us whether `isOn` is true or false, and the `setIsOn(booleanLiteral)` method, which sets the value of `isOn` to *booleanLiteral*.

So now when we create a lamp using `Lamp myLamp = new Lamp();` `myLamp` will contain the variables `isOn` and `numberOfBulbs` along with the methods `getIsOn` and `setIsOn`. We can now turn `myLamp` on and off using the commands:

```
myLamp.setIsOn(true);
myLamp.setIsOn(false);
```

This is how you access a particular method inside an instance of a class. You already saw this syntax in the `HelloWorld` program in the line:

```
System.out.println("Hello World");
```

For the most part, you don't want to allow objects to have access to variables in another object. If, however, the variable `numberOfBulbs` is accessible, you could set the number of bulbs to 3 with:

```
myLamp.numberOfBulbs = 3;
```

## References Types Versus Primitive Types

You've seen a couple of times that variables of primitive types hold the actual value and variables of reference types are just pointers to objects or arrays. Let's examine what this difference means. First, consider the following code snippet to see how this situation works for primitive types:

```
int a,b;
a=3;
b=a;
a++;
```

Here the two variables have the primitive type `int`. Variable a is given the value 3. Then, by setting b equal to a, b is given the same value that a has. This means that b now has the value 3. We then use the increment operator to add one to a so a has the value 4 while b still has the value 3.

Now let's follow the same pattern with reference types:

```
Lamp myLamp, anotherLamp;
myLamp = new Lamp(true);
anotherLamp = myLamp;
anotherLamp.setIsOn(false);
```

This is the same pattern we followed in the example using primitive types. Here `anotherLamp` and `myLamp` have the reference type `Lamp`. This means that they will point to instances of `Lamp` objects. Then `myLamp` is initialized to point to a newly created `Lamp` that is turned on. Okay, now watch carefully. This time when `anotherLamp` is set equal to `myLamp`, they are now just two different names for the same `Lamp`. In the next line, `anotherLamp` is turned off. This will mean that `myLamp` is automatically turned off because they are the same `Lamp`. It's as if my wife and I each have remote controls for the same television set (bad idea). When I turn to channel 5, the television that she is controlling turns to channel 5 as well.

The point is that what is being passed around isn't the value of a particular lamp but its address. In general, whenever you assign an object to a variable or pass an object to a method or constructor, it is done by reference.

## Null References

Technically, the type of the expression `null` is the null type. But the null type doesn't have a name, so you can't declare a variable of the null type or cast some other object to the null type. The `null` reference is used to specify an object that has no instance. The default value for a variable of reference type is `null`.

Here's where the television remote control analogy falls apart. Once you have lost the reference to an object, there is no way to reconnect to it. You can't just go out and get another remote control and reprogram it. So, once you've set a reference variable to `null`, you may have left your object with no references to it. Since you can't use that object any more, it is eligible to be garbage collected.

## The Class Object and Operators on Reference Types

As you will see, you get more bang for your buck in Java by reusing your objects. Two favorite ways of doing this are composition and inheritance. In *composition*, you build a car object out of a tire, seat, window, steering wheel object that you have already created. In *inheritance*, you look to extend or specialize objects that you already have. You might decide that a flashlight is a special kind of lamp. Then by using inheritance, you automatically get all of the functionality defined in Lamp.

There is some functionality that you would like to be present in all objects that you create in Java. To give you this, all objects inherit (either directly or through a chain of inheritance) from a special Java class called Object. One example of this functionality is the ability to copy or clone an object.

### Copying objects

If your object supports the copy() or clone() methods, you can use them to copy the value of one object into another. For our lamps, you would use either of the following.

```
anotherLamp.copy(myLamp); //copy myLamp into anotherLamp
anotherLamp = myLamp.clone(); /*clone myLamp and set
    anotherLamp equal to the clone
(i.e. to point to the clone)*/
```

When using copy(), both objects are instances of the same class. The value of all instance variables of the object you pass as an argument to copy() are copied into the instance variables of the object on the left side of the dot notation. If an instance variable contains the reference to an object, only the reference is copied, not the object itself.

With clone(), a new instance is created and the value of all instance variables of the current object are copied into the new one. Just as with copy(), if an instance variable contains the reference to an object, only the reference is copied (not the object itself). If the two objects aren't of the same type, you must perform a cast:

```
objectVariable1 = (objectVariable1) objectVariable2.clone();
```

Not all objects support copy() and clone(). When they are supported, you may need to cast objects from one type to another in order to carry out the method. Casting objects is possible as long as the object you're casting is related (by inheritance) to the object it's being cast to. This means you can cast an object only to an instance of its superclass or subclass. To perform the cast, use the cast operator to enclose the name of the class you are casting the object to in parentheses:

```
(ClassName) theObject;
```

When a cast is performed, a new instance of the specified class is created, which has the contents of the object. The original object isn't altered and can be used exactly as it was before the cast was performed. In addition to explicit casts, variables can contain references to objects whose runtime type can be converted to the variable's compile-time type through assignment conversion.

### Testing for equality

Since we are dealing with objects by reference rather than by value, the following code will tell you whether the two variables refer to the same object:

```
objectVariable1 == objectVariable2;
```

Similarly, you could use the != method to compare what two reference variables point to. To find out whether two objects (i.e., what the variables actually point to) are equal, use the equals() method:

```
objectVariable1.equals(objectVariable2);
```

### Other operators on references to objects

Objects inherit several methods from the Object class. Use getClass() to get the class that the object is an instance of. To retrieve the class name as a String, use the following:

```
anyObject.getClass().getName();
```

As with the primitive types, we have the string concatenation operator +. If you have a String followed by + followed by a reference to an object, the reference is converted to a String using the object's toString method, which returns a String representation of the object. The result of the + operator will be the concatenation of the two strings. References also have the conditional operator ? : that also acts as it did for primitive types.

Primitive types didn't have the instanceof operator. To test if an object is an instance of a particular class, use:

```
anyObject instanceof ClassName;
```

This will return true if the object is an instance of the class and false if not.

Other available methods not covered here are hashCode (used in hash tables), wait, notify, notifyAll (used in concurrent programming—for more details, see Chapter 14), and finalize (used in garbage collection).

# Summary

This chapter presented some of the foundations for the Java language. Once you have a feel for what is contained here, you probably will use it more like a reference as you are programming. When you come back, you'll find that these key concepts were presented in this chapter:

✦ Java is a tokenized language: the lines of code that you write are translated by the compiler into discrete elements known as tokens. Working from left to right, the compiler discards all comments and white space. What remains is separated into one of five possible tokens: keywords, identifiers, literals, separators, and operators.

✦ Keywords are character sequences formed by ASCII letters that are reserved by the Java language for special purposes. You cannot use them for anything other than their intended purpose.

✦ An identifier is a sequence of Unicode characters that you use to name a class, method, or variable. Identifiers can be of any length, and they can contain both letters and digits. However, they must begin with a letter, not a digit. You can use any name you can think of for an identifier, provided it doesn't begin with a digit and is not the same as a keyword. Because identifiers are Unicode, they can even include non-Latin letters and digits.

✦ Literals are explicit values, such as 18345 or "Hello World!", that are specified directly in your Java code. Java supports three categories of literals: those that are numbers (integer and floating-point literals), boolean literals (`true` and `false`), and those that are composed of characters (character literals and string literals).

✦ Types are used to identify the information stored in variables and returned by methods (on those occasions when a method does in fact return data when called). The information stored in a variable or returned by a method is known as the value of the variable or return. In essence, you create variables that have a certain type. The type of a variable also indicates the built-in operators available to that variable.

✦      ✦      ✦

# About Variables, Methods, Expressions, and Controlling Flow

In Chapter 6, we looked at the Java programming language from the perspective of the compiler. You learned about the various kinds of tokens and types and how they are interpreted in Java.

In this chapter, we will continue to look at fundamentals of Java programming, but this time, more from the point of view of the programmer. We will look at the building blocks for writing a Java program: variables, methods, expressions, and various control-flow statements, and we will revisit operators. In a way, we're assembling our tools so that we won't have to think about these details when we are worried about getting objects to communicate with each other.

## Variables

We think of a variable as holding information for us. When we write cupsOfCoffee=5 or isAwakeYet = false or myLamp = new Lamp(), we think of a box named cupsOfCoffee that is holding the value 5, a box named isAwakeYet that is holding the value false, or a box named myLamp that is holding a reference to a Lamp. A *variable* is just a storage location for a specific type; it points to some place in memory and knows how big a chunk to look at. In Chapter 6, we saw that the two basic types are primitive type and reference type. For primitive types, the storage location actually holds the value; for reference types, the storage location holds a pointer to where the actual object or array is being stored. Unlike C and C++, we can't actually get the address of the storage location that the variable points to or manipulate it in clever ways.

## Uses of variables

You use variables in Java to store values. This section summarizes situations in which you would want to use variables and then addresses each later in this chapter in context. Let's stick with the Lamp example from Chapter 6:

✦ Instance variables and array components: Suppose you want each specific Lamp to know whether it is on or not. Each Lamp will then contain a variable isOn, which is a boolean. So the code

```
Lamp aLamp = new Lamp( true );
Lamp bLamp = new Lamp( false );
```

might create two lamps, one of which is on and the other of which is off. In other words, aLamp.isOn is true while bLamp.isOn is false. Here, isOn is called an instance variable because it is a field that exists as part of an instance of a class (that is, part of an object).

Similarly, a lamp may contain an array of a user-defined type called LightBulb. A LightBulb might consist of an int that indicates the wattage of the LightBulb and a boolean that indicates whether the bulb is burned out or not. The array contains components of type LightBulb, which are effectively unnamed variables. Arrays will be covered in depth in Chapter 8, "Creating and Using Arrays and Strings."

✦ Class variables: Remember, we think of a class as a template for producing objects. A class even contains special methods called constructors that tell us how our objects are made. What if we wanted to keep track of how many Lamps we have made so far? It would be nice to create a variable that belonged to the Lamp class and not to any specific instance. On the other hand, we may want to access this variable through a specific Lamp object. Java's solution is the class variable. This is a field that is declared within a class declaration just as you would declare an instance variable with the addition of the keyword static. So within the class Lamp, you might see

```
static int numberOfLamps=0;
```

When the first Lamp is created, the numberOfLamps variable will be created and initialized to 0. As each Lamp is created, we could set up the constructor to increment the numberOfLamps. When we discuss interfaces, you will see that you can also create class variables there.

✦ Method parameters and constructor parameters: Imagine methods that tell you whether a specific Lamp is on or not and that turn a specific Lamp on or off. The code for these methods could be

```
public boolean getIsOn()
{
    return isOn;
}
public void setIsOn( boolean turnLampOn )
```

```
{
  isOn = turnLampOn;
}
```

For now, lets ignore the words before the method name getIsOn(). Notice that the method doesn't need to be given any information to perform its task. All it does is return the value of the boolean that indicates whether this specific Lamp is on or not. On the other hand, the setIsOn method needs to know whether the specific Lamp is being turned on or off. It takes an argument and the argument has a type boolean. So turnLampOn is a variable that is a parameter for the method setIsOn. Constructors are special kinds of methods used for building objects. Look back at the example Lamp aLamp = new Lamp( true ). The constructor is taking a boolean as an argument, so when you write the constructor, you will have a variable that stores the value being passed to it. In short, the way you pass information to a method or constructor is with parameters. These parameters are variables.

✦ Local variables: The separators { and } contain a *block* of code. For example, the body of a method is a block. The following if statement contains a block of code that is executed if it is true that the value of myAge is less than 16.

```
if( myAge<16 )
{
  int ageIncrement = 1;
  myAge = myAge + ageIncrement;
  System.out.println( "I'm too young to drive." );
}
```

This example is a poor one for many reasons. Its purpose is to show that you can create variables inside of a block that exist from the time they are declared to the time the block is exited. You can also create local variables within a for statement

```
for ( int count = 1; count < 6; count++)
{
  sum = sum + count;
}
```

Here, the variable count ceases to exist when we exit the block controlled by the for statement.

✦ Exception-handler parameters: We will look at Java's mechanism for handling exceptions in Chapter 11, "Exceptions and Error Handling." When we do, you'll see that in order to report on what is going wrong and where, a new variable is created.

## Declaring variables

To use a variable, you first have to declare it. A variable declaration consists of two parts:

✦ A data type: This determines the legal range of values a variable may contain, which operations may be applied to the variable, and how such operations are performed.

✦ An identifier: An identifier is used to associate a name with a variable:

```
type identifier [, identifier];
```

Any number of variables can be declared on a single line, each of the same type, as long as each identifier's name is unique and separated from the others by a comma. A semicolon is used to signal the end of a variable declaration.

Here, we declare an integer variable and give it the name `horizontal`:

```
int horizontal;
```

And here, we declare several integer variables, all on the same line:

```
int horizontal, vertical, x, y, z, days, ageInDays;
```

However, we could have broken this declaration into a number of declarations:

```
int horizontal;
int vertical;
int x;
int y;
int z;
int days;
int ageInDays;
```

How you declare your variables depends mainly on personal taste, although most programmers would have chosen the first example for ease of readability.

There is an exception for declaring arrays. You'll learn more about this in the section "Initializing Arrays," but suppose you are creating variables x and y that are `int`s and an array of `int`s called `emailsReceived`. You could write

```
int x,y, emailsReceived[];
```

You wouldn't want to do this because there is a fundamental difference between the nature of x and y and the nature of `emailsReceived[]`. You certainly could declare these variables as

```
int x;
int y;
int emailsReceived[];
```

We would prefer that you declare these variables as

```
int x,y;
int emailsReceived[];
```

This style more clearly separates your intent. It groups variables together that should be seen as the same and separates variables from those that are somehow different. Remember from Chapter 6 that these are differences that the compiler doesn't care about. These coding standards are to help you and others understand your code.

For completeness, it is also legal to use the keyword `int` only once and write either

```
int x,
  y,
   emailsReceived[];
```

or

```
int x,y,
emailsReceived[];
```

You should choose and stick with a consistent style. Your decision should be based on clarity, readability, or on understanding that the style preferred by the person signing your check is probably a good choice for this project.

## Declaring Primitive Variables

You declare a variable of primitive type similar to the `int` example just shown. Your programs will likely use a large number of different primitive variables. Any variable that you declare of type `byte`, `short`, `int`, `long`, `float`, `double`, `char`, or `boolean` is a primitive variable. The following are examples of variable declarations for each primitive type:

```
byte x;
short daysInMonth;
int counter;
long bacteriaCount;
float accountBalance;
double exactBalance;
char middleInitial;
boolean quit;
```

### Declaring Reference Variables

Reference variables are used to store references, or pointers, to objects. (Keep in mind that we're not referring to pointers such as those used in C and C++ here, but simply the concept of pointing to an object in memory.) These objects can be class instances, class instances that implement interfaces, or arrays.

An *interface* is a collection of methods that are not implemented in code; interfaces are explained in detail in Chapter 9, "Classes, Interfaces, and Packages."

Here are examples of reference variable declarations for arrays and class instances:

```
int highScores[]; /* array of integers */
int[] lowScores; /*also an array of integers */
Lamp aLamp; /* aLamp is a reference variable containing the
    address of a Lamp */
```

Notice the two forms of declaring an array. They are equivalent. In the first line, you are announcing that highScores is an array that will hold entries of the type int. In the second line, you are announcing that you are declaring an array of ints with the name lowScores.

## Initializing and storing values in variables

Once a variable has been declared, a value may be stored in it. This may be done either at the time a variable is declared — a process known as *initialization* — or any time after it has been declared, through assignment. In either case, any value assigned at any time to a variable must be of the same type as the variable itself or of a type that can be converted to that type through a cast that involves narrowing, widening, or converting to a String. These types are said to be *consistent*.

### Initializing Primitive Types and Object References

You've already seen how to declare variables that hold primitive types and reference types. You cannot create a variable that has the null type. The only way to get this type of variable is to assign a reference type variable the value null. The other exceptional variable type is the reference type that holds an array. Arrays are discussed in the next section.

For all other reference types and for all primitive types, you can initialize them once they have been declared. These are examples of variables that we've already declared being initialized:

```
counter = 1043;
bacteriaCount = 12239493;
accountBalance = 533.35;
middleInitial = 'E';
quit = false;
aLamp = new Lamp();
```

You can also initialize these variables in the same line in which you are declaring them. These are examples of variables being initialized at the time of declaration:

```
int counter = 1043;
long bacteriaCount = 12239493;
float accountBalance = 533.35;
double exactBalance = 464.3243003;
char middleInitial = 'E';
boolean quit = false;
String helloString = "Hello World!";
AudioClip m = getAudioClip(getCodeBase(), "audio/hello.au");
```

In each of these examples, a value consistent with the variable's data type is assigned to it at the time of declaration. These variables have been initialized. From the moment they are created, they contain a value.

## Initializing Arrays

In the case of arrays, each element may contain a value. We said that highScores and lowScores were each arrays of integers. We know that because they were declared

```
int highScores[];
int[] lowScores;
```

How many ints does highScores contain? We haven't yet said. We could declare it to hold twelve ints by now writing

```
highScores - new int[12];
```

As with the other types of variables, we can declare and initialize an array all at once

```
int[] averageScores = new int[12];
```

Wait a minute. We didn't really initialize the array in the same sense that we seemed to initialize the variables in the previous sections. We don't know what the value of each entry in the array is. What we've done, in a way, is set aside space for an array of twelve integers. The first element of the array is an integer. We can refer to that element as averageScores[0]. The second element of the array, averageScores[1], is also an integer as is every element including the last element. Similarly, for every element up to the last element, averageScores[11].

There are two notes. First, the numbering of positions begins with 0 just as it did in C and C++. Second, this previous line of code declared averageScores to be an array with twelve entries each of which would be an int. This last step is declaring each position of the array so that now we can just assign a value to it.

You could assign values to elements of an array at the time that you declare it. Use code similar to the following:

```
int[] perfectSquares = {0,1,4,9,16,25};
```

You could also initialize this array after declaring it, as shown in this example:

```
int[] perfectSquares = new int[6];
for ( int count = 0; count < 6; count++)
{
   perfectSquares[count] = count * count;
}
```

As you can see, the for loop also contains a variable declaration. We declare an index, i, that is used to access each element in the array. Before using i, we initialize it to zero (0), since the first element in every array is at position zero. (Arrays in Java are zero-based, just as C/C++ arrays are.) Each time through the loop, the i^{th} element in the array is initialized to the value of its square. After six iterations, each element in the array has been initialized to its square. You'll see many more examples of arrays in Chapter 8, "Creating and Using Arrays and Strings."

## Variable scope

Every variable has an *associated scope* — the portion of the program in which the variable can be called by its name. This is different from the notion of access. Access indicates which members of which objects are visible to each other and is also referred to as scope (but in a more "macro" view of the world). We'll discuss access when we discuss packages and inheritance in Chapter 9, "Classes, Interfaces, and Packages."

The scope of a variable begins immediately where it is declared, and it ends with the closing brace (}) of the block of code in which it is declared. You can access a variable only within its scope. If you attempt to access a variable outside its scope, the compiler generates an error. Here is an example of some common situations:

```
class Lamp
{
  int watts =60;//watts' scope is the class definition itself
  boolean isOn = false; //same is true for isOn

  Lamp( boolean startOn )//startOn's scope is the body of
  {                      //this constructor
    isOn = startOn;
  }

  public void setIsOn( boolean toOn )//toOn's scope is the
  {                                  //body of this method
    for( int dummy = 1; dummy<1000; dummy++)//dummy's scope is
```

```
        {                                    //the body of this for loop
          System.out.println("The count is " + dummy);
        }
        toOn = isOn;
     }
  }
```

The two instance variables `watts` and `isOn` are in scope from their declaration onwards, while the `class` is defined. The parameters of the constructor `Lamp` and the method `setIsOn` are in scope for the body of their respective method. Of course the `for` statement in the middle of `setIsOn` is there only to illustrate that `dummy` is in scope from the time it is declared through the execution of the `for` loop.

Be careful not to use a variable before it is declared. For instance, you couldn't have the following snippet:

```
class Lamp
{
  int power = watts; //no good -- watts doesn't exist yet
  int watts =60;
  boolean isOn = false;
  ...
}
```

Here is another way of writing the `setIsOn`:

```
class Lamp
{
  int watts =60;
  boolean isOn = false;

  Lamp( boolean startOn )
  {
    isOn = startOn;
  }

  public void setIsOn( boolean isOn ) //see explanation below
  {
    this.isOn = isOn;
  }
}
```

You want to change the value of the `isOn` field for a specific instance of a `Lamp`. You'll find it natural to pass in the new value as a `boolean` with the name `isOn`. But this `isOn` is a local variable and is visible only within the body of the `setIsOn` method. In addition, if that's the variable that we know by the name `isOn`, how can we refer to our instance variable by the same name?

It might help to see how this code would be called with the following snippet:

```
Lamp aLamp = new Lamp();
aLamp.setIsOn(true);
```

So aLamp is a specific instance of a Lamp and, initially, aLamp.isOn is set to false. That is to say, the value of the boolean isOn in the specific Lamp that we are refer- ring to with the reference variable aLamp has the value false. Now the second line sets its value to true.

Let's see what's happening inside the setIsOn method. It realizes that its local vari- able named isOn has the value true. The word this refers to the specific instance of the class, which in this case is aLamp. So when we call aLamp.setIsOn(true) the setIsOn method sets the isOn variable that belongs to the aLamp object to the value held by the isOn local variable. In short, aLamp.isOn has been set to true.

When we get to inheritance, we will again encounter situations in which a name can be hidden. A class may have some of the same names for instance variables as the class which it extends. We will be able to differentiate these with the keyword super.

# Methods

Variables are used to maintain an object's state; methods provide the behavior. In object-oriented programming in Java, the methods tell you what the classes do. In Java, every method must reside inside a class declaration. If you create a method outside the body of a class declaration, the code will not compile.

For those of you who are new to object-oriented programming, you can think of a method as a function. However, unlike procedural programming where functions sit out in the open (or, more accurately, are organized into files) to be called upon at any point, a method is encapsulated inside the class in which it is defined, along with the variables of that class.

## Declaring methods

To create a method, you must write a method declaration and then implement the body of it. At the least, a method is made up of the following:

   ✦ A return type
   ✦ The method name
   ✦ A method body

You can see these three elements in this code:

```
returnType name()
{
  ...
  /* method body */
  ...
}
```

## Return Types of Methods

As an example of the method skeleton, consider this code:

```
boolean getIsOn()
{
  return isOn;
}
```

It promises that what will be returned by the method will be of type `boolean`, that the method name is `getIsOn`, and that the method body consists of the one line that returns the value of the `isOn` variable. Notice that you can check that what is returned is of the correct type. The code

```
int howBright()
{
  return watts;
}
```

promises to return an `int` and it does. This helps us catch errors while we are still thinking about what we are coding. The compiler will let us know that the following is wrong:

```
boolean howBright()
{
  return 3; //this is wrong -- it's not a boolean
}
```

We are guaranteed that the result of `getIsOn` is a `boolean` and the result of `howBright` is an `int`. If we have variables

```
int power;
boolean turnedOn;
```

then we are assured that the following assignments will work:

```
power = aLamp.howBright();
turnedOn = aLamp.getIsOn();
```

In each case, these set the variable on the lefthand side of the assignment operator to the value of the primitive types returned by the righthand side of the assignment operator.

Just as a method might take no arguments, it might also not need to return any data. Use the keyword `void` as a return type if no data is being returned. For example:

```
void setIsOn( boolean isOn )
{
  this.isOn = isOn;
}
```

As you can see, when a return type is specified in the method declaration, a value of that data type must be returned. When a return statement is executed, control transfers out of the method and back to the caller of that method. Before the transfer of control is complete, the data being returned is placed on the stack, where the calling method can retrieve it.

The `return` command does not have to be the last line in a method. In fact, there can be more than one `return` in a method. The last task for a method with a non-`void` return type must do is `return` a value or a reference.

Even though a `return` statement is required if the method declaration specifies a return type, the value returned doesn't have to be what you might consider a "valid" value. For instance, when a string return type is specified, a value of `null` can be returned. Likewise, zero (0) and negative values can be returned for integral data types. Although you must return a data type if one is declared, any value in the legal range for that type is acceptable.

As a preview of coming attractions, when returning an object, that object's class must either be the same as the class specified in the method declaration or a subclass of it. If a method returns an interface, the object returned must implement that interface.

## Options in Method Declarations

Here is an example of a bare-bones method declaration:

```
returnType name()
{
  ...
  /* method body */
  ...
}
```

This declaration can be enhanced with one or more of many optional parts.

Before the `returnType` you could have had an access specifier (`public`, `private`, or `protected`), or any of the keywords `static`, `abstract`, `final`, `native`, or `synchronized`. We will discuss access specifiers and the keywords `static`, `abstract`, and `final` in Chapter 9 when we discuss classes. The `native` keyword specifies that the method is code written in another language, such as C, C++, FORTRAN, or assembly language that is platform dependent. The `synchronized` keyword will be discussed in Chapter 14 when we discuss threads.

There are other possible additions to the method skeleton. The parentheses could contain a parameter list where each parameter is given by a type and an identifier. As an example

```
boolean changeBulb( int watts )
{
  this.watts = watts;
  isOn = true;
  return isOn;
}
```

Finally, the method could throw an exception. In that case, following the `method Name([parameter list])` right before the opening bracket indicating the start of the method's body, you would have the keyword `throws` followed by an exceptions list. The keyword `throws` will be discussed in Chapter 11's discussion of exceptions.

## Overloading Methods

When choosing a name for your method, any valid Java identifier will do. However, if you choose the same name as another method in the class, you'll have to supply a different parameter list to differentiate between the two. The method name along with the number and types of the methods parameters is called the method's *signature*. Having more than one method with the same name is known as method overloading, and it is permissible only so long as the signature is unique.

Suppose we have a `Rectangle class`. We can define a `calculateArea()` method that finds the area by multiplying base times height for a rectangle and that just squares the length of a side if the `Rectangle` is a square. We can overload the `calculateArea()` method by simply providing a different parameter list for each one:

```
int calculateArea( int side )
{
  return side * side;
}

int calculateArea( int base, int height )
{
  return base * height;
}
```

Since each of these method declarations has a different set of parameters, they can all be included in the same class file. When one of them is called, Java checks the type and number of parameters and invokes the appropriate method.

## Class and Instance Methods

Just as there are class variables and instance variables, there are class methods and instance methods. By default, all methods are instance methods, unless one is specified as a class method using the static keyword:

```
static void increaseLampNumber(int sizeOfIncrement) {
...
}
```

As with class variables, class methods are shared by all objects instantiated via that class. And, just as with class variables, they can be used at any time without first instantiating an object of that class. An example of this is seen in the Math class, where all variables and methods are declared static. You can use any of Math's methods without first creating an object of that class:

```
int maxOfTwoNumbers = Math.max(x,y); //returns max of x and y
double myRandomNumber = Math.random(); // returns random number
double mySine = Math.sin(45.56); /* returns trigonometric sine
 of the angle passed in */
```

Aside from this convenience, class methods operate on class variables. In contrast, an instance method operates on instance variables: When an instance method accesses an instance variable, it is accessing the one for that particular object. Since each object shares the same class variables, it makes sense to declare methods as static if they operate on class variables, or have no need to operate on instances of a class.

## Method Constructors

A constructor is a method that has the same name as the class in which it is declared. The purpose of a constructor is to provide a way for new objects to be initialized in a special way. If a constructor isn't provided, as in the case of Lamp in the following code, an object of that class can still be created.

```
class Lamp
{
  int watts =60;
  boolean isOn = false;

  ...
}
```

Now if we create Lamp aLamp = new Lamp() the default constructor is called. When no constructors are specified, Java provides you with a constructor that takes no arguments and that creates the object with the given instance variables initialized to either default values or values provided in the class definition. In the case of Lamp, a new Lamp is created by the name of aLamp. It has a variable named watts that is an int with initial value 60 and a variable named isOn that is a boolean with initial value false.

If a constructor had been provided, the variables could have been automatically initialized. In fact, a constructor can even call methods:

```
class Lamp
{
  int watts;
  boolean isOn;

  Lamp( boolean startOn )
  {
    setIsOn( startOn );
    watts = 75;
  }

  public void setIsOn( boolean isOn ) //see explanation below
  {
    this.isOn = isOn;
  }
}
```

Once you have explicitly created a constructor, Java no longer provides the default constructor for you. If you want to create a Lamp aLamp = new Lamp();, you have to write a constructor that takes no arguments. In this case, you would be setting the values of isOn and watts without any input from the user. You could decide that the Lamp will start with isOn = false and watts = 75. You can accomplish this with a constructor that calls the existing constructor and passes in the value false for the argument. We need to use the this keyword to accomplish this task:

```
class Lamp
{
  int watts;
  boolean isOn;

  Lamp( boolean startOn )
  {
    setIsOn( startOn );
    watts = 75;
  }

  Lamp()
  {
  this( false ); //using "this" to invoke original constructor
  }              //it would be tempting to write Lamp(false)
                 //but you are referring to this instance

  public void setIsOn( boolean isOn ) //see explanation below
  {
    this.isOn = isOn;
  }
}
```

So, just as with regular methods, constructors can be overloaded. We can create as many constructors as needed, provided they each have a unique parameter list. And if you ever need to invoke one constructor from within another, you can do so using the `this` keyword.

# Expressions

*Expressions* are statements that, when executed, result in a value. When programming, we use expressions all the time, sometimes without even realizing it. Java expressions are similar in syntax to those of C and C++. The following are examples of Java expressions:

```
65 + 5 /* produces a value of 70 */
(i < 10) /* produces true or false, (depending on i's value) */
5 * 100 /* produces 500 */
x = 25 - 5; /* subtracts five from 25, then places the result
                        (20) in the x variable */
```

Expressions are typically composed of several smaller expressions, or subexpressions, connected by operators. For instance, consider the following lines of code:

```
int x = 100, y;
y = (x/4) + 3;
```

The first line of code, where our variables are declared, actually contains an expression in the assignment of 100 to the x variable. The integer literal 100 is an expression, albeit a simple one. When the compiler looks at this line, it sees something like "evaluate the expression to the right of the assignment operator, =, and place its value in the variable on the left." Since the expression is the integer literal 100, it evaluates to 100 and is then stored in the x variable.

Now take a look at the next line. The complete expression would be:

```
y = (x/4) + 3;
```

However, this expression is made up of several subexpressions. You might recognize one right off the bat:

```
x/4
```

While you would be correct in seeing that x/4 is a subexpression), there are even subexpressions *inside* this subexpression. The *x* variable is a subexpression that evaluates to 100, and the integer literal 4 is another subexpression that evaluates to 4. After each of these is evaluated and the division operation is performed, the result is 25. To this, the value 3 is added—yet another subexpression! And finally, the entire value (28) is placed inside the *y* variable. As you can see, there are many levels of expressions, even in what appear to be simple statements.

# Operators

Since Java expressions are typically identifiers and literals linked together by operators, it's important to understand exactly how operators work. Java supports both unary and binary operators. Unary operators are those that act on a single operand, while binary operators act on two operands. As we discussed in Chapter 6, in Java, the unary minus and binary minus use the same character (-). A calculator has separate buttons for the two operators. The unary minus is what you use to take the opposite of a number. For example, -3, or used with another operator, 5*(-3). There is also the binary minus used to subtract the number following the minus sign from the number preceding the minus sign: 6-2 would be 4.

The unary postfix increment operator also requires only one operand (x, in this case): x++;(for consistency choose the same solution, it doesn't matter if you keep them all or eliminate them all) You can use the binary addition operator to get the following equivalent expression: x = x + 1; In this case, the binary addition operator acts on two operands (x and 1). Once the righthand side of the assignment operator is evaluated, the result is stored in the x variable on the left.

## Operator precedence

Expressions are evaluated from left to right, according to the precedence of the operators in the expression — that is, the rules that determine which operators are executed first. The result of an expression is either a variable, a value, or nothing. You should write your expressions to avoid possible ambiguity of what is being evaluated for someone reading your code.

By following a precedence order, Java guarantees that a particular expression will produce the same results every time it is executed. Consider this expression:

```
x = 15 + 3 * 2 - 14;
```

Without a precedence order, which subexpression is evaluated first? Should it be 15 + 3, 3 * 2, or 2 - 14? For that matter, once the first subexpression is evaluated, which is next? Here again, it's less important what the order is than that everyone agree on the order. You probably learned order of operations in high school. We were taught with the mnemonic "Please Excuse My Dear Aunt Sally" to remind us that the order is parenthesis, exponents, multiplication and division, addition and subtraction. This was so that you interpreted 6+3*7 as giving you 27 — the same way everyone else did. If you were meant to add the 6 and 3 before multiplying, the expression would have been written as (6+3)*7.

In Java, there is a clearly defined sequence in which the parts of an expression are evaluated. Java operators are arranged and executed in order of precedence. Table 7-1 lists all Java operators according to their precedence order. You'll see that parentheses are first in this table. They aren't really an operator, since they don't perform an operation on data types, but they appear in the table to emphasize that they're given top priority during evaluation. (See "Forcing Order" later in this chapter.)

## Table 7-1
## Java Operator Precedence

| Precedence | Associativity | Operator | Description |
|---|---|---|---|
| First | N/A | ( ) | parentheses (forcing order) |
| Second | R-to-L | ++ | pre/post increment (unary) |
| | R-to-L | -- | pre/post decrement (unary) |
| | R-to-L | ! | logical complement (unary) |
| | R-to-L | ~ | unary bitwise logical negation |
| | R-to-L | + | addition (unary) |
| | R-to-L | - | subtraction (unary) |
| | | (className) | cast object to class type |
| Third | L-to-R | * / % | multiplication, division, and remainder |
| Fourth | L-to-R | + - | addition and subtraction |
| Fifth | L-to-R | << | shift left |
| | L-to-R | >> | shift right (sign extension) |
| | L-to-R | >>> | right shift (zero extension) |
| Sixth | L-to-R | < <= | "less than" and "less than or equal to" |
| | L-to-R | > >= | "greater than" and "greater than or equal to" |
| | L-to-R | instanceof | is the object an instance of this class |
| Seventh | L-to-R | == | equality |
| | L-to-R | != | nonequality (not equal) |
| Eighth | L-to-R | & | bitwiseAND, booleanAND |
| Ninth | L-to-R | ^ | bitwise EXCLUSIVE OR (XOR), boolean EXCLUSIVE OR (XOR) |
| Tenth | L-to-R | \| | bitwise OR, boolean OR |
| Eleventh | L-to-R | && | AND (boolean conditional "short-circuit") |
| Twelfth | L-to-R | \|\| | OR (boolean conditional "short-circuit" |
| Thirteenth | R-to-L | ? : | ternary conditional |
| Fourteenth | R-to-L | = | assignment |
| Last | R-to-L | *= /= %= += -= <<= >>= >>>= &= ^= \|= | assignment (and operation) |

In Java, operations whose operators have the highest precedence are performed first, with lower precedence operators following in sequence. When operations of the same precedence occur within the same expression, they are processed according to operator associativity. You can get around this precedence order or the associativity rules by using parentheses.

Here's another math flashback. Remember when you learned that addition was associative? Consider the expression 5 + 6 + 3. The plus sign ("+") can add two numbers at a time so we can't really understand this expression unless we break it up. We could interpret the expression as (5 + 6) + 3 or as 5 + (6 + 3). The first would mean that the first plus sign ("+") is adding the numbers 5 and 6 and then the second plus sign ("+") is adding that result to 3. The second would mean that the first plus sign ("+") is adding 5 to the result of the second plus sign ("+"), which adds the 6 and 3.

If you look up the plus sign ("+") in Table 7-1, you see that associativity is L-to-R so Java interprets 5 + 6 + 3 as (5 + 6) + 3. The rule tells us which operation to perform first. An operator's associativity determines whether it is evaluated from right to left (R-to-L) or left to right (L-to-R). See the next section, "Forcing Order," to learn how to bypass an operator's natural associativity.

Let's use the table to calculate the results of our example: `x = 15 + 3 * 2 - 14;` The multiplication operation is performed first because it has highest precedence, and then the next two operations, addition and subtraction, are carried out from left to right because of associativity, and then the assignment operation is performed:

`15 + 3 * 2 -14` becomes `15 + 6 - 14` becomes `21-14` becomes `7`. Finally, the equal ("=") sign is evaluated and the value of `7` is assigned to the `x`.

## Forcing order

If the natural order of evaluation isn't desired, you can use parentheses to control the order of evaluation. For instance, suppose you wanted the subexpression 2 - 14 to be evaluated first. You could ensure this by placing it inside parentheses:

```
x = 15 + 3 * (2 - 14);
```

In this case, the order has been changed to first evaluating the `2-14` because it is in parentheses, then the multiplication, then the unary minus, then the addition, and finally the assignment. The result is that `x` has the value `15 + 3 * -12=15+ - 36 = -21`.

We could have added another pair of parentheses to force the multiplication operation to take place last:

```
x = (15 + 3) * (2 - 14);
```

In this case, the subexpressions inside the parentheses are of the same precedence. As a result, they are carried out from left to right. The result is that x has the value 18 * (2-14) = 18 * -12 = 216.

And, of course, parentheses can be nested. We could, for example, group these three subexpressions by surrounding them with parentheses and add another subexpression to the mix. Here are a few examples, each producing a different data type:

```
x = ((15 + 3) * (2 - 14)) + 1; /* x has an integer value */
x = ((15 + 3) * (2 - 14)) + 1.2; /*x is a floating-point value */
x = ((15 + 3) * (2 - 14)) > 1;    /*x is a boolean value */
```

# Types of operators

In Chapter 6, we looked at operators for integer types, floating-point types, and booleans. We looked at the string concatenation operator (+) but will now summarize and expand the description. For completeness, we'll also cover Array operators here. Strings and arrays are the subject of Chapter 8, "Creating and Using Arrays and Strings."

## String Operators

As you know, strings in Java are actually String objects. If the arithmetic addition operator (+) is used when one (or both) of the operands is of type String, the operation is considered a string concatenation. If only one of the operands is of type String, the other operand is converted into a string before the concatenation is carried out.

When a nonstring operand is converted to a string, the process is carried out according to the compile-time type of the operand.

If the value of the operand is null, then the literal string null is used. If the value is other than null, the toString() method of the operand is invoked. This method returns a reference value of type String, which is used (unless this value is null, in which case the literal string null is used). Since the class Object defines a toString() method, this method is always available when dealing with objects, even if the operand itself doesn't implement a toString() method.

If the operand is of the primitive integral type, it's converted into a string representing the value in decimal notation. If the value of the operand is negative, the string is preceded by a minus sign. If the value is nonzero, the first digit is nonzero. If the value is zero, the single digit 0 is produced.

If the operand is of type char, it's converted to a string containing the single character of the char.

If the operand is of type `boolean`, it's converted into a string containing the boolean's value (either the literal string `true` or the literal string `false`).

## Array Operators

When operations are performed on arrays, they return the value of a specific element in that array. However, unlike the data types we've been dealing with thus far, an array must be allocated using the new operator before it can be assigned to a variable:

```
int a[] = new int[15];
```

In the preceding example, an array of 15 integer elements is created and assigned to the variable a. Once this operation has taken place, we can store and retrieve values in the array elements using the following syntax:

```
arrayVariable[expression]
```

For instance, each of the following lines of code accesses the same element in the array:

```
int x = 5, y = 2, z = 10; /* initialize integer variables */
a[10] = 82569; /* store 82569 in 11th element */
a[z] = 4370; /* store 4370 in 11th element */
a[x*y] = 111791; /* store 111791 in 11th element */
a[x+5] = 592; /* store 592 in 11th element */
int i;
i = a[10]; /* retrieve 11th element */
i = a[x+5]; /* retrieve 11th element */
i = a[100/z+1] /* retrieve 11th element */
i = a[a.length - 5]; /* retrieve 11th element */
```

In the last example, we used the instance variable length in the expression. Since `a.length` returns the number of elements in the array, this is a valid expression.

Remember that Java arrays are zero-based, like C/C++ arrays. In this example, as with all arrays, the first element is accessed with an index value of zero: a[0]. Since we have 15 elements in this particular array (from index 0 to 14), the last element is referenced with an index value of 14: a[14]. This means that using the subscript 10, as we do here, actually accesses the 11th element.

In any case, if an array index is negative or greater than the number of elements in the array minus one (14, in our example), an `ArrayIndexOutOfBoundsException` is thrown. In the previous example, the size of the array is 15 so the expressions a[15] or a[26] would be using an index value that is too big, so an `ArrayIndexOutOf BoundsException` is thrown.

Array index values can be of `byte`, `short`, `int`, or even `char` types. However, array indexes of type `long` are not permitted. To use a type `long`, it must be cast into the `int` type, as the following example shows:

```
long myLong = 10;
a[myLong]; // illegal, since array indexes can't be long
a[(int) myLong]; // legal, since the long is cast into an int
```

### Object Operators

In Java, a special operator exists that allows you to determine whether an object is an instance of a particular class, subclass, or interface. Using the `instanceof` binary operator, you can test objects to compare them against a specific class or interface type:

```
if (theObject instanceof ClassName) {
}
```

# Control-Flow Statements

To direct the flow of program execution, Java supports several control-flow statements. These are similar to their C and C++ counterparts, so they look and act as you would expect if you're already familiar with either of these languages.

## The if statements

Java supports an `if` and an `if else` statement. The syntax for the most basic `if` statement is

```
if (booleanExpression )
{
  ...  //body is executed if the boolean expression is true
}
```

The body of the `if` statement is executed if the *booleanExpression* evaluates to true. If the *booleanExpression* evaluates to `false`, the body of the code that makes up the `if` statement is skipped. Consider the `if` statement in the following code snippet:

```
if (x < 10)
{
  System.out.println("The if block is being executed.");
}
System.out.println("I'm no longer in the if statement.");
```

When the preceding statement is encountered, the `boolean` expression `x < 10` is evaluated. If the value of x is greater than or equal to 10, then the body of the `if` statement is skipped and the program continues execution after the closing brace (`}`), and your output is:

```
I'm no longer in the if statement.
```

If the value of x is less than 10, then the `if` block is executed and your output is:

```
The if block is being executed.
I'm no longer in the if statement.
```

Notice that the `print` statement following the body of the `if` statement is executed whether the *booleanExpression* evaluates to `true` or to `false`.

Sometimes you want the body of the `if` statement to be executed if the *boolean Expression* is `true` and for another block of code to be executed if the *boolean Expression* is `false`. To accomplish this, we use a second form of `if` statement that also uses the keyword `else` directing program execution along one of two distinct routes:

```
if (booleanExpression )
{
   ...  //body is executed if the boolean expression is true
}
else
{
   ...  //body is executed if the boolean expression is false
}
```

If the `boolean` value evaluates to `true`, the block of code immediately following is executed. If the expression evaluates to `false`, the `else` block is executed. Let's look at a modified version of the previous example. Consider the `if else` statement in the following code snippet:

```
if (x < 10)
{
   System.out.println("The if block is being executed.");
}
else
{
   System.out.println("The else block is being executed.");
}
System.out.println("I'm no longer in the if statement.");
```

When the preceding statement is encountered, the `boolean` expression `x < 10` is evaluated. If the value of x is greater than or equal to 10, then the body of the `if` statement is skipped and the program continues execution at the else block; the program will then exit the else block and continue execution. Your output is:

```
The else block is being executed.
I'm no longer in the if statement.
```

If the value of x is less than 10, then the if block is executed and the program skips the else block and continues executing after the closing brace of the else block. Your output is:

```
The if block is being executed.
I'm no longer in the if statement.
```

At no time will both the if block and the else block be executed, since the value of the boolean expression directs flow of execution in only one of two possible directions, not both. A common use of if else statements is to nest if statements as follows.

```
if ( booleanExpression )
{
   ...  //executed if this boolean expression is true
}
else if ( anotherBooleanExpression )
{
   ...  //executed if 1st boolean expression is false
        //and 2nd boolean expression is true
}
else
{
   ... //executed if both boolean expressions are false
}
```

Let's say that students at a school have to register for between 16 and 20 credit hours. Then we could use the following code to indicate their status:

```
if ( credits < 16 )
{
  System.out.println( "Please select more courses.");
}
else if( credits > 20 )
{
  System.out.println( "Please select fewer courses.");
}
else
{
  System.out.println( "You may register.");
}
```

If the number of credits that the student has selected is less than 16, then credits < 16 is true, the first if block is executed, and the student is told to select more courses. If `credits < 16` is `false`, then the first `else` block is executed. This block itself consists of an `if` statement. We know for sure that if we are at this point, then the number of credits is 16 or more, so we test whether `credits > 20` is `true` or `false`. If it is `true`, then the students are told to select fewer courses. If it is `false`, then we execute *that* `if` statement's `else` block (the second `else` block). At this point, we know that both `credits < 16` and `credits < 20` are `false`, so `credits` must be between 16 and 20 including the endpoints. In this case, the student is told to go ahead and register.

## The switch statement

The switch statement is used when you have to perform different actions depending on the actual value of some expression. The general format is as follows:

```
switch ( expression )
{
  case Constant1:
    ...
    // evaluated if expression has the value
    // of Constant1
  break;
  case Constant2:
    ...
    // evaluated if expression has the value
    // of Constant2
  break;
  case Constant3:
    ...
    // evaluated if expression has the value
    // of Constant3
  break;
  .
  .
  .
  default:
    ...
    //evaluated if expression has none of the
    //specified values
  break;
}
```

Upon entering a switch statement, the *expression* is evaluated. Unlike the `if` statement, the expression is not a `boolean`. The data type of the expression must be either `char`, `byte`, `short`, or `int`. The value of the expression is then converted to the `int` type, as are all the case constants.

Beginning with the first `case` statement, the value of the expression is compared to the value of the `case` constant. If the two values are equal, any code following the colon is executed, until the break statement is reached. If the expression doesn't match the case constant, it is compared to the next one. This process continues until the default case is reached, at which point the code for this case is executed.

When a case is executed, the break statement is used to stop the flow of execution. When a break statement is reached, execution stops immediately and resumes after the closing brace (}) of the entire switch body. Since execution terminates when the first break is encountered, the default case will be executed only if no match is found between the value of the switch expression and all other cases.

Be certain to end each case with a break statement. If you don't, all cases following the matching one will be tested as well. This is an undesirable condition known as *fall-through*. In particular, you could end up executing the default case without meaning to. On the other hand, if several cases are supposed to execute the same block of code, you can use the omitted break command to make sure that all of the cases fall through properly. For example:

```
switch ( age )
{
  case 0:
  case 1:
    fare = 0; //evaluated if age = 0 or 1
  break;        //stop falling through
  case 2:
    fare = 100; // evaluated if age =2
  break;
  default:
    fare = 200; //evaluated if age>2
  break;
}
```

The switch statement is particularly useful when a number of cases exist. You can use as many cases as you need, without making a mess of the code. And, if none of the cases match the value of your expression, you can rely on the default case being executed.

## The while and do-while loops

Java while and do-while loops are identical to those in C:

```
while ( booleanExpression )
{
  ... //body of while loop
}
```

In the while loop, the booleanExpression is evaluated. If the expression evaluates to true, the loop is executed. If the expression evaluates to false, it doesn't execute and we exit the loop. Each time through the body of the `while` loop, the expression is reevaluated. We call it a `while` loop because the loop is executed while the expression is `true`. For example:

```
while( x < 10 )
{
  x++;  //increase x by one
  System.out.println("Executing the while loop.");
}

do {
  ...
} while (boolean expression);
```

With the `do-while` loop, the body of the loop executes once before the expression is ever evaluated. This ensures that the loop code is executed at least once, regardless of how the expression evaluates. The general form is:

```
do
{
  ...//the body of the do while loop
} while ( booleanExpression )
```

For example:

```
do
{
  System.out.println( "Executing while loop. And x =" + x );
  x++;  //change x or we'll be stuck in the loop forever!
} while( x < 10 );
```

The `while` loop is the most popular of the two, although the `do-while` loop has the advantage of executing your code at least once, no matter what the expression evaluates to. Be sure to change your expression value either inside the body of the `while` or `do-while` loop, or in the expression itself. If the value never changes, the expression always remains true and the loop executes indefinitely.

## The for loop

The `for` loop repeats program execution as controlled through a series of expressions, terminating when a certain condition is no longer met. It continues looping until the specified boolean condition evaluates to `false`, at which point the loop is broken and execution resumes after the loop body:

```
for(initializerExpression; booleanExpression; updateExpression)
{
  ... //body of for loop
}
```

The `initializerExpression` is one or more expressions that are evaluated from left to right. Usually this is where you initialize the loop variable. The execution of a for loop begins with the evaluation of the *initializerExpression.*.

Next, the *booleanExpression* specifies the condition that must be met for the loop body to be executed. If the *booleanExpression* is `true`, then the body of the loop is executed. If it is `false`, the loop is exited.

The *updateExpression* specifies how the loop variable is to change each time through the loop. Each time the body of the `for` loop finishes executing, the *update Expression* is called. Then we check the value of the *booleanExpression* and continue. A standard use of a `for` loop would be:

```
for( int x = 0; x < 4; x++)
{
   System.out.println("Inside the for loop x = " + x);
}
```

The first expression, x=0, sets the loop variable to zero. The loop executes until the second expression, x<10, evaluates to `true`. The output is:

```
Inside the for loop x = 0
Inside the for loop x = 1
Inside the for loop x = 2
Inside the for loop x = 3
```

And the final expression, x++, increments the loop variable by one every time through the loop. Note that unlike C but as in C++, Java supports the declaration of loop variables inside the initialization portion of the loop statement.

## The jump statements

In addition to the `if`, `switch`, `while`, and `do-while` control-flow constructs, Java supports four additional statements: `break`, `continue`, `return`, and `throw`. These are considered *jump statements* because they allow the flow of program execution to jump out of the loops in which they are found or to branch out in directions not seen with the standard control-flow statements we've already discussed.

The `return` statement is used to return program execution to the caller of a code segment, such as when a method has been invoked. At any point in the method, a `return` statement can return the flow of control back to the caller of that method. The `throw` statement is used to signal a runtime exception that interrupts the flow of program execution while a handler is sought to deal with that exception. We will discuss this further in Chapter 11, "Exceptions and Error Handling."

## The break Statement

The format for break is break *label*; where the *label* is optional. You've seen the break statement used without a label in the switch statement. In that case, the break statement caused the program to exit the switch statement. In general, a break statement without a label will exit from the loop that most immediately contains it. If the break statement has a label, the program will continue executing after the block of statements controlling it that has the same label.

Here's an example:

```
int x=0;
enterLoop:   //this is a label
while(x++ < 10)
{
  System.out.println("Inside while loop, iteration:" +x );
  switch(x)
  {
    case 0:
      System.out.println("Inside switch, x=" +x);
    break;
    case 1:
      System.out.println("Inside switch, x =" +x);
    break;
    default:
      if (x==5 )
      {
        System.out.println("Break out of switch & while loop");
        break enterLoop; //break to enterLoop label
      }
    break;
  }
  System.out.println("Out of switch, back in while loop.");
}
```

Each time through the while loop, the switch statement is encountered. Up until the time x is equal to 5, standard break statements are used to break out of the switch statement and back into the while loop. However, when x is equal to 5, the following line of code is executed:

```
break enterLoop
```

When this happens, not only does the break occur for the switch statement, but also for the entire while loop. If this labeled break were not present, the while loop would execute ten times. However, it only executes five times, since the labeled break kicks the flow of control out of both the switch and while loop.

### The continue Statement

While the break statement is used to break out of the loop, a labeled continue statement redirects it to the label itself. This means that the labeled continue statement transfers control of program execution to the iteration following the label:

```
int x=0;
enterLoop://the Label in question
while (x++<5)
{
  System.out.println ("Inside while loop, iteration: " + x);
  for (int i=0; i<10;i++)
  {
    System.out.println ("Inside for loop, iteration: " + i);
    if (i == 5)
    {
      System.out.println ("Transfer flow out of for loop!");
      continue enterLoop; /* jump to enterLoop label when i
                             is 5 */
    }
  }
  System.out.println ("Out of for loop, back in while.");
}
```

Here, we've created a for loop inside a while loop. Each time through the while loop, the for loop is executed until i equals 5, at which point program execution jumps out of the for loop and goes to the first statement inside the while loop:

```
System.out.println ("Inside the while loop, iteration: " + x);
```

When this happens, the final output line in the while loop isn't executed, since the flow of execution has been rerouted to its beginning. However, if we hadn't included a label, the break statement alone would have rerouted the execution to the first line of code following the for loop. In that case, the final output line would have been executed.

# Summary

This chapter gave you more of the puzzle pieces you need to start building your own Java applications. With the knowledge you have gained in this chapter (and will be gaining in Chapter 9), you should be well on your way to creating simple applications using Java. Key points to remember about this chapter include:

✦ Variables are used to store values in Java. When a value is stored in a variable, you can use it for a wide range of purposes. One such purpose is to represent an object's state. Variables are also used to perform calculations, control the flow of program execution, and affect the overall state of a program. They are a fundamental part of programming languages; without them, we'd be hard pressed to develop software.

✦ Any variable that you declare of type `byte`, `short`, `int`, `long`, `float`, `double`, `char`, or `boolean` is a primitive variable. Reference variables are used to store references, or pointers, to objects (which can be class instances, class instances that implement interfaces, or arrays).

✦ A method is what gives a class behavior. Methods cannot exist outside of a class. Methods may return a data value of a given type or no value at all (in which case, the return type is void). They may also require some input, which we pass through parameters. The method's name along with the number and type of its parameters is called its signature.

✦ Expressions are statements that result in a value when executed. When programming, we use expressions all the time, sometimes without even realizing it. Java expressions are similar in syntax to those of C and C++.

✦ The types of operators that can be used in an operation depend on the data type of the operands involved. For instance, the operators used in an integer operation are different from those used in a boolean operation.

✦ To direct the flow of program execution, Java supports several control-flow statements. These are similar to their C and C++ counterparts, so they look and act as you would expect if you're already familiar with one (or both) of these languages. Control-flow statements include `if`, `switch`, `while/do`, `for`, and `break/continue`.

✦     ✦     ✦

# Creating and Using Arrays and Strings

In this chapter, we will look at how Java implements strings and arrays. With arrays, we can store and retrieve any type of data we'd like in each element, even other arrays. However, since we create arrays with an explicit dimension, there's no way of extending their size when we run out of elements. As a result, at the end of the chapter, we will turn to the Vector class, which provides us with growable arrays.

In the middle we'll look at strings. By now you know that in Java, strings aren't merely arrays of characters; they're first-class objects (meaning they can't be subclassed). In fact, Java offers two classes for dealing with strings: String and String Buffer. In this chapter, we'll learn about the String and StringBuffer classes. It's actually a bit confusing since String sometimes feels like a primitive type. You can create a String by typing:

```
String myString = "How are you today?";
```

You'll see that this is actually a shortcut for using a constructor to create a new String.

One of the uses for strings is to pass information to an application or an applet. These parameters are passed in as strings. We'll therefore need a way of converting information that comes in as a String into the type we are looking for. To perform this conversion, we will use the wrapper classes provided in the java.lang package.

Finally, we will take a look at some of the additional structures in which Java allows us to store data. Just as StringBuffers offer more flexibility (at a cost) than Strings, Vectors will be more flexible than Arrays. Hash tables will allow us to key the data as in a dictionary.

# Arrays

In Java, arrays are truly first-class objects. Not only are they impossible to subclass, but you won't even find a class definition for them. Instead, Java knows internally about arrays and how to treat them, just as it knows how to deal with primitive data types without offering a class for each. Arrays are capable of holding any type of data we need, even other arrays. The only restriction is that each element in the array must be of the same type. You can't, for example, have an `int` in one element of an array and a `char` in another. All of the elements in a given array must be of the same type.

As you might recall from Chapter 6, to declare an array, we need to specify the following: a variable through which we'll access the array and the data type of the elements the array will contain.

When you see the braces attached to a variable, you know immediately that it's actually an array of elements instead of a single element:

```
int myIntegers[]; // declare an array of integers
char myCharacters[]; // declare an array of characters
float myFloats[]; // declare an array of floating-point numbers
String myStrings[]; // declare an array of String objects
StringBuffer myStringBuffs[]; // declare array of StringBuffers
```

However, there is another way to declare arrays in Java:

```
int[] myIntegers; // declare an array of integers
char[] myCharacters; // declare an array of characters
float[] myFloats; // declare an array of floating-point numbers
String[] myStrings; // declare an array of String objects
StringBuffer[] myStringBuffs;// declare array StringBuffers
```

Here, we've declared exactly the same arrays but used a slightly different notation to do so. Some programmers prefer this approach because they don't have to look at the variable name to see that they're dealing with an array. Instead, they can quickly scan the data type listing to see which elements are arrays and which are standard variables.

Although it may not seem like a big deal, consider the following:

```
int myInt, aInt, myInt, theInt, anotherInt, anyInt; // ints
float myFloat, aFloat, myFloater, theFloats[], floating,
  anyFloat; // floats
```

Granted, it takes only a moment to scan the list of variables to see that `theFloats[]` is an array. However, it's much more apparent in the following variable declaration:

```
int myInt, aInt, myInt, theInt, anotherInt, anyInt; // ints
float myFloat, aFloat, myFloater , floating,
  anyFloat; // floats
float[] theFloats; // array of floats
```

By scanning the data types, you can see immediately which ones are arrays, thanks to the pair of brackets immediately following the data type. Using this notation saves the time of scanning through each variable in search of brackets. Although insignificant when you're wide awake and dealing with a relatively small group of variables, it's quite significant at the end of a long day, with half a page of variables to wade through.

## Instantiating arrays

To use an array, once you've declared it, you must first instantiate an Array object. Without an Array object, you have only an empty array variable.

To create an Array object, we typically use the new operator:

```
int myIntegers[]; // array declaration
 . . .
myIntegers = new int[25]; // instantiation
```

While this example illustrates the fact that array declaration and instantiation are two distinct steps, as with standard Java objects, they're often more closely associated in practice. Usually, the array declaration and instantiation happen at the same time:

```
int myIntegers[] = new int[25]; // declare and instantiate
```

When creating an Array object, we supply what is known as a *dimension* for that array. In the preceding examples, the dimension is 25. As a result, the array has 25 elements in it. If we supplied a dimension of 2,483, the array would have 2,483 elements.

## Autoinitialization

So, when an Array object is instantiated as shown, it contains the number of elements you specify as the dimension. The array is effectively empty at this time, and each element is initialized to a default value depending on the type of the variable.

With integral arrays, each element is initialized to zero (0). Each element in an array of booleans, on the other hand, is automatically initialized to false. In all other cases, such as with String objects and other compound data types (that is, any nonprimitive), each element is initialized to null.

## Inline initialization

In cases where you already know the elements you'd like to have in an array, you can save the time and effort of placing each into their position by providing them at the time of declaration:

```
int[] myIntegers2 = {123, 354, 235, 6255, 1, 35, 42563};
```

In this case, you don't have to explicitly dimension the array. We can have a good deal of work done for us by setting the array equal to the elements surrounded with curly braces, each separated by a comma.

In the last example, the compiler sees that we want to add seven elements and, therefore, does the rest of the work automatically. The array is created and each element is added. We don't have to dimension the array and we don't have to fill it ourselves (more on filling arrays in a moment).

This applies to arrays of any type; as long as you know what elements you want, you can add them inline at the time of declaration:

```
String[] myStrings = {"Hickory", "Dickory", "Dock"};
float[] myFloats = {253.35, 2.0, 644.13, 35612., 6.7};
char[] myCharacters = {'H', 'e', 'l', 'l', 'o'};
```

Of course, as with any array, the data in each element in a given array must be of the same type. For example, you can't add a `String` object to an array of floating-point numbers.

# Setting and retrieving array elements

In certain circumstances, we can fill an array inline at the time it's declared. Where possible, this is helpful, since we don't have to do it ourselves. Unfortunately, it's not usually possible to do this. Often, we're not certain which elements are going to be in an array at the time it's created. In these cases, we must fill the array later.

## Setting Elements

To fill an array or a portion of an array, we access a particular element in it with an index value and set it equal to whatever we want to be stored in it. Of course, the data we're trying to stuff into an array element must be the same type as the array is declared to hold:

```
int[] myInts = new int[25]; // create array with 25 elements
myInts[1] = 2353; // set element at index 1 to 2353
```

In this code, we're stuffing the `int` value of 2353 into index 1 of the array. Because this is an array of integers, the assignment is legal. To attempt a string assignment, on the other hand, would prevent your code from compiling.

**Note**    The term *index,* or *subscript,* is used to refer to a particular position in an array. If we supply the value of 5 as an index or subscript for an array, we're said to be accessing the array at index 5, yet retrieving the value stored at position 6. This is because indexing begins at zero (0). When you supply an index/subscript value of 5, you'll actually receive the sixth item in the array.

As you may recall from Chapter 6, array indexing begins at zero (0). C and C++ programmers are already familiar with this approach, although it can sometimes result in problems. If you're not careful, you might attempt to access an element beyond the legal range of index values.

In our example, the legal range of index values is 0 to 24. The first item in the array is set or retrieved using:

```
myIntegers[0]
```

while the last item is available with:

```
myIntegers[24]
```

If you attempt to access an element with an index of 25, you're in for trouble:

```
myIntegers[25]; // ILLEGAL - INDEX OUT OF RANGE!
```

Although the compiler will let this pass, the runtime system throws an ArrayIndex OutOfBoundsException exception. This is one of the particularly nice points about both arrays and strings in Java; the system catches oversights such as this and throws an exception. This bug is caught the first time the line of code is executed.

At times, you may want all items in an array to be set to the same value. In this case, it's much easier to use a loop than to set each manually:

```
int highScores[] = new int[25]; /* declare array of 25
                                       integers */
for (short i=0; i < 25; i++)
{
   highScores[i] - 9999, /* initialize each array element
                          to 9999 */
}
```

This approach can be used even in cases where each element is different. As long as you can get the data you need for each element while inside the body of the loop, you can fill an array with this technique. For example, you might fill an array with characters typed by the user:

```
char keyStrokes[] = new char[500]; /* declare array of 500 characters */
char keyChar; // variable to hold keyboard input
for (short i=0; i < 500; i++)  // load up to 500 characters
{
  keyChar = System.in.read(); /* Get character from standard
                                  input stream */
  if (keyChar == -1) /* has user attempted to break out of
                        the process? */
    break; // break out of loop
  else
    keyStrokes[i] = keyChar; // stuff keyboard input into array
}
```

## Retrieving Elements

To retrieve an element in an array, you do the opposite of setting an element. Rather than stuffing an item into an element, you set a variable equal to that element:

```
myVariable = myIntegers[4]; // get 5th item in array
myString = myStrings[10]; // get 11th item in array
```

If you find yourself not adapting to the index being one less than your position in the array, you may find it helpful to subtract 1 from the value representing the item you want. For example, if you want to retrieve the tenth item in an array, you can use either of the following approaches:

```
theNum = myIntegers[9]; // explicit
theNum = myIntegers[10-1]; // using "off by one" technique
```

Your code will probably be easier for others to read if you will learn to use the explicit call:

```
public class test
{
  public static void main (String [] args)
  {
    int [] stuff = new int [20];

    for (int i = 0; i < 20; i++)
      stuff [i] = 9999;

    System.out.println("  Explicit ... "+stuff [9] + "\n");
    System.out.println("Off by one ... "+stuff [10-1] + "\n");
  }
}
```

And then, using javap –c to disassemble the code, this is what is produced:

```
  32 ldc #2 <String "  Explicit ... ">
  34 invokespecial #10 <Method
java.lang.StringBuffer(java.lang.String)>
  37 aload_1
  38 bipush 9
  40 iaload
  41 invokevirtual #11 <Method java.lang.StringBuffer
append(int)>
  44 ldc #1 <String "\n">
  46 invokevirtual #12 <Method java.lang.StringBuffer
append(java.lang.String)>
  49 invokevirtual #15 <Method java.lang.String toString()>
  52 invokevirtual #14 <Method void println(java.lang.String)>
```

```
55 getstatic #13 <Field java.io.PrintStream out>
58 new #6 <Class java.lang.StringBuffer>
61 dup
62 ldc #3 <String "Off by one ... ">
64 invokespecial #10 <Method
java.lang.StringBuffer(java.lang.String)>
67 aload_1
68 bipush 9
70 iaload
```

The interesting thing is bytes 38 and 68 where the value "9" is explicitly used. Hence, the compiler performed the calculation.

### Array Length

To determine the number of elements in an array, use the `length` variable. This seems a little inconsistent with the Java way of naming methods". It seems that we should be calling a `length()` or a `getLength()` method. If you have an array called `myArray`, you would get the length using:

```
int len = myArray.length; /* get the length and assign to
                             a variable */
```

Again, the length used here is a variable, not a method, as is seen with `String` and `StringBuffer` objects.

## Array of Arrays

Although Java doesn't support multidimensional arrays, it offers essentially the same capability by allowing us to create an array of arrays:

```
int grid[][] = new int[10][10];
grid[0][0] = 1230;
grid[0][5] = 4;
grid[9][5] = 355;
System.out.println("Grid value at 0,0 is " + grid[0][0]);
System.out.println("Grid value at 0,5 is " + grid[0][5]);
System.out.println("Grid value at 9,5 is " + grid[9][5]);
```

In the preceding snippet of code, we created two arrays of integer values, both accessible through the grid variable. Although we created each array with ten elements, they didn't have to be of the same dimension:

```
int grid[][] = new int[15][10];
grid[14][9] = 2265;
System.out.println("Grid value at 14,9 is " + grid[14][9]);
```

We can create as many arrays as necessary, each accessible through the single variable:

```
int grid2[][][] = new int[15][10][5];
grid2[0][0][0] = 4630;
grid2[4][5][1] = 7345;
grid2[9][5][0] = 35;
grid2[14][9][0] = 6465;
grid2[14][9][4] = 16547;
System.out.println("Grid2 value at 0,0,0 is " + grid2[0][0][0]);
System.out.println("Grid2 value at 0,5,1 is " + grid2[4][5][1]);
System.out.println("Grid2 value at 9,5,0 is " + grid2[9][5][0]);
System.out.println("Grid2 value at 14,9,4 is " + grid2[14][9][4]);
```

And we can even use an array of arrays in another array of arrays, to give us as many dimensions as we'd like.

## Exceptions

Thanks to arrays being objects, we're alerted any time something illegal is done with them. Rather than allowing such activity to slip through the cracks, Java lets us know right away when our program is doing something it shouldn't. Although we'll look at exceptions more carefully later, the two exceptions you're most likely to encounter when dealing with arrays are `ArrayIndexOutOfBoundsException` and `ArrayStoreException`.

Whenever an attempt is made to access an item with an index that is out of the legal range, whether that index is too low (negative) or too high, an `ArrayIndexOutOf BoundsException` is thrown. If, however, you attempt to store an element in an array that's of a type different than was declared for the array, you'll receive an `ArrayStoreException`.

# Strings (java.lang.String)

Java strings aren't like the ones we're accustomed to in C and C++. In those languages, strings are simply a null-terminated array of characters. Java strings, however, are sequences of characters which are actually objects defined by the `String` class. This means that, once again, you won't be able to use some of your favorite shortcuts. We will use the String class to create strings and to access various parts of immutable strings. If you need to change or add on to your string, you should be using a string buffer (described in the section "String Buffer" later in this chapter).

**Note**    As with arrays, we begin counting `String` elements with the number 0. So the first element has index 0, the second element has index 1, and so on. The index number is always one less than the number of the element. If you had the code `String myString = "This is an example.";`, then you can see that the letter "a" is in the eighth slot. This means that `myString[7]` is a. If you are new to this counting scheme, you might find it helpful to think of this as `myString[ 7 - 1 ]` is a.

Instead of having direct access to the individual elements of your string, you will use the methods provided by the String class. This additional structure will mean that it will be harder for you to mishandle strings. For example, bounds-checking is performed on Java strings at both compile and runtime. If we attempt to access portions of a string outside the legal bounds, an exception is thrown, which we can catch and handle. (See Chapter 11 for details on exceptions.)

C and C++ strings, in contrast, don't support such well-defined behavior. In these languages, it's quite easy to overrun the boundaries of the array in which our characters are stored. Since no error checking is performed with C/C++ strings, we're free to go right past the end of the array. Sometimes, the error is immediately apparent and sometimes it's not, in which case, it can be difficult to track down and eliminate the programming error.

# Creating Strings

Sometimes strings feel like a primitive type. Like the primitive types, strings are associated with literals. Remember from Chapter 6, "Java Syntax: Tokens, Types, and Values," that string literals are basically a sequence of character literals. Also, you can create a string in the same way that you would create a primitive. The line

```
String pickUpLine = "Come here often?";
```

declares a `String` by the name `pickUpLine` and initializes it to the value `"Come here often?"`. This looks a lot more like what we do in the case of a primitive type, as in

```
int drinkNumber = 7;
```

than what we do in the case of a reference type, for example

```
Drink myDrink = new Drink("Shot of Tequilla");
```

The syntax used to declare and initialize `pickUpLine` is mainly a convenience for programmers. There are many ways to create a `String`.

## Constructors

We can create strings in many ways from many initial pieces of information. Let's look at the various constructors provided with the `String` class. The general format for using them to create a `String` would be

```
String myString = new String( with a possible argument list);
```

and the format for a constructor is

```
public String( insert arguments here );
```

We can create a `String` in many ways, including from nothing, from another `String` and from an array of characters. The constructors are as follows:

✦ `String()`: Constructs a new, empty string.

✦ `String( String aString )`: Constructs a new string that is a copy of the string `aString`. Notice that the code

```
String pickUpLine = "Come here often?";
```

is equivalent to writing `String pickUpLine = new String`

`("Come here often?");`

✦ `String(char arrayOfChars[] )`: Constructs a new string and initializes it to the specified array of characters. The resulting string and the `arrayOfChars` array are not linked in any way. We are just using the `arrayOfChars` to initialize the string.

✦ `String( char arrayOfChars[], int startingCharacter, int lengthOf Subarray )`: Constructs a new string in the same way as the previous constructor. The difference is that this time, instead of copying the entire array, it just copies `lengthOf Subarray` elements beginning with index `startingCharacter`.

✦ `String( Stringbuffer aStringbuffer )`: Constructs a new string by copying the contents of the given stringbuffer. Again, we'll discuss `stringbuffer`s in the next section.

✦ `String( byte[] arrayOfASCIIs, int hiByte)`: Constructs a new string from an array of 8-bit integers (for example, ASCII characters). The byte array will be transformed into Unicode chars using `hiByte` as the upper byte of each character.

✦ `String( byte[] arrayOfASCIIs, int hiByte, int startingCharacter, int lengthOfSubarray)`: Constructs a new string in the same way as the previous constructor copying `lengthOfSubarray` elements beginning with index `startingCharacter`.

All but the first two constructors are created from reference variables that could be `null`. If they are, then Java will throw a `NullPointerException`. The two constructors that allow you to specify the index at which the copy begins and the number of elements being copied, could be trying to refer to elements that are outside of the bounds of the array. These constructors can throw an `IndexOutOfBoundsException`. Exceptions will be covered in Chapter 11, "Exceptions and Error Handling."

We can make a copy of a `String` using

```
String aString = new String(myString); /* creates copy of myString */
```

We can also assign one String object to another. The following assignment is the functional equivalent of the preceding constructor:

```
anotherString = myString; // copy myString into anotherString
```

## Methods That Create Strings

Sometimes you are working with strings and the result of the operation is another String. Because String creates an immutable object, you can't just change the string you are working with. You have to create a new String. Of course, you can reassign your reference variable so that it now points at the new String you have created.

All objects inherit from the Object class and therefore have a toString method. If the object is a String to begin with, this method just returns a reference to the String. For example, if we have String pickUpLine - "Come here often?" then pickUpLine.toString() returns a reference to pickUpLine.

### Substrings

You can create a new String by copying an existing String starting with a given index to the end of the String using

```
    public String substring( int beginIndex )
```

or to a fixed position using

```
    public String substring( int beginIndex, int endIndex )
```

So using the String pickUpLine, which had the value "Come here often?", pickUp Line.substring(2) would return "me here often?" and pickUpLine.substring (5,7) would return "her".

### Manipulation

Java provides several methods to create strings by manipulating existing strings. For example, the methods toLowerCase() and toUpperCase() create a new String where the toLowerCase() or toUpperCase() methods have been applied to each character. Note that if this doesn't change anything in the String, then a reference to the existing String is returned rather than creating a new String. As an example, "Come here, George".toLowerCase() returns "come here, george", while "Come here, George".toUpperCase() returns "COME HERE, GEORGE".

The `replace` method can be used to create a new `String` with a specified character replacing another specified character. If nothing is changed, then this method returns a reference to the existing `String` rather than creating a new one. So our `pickUpLine` "Come here often?" can become a programmer-specific pickup line by replacing the "m" with a "d". The following snippet

```
String pickUpLine = "Come here often?";
String newPickUpLine = pickUpLine.replace('m','d');
System.out.println(newPickUpLine);
```

creates a new `String` called `newPickUpLine` which is a copy of `pickUpLine`, except that all occurrences of m are replaced by d. The new `String` is then displayed as "Code here often?". Note that the methods that would normally alter the contents of the string—such as `replace()`—don't. Instead, they return a new `String` object.

The `trim` method basically is used to trim white space from the beginning and end of a `String`. If the `String` contains nothing but white space, then a new empty `String` is returned. If there is no leading or trailing white space, then no new `String` is created but a reference to the current `String` is returned. Otherwise, the substring of the `String` between and including the first non–white space character and the last non–white space character is returned. For example, "       Come here    often?".trim() returns "Come here    often?". Note that the extra white space characters between here and often remain.

The `concat` method has the form `concat( String tailEnd )`. It creates a new `String` with the initial value from concatenating the `String` and the `String` `tailEnd`. For example, "Come".concat(" here") returns "Come here". If the `String tailEnd` is null, then a reference to the initial `String` is returned.

### The valueOf method

For the most part, the `valueOf` method creates a `String` representation of its argument. The general format of the method is

```
public static String valueOf( argument (s list) )
```

Recall from Chapter 7, "About Variables, Methods, Expressions and Controlling Flow," that `static` means that the method belongs to the class and not any particular instance. Note that the return type is `String`. If you want a method that takes, for example, the `String` "123" and returns the int 123, you will have to use the wrappers described later in this chapter.

The primitive types can each be used as arguments for the `valueOf` method. For example, `valueOf( boolean b )` creates and returns the `String` "true" if b is "true" and "false" if b is false. Also, `valueOf( char myChar )` creates and returns a `String` containing only the character myChar. Use `valueOf` to change any numeric primitive type (int, long, float, and double) to a `String`. For example, valueOf(7) returns "7", valueOf(1243L) returns "1243", valueOf(123.56) returns "123.56", and valueOf(1532.89D) returns "1532.89".

There are two valueOf methods that create strings from character arrays.

```
valueOf( char[] charArray )
```

creates and returns a String from the contents of charArray. The variation

```
valueOf( char[] charArray, int beginIndex, int substrLength )
```

creates and returns a String from substrLength characters of charArray beginning at index beginIndex. These methods throw a NullPointerException if the charArray is null. An IndexOutOfBounds exception is thrown by the second method if you are trying to copy elements beyond the ends of charArray.

The final valueOf method takes an Object as its argument. Remember, all objects in Java inherit from Object. The code valueOf( Object myObject ) returns "null" if myObject is null and otherwise uses the toString method that the object myObject knows about.

### The intern method

You'll notice that in many of the preceding methods, if nothing was changed, then no new String was created. All that happens is that a reference to the current String is returned. What's going on is that the class String keeps track of this set of strings. Java provides the intern method, which returns a String that is equal to the calling String but is guaranteed to be from the unique string pool.

## Using strings

Remember that when it comes to classes, the methods tell you what the objects can do. This makes it easy for us to see what strings can be used for. We have already discussed String literals and the operation of concatenations.

### String Literals

Recall that String literals are characters surrounded by double quotation marks (" "). We've been using them all along, most obviously when we create a String object:

```
String myString = "You're looking at a string literal";
```

In fact, we use string literals in method calls all the time:

```
drawString("Hello World", 100, 100);
getImage(getCodeBase(), "images/world.gif");
getAudioClip(getCodeBase(), "audio/hello.au");
```

```
setTitle("Widget Window");
new Menu("Edit");
new Button("Click Me");
```

Anywhere a String object is used, we can substitute a string literal. This is because the compiler actually instantiates a String object from our literal. String literals can be any number of characters surrounded by double quotation marks, even no characters at all like "" giving you the empty String.

## String Concatenation

Java supports the use of a concatenation operator that joins two or more strings together to form one string:

```
String myString1 = "Hickory";
String myString2 = "Dickory";
String myString3 = "Dock";
String allInOne = myString1 + myString2 + myString3;
```

We can also concatenate string literals:

```
String allInOne = "Hickory" + "Dickory" + "Dock";
```

The result is one string containing the contents of all three. In this case, we assign the result to a string variable. If we were to take a peek at the contents of allInOne, it would be the String "HickoryDickoryDock". Notice no spaces were specified, so none were inserted. The string concatenation operator can join String literals and objects broken up over several lines:

```
String brokenString = new String("This string literal is" +
  "split over two lines");
String brokenString = "The string literal is also " +
  "split over two lines";
drawString("Hello " +
  "World", 100, 100);
```

# Character constants

When specifying string literals, we can include escape sequences that represent characters such as tabs, carriage returns, and form feeds:

```
String myString = "There is a tab here \t o.k.";
String myString = "Here's a carriage return \r o.k.";
String myString = "There's a new line \n here.";
String myString = " \"Mouse\" is in double quotes";
```

In addition, we can include Unicode escape sequences:

```
String myString = "Here is a trademark symbol:\u2122.";
```

When adding Unicode escapes, however, keep in mind that just because you can do it doesn't mean users will see what you intend. If the system on which your program is executed doesn't support the full suite of Unicode characters, or the font used during output doesn't support that character, they'll never see what you specify. As a result, be frugal with Unicode and test your programs on as wide a range of systems as possible, if you do utilize it in this way.

## Locaters

Often you are trying to figure out if your string contains a character or comparison string. If it does, you may want to know where it is located. The methods that help with this are `indexOf` and `lastIndexOf`.

### The indexOf method

The `indexOf` method returns an `int`, which specifies the index of where the item you were searching for begins. Remember that strings are indexed starting with 0, so the index number will always be one less than the position number. The general form of the `indexOf` method is

```
public int indexOf( argument(s list) )
```

This method comes in four flavors depending on the signature.

✦ `indexOf( int myChar )` looks through the `String` for the first element that is a `char` with the value `myChar`. If it finds the element, it returns the index of the element. If it doesn't find it, the number -1 is returned.

✦ `indexOf( int myChar, int fromIndex )` looks through the `String` from index `fromIndex` onward for the first occurrence of a character with the value `myChar`. As with the previous method, if it finds the element, it returns the index of the element and if it doesn't find it, the number -1 is returned.

✦ `indexOf( String myString)` looks through the `String` searching for the `String` `myString`. If it finds `myString`, the index of the first character of the first occurrence of `myString` is returned; if it doesn't find it, the number -1 is returned. If `myString` is `null`, then a `NullPointerException` is thrown.

✦ `indexOf( String myString, int fromIndex )` behaves like the last method except that it starts searching from index `fromIndex`.

### The lastIndexOf method

These behave exactly the same as the four `indexOf` methods, except that the index of the last occurrence is returned instead of the index of the first occurrence. The general form is

```
public int lastIndexOf( argument(s list) )
```

The specific method calls are `lastIndexOf( int myChar)`, `lastIndexOf( int myChar, int fromIndex )`, `lastIndexOf( String myString )`, and `lastIndexOf( String myString, int fromIndex )`.

## Comparison Methods

The following methods are used to compare strings or parts of strings to other strings or parts of strings.

### The equals, equalsIgnoreCase, and compareTo methods

The method `equals` is used to compare an object to the `String`. It returns `true` if the object is a non-null `String` object that has the same characters in the same order as your `String`. The expression `"MeToo".equals("meToo")` returns `false`.

But can't we check for equality using the `==` operator? Sure, and in most cases you'll get the result you'd expect. However, you need to be extremely cautious. To test the concept of testing for equality, try this:

```
String numString1 = new String().valueOf(12345);
String numString2 = "12345";
if (numString1 == numString2)
   System.out.println(numString1 + " and " + numString2 + " ARE EQUAL");else
   System.out.println(numString1 + " and " + numString2 + " ARE NOT EQUAL");
```

Even though they look equal, and they are when using the `equals()` method, the internal representation of these two String objects is different. The result is an equality evaluation of `false`. The reason is that we've supplied an `int` to `valueOf()`, which is different from supplying characters:

```
String numString1 = new String().valueOf("12345");
String numString2 = "12345";
if (numString1 == numString2)
   System.out.println(numString1 + " and " + numString2 + " ARE EQUAL");else
   System.out.println(numString1 + " and " + numString2 + " ARE NOT EQUAL");
```

Now, this would indeed evaluate to `true`. We didn't supply `valueOf()` with an `int` this time; we supplied a `String` literal. As a result, the `==` operator recognizes these as being the same. However, no matter which way you create a string using `valueOf()`, it won't be the same as one returned as the result of the `trim()` method, as far as the `==` operator is concerned. To be safe, it's best to use the `equals()` method whenever you're evaluating String objects for equality.

The method `equalsIgnoreCase( String comparisonString )` returns `true` if the two `Strings` contain the same characters, ignoring case, in order. So the expression `"MeToo".equalsIgnoreCase("meTOO")` returns `true`. The method `equalsIgnoreCase` is used to compare whether or not two strings are equal.

The `compareTo` method is used to order strings. The method `compareTo( String comparisonString )` returns an int. The expression `myString.compareTo( comparisonString )` returns zero if `myString.equals( comparisonString )` returns `true`. The int will be negative if `myString` lexicographically precedes `comparisonString` and will be positive if `myString` lexicographically follows `comparisonString`.

### The regionMatches method

The `regionMatches` method allows you to compare a substring of your `String` with a substring of the `String` passed in as an argument to the method. It comes in two flavors. The first has the following signature:

```
public boolean regionMatches( int thisBeginIndex, String
    comparisonString, int compBeginIndex, int lenOfSubstring)
```

It returns `true` if the substring of our `String` of length `lenOfSubstring` starting at index `thisBeginIndex` is identical to the substring of `comparisonString` of the same length starting at index `compBeginIndex`. It returns `false` if either the indices or the length are beyond the bounds of either `String`. If the `comparisonString` is `null`, a `NullPointerException` is thrown.

The other version of `regionMatches` allows you to specify whether the comparison should be case sensitive or not.

```
public boolean regionMatches( boolean ignoreCase, int
    thisBeginIndex, String comparisonString, int compBeginIndex,
    int lenOfSubstring)
```

If `ignoreCase` is `true`, the substrings will be compared without regard to case; if `ignoreCase` is `false`, a case-sensitive comparison will be performed.

### The startsWith and endsWith methods

The method `startsWith( String startingString )` returns `true` if our `String` starts with the `String startingString` and `false` if it doesn't. If `startingString` is `null`, the method throws a `NullPointerException`. For example, `"Come here often?".startsWith("Comet")` returns `false`. Similarly, the method `endsWith( String endingString )` returns `true` if our `String` ends with the `String ending String` and `false` if it doesn't. You can find out if the `startingString` appears starting at position `startingIndex` in our `String` with the method `startsWith (String startingString, int startingIndex )`.

## Accessor Methods

Although a `String` is immutable, you may want to access parts of strings as well as to change them. You also might want simple information, such as how many characters are in a given `String`. For this, use the `length` method. `"Talk to me".length()` returns 10.

The hashCode() method returns a hash code for the string. This is a large number based on the values of the characters of the string and their index.

To find out which character is in a given position, use charAt( int index). For example, "Talk to me".charAt(3) would return the character 'k'. Remember that the index begins at zero.

The getChars method doesn't return anything. It copies characters from a String to a given character array. The name of the array is passed into the method as one of its arguments. The method is getChars( int startIndex, int endIndex, char targetArray[], int targetStartIndex ). Characters in the String between startIndex and endIndex are copied to the targetArray beginning with index targetStartIndex. If the targetArray is null, then a NullPointerException is thrown. If any of the indices being referenced by the three ints is out of bounds, an IndexOutOfBoundsException is thrown.

The getBytes method is almost the same as the getChars method, except that it copies the eight low-order bits of each character from the String into an array of bytes. The method is getBytes( int startIndex, int endIndex, byte targetArray[], int targetStartIndex ), where the various variables are as they were in the getChars method.

The toCharArray method does what you might have expected of the getChars method. It takes no arguments and creates a character array of the same length as the String containing the same characters as the String in the same order. Suppose you wanted to output a string in reverse. You can do it as long as you know the length of the string:

```
String myString = "Hickory, Dickory, Dock";
int len = myStr.length(); //get # of chars in array
for (; len>0; len−)
  {
  System.out.print(myStr.charAt(len-1)); //output char
  }
  System.out.println(); // flush output
```

Notice the parameter to charAt()? Again, since String objects are stored in the same fashion as arrays, you need to be aware that the first character begins at zero (0), and the last character is at the position "length of the array minus one."

# StringBuffer (java.lang.StringBuffer)

As you just saw, String objects are immutable. Instead of modifying them, you create a completely new String object that receives the result of whatever you want to do to the original. In this way, the original string is preserved, pristine, untouched.

A `StringBuffer`, like a `String`, contains a sequence of characters. StringBuffer objects, however, allow you to create mutable strings. The cost is that StringBuffer objects are typically less efficient than `String` objects. They are usually used to create `String` objects. The methods in the StringBuffer class make it easy to create and grow a string. A StringBuffer is created with a set capacity.

As it turns out, the Java compiler uses StringBuffer objects to implement the string concatenation operator we saw earlier:

```
"This string literal is"+
"split over two lines";
```

The string concatenation compiles like this:

```
new StringBuffer().append("This string literal is ").
  append("split over four lines").toString();
```

Although this might be a bit messy at first glance, begin reading carefully from left to right. You'll see that a new StringBuffer object is created, to which each string literal is appended using the `append()` method. Finally, the results contained in the StringBuffer object are converted into a String object by way of the `toString()` method.

## Creating StringBuffers

There are three constructors for StringBuffers:

✦ `StringBuffer()` creates a StringBuffer that contains an empty character sequence and whose capacity is initialized to 16: for example, `StringBuffer myBuffer = new StringBuffer();`

✦ `StringBuffer( int givenCapacity )` creates a stringBuffer that contains an empty character sequence that has the capacity `givenCapacity`. If `givenCapacity` is negative, the constructor throws a `NegativeArraySize Exception`. To create an empty StringBuffer that has capacity of 50 characters, use `StringBuffer myBuff2 = new StringBuffer(50);`

✦ `StringBuffer( String aString )` creates a stringBuffer that contains the String `aString` and has the capacity 16 plus `aString.length()`. So the following StringBuffer has capacity 21: `StringBuffer myBuff3 = new String Buffer("Hello");`

Although it may be tempting to create empty buffers of unspecified length, it's much more efficient to specify the length if possible. When you don't, or if you use a `String` object when creating a StringBuffer, memory must be allocated whenever something is appended to the buffer. When the size is known, as in the last two examples, the buffer allocates the memory in advance and doesn't need to allocate more, unless it grows beyond that size. We'll continue to look at the length and capacity of a StringBuffer in the next section. To sum up this discussion, the following is discouraged:

```
StringBuffer myBuffer = new StringBuffer();
myBuffer.append("There once was a mouse from Nantucket");
```

In favor of this:

```
StringBuffer myBuffer =
    new StringBuffer("There once was a mouse from Nantucket");
```

Or this:

```
StringBuffer myBuffer = new StringBuffer(37); /* exactly what we need */
myBuffer.append("There once was a mouse from Nantucket");
```

Or even this:

```
StringBuffer myBuffer = new StringBuffer(50); /* a little more than we need */
myBuffer.append("There once was a mouse from Nantucket");
```

## Length and capacity of a StringBuffer

The length of a StringBuffer is the number of characters being stored by it. You can find the length and capacity of a StringBuffer with the methods `length()` and `capacity()`.

You can increase the capacity of the StringBuffer with the method `ensureCapacity( int minCapacity )`. This method is called by many of the other methods. The new capacity will be either `minCapacity` or two more than twice the old capacity—whichever is greater.

You can change the length of the character sequence stored in the StringBuffer with the method `setLength( int newLength )`. If `newLength` is less than the old length, then only the first `newLength` characters are kept. If `newLength` is greater than the old length, then this method calls `ensureCapacity( newLength )` and pads the old string with (`newLength` - the old length) copies of the null character '\u0000'. If `newLength` is negative, then an `IndexOutOfBoundsException` is thrown. Notice you can use this method to shorten a StringBuffer.

## Adding onto and changing elements in a StringBuffer

Once you have created a StringBuffer, you can either add to the end of a StringBuffer using `append()` or insert at a given position using `insert()`.

## The append Method

The method `append( String additionalString )` calls `ensureCapacity( )` with an argument equal to the sum of the original StringBuffer length and the length of `additionalString`. It then appends the characters of `additionalString` to our StringBuffer. Interestingly enough, if `additionalString` is `null`, then the string "null" is appended to our StringBuffer.

There are two methods used for appending a character array to a StringBuffer. The first is `append( char[] charArray )`, which appends the character array to the StringBuffer. The length of the StringBuffer is increased by the length of `charArray` and `ensureCapacity()` is called with this length as its argument. The variation on this method appends `substringLength` elements of the `charArray` starting with index `beginIndex` to the StringBuffer. The format is `append( char[] charArray, int beginIndex, int substringLength )`. Both methods can throw a `Null PointerException` and the second can throw an `IndexOutOf BoundsException`.

The `append` method works in a straightforward way on primitive types. The method

```
append( primitiveType p )
```

converts the argument *p* to a `String` the same way that `String.valueof` works. This string is then appended to the StringBuffer object. This works whether *p* is a `boolean`, `char`, `int`, `long`, `float`, or `double`. The behavior is also the same if the argument is of type `Object`.

Here are examples of `append` with a `boolean`, `int`, `long`, `float`, `double`, and an object. Let `myBuff` contain the `String` and assume after each example we're going back to our original value for `myBuff` —; otherwise, the new element would be appended to the already altered StringBuffer:

```
myBuff.append(false); // results in "Hickoryfalse".
myBuff.append(13565); // results in "Hickory13565"
myBuff.append(35356253565L); // results in "Hickory35356253565"
myBuff.append(4564.62); // results in "Hickory4564.62"
myBuff.append(4.76645D); // results in "Hickory4.76645"
Button myButton = new Button("Click Me");
myBuff.append(myButton); // append the button object
```

Before the appending takes place, the Button object is converted into a string. As a result, myBuffer would be:

```
"Hickoryjava.awt.Button[0,0,0x0,invalid,label=Click Me]"
```

### The insert Method

There is an `insert` method corresponding to each of the `append` methods, except the `append( char[] charArray, int beginIndex, int substringLength )` method. The general form is

```
insert( int beginIndex, appendArguments )
```

where `beginIndex` is the index of the position at which the first character is inserted and *appendArguments* are the argument lists we saw with the `append` methods.

Instead of placing the new pieces of the string at the end of the StringBuffer, the `insert` method places the new element beginning at index `beginIndex` and moving the remaining part of the StringBuffer so that it continues after the end of the inserted portion. In other words, make room for the new piece at the specified position and insert it. If the index specified is not legal, then `insert` throws an `IndexOutOfBoundsException`.

### The reverse Method

Just for the fun of it, the StringBuffer class contains the `reverse` method. This method replaces the character sequence contained in the StringBuffer with the same sequence in reverse order.

### The Various Char Methods

Java allows you to access and change a `char` at a specified position. The method `charAt( int index )` returns the character with that index in the StringBuffer. Remember, index numbering begins at zero (0). There is a corresponding command to change the `char` at a specified position. The `setCharAt(int index, char newChar)` changes the `char` at index `index` to `newChar`.

To copy a portion of your StringBuffer into a character array, use the method `getChars( int startIndex, int endIndex, char targetArray[], int targetStartIndex )`. This works in the same way that the `getChars` method worked for `String`. Characters in the StringBuffer between `startIndex` and `endIndex` are copied to the `targetArray` beginning with index `targetStart Index`. If the `targetArray` is null, then a `NullPointerException` is thrown.

In each of these methods, if any of the indices being referenced is out of bounds, an `IndexOutOfBoundsException` is thrown.

# Wrappers

You will often receive data as a `String`. How can you convert the information so that you can use it as, for example, a number. Say you have

```
String myString = "147";
```

You know that 147 is an integer, so why not write code like

```
for( int count = 0; count < myString; count++) //don't do this
{
   System.out.println( "this won't work" );
}
```

The `String myString` is just a sequence of characters. What should it mean to compare an `int` to this `String`? So what we need to do is convert `myString` to an `int`. As we saw before, the `valueOf()` methods go the other way; they create a `String` from another type. Type wrappers give us exactly what we're looking for: a way to extract numerical values from String objects.

In the previous two chapters, we talked about the difference between primitive types and reference types. To treat a primitive type as an object, we have to wrap it in an object — we are providing more functionality and losing the efficiency benefits we had.

For example, if we have an `int` value of 235, that value isn't an object; it's a primitive data type. To treat it as an object, we must first wrap an `Integer` object around it. Now, don't confuse the `Integer` class (java.lang.Integer) with an `int` data type: they're two different beasts. The `Integer` class defines the methods we'll use to treat an `int` as an object. As such, it's known as an integral type wrapper; it allows us to wrap an object around numeric data types.

To use a type wrapper, you supply it with a value. What you receive in return, is an object that may be treated like any other object. You can send it messages to invoke methods and pass it as a parameter to other methods. The code

```
Object myIntObject = new Integer(235); // create Integer object
```

gives us an object that can be treated like any other object. So far, we've only gotten from an `int` to an object. Remember that our original goal was to get from a `String` to an `int`. Wrapper classes allow us to do just that. First, we use the `Integer` constructor that takes as its parameter a `String`. Once we've created an object using this type wrapper, we can use the `intValue()` method to retrieve from it the `int` value we need:

```
String myInt = "235";
int  theInt = new Integer(myInt).intValue(); // get that int!
    for (int i=0; i<theInt; i++) { // and use it . . .
        System.out.println("Iteration: " + i);
    }
```

We've finally solved our problem of treating a `String` object as a primitive data type: we don't actually treat it as a primitive. Instead, we wrap an Integer object around the `String` object, then use the `intValue()` method to extract the primitive. Note that you can't just cast the `String` object to an Integer:

```
int theInt = ((Integer) myInt).intValue(); // ILLEGAL!
```

There are wrapper classes for every primitive data type. Since there are several primitive data types, there are several type wrapper classes. In addition to the constructors and methods that we'll see in the next few subsections, each wrapper class contains constants indicating the minimum value and maximum value that can be taken by literals of the corresponding type. These are represented as `MAX_VALUE` and `MIN_VALUE`.

# java.lang.Boolean

A `Boolean` is a wrapper class for the primitive type `boolean`. It is fairly typical of the other wrapper classes. `Boolean`s can be constructed from `boolean`s or `String`s. The constructor `Boolean( boolean value )` would take a `boolean` with value either `true` or `false` and create a `Boolean` object initialized to this value. You could instead use the constructor `Boolean( String string)`. Here, `string` is either the `String` "true" or the `String` `false`. A `Boolean` is constructed with its value initialized to the value specified by `string`. The point here is that you could take text input and create a `Boolean` (and later, a `boolean`) with it.

Once you have created a `Boolean`, you can use many of the same methods that you saw in `String`. You can use `booleanValue()` to return the `boolean` represented by the `Boolean`. This may seem confusing, but remember, a `boolean` is a primitive type and a `Boolean` is an object — they behave very differently and are stored very differently. What we have just seen, is that, given either of them, we can create the corresponding instance of the other type.

You can use `equals` to compare the `Boolean` to a specified object and return a hash code for the object using `hashCode()`. As you would expect, `toString` returns a new `String` object representing this `Boolean`'s value. The `valueOf( String string )` returns `true` if `string` is equal (forgetting about case) to "true." The method `getBoolean( String string )` returns `true` when the system property whose name is `string` is `true`.

# java.lang.Character

There is only one constructor for the class `Character`. It takes a `char` and creates a `Character` object. On the other hand, this class has many methods. The `hashCode()`, `equals()`, `toString()`, and `charValue()` act exactly as we would expect from our experience with `String` and `Boolean`.

There is a group of methods used for testing whether a condition is met. These methods all return `boolean`s. The method `isDefined(char myChar)` returns `true` when `myChar` is a legal Unicode character. The methods `isLowerCase(char myChar)` and `isUpperCase(char myChar)` clearly return `true` when the case of their argument is the case they are testing for. Unicode has another case called `titlecase` and Java has a corresponding third method called `isTitleCase(char myChar)`. The `isDigit(char myChar)` and `isLetter(char myChar)` methods return `true` when `myChar` is the digit or letter that is being tested for. To find out if `myChar` is either one, use `isLetterOrDigit(char myChar)`.

In Chapter 6, "Java Syntax: Tokens, Types, and Values," we saw that an identifier had to start with a Java letter. This meant an ordinary letter, the dollar ("not really$") sign, or the underscore ("_"same). We can, therefore, test whether `myChar` is a Java letter or digit using the methods `isJavaLetterOrDigit` and `isJavaLetter`. Java also has methods that allow us to modify characters by changing their case. We have the methods `toLowerCase`, `toUpperCase`, and `toTitleCase`.

# java.lang.Number

There are four classes `Integer`, `Long`, `Float`, and `Double` that are wrappers for the primitive types `int`, `long`, `float`, and `double`. They each inherit from the abstract class `Number` and each implement the methods `intValue()`, `longValue()`, `floatValue()`, and `doubleValue()`. These methods convert the number to the appropriate type and return it.

This solves our problem of starting with a `String` and converting it to an `int`:

```
String myInt = "235";
int i = new Integer( myInt ).intValue();
```

Other methods common to the four classes include `toString()`, `equals()`, `hashCode()`, and `valueOf()`. These behave much as they did in `String` and `Boolean`. The `compareTo()` method compares two numbers to see what their order is in the same way that the `compareTo()` method worked for `String`. Also, as mentioned previously, each has constants `MIN_VALUE` and `MAX_VALUE` that contain the smallest and largest allowable value of that type. Let's look at some of the other methods in the specific `Number` classes.

## java.lang.Integer

You can construct an `Integer` object from an `int` or from a `String`. You will get an `Integer` object that is initialized either to the value of the `int` or to the value that corresponds to the value of the `String`. In addition, there are `static` methods for converting an `int` to a `String` in hex, octal, or binary. They are, respectively, `toHexString( int i )`, `toOctalString( int i )`, and `toBinaryString( int i )`.

We could answer our question about converting a String into an int using either of the two static methods parseInt(). The first is parseInt( String string ). It takes a string whose characters are all digits 0 through 9 and whose first digit may also be the minus ("-") sign. It returns an int with the value equal to the number represented by string. There is also a parseInt( String string, int radix ) method. Now the string must contain legal digits in the given radix and what is returned is the int that corresponds to what is represented by string in the given radix.

For example, if radix is 2, then the only allowable digits are 0 and 1. This would mean that parseInt( "11011", 2 ) would return the value 27. If the radix is 16, then the allowable digits are 0 through 9 followed by a through f (where the letters are not case sensitive). So parseInt("1b",16) would also return the value 27.

The getInteger method returns an Integer and not an int. The Integer wraps the value of an integer representation of the value of a system property that we input as string. The method call is getInteger( String string ). You can also supply an int as the default value as a second argument using getInteger( String string, int val ). Finally, you can supply the default value as an Integer using getInteger( String string, Integer val ).

## java.lang.Long

The methods in this class are what you would get if you made the appropriate changes to the names of methods, return types, signatures, and behaviors to the methods in the class Integer. Instead of parseInt() and getInt() methods, there are parseLong() and getLong() methods. Instead of these methods returning ints, they return longs.

## java.lang.Float

You can construct a Float object from a float, from a double, or from a String. You will get a Float object that is initialized either to the value of the float, to the value you would get if you cast the double to a float, or to the value that corresponds to the value of the String. There are static methods floatToIntBits( float aFloat) and intBitsToFloat( int someBits ) used for converting between floating-point values and the bit representation.

In addition to the constants MAX_VALUE and MIN_VALUE, the Float class also contains the constants NEGATIVE_INFINITY, POSITIVE_INFINITY, and NaN. The last stands for Not-a-Number. There are methods for testing whether a quantity is infinite or not a number. The method isNaN() returns a boolean that is true when the value of the Float is NaN. There is also a static method isNaN(float aFloat) that returns a boolean that is true when the value of the argument is NaN. Similarly, there is the method isInfinite() and the static method isInfinite (float aFloat), which return true if the Float in the first case and the float in the argument in the second case is positive or negative infinity.

### java.lang.Double

As with `Long` and `Integer`, make the appropriate changes to the `Float` methods and constants and you will get the `Double` class. You can construct a `Double` from a `double` or from a `String` but not from a `float`. Everything else corresponds nicely, including the pair of methods `doubleToLongBits(double aDouble)` and `longBitsToDouble( long aLong )`, which convert between `doubles` and their bit representation.

# Command-Line Arguments and Applet Tag Attributes

We're now ready to combine much of what we've learned to add flexibility to your applications and applets. Until now, the Java programs we've written have been very inflexible. That is to say, the data these programs use is hard-coded and can't be changed, except by a programmer.

The original HelloWorld application will always output the words "Hello World!" to the screen until the program has been altered by the programmer to say something else. The MediaHelloWorld applet you created will always use the same audio and image files until it is rewritten to use others. In both cases, the programs require fiddling around with the source code and must be recompiled before changes to the data they use can be put into effect.

In some cases, this lack of flexibility may be exactly what you want. Perhaps there is a portion of the data your program uses that you want never to change unless the program itself is updated. Such is the case with copyright notices and developer credits, which remain constant throughout the life of a particular software version release. However, more often than not, the data your programs use will change regularly.

In the case of an application, you may well want your program to act in a certain way, depending on what input is provided by the user at the time of execution. For this, you have the option of using Java command-line arguments. With command-line arguments, you can specify any number of parameters to the application at the time it is executed.

If you're a C/C++ programmer with experience developing programs executed from the command line, the notion of command-line parameters will come as no surprise. If not, the following chapter will be of particular interest.

But how does this affect applets? From a practical standpoint, the answer lies in the Web server. Unless the directory structure of your Web site never changes and the files your applet relies on are always in the same place, applet flexibility is a tremendous advantage when it comes to maintaining a site. Most Web sites grow continually, with new content being added on a regular basis. If the data files your applet requires are hard-coded, as ours have been, maintaining a Web site becomes a nightmare.

If you think of the Web server as a giant, universally accessible hard disk, it may help drive home the point that you're more likely than not to be reorganizing files and directories regularly. How many times have you moved files and directories around on your local hard disk to keep it organized? This will eventually become necessary on your Web server if it isn't already. And if you have to update source code, recompile it, and then upload the result for each applet at your site merely to reflect changes in the server directory layout, you'll certainly appreciate the ability to pass parameters to applets.

Couple ease of maintenance with an ability to create very robust applets that can be customized without touching the applet or applet source code, and you have extremely compelling reasons to build flexible applets. And, thanks to applet attributes, your applets can be as flexible as you choose.

# Java command-line arguments

Java command-line arguments are arguments that are passed to a Java application when it is invoked from the command line. If you created the HelloWorld application discussed in Chapter 5, "Stepping Through Code," you're already familiar with executing Java applications at the command line:

```
c:\> java HelloWorld
```

Although you are free to pass any number of command-line arguments to a Java application, it's up to the application to make use of them. If an application hasn't been written to handle command-line arguments, it will execute as it normally would and ignore the arguments altogether. HelloWorld, as we wrote it, doesn't know what to do with command-line arguments. If we provided them, nothing would happen.

On the other hand, you want to avoid attempting to access an element that does not exist. This would cause the runtime system to throw an `ArrayIndexOutOfBoundsException` exception.

## Java Command-Line Arguments: Number and Type

All arguments are passed to your application through an array of strings in the `main()` method. You simply take them out of the array and do with them as you wish. Remember the signature of a typical `main()` method in Java:

```
public static void main (String args[]) { ... }
```

Programmers who have worked with C/C++ command-line arguments are already familiar with the concept of receiving parameters through the main() function. Command-line arguments in Java differ from their C and C++ counterparts in two major ways: number and type. C/C++ uses two variables to pass arguments to applications; Java uses only one, and the data type of the variable containing the parameters is not the same.

As you can see from the signature of the main() method, Java uses one argument variable args, which is an array of strings that contain the command-line arguments. Refer to Chapter 8, "Creating and Using Arrays and Strings," for more information as you need it. You can get the number of command-line arguments by referencing the length instance variable of our array. Here the command is args.length.

Because each element in the args array is a command-line argument, the length of the array is equal to the total number of command-line arguments the user provided when executing the application. By referencing the number of elements in the array, as shown previously, your Java applications will know exactly how many command-line arguments were provided when executed.

In addition to eliminating the need for a variable to hold the number of command-line arguments passed to your application, in Java, you deal directly with the array of String objects. To access a command-line argument, you only need to access a particular element in the args array. Suppose, for instance, that you wanted to get the third command-line argument provided by the user. Since all array indexing begins with 0, this would do the trick:

```
String theArg;  /* variable to hold argument */
theArg = args[2]; /* retrieve third argument */
```

**Note**    The fact that all arguments are passed in as strings is a big part of why we needed the preceding section on Wrapper classes. We need some mechanism for transforming data from a string to the type that we need to properly use the data.

## Java Command-Line Argument Conventions

The Java language adheres to UNIX conventions for command-line arguments, defining three different types:

✦ Word arguments

✦ Arguments that require arguments

✦ Flags

Adhere to the conventions listed in the next three sections when dealing with command-line arguments.

## Word arguments

Word arguments, such as `verbose`, must be specified precisely on the command line. As a result, `ver` would not be valid if you wanted to invoke the `verbose` option: only `verbose` would work!

Typically, your program will test to see if a particular word argument has been specified and set a flag accordingly. In the following code snippet, we've tested for the `verbose` word argument and set the `verb` flag accordingly:

```
if (argument.equals("-verbose"))
{
  verbose = true;  // turn the verbose flag (verb) "on"
}
```

## Arguments that require arguments

In many cases, you'll want to use arguments that, themselves, require additional information. You might, for example, want to use a command-line argument such as `file` to redirect output of the program into a file. The `file` option alone, however, isn't enough. A file name must also be supplied.

In this case, you need to read in the file name following the `file` argument. That is, you must parse the command line to retrieve the additional information:

```
if (argument.equals("-file"))
{
  if (nextarg < args.length)
  {
    filename = args[nextarg++]; // set the "filename" variable
  }
  else
  {
    System.err.println("Follow -file with a filename!");
  }
}
```

In this example, we test to see whether the user actually supplied an argument following `-file`. If so, it's retrieved and assigned to a variable. If not, a message is output to the user telling him or her how to use this argument.

## Flags

Single-character codes used to modify the behavior of a program are known as flags. You might, for example, want to supply a help option in your program. In this case, you would use the `?` flag. Of course, you could also implement a `help` word argument. In fact, you might want to use both.

Typically, flags can be specified separately and in any order. For example, either `?`, `z`, or `z -?` work just fine. In addition, flags can typically be concatenated and specified in any order. Thus, `z?` and `?z` are also fine.

### Other conventions

In addition to the conventions described in the three previous sections, there are a few others that you should be aware of when developing Java applications:

✦ You can assume the user will precede all options, flags, or series of flags with the hyphen (-) character.

✦ The names of files your program will use (operate on) are typically the last argument on the command line.

✦ Your application should output a usage statement whenever a command-line argument can't be recognized; it should have the following form:

```
usage: application_name [ optional_args ] required_args
```

## Enhancing the HelloWorld Application with Command-Line Arguments

Recall the HelloWorld application:

```
//version #1
class HelloWorld
{
  public static void main (String args[])
  {
    System.out.println("Hello World!"); //the print statement
  }
}
```

We are going to enhance it in two ways. First, we'll look to pass the String to be printed in as an argument. Next, we'll pass in the number of times that we'd like to print it.

### Passing in the string to be printed

Let's change HelloWorld so that we can pass the String to be printed in as an argument.

```
//version #2
class HelloWorld
{
  public static void main (String args[])
  {
    System.out.println( args[0] ); //the print statement
  }
}
```

Compile it as before by typing `javac HelloWorld.java` at the command line. Now when it is time to run the program, you need to provide input.

Run the program with the argument "Hello" by typing

```
java HelloWorld Hello
```

The output from the program is

```
Hello
```

Run the program with the argument "Hello World" by typing

```
java HelloWorld Hello World
```

The output from the program is

```
Hello
```

Hey, wait a minute, what happened? Java uses white space as the separator for arguments. It sees `Hello` as the first `String`, which it is storing as `args[0]`, and `World` as the second `String`, which it is storing as `args[1]`. If you want "Hello World" to be a single argument, then use the double quotes and type

```
java HelloWorld "Hello World"
```

This time the output from the program is

```
Hello World
```

### Passing in an integer

Let's make another change to our program and input the number of times that we'd like the `String` that the user provides to be printed. Here we will use the `Integer` wrapper class to convert the `String` being input to an `int`.

```
//version #3
class HelloWorld
{
  public static void main (String args[])
  {
    String stringToBePrinted = args[0];
    int numberOfTimes = new Integer(args[1]).intValue();
    for(int i = 0; i < numberOfTimes; i++)
    {
      System.out.println( stringToBePrinted );
    }
  }
}
```

Compile this program as before by typing `javac HelloWorld.java` and then run it by typing in a `String` followed by an `int`. For example,

```
java HelloWorld "Hi There" 3
```

results in the following output:

```
Hi There
Hi There
Hi There
```

### Other Issues in Dealing with Arguments

We could have elected to not use the `stringToBePrinted` variable in version #3. After all, that's the way we did it in version #2 — there we just continued to use the variable `args[0]`. There are times when the order of the arguments may not be set in stone. If, for example, you are reading in various flags, the user may not enter them in the order you expect. You will then have to write some sort of parser and store the relevant pieces in named variables.

As we saw in version #2, adding extra inputs that are never used by the program doesn't cause the compiler to signal an error. Of course, this is not behavior that should be encouraged.

On the other hand, we have a real problem if the application depends on input that it isn't getting. In either version #2 or #3, if not enough command-line arguments are passed in at runtime, you will see the error:

```
Exception in thread "main"
java.lang.ArrayIndexOutOfBoundsException at HelloWorld.main(
HelloWorld.java, Compiled Code)
```

If the arguments are typed in the wrong order, or if it is clear that there is a type mismatch, you will also see an exception thrown. For example, if you type

```
java HelloWorld Hi There 3
```

then `args[0]` is `"Hi"`, `args[1]` is `"There"`, and `args[2]` is `"3"`. The application never uses `args[2]`, so this doesn't cause an official problem. The program does, however, expect to be able to create an `int` from `args[2]` and instead of encountering the `String` `"3"`, it finds the `String` `"There"`. It throws a `NumberFormatException`.

## Passing information to applets

Command-line arguments are supplied on the command line at the time of executing an application. On the other hand, an applet is downloaded from the Web and passed to the Java runtime environment for execution. We'll need to use a different mechanism for supplying applets with user-defined information.

The following code illustrates the basic structure of the <APPLET> tag:

```
<APPLET standard-attributes>
applet-parameters
alternate-context
</APPLET>
```

The `standard attributes`, including items such as the HEIGHT and WIDTH, which are specified in all the HTML documents we've created so far, are actually applet attributes just as the name of the class file we specify for CODE is:

```
<APPLET CODE="MediaHelloWorld.class" WIDTH=200 HEIGHT=150>
```

At a minimum, these three attributes must be included in the <APPLET> tag. They are required; whereas, the majority of applet attributes are optional. CODE is the name of a java class file that inherits from the Applet class. WIDTH and HEIGHT specify the initial dimensions of the Applet in pixels.

**Note**     The identifiers used to specify applet tags (such as CODE, HEIGHT, and WIDTH) are not case sensitive. They can be in uppercase, lowercase, or a mixture of both. For the sake of readability, however, it's a good idea to use uppercase. The values you provide for these attributes, such as MediaHelloWorld.class in the previous example, are another matter. Be certain to use the proper case: MediaHelloWorld.class is not the same as MEDIAHELLOWORLD.CLASS!

The `applet parameters` are our way of passing information, such as the URL of a file on the Web or a text string to display when executed, to an applet. They take the place of command-line arguments for passing information to an application.

We will use the keyword PARAM to pass in the applet version of command-line arguments. These applet parameters appear as a pair of name and value attributes inside a <PARAM> tag:

```
<PARAM NAME=hello VALUE="Hello World!">
```

The `alternate applet` context allows you to include any type of HTML code between the last applet parameter and the </APPLET> end tag. It is displayed by browsers that are not Java-savvy and won't be visible to users viewing the document with a browser that is capable of dealing with Java applets.

Alternate applet context can contain any type of HTML code you wish, such as text, tags, or both. This is an example of text-only applet context:

```
<APPLET CODE="MediaHelloWorld.class" WIDTH=90 HEIGHT=50 ALIGN=top>
...This page requires a Java-savvy browser.
</APPLET>
```

The line immediately preceding the </APPLET> end tag will appear as standard HTML text to a browser that doesn't support Java. In most cases, it's a good idea to include alternate applet context when creating your HTML pages, even if it's nothing more than a "You need a Java browser to see this page!" message. If you don't, those users who view your pages using a browser that doesn't support Java will have no idea that they are missing out on something.

## Optional Attributes

Applet attributes are specified in the <APPLET> HTML tag, and they provide information that either the browser, the Java runtime system, or the applet itself will use to execute properly. To use an optional attribute, you simply include its name and an associated value within the <APPLET> start tag. The start tag begins with <APPLET and ends with a closing angle bracket (>).

The standard attributes are special settings that the browser and runtime system use to execute your applet according to your specifications. You can supply optional attributes after the required ones, as long as they are inside the closing angle bracket:

```
<APPLET CODE="MediaHelloWorld.class" WIDTH=200 HEIGHT=150 ALIGN=top>
```

The ALIGN attribute let's you specify where your applet is placed on the page with respect to the text around it. You can specify it to be left, right top, texttop, middle, absmiddle, baseline, bottom, or absbottom. ALT is the alternate text to be displayed by a text-only browser. You can set the base URL for your applet using CODEBASE. The default is the URL of the HTML document that calls the applet. The HSPACE and VSPACE attributes let you specify the horizontal and vertical space around your applet for certain settings of ALIGN. Other applets embedded in the same page will refer to your applet by the NAME setting. You can preload one or more archives (say, JAR files) using the ARCHIVE attribute. Finally, OBJECT is the name of a class containing a serialized version of an applet. When a serialized applet is loaded, its `init()` method isn't invoked but its `start()` method is.

Note that the start tag can extend over several lines. As long as the opening and closing angle brackets are present, the start tag can span as many lines as needed. Also, the attributes can appear in any order, although it's a good idea to place the required three immediately following the word *APPLET*:

```
<APPLET CODE="MediaHelloWorld.class"
WIDTH=200
HEIGHT=150
ALIGN=top>
```

## Applet "Parameter" Attributes

For the example

```
<PARAM NAME=hello VALUE="Hello World!">
```

the parameter called `hello` is specified as having the value `"Hello World!"`. To retrieve this value from within an applet, we must use the `getParameter()` method defined in the Applet class:

```
String  helloStr = getParameter ("hello");
```

Here, we've declared a String variable, `helloStr`, into which we've received the value of the hello parameter. After this line of code is executed, `helloStr` will contain the string "Hello World!" Of course, we could have just as easily declared the variable on one line and retrieved the parameter on another:

```
String  helloStr; /* declare the variable first */
helloStr = getParameter ("hello"); /* and then get the
parameter */
```

Functionally, these two approaches are equivalent. Yet in both cases, we're assuming an applet parameter specifying a value for hello exists in the HTML document. We're expecting something like this:

```
<APPLET CODE="HelloWorldApplet.class" WIDTH=90 HEIGHT=50
ALIGN=top>
<PARAM NAME=hello VALUE="Hello World!">
</APPLET>
```

This HTML code clearly specifies a hello parameter with the value of "Hello World!" But what if the second line of code didn't exist? What if you forgot to include it when creating the HTML document, yet included the code in your applet to retrieve a hello parameter? In this case, your `helloStr` variable would be set to `null`, since the `getParameter()` method would fail to find the hello parameter and return null instead of a valid string.

It's a good idea to test for null values when processing applet parameters and act accordingly. In some cases, such as with the code presented here, you may provide default values to allow your applet to continue executing where it would otherwise fail to run properly.

Like with the identifiers used to specify attributes (CODE, HEIGHT, WIDTH, PARAM NAME, VALUE, and so on), you can use either uppercase or lowercase letters when associating a value with the PARAM NAME. As you can see, the word *hello* is all lowercase characters. We could just as easily have used all capital letters (HELLO), or a combination of both (Hello).

Since the `getParameter()` method isn't case sensitive, it really doesn't matter how we name an applet parameter. The Java code `getParameter("hello")` will find and return the value associated with hello, HELLO, or even Hello. However, to make your HTML code easier to read, it's a good idea to use uppercase letters for the attribute identifiers (CODE, HEIGHT, and so on) and lowercase for the actual parameter (such as hello in our example).

## All Applet Parameters Are Strings

We can rewrite the HelloWorldApple code similar to version #3 of the HelloWorld application:

```
import java.awt.Graphics;
import java.applet.*;

public class HelloWorldApplet extends Applet
{
  public void init()
  {
    resize(200,150);
  }
  public void paint( Graphics g)
  {
    String stringToBePrinted = getParameter("inputString");
    int numberOfTimes = new Integer( getParameter(
      "repetitions" ) ).intValue();
    for (int i = 0; i < numberOfTimes; i++)
    {
      g.drawString(stringToBePrinted, 50,90 + 10 * i);
    }
  }
}
```

Notice that, as in HelloWorld version #3, we are expected to pass in the name of the String being printed and the number of times we are to print it. This means we need to modify the HTML document to include the PARAM commands.

```
<HTML>
<HEAD>
<TITLE> Hello World Applet Test </TITLE>
</HEAD>
<BODY>
Here is our applet:
<APPLET CODE="HelloWorldApplet" WIDTH=200 HEIGHT=150>
<PARAM NAME = repetitions VALUE = 3>
<PARAM NAME = inputString VALUE = "Hello World">
</APPLET>
</BODY>
</HTML>
```

Then your browser will display the applet with Hello World written three times. Note that again we had to convert the parameter input from a String to an int.

# Collection Classes from the java.util Package

Arrays are the answer to many questions — but it is nice to have other ways of collecting data. In the java.util package, you'll find classes for dealing with hash tables, stacks, vectors, and bit sets. While each of these has a specific function, you'll find they each provide a mechanism for storing and retrieving data.

## Interfaces

The interfaces promise that any class implementing the interface will provide the specified functionality. The interface does not say anything about how this functionality will be provided.

### The Collection Interface

The most general functionality is specified in the `Collection` interface. Its (empty) methods are the following:

✦ `contains( Object myObject )` returns `true` if the collection contains `myObject`.

✦ `containsAll( Collection myCollection )` returns `true` if the collection contains all of the elements of `myCollection`.

✦ `equals( Object myObject )` returns `true` if the collection is equal to `myObject`.

✦ `hashCode()` returns the `hashCode` of the collection.

✦ `isEmpty()` returns `true` if the collection contains no elements.

✦ `iterator()` returns an instance of the `Iterator` class, which can be used to iterate through the elements of this collection.

✦ `size()` returns the number of elements in the collection.

✦ `toArray()` returns an array containing the elements in the collection.

✦ `toArray( Object[] arrayName )` does the same as `toArray()`, but the array's type is that of `arrayName`.

`Collections` also includes the following optional methods.

✦ `add( Object myObject )` adds `myObject` to the collection if it isn't already there.

✦ `remove( Object myObject )` removes one instance of `myObject` from the collection.

✦ `addAll(Collection myCollection )` adds all of the elements of `myCollection` to the collection.

✦ `removeAll( Collection myCollection )` removes each of the elements of `myCollection` from the collection.

✦ `retainAll( Collection myCollection )` removes all of the elements from this collection that aren't contained in `myCollection`.

✦ `clear()` removes all of the elements from the collection.

## Interfaces That Extend Collections

The interfaces `List`, `Set`, and `SortedSet` extend the interface `Collections`.

A `List` allows the user to insert elements at specified places in the `List`. A `List` will also allow you to add an element that is equal to an element the `List` already contains. A `List` also allows you to insert or remove one or more elements at a specified position.

As an example, imagine that you are driving somewhere and have the instructions "Take a right. Go straight for three blocks. Take a right. Go straight for six blocks." You wouldn't want the `List` to say, "hey you already turned right, I'll delete the second 'Take a right' instruction." Similarly, if you later realize that after going straight for three blocks they need to get in the right lane to take a right, you'd like to add "Get in the Right Lane" at a specific point.

A `Set`, on the other hand, only keeps one copy of each element. The methods need to support this. For example, say you ask someone to name all seven days of the week and have them say Sunday, Monday, Tuesday, Sunday, Monday, Tuesday, and Sunday. She is pleased because she gave you seven names, all of which were dwarfs. You certainly don't want to reward her because really she only gave you three distinct pieces of information. You want to make sure that a constructor would eliminate the redundant data.

A `SortedSet` is a specific extension of `Set` that forces the iterator to go through the elements in a natural order. You need to be able to use the `compareTo()` method to place the elements in the appropriate order. Remember that `compareTo()` is able to decide if two elements are equal or if one precedes the other.

## Other Interfaces from java.util

For completeness, the other interfaces in java.util are listed. The `Map` is kind of like a dictionary (and replaces the `Dictionary` class). It links keys to values so that you can quickly look up values. A key together with its value is a `Map.Entry`. Just as `Sets` can be `SortedSets`, so too a `Map` can be a `SortedMap`. This is a `Map` that is also sorted so that its keys are in ascending order.

There are interfaces that are used to handle the elements in a `Collection`. The `Comparator` is the interface that imposes a total ordering (i.e., each pair of elements can be compared). You can make up many different orderings on sets, but you should be careful if you're not choosing the natural order. For example, you could decide to order strings by the value of their Unicode string instead of in the usual lexicographical order. This would mean that writing the words "apple, Banana, coffee" in this order would be "apple, coffee, Banana" since the capitol "B" places it at a value higher than the "c" that starts "coffee."

The interface `Iterator` helps you move through the elements in a `Collection`. A `ListIterator` specializes this behavior to a `List`. An `Enumeration` will provide a sequence of elements in a `Collection` one by one.

Two of the interfaces provided in java.util have nothing to do with `Collections`. You will see the `EventListener` and `Observer` classes when Java's event model is described in the next part of this book.

# Abstract Classes for the Collections

The package java.util includes the classes `AbstractCollections`, `AbstractList`, `AbstractMap`, `AbstractSequence`, and `AbstractSet` as a bridge between the interfaces and concrete classes. `Dictionary` is also an abstract class for anything that needs keyed values. `Calendar` is an abstract class used to convert `Date` objects to and from variables that store individual fields of information.

These classes are just skeletons that provide minimal functionality guaranteed by the interfaces. It is easier to extend these classes than to implement the interface. You will see this again with the Java event model.

# Concrete Classes for the Collections

In this section, we will quickly list some of Java's collection classes and then take some time with `Hashtable`, `Vector`, and `StringTokenizer`.

Java provides for the following concrete collection classes: `Arrays`, `Collections`, `Dictionary`, `HashMap`, `HashSet`, `Hashtable`, `LinkedList`, `ListResourceBundle`, `ResourceBundle`, `Stack`, `TreeMap`, `TreeSet`, `Vector`, and `WeakHashMap`.

## Hashtable

Now that there have been some changes in the interfaces of the java.util package, the class `Hashtable` extends the class `Dictionary` while implementing the interfaces `Map`, `Cloneable`, and `Serializable`. That's a lot of functionality in one class. A hash table maps keys to values, values that can be any Java object. Whatever object you use as a key, however, must implement the `hashCode()` and `equals()` methods.

In the following code, we create a hash table to track the amount of stock a store might have. We use the names of the items in stock as keys, and give each a value:

```
Hashtable stockLevels = new Hashtable();
stockLevels.put("Radios", new Integer(4343));
stockLevels.put("Bikes", new Integer(523));
stockLevels.put("Chairs", new Integer(3563));
stockLevels.put("Bananas", new Integer(646));
    // now retrieve the number of Bananas in stock:
Integer n = (Integer)stockLevels.get("Bananas");
if (n != null)
{
  System.out.println("Yes, we have " + n + " bananas.");
}
```

A particularly powerful feature of hash tables is their ability to store more than one type of data. While `String` and `StringBuffer` objects can contain only characters, and arrays can have only elements of the same type, we can mix and match the data types stored in a hash table.

Even though we stored values of `Integer` objects in the preceding example, each could have been a different data type. If, for example, we wanted to store a string as the Banana value, we might have written the following:

```
stockLevels.put("Bananas", new String("lots o' naners"));
```

However, when retrieving this element, we'd have to get it as a `String` object. If we attempted to extract it as an `Integer` object, as we did earlier, a `ClassCastException` would be thrown (since a `String` can't be cast into an int). As a result, we would use something like the following to output the value of the Bananas key:

```
System.out.println(stockLevels.get("Bananas"));
```

`Hashtables` have a capacity and a load factor. The load factor is a number between 0 and 1. It tells you how full a `Hashtable` can get before its capacity is increased. If you don't specify the load factor when creating a `Hashtable`, it is set to `.75`. This means that when the number of entries reaches 75 percent of the capacity, the capacity will be increased using the `rehash()` method.

## Vectors

Although arrays are nice and convenient to use, sometimes you need the ability to grow them. However, as you know, arrays must be dimensioned to a certain size before they are used. And once set, you can't change that dimension.

*Vectors*, on the other hand, are growable arrays. Rather than being constrained to a specific number of elements, you can expand them as needed. In the following example, we'll create an empty Vector and add two elements to it:

```
Vector myVector = new Vector(); // create a vector
String myString = "Obla-de, obla-da"; // any 'ol String
Button myButton = new Button("life goes on"); // a Button

/* Add objects to our vector: */
myVector.addElement(myString);
myVector.addElement(myButton);

/* Now retrieve the button (notice the cast): */
anotherButton = (Button) myVector.lastElement();
```

Notice how we managed to cram a Button object and a String object into the Vector object? Anything you put into a vector is first converted into a plain vanilla object, meaning you can put anything you'd like into it. But to get something out, you have to know what to cast it to! This is seen in the last line of the preceding code, where we retrieve the last item as a Button; because it was a Button object going in, we need to cast it to a Button object coming out.

**Caution**    The flexibility of vectors make them attractive to work with. The cost is that you need to be careful because your objects lose their type when they are placed in a vector. The client using the data may need to be told the type of the data.

You can take a great deal of work off the runtime system by creating your vectors with an initial storage capacity; if you don't, each new element that is added forces the vector to expand—a significant effort on Java's part and one to avoid if at all possible.

## Stacks

A common data storage mechanism used by many programmers is the Stack, which allows you to push() objects onto it and pop() objects off when they need to be retrieved. Stacks follow a last in, first out (LIFO) ordering, meaning the last object you push() onto the stack will be the first one you receive when you call pop().

You can also peek() at the object on top of the Stack and search() for an object and be told how far down the Stack it is.

The Stack class is a subclass of Vector, meaning you don't have to worry about how many items a Stack object will contain. You can simply create one and begin using it without worrying about how many items you'll eventually push() onto it.

## StringTokenizer

At times, you'll need to retrieve the chunks of information stored in a String object. Such chunks, or tokens, must each be separated by a delimiter, such as a comma or a space. When you have such elements in a string, you can retrieve them using the StringTokenizer class.

For example, suppose you've stored a series of words into a string, as we've done in earlier examples:

```
String myString = "There once was a";
```

Since each of the words is separated by a space, you could retrieve them as follows:

```
StringTokenizer tokens = new StringTokenizer(myString);
while (tokens.hasMoreTokens())
{
   System.out.println(tokens.nextToken());
}
```

When executed, the preceding code would output each word in the string on its own line:

```
There
once
was
a
```

Since the default delimiter for `StringTokenizer` is a space, we didn't have to do anything special to retrieve these words. If we were dealing with a delimiter other than a space, we could specify that delimiter when creating the `StringTokenizer` object or when reading tokens.

# Summary

Now you understand how to add strings and arrays to your Java applications. You can also use these strings to pass information to applications and applets. Key concepts to remember from this chapter include these:

✦ Java strings aren't like the ones we're accustomed to in C and C++. In those languages, strings are simply an array of null-terminated characters. Java strings, however, are actually objects defined by the `String` class. As a result, they feature a number of methods that are used to access their contents. With Java, strings are first-class objects that support a well-defined set of methods.

✦ In Java, arrays are truly first-class objects. Not only are they impossible to subclass, but you won't even find a class definition for them. Instead, Java knows internally about arrays and how to treat them, just as it knows how to deal with primitive data types without offering a class for each. (Keep in mind that type wrappers for primitives are different from the primitives themselves; there are type wrapper classes, but no primitive classes.) Unlike `String` and `StringBuffer` objects, which can contain only character data, arrays are capable of holding any type of data we need, even other arrays. The only restriction is that each element in the array must be of the same type.

✦ Java provides two distinct string classes: `String` and `StringBuffer`. The `String` class is used to create `String` objects, which are immutable; their contents can't be altered once characters have been stored in them. `StringBuffer`, on the other hand, is specifically for strings that are mutable or able to be changed even after characters have been stored in them.

✦ The java.lang package also contains wrapper classes. These are there for wrapping the full functionality of an object around a variable of primitive type. These wrappers can also be used for converting from strings to specific data types.

✦ Java command-line arguments are arguments that are passed to a Java application when it is invoked from the command line. Applications accept arguments on the command line, much like C/C++ programs. The program then stores them in the `args` `String` argument of the `main` method.

✦ Applets live on the Web and are downloaded by a Java-savvy browser before they are executed. Applets accept special attributes supplied in the <APPLET> HTML tag. Those included in the tag PARAM can be accessed by the applet using the `getParameter` method.

✦ The `Hashtable` class has the ability to store more than one type of data. While `String` and `StringBuffer` objects can contain only characters, and arrays can have only elements of the same type, we can mix and match the data types stored in a hash table.

✦ Vectors are growable arrays. Rather than being constrained to a specific number of elements, you can expand them as needed.

✦ A common data storage mechanism used by many programmers is the stack, which allows you to `push()` objects onto it and `pop()` objects off when they need to be retrieved. Stacks follow a last in, first out (LIFO) ordering, meaning the last object you `push()` onto the stack will be the first one you receive when you call `pop()`.

✦    ✦    ✦

# Classes, Interfaces, and Packages

**T**o write Java programs, you must be able to create and manage objects. As you know, objects are instantiations of classes, which you can think of as the code templates or blueprints for objects.

In this chapter, you'll also see how classes and interfaces can be organized into packages. Packages allow you to group classes and interfaces together as you see fit, helping to manage what might otherwise become overwhelming, allowing you to create well-organized repositories of Java code.

## Classes

A Java program is basically a collection of interacting objects. Classes are the templates, or blueprints, from which objects are created. You can think of classes as data types. When objects are created or instantiated from the same class, they are considered to be of the same type.

Each object is an instance of a class. The class that an object is instantiated from determines the type of that object. If two objects are instantiated from the same class, they are considered to be of the same type. You can use the `instanceof()` method to find out whether an object is instantiated from a particular class.

When writing Java programs, you use a number of classes that are supplied with the Java development environment. You can use them as they are or adapt them to your needs. You can also use classes developed by other Java programmers or create them yourself.

To create a class, declare it and code the body of the class:

```
class declaration
{
  ...
  /* class body (typically variables and methods) */
  ...
}
```

Although this is an oversimplified example, it enables you to see the two parts of a class implementation clearly:

✦ The *class declaration* includes the name of the class, what type of access other objects will have to it, and what superclasses (and interfaces) it inherits state and behavior from.

✦ The *body* is where the specific state and behavior of the class are defined, through the implementation of variables and methods.

In Java, only one public class declaration is allowed in each source file. You can, however, have any number of nonpublic classes in one file. Although this is technically possible, it's not recommended. It's best to create a separate source file for each class and use the package mechanism, discussed in detail in the "Packages" section at the end of this chapter, to organize and use them.

## Class declaration

The syntax of the `class` declaration is

```
[modifiers] class ClassName [extends superClass] [implements
interfaces]
```

The elements in the `class` declaration in brackets (`[ ]`) are optional. You can declare a `class` by simply providing the keyword `class`, followed by a name, as shown in the next piece of code. Here we have declared `SimpleClass`, an example of the simplest `class` signature you can declare:

```
class SimpleClass()
{
}
```

The optional portions of the declaration allow you to specify the visibility of the `class` as well as a superclass that it can extend and interfaces that it can implement. The `class` name you specify must be a valid identifier. (See Chapter 6, "Java Syntax: Tokens, Types, and Values," for information on Java identifiers.) Class names usually begin with a capital letter. Names of variables and the names of objects, on the other hand, typically begin with a lowercase letter. In each, the first letter of each word that follows is usually capitalized. For example,

```
ThisIsAClass
thisIsAnInstanceOfTheClass
thisIsAVariable
```

## Modifiers

Class modifiers declare whether a class is `abstract`, `final`, or `public`.

### abstract

An `abstract` method is one that has no implementation. A class that has at least one `abstract` method in it must be declared to be `abstract`. The purpose of having an `abstract` class is to allow it to declare methods, yet leave at least some of them without an implementation. As such, the subclasses of an abstract class are required to provide implementation for the `abstract` methods.

You should declare a class as `abstract` when you know that its subclasses will implement a certain method differently. Take, for instance, a method such as `makeMusic()`. In an orchestra program, several of the program's classes (such as `Violin`, `Trumpet`, `Triangle`, and others) will implement a `makeMusic()` method, but each might implement it differently. It makes sense in this case to declare the parent class as `abstract`, allowing all subclasses to implement the `abstract` methods declared in the parent classes they wish:

```
abstract class MyInstrument
{
    ...
}
```

In the preceding example, only the `class` declaration is shown. To be a complete and valid `class` implementation, you'd also need to declare at least one `abstract` method such as `makeMusic()`. Since you're concentrating only on the `class` declaration here, we've omitted the `abstract` method declaration.

If you declare a `class` as `abstract`, at least one of the methods in that `class` must also be `abstract`. The compiler kicks out an error message and refuses to compile an `abstract` `class` that has no `abstract` methods in it.

More importantly, you cannot create an instance of an `abstract` `class`. You must create a subclass and then create an instance of that subclass (provided that the subclass isn't `abstract`). You will recognize that a subclass of an `abstract` `class` is not itself `abstract` if it has completed the implementation of the methods of the parent class.

For example, you might have declared a ShowDown class as abstract, in addition to one or more of the methods in that class, as shown here:

```
public abstract class ShowDown
{
  int  aVar; // an instance variable

  public abstract void Encounter(); // abstract method
  public abstract void SizeUp(int dude); // abstract method
  void aRegularMethod()
  {             // a standard method, not abstract
    ...         // implementation here...
  }
}
```

In this case, an object of type ShowDown could never be instantiated. As an abstract class, it can only be subclassed. And whenever subclassed, the two abstract methods, Encounter() and SizeUp(), must be implemented by the subclass.

An abstract class is a nice intermediate between a standard class and an interface. Since it can actually implement methods, it is useful when a class must be created that needs to rely on the subclass for the implementation of one or more methods. Other than containing abstract methods, and the fact that an object can't be created directly from them since one or more of the methods are empty, abstract classes behave like standard classes.

### final

The final modifier specifies a class that can have no subclasses. As final classes can't be subclassed, additional variables and methods can't be added, and more importantly, methods can't be overridden and implemented differently from the way the author of the class intended.

For example, Java's String class (see Chapter 8) is a final class. Whenever you use a String, you're dealing with an object that is instantiated directly from the String class, as defined in the java.lang package. As a final class, you can be certain you're always dealing with objects defined in the String class, not something that is defined by a subclass of the String class.

This may not make sense yet. We haven't looked at polymorphism yet, so we haven't explored situations where we can call objects that are instances of a subclass as if they were instances of the parent class. A final declaration ensures that the object has exactly the behavior we know about.

To specify a final class, use the keyword final just before the keyword class. For example, the String class defined in java.lang.String is declared as follows:

```
public final class String
{
  ...
}
```

As you can see, the `final` modifier is preceded by yet another modifier: `public`. The `public` modifier, discussed next, specifies the scope of the `String` class; it specifies which other objects can access it. The `public` and associated modifiers are sometimes called access modifiers; they specify the access for a `class`.

It doesn't make sense for a `class` to be both `final` and `abstract`. When a class is `abstract`, it leaves implementation of certain methods up to its subclasses. However, because a `final` class can't be subclassed, the two can't coexist. The compiler generates an error any time an attempt is made to declare a class as both `abstract` and `final`.

### public

The `public` modifier specifies that a class can be used by objects outside the current package. (See the "Packages" section later in this chapter.) By default, when no access modifier is specified, classes can be used only within the `package` in which they are declared.

For example, the `String` class is declared `public` because other classes and objects outside its package, such as classes and methods in your programs, need to have access to it. Thus, Java's String class is declared as public:

```
public final class String
{
    . . .
}
```

When specifying a class as `public`, you should provide the `public` keyword first in the declaration, as shown here. If your `public` classes also happen to be `final` or `abstract`, be sure these words come after `public`. Although you don't have to follow this convention, doing so will make your class declarations consistent with Sun's and those of your fellow developers.

### extends Superclass

One of the most powerful features of any object-oriented programming (OOP) language is the ability to reuse existing code. In the early days, the push was to accomplish this through inheritance. For instance, rather than writing a class from scratch, you can benefit greatly by inheriting the variables and methods defined in another class that has the basic properties you require. When you do this, you create what's known as a subclass of the original class. The class you inherit from is known as the *superclass*.

For example, in Chapter 8, we talked about java.lang.Number, java.lang.Integer, java.lang.Long, and other associated classes. The class `java.lang.Integer` has a superclass java.lang.Number. The class `java.lang.Number` has abstract methods `intValue()`, `longValue()`, `floatValue()`, and `doubleValue()`. This guarantees that java.lang.Integer will have methods with the same name and signature. The fact that they are abstract in the parent class (that is, the superclass) means that java.lang.Integer will have to implement the methods if they are to do anything. The declarations for the two classes are:

```
public abstract class Number
{
...
}
```

and

```
public final class Integer extends Number
{
...
}
```

Notice that Number is an abstract class, while Integer is both public and final and it has Number as a superclass (since it extends Number).

In Java, all classes are descendants of the Object class. The Object class is at the top of the inheritance tree, or class hierarchy. Every other class, either directly or indirectly, subclasses the Object class. Even those classes at the bottom of the hierarchy are descendants of the Object class; they subclass any class that, through a long chain of subclasses, can eventually be traced back to the top of the tree.

This might not seem right. After all, we've seen classes that don't use the word extends in their declaration. Any class that doesn't explicitly use the word extends in its declaration is assumed to have Object as its superclass. In other words, we could rewrite the Number declaration as:

```
public abstract class Number extends Object
{
...
}
```

As you now know, almost any class can be subclassed as long as it's not specified as final. The process of subclassing is a natural and powerful feature of Java, allowing your classes to inherit functionality that you would otherwise have to write yourself.

To inherit properties from an existing class, that class must be explicitly specified using the extends keyword. In Java parlance, our subclass is said to "extend a superclass." As you've seen in earlier chapters, our applet version of "Hello World!" inherited a great deal of functionality by simply extending the Applet class:

```
public class HelloWorldApplet extends java.applet.Applet
{
    ...
}
```

In this case, we specified java.applet.Applet; the Applet `class` is defined in the `java.applet package`. However, if the Applet class wasn't part of a `package`, we would have used the following syntax:

```
public class HelloWorldApplet extends Applet
{
    ...
}
```

In this case, the `Applet class` is expected to reside in the same directory as the HelloWorldApplet `class` itself. Since a `package` wasn't specified (such as java.applet), the Java compiler doesn't have a clue where to look for the superclass. As a result, it expects to find the `class` inside the same directory as the program itself. We'll look at packages more later in this chapter.

## implements Interfaces

In addition to specifying a superclass, you can specify one or more interfaces in your class declaration. An *interface*, discussed in more detail in the section "Interface" later in this chapter, declares a set of constants and methods but doesn't actually implement any of the methods. Similar to an abstract class, an interface requires other classes to provide the implementation for its methods; it does not provide them itself.

However, with an abstract class, only one of the methods in it is required to be abstract. The remaining methods can be fully functional, meaning your class inherits the functionality of all methods except the ones defined as abstract. With an interface, none of the methods are implemented, leaving this responsibility up to the classes that use it.

When a class implements an interface, it must provide implementations for all of the methods declared in that interface. And, unlike the act of subclassing an abstract class, a class can implement any number of interfaces. In other words, Java supports only single inheritance (meaning you can't subclass more than one class), whereas you can implement any number of interfaces.

Some have said that this is your way around Java's prohibition of multiple inheritance. It really is a different animal. Because you are specifying the implementation, you can't create the same problems that arise if you inherit from two classes, each of which implements a method with the same signature in two different ways. In that case, you wouldn't know which method you were invoking in the subclass. When you use more than one interface with the same method and signature, you are providing a single implementation, so there is no confusion. We'll revisit this idea in Chapter 10, "Inheritence, Composition, and Polymorphism."

To implement an interface, declare your class as usual with the keyword implements followed by the name of the interface. The implements clause should come after the extends clause, if one exists, or immediately following the class name otherwise:

```
class Triangle extends MyGraphics implements Brushes
{
```

```
    ...
    // each method declared in Brushes must be implemented here
    ...
}
```

The preceding example illustrates the declaration of a class named `Triangle`, which is a subclass of `MyGraphics`, and implements the `Brushes` interface. Since `Triangle` specifies the use of the `Brushes interface`, it must also override and implement each of the methods declared in that interface.

Following is the same example, this time without explicitly specifying a superclass:

```
class Triangle implements Brushes
{
    ...
    // each method declared in Brushes must be implemented here
    ...
}
```

In this case, `Triangle` is a direct descendant of the `Object class`; it is said to be a subclass of `Object`. However, it specifies the same `interface`, so it must provide the implementation for each of the methods of `Brushes`.

In the case of multiple interfaces, a comma is used to separate the names of the interfaces:

```
class Triangle implements Brushes, Paints, Surfaces
{
    ...
    /* every method in Brushes, Paints, and Surfaces must
       be implemented in Triangle */
    ...
}
```

Just as with a single `interface`, the `Triangle` class must implement the methods of each one it specifies. In this case, `Triangle` must implement all the methods declared in `Brushes`, `Paints`, and `Surfaces`.

## Class body

So far, we've only discussed the class declaration. The body is where the variables and methods of a class are declared and defined, bringing it to life with variables (state) and methods (behavior). We introduced variables and methods in Chapter 7. This time, we will concentrate more on their role as a part of a class.

## Nonmember and Member Variables

In Java classes, there are two kinds of variables:

✦ Nonmember variables: These are not associated with the class (such as local variables used in methods and variables used as parameters for methods).

✦ Member variables: These are directly associated with the class and objects made from it.

The following example will help you see the differences:

```java
public class StayAfterSchool
{
  String whatToWrite;
  int numberOfTimes;

  public StayAfterSchool()
  {
    whatToWrite = "I will not chew gum in class.";
    numberOfTimes = 100;
    writeOnBoard( whatToWrite, numberOfTimes );
  }
  public void writeOnBoard( String s, int i )
  {
    for( int count = 0; count < i; count++)
    {
      System.out.println(s);
    }
  }

  public static void main( String[] args )
  {
      new StayAfterSchool();
  }
}
```

### Nonmember variables

Variables that are part of a method parameter list or that are declared inside a class method are not considered member variables. Although they may be critical to the object, they aren't considered part of the object's formal state. In our previous example, the variables s and i pass information that is needed for the output (printing "I will not chew gum in class" one hundred times), but the variables are not part of what a StayAfterSchool class is or knows. Similarly, we need the count variable to iterate through the for loop, but it is not part of what a StayAfterSchool class is or knows.

### Member variables

All member variables are declared within the body of the class, not inside a method or as a parameter to a method. In our example, the member variables are whatTo Write and numberOfTimes. Member variables come in two flavors:

✦ Class variables

✦ Instance variables

The variables whatToWrite and numberOfTimes are instance variables. They belong to a specific object. You can imagine that we might have more than one child being punished. Maybe we'd like to keep track of the number being punished. If we use instance variables, we can assign the first child the number 1, the second 2, and so on. But really, we just want to know the total. We create a class variable called numberPunished. You can tell that it is a class variable because it has the keyword static. A class variable belongs to the class but can be accessed through any instantiation of that class.

Our revised version of the code shows three students being punished. You now have to pass the information of what the student is writing and how many times, so we have rewritten the constructor.

```java
public class StayAfterSchool
{
  String whatToWrite;
  int numberOfTimes;
  static int numberPunished;

  public StayAfterSchool(String writeThis, int thisManyTimes)
  {
    numberPunished++;
    whatToWrite = writeThis;
    numberOfTimes = thisManyTimes;
    writeOnBoard( whatToWrite, numberOfTimes );
  }
  public void writeOnBoard( String s, int i )
  {
    for( int count = 0; count < i; count++)
    {
      System.out.println(s);
    }
  }

  public static void main( String[] args )
  {
      new StayAfterSchool("I won't chew gum.", 100);
      new StayAfterSchool("I won't run in the hall.", 50);
      new StayAfterSchool("I won't barf in my desk.", 25);
      System.out.println("There are " + numberPunished +
        " students being punished.");
  }
}
```

This code will output "I won't chew gum." one hundred times, followed by "I won't run in the hall." fifty times, followed by "I won't barf in my desk." twenty-five time, followed by "There are 3 students being punished."

## Member Variable Declarations

In Chapter 7, we looked at the various types of variables that we could define. Here is a summary of the possible member variable declarations (items in square brackets are optional):

```
[accessSpecifier] [static] [final] [transient] [volatile] type variablename
```

Let's look at each part of the variable declaration.

### accessSpecifier

Java supports five levels of access for variables and methods. The keywords are

- ✦ `private`: Access is only allowed from within the same class. The standard Java practice is that instance variables should be private (only a class or object is able to manipulate its state). Access to these private variables is usually provided by `public` methods.

- ✦ `protected`: Access is allowed from within the package containing the class where this element is declared. Access is also allowed from subclasses that are in separate packages.

- ✦ `public`: Access is allowed for anything that can get to our class. If you can find it, you can use it.

- ✦    : Access is allowed only from within the package containing the class. Notice there is no keyword for this. It is often referred to as *friendly* and is the default behavior if there is no explicit access specifier.

### static

We have already seen an example of the keyword `static`, which specifies that a variable is either a class variable or an instance variable. Let's focus, for a minute, on the difference between class variables and instance variables.

*Class variables* occur only once per class, no matter how many instances of that class are created. Memory for class variables is allocated by the Java runtime system the first time a class is encountered, and only then.

In contrast, *instance variables* are allocated once for every instance of a class. Whenever an instance of a class is created, the system allocates memory for all instance variables in that class. In essence, class variables are shared by all instances of a class while each object gets its own copy of instance variables.

Class variables are distinguished from instance variables by the keyword `static`, as the following example illustrates:

```
class Bogus
{
   static int myClassVar; // declare class variable of type int
   int myInstanceVar; // declare instance variable of type int
   ...
   /* Method Declarations would follow... */
   ...
}
```

When the keyword `static` precedes the data type in a variable declaration, that variable becomes a class variable. In this example, memory for `myClassVar` is allocated only once, regardless of how many instances of class `Bogus` are created. In contrast, `myInstanceVar` is created anew each time an instance of `Bogus` is created.

As a result, the variable `myClassVar` is the same, no matter what object of type `Bogus` accesses it. For example, suppose the value 3 were stored in `myClassVar`. Every time this variable was retrieved, regardless of when or how, it would contain 3 in all cases (at least until a value other than 3 was stored in it). When a class variable is altered (that is, changing `myClassVar` to 15), all instances of that class see the change. All instances of a particular class share the same class variables.

Since all the instances of a particular class share the `static` variables that are declared in that class, these variables can be referenced directly without requiring that an object first be instantiated. For example, to access the `static` variable declared in our `Bogus` class, you can simply do the following:

```
int i = Bogus.myClassVar; // set i equal to the class variable
```

As you can see, you've accessed the class variable directly and assigned it to `i` without first having to instantiate a `Bogus` object using the `new` operator. While this may seem new to you, in truth, you've been dealing with class variables all along. Remember outputting data via `System.out.println()`? Since `out` is a `static` variable declared in the `System class`, you don't have to bother creating an instance of that class before accessing this variable. Instead, you conveniently access the `out` class variable directly.

In contrast, because a new `myInstanceVar` variable is created with each instantiation, each `Bogus` object has its own copy. This means the value of `myInstanceVar` is different from object to object; each has its own copy of the variable, unlike `myClassVar`, which is shared by all. You have to access an instance variable through an instance of the class:

```
Bogus freshBogus = new Bogus(); // create an instance of Bogus
                    // set i equal to an instance variable:
int i = freshBogus.myInstanceVar;
```

Here, we've created a `Bogus` object, through which we access the instance variable `myInstanceVar`. In this case, the instance variable was available directly. In some cases, however, instance variables may be declared `private`. If this is the case, the only way to access them is through an object's methods. Such data hiding is vital to an object-oriented language such as Java, as it prevents direct access to the internal representation of an object and enforces a "black box" approach to software development.

### final

Regardless of whether a variable is a class or instance variable, it can also be declared as `final`. A variable that has been declared as `final` can never be changed once a value is assigned to it. You can think of `final` variables as `constants`: Once they're set, they can't be altered. As such, they can be used like #define statements are in C/C++. (Remember, Java doesn't support #define statements.) Attempting to alter the value of a `final` variable is illegal and invokes an error message from the compiler.

By convention, constant names in Java are spelled in all capital letters. If the name contains more than one word, they are linked by an underscore. Thus, you might declare the value of pi or a person's normal body temperature using constants as follows:

```
final double PI = 3.14159265359;
final double NORMAL_BODY_TEMPERATURE = 98.6;
```

Class variables are often used to declare constants that all objects of that class will share. It's more efficient to use a `static` (class) variable than an instance variable in this case; memory is allocated only once. To declare a class variable as a constant, simply precede the `static` keyword with `final` (by convention, Java constant names are uppercase):

```
final static double PI = 3.14159265359;E
```

Note that finals can be declared without being initialized. Once they are assigned a value, though, they cannot be changed. This allows you to now create calculated constants, which cannot be changed once they have been assigned a value.

### transient

Transient is meant to specify variables that are not part of the persistent state of the class. When you serialize an object, you want to record information that includes its current and persistent state. Variables that have the `transient` keyword will not be serialized with the object.

### volatile

Volatile specifies a variable whose value is vulnerable to thread access. It is read from memory each time it is used and stored to memory after each occasion, to ensure data integrity. You cannot declare a variable to be both `final` and `volatile`. When you read Chapter 14, "Threads," you'll learn more about `volatile` when you study threads.

## Setting and Retrieving Member Variables

As you know, your member variables can be retrieved and set directly, using the dot notation:

```
Bogus freshBogus = new Bogus(); // create an instance of Bogus
freshBogus.myInstanceVar = 1827; /* set variable using dot
                                    notation */
int i = freshBogus.myInstanceVar; // get using dot notation
```

Or you can set and retrieve variables using methods defined for doing just that:

```
Bogus freshBogus = new Bogus(); // create an instance of Bogus
freshBogus.setIt(1827); // set variable using setIt() method
int i = freshBogus.getIt(); // retrieve using getIt() method
```

Of course, the preceding example assumes that the two methods, `setIt()` and `getIt()`, are defined in the body of the `Bogus` class, for the purpose of setting and retrieving the `myInstanceVar` variable. The only way to know if a method exists for setting or retrieving an object's value is to read the documentation or source code of the class.

## Setting and Retrieving Class Variables

In the previous examples, the class's instance variable was accessed. This is apparent by looking at the name of the variable (`myInstance`), and, more importantly, by the fact that we had to instantiate a `Bogus` object to get to the instance variable. In the case of class variables, however, we don't have to bother creating an object:

```
Bogus.myClassVar = 111791; // set class variable w/o
// instantiation
int i = Bogus.myClassVar; // retrieve w/o instantiation
```

As you can see, we can get and set a class variable without bothering to instantiate an object. However, we can also access class variables through objects, just as we do instance variables:

```
Bogus freshBogus = new Bogus(); // create an instance of Bogus
  // set class variable using dot notation:
freshBogus.myClassVar = 111791;
int i = freshBogus.myClassVar; // retrieve using dot notation
  // set variable using setClassVar() method:
freshBogus.setClassVar(111791);
  // retrieve using getClassVar() method:
int i = freshBogus.getClassVar();
```

If you access class variables through an object, as shown here, you'll get the same results as if you accessed them directly with the class name and dot notation, as illustrated in the first example. To make your programs easier to read and less confusing ("Am I dealing with a class or instance variable here?"), it's a good idea to avoid accessing class variables through objects.

## Variable Scope

Member variables can be referenced anywhere in the body of your class, even inside methods, as shown in Chapter 7. As you may remember, however, a member variable is "hidden" when a variable of the same name is declared inside a method. For details on variable scope, refer to Chapter 7.

### Reusing variable names as arguments and the this keyword

Recall our StayAfterSchool code. We had a String named whatToWrite which held a reference to the String that we had to output a numberOfTimes. We set its value by passing it to the StayAfterSchool() constructor where it was referred to as writeThis. After whatToWrite was set equal to writeThis, the String was passed into the writeOnBoard() method where it was referred to as s:

```
public class StayAfterSchool
{
  String whatToWrite;
  int numberOfTimes;

  public StayAfterSchool( String writeThis, int soManyTimes)
  {
    whatToWrite = writeThis;
    numberOfTimes = thisManyTimes;
    writeOnBoard( whatToWrite, numberOfTimes );
  }
  public void writeOnBoard( String s, int i )
  {
    for( int count = 0; count < i; count++)
    {
      System.out.println(s);
    }
  }

  public static void main( String[] args )
  {
      new StayAfterSchool("I won't chew gum.", 100);
  }
}
```

It might seem a bit confusing that this same String is being called by different names. It's kind of like when you drop your sister off at your mother's house. She's your sister. Your daughters and sons know her as their aunt. Your mother knows her as her daughter.

That might make you understand why it makes sense to call the same String by different names. But what if you wanted to call it by the same name? Really, you, your mother, and your daughters and sons call your sister by her first name.

Why can't you just call the String inside of the constructor whatToWrite? The answer is that you can — but then there are two whatToWrite variables. One is a local variable inside of the constructor and the other belongs to the object. How do you talk to the one that belongs to the object from inside the constructor? What you'd like to do is use the dot notation, but you don't know the name of the object. You do know that the object we're talking about is the one to which the constructor belongs. In other words, as far as the constructor is concerned, you are talking about this current instantiation of the class.

That is the point of the keyword this. It enables you to refer to this instance of the class. You can then rewrite the previous code as follows:

```
public class StayAfterSchool
{
  String whatToWrite;
  int numberOfTimes;

  public StayAfterSchool( String whatToWrite, int
numberOfTimes)
  {
    this.whatToWrite = writeThis;
    this.numberOfTimes = thisManyTimes;
    writeOnBoard();
  }
  public void writeOnBoard()
  {
    for( int count = 0; count < numberOfTimes; count++)
    {
      System.out.println(whatToWrite);
    }
  }

  public static void main( String[] args )
  {
      new StayAfterSchool("I won't chew gum.", 100);
  }
}
```

Notice that we've also changed the writeOnBoard() method to not take any arguments. In the body of the writeOnBoard() method, the whatToWrite variable is not hidden by any local variable, so you don't need to use this.whatToWrite, although it wouldn't be wrong.

### Shadowed variables and the super keyword

An interesting situation, known as variable shadowing, occurs when a subclass declares a member variable having the same name as a member variable in its superclass. As you might recall, this situation is known as overriding if methods are involved; when you're dealing with variables, it's called shadowing.

Remember the `Bogus` class:

```
class Bogus
{
  static int myClassVar;
  int myInstanceVar;
  ...
}
```

Consider, if you will, the following class declaration, which subclasses the `Bogus` class:

```
class UltraBogus extends Bogus
{
  double myInstanceVar; /* shadows myInstanceVar in
                           class Bogus */
  int    good, bad, ugly; // UltraBogus instance variables
}
```

As you can see, although a `myInstanceVar` variable is declared in `UltraBogus`, it is not of the same data type as the one in `Bogus`. (This is a `double`, whereas `Bogus` declared an `int`.) Nonetheless, it shadows the `myInstanceVar` variable declared in `Bogus`.

Any reference to `myInstanceVar` in the context of `UltraBogus` (whether in the class body or through an object) refers to the one declared in `UltraBogus`. After all, how would Java know which one you're talking about unless it automatically uses one or the other? It wouldn't, so it chooses the variable declared in the subclass over the one in the superclass. To access the `Bogus` variable of the same name, you have to use the `super` keyword.

The Java variable `super` refers to the parent class, or superclass, of an object. It is useful in many cases to use `super` to invoke methods in an object's parent class. It is also helpful when you need to access a member variable in a superclass that has been shadowed by a variable in the subclass.

## Declaring Methods

A method declaration has many optional parts. In the following method declaration summary, each of the items in square brackets is optional:

```
[accessSpecifier] [static] [abstract] [final] [native]
[synchronized] returnValue methodname ([paramlist]) [throws
exceptionsList]
```

At a minimum, a method declaration must include a return type and a name for the method. We looked at this `returnValue` and parameter list in Chapter 7. Recall that when a return type is specified in the method declaration, a value of that data type must be returned. Also, you can overload a method by using the same name with different numbers and types of parameters.

Beyond that, each option allows you to control how your method will act and to what extent it may be used. The access specifier was discussed in the previous section on variables. The keywords `static`, `abstract`, and `final` were also described previously. The keyword `throws` means that the method can create an exception. These are described in Chapter 11, "Exceptions and Error Handling."

## Method Constructors

We looked at constructors in Chapter 7, but there are a few more points to discuss here. The first is to note that your constructor does not return anything but you do not use the keyword `void` as a return type. This is an easy mistake to miss when you are debugging code. You can see that your constructor isn't being called and yet everything about it looks right. The number of arguments matches; it is set up to create objects in just the right way. Check to make sure you don't have `void` before the name of the method.

Java could throw an exception if you had any method other than a constructor with the same name as the class. This would quickly point you in the direction of what needs to be fixed. It is not part of the Java implementation.

Just as with regular methods, constructors can be overloaded. You can create as many constructors as needed, provided they each have a unique parameter list. And if you ever need to invoke one constructor from within another, you can do so using the `this` variable.

Let's consider the `StayAfterSchool` class again. If no `String` is specified, then you could just have the student write "I will not do that again." If no `String` or `int` is specified, then you could have the student write that phrase 100 times. You do this by having one constructor call another one using the `this` variable.

```
public class StayAfterSchool
{
  String whatToWrite;
  int numberOfTimes;

public StayAfterSchool( String whatToWrite, int
  numberOfTimes) //constructor 1
  {
    this.whatToWrite = writeThis;
    this.numberOfTimes = thisManyTimes;
    writeOnBoard();
  }
  public StayAfterSchool( int numberOfTimes )
  {                            //constructor 2
    this( "I will not do that again.", numberOfTimes );
  }
```

```
public StayAfterSchool() //constructor 3
{
  this( 100 );
}

public void writeOnBoard()
{
  for( int count = 0; count < numberOfTimes; count++)
  {
    System.out.println(whatToWrite);
  }
}

public static void main( String[] args )
{
    new StayAfterSchool();
}
}
```

Here the output is "I will not do that again." written one hundred times. The call to `new StayAfterSchool()` results in constructor 3 being called. This in turn calls `this( 100 )`, which looks for a constructor taking an `int` as its only input. That means that constructor 2 is called. This in turn calls `this("I will not do that again.", 100 )`, which looks for a constructor taking a `String` and an `int`, so constructor 1 is called.

Like with standard methods, you can invoke a constructor in the class's superclass using the `super` keyword. Often you have a subclass that has more functionality than its superclass. This means that the subclass's constructor might first want to call the superclass constructor and then perform more tasks. For example, a sketch of the code is:

```
public class aSubClass extends a SuperClass
{
  public aSubClass()
  {
  super();
  aSubClass.doSomething();
  aSubClass.doSomethingElse();
  }
  ...
}
```

## The finalize() Method

While a constructor method initializes an object, a `finalize()` method may be created that is used to help optimize the disposing of an object. It is called just before Java's automatic garbage collection mechanism reclaims an unused object, allowing your object to close any files or streams it has opened, and perform similar house-keeping tasks:

```
finalize()
{
    ...
}
```

When an object is no longer used, meaning there are no longer references to it, it is marked for garbage collection. Unfortunately, you have no guarantee of exactly when an object will be garbage collected or if your finalize() method will ever be called. As a result, you should use a finalize() method only to optimize the disposing of your object. But you should never depend on it to be executed, and your programs should never rely on it to work properly. It's interesting to note that you can manually invoke an object's finalize() method just as you would call any other method. However, calling this method does not force garbage collection for that object. Instead, you can force garbage collection for the entire program using this System method:

```
System.gc();
```

You can also invoke the finalize() method for all recently released objects by calling this System method:

```
System.runFinalization();
```

These methods are particularly useful if a Java program is being run with the garbage collector disabled. This is done by invoking an application at the command line with the -noasynchgc flag, as follows:

```
C:\> java -noasynchgc ProgramName
```

# Inner Classes

Inner classes are primarily used for defining simple helper classes, which are intended to be used for a specific function in a particular place in a Java program. Inner classes are not for use as top-level, general-purpose classes. With inner classes, you can define these specific-use classes right where they are utilized — helping to make your application more understandable.

One of the most common places to find inner classes is when you are working with event handling for graphical user interfaces (GUIs), as you will see in the next part of the book. Although you'll see their power when you get to that part and start constructing event listeners and adapters, we'll just quickly introduce inner classes here. An example to keep in mind is that you may want to put the class responsible for responding to a button being pressed inside the component on which the button sits. It will turn out that not only are inner classes the right way to handle this situation, but your instance of the class doesn't even need a name. It is called an anonymous inner class.

There are four different types of inner classes: nested top-level classes, member classes, local classes, and anonymous classes — which are actually extensions of the local class type. Okay, so that's great.

## Nested top-level classes and interfaces

A *nested class* is just what it sounds like — a class within another class. Nested top-level classes must be declared as static, and they can be nested only within other top-level classes. You define a nested class like this:

```
public class TopClass
{
  public static class NestedClass
  {
      ...
    }
    ...
}
```

As you can see, you can now define classes within other classes. Why would you want to do this? Well, if the nested class is used only within the top class, defining it as a nested class makes it clear that this is the only place this class is used.

Nested classes can be nested to any depth, which just means that you can keep nesting classes as many times as you want! Don't go too crazy with this capability — nesting your classes too deep can make your code nearly impossible to understand. The best recommendation is to nest classes only one level deep, unless you have a compelling reason to do otherwise.

## Member classes

Nested classes are defined within top-level classes. Because they are essentially static classes, however, they really aren't any different from top-level classes. *Member classes* are different though, because they aren't declared as static. Member classes are truly members of the containing class; they are defined in the same manner as nested classes, except the static option is omitted. Member classes can be defined as public, protected, or private.

One of the nicest features is that methods of a member class can access the fields or methods of enclosing classes — even private fields and methods. Without inner classes, you have to "introduce" the two classes to each other. The restrictions on member classes are that they cannot have the same name as any containing class or package, and they cannot contain any static fields, members, or classes.

## Local classes

Local classes are classes defined within a block of code. They are visible only within the block of code in which they are defined. Local classes are analogous to local variables — they are defined just where they are used. There are two important features of local classes:

✦ They are visible only in the block of code where they have been defined.

✦ They can use any final local variable or method parameters in the block of code where they are defined.

A local class is defined as follows:

```
public class TopClass
{
  public void methodA
  {
    class LocalClass
    {
      ...
    }
    ...
  }
  ...
}
```

This is a trivial example of a local class with the class bodies omitted for simplicity. As illustrated in this example, the LocalClass class is visible only within the methodA() method. LocalClass can access any methods and fields of the TopClass class.

Like member classes, local classes cannot contain any static fields, methods, or classes.

## Anonymous classes

The last type of inner classes are anonymous classes — a special case of local classes. The main difference between local and anonymous classes is that anonymous classes don't have any name. So, how can a class without a name be useful and used? Let's take a closer look at how an anonymous class is defined:

```
class A
{
  AnonymousClass method1
  {
    return new AnonymousClass()
    {
      int i = 0;
      public int increment() { return(i++); }
```

```
    public int decrement() { return(i--); }
  }
 }
}
```

In this example, method1 creates and returns the anonymous class — Anonymous Class. Anonymous classes are created by calling a class body definition after the new command. In this case, an anonymous class is created that defines two methods, increment() and decrement().

Another important feature of anonymous classes is their use as instance initializers, which are similar to static initializers found in the 1.0 JDK. An instance initializer is simply a block of code that is embedded inside a class definition. Here is an example of an instance initializer:

```
class A
{   // Example of an instance initializer...
  int[] array1 = new int[5];
  {
    for(int i=0; i<5; i++)
      array1[i] = i * 100;
  }
}
```

Instance initializers are executed in the order they appear. They are run after any superclass constructors, but before the constructor of the current class.

When should you use an anonymous class over a local class? Well, if your class fits any of these descriptions, it might be appropriate:

✦ Only one instance of the class is ever used.

✦ The class is used immediately after it's defined.

✦ The class is small. (Sun recommends four lines or fewer.)

✦ Naming the class doesn't make your code easier to understand.

There are four important restrictions to keep in mind when you're using anonymous classes:

✦ Anonymous classes can't have constructors.

✦ Anonymous classes cannot define any static fields, methods, or classes.

✦ Anonymous classes cannot be public, private, protected, or static.

✦ You can only ever create one instance of an anonymous class.

You have used classes anonymously already (but not inner classes). For example, you could rewrite our `StayAfterSchool` program so that what is written and how many times it is to be written are passed in as command-line arguments:

```java
public class StayAfterSchool
{
  String whatToWrite;
  int numberOfTimes;

public StayAfterSchool()
  {
    whatToWrite = args[0];
    numberOfTimes = new Integer( args[1] ).intValue();
    writeOnBoard();
  }

  public void writeOnBoard()
  {
    for( int count = 0; count < numberOfTimes; count++)
    {
      System.out.println(whatToWrite);
    }
  }

  public static void main( String[] args )
  {
      new StayAfterSchool();
  }
}
```

The user would run the program by typing:

```java
java StayAfterSchool "I won't run in the halls", 140
```

Look at the line where `numberOfTimes` is initialized. As you learned in Chapter 8, "Creating and using Arrays and Strings," you can create a `new Integer` object from the `String` corresponding to the second argument. You then extract its integer value using the `intValue()` method. The variable `numberOfTimes` points to the `int`. There is no variable that points to the `Integer` object. It can't be accessed again. It was used for a single purpose and is now discarded. It was an anonymous object.

# Interfaces

By this point in the chapter, you're probably pretty comfortable with the concept of an interface. After all, you've seen how to declare interfaces in a class using the `implements` keyword. And you've seen how to declare abstract classes and abstract methods, which are similar in nature to an interface.

One of the big ideals in Java is that you program to an interface and not to the implementation. That use of the word interface is the same as the I in GUI. It's what you see and interact with. When you use an Automated Teller Machine and press the keys that instruct it to give you $50, you don't really care how they are coming up with and dispensing the money. It could be a robot dealing twenties and tens off of a deck of bills, or it could be a monkey running around finding the money on the floor. All you can see is the interface. You press some buttons to tell the machine that you want the money and it dispenses money to you through some slot.

The concept of a Java interface is completely consistent with this idea. It is a way of specifying how a user will interact with any class that implements this interface. It promises that certain methods will be available and yet it leaves their implementation for a later day. It also provides appropriate constants (`public`, `static`, and `final` variables).

You could view an interface as an entirely abstract class; not a single method declared in an interface can be implemented by the interface. All methods in an interface must be implemented by the class that implements them.

Here is the syntax for declaring an interface (items in square brackets are optional):

```
[public] interface name [extends interface1, interface2, ...]
{
   ...
}
```

As you can see, an interface can extend any number of other interfaces. And, if you recall, a class can extend any number of interfaces. In an interface, all variables are automatically treated as `public`, `static`, and `final`. You can explicitly specify each, if you want, but it really doesn't matter. If you were to specify a variable as `protected`, for instance, the compiler would generate an error.

The same is true for an interface's methods, which are automatically treated as `public` and `abstract`. You can explicitly declare your interface methods as `public` and `abstract`, but it really doesn't matter since the system will do it for you automatically. Consider for a moment a `ShowDown` interface:

```
public interface ShowDown
{
   int SHERIFF = 60000; // all variables are public, static, &
                        //        final
   void Encounter();  // all methods are public and abstract
   void SizeUp(int dude); //  all methods are public & abstract
}
```

You'll notice that we didn't bother to declare the constant variable `SHERIFF` as being `final` and `static` because it's automatically treated as `public`, `static`, and `final` when implemented as an `interface`. The same goes for `ShowDown`'s methods. There's no need to declare them as `public` because they already are when implemented as an `interface`. And since each method is also `abstract`, we're relying on the subclass to do the implementation — don't even bother with the body of methods declared in an interface.

We only need to provide the name and parameter list of interface methods. The curly braces ({ }) of the body block aren't even needed. In fact, if you included them, the compiler would generate an error, regardless of whether you actually provided code for the body:

```
void SizeUp(int dude)
{    // illegal! Can't include braces!
}
```

With interfaces, you need to remove the method block entirely and replace it with a semicolon, as follows:

```
void SizeUp(int dude); // this is fine
```

Even though all the variables and methods in an interface are implicitly prefixed with access specifiers and modifiers, the same is not true with the interface declaration itself. If you don't specify your interface as being public, Java doesn't automatically make it public. Instead, the scope of your interface is "friendly," making it available only in the package in which it is created. As a result, you may want to explicitly declare a package for your interfaces. (See the next section, "Packages," for more details.):

```
package numberville; // make part of numberville package
interface ShowDown
{ /* not public; making class available
                    only to the numberville package */
  int SHERIFF = 60000;
  void Encounter();
  void SizeUp(int dude);
}
```

# Packages

After writing a few Java programs and creating a number of classes in the process, you'll probably find yourself wanting to reuse some of the classes in new projects. And this is exactly what you're supposed to do: why rewrite when you can reuse? The answer is that it is a lot harder to write classes that are flexible and powerful enough to reuse than people originally thought. But you will be using yours or other people's work in your code that has been organized into libraries. In fact, you've already been introduced to what Java calls packages.

Packages allow classes to be grouped according to their purpose, much like you might group files inside a directory on your computer's hard disk. In fact, the packaging corresponds to the directory structure. Packages can also contain interfaces, but rather than having to say "classes and interfaces" every time we talk about packages, we'll simply use the term classes, with the understanding that interfaces are implied.

# Using packages

In Chapter 8, we looked at `String`, `StringBuffer`, `Integer`, and other classes that are members of the `java.lang` package. When you begin to introduce GUI elements into your programs, you will need classes in the `java.awt` and `javax.swing` packages.

There are a few ways to access classes that are in packages. The most basic method is to import a package in the beginning of your program files before any other code. (It's okay if they come after comments and white space such as character returns and linefeeds.):

```
import java.applet.*;
import java.awt.*;
import java.net.URL;
import java.net.MalformedURLException;
public class YourClass
{
   ...
}
```

As you can see, we have imported four packages (or, more precisely, the public classes of four packages) using two different techniques. In the first two lines of code, we used the asterisk (*) to effectively tell the compiler to "Give me access to all of the public classes in this package":

```
import java.applet.*; // import all public classes in
                      // java.applet package
   import java.awt.*;   // import all public classes in
   // java.awt package
```

In the second two lines, we explicitly state the name of the `public` classes to import:

```
   // import URL class in the java.net package:
import java.net.URL;
// import MalformedURLException class in the java.net
//package:
import java.net.MalformedURLException;
```

You can only import the public classes in a package, and only those public classes that are directly part of that package. You can't, for example, import the `java.awt` sub-packages, `java.awt.image` and `java.awt.peer`, using the following import statement:

```
import java.awt.*; // import public classes in java.awt,
                   // but not subpackages!
```

This is initially confusing because you think that this `import` statement means `import` any public package whose name begins with `java.awt`. This example imports only the public classes that are directly part of the `java.awt` package. If you want to import the classes in a subpackage, you have to specify each subpackage explicitly:

```
import java.awt.image.*;  // import public classes in
   // image subpackage of java.awt
import java.awt.peer.*;   // import public classes in peer
   // subpackage of java.awt
```

It may be easier to think of this in terms of the corresponding directory structure. There is a directory called `java` inside of which is a directory named `awt`. This directory contains some `public` classes. Those classes are available when you specify `import java.awt.*`. This directory also includes other directories such as `image` and `peer`. The command `import java.awt.*` does not make the contents of `java.awt`'s subdirectories available. You must specifically specify them using the `import java.awt.image.*` and `import java.awt.peer.*` commands.

In our example, we could just as easily have used the asterisk to import all the classes in the `java.net` package, instead of specifying the specific classes, as we just did:

```
import java.net.*; // import all public classes in the
// entire java.net package
```

Although you might initially think this is excessive, since we only use the URL and `MalformedURLException` classes, it's really not. Even though it seems that the entire `java.net` class is imported, in truth, only those classes that are used in the program are imported; Java links in classes only when they are actually used. There used to be arguments about efficiency regarding whether to use the asterisk (*) to import a single class within a package. Now the argument is more a matter of programming style.

Note that we could have used asterisk notation to import all public classes in the `java.net` package (import java.net.*); we explicitly specified the URL and `Malformed URLException` classes to make it clear to the reader of this program what portions of the `java.net` package are used. In general, it's better programming style to explicitly import the classes you use in a program (as we've done with URL and `MalformedURL Exception`) rather than using the asterisk approach. Clearly identifying the classes you import in this way makes it much easier for others to maintain your code; they won't have to search through your program to find out which classes in a package you use.

Any time you want to use a class, you need to import the package it is part of (or reference it explicitly in your code, as described shortly). You know from your experience in Chapter 8 that this isn't always true. There, we used `String` and `StringBuffer` without importing anything. You don't need to import the `java. lang` package; these classes are fundamental to Java and are automatically imported regardless of whether you explicitly import them or not.

# Explicit class references in imported packages

Once a package has been imported, the public classes in it can be used as often as desired in your code. This is all well and good, but what if you need to use a class only once? In this case, you can explicitly reference the class, without having to import the package it is part of. For example, suppose you didn't want to bother importing the URL class in our earlier example. If you precede all references to URL with the java.net package, you wouldn't have to:

```
java.net.URL imageURL=null; /* explicitly reference to declare
variable...*/
try
{
  imageURL = new java.net.URL(imageString); /* and once again
in the code*/
}
catch (MalformedURLException e) { ; }
```

Since you've explicitly specified the java.net package immediately before the URL class name, Java knows exactly what package the URL class is part of. And, as a result, we don't have to import the java.net package at all. Contrast the preceding code snippet with how it was written originally:

```
import java.net.URL;  // import the URL class
URL  imageURL=null;
try
{
  imageURL = new URL(imageString);
}
catch (MalformedURLException c) [ ; }
```

If it weren't for the fact that the URL class name is pretty descriptive, we wouldn't have any idea where it comes from just looking at the implementation: you can't tell that URL is part of the java.net package by merely looking at the code. This is a downside to importing packages; you can't easily see where a class is coming from by looking at the code alone. Instead, you have to have an understanding of what classes are in each package and make an educated guess whenever a class name appears in code.

Unless you have a large number of references to a particular class in a program, it's often more helpful to precede the class with its package rather than import that package. However, there is a tradeoff between readability and ease of coding. It's much easier to simply type **URL** than it is to type **java.net.URL**. As result, you may prefer to import packages, rather than reference them explicitly.

## Naming conflicts

One of the main benefits of explicitly referencing packages, apart from the clarity of code produced as a result, is the fact that class names won't conflict, as they could when using an `import` statement. At some point, you're going to create a class with the same name as one that exists in another class. For example, how many understandable yet unique identifiers can you come up with for a `Sort` class?

Suppose, for a moment, that your `Sort` class is part of a package called `utility Package`. Now, what if you imported that package and another one that also happens to have a class named `Sort`?

```
import utilityPackage; // contains your Sort class
import anyOtherPackage; // also contains a Sort class
Sort mySort = new Sort(); // which Sort class is
// instantiated?
```

As you can see, you've got a problem here. Which `Sort` class is instantiated when this code is executed? Since that can't be determined, the compiler kicks out an error and refuses to compile the code. You can avoid this, however, by using an explicit class reference directly in the code:

```
utilityPackage.Sort mySort = new utilityPackage.Sort();
```

Here we resolved any potential conflict by explicitly declaring the `package` name along with the class. There will be no confusion to a person reading your code, or when the compiler tries to create a `Sort` object. It's clear just by looking at the code that the object we're talking about comes from `utilityPackage`.

Package names are arranged in levels, with each level separated from the next with a period. Consider, for example, the `java.applet` package. It's comprised of two levels: the first level is `java` and the second is `applet`. The `java.awt.image` package, on the other hand, is made up of three levels, with `image` being the third level.

When you create your own packages, it's up to you to decide on the names and number of levels. Just remember that packages are directly related to the directory structure containing the classes they're composed of — when you create your own packages, you do so based on the directory layout containing the classes to be included in these packages.

## Creating packages

It's easy to create your own packages, something you'll almost certainly want to do at some time or another. To create a package (that is, to add a class to a package), simply use the following statement as the first line of code in your source code file:

```
package packageName;
```

Suppose, for example, you wanted to create a new package called `punishment` to organize all the classes that might be used to dole out punishment. We could easily do this by placing the following statement in every class file that we wanted to be part of the package:

```
package punishment;
```

Be sure to place your package statements first, before all other statements in your program. A `package` statement should come before all other code, including `import` statements.

For instance, the file StayAfterSchool.java would be inside of the punishment directory and it would look like this:

```
package punishment; // StayAfterSchool becomes part of the
                    // punishment package
public class StayAfterSchool
{
   ...
}
```

Now, whenever you need to use the `StayAfterSchool` class, you need only import the `punishment` package or explicitly specify it when creating a `StayAfterSchool` object. Furthermore, you could continue to create classes and easily add them to the `punishment` package using only one line of code: `package punishment`.

Once you specify that `StayAfterSchool` is part of the `punishment` package, you won't be able to run it from within the `punishment` directory. You need to be outside of the `punishment` directory so that the VM can see the class `StayAfterSchool` inside of the package `punishment`.

# Summary

This chapter introduced the concept of creating and using objects in your Java applications. This is the final big puzzle piece required to start developing your own Java applications. The upcoming chapters will continue to take a closer look at fundamentals required to develop your own Java applications. Key concepts to remember about this chapter include the following:

✦ Classes are templates, or blueprints, from which objects are created. As such, we often think of classes as data types. When objects are created or instantiated from the same class, they are considered to be of the same type. All objects are an instance of a class.

✦ All member variables are declared within the body of the class, not inside a method or as a parameter to a method. They are used to maintain the state of an object.

✦ While variables are used to maintain an object's state, methods provide the behavior. For those of you who are new to object-oriented programming, you can think of a method as a function. However, unlike procedural programming where functions sit out in the open (or, more accurately, are organized into files) to be called on at any point, a method is encapsulated inside the class in which it is defined, along with the variables of that class.

✦ No method declared in an interface can be implemented by the interface. All methods in an interface must be implemented by the class that "implements" them.

✦ Inner classes are introduced to keep a helper class close to what it helps and to provide it with access back to the class that needs it.

✦ To make it easier to reuse code and organize classes, Java supports a mechanism called packages. Packages allow classes to be grouped according to their purpose, much like you might group files inside a directory on your computer's hard disk.

✦ It's easy to create your own packages, something you'll almost certainly want to do at some time or another. To create a package (that is, to add a class to a package), simply use the package statement as the first line of code in your source code file.

✦    ✦    ✦

# Inheritance, Composition, and Polymorphism

**O**ne of the big selling points for object-oriented programming (OOP) is that you can reuse code. The idea is that if you build well-designed, powerful, flexible, and extensible objects, then you will just be assembling software components in the same way that a computer is built by assembling hardware components. It turns out that writing reusable software components is a lot harder than people thought it would be.

Initially, the wisdom was that inheritance was the best way to reuse your work. The idea was that a subclass would just extend the functionality of a superclass with very little tweaking. However, the features that make this setup desirable also create problems for you. The behavior of subclasses is tied to superclasses and their superclasses and so on, so little changes high up the hierarchy can have large ripple effects.

When Java was first released, much was made of the fact that it didn't support multiple inheritance. The point is that each class can have only one superclass. Early authors pointed to interfaces as a way of doing multiple inheritance in Java. That really isn't the purpose of interfaces. The idea is to abstract the part of the code with whichpeople need to interact . They often don't need to know or understand the implementation of a method.

We'll also look at polymorphism. Some developers draw a line in the sand and say that if you're not using polymorphism, then you aren't really doing object-oriented programming. This is an extreme point of view, but after you've thought about the benefits, you'll probably find yourself incorporating polymorphism many places in your code.

**Tip**    If you haven't downloaded the documentation for the current API's from Sun's Web site (http://java.sun.com/docs), either download or view it online soon. You can get quite a feel for these concepts by looking at classes in the packages from Sun that support them. Look for classes that "extend" a class and/or "implement" an interface. Look at how the methods and fields are listed. You can get a good understanding of how Sun wants you to use the language by looking at how they constructed these libraries.

# Reuse

The goal behind reuse was the following: you put so much effort into creating these objects and methods, why start from scratch each time? Why not find ways to use the classes and methods you have created in other projects or in other places in this project? If you've worked with other people or are fairly self-aware, you know that people tend to establish signatures in the way that they solve problems. They are reusing their experience by tending to use the same tool set on each project. That's not what we're talking about.

By reuse, we mean explicitly using classes you created before with little or no alterations. Imagine that you are a big car manufacturer with many different lines of cars. You may want to use the same engine in two of your different model lines. Rather than go through all the time and expense of having an independent design team work with the same requirements, why not just reuse what you already have? In software, this is more desirable than in building cars. With cars, you are also selling an image and consumers want to believe that there are differences between two given models.

You could, however, imagine an announced partnership. In this partnership, the engineers from model XX and model YY are working together to create a superior engine that will be in the new cars from each company. Here you are designing an engine to be used by two different groups. You've got to take a lot more into account so that you meet the needs of each group. You can see that if there were more groups, this process would become more difficult.

We're asking you to imagine that you have been asked to design an engine that works great in your car and will probably work great in other cars that you haven't even thought about yet. This is a lot harder than just designing the engine for your car.

Designing classes with the intention of reuse is very hard. It does mean, however, that your software will probably be better designed and easier to maintain. Look for high cohesion in your code: your classes and methods should do very specific, easy-to-describe tasks. If you have a `CoffeeMaker` class, then a `pourOneCup()` method is easy to describe and to implement. If the `coffeeMaker` contains at least a cup of coffee, then it should pour one cup of coffee. Similarly, `brewOnePot()` should be a simple method that brews a pot of coffee (perhaps after dumping out the old batch).

This is not to say that your methods must be limited to brewing only a full pot or pouring a single cup. You could have a brewSomeCoffee( int howMuch ) method that brews the amount passed in. You must know, however, whether the number being passed in is the number of ounces or the number of cups. This is an example of being vigilant about the coupling of a method. Make sure that a method knows no more or no less than what it needs to know.

A method called pourManyCups( int howMany ) would naturally take the number of cups it is to pour as its argument. Consider this code:

```
public class CoffeeMaker
{
  private int coffeeRemaining;
  public void pourOneCup()
  {
    if (coffeeRemaining > 0)
    {
      System.out.println( "pouring one cup" );
      coffeeRemaining--; //measured in whole cups
    }
    else System.out.println( "sorry, not enough coffee" );
  }
  public void pourManyCups( int howMany )
  {
    for (int i =  0; i < howMany; i++)
    {
    pourOneCup();
    }
  }
  public void brewThisMuch( int howManyCups )
  {
    cofeeRemaining = howManyCups;
  }
}
```

The pourManyCups() method uses the pourOneCup() method for its functionality. Each method does very little by itself. This is what you are looking for at the class level. The two key ways to build on existing functionality is with inheritance and with composition. We'll also see that it is sometimes best to build on a foundation with no explicit functionality. This sounds nuts for now, but you'll see its power when we discuss interfaces.

Before moving on to inheritance, let's see what happens when we create and pour from a CoffeeMaker using the CoffeeTester class:

```
public class CoffeeTester
{
  CoffeeMaker myCoffeeMaker;

  public static void main( String args[] )
  {
```

```
        CoffeeTester c = new CoffeeTester();
        c.myCoffeeMaker = new CoffeeMaker();
        c.myCoffeeMaker.brewThisMuch( 3 );
        c.myCoffeeMaker.pourManyCups( 5 );
    }
}
```

Here we get the output:

```
pouring one cup
pouring one cup
pouring one cup
sorry, not enough coffee
sorry, not enough coffee
```

# Inheritance

In Chapter 9, we looked at some of the syntax behind inheritance. Now we'll consider how and why you might implement inheritance. The standard rule of thumb is that you look to extend a class through inheritance if it can be said that an object created by the new class has an "*is-a*" relationship with an object created by the original class. For example, a drip coffee maker, an espresso machine, a vacuum coffee pot, a percolator, and a French press are all extensions of a CoffeeMaker. You could say that a drip coffee maker *is a* CoffeeMaker, that an espresso machine *is a* CoffeeMaker, and so on.

## Parent class and subclass

Let's start from our CoffeeMaker. Maybe we would like to create a more polite coffee maker that checks to make sure that it can pour everyone a cup of coffee before it begins to pour coffee. Let's define a class NiceCoffeeMaker that's the same as CoffeeMaker except that it makes sure it has enough coffee for everyone before pouring for anyone:

```
public class NiceCoffeeMaker extends CoffeeMaker
{
  public void pourManyCups( int howMany )
  {
    if ( coffeeRemaining < howMany)
    {
      System.out.println( "Sorry, I'm short by " +
        (howMany - coffeeRemaining) +  " cups." )
    } else
    {
      for (int i =  0; i < howMany; i++)
      {
        pourOneCup();
      }
```

```
      }
    }
}
```

Let's take this out for a drive with CoffeeTester2:

```
public class CoffeeTester2
{
   NiceCoffeeMaker myCoffeeMaker;

   public static void main( String args[] )
   {
     CoffeeTester2 c = new CoffeeTester2();
     c.myCoffeeMaker = new NiceCoffeeMaker();
     c.myCoffeeMaker.brewThisMuch( 3 );
     c.myCoffeeMaker.pourManyCups( 5 );
     System.out.println("\n");
     c.myCoffeeMaker.brewThisMuch( 5 );
     c.myCoffeeMaker.pourManyCups( 3 );
   }
}
```

This time, we are making a NiceCoffeeMaker. We ask it to brew three cups. You'll notice that the NiceCoffeeMaker doesn't have a brewThisMuch() method. Because NiceCoffeeMaker extends CoffeeMaker, it uses CoffeeMaker's brewThisMuch() method. This stores the amount being brewed in the coffeeRemaining variable defined in CoffeeMaker but included in NiceCoffeeMaker. If you had defined a variable coffeeRemaining in the NiceCoffeeMaker class, it would not have been visible from the brewThisMuch method, so the information of how much was brewed would not have been stored in the right variable.

Now when we tell myCoffeeMaker to pour five cups, it uses the pourManyCups() method in the class NiceCoffeeMaker because myCoffeeMaker is a NiceCoffee Maker. To summarize, a method or variable in the derived class that also exists in the superclass with the same signature or type, will override the corresponding method from the superclass. The message is that you keep all of the functionality of the parent class except for those variables or methods that are deliberately overridden. The output generated from running CoffeeTester2 is:

```
Sorry I'm short by 2 cups.

pouring one cup
pouring one cup
pouring one cup
```

Although the implementation of NiceCoffeeMaker's pourManyCups() method is different than that of CoffeeMaker, their interface is exactly the same. In other words, the user calls the functions using the same sorts of parameters and can treat the methods the same, as the output will be consistent.

# Risks of extending or hiding functionality in a subclass

Another use of inheritance is to extend the functionality in the derived class or to override some functionality of the superclass. Let's look quickly at these ideas.

First, to indicate that a class is a subclass, we use the keyword `extends`. The subclass is a special case of the superclass. This means that we know more specifically about its state and behavior and should, perhaps, act accordingly. This may mean that a subclass has functionality that the superclass didn't have. For example, consider the code for `NicerCoffeeMaker`:

```java
public class NicerCoffeeMaker extends CoffeeMaker
{
  public int timeBrewed;
  public void pourManyCups( int howMany )
  {
    if ( coffeeRemaining < howMany)
    {
      System.out.println( "Sorry, I'm short by " +
        (howMany - coffeeRemaining) +  " cups." )
    } else
    {
      for (int i =  0; i < howMany; i++)
      {
        pourOneCup();
      }
    }
  }
  public void isOld(int currentTime)
  {
    if ((currentTime - timeBrewed)> 45 )
    {
      System.out.println("This coffee is too old.");
    }
  }
}
```

Here the `NicerCoffeeMaker` has a way of checking whether the coffee is too old to drink or not. There is no corresponding method in the superclass. Although a `NicerCoffeeMaker` is a `CoffeeMaker`, we can't forget that it's a special type because it has functionality that our other `CoffeeMaker`s don't have.

Again, this is not the same as removing functionality. What if we decide to create a `CoffeeMaker` that makes one cup? It would never need to `pourManyCups()` or brewThisMuch(). We could also insist that every time you want to pourOneCup(), you first have to brew a single cup. The class could look like this:

```
public class OneCupCoffeeMaker extends CoffeeMaker
{
  public void pourManyCups( int whoCares )
  {
  }
  public void brewThisMuch( int soWhat )
  {
  }
  public void pourOneCup()
  {
    super.brewThisMuch( 1 );
    super.pourOneCup();
  }
}
```

We have overridden the pourManyCups() and brewThisMuch() methods. This makes inheritance, in this case, a bit puzzling. We're saying that a OneCupCoffee Maker *is-a* CoffeeMaker but that it doesn't do everything that a CoffeeMaker does. In addition, we have changed the way pourOneCup() works. We have implemented the method using methods in the superclass, which we have explicitly called with the keyword super. We can test it with the code:

```
public class CoffeeTester3
{
   CoffeeMaker myCoffeeMaker;

   public static void main( String args[] )
  {
    CoffeeTester3 c = new CoffeeTester3();
    c.myCoffeeMaker = new OneCupCoffeeMaker();
    c.myCoffeeMaker.pourOneCup();
  }
}
```

The output is:

```
pouring one cup
```

Adding or deleting functionality in subclasses means that the user interacts with and has different expectations of subclasses than of the original class. In some cases, this seems quite natural. After all, you wouldn't expect to be able to brew five cups in a one-cup coffee maker. On the other hand, this might be telling you that inheritance isn't the best solution for your problem.

# The fragile side of inheritance

Inheritance seems like a great idea. You have the basic functionality contained in a superclass and you just customize to your specific needs. Let's think about our CoffeeMaker again. When we extended it to a OneCupCoffeeMaker, we decided that whenever we needed a cup of coffee, we should brew it fresh. It wouldn't be reasonable to have this behavior in a CoffeeMaker, but maybe if there wasn't enough coffee, we want to automatically brew some more.

Let's adapt the pourManyCups() method so that it pours what it can and then brews what is still needed. For this, we would like users to pour coffee using only pourManyCups(). If they just want one cup, we want them to use pourManyCups ( 1 ). This means that we will make pourOneCup() **private.** Here is the modified CoffeeMaker **class:**

```
public class CoffeeMaker //this has been modified
{                        //put in a different folder
  private int coffeeRemaining;
  private void pourOneCup()
  {
      System.out.println( "pouring one cup" );
      coffeeRemaining--; //measured in whole cups
  }
  public void pourManyCups( int howMany )
  {
    if (howMany > coffeeRemaining)
    {
      brewThisMuch( howMany - coffeeRemaining);
    }
    for (int i =  0; i < howMany; i++)
    {
    pourOneCup();
    }
  }
  public void brewThisMuch( int howManyCups )
  {
    cofeeRemaining = howManyCups;
  }
}
```

Maybe we've decided that this makes more sense for a CoffeeMaker, but we have now broken a lot of code. The NiceCoffeeMaker is no longer very nice:

```
public class NiceCoffeeMaker extends CoffeeMaker
{
  public void pourManyCups( int howMany )
  {
    if ( coffeeRemaining < howMany)
    {
      System.out.println( "Sorry, I'm short by " +
```

```
            (howMany - coffeeRemaining) +  " cups." )
      } else
      {
        for (int i =  0; i < howMany; i++)
        {
          pourOneCup();
        }
      }
    }
  }
}
```

First of all, it won't compile. But let's assume for a moment that it will. Suppose that coffeeRemaining = 3 and the user requests five cups. A NiceCoffeeMaker would respond:

```
Sorry I'm short by 2 cups.
```

A CoffeeMaker would brew the additional two cups and pour all five cups.

Now, why won't NiceCoffeeMaker compile? It calls the pourOneCup() method of CoffeeMaker, which is now private and therefore not visible to NiceCoffeeMaker. By making pourOneCup() either public or protected, we can make it visible again. In this case, we can compile the NiceCoffeeMaker but it is no longer the nice one.

You can test for this response by running CoffeeTester and CoffeeTester2 after you have changed the pourOneCup() access to protected.

The point is that even making a small, seemingly minor, change in the parent class broke the subclasses and changed the intent of the hierarchy. Imagine that you have larger, more complicated trees of classes. It becomes harder to trace all of the classes that might depend on the class you are trying to change.

Take a look at the documentation for a class such as JPanel in the swing package of the standard Java2 API. Although we aren't going to cover Swing until later in the book, take a look at which methods it inherits from each level in its hierarchy. JPanel has a great deal of functionality. Some of it is because it is a JPanel. Some of it is because a JPanel is a JComponent and a JComponent has methods that JPanels inherit. But a JComponent is a Container that has methods. This continues up the ladder until you get to the class Object from which all classes in Java originally inherit.

# Polymorphism

Not to start a religious battle, but many people will say that you aren't doing object-oriented programming unless you are using polymorphism. Others will point out that you can use polymorphism without being much of an object-oriented programmer. In any case, polymorphism is a powerful tool that you should add to your arsenal.

This time, we'll start with a less functional `CoffeeMaker` that can only pour one cup. It's all we need for this example. Notice that the `pourOneCup()` method doesn't do anything. That is because we will never call it. We will only call a `pourOneCup()` method for a specific type of coffee maker. In other words, we will only call `pourOneCup()` from a subclass of `CoffeeMaker`.

**Note**    Why would we want to include a method in the parent class that we never plan to use? This is the key to polymorphism. We are leaving a signal that every class that derives from `CoffeeMaker` must have a `pourOneCup` method. We could be more insistent by making the method (and therefore the class) abstract. In that case, subclasses wouldn't compile unless they implemented the method. We will see that another solution is to use interfaces.

So as not to complicate this example with side issues (like having you scurry to remember what an abstract method or class is), we'll just create a class with a method that has an empty body:

```
public class CoffeeMaker
{
  public void pourOneCup(){}
}
```

We will inherit several types of `CoffeeMaker`s from it. There will be a `DripCoffeeMaker`, a `FrenchPress`, and a `VacuumCoffeeMaker`. Let's start with the `DripCoffeeMaker`:

```
public class DripCoffeeMaker extends CoffeeMaker
{
  public void pourOneCup()
  {
    System.out.println("Here's a cup of Drip coffee.");
  }
}
```

We can test this with the following `CoffeeTester` class:

```
public class CoffeeTester
{
  DripCoffeeMaker brewer;

  public static void main( String args[] )
  {
    CoffeeTester c = new CoffeeTester();
    c.brewer = new DripCoffeeMaker();
    c.brewer.pourOneCup();
  }
}
```

The result is this message:

```
Here's a cup of Drip coffee.
```

There's nothing surprising here. This is just one class extending another class. We create an instance of the subclass and ask it to pourOneCup(). All that we've used is the subclass overriding a method in the superclass. Let's look at CoffeeTester2. There is one slight change — but it gets right to the point we're making:

```
public class CoffeeTester2
{
   CoffeeMaker brewer;

   public static void main( String args[] )
   {
     CoffeeTester2 c = new CoffeeTester2();
     c.brewer = new DripCoffeeMaker();
     c.brewer.pourOneCup();
   }
}
```

Surprisingly, the result is still displaying this message:

```
Here's a cup of Drip coffee.
```

In this version, the brewer is of type CoffeeMaker, even though it is created using the constructor for DripCoffeeMaker. This is possible because a DripCoffeeMaker *is-a* CoffeeMaker. What we're saying is that we will make a DripCoffeeMaker but all that is important to the outside world is that it is a CoffeeMaker. The difference is in the line

```
c.brewer.pourOneCup();
```

Here we are telling a CoffeeMaker to pourOneCup(). This is legal, because the CoffeeMaker has a method called pourOneCup(). That is why we needed this method in the superclass. But the method in the superclass doesn't do anything. How did the command

```
c.brewer.pourOneCup();
```

result in the DripCoffeeMaker's pourOneCup() method being called? The point is that brewer was created as a DripCoffeeMaker so it knows that pourOneCup() results in displaying Here's a cup of Drip coffee. This is the heart of polymorphism.

To sum up:

✦ You can declare that you are creating a reference variable of type `Coffee Maker` while, in fact, you are assigning that variable to an instance of `Drip CoffeeMaker` because a `DripCoffeeMaker` *is-a* `CoffeeMaker`. **This is called** *upcasting*.

✦ You can call `brewer.pourOneCup()` because the world views `brewer` as a `CoffeeMaker` and a `CoffeeMaker` knows that it has a `pourOneCup()` method.

✦ The `brewer` uses the `pourOneCup()` method associated with the `DripCoffeeMaker` because the `brewer` knows that, despite how the outside world looks at it, in its heart, it is truly a `DripCoffeeMaker`.

Now let's create other types of `CoffeeMakers`. We create a French press:

```
public class FrenchPress extends CoffeeMaker
{
  public void pourOneCup()
  {
    System.out.println("Here's a cup of French Press coffee.");
  }
}
```

We also create a vacuum pot:

```
public class Vacuum extends CoffeeMaker
{
  public void pourOneCup()
  {
    System.out.println("Here's a cup of Vacuum coffee.");
  }
}
```

Now let's test all three subclasses with `CoffeeTester3`:

```
public class CoffeeTester3
{
   CoffeeMaker brewer;

   public CoffeeTester3()
  {
    brewer = new DripCoffeeMaker();
    brewer.pourOneCup();
     brewer = new FrenchPress();
    brewer.pourOneCup();
     brewer = new Vacuum();
    brewer.pourOneCup();
   }
```

```
      public static void main( String args[] )
      {
        new CoffeeTester3();
      }
    }
```

The variable `brewer` is declared to be a reference variable that points at a `Coffee Maker`. In its lifetime, it points at a `DripCoffeeMaker`, a `FrenchPress`, and a `Vacuum`. In each case, `brewer` knows just how to `pourOneCup()`. The output is

```
Here's a cup of Drip coffee.
Here's a cup of French Press coffee.
Here's a cup of Vacuum coffee.
```

Finally, we take this process one step further. You could argue that `brewer` knows what it's going to be because the various roles are hardcoded in. Let's generate `CoffeeMaker`s at random using the `coffeeMakerMaker()` method and ask them to `pourOneCup()`:

```
    public class CoffeeTester4
    {
      CoffeeMaker brewer;

      public CoffeeTester4()
      {
        for( int counter = 0; counter <10; counter++)
        {
          brewer = coffeeMakerMaker();
          brewer.pourOneCup();
        }
      }
      public CoffeeMaker coffeeMakerMaker()
      {
        int i = (int) (Math.random() * 3);
        switch(i)
        {
          case 0:
            return new DripCoffeeMaker();
          case 1:
            return new FrenchPress();
          default:
            return new Vacuum();
        }
      }
      public static void main( String args[] )
      {
        new CoffeeTester4();
      }
    }
```

Let's think about the two lines:

```
brewer = coffeeMakerMaker();
brewer.pourOneCup();
```

What is returned by the method `coffeeMakerMaker()` is a `CoffeeMaker`. We don't know when we write or when we compile this code what kind of `CoffeeMaker` will be returned. It will be a random process determined at runtime. In fact, it should be different each time we execute `CoffeeTester4`. Therefore, asking the `brewer` to `pourOneCup()` means that we know only that a `CoffeeMaker` will be able to execute the `pourOneCup()` method. The fact that the appropriate `pourOneCup()` method is executed tells us that the `brewer` always knew what it was. The following is my output for one run of `CoffeeTester4`:

```
Here's a cup of Drip coffee.
Here's a cup of Vacuum coffee.
Here's a cup of French Press coffee.
Here's a cup of Drip coffee.
Here's a cup of Drip coffee.
Here's a cup of French Press coffee.
Here's a cup of Vacuum coffee.
Here's a cup of French Press coffee.
Here's a cup of Drip coffee.
Here's a cup of French Press coffee.
```

Look for places to use polymorphism in your design. You can see how powerful it is to design the hierarchies with the promise of functionality made in the superclass so that any derived class can be substituted. What should also be clear from this example is how easy it is to add more subclasses. We could create a `Percolator` class and just add a case to the `CoffeeTester4` so that `Percolator`s are being created as well.

# Composition

Having seen inheritance and polymorphism, you may be tempted to use it everywhere. In fact, that was the push in early object-oriented design. You run into problems pretty quickly if you try to use this for everything.

## The diamond problem

One of the problems you'll run into is the so-called diamond problem. This is a reason that Java supports only single inheritance. Suppose you have a `Doll` class:

```
import java.awt.Color;
public class Doll
{
  protected Color hairColor;
  protected int hairLength;
}
```

An instance of Doll basically has hair of a specified length and color. Now you want to have a talking doll so you create a `TalkingDoll` class that extends `Doll`:

```
public class TalkingDoll extends Doll
{
  public void talk()
  {
    System.out.println( "I can talk." );
  }
  public void setHairColor( Color hairColor )
  {
    super.hairColor = hairColor;
    hairLength = 8;
  }
}
```

Now suppose you want a doll that can wet (just play along on this one). A `Wetting Doll` shouldn't have long hair, for obvious reasons:

```
public class WettingDoll extends Doll
{
  public void wet()
  {
    System.out.println( "I'm wetting right now." );
  }
  public void setHairColor( Color hairColor )
  {
    super.hairColor = hairColor;
    hairLength = 3;
  }
}
```

At this point, you might think that it should be easy to create a doll that both talks and wets. Just create a `TalkingWettingDoll` like this:

```
public class TalkingWettingDoll extends TalkingDoll,
  WettingDoll  //this won't work
{
}
```

Because `TalkingWettingDoll` extends `TalkingDoll`, it should be able to `talk()`, and because it extends `WettingDoll`, it should be able to `wet()`. You can't do this in Java because Java doesn't support multiple inheritance. You can inherit only from one class.

Therefore, what would happen if you created a `TalkingWettingDoll` named `susie` and you tried to set `susie.setHairColor( Color.red )`. Would `susie`'s hair be long or short? This is the so-called *diamond problem*. To avoid this problem, there is no multiple inheritance in Java. In the next section, we will see how interfaces solve this problem. Now we'll look at what composition can do for us.

# Using composition

You think of composition as assembling the pieces you need into a whole that has all of the accumulated functionality. Let's create a doll that talks and wets using composition.

Again, we begin with a `Doll` class:

```
import java.awt.Color;

public class Doll
{
  protected Color hairColor;
  protected int hairLength;

  protected void setHairLength( int hairLength )
  {
    this.hairLength = hairLength;
  }
  protected void setHairColor( Color hairColor )
  {
    this.hairColor = hairColor;
  }
}
```

It can't do a lot. It has hair with color and length that can be set by objects made from this class and its subclasses. Let's also create a `Talker` that talks:

```
public class Talker
{
  public void talk()
  {
    System.out.println(" I can talk." );
  }
}
```

Add to the mix a `Wetter` that wets:

```
public class Wetter
{
  public void wet()
  {
    System.out.println(" I am wetting right now." );
  }
}
```

Now let's create a `TalkingWettingDoll` by inheriting from `doll` and including a piece that knows how to talk and a piece that knows how to wet:

```
public class TalkingWettingDoll extends Doll
{
```

```
    Talker t = new Talker();
    Wetter w = new Wetter();

    public void setHairLength( int hairLength ){
     if (hairLength <3) super.setHairLength( hairLength );
    else super.setHairLength( 3 );
    }
    public static void main( String args[] )
    {
      TalkingWettingDoll tW = new TalkingWettingDoll();
      tW.t.talk();
      tW.w.wet();
    }
  }
```

So when you want the TalkingWettingDoll to talk, you just ask the Talker t to talk(). Similarly, for wetting, ask the Wetter w to wet(). Running the Talking WettingDoll results in the display reading:

```
I can talk.
I am wetting right now.
```

We have made the doll from pieces that know how to do what we need the whole to do. This is composition. Remember that variables hold what an object knows and methods are what an object can do. Our doll example showed how to use composition to increase functionality. We could also use composition to hold pieces of information as well.

# Interfaces

One of the points from polymorphism was the importance of identifying a method and its signature in the parent class. This meant that, in some sense, the different implementations of the method defined in the subclasses were interchangeable. In our case, it didn't even matter that the body of the method was empty in the parent class. We never intended to call that method. We were just using it to announce to the users of our classes that a CoffeeMaker or any of its subclasses would be able to respond to the pourOneCup() method.

What we were defining, really, was an interface. This instructs a client of a method how to call the method. An interface is what we care about when we use an automated teller machine (ATM) to withdraw money from our account. We can see which buttons to press, and we can see the slot where the money comes out. We don't really care how an ATM takes the money from our account and gives it to us. It could be an electronic debit to our account followed by an automatic dispensing of the bills. It could be that someone runs to the vault and takes the bills out of our specific pile. We don't care.

Java allows us to specify the interface and then to use the classes that implement the interface in a polymorphic way. Let's start by defining an interface for objects that can talk:

```
public interface ITalk
{
  void talk();
  void blink( int i ); //for illustration
}
```

The method `talk()` is automatically `public`. Any method declared in an interface is `public`, so you don't have to explicitly use the keyword `public`. Also, we know that objects that talk don't necessarily blink. The `blink()` method is included to show you that interfaces don't give you the same diamond problem we encountered with multiple inheritance.

Now define an interface for objects that can wet:

```
public interface IWet
{
  void wet();
  void blink( int j); //for illustration
}
```

`Doll` is still just:

```
import java.awt.Color;

public class Doll
{
  protected Color hairColor;
  protected int hairLength;

  protected void setHairLength( int hairLength )
  {
    this.hairLength = hairLength;
  }
  protected void setHairColor( Color hairColor )
  {
  this.hairColor = hairColor;
  }
}
```

We can define a `NewTalkingWettingDoll` as follows:

```
public class NewTalkingWettingDoll extends Doll implements
  ITalk, IWet
```

```
  {
    public void talk()
    {
      System.out.println( "I can talk." );
    }
    public void wet()
    {
      System.out.println( "I am wetting now." );
    }
    public void blink( int k )
    {
      for(int count=0; count<k ; count++)
      {
        System.out.println( "I have no problem blinking." );
      }
    }
  }
}
```

There are lots of points to notice. First, we can extend a class while implementing an interface. NewTalkingWettingDoll *is-a* Doll, but it also promises to implement what has been detailed in both the interface ITalk and the interface IWet. This brings us to the second point to notice: NewTalkingWettingDoll implements more than one interface. This doesn't create the problems that we had with multiple inheritance because we will be implementing blink() only once even though both interfaces guaranteed that we would. There is no room for confusion because there aren't two separate implementations to choose from.

The last point is not something you would necessarily notice. Every method in either of the interfaces has been implemented. You can't leave anything out. That's the promise of interfaces. This can sometimes be a pain. When you look at responding to actions from the mouse and keyboard, you will learn about interfaces called MouseListener and KeyListener. You will learn about *Adapters*. These implement every method in the interface with an empty body. This makes it easy for you to create a class that just listens for a couple of keys to be pressed. The down side is that this brings you back to the restriction of inheriting only from one class (that is, if you extend an adapter, you can't be extending something else). The up side is that you usually do this in inner classes that exist only for the purpose of listening for certain user-generated events.

Now we can use interfaces in polymorphism. Anything that implements ITalk will be able to respond to the method calls talk() and blink( 7 ) in the same way that classes that extended CoffeeMaker could respond to pourOneCup().

# Summary

In this chapter, we looked at how you can design objects to more effectively use and reuse your work. One of the mantras of object-oriented programming is that you separate the interface from the implementation. You have seen that once you have identified the interface, you can take advantage of this commonality with polymorphism. In this chapter, you learned the following:

✦ Inheritance is appropriate when you can say that objects created by the sub-class have an *is-a* relationship to objects of the parent class. The advantage is that you can treat objects of the subclass as if they were objects of the parent class. This upcasting makes it easy to take advantage of polymorphism.

✦ Inheritance can cause trouble because changes in the superclass may have wide- ranging effects. These effects can be both in subclasses and in classes that access the subclasses. You may be using a class that uses a class that inherits from the class that has been changed. Even this class must make sure the changes don't affect it.

✦ Polymorphism takes advantage of interfaces or inheritance where the methods have a common interface. It allows one object to substitute for another object at runtime. You may now know which specific type of object will be passed into a method when you write and compile the program. As long as that object either extends the appropriate class or implements the appropriate interface, you know that you are allowed to pass it in.

✦ Composition offers another way of assembling the pieces that you need into one class. You add state information and functionality by providing reference variables that point to the classes that contain what you need.

✦ An interface allows you to publicly announce what you have agreed to take as inputs to relevant methods in classes that implement this interface. It is like a contract with the user that they know how a method is supposed to behave. The user knows how to call the method and what will be returned.

✦    ✦    ✦

# Exceptions and Error Handling

**O**ne of the goals of Java designers is that more mistakes
will be caught while the programmer is still thinking
about the piece of code containing the mistake. The idea is
that as many problems as possible should be caught at compile time. The next best solution is that those that can't be
caught by the compiler should be caught early on while running your programs. This way, you aren't sitting in your room
months from now wondering what you were thinking when
you set up a particular method in such a nonintuitive way.

Three kinds of safety checks will help you catch and avoid
errors in your code: those that Java enforces, those that Java
assists with, and those that are left up to you. In a nutshell:

◆ The first type consists of those that the compiler enforces
for you. For example, you've seen that strong type checking means that the compiler will make sure that if a method
needs an int as its argument and you pass in a boolean,
then you will be told that there's a problem. Although
beginning programmers get frustrated with such error
messages, it is the compiler protecting you from yourself.

◆ A second level of defense includes exceptions. For several chapters now, you've seen that certain methods
throw exceptions, and you've been told that we'd cover
exceptions in Chapter 11. Now that we're here, you'll see
that exceptions are Java's way of helping you respond
correctly to exceptional situations. This encourages you
to anticipate situations that your program is not meant
to handle but that could occur.

◆ The third kind of defense is completely on your shoulders. Testing your code as you write it and as you add
functionality will help you uncover where problems were
introduced. Writing code that is easy to understand,
maintain, and extend is also your responsibility.

Let's start by looking at exceptions and then quickly review
the other protections you should know about.

# Exceptions

Java features a general-purpose error-processing system known as an *exception mechanism*. The exception mechanism is composed of two parts: throwing exceptions and catching them. To throw an exception means to signal an error, while to catch one is to trap and handle an error that has been thrown. While new to C programmers, C++ programmers will find Java's exception mechanism very similar to that of C++.

The term *exception* is short for *exceptional event*. Exceptional events are those that disrupt the normal flow of program execution. Exceptions provide a uniform approach to signaling and processing errors, removing much of the burden of traditional error processing.

You can think of the exception mechanism as being made up of three parts. Each part is tied to one of the following Java keywords.

✦ `throws`: A method `throws` an exception if the exception is one of the exceptional events that could be true during the evaluation of the method. The syntax is

```
scope returnType methodName( argumentList )throws
ExceptionList
```

Here the `ExceptionList` is a list of exceptions that could be thrown by the method. The items on the list are separated by commas.

✦ `throw`: This is the spot in the method where the exception is actually created and the program flow is altered. For example, if you are trying to divide `x/y` and want to make sure that you're not dividing by zero, you might check, and if the denominator is zero, then create an `ArithmeticException`.

```
if ( y == 0 )
{
   throw ArithmeticException
} ...
```

✦ `try-catch`: You put all of the code that might throw an exception into a `try` block and you put each exception and how you want it handled in a `catch` block that immediately follows the `try` block.

## Examples of exceptions

In your early days of programming with Java, you probably encountered exceptions. It might be helpful to review some of these to keep in your mind as examples. You didn't write any code to `throw` or `catch` these exceptions. They are provided as part of Java, so there is something a bit different about them. These are called *Java Runtime Exceptions*. Their syntax is a bit different, but they are a good place to start.

## An Array Index Exception Example

As was mentioned in Chapter 8, "Creating and Using Arrays and Strings," a common mistake when dealing with arrays is to forget that the indexing starts with zero. An array with ten elements will have indices 0,1,2, . . ., 9, so there is a problem with the following code snippet:

```
int[] intArray = new int[10]; //don't do this
for ( int count = 1; count <= 10; count++)
{
  int[ count ] = count;
}
```

You have declared an array called `intArray` that will hold ten `int`s. You then start assigning the various positions of the array beginning with the second slot (index = 1). Really nothing goes wrong until `count` has the value 10. You are now trying to access the eleventh element in an array that holds only ten elements. Your index is greater than the greatest possible value. You will throw an `ArrayIndexOutOfBoundsException`.

## The Class Not Found Exception Example

Our first program in this book, `HelloWorld`, was written before we introduced you to packages. Suppose our code was changed to include the package declaration `firstSteps`:

```
package firstSteps;
public class HelloWorld
{
  public final void main( String args[] )
  {
    System.out.println( "Hello World.");
  }
}
```

This program must be saved as a file called "HelloWorld.java," which is located in the directory, firstSteps. Go ahead and compile the file. Then run it from within the firstSteps directory using the command line:

```
java HelloWorld
```

You will see a `ClassNotFoundException`. The Java runtime knows that it is supposed to find a class file named "HelloWorld.class" inside of a directory called firstSteps. It's looking for the directory firstSteps and can't find it because it's already on the inside of the directory. If you move up a level and try to run the application, you will have to type:

```
java firstSteps/HelloWorld
```

Before you complain, look again at the `ClassNotFoundException`. It also has information that it was looking for the class `firstSteps/HelloWorld`. This gives you helpful information about what was wrong and points you in the direction of fixing it.

### The Reference Variable Not Referring to Anything Exception Example

Here's another common exception you may have encountered when building arrays of reference variables. Let's say that you have a class called `Car` and you would like to have a class called `ParkingLot` that contains an array of ten `Cars`. You could try to proceed as follows:

```
Car[] arrayOfCars = new Car[ 10 ];
arrayOfCars[0].getType();//this doesn't work
```

The problem is that the first line of code declares that `arrayOfCars` is an array that will hold ten elements in it and each element will be a `Car`. But these are reference variables. The element `arrayOfCars[0]` isn't really a `Car`; it is a reference to an instance of `Car`. So now you can see that the problem is that you have never created a new instance of `Car` and made `arrayOfCars[0]` its handle. The previous code snippet would throw (as perhaps you've experienced) a `NullPointerException` because `arrayOfCars[0]` has been declared to be a reference variable — but it doesn't reference anything yet. What you need to do instead is something like:

```
Car[] arrayOfCars = new Car[ 10 ];
arrayOfCars[0] = new Car( "Gremlin" );
```

# Using exceptions for error handling

In languages other than Java, such as C, each function is responsible for signaling success or failure during its execution. In many cases, this is done by returning an integer value that the caller can test. Typically, if the return value of a function is zero, the function has been executed without error. If a nonzero value is returned instead, an error may have occurred during execution. It is up to the programmer to intercept, interpret, and act on these often cryptic error indicators.

However, not all routines return error codes and those that do, don't necessarily report errors in the same way. Some may return an error code; others might return a null value, and still others might set a global error variable. Such inconsistencies place a substantial burden on the programmer, who must learn the error-reporting mechanism employed by each routine and write the appropriate code to test for such errors.

As a result, many programmers save time by testing only for errors generated by critical routines, not bothering with the others. In some cases, the programmer may not fully understand the routine in question, so errors are handled incorrectly. In either case, the integrity of the program suffers and error checking becomes a nuisance, if not a nightmare.

Using exceptions, Java provides developers with a consistent and relatively simple mechanism for signaling and dealing with errors. Exceptions provide methods with a way to stop program execution when an error is encountered, while allowing the method to notify its caller that a problem has occurred. If the caller chooses, it may ignore, or "duck" the exception, in which case the exception is passed down the call stack until it is dealt with.

## A Motivating Example

For instance, say that you have written the front end for a database of people selling an item that you've been looking for. You want to sort your list by price and retrieve the name of the person offering the item at the cheapest price and save it in another database you are building of the year's best buys. So your Java program goes to the first database and gives the command for — hey, wait a minute. What if it couldn't find the database? Your program shouldn't crash or hang. You would like some graceful way of handling this situation that also provides the user with useful information.

Now suppose your program found the database but there were no people offering the item that you're looking for. Again, your program should accommodate this. Maybe you found what you were looking for and went to save it in the second database but couldn't find that database. Maybe you could find the second database but didn't have permission to write to it.

You'll notice that it would be quite inconvenient and unwieldy to have each method test for successful execution at the time that method is called. It would be as if every sentence in a story contained a long and involved aside. You would soon lose the thread of the story. In addition, you'll notice in the previous example that there are two places where you are testing for the same situation: could you find the database you were looking for? Java encourages you to tell your story in one nice chunk called a `try` block and then to write a `catch` block for each problem that could reasonably happen.

## Who Handles the Exceptions

Before talking about how we create and check for exceptions, let's take a minute to look at how the responsibility is passed. If you've done graphics programming, this might remind you of how events bubble up through the system until some graphics element handles them. The differences here are what the exception "bubbles up" through and that you can't end up with an exception that no one is willing to handle.

A call stack is nothing more than the sequence of methods that have been invoked. For instance, if a method named `drawShape()` calls another method named `draw Circle()`, we'd have a pretty simple call stack. Here, `drawShape()` calls the `draw Circle()` method. The `drawShape()` method is said to be at the bottom of the stack, while `drawCircle()` is at the top. However, `drawCircle()` might invoke another method named `draw()`. This would then sit at the top of the call stack. And `draw()` might call another method, named `paint()`, as the call stack continued to grow.

The relevance to exceptions is that if an exception occurred in paint(), it could possibly be ignored by every method. As a result, the exception would be passed all the way down the call stack from paint() to draw() to drawCircle() to drawShape(). In other words, if an exception isn't handled by a method, it's passed down the call stack to the method below it. Somewhere along the way, the exception has to be caught and dealt with. If it isn't, the program is aborted. If you attempt to write a Java program that would result in such a situation, the compiler warns you about it.

## Throwing exceptions

Before an exception can be caught, it must be thrown. Exceptions can be thrown by any Java code: your own code, code in the packages that come with the Java development environment, or code in packages written by others. Even the Java runtime system can throw exceptions that your programs must catch.

When an exception is thrown, the Java runtime system receives a signal that an error has been generated. Exceptions are thrown to notify the system that an error has occurred. As soon as an exception is thrown, the runtime system searches for the matching catch clause to handle it.

### Throw Syntax

Exceptions are thrown using the following Java syntax:

```
throw new AnyExceptionObject();
```

Regardless of what code raises an exception, it's always done using the throw statement.

The throw statement takes a single argument: a throwable object. Throwable objects are instances of any subclass of the Throwable class defined in the java.lang package. In our previous example, we instantiated a throwable object:

```
new AnyExceptionObject(); // instantiate a throwable object
```

If you attempt to throw an object that isn't throwable, the compiler emits an error message and refuses to complete the compilation process. Exception objects you'll encounter are derived from either the Exception class or the Error class. These classes are subclasses of Throwable (java.lang.Throwable) and, therefore, produce objects (or are extended by other classes) that are considered throwable.

When we wanted to transform a String into the int being represented by the String, we used the method intValue() in the Integer class. We could have also used the parseInt() method. For example:

```
int intExample = Integer.parseInt("27");
```

creates an `int` named `intExample` and gives it the value 27, which it gets from the `parseInt()` method operating on the `String` `"27"`.

The syntax for the `parseInt()` method is:

```
public static int parseInt( String aString ) throws
    NumberFormatException
```

Notice that the formal definition of the method promises that `parseInt()` throws a particular type of exception. You'll find such examples all over the Java Library (lower case).

Let's see how the exception is thrown with the following method declaration:

```
public static int myDivide(int x, int y) throws
    ArithmeticException
{
    if (y==0)
        throw new ArithmeticException();
    else
        return (x/y);
}
```

In the method signature, we declare this method as being capable of throwing `ArithmeticException`:

```
throws ArithmeticException
```

Remember, when we `throw` an exception, we are creating an object. So far, we've used the default constructor to `throw` exceptions. You can also use a constructor that takes a `String` as its argument. This `String` can be retrieved using the `getMessage()` method.

The Java language requires that methods either catch or declare all nonruntime exceptions they can throw. Runtime exceptions are explained in a minute. You also aren't required to catch or declare `Errors`. With the previous line of code, we declared that our `myDivide()` method throws the `ArithmeticException`, satisfying this requirement.

However, throwing exceptions is only half the battle. To write effective Java programs, you must be able to catch exceptions as well. That is covered in the next section, "Catching exceptions."

## Runtime Exceptions

One of the subclasses of the `Exception` class is the `RuntimeException` class. You've already seen that runtime exceptions are not checked. You don't have to write `try` and `catch` blocks for them. They include the `IndexOutOfBound` sException and NullPointerException used in examples. If you divide by zero, you'll encounter the ArithmeticException. In Chapter 8, "Creating and Using Arrays and Strings," you learned about passing in arguments to an application using the args array ( as in main( String[] args ) ). You then needed to convert these arguments to numbers. If your String doesn't have the appropriate form, you will get a NumberFormatException.

There are other runtime exceptions. These can't be checked by the compiler — it would be too costly (and in many cases impossible) to prove to the compiler that your code would never throw one of these exceptions. For example, if you are reading in data that you will then be calculating with, you can't know that you will never be dividing by zero. This is best left to runtime. Other than members and descendents of the class RuntimeException, all other members of the Exception class are checked exceptions.

For example, if you want to find the square root of a number x, you can write

```
float sqrtExample = Math.sqrt(x);
```

Here, x is cast to a double and then the square root of x is calculated and stored in the variable sqrtExample. The syntax of sqrt is

```
public static native double sqrt(double x)
```

The point is that if x = -3, for example, sqrt would throw an ArithmeticException even though the syntax does not specify that sqrt throws any exception.

You may be tempted, therefore, to avoid having to read the rest of this chapter by just making all of the exceptions that you write descendents of RuntimeException. However, you would be perverting the system by creating ways of dealing with errors using a mechanism that may hide your own errors from you.

In cases where you wish to define your own methods, you simply create a new class that is a subclass of Exception. Here is the program with the myDivide() method using a custom exception:

```
class MyOwnException extends Exception {
}
public static int myDivide(int x, int y) throws
  MyOwnException
  {
    if (y==0)
      throw new MyOwnException();
    else
      return (x/y);
}
```

You can even create hierarchies of exceptions so that AnotherOfMyExceptions can extend MyOwnException. This means that you can apply the benefits of inheritance we covered in Chapter 9 to exceptions.

# Catching exceptions

When an exception is thrown, the Java runtime system immediately stops the current flow of program execution and looks for an exception handler to catch it. Searching backward through the call stack, a corresponding handler is sought starting with the method where the error occurred.

The search continues down the call stack until a method containing an appropriate exception handler is found. The first handler encountered that has the same type as the thrown object is the one chosen to deal with the exception.

If the exception travels all the way down the call stack with no handler catching it, the program aborts execution. Typically, an error message is output to the terminal display in such cases. This, of course, assumes the exception is a runtime exception that can't be seen by the compiler.

Dividing a number by a variable that happens to be zero, accessing an array element using an index value (subscript) that is beyond the legal range, accessing null objects, and similar dynamic activities produce runtime exceptions that aren't recognized at compile time. As a result, the compiler can't force you to catch such exceptions, since it doesn't even realize they exist. And, in cases where a runtime exception propagates to the bottom of the call stack, your program is aborted.

## The try-catch Clause

To catch an exception, you must write an exception handler using the try-catch clause. For instance, suppose you wanted to use the original `myDivide()` method created earlier. To catch the exception that might result, you'd write the following try-catch clause:

```
try
{
   int y = myDivide(10,0);
}
catch (ArithmeticException e)
{
   System.out.println("Whoops - There it is!");
}
```

### The try block

The first part of a try-catch clause, the try block, encloses those statements that may throw an exception. Here is the syntax of a typical try block:

```
try {
   ...
   /* statements capable of throwing an exception */
   ...
}
```

The only code in our example capable of throwing an exception is the `myDivide()` method. However, you can include in the try block any number of legal Java statements that have the potential to throw an exception. As you can see, we intentionally supply `myDivide()` with parameters that will cause an exception to be thrown. Specifically, the second integer passed to the method is zero.

If we had additional lines of code following `myDivide(10,0)`, they wouldn't be executed. Instead, `myDivide()` would throw an exception that would immediately stop program execution at that point, which would then drop into the catch portion of the try-catch clause.

### The catch block

Following the try block, are one or more catch blocks that you can use to trap and process exceptions. This is the catch block syntax:

```
catch (ThrowableClassName variable) {
    ...
}
```

Although we supplied only one catch block in the `myDivide()` exception handler, any number could have been provided. However, since the `myDivide()` method throws only one exception, we have to catch that one. In our example, we merely output a line of text to prove that our exception was indeed caught. In the case of multiple catches, the try-catch clause has this syntax:

```
try {
    ...
}
catch (ThrowableClassName variable)
{
    ...
}
catch (ThrowableClassName variable)
{
    ...
}
catch (ThrowableClassName variable)
{
    ...
}
catch (ThrowableClassName variable)
{
    ...
}
```

For instance, suppose `myDivide()` was capable of throwing two different exceptions. In this case, we would provide a catch block for each of the possible exceptions:

```
try {
    int y = myDivide(10,0);
} catch (ArithmeticException e) {
```

```
      System.out.println("Have caught an ArithmeticException.");
   } catch (MyOwnException e) {
      System.out.println("Have caught MyOwnException.");
   }
```

The exception that is thrown is compared to the argument for each catch block in order. (The catch argument can be an object or an interface type.) When a match is found, that catch block is executed. If no match is found, the exception propagates down the call stack, where it is compared against potential exception handlers until a match is found. And, as always, if no match is found, the program is aborted.

You can access the instance variables and methods of exceptions, just as for any other object. With this in mind, you can invoke the exception's `getMessage()` method to get information on the exception — `getMessage()` is a method defined in the `Throwable` class:

```
System.out.println(e.getMessage());
```

The `Throwable` class also implements several methods for dealing with the call stack when an exception occurs (such as `printStackTrace()`, which outputs the call stack to the display). The `Throwable` subclass that you, or anyone else, creates can implement additional methods and instance variables. To find out which methods an exception implements, look at its class and superclass definitions.

### The Exception class
Because exceptions are subclasses of the `Exception` class, you can catch all of the exceptions that you haven't explicitly specified with the code

```
catch (Exception e )
{
  ...
}
```

This should be at the bottom of your set of `catch` blocks, as it will catch everthing. Subclassing the `Exception` class allows you to handle the specific exception in a more tailored way.

### Additional methods and instance variables
When you throw an exception, you are creating an object. This means that you can add to what the object knows and does by adding instance variables and methods. For example, suppose you want a new exception called `MyDivideByZeroException`.

You can define

```
public class MyDivideByZeroException extends
  ArithmeticException
  {
    int myNumerator;
```

```
      public MyDivideByZeroException( int top )
      {
        myNumerator = top;
      }
      public int getMyNumerator()
      {
        return myNumerator;
      }
    }
```

Now, if you redesign myDivide() to throw a MyDivideByZeroException instead of an ArithmeticException, you could print out the dividend (numerator) of the expression.

## The finally block

Unlike C++, Java's try-catch clause supports the use of an optional finally block. If defined, this is guaranteed to execute, regardless of whether or not an exception is thrown. As a result, you can use it to perform any necessary clean-up operation (closing files and streams, releasing system resources, and so on) that your methods require before the flow of control is transferred to another part of the program. Restoring the system the way it needs to be left is really the purpose of the finally block.

This is the syntax of the finally block:

```
finally
{
  ...
  /* statements here are executed before control transfers */
  ...
}
```

In the context of our myDivide() example, a finally block might look like this:

```
try
{
  int y = myDivide(10,0);
}
catch (ArithmeticException e)
{
  System.out.println("Have caught an
    ArithmeticException.");
}
catch (MyOwnException e)
{
  System.out.println("Have caught MyOwnException.");
}
finally
{
```

```
    System.out.println("cleaning up...");
    // do any clean-up work here
}
```

Upon executing the `finally` block, control is transferred out of the try-catch clause. Typically, whatever event caused the `try` statement to terminate (fall-through; the execution of a break, continue, or return statement; or the propagation of an exception) dictates where the flow of control will resume.

The `finally` block could also execute a jump statement. This would cause another unconditional control transfer outside its block, or cause another uncaught exception to be thrown. In either case, the original jump statement is abandoned, and the new unconditional control transfer (or exception) is processed.

All jump statements (`break`, `continue`, `return`, and `throw`) transfer control unconditionally. Whenever one causes control to bypass a `finally` block, the control transfer pauses while the finally part is executed and continues if the finally part finishes normally.

## Catch or declare

Java requires that methods either catch or declare all nonruntime exceptions that can be thrown within the method's scope. This means that if a method chooses not to catch an exception, it must declare that it can throw it.

Sometimes, it's not a good idea to catch exceptions. For example, if you catch an exception deep down in the call stack, you might not know how or why your method is being called. What would you do with the exception, once caught?

Since you don't know enough about what caused your method to be called, you might not be able to adequately handle the exception. In that case, it would be better to pass the exception back down the call stack: you should declare the exception rather than catch it.

To declare an exception, simply add the `throw` statement to your method signature, followed by the exception name. To declare more than one exception, separate each name by a comma.

Suppose, for example, you wanted to define a new method that calls the `myDivide()` method we created earlier. Instead of implementing an exception handler for `myDivide()` in our new method, we can declare the potential exceptions to pass them down the call stack:

```
public void myMath() throws ArithmeticException, MyOwnException
{
    ...
}
```

Some programmers realize that it takes a lot less time to declare an exception than it does to write an appropriate exception handler, and they are often tempted to simply pass the buck rather than deal with it. As a general rule, this is a bad idea. However, sometimes it is appropriate to declare an exception rather than handle it. For a detailed discussion of this topic, see "Handling Errors Using Exceptions" in the Java Language Tutorial (available on the JavaSoft Web site at `http://java.sun.com/docs/books/tutorial/index.html`), specifically the section named "Runtime Exceptions — The Controversy."

# Reducing Errors in Your Code

Exceptions force you to think about what exceptional situations your code may encounter. This encourages you to build robust code. You provide the user with ways to recover from anticipated situations. At first you may be tempted to use exceptions to control the flow in your program. This is not the point of exceptions. They aren't there to handle everyday events. For example, if an input to an automated teller machine (ATM) program is positive, you might consider it to be a deposit, and if negative, you might consider it to be a withdrawal. You wouldn't want to decide that the main flow of the program is for deposits and then create an exception to handle the negative numbers. You might want to have a `NotEnoughCashException` to handle a request for a withdrawal that exceeds the balance. It is natural to handle this exceptional situation and return the user to a menu allowing him or her to withdraw a smaller amount or to make another selection.

Understanding exceptions takes us into the realms of the other two ways of reducing errors in your code: responding to compiler warnings and writing and documenting better code.

## Compiler warnings

In Chapter 6, "Java Syntax: Tokens, Types, and Values," we discussed Java being a strongly typed language. Each variable has to be declared. You think if you write

```
myInteger = 6;
```

that it should just be obvious that `myInteger` is an `int`. For reference variables, the situation appears even more confusing. You announce to the world that your new variable will point at a specific type of object and now you have to go about creating that object, or finding one for it to point to.

For methods, Java is similarly helpful. Consider the simple method:

```
public int squareTheInput( int anInt )
{
  return anInt * anInt;
}
```

Your code promises to return an `int`. This is easy to check. For example, you couldn't have written

```
public int squareTheInput( int anInt )
{
   return "How are you"; //doesn't work
}
```

You promised to return an `int` and then you go ahead and return a `String`. The compiler will let you know that something is wrong. You also couldn't call this method from somewhere else using the call

```
squareTheInput( 2.3 );
```

The compiler will look around for a method with the signature:

```
public int squareTheInput( float aFloat )
It won't find it and will tell you that no method with the
signature
squareTheInput( float aFloat )
```

was found. You may think that you are making the same call: just multiply the input by itself and return it. It only knows how to do this with `int`s and not with `float`s.

You have seen these checks before. You may have also encountered a message from the compiler that you didn't know how to deal with. You may have used a method that required you to `throw` or `catch` an exception and you didn't yet know how to do that.

Let's go back to the `myDivide()` method:

```
public static int myDivide(int x, int y) throws
   MyOwnException
   {
     if (y==0)
       throw new MyOwnException();
     else
       return (x/y);
   }
```

Let's say you define another method that uses `myDivide()`:

```
public static int myReciprocal( int x )
{
   return myDivide( 1, x );
}
```

You have a problem because myReciprocal() could end up trying to divide by zero in the same way that myDivide can. Unfortunately, you could lose sight of the fact that myDivide() is prepared to catch the exception. There's nothing in our code to indicate that myReciprocal() could throw an exception. Consider the following simple application:

```java
public class TestDrive
{
  public static void main( String[] args)
  {
    int i = new Integer( args[0] ).intValue();
    System.out.println( "The reciprocal of " + i + " is " +
      myReciprocal( i ));
  }
  public static int myDivide(int x, int y) throws
    MyOwnException
    {
      if (y==0)
        throw new MyOwnException();
      else
        return (x/y);
    }

  public static int myReciprocal( int x )
  {
    return myDivide( 1, x );
  }
}
```

TestDrive is set to take an argument from the command line and transform it into an int i  and then take the reciprocal of i. You can't know ahead of time what the value of i will be. It could even be zero. You will get an error message when you go to compile this code. It will tell you that myReciprocal() must either catch the exception MyOwnException or specify that it throws the exception MyOwnException. The specific place where this problem is flagged is when myDivide() is called from within myReciprocal.

# Your role

Java does all that it can to help you write cleaner, more error-free code. Here are a few quick suggestions on how you should help yourself.

## Document Your Code

The people who will look to find a way around exceptions and who get annoyed with the compiler for generating error messages about their code will also avoid writing good documentation. They probably also aren't reading this paragraph or much of this chapter. So to the rest of you, good job. Keep writing helpful comments explaining what each method and each variable are for. You can't write too many comments.

## Coupling and Cohesion

You shouldn't need to write too much documentation if you keep in mind the goal of low coupling and high cohesion. Think of high cohesion as meaning that a method should do a very limited, easy to describe task. Although not given a great name, `myDivide()` is highly cohesive. It divides the first argument by the second. This makes it useful to us in other settings. Maybe we have two points, `p` and `q`, and two methods, `rise(p,q)` and `run(p,q)`, that calculate the difference of the y and x coordinates. Then we can define `slope(p,q)` to return `myDivide( rise (p,q), run(p,q) )`.

Think of coupling as working on a need-to-know basis. If a method doesn't need to know values of certain variables, then they shouldn't be passed in as parameters. When you unnecessarily tie a method to other methods, classes, and variables that it doesn't need to be tied to, you make it less flexible and also much harder to maintain.

## Stubs and Test Suites

When you write your code, write stubs and then add functionality. For example, you will soon be writing GUI applications with all sorts of widgets that perform many tasks. It will be easy to lose your way. Let's say that your application has a button that will order lunch for you when it's been pressed. Initially, the method that you call should have a simple body such as

```
System.out.println("The order lunch button was pressed.");
```

This way, you can easily test that when the button is pressed, it is calling the right method. Later, you can add the functionality to the button. This helps you know where you have introduced mistakes as you iterate through the development process.

Notice that testing your code was built into the development process. As you design what your solution will do, create test cases that you can run against your code as it progresses. Search out exceptional cases and test them.

It's easy to get lost in the development process just thinking about people who use your system correctly. If you design a juice dispenser designed to sell cans of juice for seventy-five cents, you may think "they insert seventy-five cents or more and select a drink." Make sure you test what happens if you don't put in enough money but still select a drink. Test what happens if you put in too much money and then select a drink (oops, guess we need a coin return).

# Summary

Programmers who have programmed in Java and then, because of job requirements, returned to other languages, say that programming in Java has made them better programmers. The language has forced them to take care of some areas and provided a helpful environment for taking care of others. You should now appreciate what exceptions can do to help those using your program. In a nutshell, you've learned the following:

✦ Java is a strongly typed language. The compiler will catch when a method's call doesn't match up with its definition. The compiler will also indicate incompatible assignments and when an exception is not caught or specified.

✦ Java features a general-purpose error processing system known as an exception mechanism. The exception mechanism is composed of two parts: throwing exceptions and catching them. To throw an exception means to signal an error, while to catch one is to trap and handle an error that has been thrown.

✦ The programmer must catch or specify all checked exceptions. These are all subclasses of the `Exception` class that aren't also subclasses of the `RuntimeException` class.

✦ You contain all of the code that might throw an exception in a `try` block and handle each type of exception in its own `catch` block. When you declare a method, you announce whether it `throws` one or more exception.

✦ Java can't do everything for you. You need to maintain well-designed, easy-to-read code with plenty of comments. You should look for low coupling, high cohesion, and write test suites to test your code along the way.

✦    ✦    ✦

# Accelerating into the Curve: Core Class Libraries

P A R T

III

◆ ◆ ◆ ◆

**In This Part**

**Chapter 12**
Collections, Utilities, and Data Structures

**Chapter 13**
Input/Output: Java Streams

**Chapter 14**
Threads

**Chapter 15**
Networking

**Chapter 16**
JDBC: Java API for Database Connectivity

◆ ◆ ◆ ◆

# Collections, Utilities, and Data Structures

In Chapter 8, we introduced you to the basics of the java.util package. We covered most of the essential utility classes for dealing with primitive manipulation and elementary data handling such as dates and resources. In this chapter, we will explore the rest of the package and show you the wide range of data structures that are available for your application.

The java.util package provides a standard set of generic data structures termed the Collections APIs. Almost every language has them in some form. If you've come from the C++ world, these are the equivalent of the Standard Template Library (STL). These have morphed over the years from a very simplistic package in JDK 1.0 to the very comprehensive system you see now.

## The Role of Collections

A study of the computer sciences over the years has produced a wide variety of research into the elementary arrangement of data for specific needs, regardless of what the actual data is. Standard structures typically include trees, sets, maps and queues. In most well-established languages, when you needed to write, say, a first in, first out (FIFO) queue, that meant you had to code the entire set of data structures and manipulation functions every time you needed it. If you needed three different queues in your application, you had to write the same piece of code three times. Obviously, this is a frequent source of bugs and memory leaks.

With the arrival of Java 2, Sun acknowledged the fundamental requirement of having a built-in set of implementations of these data structures. One of the niceties of having an object-oriented language (OOP) like Java is that, as long as the base classes are written correctly, you can effectively store any kind of data and manipulate it, write the manipulation classes once, and reuse them as often as you need.

There are four basic areas that all data structures can be classified into: trees, maps, sets, and lists. Java provides direct implementations for all of these except trees. The term *collection* refers to all of these generic structures. In the next few sections, we'll define in more detail what each of these are; then, we'll look at how Java implements them.

Note    We gloss over many of the important implementation details in this chapter. If you want to understand more about the algorithms involved in creating these data structures, then you should invest in a copy of *Introduction to Algorithms* by Cormen, Leiserson, and Rivest (MIT Press). A hefty tome, and not for the mathematically challenged, this book is regarded as the industry bible on almost all of the fundamental computer science algorithms.

## The list

Conceptually, the list is probably the easiest to picture. As its name suggests, a *list* is a single ordered collection of elements (sometimes called a sequence). You can add an item to the start of the list, to the end, or in the middle. You can remove items too, and the list will automatically adjust.

Lists come in many forms, such as linked lists, circular lists, and various forms of queues such as the FIFO and the *stack* — a Last in, First Out style of queue. Lists have a simple, basic property: no matter how many times you access the contents, the order is always maintained. As long as you don't add or remove anything, the first element will always be the same object.

## The map

A *map* is a data structure that contains two halves — a key and a value. For every key there is a corresponding value, or a key maps to a value. Ask the data structure for an item by specifying the key, and it will return the corresponding value.

Maps are not limited to a one-to-one relationship between keys and values. In many cases, a single key may map to many different values or a single value may be referenced by many different keys. The most common example of this is a relational database, such as Oracle or Ingres. Inside the database, there are lots of tables that map one piece of data to another. You then use a language like SQL to specify the key, and it will return you all of the corresponding data.

How keys are mapped to values depends on the implementation of your map. Sometimes, you need to keep many values for a single key, while other times, you require only one. The mapping function depends on the data structure.

## The set

*Sets* are similar in some respects to lists. They contain many values, but in sets, every value is guaranteed to be unique. A set may not contain two copies of a particular value. If you remember back to your math classes, this is identical to the mathematical Set entity.

Like maps, how a set decides whether two values are the same depends on the implementation. Sometimes a straight comparison is used, while other times, a hashing function may be used.

## The tree

A *tree* data structure, like a map, contains a series of key/value pairs. Where they differ is how data is stored for quick retrieval. In general, a map is considered to be a simple structure like an array or linked list internally. On the other hand, a tree stores the information in a hierarchical fashion. The hierarchy is defined by the keys of the key/value pairs and can have many different arrangements, as shown in Figure 12-1.

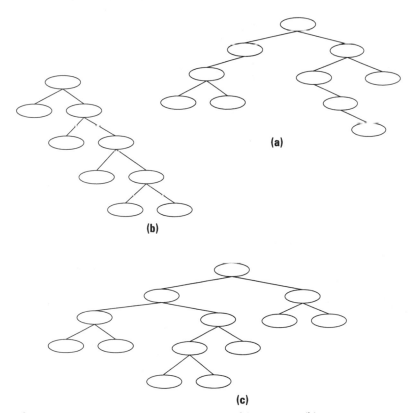

**Figure 12-1:** Various types of trees: (a) a binary tree, (b) a sparse tree, and (c) a red-black tree

**Note**    In the Java implementation of data structures, the distinction between trees and other data structures is somewhat blurred. Both maps and sets can be implemented using an underlying tree structure.

## More than just data

The role of a collection of data structures is to make life easy for you, the programmer. So, while we may use a collection like a list just to store some data internally to the program, other times we want to show the application user that data too.

A list is a list, no matter how we create it or use it. If you look at your closest GUI-based application, you're probably staring at more than a dozen lists immediately. Each of those toolbars could be described as a list. So, for example, we could arrange the icons alphabetically in our toolbar list by representing it as the List base class and passing it to a list sorter. We could also create a generic toolbar class that constructs its look and feel by simply passing it a list. Another example would be one of those pull-down list boxes. The applications of the collections data structure is much wider than just pure data storage. As you travel through the rest of this book, examine all the different places where the collections API pops up — particularly in the Swing sections later on.

# The java.util Package (Continued)

Now that you understand the basic definitions of the various types of collections, we need to look at Java's prepackaged implementations that you can use.

Most of the basic definitions of the various data structures are described by interfaces in the java.util package. With these interfaces, a set of abstract class implementations are then constructed. From these abstract classes, concrete implementations are then provided. Following the structures can be very messy, so we've provided a diagram showing all the relationships in Figure 12-2.

## Beginning the Collection

At the bottom of the heap is the Collection interface (note the lack of an *s* at the end of *collection*). This defines a set of basic capabilities for all of our data structures. The methods are outlined in Table 12-1.

As you can see from this table, most of the methods are fairly general. The only method that deserves to be singled out is the toArray() method that takes an

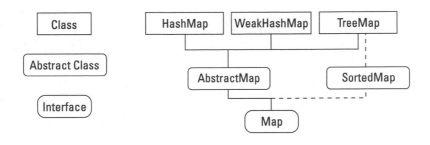

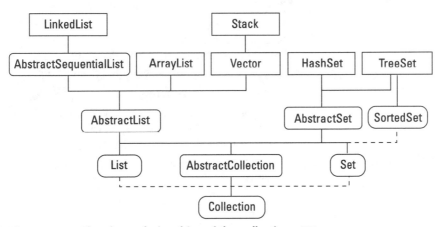

**Figure 12-2:** The class relationships of the collections APIs

array of objects as an argument. Unfortunately, the javadoc API documentation is not particularly clear about what it all means, so we'll explain it here.

Say we have a list where we store a bunch of Strings and we want to get those Strings out so that we can print them. Something like this pseudocode:

```
List stringList = new List();
// add lots of Strings to the list
// now make an array and print it out
String[] stringArray = (String[])stringList.toArray();
for(int i = 0; i < stringArray.length; i++)
   System.out.println("String " + i + " is " + stringArray(i);
```

## Table 12-1
## The Collection Interface

| Method | Description |
|---|---|
| `boolean add(Object)` | Adds the given object to the collection. This may or may not add the object twice depending on the implementation. If the collection has changed, then `true` is returned |
| `boolean addAll (Collection)` | Adds all of the objects in the given collection to this collection. If the collection has changed as a result, then `true` is returned. |
| `void clear()` | Clears all of the objects from this collection. |
| `boolean contains (Object)` | Checks to see if the collection contains the nominated object. It should check equality using the `.equals()` method of the passed object for comparison. |
| `boolean containsAll (Collection)` | Checks to see if this collection contains all the objects in the nominated collection. |
| `boolean equals (Object)` | Checks for equality of this collection with another. It should have exactly the same behavior as `java.lang.Object equals()` method. |
| `int hashCode()` | Gets the hash code value for this collection. It should have exactly the same behavior as `java.lang.Object hashCode()` method. |
| `boolean isEmpty()` | Checks to see if this collection contains any elements. |
| `Iterator iterator()` | Fetches an iterator that allows you to traverse through all of the elements of this collection. |
| `boolean remove (Object)` | Removes the nominated object from this collection. If the collection contains multiple copies of this object, only the first is removed. |
| `boolean removeAll (Collection)` | Removes all of the elements from this collection that are common to both collections. |
| `boolean retainAll (Collection)` | Removes from this collection all objects that are not also contained in the nominated collection. |
| `int size()` | Fetches the number of elements in this collection. |
| `Object[] toArray()` | Copies the reference of all the objects from this collection into an array and returns the array. |
| `Object[] toArray (Object[])` | Copies the reference of all the objects from this collection into the nominated array if it is large enough. If not, the type of the object used in the parameter is used to generate the return value, allowing correct casting of objects. |

If you did this in normal code, the forth line would generate a `ClassCastException`. Why is this? Haven't we stored everything as Strings? Well, not exactly. We don't know how the collection has stored the items internally. To generate a return value for the standard `toArray()` method, it creates a new array of objects and copies all of the data elements into it. You could imagine it doing the following:

```
public Object[] toArray() {
    Object[] values = new Object[size()];
    System.arraycopy(internalData, 0, values, 0, size());
    return values;
}
```

As you can see from this, the internal representation is not an array of Strings (`String[]`) but an array of objects (`Object[]`). There is a very big difference in Java between the meaning of these two representations of the same data.

Therefore, the second `toArray()` method is provided. In this variant, it will create an array of the object type that you pass to it and return that. This then allows you to cast the object to the correct type and use the data appropriately. Explaining how Java does this internally is beyond the scope of this book. However, to continue with getting our example working, we have two alternative approaches. The first is to create an array of exactly the size that we need and let the collection fill in the values:

```
String[] stringArray = new String[stringList.size()];
stringList.toArray(stringArray);
```

The second option is to tell the method the type of items that you want, but use the return value from the method instead:

```
String[] stringArray;
stringArray = (String[])stringList.toArray(new String[0]);
```

As you can see, the second example creates a zero-length array of the type of object that we want. Basically, this acts as a marker to the collection to tell it which type of object to create and lets it do all the hard work.

In reality, there is no real difference between the end results. However, under the covers, there is quite a difference. For the second example, there is a lot more work that the collection must do. First, it needs to see if the passed array is big enough to just copy the data straight into it. If not, then it must determine the type of the array, create a new instance of it that is the correct length, and then finally copy all the values over. A whole lot more work is done, generating lots of extra garbage and making your program run that little bit slower.

# Iterations

One particularly nice feature of the collections classes is the ability to grab a generic data structure that allows us to traverse through all of the data kept by the collection. The Iterator class provides us a way to move through all of the data as we need it. The idea of an iterator is to provide a clean interface for all the data when we want to traverse through *all* of it in one go.

**Caution**    The statement about an iterator being used for all elements is very important. If you attempt to modify the collection, such as adding or removing an object while another part of your code is using an iteration, it will generate a ConcurrentModification Exception. That means that you can't use an iteration to grab, say, the first few objects and then forget about the rest (such as making the reference to the iterator null). The internals rely on you reaching the end of the iteration (hasNext() returns false) to turn off any checks that might generate this exception.

The Iterator interface is very simple and is described in Table 12-2. Basically, it allows you to move in one direction through the elements provided until the end of the collection is reached. Once you are there, you cannot rewind or do any other operations.

| Table 12-2 | |
| :--- | :--- |
| **The Iterator Interface** | |
| *Method* | *Description* |
| boolean hasNext() | Checks to see if there are any more items that this iterator will allow us to fetch. |
| Object next() | Fetches the next element from the iteration. The object may be cast to whatever type it really represents. |
| void remove() | Removes the last element that next() fetched from this iteration. |

# Keeping a List

Next on the order of the hierarchy is the List interface. Extending from the Collection, it adds a few new methods to add and remove items from specific positions in the list. Lists, to some extent, act just like a glorified array. You can set an index, remove an index, and shuffle them around, just like an array, but without you having to write all the code.

Lists also have a special iterator available to them called ListIterator. To the basic forwards traversal capabilities of the base class, ListIterators allow you to move backwards through the list as well.

**Note** Lists are also zero based like arrays. That is, the first element of the list has an index value of zero, not one.

Java defines three basic types of lists: `ArrayList`, `LinkedList`, and `Vector`.

An `ArrayList` is a list that uses an array as the underlying data structure. This makes it easy and very quick to access elements at any position. Where it suffers is when you want to change the size of the list by adding new elements. Internally, it must allocate a new array and copy over all of the data to the new array before it can add your element. `ArrayList` is best in fixed or well-controlled, sized applications.

`LinkedLists` uses a collection of linked objects to represent each element in the list. If you don't understand what this means, have a look at Figure 12-3. This makes accessing arbitrary index values rather slow, but adding and removing elements is very quick and painless. `LinkedLists` is very useful if you have rapidly changing data in the list or if you need to traverse only the entire list.

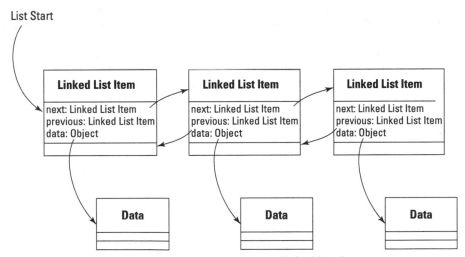

**Figure 12-3:** A graphical representation of what a linked list data structure may look like

`Vector` is just another type of `ArrayList`. It uses an array internally to store data. The main reason for its existence is that it is a holdover from earlier versions of Java that has been retrofitted for use with the collections API. The biggest advantage (and also probably the biggest disadvantage) is that all the methods are synchronized, allowing `Vector` to be shared among multiple application threads.

**Cross-Reference**  Threading and synchronization are covered in Chapter 14, Threads.

## Mapping

Unlike the other collections classes, the Map interface is not derived from the Collection interface. This is because a map provides a different set of capabilities. It is not concerned with storing single objects, but rather, the relationships between objects.

Maps in Java are restricted to a one-to-one mapping of key-value pairs. The variations then are based around how a map determines what each key is and how it is stored in the mapping. Java provides four maps — HashMap, HashTable, TreeMap, and WeakHashMap.

HashMap provides a mapping by using the hash value of the key to store it in the table of information. To obtain the hash value, it calls the hashCode() method on the key object and uses that value to insert or replace the value in the current table. Probably the most used of the maps, this is typically used for storing relationships such as a String description string to the actual data object, for example, in a pick list in a GUI component. A HashMap provides a constant time lookup for an object in the table regardless of how many items are stored in the table.

HashTable does the same thing as HashMap. Like Vector is to ArrayList, so is HashTable to HashMap. HashTable is a holdover from older versions of the Java API and is thread safe.

TreeMap provides the combination of a tree and a map. Data is stored internally in a tree structure rather than a table. To traverse the tree, the key value is used to descend the branches until the appropriate leaf is found. As mentioned earlier in the chapter, trees form a type of data structure in their own right. There are many different tree structures that could be used to implement this class, but in this case, it uses a Red-Black tree. Adding, removing, and searching the tree increases in a logarithmic amount of time compared to the number of entries.

Finally, WeakHashMap is another form of the HashMap class that does a lot of its own self-culling. Once every other part of your application has dropped a reference to the value that you are storing in the map, the map itself will also drop that value. To do this, it makes use of the Weak Reference capabilities provided by Java. This is way beyond the scope of this book, so we won't delve any further into this class.

# Using Collections

To use a collection, just think of anywhere that you want to store a bunch of related data and you've probably found a use for the collection classes. With this built-in capability, it is now much easier to use these classes rather than to write your own handlers unless you really need something special.

## Using Lists and Iterators

There is nothing particularly tricky to using collections in day to day use. In Chapter 8, "Strings, Arrays, and Characters," you saw an example of `StringTokenizer` being used to strip down a string into individual words. This time, instead of printing them out, we can store them for later use:

```
String myString = "There once was a mouse from Nantucket";
LinkedList list = new LinkedList();

StringTokenizer tokens = new StringTokenizer(myString);

try {
  while(tokens.hasMoreTokens())
    list.add(tokens.nextToken());
}
catch(NoSuchElementException nse) {
}

// now print the list out
Iterator itr = list.iterator();
while(itr.hasNext())
  System.out.println("Token: " + itr.next());
```

This will result in the same output as you saw for the previous example, except now, you have a copy of each word to use some other time in your application.

## Using Sets

Using sets is not that much different than using lists. As noted earlier in the chapter, the key difference is that a set can only ever contain one of each value, whereas a list can contain multiple copies.

To illustrate this, we'll modify the list example a little bit:

```
String myString = "one two two three three three";

HashSet set = new HashSet();

StringTokenizer tokens = new StringTokenizer(myString);

try {
  while(tokens.hasMoreTokens())
    set.add(tokens.nextToken());
}
catch(NoSuchElementException nse) {
}

// now print the list out
System.out.println("The contents of the set are: ");
```

```
Iterator itr = set.iterator();
while(itr.hasNext())
  System.out.println("Token: " + itr.next());
```

Compiling and running this code results in the following output:

```
The contents of the set are:
Token: one
Token: two
Token: three
```

As you can see, only one copy of each word is actually kept in the set, regardless of how many times we attempt to add it.

## Using Maps

As you are now aware, maps work quite differently than a list or set. To put in a value, we need to provide two pieces of information—a key and the value, rather than just the value itself.

The most common use of using mapping structures is when you want to look up complex pieces of information based on something simple. For example, say we have a library, and we keep all of the information about a book in the data structure:

```
class Book {
  String title;
  String author;
  String isbn;
  String location;
  String summary;
}
```

Now in the library, we provide an application to allow a borrower to look up the book. We need to name each book using something that is guaranteed to be unique. If we assume a really small library where every book has a different title, we could use that as a key. (We really should use the ISBN number, which *is* guaranteed to be unique, but how many people will remember this number rather than a title?) So we create our library catalogue:

```
Book book1 = new Book();
book1.title = "The first book";
book1.author = "Justin Couch";

// etc
```

We now need to enter these into our "database" somehow. To make our search quick, we can use a map where the key is based on the title but the value is actually the whole book class instance that describes everything we want to know.

```
HashMap database = new HashMap();
database.put(book1.title, book1);
database.put(book2.title, book2);
```

. . .

**Note**

The key value can be any object you like; it doesn't have to be a String, although this is what is most typically used. Strings are really handy because they are normally displayed on the screen for the user to read when trying to access the complex information underneath.

Now we have a complete database of all our books. Of course, now our borrower wants to come along and find our book on the shelves. Somehow, our application asks the user for the name of the book to print information on:

```
String bookName =  // get from the user the name

// get the book from the database based on our name
Book book = (Book)database.get(bookName);

if(book != null) {
   System.out.println("   Title: " + book.title);
   System.out.println("  Author: " + book.author);
   System.out.println("Location: " + book.location);
   System.out.println("    ISBN: " + book.isbn);
   System.out.println(" Summary: " + book.summary);
}
else
   System.out.println("Unable to locate book " + bookName);
```

The get() method is used to retrieve an object from the database. This method always returns an Object instance, so you will need to cast it to the appropriate object type. See how our value depends on the key. If the user types in the wrong name or it doesn't exist in the database, the attempt to fetch the book will return null. Even if the name is correct but there are different numbers of spaces or capital letters, we won't find the book. Depending on the way that you want to access information, this can be an advantage or a disadvantage.

Sometimes, you want to give the user the list of options available. To do this, we need to show them the list of keys. The keySet() method returns a Set that contains every single key in the database. With this, you can then use the Iterator to do something with the keys. For example, you might put these in a `ComboBox` or other form of pick list that the user can make use of:

```
Set bookTitles = database.keySet();
Iterator itr = bookTitles.iterator();

System.out.println("The list of book titles are:");
While(itr.hasNext())
  System.out.println(itr.next());
```

# Manipulating Collections

Creating and using collections is only half the story. Frequently, you will need to do more than this. Many of the basic tasks that you would use with any of the previous data structures have been provided with the `Collections` class, which is not the same as the `Collection` interface. (Blame Sun for this very confusing naming.) In the next few sections, we'll look at the various capabilities provided by the `Collections` class.

## Sorting

One of the most common operations that you will need to perform is sorting the values in the list. Whether this be an alphabetical sort, a numerical sort, or by some other discriminator, the same basic principle applies. There are many different sorting algorithms, some more efficient than others. To save you the hassle of having to know these, a basic sort capability is provided in the `Collections` class. This takes care of all the messy details and leaves you with a sorted version.

By nature, `Maps` and `Sets` are sorted. The act of placing an object into these data structures causes them to be sorted according to the underlying implementation. Therefore, only `Lists` may be sorted.

The `Collections` class provides two ways of sorting, one that takes only a `List` and another that needs a `List` and a `Comparator`. The first sort uses what is called *natural order* of the elements. For example, if we sorted the words generated from the previous example using

```
System.out.println("\nList after default sorting");
Collections.sort(list);

itr = list.iterator();
while(itr.hasNext())
  System.out.println("Token: " + itr.next());
```

the resulting output would be:

```
List after default sorting
Token: Nantucket
Token: There
Token: a
Token: from
Token: mouse
Token: once
Token: was
```

Note that the words starting with a capital letter are higher in the sort order than those starting with lowercase.

If we wanted to change this behavior so that the sort was case insensitive, we would need to use the alternative form of the sort() method and provide our own comparator. Providing our own comparator requires that we implement the Comparator interface. There are two methods that must be provided: compare() and equals(). The equals() method is the standard equals() that most classes implement, which we return true only if the passed argument is also an instance of our comparator class. The compare() method is more interesting.

Compare() takes two arguments, which are the objects that we need to see if they are equal. From this, we return a positive number if the first is greater than the second, zero if they are identical, and negative if the first is less than the second. Since we know that we are always dealing with Strings, we can use the compareToIgnores Case() method of String and just return the value, so we end up with a simple caseless comparator that looks like this:

```
class AlphaComparator
  implements Comparator {
  public int compare(Object o1, Object o2) {
    return ((String)o1).compareToIgnoreCase((String)o2);
  }

  public boolean equals(Object obj) {
    return (obj instanceof AlphaComparator);
  }
}
```

Now, in our example code, we change one line from

```
Collections.sort(list);
```

to

```
Collections.sort(list, new AlphaComparator());
```

and we get the following output:

```
List after corrected sorting
Token: a
Token: from
Token: mouse
Token: Nantucket
Token: once
Token: There
Token: was
```

This is exactly what we wanted.

## Controlling changes

Sometime you want to pass your list, map, or set to someone else, yet you don't want him or her to modify it. Effectively, you want a read-only data structure. The `Collections` class provides this convenience capability for you too.

For each of the types of data structures, there is a method called `unmodifiable<data type>`. So if we wanted to give a caller a read-only version of our list, we could do this:

```
LinkedList list = new LinkedList();

// fill the list with the string tokenizer
List fixedList = Collections.unmodifiableList(list);
return fixedList;
```

This now ensures that the caller knows exactly what we know but does not let that person interfere with the contents of our internal data structures.

## Randomizing a List

The opposite of a sort is randomizing the list. Like sort, this functionality is restricted to lists only. To randomize, we use one of the `shuffle()` methods, changing

```
Collections.sort(list);
```

to

```
Collections.shuffle(list);
```

and we may get the following output:

```
List after random sorting
Token: from
Token: There
Token: mouse
```

```
Token: once
Token: was
Token: Nantucket
Token: a
```

With each run of the application, or even of the shuffle method, we get a different output.

## Reversing List contents

Sometimes, the list that you have needs to be reversed in order. For example, you have a mail folder sorted from oldest to newest, but you want it in the other order. To do this, use the reverse() method. Following the example thread, change

```
Collections.sort(list);
```

to

```
Collections.reverse(list);
```

and we may get the following output:

```
List after reverse sorting
Token: Nantucket
Token: from
Token: mouse
Token: a
Token: was
Token: once
Token: There
```

## Making Copies

Copying a list or making a number of copies of an object can also be performed using the Collections class using the nCopies() and copy() methods.

Using the nCopies() method allows you to create a number of identical copies of the given object and is returned as a list. You might want to use this to create an empty table or fill some data structure before putting meaningful data into it. A call of

```
MyObject myObject  = new MyObject();
List objectList = Collections.nCopies(20, myObject);
```

will create 20 copies of your object and put them into objectList. What this really does is create 20 references to your one object, rather than cloning it 20 times. Also, you will need to be careful because this list is immutable; that is, you cannot change the contents or its size.

If you need to copy items between lists, you can use the `copy()` method. This copies the entire contents of one list into another list. This is quite different from the `addAll()` method that you saw earlier. This time, the index positions of the source list are kept when putting them into the destination list. Values previously at those positions are gone. Where they go is not exactly specified. Depending on the implementation, it might shuffle them up the list or it may just completely replace the items.

If copying items in your list is not exactly what you wanted, then maybe the `fill()` method will work better. This takes your list and replaces every item in it with your nominated object. Of course, lists are agnostic to the data provided, so that object could well be null, which would result in a list of empty objects.

## Searching

If you were to look for an object in the list, you might decide to start at the beginning and check each object to see if it matches. The problem with this is that it is very inefficient. If we double the length of our list, we double the time it takes to search. For very big lists, that can be a significant amount of time and makes your application run slow. There are many different and more efficient ways of searching a list.

One of the more efficient methods is to use a *Binary Search*. Basically, this takes the middle item of the list and checks to see if the object we are looking for is less than or greater than the middle object. If it is less than the middle object, we take the lower half of the list and find the middle item from the first item to the original middle. Then we do the same less than/greater than check again. This keeps going until we find the actual object, or we can't divide any further. (The object wasn't found.)

Java provides this search method using the `binarySearch()` method of the `Collections` class. To use it, all you have to do is pass it the list and the object you are looking for. In return, you get the index of the object in the list, or –1 if the object doesn't exist in that list. This acts in exactly the same way as the `Arrays` class `binarySearch()` method that you saw in the previous chapter. This routine also requires that the list is sorted first, so it internally calls the `sort()` method on your list before doing the search.

Of course, like the sort routines, by providing our own comparator, we can search the list by any means that we want. We could use `AlphaComparator` that we created earlier as the basis for doing a case-insensitive search of the list of words.

## Miscellaneous Methods

The `Collections` class provides a number of other simple methods for finding various items in the list. For example, you might want to find the minimum value in the list using the `min()` method. Providing the complement to this is the `max()` method that finds the maximum value.

If you have been around the computing industry for even a short time, you have probably heard of the term *"design patterns."* These are ways of looking at your code requirements and breaking it up into various tried-and-true models. If you look at Java, you will see that the APIs are designed along a number of very familiar design patterns. One of the most common of these is called the *singleton*. This means that throughout the application, there is only ever one instance of your class. This is useful if you want to create only one network connection to your server, but you have many different parts of the application use it. Using the `singleton()` method, you can ensure that this happens with your classes. The Set returned allows only one instance of your class to be used.

# Keeping Property Lists

There is one particular data structure that you are likely to be constantly using in your applications — a list of properties. These properties might describe anything: the attributes of a chair (color, style, supplier, and so on), or the information about a user's identification.

As you might have guessed from this introduction, this sounds very much like a map data structure. In fact it is, but just very highly structured. The `Properties` class in Java serves a very special purpose. Derived from `HashTable`, extra methods are added that give you a whole lot more flexibility to describe your application's data. The one difference between a normal `HashTable` and `Properties` is that the key for accessing information from `Properties` is always a `String` (`HashTable`/`HashMap` may use any `Object`).

## Why use Property lists?

If this were the only difference, there would not be much point in having a separate class. Where the class comes into its own is dealing with information loaded from disk. Almost the entire reason for existence of this class is to provide a convenient way of loading and saving text-based data to disk.

Why might this be so important, you ask? Let's say you have a simple application that runs on your local network. Suddenly, the boss comes in and wants to make it available to your Japanese customers. The problem is, all the text labels are in English and they'd like it in Kanji. If you'd taken the easy route and declared

```
JLabel l1 = new JLabel("Go Now");
```

you'd be in trouble. This means making two separate lots of code, one for each language. For each version of the applet, you'd need a separate code base. Imagine how quickly this can become a code maintenance nightmare when trying to add new features or fix bugs. The simple way around this is to declare all of the text information in a separate file and create all of the labels based on this external file. To change languages, just fill out the appropriate items in the text file and hey, presto, instant version of the application for a new language. No recompiles, no messy maintenance nightmares.

## Loading Properties from disk

In its most simple form, the `Properties` class takes an `InputStream` from which it processes data and places it in the internal map. Generally, this stream is a file on the local disk with all of our data in it.

Streams are covered in detail in Chapter 13, "Input/Output: Streams." For these examples, we'll just show you the code without explaining what is happening.

To load the data into the `Properties` class, the data must exist in a particular format. If you have explored the installation directories of the JDK, you may have seen files lying around that end with `.properties`. These are what the JDK uses internally to load its information. Each line of the file defines a new property. The line is divided into two parts. Everything before a semicolon (;), equal (=) sign, or white space defines the key. Everything after it defines the value. A line starting with the pound (#) character or exclamation (!) mark is treated as a comment.

Only lines starting with a pound (#) sign and an exclamation (!) mark are treated as comments. If you have a key/value defined and then add a pound sign to the end of that line, it is treated as part of the value, not as a comment.

Let's look at the following example file:

```
# Lines like this are comments
#
key : value
simple_key: simple_value
a property definition with spaces
dots.dont.mean.anything = at all
```

As you can see, you can pretty much use anything. Just remember that the values are always treated as text. Therefore, if you put a numerical value in there, your application code must parse the string and turn it into a real number (`int`, `float`, `boolean`, and so on).

To load this file, we would need to use the following code:

```
String path = "c:\\myexamples\\example.properties";
try {
    InputStream is = new FileInputStream(path);

    Properties props = new Properties();

    // now load the file contents
    props.load(is);
    is.close();
}
catch(IOException ioe) {
    // print out a warning here
}
```

Following this, you now have a completely loaded `Properties` class. You can fetch values from this just like you would any other map-derived class, or you can use the explicit `setProperty()` and `getProperty()` methods.

## Saving Properties to Disk

If you can load properties from disk, then saving them is just as important. While you might not use this feature to keep the latest names of the labels for buttons, you can use it to save user preference information. For example, you might use this to store the user settings for the various colors, window size/spacing, or default values.

When writing out property information, we basically follow the reverse process for reading them. We need an OutputStream to write the information to, the Properties list that we want, and we can also supply an option header (e.g., for copyright information, etc).

Say we want to write out the information saved from the previous example:

```
String comment = "(c) Dodgy Brothers Software 1900";
String path = " c:\\myexamples\\user.properties";

try {
    OutputStream os = new FileOutputStream(path);

    props.store(os, comment);
    os.close();
}
catch(IOException ioe) {
    // print out a warning here
}
```

## Using Properties in Applets

In the previous examples, we've used references to files to fetch the property information. When it comes to using applets, there is an extremely good chance that you can't read files from the local user's hard disk.

**Caution**

This section shows you how to read property information from within an applet. Before we start, however, you should know that the concepts presented are advanced, and it takes quite a bit of background knowledge to understand what is really happening. As such, we are going to present you with code, tell you a bit about it, and attach a "no warranty" tag to it. The code is available online for you to look through. However, if you don't stray too far from what is presented, you should have no problems using this code as much as you like.

The key to understanding how to deal with applets is knowing that all the classes are fetched from the same place. Now we don't really care what that "same place" is, just that all of the classes and anything else needed will always be there for us. For example, if our code is delivered in a JAR file (see Chapter 25, "Deploying Applets and Applications," for more information), then everything is contained in that file without us having to tell the JVM anything special at the code level. (There is always something in the HTML or environment.)

Once you understand this little piece of information, all you need to do is work out how to fetch the property file relative to wherever the applet started. For this, the ClassLoader class fills the appropriate requirements.

**Note**    ClassLoader **is part of the** java.lang **package, so you don't need an explicit** import **statement to be able to use it.**

Modifying our earlier property file reading example, now we want to read the file called example.properties using the ClassLoader. Naturally, we need this as a stream so that we can pass the stream to the load() method of the Properties class. To do this, we use the getResourceAsStream() method with the name of the file that we want:

```
private static final String SOURCE_FILE =
    "example.properties";

try {
    ClassLoader cl = ClassLoader.getSystemClassLoader();
    InputStream is = cl.getResourceAsStream(SOURCE_FILE);


    // now process the property information as normal
Properties props = new Properties();

    // now load the file contents
    props.load(is);
    is.close();

    // etc
```

That's about it. Now, whenever the applet starts, it reads the properties from the same code base that the applet starts with, so you can immediately get running with configurable applets.

**Tip**    The previous code works just as well for applications as it does for applets. This allows you to specify all of your configurable parts of your code relative to the main application directory without having to know where the application is actually installed.

# Summary

As you can see, there are a lot of labor-saving classes provided by the `java.util` package. In probably 80 percent of your applications, everything you need is here with all of the major data structures presented. If you are ever in need of some data handling, check here first because it probably has already been written for you!

Key points that you have learned in this chapter include the following:

✦ Java provides a standard set of all the commonly used data structures in the `java.util` package.

✦ You can create and access information from various types of data structures.

✦ Using the `Collections` class, you can sort, shuffle, randomize, and control people's access to your important data.

✦ You can create your own custom comparators for controlling how to look and sort through your data.

✦     ✦     ✦

# Input/Output: Streams

**S**treams can be thought of as flowing buffers of data, providing our programs with a relatively easy mechanism for reading and writing data. You may already know of at least one way of sending data using streams; you've been using the system input stream all along. As you'll see throughout this chapter, System.out is only a very small way in which to use streams. In this chapter, you'll also learn how to create and use input and output (I/O) streams. You will also learn about FilterInputStream and FilterOutputStream, which provide an enhanced I/O mechanism for streams. Object serialization, which allows any Java object to be written to an output stream and then recreated later by reading the object back from the input stream, will also be covered.

## About Streams

Streams are a conduit for sending and receiving information in Java programs. When sending a stream of data, it is said that you are *writing a stream*. When receiving a stream of data, you are said to be *reading a stream*.

Whenever a stream is being written or read, it blocks all other activity of your application. This is not a major issue, however, if you use threads. As you'll see in Chapter 14, "Threads," you can place input and output streams in a separate process to allow other program execution to continue while these processes are reading and writing. If an error occurs when reading or writing a stream, an IOException is thrown. As a result, you must surround your stream statements with a try-catch clause, to handle any of the potential exceptions. (For details on exceptions, see Chapter 11, "Exceptions and Error Handling.")

Java has not only a standard system stream, but also a more complex and complete set of streams dedicated entirely to input/output: the `java.io` package. Before we get into this package, however, we'll look at standard system input/output to set the stage.

# Standard System Streams (java.lang.System)

The `java.lang.System` class defines a standard input and a standard output stream. So far, we've been using output streams to output data to the display monitor in our applications.

There are three types of standard streams:

1. The standard output stream (accessed through the `System.out` class variable); this is typically the display, or the monitor, of the machine on which your program is running and is normally used to communicate textual information with the user.

2. The standard input stream (accessed through the `System.in` class variable); this usually comes from the keyboard and is often used for reading character data.

3. The standard error stream (accessible through the `System.err` class variable).

Let's take a look at each.

`System`'s class constructor is private, preventing the class from being instantiated. It also cannot be subclassed, since it has been declared as final (with all methods and variables specified as static). Since `System` methods and variables are static, you simply refer to them directly, as we've been doing throughout the book. (For details on the private, final, and static modifiers, see Chapter 9, "Classes, Interfaces and Packages.")

## Standard output (System.out)

So far, this book has used the standard output in all of its Java applications. You haven't, however, seen how to use standard output in applets, since we paint and draw information upon the applet canvas rather than sending output directly to `System.out`. Standard out, as you may recall, is often the display or the monitor, and is used in applications to output information directly to the console. With applets, we already have a surface to draw on; with applications, however, we typically output information to the command line. This is done by sending either a `print()` or `println()` method to the `System.in` variable:

```
System.out.print ("Hello World"); // print
System.out.println("Hello World"); // print line
```

The `print()` method sends information into a buffer. This buffer is not flushed until an end-of-line character ('\n') is sent via `print()`, or the `println()` method is called. As a result, all of the information is printed on one line until an end-of-line character is encountered or the `println()` method is invoked. By contrast, `println()` takes the information provided and prints it on a line followed by a carriage-return/line feed.

## Standard input (System.in)

The second standard stream is `System.in`, which hasn't been used yet in this book; however, there's no time like the present.

Let's assume you wanted to read information from the keyboard. In an applet, you already know how to do this: you would add a `KeyListener` and process the key presses through the `keyPressed` method. In an application, you don't usually have the luxury of dealing with those types of events (unless a GUI is created for the application; see Part IV "Looking out the Windshield: User Interaction" for details). What you do have, however, is access to the standard input stream by sending the `read()` method to the `System.in` variable:

```
int keyInput;
int i = 0;
try {
  while ((keyInput = System.in.read()) != -1) {
    i++;
    System.out.println(i + " = " + keyInput);
  }
}
catch (IOException e) {
  ...
}
```

As you can see, this fragment of code simply reads in character input from the keyboard, incrementing the counter each time through, outputting the character that is read to standard out, along with the character count, and then repeating the process. This loop can be broken only when the read returns -1. With `read()`, a -1 is returned only when an end-of-file character is received.

**Tip**

End-of-file characters are generated in different ways for UNIX and DOS/Windows-based machines. With UNIX, Ctrl+D (^D) must be used (holding down the Control and D keys at the same time). In DOS/Windows environments, Ctrl+Z (^Z) is used.

## Standard error (System.err)

Although you'll use `System.out` most of the time, you may wish to use the standard error output stream, rather than sending output to `System.out`, as we've just done. The system output can be redirected to another place other than the console, such as a file. If this happens, any really important error messages are sent to that file so the user might miss them. Using `System.err` provides a separate output stream for those really important error messages.

The error stream is identical to the standard output. To send output to it, you would use almost the same code as the earlier examples using `System.out`, just changing `out` to `err`. To ensure that output goes to the display screen, you could simply send your data to the system-error variable like this:

```
System.err.println("Warning!");
```

Now the data doesn't run the risk of being "hidden" when output; it is always sent to the display.

# java.io Streams

Although the system streams are very handy, they really aren't robust enough to be of much use when dealing with substantial I/O. For the full power of streams, you need to turn to the `java.io` package. As you can see from the diagram in Figure 13-1, this package supports two streams — one input and one output stream — from which all other streams are subclassed.

`java.io.InputStream` and `java.io.OutputStream` are actually abstract classes. They are implemented in the subclasses shown in Figure 13-1. However, they are the parent classes of all other streams, and as such, they have a common element that all streams share. To better understand the types of streams that are supported by the `java.io` package, you'll need to take a closer look at the `InputStream` and `OutputStream` classes.

## Classes of Streaming

Java divides streams into two classes — `Readers/Writers` and `InputStream/Output Stream`. The stream-based classes were the original method of dealing with data while the reader system was introduced with JDK 1.1. There is a subtle yet very important difference between them.

In the shrinking world of the global Internet, almost anyone can use your software — that may be someone from India, China, or Europe. It is quite probable that they don't use English on their screen. Making your software cope with these differences is called Internationalisation. The standard English character set — typically represented as the ASCII characters — has just under 200 different items. These 200 items include punctuation, numbers, letters, and other important features like indicators for the end of a file (stream). However, Russian Cyrillic, Japanese Kanji, and Arabic don't use the same characters as we do, yet they still want to use software.

With 200 odd characters, we can easily represent this with a single byte, which gives us 256 options. It is said that an average Japanese person needs to know roughly 3,000 different characters just to have a coffee and be able to read the paper in the morning. One byte is obviously not enough. Enter the Unicode character set, which uses two bytes to represent a character. The fundamental difference between readers and input streams is the ability to deal with one- or two-byte characters. If you are writing a word processor and reading information from a file, you can see how quickly this little distinction becomes important for representing non-English text.

## InputStream

InputStream is an abstract class that defines how data is received. Where this data comes from really doesn't matter; what's important is that it is accessible. In fact, the data can come from just about anywhere. It may come from the keyboard, from a file on your local file system, or from across the Web — the program doesn't care. This is the strength of streams: it isn't necessary to know where the data is coming from or where it's going to use it.

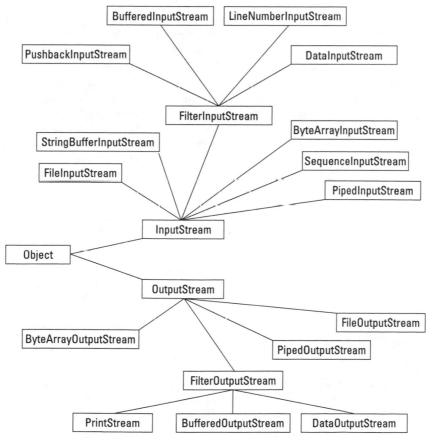

**Figure 13-1:** All Java streams descend from one of two parent classes in the java.io package: InputStream or OutputStream.

## InputStream Methods

The InputStream object provides a number of methods that allow you to create, read, and process input streams. Table 13-1 lists a few methods that operate on input streams and how they might be used. In all these methods, an IOException may be thrown to indicate than an error occurred in the underlying implementation or source of the stream.

### Table 13-1
### Class java.io.InputStream

| Method | Description |
| --- | --- |
| public abstract int read() | Reads a byte of data. This method blocks (does not return) if no input is available. |
| public int read(byte[]) | Reads into an array of bytes. This method blocks until some input is available. Returns the actual number of bytes read; -1 is returned when the end of the stream is reached. |
| public int read(byte[] int, int) | Reads into an array of bytes starting from the given offset into the array and for the specified maximum number of bytes. This method blocks until some input is available. Returns the actual number of bytes read; -1 is returned when the end of the stream is reached. |
| public int available() | Returns the number of bytes that can be read without blocking at the time of calling. |
| public long skip(long) | Skips *n* bytes of input. Returns the actual number of bytes skipped. |
| public void mark(int) | Marks the current position in the input stream. A subsequent call to reset() repositions the stream at the last marked position so that subsequent reads can reread the same bytes. The stream promises to allow readlimit bytes to be read before the mark position is invalidated. |
| public void reset() | Repositions the stream to the last marked position. |
| public boolean markSupported() | Returns a boolean indicating whether or not this stream type supports mark/reset. Returns true if this stream type supports mark/reset; false otherwise. |
| public void close() | Closes the input stream. Must be called to release any resources associated with the stream. |

Stream marks are intended to be used in situations where you need to read ahead a little to see what's in the stream for parsing purposes. If the stream is of the type handled by the parser, it just chugs along happily. If the stream is not of that type, the parser should toss an exception when it fails — which, if it happens within readlimit bytes, allows the outer code to reset the stream and try another parser.

### read()

The previous table contains three read() methods, each of which takes a different set of parameters; the most basic is the one we've been using with the system input stream. This read() method simply reads one byte from the input stream. The other two methods let you specify either an array of bytes or a portion of an array of bytes:

✦ read(): Reads a single byte from the stream

✦ read(byte[]): Reads a number of bytes at once. The maximum number is the length of the provided array

✦ read(byte[], int, int): Reads a portion of the stream into the array at the given offset and number of bytes

In the second example, read() tries to fill up the entire array we've passed to it. If it's not successful, meaning there were fewer characters in the stream than there were indexes in the array, -1 is returned. This indicates that the end of the stream has been reached. It will block if it can't fill the array, but the end of the stream has not been reached. The number returned is the number of bytes actually read.

However, -1 doesn't indicate an error; it simply lets us know that the process didn't run all the way through. If an actual error had occurred, an IOException would have been thrown.

In the third example, we specify the location in the array to begin writing the stream, along with how many elements in the array to actually fill. This is useful when you have an array that you want partially filled with data. You can begin reading data at any index and continue for the remainder of the array or just a portion of it. Like the second example, the number returned is the number of bytes read. For example, to completely read a stream:

```
int i, bytesRead;
byte[] byteArray = new byte[1024];
while((bytesRead = anyStream.read(byteArray, 0, 1024)) != -)
   // do something with the array of bytes
```

### available()

The available() method enables you to find out how many bytes there are in a stream that can be read without blocking. Unfortunately, a number of the stream classes don't support calculation of the correct values for available(). As a result, unless you're certain that the stream you're using supports available(), you can't guarantee this method will return a valid number. Sometimes, zero is returned; at other times, the actual number of bytes in the stream is returned. It's a good idea to avoid using `available()`, if possible, unless you're certain of exactly what you're doing.

### skip()

At times, you'll want to skip over a number of bytes in a stream. This is easy enough; just invoke the `skip()` method. Supply it with a numeric parameter, telling it how many bytes to skip over, and the stream begins reading again at the position after that skip. This assumes, of course, that you are in the process of reading a stream:

```
anyStream.skip(200); // skip over next 200 bytes
```

**Tip**     Although you may be tempted to provide an actual `long` value to the `skip()` method, you should keep the range of your values to those of an `int`. This is because Java actually converts your long integer into an `int`. In future releases, `skip()` may indeed use a `long`, but for now, assume that it uses an `int`.

### mark() and reset()

At times, you may want to revisit a particular position in a stream and return to read there once again. This is possible by marking that position in the stream using the `mark()` method. When you want to return, simply call `reset()`:

```
// mark the current byte as special, with a limit of 256 bytes
anyStream.mark(256);

... do something ...

// return to the marked byte, and begin from there
anyStream.reset();
```

As you can see in the preceding example, we've marked the current byte in the stream in the first line. At the time, we've said that we have an interest in resetting the stream up to a maximum of 256 bytes from the current position. When we call `reset()` on that stream, we rewind back to the original marked position. Note, however, that if we read more than 256 characters between the time that we've set the `mark()` and called `reset()`, a problem occurs. This is because the stream must keep track of the number of bytes you supply in `mark()`. If you read more than that number, it can't guarantee you can go back to the same position. Suppose you read beyond the 256 characters; that is, you read 257 characters after setting the mark. The memory allocated for that mark may not be available, in which case, when you call `reset()`, an exception may be thrown.

Keep this in mind whenever you use `mark()` and `reset()`. Make certain that, once you mark a stream, you don't read more characters than you marked, minus one if you need to reset. For instance, if you set a mark at 1000, read only up to 999 more characters before calling `reset()` or update the mark to the new position.

Not all stream types support `mark()`. To test whether it can, call the `markSupported()` method.

### close()

Streams support the notion of being *closed*; that is, when you're done with them, you can close them down. This is easily done by sending the `close()` method to a stream:

```
anyStream.close ();
```

Although the garbage collector in Java is supposed to take care of this for you, it's a good idea to do it yourself. Since you can't guarantee when the garbage collector will come around and close an unused stream for you, you might attempt to reopen it before the garbage collector has finished with it.

By closing the stream yourself, you guarantee it to be closed. The next time you try to open it, you won't run into this potential problem:

```
try {
    ... work with the stream ...
}
catch (Exception e) {
    anyStream.close(); // close this stream
}
```

From the snippet just given, you can see that the best place to close a stream may be the `finally` clause in a `try-catch` clause. The `finally` clause is always a good way to close a stream, because it's the last thing called in a `try-catch` clause. And, as you know, since streams may generate or throw off exceptions, you need the `try-catch` clause anyway. So, why not simply close a stream in the `finally` clause when you're done using it? It's a good, safe way to ensure that your stream is closed before going on with the rest of your program.

**Tip**    In most of these examples, I haven't bothered to use the `try-catch` clause for the sake of brevity and clarity. Since working with streams can result in exceptions being thrown, you'll need to write your stream code using exception handlers.

## Readers

When dealing with text, the standard byte streams are usually inappropriate if you need to deal with internationalization concerns. Non-English characters, such as Japanese Kanji, take more than a single byte to represent. To deal with this, the `Reader` and `Writer` classes are available for use with text process. They are used in basically the same manner as their byte-stream counterparts. The `Reader` and `Writer` classes automatically provide the appropriate Unicode character conversions, making your applications and applets more portable between locales (character sets). The `InputStreamReader` class (see Table 13-2) reads bytes from a data source and converts them to their appropriate Unicode character counterparts.

One area to be cautious of is knowing exactly when you are dealing with a text stream and when you aren't. If you accidentally use a Reader to read a binary stream, you can run into some really hard-to-track problems in your data, as almost every second byte will be treated as the upper byte of a Unicode character.

Using a reader is almost identical to using an input stream. The methods are the same, but the way it treats the underlying stream is not. Readers handle internationalized text so that you can be assured everything works correctly when needing to display strings.

### Swapping Between Readers and InputStreams

Frequently, you end up finding that your code will have a stream when you really want a reader. The InputStreamReader class is used as the translator between these two. As readers are more general and more capable than input streams, there is the ability to move from a stream to a reader but not the reverse.

| Table 13-2<br>java.io.InputStreamReader | |
|---|---|
| **Constructor** | **Description** |
| public InputStreamReader (InputStream) | Creates an input stream reader that uses the default character encoding. |
| public InputStreamReader (InputStream, String) | Creates an input stream that uses the character encoding specified. |
| **Methods** | **Description** |
| public void close() | Closes the input stream. |
| public String getEncoding() | Returns the name of the encoding currently used. |
| public int read() | Reads a single character. |
| public int read (char[], int, int) | Reads a number character into a buffer starting at the given offset and for the maximum number of items. |
| public boolean ready() | Determines whether the input stream is ready to be read. |

# OutputStream

The OutputStream class is an abstract class that defines how all streams are written. It performs the opposite of the InputStream. Where there is a read() method for the input, there is a corresponding write() method for the output.

## OutputStream Methods

The `OutputStream` object provides methods to create, write, and process output streams. Every type of stream uses the methods shown in Table 13-3. Let's take a closer look at each.

| | |
|---|---|
| **Table 13-3** | |
| **The java.io.OutputStream class** | |

| Methods | Description |
|---|---|
| `public void write(int)` | Writes a byte. Takes the bottom byte from the `int` (values between 0 and 255) and writes that to the stream. This method blocks until the byte is actually written. |
| `public void write(byte[])` | Writes an array of bytes. This method blocks until the bytes are actually written. |
| `public void write(byte[], int, int)` | Writes a subarray of bytes from the given offset and length. |
| `public void flush()` | Flushes the stream. This writes any buffered output bytes. |
| `public void close()` | Closes the stream. This method must be called to release any resources associated with the stream. |

### write() and flush()

The three `write()` methods write bytes to a stream. Use the one that makes sense for your program. (See the descriptions in Table 13-3.):

✦ `write(int)`: Writes a single byte

✦ `write(byte[])`: Writes an array of bytes

✦ `write(byte[], int, int)`: Writes a particular section of an array of bytes

You'll note that these are similar, at least in their parameters, to the `read()` methods defined in `InputStream`. This is no surprise, since `OutputStream` can be considered the reverse of `InputStream`. While `InputStream` allows you to read bytes in from a stream, `OutputStream` sends bytes to a stream. Drawing from our previous `Input Stream` examples, you might use the following to write a stream:

```
byte myByte = System.in.read(); // read a keyboard character
anOutputStream.write(myByte); // write it to a stream
anOutputStream.write(byteArray); // write array into a stream
anOutputStream.write(byteArray, 25, 100); /* write portion of
                                            an array */
```

### flush()

The `flush()` method is used to write bytes that may be in memory to the stream. This may be necessary, for instance, when a stream is being built up in memory and needs to be flushed out to the disk.

This can also happen when the stream you are creating is being written to the network. In this case, while the stream may be written to memory, the `flush()` method will actually send it:

```
anOutputStream.flush();
```

### close()

After you've opened an `OutputStream`, it's a good idea to close it. Just as with its `InputStream` counterpart, don't rely on the garbage collector to come around and close it for you. It's best to explicitly close any stream you're using when you're done:

```
try {
    ... work with the stream ...
}
finally {
  anOutputStream.flush();
  anOutputStream.close(); // close this stream when done
}
```

`Close()` also normally calls `flush()` before really closing the stream to make sure everything has been written. However, to be sure, you should always explicitly call flush just before calling `close()` to make sure.

## Writers

When writing text to an output, internationalization is just as much a concern as it is for reading text. Even though you may have written your word processor with English menu items, the user could still be putting non-English characters into his or her document. To ensure that you keep things the way that the author intended, you should use Writers. Like the reader, when you present a character to it, it is written to the file using the appropriate single or two-byte representation.

All writers are based on the `Writer` class. Again, mirroring the `Reader`/`InputStream` coupling, the `OutputStream`/`Writer` shared exactly the same method definitions. Swapping between the two should be no more than changing the line of code that is used to construct the object.

### Swapping Between OutputStreams and Writers

Like the input side, the output also tends to find you needing one where you really want the other. In yet another parallel, the OutputStreamWriter class provides the code glue between an OutputStream and a Writer.

The OutputStreamWriter class (see Table 13-4) writes characters to an output stream, translating the characters into bytes as specified by the character encoding scheme. This ensures that characters are written in the appropriate format according to the translation scheme specified.

| Table 13-4 java.io.OutputStreamWriter | |
|---|---|
| **Example** | **Description** |
| public OutputStreamWriter (OutputStream) | Creates an output stream writer that uses the default character encoding. |
| public OutputStreamWriter (OutputStream, String) | Creates an output stream that uses the character encoding specified. |
| public void close() | Closes the output stream. |
| public void flush() | Flushes the stream to ensure all buffered data is moved to the final output. |
| void write(int b) | Writes a single character. |
| public int write(char[], int, int) | Writes an array of characters into buffer. |
| boolean ready() throws | Determines whether the input stream is ready to be read. |

# Special-Purpose Streams

As you know, the InputStream and OutputStream classes are the parents for all other streams in the java.io package. They define the basic behavior each stream supports. However, there are a number of special-purpose streams supported in java.io that allow you to do specific stream work. Since you already know how the InputStream and OutputStream methods are used, it's time to take a look at each of their special-purpose "children." (Take a look back at Figure 13-1, where the class hierarchy is laid out.)

# File input

One of the most useful things you'll do with streams is read and write files with them. Two special classes, `FileInputStream` and `FileOutputStream`, make this process a breeze. As you can see in Table 13-5, there are several constructors — three of which allow you to create an input stream from a file.

| Table 13-5 <br> java.io.FileInputStream Constructors | |
|---|---|
| *Signature* | *Description* |
| `public FileInputStream` | Creates an input file with the specified name (name is `(String)`system-dependent). |
| `public FileInputStream (File)` | Creates an input stream from the specified file object. |
| `public FileInputStream (FileDescriptor)` | Creates an input file from the specified file descriptor object. |

The first constructor takes a string that is the actual pathname of a file. The pathname that you provide is system-dependent. You can use UNIX conventions for UNIX-based files, DOS conventions for DOS- and Windows-based files, and Macintosh conventions for Macintosh-based files; and, as Java is ported to other platforms, these will each have their own conventions.

## File and Applets

Due to the security restrictions with applets, Files cannot be read or written. The only exception to this is if you are using a signed, trusted applet, and then the user must also grant you permission to run the code.

To enable file reading and writing within an applet, you need to check for the `java.io.File Permission` of `"read"` or `"write"` respectively. As an applet, you will also need to nominate these permission requirements in your JAR file manifest. If you need more information about how to set and read security settings, please refer to Chapter 25, "Deploying Applets and Applications."

However, since Java automatically converts a path to accommodate whatever platform it is running on, you can use the one most convenient for you. The examples of the different styles needed can be seen below

```
InputStream myUNIXFile =
  new FileInputStream("/java/code/HelloWorld.java");

// DOS slashes are escaped! (see note)
InputStream myDOSFile =
  newFileInputStream("c:\\java\\code\\HelloWorld.java");

InputStream myMacFile =
  newFileInputStream(":java:code:HelloWorld.java");
```

**Note**  In Java (and most other languages, for that matter), the backslash character ( \ ) is used to escape another character, or to tell the compiler to use the special meaning. For example "\t" says that this should be a tab character and "\n" is a new line. To tell the compiler that you really want the backslash character to appear in the string, you must escape it to use it. Hence, you will see the double backslash ( \\ ) construct quite frequently when dealing with Windows file names in any code.

In addition, you can create a FileInputStream using a FileDescriptor (defined in the java.io.FileDescriptor class). Once you've opened a file, it has what's known as a descriptor associated with it. You can get the FileDescriptor for a file you've just opened using the getFD() method. Once you have a FileDescriptor, you can hang onto it and use it to reference the file later:

```
InputStream myFile =
newFileInputStream("/java/code/HelloWorld.java");
FileDescriptor myDesc = myFile.getFD(); // get descriptor
...
InputStream myFile2 = newFileInputStream(myDesc); // new stream
```

This is particularly useful when you're creating applications that need to access information in a file, and you know which file you'll be using (such as a temporary data file that your program creates). However, sometimes you'll want to use files that come from a server.

This is common when using applets; in fact, this is the best way to handle files when dealing with applets. Since applets are prevented from accessing files on the local machine, unless specified to do so by the user, it's best to always load applet files from the server. This is done by creating a FileInputStream using a File object as a parameter. (A File object is created using the File class defined in java.io.File.)

**Note**    When using `FileInputStream`, the `available()` method works properly. This is because files are of a known size (that is, they're not infinite). As a result, `available()` can calculate how many characters or bytes are in a file. Keep in mind, however, that not all streams support the `available()` method!

## File output

In addition to reading streams that come from files, you may want to write a stream out to a file. Table 13-6 shows the various constructors the `FileOutputStream` class supports. These are effectively the reverse of `FileInputStream`, creating an output stream instead of an input stream. The various output methods discussed earlier act as you would expect on the resulting stream.

| Table 13-6 java.io.FileOutputStream Constructors | |
|---|---|
| **Signature** | **Description** |
| `public FileOutputStream (String)` | Creates an output file with the file name. (File name is system-dependent.) |
| `public FileOutputStream (String,boolean)` | Creates or appends to an output file with the file name. (File name is system-dependent.) If the boolean parameter is true, then you may append to the file. |
| `public FileOutputStream (File)` | Creates an output file using the `File` object passed to it. |
| `public FileOutputStream (FileDescriptor)` | Creates an output file from the specified `FileDescriptor` object. |

Listing 13-1 illustrates how to open a connection to the Web using a URL and retrieve the contents of whatever the URL points to. The object (page, graphic, sound file, and so on) is pulled off the Internet and is placed in a file inside the directory of your choice. Keep in mind that this is an application, not an applet, so it is invoked from the command line:

```
> java GetURL stuff http://www.pepsi.com
```

In this example, the home page at `http://www.pepsi.com` is retrieved and placed inside the stuff directory (located inside the same directory as the `GetURL` application). The program uses an input stream to download the data and a `FileOutputStream` stream to spit the contents out to a local file.

## Listing 13-1: **GetURL.java: An Example of FileOutputStream in Action**

```java
// Usage: java GetURL dir URL [ URL ... ]
import java.net.*;
import java.io.*;

class GetURL {
  static final int BUF_SIZE = 4000;
  // size of buffer for copying

  public static void main (String args[]) {
    int   dx, tail, numb, dir_idx = 0;
    boolean  noisy = false;
    byte     buffer[] = new byte[buf_size];
    String   outfile;
    URL      url;

    InputStream in;
    FileOutputStream out;

    // Get command-line options
    while (dir_idx < args.length  &&
           args[dir_idx].startsWith("-")) {
      if (args[0].equals("-noisy")) {
        noisy = true;
      }
      else {
        System.err.println("Unknown option: "+args[0]);
        return;
      }
      dir_idx++;
    } // end of while loop

    // Check for correct number of command-line arguments
    if (args.length < dir_idx+2) {
      System.err.println("Usage: java GetURL [-noisy] " +
                         "directory URL [URL ...]");
      System.err.println("      copies the files specified " +
                      " by the URL's into directory");
      return;
    }

    // Get the files
    for (idx = dir_idx+1; idx < args.length; idx++) {
      // Open the URL
      try {
        url = new URL(args[idx]);
      }
```

*Continued*

**Listing 13-1** *(continued)*

```
catch (MalformedURLException e) {
  System.err.println("Error: malformed URL " +
                        args[idx]);
  System.err.println(e.getMessage());
  continue;
}

try {
  in = url.openStream();
}
catch (IOException e) {
  System.err.println("Error: couldn't access " +
                        args[idx]);
  System.err.println(e.getMessage());
  continue;
}

// Extract file name and open file
tail  = args[idx].lastIndexOf('\\');
if (tail == -1) {
  tail = args[idx].lastIndexOf('/');
}

outfile = args[idx].substring(tail + 1);

try {
  out = new FileOutputStream(args[dir_idx] + '/' +
                                outfile);
}
catch (IOException e) {
  System.err.println("Error: couldn't create " +
                        args[dir_idx] + '/' + outfile);
  System.err.println(e.getMessage());
  continue;
}

// Get the file
if (noisy) {
  System.out.println("Copying "+outfile+"...");
}

try  {
  while ((numb = in.read(buffer)) != -1)
    out.write(buffer, 0, numb);
}
catch (IOException e) {
  System.err.println("Error: IOException during copy");
  System.err.println(e.getMessage());
  continue;
}
```

```
        // Cleanup
        try {
          in.close();
        }
        catch (IOException e) {
        }

        try {
          out.close();
        }
        catch (IOException e) {
        }
      } // end of for loop loading for each stream.

    if (noisy){
      System.out.println("Done");
       }
    }
  }
```

## Files and directories

The `java.io.File` class supports objects that reference disk files. With this class, you can create files, rename them, and delete them. Typically, you would use it to create a file object and then pass it to a `FileInputStream` or `FileOutputStream` constructor to create a stream linked to the file. Using the stream to perform I/O, you would use the File class methods to rename the file as needed, or delete it altogether when it is no longer required.

The `File` class offers three constructors and a number of methods for dealing with files, as shown in Table 13-7.

| Table 13-7 |
| :---: |
| **The File Class** |

| Constructor | Description |
| --- | --- |
| File(String) | Creates a `File` object using the directory path passed to it. |
| File(String, String) | Creates a `File` object using the directory path and file name passed to it. |
| File(File, String) | Creates a `File` object using a directory `File` object (File) and file name. |

*Continued*

## Table 13-7 *(continued)*

| *Method* | *Description* |
|---|---|
| `public boolean canRead()` | Returns `boolean` indicating whether you can read this file. |
| `public boolean canWrite()` | Returns `boolean` indicating whether a writeable file exists. |
| `public void delete()` | Deletes specified file. |
| `public boolean equals(Object)` | Compares this object against the specified object. |
| `public boolean exists()` | Returns `boolean` indicating whether a file exists. |
| `public String getAbsolutePath()` | Gets absolute path of file. |
| `public String getName()` | Gets name of file. |
| `public String getParent()` | Gets name of parent directory. |
| `public String getPath()` | Gets path of file. |
| `public int hashCode()` | Computes hash code for file. |
| `public boolean isAbsolute()` | Returns `boolean` indicating whether file name is absolute. |
| `public boolean isDirectory()` | Returns `boolean` indicating whether a directory file exists. |
| `public boolean isFile()` | Returns `boolean` indicating whether a normal file exists. |
| `public long lastModified()` | Returns the last modification time. |
| `public int length()` | Returns the length of the file. |
| `public String[] list()` | Lists the files in a directory. |
| `public String[] list (FilenameFilter)` | Uses the specified filter to list files in a directory. |
| `public void mkdir()` | Creates a directory and returns a `boolean` indicating the success of the creation. |
| `public void mkdirs()` | Creates all directories in this path. |
| `public void renameTo(File)` | Attempts to rename the file and returns a `boolean` indicating if successful. |
| `public void toString()` | Returns a `String` object representing the file's path. |

In Java, a directory is simply treated as a File object that has additional information—a list of names that may be examined with the list() method. The following
code creates a file, in the java/code directory, and then queries it using several of
the File class methods:

```java
import java.io.File;
class FileQuery {
  public static void main(String args[]) {
    String dirname = "/java/code"; // directory must exist!
    String filename = "readme.txt";

    File myFile = new File(dirname, filename);
    System.out.println("File Name:" + myFile.getName());
    System.out.println("Is it a directory? " +
                       myFile.isDirectory());
    System.out.println("Is it a real file? " +
                       myFile.isFile());
    System.out.println("File Path:" + myFile.getPath());
    System.out.println("Absolute Path:" +
                       myFile.getAbsolutePath());
    System.out.println("Is file Readable? " +
                       myFile.canRead());
    System.out.println("Is file Writeable? " +
                       myFile.canWrite());
    System.out.println("Modified on: " +
                       myFile.lastModified());
    System.out.println("Size (in bytes):" + myFile.length());
    System.out.println();

    System.out.println("--- Directory listing ---");
    File dir = new File(dirname);
    if (dir.isDirectory() == false) {
      System.out.println(dirname + " is not a directory");
    }
    else {
      System.out.println("Directory of " + dirname);
      String d[] = dir.list();
      for (int i=0; i < d.length; i++) {
        System.out.println(d[i]);
      }
    }
  }
}
```

When it comes to path separators, you can use whatever is most convenient for
you. Java converts between the Windows and UNIX path separators automatically,
so you don't have to worry about how to enter them. Of course, if you choose to
use the Windows (DOS) convention of backslashes, you'll have to enter them as
escape codes, since the compiler can't handle them in strings directly. Therefore,

the preceding code uses UNIX-style path separators (forward slashes) even though it was written on a Windows machine; using a backslash with escape codes ("\\") isn't quite as clean when it comes to reading the source. However, the following would have been fine:

```
String dirname = "\\java\\code";
```

Keep in mind that the directory must exist for this code to work properly. However, you can always augment the code to include the File class mkdir() or mkdirs() methods if you want the directory (or directories) to be created on the fly, if they don't already exist. You may also delete the named file by calling delete() on the reference you have.

**Note**    At runtime, a NullPointerException is thrown if you call list() on an object that isn't actually a directory.

At times, you may want to exclude certain files from a directory listing. For instance, suppose you only wanted to view .txt files. To do this, you'd implement the FilenameFilter interface found in java.io. To do this, create an object that implements the interface and the abstract accept() method it defines. In this method, you define which files will be accepted. By passing the resulting object to the list() method, only those items that match the criteria are returned.

For example, here's a class that allows you to filter files based on the extension of the file name:

```
public class ExtensionFilter implements FilenameFilter {
  private String extension;
  public ExtensionFilter (String e) {
    this.extension = "." + e; // tack on constructor param
  }

  public boolean accept(File dir, String fileName) {
    // accept only these files
    return fileName.endsWith(extension);
  }
}
```

To use this filter in our earlier example, you'd first create an object with it, passing in the extension you'd like all files to have in order to be listed. By passing the resulting object to list(), only files that are accepted by the filter (that is, files that cause the accept method to return a boolean value of true) are listed:

```
FilenameFilter textFiles = new ExtensionFilter("txt");
// create filter object
String[] d = dir.list(textFiles); // use it in list()
```

### FileWriter and FileReader

FileReader (see Table 13-8) and FileWriter classes (see Table 13-9) are provided for dealing directly with text files. Both the FileReader and FileWriter classes operate in the same manner as their FileInputStream and FileOutputStream counterparts.

**Table 13-8**
**java.io.FileReader Constructors**

| Signature | Description |
|---|---|
| public FileReader(String) | Creates an input file with the specified name. (Name is system-dependent.) |
| public FileReader(File) | Creates an input file from the specified file object. |
| public FileReader (FileDescriptor) | Creates an input file from the specified file descriptor object. |

**Table 13-9**
**java.io.FileWriter Constructors**

| Signature | Description |
|---|---|
| public FileWriter(String) | Creates an output file with the file name. (File name is system-dependent.) |
| public FileWriter (String, boolean) | Creates or appends to an output file with the file name. (File name is system-dependent.) |
| public FileWriter(File) | Creates an output file using the File object passed to it. |
| public FileWriter (File Descriptor) | Creates an output file from the specified File Descriptor object. |

# Strings

At times, you may wish to create a stream using strings. This is simple enough, using the StringBufferInputStream class. You provide a String object as the parameter, and as you might expect, you'll be given a stream containing its contents:

```
String myString = "If a chicken and a half lays an egg and " +
                  "a half in a day in a half, how much time " +
```

```
                        "does it take a one-eyed grasshopper to " +
                        "poke a hole through a donut?";
InputStream riddle = new StringBufferInputStream(myString);
```

Since all `String` objects have a length (they aren't infinite!), `available()` works perfectly on it. However, `reset()` sets the buffer back to the beginning, not to a previously set mark as you might expect. Win some, lose some.

## Byte arrays

The `ByteArrayInputStream` class allows you to create input streams using arrays of bytes, as Table 13-10 shows.

<table>
<tr><td colspan="2" align="center">Table 13-10<br>**java.io.ByteArrayInputStream Constructors**</td></tr>
<tr><td>*Signature*</td><td>*Description*</td></tr>
<tr><td>`public ByteArrayInputStream (byte[])`</td><td>Creates a byte array input stream from the array of bytes passed to it.</td></tr>
<tr><td>`public ByteArrayInputStream (byte[], int, int)`</td><td>Creates a byte array input stream from the array of bytes passed to it where the stream starts from the first int value and goes for the second int's number of bytes</td></tr>
</table>

The `ByteArrayOutputStream` class, seen in Table 13-11, allows you to create output streams based on arrays.

<table>
<tr><td colspan="2" align="center">Table 13-11<br>**java.io.ByteArrayOutputStream Constructors**</td></tr>
<tr><td>*Signature*</td><td>*Description*</td></tr>
<tr><td>`public ByteArrayOutputStream()`</td><td>Creates a byte-array output stream.</td></tr>
<tr><td>`public ByteArrayOutput Stream (int size)`</td><td>Creates an array output stream of the specified size.</td></tr>
</table>

Because arrays are of a known size, the available() method works as you would expect. However, the reset() method returns the stream to the beginning because marks are not available. (See Listing 13-2.) When you create a ByteArrayOutput Stream, the buffer continues to grow as data is written to it. Once a byte array buffer has been filled, that data can then be retrieved using the methods toByte Array() and toString(). This is useful when you want to extract the contents of a ByteArrayOutputStream and assign them to an array or to a string.

The following program, Flip, creates a ByteArrayInputStream stream using an array of characters that together form the words "HELLO WORLD!" in uppercase letters. It then extracts each character in a loop for output; if the convert variable is true, the character is converted to lowercase before being printed. Since the reset() method returns the stream to the very beginning, Flip alternates between uppercase and lowercase output indefinitely (or until terminated by the user), as seen in Figure 13-2.

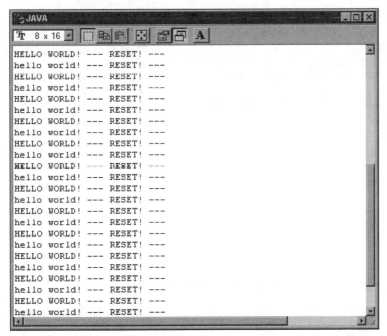

**Figure 13-2:** Flip takes advantage of ByteArrayInputStream's reset() method to toggle between uppercase and lowercase output.

Listing 13-2: **Flip.java: An Example of ByteArrayInputStream in Action**

```java
import java.io.*;
import java.util.*;

class Flip {
  public static void main(String args[]) {
    byte[] myBytes =
      {'H','E','L','L','O',' ', 'W','O','R','L','D', '!'};
    ByteArrayInputStream myStream =
      new ByteArrayInputStream(myBytes);

    // Process the stream
    int c;
    boolean convert = false;

    // enter infinite loop! User can only terminate
    // with key combination (ctrl-c for Windows)
    while (true) {
      while ((c = myStream.read())!= -1) {
        if (convert)
          System.out.print(Character.toLowerCase((char)c));
        else
          System.out.print((char)c);
      }

      convert = !convert; // reverse value of convert
      System.out.println(" - RESET! - ");
      myStream.reset();
    }
  }
}
```

# CharArrayReader and CharArrayWriter

The classes CharArrayReader (see Table 13-12) and CharArrayWriter (see Table 13-13), are used to deal with arrays of characters rather than arrays of bytes, which most streams use. Both the CharArrayReader and CharArrayWriter classes operate in the same manner as their ByteArrayInputStream and ByteArrayOutput Stream counterparts.

## Table 13-12
### java.io.CharArrayReader Constructors

| Signature | Description |
|---|---|
| public CharArrayInput Stream(char[]) | Creates a character array input stream from the array of bytes passed to it. |
| public CharArrayInput Stream(char[], int, int) | Creates a character array input stream from the array of bytes passed to it. |

## Table 13-13
### java.io.CharArrayWriter Constructors

| Signature | Description |
|---|---|
| public CharArrayOutput Stream() | Creates a character array output stream. |
| public CharArrayOutput Stream(int) | Creates a character array output stream of the specified size. |

# Sequences

You are able to join streams using the SequenceInputStream class. Much like concatenating strings, SequenceInputStream allows you to specify two different streams that will be used to create a third — the result of the first two streams being joined. As you can see from Table 13-14, SequenceInputStream also has a constructor that supports enumeration. This is useful when you have more than two streams that you want to join.

## Table 13-14
### java.io.SequenceInputStream Constructors

| Signature | Description |
|---|---|
| public SequenceInputStream (Enumeration) | Constructs a sequence input stream using the specified list (enumeration). |
| public SequenceInputStream (InputStream, InputStream) | Constructs a sequence input stream set to the two input streams passed to it. |

You might be wondering where a sequenced set of streams would be useful. One of the most common uses is to deal with streams that do not support marking. Instead of setting a read limit and then resetting, you just grab a handful of bytes and create an input stream from those. Then hook the two together like this:

```
static final int READ_AHEAD_LIMIT = 256;
InputStream originalStream;
InputStream destination = null;

if(originalStream.markSupported() {
  originalStream.mark(READ_AHEAD_LIMIT);
  // do some processing here
  // originalStream.read();
  // then reset the stream
  originalStream.reset();
  destination = originalStream
}
else {
  byte[] buffer = new byte[READ_AHEAD_LIMIT];
  // do some processing here
  // somevalue = buffer[index];
  // finished processing so "reset" the stream
  ByteArrayInputStream bis = new ByteArrayInputStream(buffer);
  destination = new SequenceInputStream(bis, originalStream);
}

someMethod(destination);
```

**Note** Enumeration **is an interface defined in the** java.util **package. It specifies a number of methods that are used to enumerate or count through a number of values. For details on enumeration, see the** java.util **package section in Sun's application programming interface (API) documentation.**

## Pipes

The java.io package supports piped streams. PipedInputStream (shown in Table 13-15) and PipedOutputStream (shown in Table 13-16) work in tandem.

These piped streams are used specifically to pass streams back and forth between two different threads. You'll learn about threads in Chapter 14, "Threads," but for now, it's worth understanding that the two piped streams work together; it's not useful to have one without the other. To use piped input and piped output, we simply create one of each kind of stream and reference them to each other, as follows:

```
PipedInputStream pipeIn = new PipedInputStream();
PipedOutputStream pipeOut = new PipedOutputStream(pipeIn);
```

Whenever a thread reads from the pipeIn, it is actually reading data that another thread is writing to pipeOut. Conversely, whenever a thread is writing to pipeOut, it is actually providing the input for another thread.

**Caution** Piped streams should never be used in the same thread because they will cause that part of your application to freeze. They should never be used to connect one input stream to another output stream to transfer data, e.g., from a URL connection to a local file.

### Table 13-15
### java.io.PipedInputStream Constructors

| Signature | Description |
|---|---|
| `public PipedInputStream (PipedOutputStream)` | Creates an input file using the piped output stream passed to it. |
| `public PipedInputStream()` | Creates an input file that isn't initially connected to anything and that must be connected to a piped output stream before being used. |

### Table 13-16
### java.io.PipedOutputStream Constructors

| Signature | Description |
|---|---|
| `public PipedOutputStream (PipedInputStream)` | Creates an output file connected to the piped input stream passed to it. |
| `public PipedOutputStream()` | Creates an output file that isn't initially connected to anything and that must be connected before being used. |

The classes `PipedReader` (see Table 13-17) and `PipedWriter` (see Table 13-18) return and use character arrays rather than raw bytes. Both the `PipedReader` and `PipedWriter` classes operate in the same manner as their `PipedInputStream` and `PipedOutputStream` counterparts.

### Table 13-17
### java.io.PipedReader Constructors

| Signature | Description |
|---|---|
| `public PipedInputStream (PipedWriter)` | Creates an input file using the piped output stream passed to it. |
| `public PipedInputStream()` | Creates an input file that isn't initially connected to anything and that must be connected to a piped output stream before being used. |

| | Table 13-18 |
| | **java.io.PipedWriter Constructors** |
| --- | --- |
| **Signature** | **Description** |
| `public PipedWriter` `(PipedReader)` | Creates an output file connected to the piped input system passed to it. |
| `public PipedWriter()` | Creates an output file that isn't initially connected to anything and that must be connected before being used. |

# Filtered Streams

The `java.io` package contains two abstract classes, `FilterInputStream` and `FilterOutputStream`, that provide an enhanced I/O mechanism for streams. These classes allow streams to be chained together, providing additional functionality to one another as they are processed. There are a number of subclasses from these abstract filter classes, each of which we'll take a look at.

## Buffered I/O

Java supports buffered streams, which are kept in memory to allow much faster access than would otherwise be possible. These particular streams, `BufferedInput Stream` and `BufferedOutputStream`, are actually the only ones that properly use the `mark()` and `reset()` methods. However, since `BufferedInputStream` and `BufferedOutputStream` are subclasses of `FilterInputStream` and `FilterOutput Stream`, respectively, you can pass on their buffered functionality to other streams using a simple stream filtering technique:

```
// create buffered String stream:
myString = "Obviously the question is false, because " +
           "ice-cream has no bones.";

StringBufferInputStream in_str =
  StringBufferInputStream(myString);
OutputStream theStream = new BufferedOutputStream(in_str);

// create buffered File stream:
FileOutputStream fos = new FileOutputStream("HelloWorld.java");
OutputStream myStream = new BufferedOutputStream(fos);
```

As you can see, we've created two different buffered streams, even though the original stream types (`StringBufferInputStream` and `FileOutputStream`) don't support buffering. We've used the filter capability of `BufferedOutputStream` to create buffered versions of each.

As a result, these streams are not only faster, but use the `mark()` and `reset()` methods properly. It can be said that we've run our two streams through a `Buffered OutputStream` filter, which passes on functionality that they normally don't have.

## Line numbers

Line-number readers understand and use the concept of line numbering; they remember each line as a stream's data is input. This is a special-purpose class that is also a subclass of `BufferedReader`. (See Table 13-19.) The older `LineNumberInput Stream` is available and uses an `InputStream` as a base. However, this is a deprecated class because it does not handle internationalized text correctly.

### Table 13-19
### java.io.LineNumberReader Constructor

| Signature | Description |
| --- | --- |
| public LineNumberReader (Reader) | Constructs a line-number input stream initialized using the input stream passed to the constructor. |
| public LineNumberReader (Reader, int) | Constructs a line-number input stream initialized using the input stream passed to the constructor. |

To retrieve the line number of a particular portion of the stream, use the `getLine Number()` method. To read lines from the stream, use the `readLine()` method, defined in `java.io.DataInputStream`. (See the section "Typed I/O" later in this chapter.) An example follows in Listing 13-3.

### Listing 13-3: **LineByLine.java: An Example of LineNumberInputStream in Action**

```
import java.io.*;

class LineByLine {
  public static void main (String args[])
    throws FileNotFoundException {

  String fileName = "letter.txt"; // name of file to open

    // - Open the streams
  FileReader fr = new FileReader(fileName);
  LineNumberReader reader = new LineNumberReader (f);
```

*Continue*

**Listing 13-3** *(continued)*

```
    // Process them line by line
    try {
      int ch;

      // print 1st line # before loop
      System.out.print("Line 1: ");

      // loop until the end of the stream
      while ((c=reader.read())!= -1) {
        System.out.print((char)c); // output each character

        // is this the last character in the line?
        // if so, print the next line number:
        if (c == '\n') {
          System.out.print("Line " +
                          (reader.getLineNumber() + 1) +
                          ":");
        }
      }
    }
    catch (IOException e) {
      System.out.println("Can't open stream!");
    }
  }
}
```

LineByLine **opens a text file using a** FileReader **stream. It passes this to the** Line
NumberReader **constructor, which returns a stream capable of understanding line
numbers. Each line in the text file is output on the command line, preceded by its
line number. (See Figure 13-3.)**

## Pushing back

PushbackInputStream **provides an interesting method called** unread(), **which
allows us to place the last character back where it was read, as if we had never
actually read it. This is useful in cases where you need to see what the next character in a buffer will be but don't necessarily want to advance the stream. With**
PushbackInputStream, **if the character is not what you want, you can put it back
using the** unread() **method.**

**Note**   `PushbackInputStream` **invalidates the** `mark()` **and** `reset()` **methods of the** `InputStream` **created with it.**

```
MS-DOS Prompt
T  8 x 16
Line 1: Jan 1, 1996
Line 2: Ret. Major Bill Grein
Line 3: US Marine Corps.
Line 4: Toys for Tots Foundation
Line 5:
Line 6: Dear Bill,
Line 7:
Line 8: I wanted to let you know how happy we are to be part of the Toys For
Line 9: Tots campaign, having successfully launched the official Web Site this
Line 10: Christmas.
Line 11:
Line 12: With the site now underway, we anticipate a tremendous response and
Line 13: greatly increased awareness for Christmas 1996.  We will continue to
Line 14: develop the Toys For Tots Web site around the year, and will have a
Line 15: Internet domain name donated to the cause.  This means that Toys for
Line 16: Tots will be a site unto itself, not a sub-site of Mantis Development
Line 17: Corporation as it is now.
Line 18:
Line 19: We're now adding multimedia to the site, using a new technology
Line 20: know as "Java". The Toys For Tots site will be featured in all
Line 21: books written by our company this year as a showcase of the Java
Line 22: "bells and whistles" technology, and in an effort to build public
Line 23: awareness of the site.
```

**Figure 13-3:** FileReader understands line numbers, a particularly useful feature for text editing of any kind.

The `PushbackReader` class processes character strings instead of byte arrays. `PushbackReader` functions in the same manner as the `PushbackInputStream` class.

## Typed I/O

Up until now, we've been dealing with streams of bytes, which are a rather ineffective way to deal with data. While it's true that they provide an efficient mechanism for spitting data out and reading data in, we have no convenient way of using specific data types, such as booleans, shorts, integers, longs, floats, and doubles.

To help us deal with typed data streams, `DataInputStream` and `DataOutputStream` classes are available. They are described in Tables 13-20 and 13-21.

**Table 13-20**
**java.io.DataInputStream**

| Constructor | Description |
| --- | --- |
| `public DataInputStream (InputStream)` | Creates a data input stream using the input stream passed to it. |

| Method | Description |
| --- | --- |
| `public read(byte[])` | Reads data into an array of bytes. |
| `public read(byte[], int, int)` | Reads data into an array of bytes from the given offset until the length has been reached. |
| `public boolean readBoolean()` | Reads a `boolean`. |
| `public byte readByte()` | Reads an 8-bit `byte`. |
| `public char readChar()` | Reads a 13-bit `char`. |
| `public double readDouble()` | Reads a 64-bit `double`. |
| `public float readFloat()` | Reads a 32-bit `float`. |
| `public void readFully(byte[])` | Reads `bytes`, blocking until all are read. |
| `public void readFully(byte[], int, int)` | Reads data into an array of bytes from the given offset until the length has been reached. Blocks until the all bytes are read. |
| `public int readInt()` | Reads a 32-bit `int`. |
| `public int readLine()` | Reads a line that is terminated with \n, \r, \r\n, or end-of-file (EOF). |
| `public long readLong()` | Reads a 64-bit `long`. |
| `public short readShort()` | Reads a 16-bit `short`. |
| `public String readUTF()` | Reads a UTF format string. |
| `public String readUTF(DataInput)` | Reads a UTF format string from the given input stream. |
| `public byte readUnsignedByte()` | Reads an unsigned 8-bit `byte`. |
| `public short readUnsigned Short()` | Reads a 16-bit `short`. |
| `public int skipBytes(int)` | Skips `bytes`, blocking until all are skipped or the end of stream is reached. The return value indicates the actual number of bytes skipped. |

## Table 13-21
## java.io.DataOutputStream

| Constructor | Description |
| --- | --- |
| `public DataOutput Stream (OutputStream)` | Creates a data output stream using the output stream passed to it. |

| Method | Description |
| --- | --- |
| `public void flush()` | Flushes the stream. |
| `public int size()` | Returns the total number of `bytes` written. |
| `public void write(int b)` | Writes a `byte`. |
| `public void write(byte[], int, int)` | Writes a subarray of bytes. |
| `public void writeBoolean(boolean)` | Writes a `boolean`. |
| `public void writeByte(int)` | Writes an 8-bit `byte`. |
| `public void writeBytes(String)` | Writes `String` as a sequence of bytes. |
| `public void writeChar(int)` | Writes a 16-bit `char`. |
| `public void writeChars(String)` | Writes `String` as a sequence of chars. |
| `public void writeDouble(double)` | Writes a 64-bit `double`. |
| `public void writeFloat(float)` | Writes a 32-bit `float`. |
| `public void writeInt(int)` | Writes a 32-bit `int`. |
| `public void writeLong(long)` | Writes a 64-bit `long`. |
| `public void writeShort(int)` | Writes a 16-bit `short`. |
| `public void writeUTF(String)` | Writes String in UTF format. |

Now, rather than having to deal with streams in terms of bytes, you can use them as standard data types. If you want to write a byte, you can write a byte; if you want to write a boolean, you can write a boolean. As you can see from the last two tables, you can read and write the data types that you are most comfortable with. In this way, you're not restricted to dealing simply with bytes.

Listing 13-4, the `GetFortuneString()` method taken from the `KzmFortune` applet found at JavaBible.com, shows how `DataInputStream` is used to read lines of text. Specifically, this method opens an input stream using a URL that points to a text file residing either locally or on the Web. If a valid stream is opened, a line of text is read from it for display in a scrolling ticker tape. Pay particular attention to the try-catch clauses surrounding the stream code.

### Listing 13-4: **How to Use the DataInputStream Object**

```
//  GetFortuneString, a method of KzmFortune
//      input: filename, the number of lines to show
//      output: message to show
//
public String GetFortuneString (String fileName, int num) {
  String line = null;
  String url_str = directoryURL() + fileName;
  String result = "NO FORTUNE";
  int cnt = 1;

  try {
    URL url = new URL(url_str);
    InputStream is = url.openStream();
    DataInputStream my_data = new DataInputStream(is);

    while ((lLine = my_data.readLine()) != null) {
      if (num == cnt) {
        result = line;
      }
      cnt++;
    }
  }
  catch (Exception e) {
    System.out.println("Error reading fortune " +
                       e.toString());
  }

  return result; // return the "fortune" string
}
```

The entire source code for KzmFortune is provided on the companion Web site JavaBible.com. Here you'll find a large number of applets that make use of streams, and you may wish to supplement this chapter by looking at them.

When you're dealing with data input streams, you must be aware that, when the end of the stream is reached, the value of -1 is returned from `read()`.

If you're dealing with data output streams, however, you're likely to run into an IOException. If the DataOutputStream methods shown in Table 13-21 are ever unable to actually write the stream out, they throw an IOException. Of course, to handle this, simply surround your data output with the try-catch clause, just as we did with the data input streams:

```
try {
    ... work with the stream ...
}
catch (IOException e) {
    // we know stream couldn't be written
}
finally {
  anOutputStream.flush();
  anOutputStream.close(); // close this stream
}
```

**Tip**
As you learned in the chapter covering exceptions (Chapter 11 "Exceptions/Error Handling"), you don't necessarily have to use the try-catch clause when dealing with these. You can, of course, explicitly say that the method in which the code appears throws the error itself.

Although this technique gets around having to capture and deal with the error yourself, that isn't a very elegant way of coping with errors. In general, you should capture all the exceptions that are thrown rather then pretend to throw them yourself.

You'll also notice that the KzmFortune example shown didn't provide a specific exception name in the catch clause. The author of this applet chose to catch all possible exceptions at once, using catch (Exception e), instead of providing a catch clause for each possible type of exception.

## PrintStream

You may be aware that you've been using the PrintStream class in some fashion already. Whenever you send the print() or println() method to the System.out or System.err class variables, you are, in fact, calling PrintStream methods. System.out and System.err are actually PrintStream variables defined in the System class:

```
// System class standard out variable
public static PrintStream out;

// System class standard err variable
public static PrintStream err;
```

PrintStream is the most commonly used output stream, and that's not surprising. This class provides a plethora of methods (see Tables 13-22 and 13-23) for outputting text, and makes doing so a pleasure. Chances are good that you're already familiar with print() and println() and their ability to handle a great number of parameters and different types; you might want to experiment with the other methods to gain full appreciation of the PrintStream class.

### Table 13-22
### java.io.PrintStream Constructors

| Signature | Description |
| --- | --- |
| public PrintStream (OutputStream) | Creates a print stream using the output stream passed to it. |
| public PrintStream (OutputStream, boolean) | Creates a print stream with optional auto flushing. true for the second argument specifies the stream, automatically flushes its output when a new line character is printed. |

### Table 13-23
### java.io.PrintStream Methods

| Method | Description |
| --- | --- |
| public void write(int b) | Writes the byte, blocking until it is written. |
| public void write(byte[], int, int) | Writes the subarray of bytes. |
| public void flush() | Flushes the stream, writing all buffered output bytes. This method overrides flush in the FilterOutputStream class. |
| public void close() | Closes the stream. |
| public boolean checkError() | Flushes the print stream, returning true if there was an error on the output stream, false otherwise. (Note: Errors are cumulative; if the print stream encounters an error, checkError() returns true on all successive calls. Thus, true is returned if the print stream has ever encountered an error on the output stream.) |
| public void print(Object) | Prints the object passed to it. |
| public void print(String) | Prints the String passed to it. |

| Method | Description |
|--------|-------------|
| `public void print(char[])` | Prints the array of characters passed to it. |
| `public void print(char)` | Prints the character passed to it. |
| `public void print(int)` | Prints the integer passed to it. |
| `public void print(long)` | Prints the `long` passed to it. |
| `public void print(float)` | Prints the `float` passed to it. |
| `public void print(double)` | Prints the `double` passed to it. |
| `public void print(boolean)` | Prints the `boolean` passed to it. |
| `public void println()` | Prints a new line. |
| `public void println(Object)` | Prints the object passed to it, followed by a new line. |
| `public void println(String)` | Prints the `String` passed to it, followed by a new line. |
| `public void println(char[])` | Prints the array of characters passed to it, followed by a new line. |
| `public void println(char)` | Prints the character passed to it, followed by a new line. |
| `public void println(int)` | Prints the integer passed to it, followed by a new line. |
| `public void println(long)` | Prints the `long` passed to it, followed by a new line. |
| `public void println(float)` | Prints the `float` passed to it, followed by a new line. |
| `public void println(double)` | Prints the `double` passed to it, followed by a new line. |
| `public void println(boolean)` | Prints the `boolean` passed to it, followed by a new line. |

**Caution**

Although these methods are extremely flexible, able to accept and output a wide variety of data types, they do not accept Unicode characters, only Latin-1 characters (ISO 8859-1). If you attempt to pass Unicode characters to `PrintStream` methods, be warned: the top 8 bits of these 16-bit characters are ignored!

# PrintWriter

The PrintWriter class operates in the same manner as the PrintStream class. Instead of creating a byte output stream, PrintWriter produces a character output stream. The PrintStream and PrintWriter classes use the same constructors and methods.

# Object Serialization

An interesting capability provided by Java and streams is the concept of *object serialization*. Object serialization allows any Java object to be written to an output stream and then recreated later by reading the object back from the input stream. The cornerstone of object serialization are the classes ObjectInput (see Table 13-24) and ObjectOutput (see Table 13-25). You can serialize objects by simply calling the writeObject() method, and recreate an object by calling the read Object() method.

Only objects that subclass the Serializable (or Externalizable) interface can be serialized. If a field in the class is declared as transient, it is not serialized. This is handy for dealing with areas that are potentially serious security areas. For example, any time that you reference a File object, this should be declared as transient to stop it from being written out to the stream.

| Table 13-24 java.io.ObjectInput | |
| --- | --- |
| **Constructor** | **Description** |
| public ObjectInput (InputStream) | Creates an object input stream using the input stream passed to it. |
| public int available() | Returns the number of bytes that can be read without blocking. |
| public void close() | Closes the input stream. |
| public int read() | Reads a byte of data. |
| public int read(byte[]) | Reads an array of bytes in array b. |
| public int read(byte[], int, int) | Reads a len number of bytes into array b, starting at the given offset and for the specified number of bytes. |
| public Object readObject() | Reads and returns an object. Throws ClassNot FoundException if an I/O error has occurred. |
| public long skip(long n) | Skips *n* bytes of input. |

<table>
<tr><td colspan="2" align="center">Table 13-25<br>**java.io.ObjectOutput**</td></tr>
</table>

| Method | Description |
|---|---|
| `public ObjectInput (OutputStream)` | Creates an object output stream using the input stream passed to it. |
| `public int close()` | Closes the output stream. |
| `public void flush()` | Flushes the output stream. |
| `public void write(int b)` | Writes a byte of data. |
| `public void write(byte[])` | Writes an array of bytes. |
| `public void write(byte[], int, int)` | Writes the number of bytes from the array, starting at the given offset. |
| `public void writeObject (Object)` | Writes object `obj` to the output stream. |

# More I/O

In addition to the streams we've covered that are supported in the `java.io` package, other streams in the `File` and `RandomAccessFile` classes offer enhanced capabilities for working with data files. We'll return to a discussion of data files in later chapters.

For now, if you want to attain greater mastery of streams, you may want to do some research farther afield on the Web. For example, consider investigating the `StreamTokenizer` class, which allows you to break an input stream and put it into a stream of tokens. This class can be particularly helpful if you are parsing languages (either programming languages or those you use in everyday life), and it clearly bears a close look if you require such functionality.

When dealing with streams, you must handle the potential exceptions that may be thrown in the process. The `java.io` package defines several exceptions, as shown in Table 13-26. To handle these exceptions, surround your stream-usage statements with a `try-catch` clause, or declare the methods that use them to throw the particular type of exception the statements are likely to generate.

| Table 13-26 java.io Package Exceptions | |
| --- | --- |
| Exception | Description |
| EOFException | Indicates that an unexpected EOF was reached during input. |
| FileNotFoundException | Indicates that a requested file couldn't be found. |
| IOException | Indicates that an error had occurred reading or writing a stream. |
| InterruptedIOException | Indicates that an interruption had occurred while reading or writing a stream. |
| UTFDataFormatException | Indicates that a malformed UTF-8 string was read in a data input stream. |

# Summary

In this chapter you learned all about Java streams as an essential aspect of input and output. More specifically, you learned the following:

✦ Streams are a conduit for sending and receiving information in Java programs.

✦ Sending a stream of data is called writing a stream.

✦ Receiving a stream of data is called reading a stream.

✦ Streams are a versatile way to manage input, output, and object serialization.

# Threads

I f you've spent any time looking at the source code of the applets included on JavaBible.com, you may have noticed that a number of them use threads. Threads are independent processes that can be run simultaneously. In this chapter, you will learn how threads operate and affect programs both indirectly and directly. You will also see how threads can be used to speed up your programs and prevent bottlenecks when long processes in your code begin.

## About Threads

In everyday life, we take the concept of threads for granted. For example, often the most critical task in your day is filled with threads: when you create a cup of coffee in the morning, you perform a number of smaller tasks in the process.

To begin, you place a pot of cold water on the stove and turn the burner on underneath it. While waiting for the water to heat up, you take the coffee beans and cream out of the refrigerator, then pour a little cream into the cup and add a teaspoon of sugar to it. Because you know exactly how much cream you like in your coffee and all your coffee cups hold the same amount of liquid, you don't have to wait until the coffee is poured before you add these coffee condiments.

As the water gradually shows signs of letting off steam, you toss a fistful of beans into the grinder and give 'em a whirl. While dumping the pulverized beans into the coffee press with your right hand, the water usually comes to a rapid boil, so you take it off the heat with your left hand and place it onto a cold burner.

Because it's a bad idea to pour boiling water directly onto freshly ground beans, lest the poor babies are scalded and produce a bitter cup of Joe (and who wouldn't be bitter after having boiling water poured over his freshly pulverized body?), you spend the next minute or so slowly swirling the cream and sugar with a teaspoon to blend the two into a perfect, granular-free mixture. By the time the sugar has completely dissolved in the cream, you become impatient and figure the water temperature has had time to come down a few degrees.

You grab the pot of water and pour it into the press, all the while stirring the mix with the same teaspoon you used to prepare the cream and sugar. At this point, you may have cradled a portable phone between your cheek and neck to get a jump on the work day — and why not? They'll never know you're still in your boxer shorts and furry slippers. If you're not on the phone by now, you're probably knocking back a fine assortment of vitamins to counteract the damaging effects of your caffeine habit.

Regardless, within a few minutes, you begin the pressing process, separating grounds from water. After pushing all the solid stuff to the bottom of the glass press, you pour the steaming liquid into your cup of waiting, sugary sweet cream. Within moments, you lift the nectar to your lips, and, for the first time that day, a smile creeps across your face and your hands stop shaking.

By the time you take your first gulp of coffee, you've accomplished a number of tasks. Each of these has a distinct beginning, an end, and a sequence of steps that happen in between before the task is complete and you move on to the next one. In a number of cases, these tasks happen concurrently.

In essence, your morning coffee ritual has a number of threads of execution. As a result, the process of creating coffee can be considered multithreaded. In fact, just about everything we do in life can be broken down into threads. Can you chew gum and avoid the cracks in the sidewalk at the same time? Chalk up two threads: one for chewing, the other for avoidance behavior. Do you brush your teeth while looking in the mirror for signs of premature aging? Chalk up two more threads, plus one more to keep your ego in check.

As you can see, our lives can be broken down into threads. And, because they're going on in our lives all the time, we can be thought of as multithreaded beings.

In software, a *thread* is a single sequential flow of control. You're already familiar with sequential flow of control; it's what happens when you execute a program. The program begins, runs through a sequence of executions, and eventually ends. At any given time in the life of a program, there's only one point of execution; that is, the lines of code you write are executed sequentially, not at the same time.

Threads, also known as *execution contexts* or *lightweight processes*, are similar to the sequential programs you're accustomed to writing; they have a beginning, a middle, and an end. During its life, a thread executes a sequence of commands and, at any given time, there's only one point of execution.

Does this sound like a program?

In fact, threads and programs are very similar concepts. Unlike programs, however, threads don't exist as discrete collections of executable commands. That is, the end user doesn't execute a thread directly. Instead, threads run *within* a program. It might help to think of them as miniprograms that exist within the lifetime of an actual program (hence the name *lightweight process*).

There is nothing new about the concept of a single thread. The excitement in this industry is about multiple threads in a single program all running at the same time and performing different tasks. As you know, having more than one thread executing at a time is known as multithreading. It's this subject that has become a popular topic in computer science circles, especially when discussion turns to Java.

Threads are the reason browsers, such as HotJava and Netscape Navigator, can download a file to your hard disk, display a Web page in one window while opening another in a new window, output one or more Web pages to the printer, and perform a number of other processes concurrently. This is exactly the behavior multiple concurrent threads offer: many things can happen at once (or, more accurately, appear to happen at once). Instead of waiting for a connection to finish before going on to the next one, a number of threads can be created, or "spawned," each of which is responsible for handling its own connection. Because a different thread is taking care of each of these processes, the processes appear to happen in parallel.

**Note**   In truth, these multiple processes don't really happen at once. Unless threads are executing on a true multiprocessing computer system (a system with more than one processor, capable of executing commands in parallel), threads must take turns using a single CPU. However, because this happens so fast, we are often convinced that things are happening simultaneously.

Rather than going from start to finish in one large program, you can think of threads as divvying up your program into little chunks, or separate tiny programs that can run concurrently. The result is a dramatic improvement in the overall speed of your program. Without threads, the program would have to follow a predetermined set of instructions and wait for each one to be completed before going on to the next.

This approach might not sound all that bad. After all, it's what we're used to. However, what if one of the steps in a program takes a particularly long time to finish? Imagine if we had to wait every time an image or sound file was pulled off the network before we could go on to the next step. This would be a long process, and the larger the file, the longer the wait would be. Thankfully, Java automatically uses threads for just such things. As a result, the rest of our program is free to execute while the files come across the wire.

We can also add threads of our own to further increase the efficiency of our programs. Using them is extremely easy in Java. All we have to do is create a new Thread object and tell it to start executing. Take a look at how we can do this with our applets.

# Getting Started with Threads

In real life, each of your activities has a beginning, a middle, and an end. Threads act the same way. We need to start them, let them run, and stop them. A lot like real life, threads will just continue to work until you act to explicitly stop them. Stop them at the wrong point or wrong way, and it can have nasty consequences for the rest of your code.

## Types of threads

Java contains two slightly different ways of implementing a thread: extending the `Thread` class or implementing the `Runnable` interface. The actual running code does not change, but there are some different capabilities depending on which option you take:

✦ `Runnable`: This is the barebones thread implementation. There is only a single method named `run()` that needs to be implemented. This is where you place all of your code that you want to have work as an independent entity.

✦ `Thread`: This is the Rolls-Royce model that contains everything. Like `Runnable`, the `run()` method is the only one that needs to be implemented by any extending class; however, it is not an abstract method, so even that is not required.

This is as much as we'll explain for the moment. We'll look at the circumstances of which implementation to use later on in the chapter in the "Runnable or Thread" section.

## Creating a new thread

Regardless of which way you implement a threaded piece of code, you still need to create an instance of the `Thread` class to make it run. This is because the class forms a kind of holder of all the information that is important to the `Thread` and to the Java runtime system. It also happens to contain all of the methods needed to register a thread with the JVM, start it, control it, and stop it.

Let's start with a class that implements the `Runnable` interface:

```
public class AnyClass implements Runnable {
...
}
```

To register this with the system, we need to create a `Thread`:

```
Runnable runnable = new AnyClass();
Thread myThread = new Thread(runnable)
```

Now we have told the system that we have a thread (other ways of constructing a new Thread object are shown in Table 14-1). At this point, no code is executed, just registered with the system. That is not such a big problem, but it is definitely not what we wanted. What we have to do is kick off the thread by telling the system that it needs to run the threaded part of the class by calling (naturally) the start() method:

```
myThread.start();
```

### Table 14-1
### java.lang.Thread Constructors

| Signature | Description |
|---|---|
| public Thread() | Constructs a new thread. Threads created this way override their run() method to do anything. An example illustrating this method is shown in the section "Using the Thread() Constructor." |
| public Thread(Runnable) | Constructs a new thread, which applies the run() method of the specified target. |
| public Thread(ThreadGroup, Runnable) | Constructs a new thread in the specified group of threads. |
| public Thread(String name) | Constructs a new thread with the specified name. Useful only when extending the Thread class. |
| public Thread(ThreadGroup, String) | Constructs a new thread in the specified thread group with the specified name. Like the ungrouped version, only really useful when extending the Thread object. |
| public Thread(Runnable, String) | Constructs a new thread with the specified name and applies the run() method of the specified target. |
| public Thread(ThreadGroup, Runnable, String) | Constructs a new thread in the specified thread group with the specified name and applies the run() method of the specified group. |

Now that we have a thread that is actually executing, we need to provide some code to run. You may have noticed that the common link between Runnable and Thread is the need to provide a run() method. In this method, you provide all of the code that must be executed. Anything contained in this method, and any method calls that are made within it, will run separately to the rest of the application.

For threads, the run() method is very special. It contains all of the code that needs to be executed. It also is not called by your application code. Note that in the previous section, we said that to start a thread, you need to call the start() method, not the run() method. There is a very good reason for this.

Say your application called the run() method of the thread. Inside that method, you spend the time rendering images to the screen to provide some animation. To do this, the run() method probably contains some sort of infinite loop that just continually paints images to the screen in some cyclic fashion. Considering that the loop is infinite, the run method never exits, and your calling code will never get to continue — ever. The entire idea of a thread is to allow lots of different pieces of code to run in parallel. By directly calling run(), obviously, this won't be the outcome.

The run() method provides a method for the VM to call directly when it is time to execute your thread. By calling start() in your code, you are telling Java that you want the registered thread instance to start running separately. Some time later, Java will then call your run() method.

# Using Threads in Applets

To use threads in applets, we need only implement the Runnable interface. The Runnable interface declares the methods that we'll need in order to implement threads in our program. The following code is the class signature for a program that uses the Runnable interface:

```
public class AnyClass extends java.applet.Applet
    implements Runnable {
...
}
```

Once we've claimed that our applet will use the Runnable interface, there are only three easy things left to do:

✦ Declare a variable to hold a Thread object.

✦ Create a run() method, the nerve center of a thread.

✦ Transfer the contents of our start() method into run() and use start() to kick off the thread.

Because these basic steps take place in all applets that support threads, you can use Listing 14-1 as the basis for future threaded applets.

## Listing 14-1: **A Basic Threaded Class Example**

```
public class AnyClass extends java.applet.Applet
  implements Runnable {

  Thread myThread; // a variable to hold our thread

  public void start() {
    if (myThread == null) {
      myThread = new Thread(this); // create Thread object
      myThread.start(); // start it
    }
  }

  public void run() {
    while (myThread != null) {
      try {
        // code that used to be in the
        //original applet start() method goes here...
      }
      catch(Exception e)
        if(myThread.isInterrupted())
          myThread = null;
      }
    }
  }

  public void stop() {
    myThread.interrupt(); // stop it
    myThread = null; // prepare for garbage collection
  }
}
```

**Note** Note that we didn't bother to import the Thread class (java.lang.Thread); the java.lang package is automatically available to all our programs, so we don't have to explicitly import it.

The start() method creates, or spawns, a new Thread object and starts it running. As you can see, this method doesn't do anything but begin the thread. It's the run() method that has the bulk of the responsibility.

The run() method contains the thread body, the sequence of code that the thread will execute. After a thread has been created and started, the runtime system calls its run() method. The code in this method is the entire reason the thread was created in the first place and is what the thread is responsible for executing.

As the thread's nerve center, `run()` is the method that defines the life of every thread. When `run()` is complete, the thread dies (more on `Thread` life and death later in this chapter). Often, `run()` contains code that takes a long time to execute (such as downloading a large file off the network). As a result, this code executes in parallel with other threads, thereby eliminating a potential bottleneck.

Typically, the `run()` method makes use of a loop control structure, as in the animation applet seen in Listing 14-2. As you can see, we've created an instance variable of the `Thread` object called kicker. In the `start()` method, we determine whether or not kicker has already been instantiated and, if it hasn't, we create a new one:

```
kicker=new Thread(this);
```

Essentially, the line instantiates a new `Thread` object with our class as the parameter (`this`). This argument, our applet, becomes the thread's target. Because a thread executes the `run()` method of its target, our new thread knows to execute the `run()` method of this applet.

After the new `Thread` object is created, it is put into motion:

```
myThread.start(); // start it
```

When a thread is sent the `start()` method, it begins to execute by invoking the `run()` method of its target. Until this point, the thread is simply instantiated and does us no good. Listing 14-2 demonstrates how to use the `start()` and `run()` methods.

## Listing 14-2: **BlinkItem.java**

```java
import java.awt.Graphics;
import java.awt.Image;

public class BlinkItem extends java.applet.Applet
 implements Runnable {

  // An array that holds the two images
  Image[] imPic = new Image[2];
  int iPicIndex=0; // Keeps track of which image is displayed
  Thread kicker;

  public void init() {
    resize(512,243);
  }

  public void paint(Graphics g) {
    // Display an error message if something
    // unexpected has happened to the images
    if(imPic[iPicIndex]==null) {
```

```
        g.drawString("Error when loading picture", 0, 172);
    }
    // Draw the current image (method won't draw a null image)
    g.drawImage(imPic[iPicIndex],0,0, this);
}

// Using the update method will get rid of some flickering
public void update(Graphics g) {
    paint(g);
}

public void start() {
    if(kicker == null) {       // If no thread is started yet
        kicker=new Thread(this);   // then create one
        kicker.start();            // and start it
    }
}
public void stop() {
    kicker.interrupt();
    kicker=null;
}

public void run() {
    boolean finished = false;
    imPic = new Image[2];      // Dimension the image array
    // Load the two images in our 'animation'
    imPic[0] = getImage(getCodeBase(), "images/Homepage1.gif");
    imPic[1] = getImage(getCodeBase(), "images/Homepage2.gif");
    for(!finished) { // Loop forever
        repaint();         // Redraw the window
        iPicIndex = (iPicIndex==0) ? 1 : 0;   // Switch image

        // The sleep method below might be interrupted and cause
        // an InterruptedException, so we'll have to catch it.

        try {
            // Wait for a random amount of time
            Thread.sleep( (int) (Math.random()*500));
        } catch (InterruptedException e){
            finished = true;
        }
    }
}
```

Because the run() method contains the body of a thread, we move the contents of our previous start() method here and simply use the original start() method to create and get the thread running.

In this applet, which is a threaded and more elegant version of the `BruteForce` animation program discussed in Chapter 17, `run()` simply loads two different images into an array and then enters an infinite `for` loop. In this loop, the images are repainted one after another.

After an image is drawn, however, the thread is told to sleep a random amount of time:

```
Thread.sleep( (int) (Math.random()*500));
```

# Thread Attributes

To use threads efficiently and without incident, you must understand the various aspects of threads and the Java runtime system. Specifically, you need to know about the following:

✦ Thread body: How to provide a body for a thread

✦ Thread state: The lifecycle of a thread

✦ Thread priority: How the runtime system schedules threads

✦ Daemon threads: What they are and how to write them

✦ Thread groups: All Java threads must be part of a thread group

## Thread body

As you now know, thread activity takes place in the body of a thread. Specifically, the thread's body is implemented in its `run()` method. You can provide a thread body by creating a subclass of the Thread class and then overriding its `run()` method, as we did with `EZThread`. Or, you can create a class that implements the `Runnable` interface. In that case, you must instantiate a Thread object and supply it with a `Runnable` object as the target:

```
kicker=new Thread(this);
```

Accordingly, we have two options when it comes to using threads. However, when writing applets, we have no such choice, because we can only extend one class. Applets must inherit from the `java.awt.Applet` class, so we must implement the `Runnable` interface.

If we don't need to extend another class, we can choose to extend the `Thread` class. However, as a general rule, unless we need to override more than the `run()` method, there's no reason to use this approach rather than implement the `Runnable` interface.

# Thread state

During the lifetime of a thread, there are many states it can enter. Off the top of your head, you can probably think of at least one of these states: the Runnable state. A thread enters this state whenever it receives the start() method.

There are three other states a thread can enter, as shown in Figure 14-1. In all, the four states are:

✦ New Thread

✦ Runnable

✦ Not Runnable

✦ Dead

Take a look at each of them in turn.

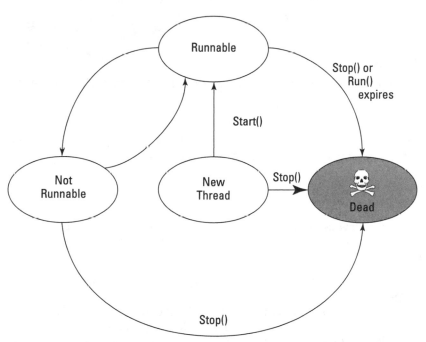

**Figure 14-1:** Threads may be in one of four states at any given time.

## Security Issues with Threads

In an applet environment, you need to be very careful. A thread that decides to go haywire can constitute a denial of service attack. Therefore, a number of restrictions can be placed on what the user can and cannot do to threads.

You can use the following permissions that are part of `java.lang.RuntimePermission` to control the security settings in your environment.

✦ `modifyThread`: Control of calls to stop, suspend, resume, rename, and set the priority of a thread.

✦ `stopThread` :If the user has been granted access to a thread through `modify Thread`, then this is a second gateway to prevent him or her from being able to stop that thread.

✦ `modifyThreadGroup`: When part of a larger group, methods on the group can be used to indirectly control threads. This prevents users performing similar operations to `modifyThread` on the group.

### New Thread

Whenever you instantiate a `Thread` object, that thread enters a `New Thread` state:

```
Thread myThread = new Thread(this);
```

At this point, no system resources have been allocated for the thread; it is only an empty object. As a result, you can only start or stop it:

```
myThread.start();
myThread.stop();
```

If you attempt to invoke any other method at this point, an `IllegalThreadState Exception` is thrown. This happens because a thread in this state has no way of dealing with methods.

### Runnable

Once a `Thread` object receives the `start()` method, it enters what is known as the `Runnable` state. You may think it should be called the "Running" state because at first, you might assume it is executing.

However, this is not necessarily true. Even though threads seem to operate and execute at the same time, the underlying system architecture determines this capability.

## Stopping Threads

Starting with Java 2, the `stop()` method has been deprecated. While this means you can still call it, you should never really do so. Calling `stop()` causes an immediate crash halt of the thread — and, hence, everything that it was doing. This can cause severe problems, such as leaving resources in an unknown state or even hanging your entire application.

The recommended way to terminate a thread is to use a flag to indicate to the body of the `run` method that it needs to exit. If your thread is blocked waiting for input (from a network connection, for example), then you can always interrupt the thread, catching the resultant `InterruptedException` and then exiting cleaning. This technique is covered more later in the chapter.

Specifically, to execute at the same time, or in parallel, more than one CPU must be available. Because true multiprocessing computers are rare, your threads are more likely to wait around while each takes a crack at a single CPU.

**Note** Simply having multiple CPUs installed in a single computer does not result in a true multiprocessing system. The system architecture (the system hardware and operating system software) must support the capability to execute commands in parallel. True multiprocessing machines are currently a high-end option; they're just beginning to be marketed for everyday desktop use. Note that Windows 95 only supports a single CPU, even if your machine has more than one, while Windows NT will make use of all the CPUs. All flavors of UNIX support multiple CPUs.

### Not Runnable

If a thread isn't in the `Runnable` state, it may be in the `Not Runnable` state. `Not Runnable` is entered when a thread is in one of four conditions:

✦ Suspended

✦ Sleeping

✦ Waiting on a condition variable

✦ Blocked by another thread

Three of these are each the result of a specific method:

✦ `suspend()`

✦ `sleep()`

✦ `join()`

The remaining condition is a result of a thread being blocked by an input/output operation. (See Chapter 13, "Input/Output: Streams.")

Because each of these is a Not Runnable condition, sending messages to a thread in one of them results in an exception being thrown. For each possible way a thread may become Not Runnable, there is a single and distinct way that it may reenter the Runnable state. Take a close look at each of these conditions and how each can be reversed.

## Suspended

Whenever a thread's suspend() method is invoked, that thread effectively goes into limbo. When suspended, the thread is not in a position to be executed; it must be awakened first by the resume() method. This is helpful when you want to suspend a thread's execution but you don't want to kill it. An example of where you might want to do this is the animator that was presented earlier in the chapter in Listing 14-2.

The suspend() and resume() methods have been deprecated because they can cause just as many problems as an outright kill using stop(). They are very dangerous and should be avoided whenever possible. The alternative is to bring the animation thread to a halt normally and create a new thread when you need to restart. The ideal way of doing this is to implement the Runnable interface rather than extend Thread so that you can keep all of the instance variables. (Threads cannot be restarted.)

## Sleeping

As you saw earlier, you can put threads to sleep for a period of time (measured milliseconds). Once a thread is put to sleep, it cannot run. Even if it has a crack at a processor, a sleeping thread won't take it. Until the "sleep time" has expired, the thread simply won't execute. When its time has passed, it reenters the Runnable state.

What if you called resume() on a sleeping thread? A nice idea, but it would do absolutely no good. When a thread is sleeping, the resume() method is ignored altogether. It's only useful for taking suspended threads out of limbo.

## Waiting for a Condition Variable

A thread can be told to wait on a conditional variable, forcing it to hang out until that condition is satisfied. After sending a thread the join() method, you must wait indefinitely until that thread's run() method has finished. Sending the join() method to a thread may be dangerous, however, if you have important things to do and are forced to wait around for a long period of time. If you refer back to Javadoc for the Thread class, you'll notice a timeout period may be supplied with two of the join() methods, in which case, the thread continues after the specified time passes, regardless of the outcome of the condition.

Whatever object is in control of the condition you're waiting on must alert waiting threads using either the `notify()` or `notifyAll()` methods. If a thread is waiting on something to happen, it can proceed only once `notify()` or `notifyAll()` has been issued, or if the (optional) timeout period has passed.

## Blocked

If a thread is blocked by an input/output operation, it has no choice but to wait around until the input/output command is finished. In this case, the thread is considered `Not Runnable`, even though it may be fully qualified to run otherwise.

If you really need to make the thread resume (such as to close it down when the application is exiting), then you have the option of closing the underlying stream. When you close the stream source (for example, a `File` or `Socket`), this will immediately cause the thread to unblock and continue executing. You need to be really careful when doing this, however, as it really should only be done when you want to exit the thread.

## Dead

Just like us, threads have a lifecycle. Once a thread's `run()` method is complete, its life is up: sorry, buddy, it's time to die!

For example, if the loop in the `run()` method for our `BlinkItem` example was to iterate only 1,000 times, the lifecycle of that thread would be 1,000 iterations of that loop. However, because the loop is intentionally infinite, the lifecycle of that thread is also infinite, as long as you don't exit the page in which it's embedded.

As soon as the page is exited, the applet's `stop()` method is called, which in turn terminates the thread. In this case, the thread does not die from "natural causes," as our `EZThread` threads do: it's murdered. The thread is killed by the `interrupt()` message being sent to it. When a thread receives this, it commits digital hara-kiri and terminates itself.

In general, you should terminate all threads whenever your applet's own `stop()` method is invoked. (Remember, don't ever call `stop()` on the threads, though.) Unless you have a very good reason, whenever someone moves out of the page in which your applet is running, you should kill all threads (or, at the very least, suspend them). It is extremely bad style to allow threads to run in the background when your applet is not actually executing.

The Thread class provides a method called `isAlive()`, enabling our program to determine whether a thread has been started and not stopped. The `isAlive()` method returns `true` if a thread has been created and started but hasn't been stopped. It returns `false` if the thread is dead, or if it has been created but not started.

## Thread Exceptions

The Java runtime system throws `IllegalThreadStateException` whenever you attempt to invoke a method that the thread cannot handle in its current state. For example, a sleeping thread can't deal with the `resume()` method. The thread is busy sleeping; it doesn't know how to react to it.

The same holds true when you try to invoke `suspend()` in a thread that isn't in its `Runnable` state. If it's already suspended, sleeping, waiting on a condition variable, or blocked by I/O, a thread won't understand how to deal with `suspend()`.

Whenever you call a thread method that may potentially throw an exception, you have to supply an exception handler to catch whatever exceptions may be generated.

As you can see in the following snippet of code, you can determine whether a thread was killed cleanly or whether an exception occurred:

```
try {
... // deal with threads here...
}
catch (ThreadDeath death) {
    // was killed... be sure to rethrow:
    throw death;
}
catch (IllegalThreadStateException itse) {
    // thread was sent a method it couldn't handle in its state
}
catch (InterruptedException ie) {
    // the thread was interrupted
}
```

If the thread surrounded by the `try-catch` clause was killed, the first exception handler captures it. In this case, we need to rethrow the `ThreadDeath` object to ensure the thread is killed cleanly. However, if the thread was sent a method it couldn't handle in its current state, the second catch clause catches it.

Finally, if the thread is unexpectedly interrupted, the `InterruptedException` exception is thrown. In this case, our last handler catches it.

As a result, when `isAlive()` returns true, you know that a thread is either in the `Runnable` or `Not Runnable` state. Unfortunately, there is no way to know which of these two states the thread is in. Conversely, you know that when `isAlive()` returns `false`, the thread is either dead or has not yet been started.

## Relinquishing Control with Yield( )

Although threads of the same priority are given equal treatment by the Java thread scheduler, it's possible for a thread to hog the CPU. Consider the following code, and assume it is part of a thread body:

```
int i = 0;
while (i++ < 500000) {
   System.out.println("Iteration: " + i);
}
```

You'll see that, once the loop is entered, there's no way other threads have a chance to run and the current thread cannot move into the Not Runnable state. So this thread monopolizes the CPU entirely and all 500,000 iterations happen without so much as a second of time going to other threads of equal priority. Unless a thread of a higher priority comes along and preempts this one, the loop completes naturally. If this is the case, you should use the yield() method to force the thread to relinquish control of the CPU:

```
int i = 0;
while (i++ < 500000) {
   System.out.println("Iteration: " + i);
   yield(); // relinquish control
}
```

Here, we still execute the loop, but we also give threads of the same priority a chance to execute. Keep in mind that threads of a lower priority must still wait until all these threads enter a Not Runnable state or die.

## Thread priority

In Java, each thread has a priority that affects the order in which it is run. Threads of high priority run before threads of low priority. This is essential because there are times when threads must be separated in this way. For example, the thread responsible for handling user input is of a higher priority than one that crunches a data file in the background.

**Note** A thread inherits its priority from the thread that created it. Unless a new priority is assigned to a thread, the thread keeps this priority until it dies.

You can set the priority of a thread using the setPriority() method, assigning it a value between the Thread class constants MIN_PRIORITY and MAX_PRIORITY refer Refer to Table 14-5. For example, we could make our BlinkItem thread the highest priority with the following line:

```
kicker.setPriority(MAX_PRIORITY); //
```

## Under the Covers

The Java runtime system's scheduler is preemptive. If the scheduler is running one thread and another thread of a higher priority comes along, the thread that is currently executed is put on the back burner and the one with the higher priority is placed in execution. In this sense, the highest priority thread is said to preempt the currently running thread.

The Java scheduler doesn't preempt the currently running thread for another of the same priority, however. And although the scheduler itself isn't *time-sliced* (that is, it doesn't give threads of the same priority a slice of time in which to execute), the system implementation of threads underlying the `Thread` class may support time-slicing.

Because you can't be certain on which systems your applets will be executed, never write your program to rely on time-slicing. That is, you should use yield() to allow threads of the same priority an opportunity to execute rather than expecting each to get a slice of the CPU pie automatically.

Because `kicker` is the only thread in this applet, changing its priority doesn't make much sense. In programs with multiple threads, however, the ability to assign priority is quite important. Certain parts of our programs vary in how critical they are, and by setting their priorities accordingly, we can ensure they are given the attention (or lack of attention) they deserve.

Java threads are scheduled using fixed-priority scheduling. This algorithm essentially executes threads based on their priority relative to one another and can be summed up in a simple rule: *At any given time, the "Runnable" thread with the highest priority will be running.*

Whenever multiple threads are ready for execution, the Java runtime system chooses whichever has the highest priority and executes it. When that thread stops running, yields (see the "Relinquishing Control with Yield( )" sidebar), or becomes `Not Runnable`, the lower priority threads have an opportunity to run. If there are two threads with the same priority waiting to be executed, the scheduler executes them in a round-robin fashion, as described earlier.

## Daemon threads

Java supports what are known as *daemon threads*. A daemon thread can be considered a head honcho, or taskmaster thread that supports other threads. The body of a daemon thread, the `run( )` method, often uses an infinite loop that waits for a request from an object or other threads. When such a request is made, the daemon thread carries it out, dispatching the appropriate methods. For example, the

HotJava browser has a daemon thread named Background Image Reader. This thread is responsible for downloading images from the network and handing them off to objects and other threads that need them.

To set a daemon thread, invoke the `setDaemon()` method with a `true` parameter:

```
myThread.setDaemon(true); // myThread is now a daemon
```

You can find out if a thread is a daemon by using `isDaemon()`:

```
myThread.isDaemon();
```

The `isDaemon()` method returns true if the thread is a daemon; otherwise, it returns false.

## Thread groups

All Java threads are part of a thread group (see Tables 14-2 and 14-3), whether or not you explicitly specify one when creating them. However, there are three constructors in the `Thread` class that enable you to specify which group a thread should be part of, if you want to specify one other than the default group:

✦ Thread(ThreadGroup, Runnable);

✦ Thread(ThreadGroup, String);

✦ Thread(ThreadGroup, Runnable, String);

| Table 14-2 Class java.lang.ThreadGroup Constructors | |
|---|---|
| **Signature** | **Description** |
| `public ThreadGroup(String)` | Creates a new thread group with the given name. Its parent is the thread group of the current thread. |
| `public ThreadGroup (ThreadGroup,String)` | Creates a new thread group with a specified name in the specified thread group. Throws `NullPointerException` if the given thread group is null. |

## Table 14-3
## Class java.lang.ThreadGroup Methods

| Method | Description |
|---|---|
| `public int activeCount()` | Returns an estimate of the number of active threads in the thread group. |
| `public int activeGroupCount()` | Returns an estimate of the number of active groups in the thread group. |
| `public void checkAccess()` | Checks to see if the current thread is allowed to modify this group. Throws `SecurityException` if the current thread is not allowed to access this thread group. |
| `public final void destroy()` | Destroys a thread group. This does not stop the threads in the thread group. Throws `Illegal ThreadState Exception` if the thread group is not empty or if it was already destroyed. |
| `public int enumerate (Thread[])` | Copies, into the specified array, references to every active thread in this thread group. You can use the `activeCount()` method to get an estimate of how big the array should be. The return value is the number of items actually filled in. |
| `public int enumerate (Thread[], boolean)` | Copies, into the specified array, references to every active thread in this thread group. The boolean can be used to control whether the copy should recourse all children thread groups of this thread group. You can use the `activeCount()` method to get an estimate of how big the array should be. The return value is the number of items actually filled in. |
| `public int enumerate (ThreadGroup[])` | Copies, into the specified array, references to every active subgroup in this thread group. You can use the `activeGroupCount()` method to get an estimate of how big the array should be. |
| `public int enumerate (ThreadGroup[], boolean)` | Copies, into the specified array, references to every active thread in this thread group. You can use the `activeGroupCount()` method to get an estimate of how big the array should be. |
| `public final int getMaxPriority()` | Gets the maximum priority of the group. Threads that are part of this group cannot have a higher priority than the maximum priority. |
| `public String getName()` | Gets the name of this thread group. |

| Method | Description |
| --- | --- |
| `public ThreadGroup getParent()` | Gets the parent of this thread group. |
| `public boolean isDaemon()` | Returns the daemon flag of the thread group. A daemon thread group is automatically destroyed when it is found empty after a thread group or thread is removed from it. |
| `public void list()` | Lists this thread group. Useful only for debugging. |
| `public boolean parentOf (ThreadGroup)` | Checks to see whether this thread group is a parent of, or is equal to, another thread group. |
| `public void setDaemon (boolean)` | Changes the daemon status of this group. |
| `public void setMaxPriority (int)` | Sets the maximum priority of the group. Threads that are already in the group can have a higher priority than the set maximum. |
| `public String toString()` | Returns a string representation of the thread group. |
| `public void uncaught Exception(Thread, Throwable)` | Called by the JVM when a thread in this group stops because of an uncaught exception. |

Thread groups are particularly useful because you can start or suspend all threads within them, meaning you don't have to deal with each thread individually. Thread groups provide a general way of dealing with a number of threads at once, saving you a great deal of time and effort tracking them down individually.

The following snippet creates a thread group called `genericGroup`. Once we've created the group, we then create a few threads that are part of it:

```
ThreadGroup genericGroup =
  new ThreadGroup("My Generic Threads");
Thread aThread = new Thread(genericGroup, this);
Thread aThread2 = new Thread(genericGroup, this);
Thread aThread3 = new Thread(genericGroup, this);
```

You don't necessarily have to create the group of which your threads are a part. You can use one created by the Java runtime system or one created by the application in which your applet is running. If you don't specify a particular thread group when creating a new thread, as we have in the preceding examples, the thread becomes part of Java's main thread group. This is sometimes referred to as the current thread group.

**Note**    With applets, the default group may not be the main group. It's up to the browser to give the thread a name. To find out what the name is, use the `getName()` method. (Refer to Table 14-4.)

To find out which group a thread is in, use the `getThreadGroup()` method defined in the Thread class. This method returns a thread group to which you can send a variety of methods that act on each member of the group. As you may recall, Table 14-2 shows the various methods that operate on groups.

**Tip**    Thread groups support the notion of access privileges. If you don't specify an access privilege for a group, the threads in that group are allowed to query and find out information about threads in other groups. If you don't have the right privileges, then attempting to read the details about other threads will throw security exceptions.

By default, the threads you create don't have a specific security level assigned to them. As a result, any thread in any group is free to inspect or modify threads in other groups. You can, however, use the abstract `SecurityManager` class (`java.lang.SecurityManager`) to specify access restrictions for thread groups.

To specify access restrictions, you would create a subclass of the `SecurityManager` class and override those methods that are used in thread security. Keep in mind, however, that most browsers (such as Netscape) won't allow you to change or alter security managers, so this procedure applies only to applications.

| Table 14-4 java.lang.Thread Methods | |
|---|---|
| **Method** | **Description** |
| `public static Thread currentThread()` | Returns a reference to the currently executing `Thread` object. |
| `public static void yield()` | Causes the currently executing `Thread` object to yield. If there are other runnable threads, they will be scheduled next. |
| `public static void sleep (long)` | Causes the currently executing thread to sleep for the specified number of milliseconds. Throws `InterruptedException` if another thread has interrupted this thread. |
| `public static void sleep (long, int)` | Sleeps, in milliseconds and additional nonoseconds. Practically useless because no VM implementations support millisecond accuracy. Throws `InterruptedException` if another thread has interrupted this thread. |
| `public void start()` | Starts this thread. This causes the `run()` method to be called. This method returns immediately. Throws `IllegalThreadState Exception` if the thread was already started. |

| Method | Description |
|---|---|
| `public void run()` | The actual body of this thread. This method is called after the thread is started. You must either override this method by subclassing class `Thread`, or you must create the thread with a runnable target. |
| `public void interrupt()` | Sends an interrupt to a thread. |
| `public static boolean interrupted()` | Asks whether you have been interrupted. |
| `public boolean is Interrupted()` | Asks whether another thread has been interrupted. |
| `public void destroy()` | Destroys a thread without any cleanup. In other words, this method just tosses its state; any monitors it has locked remain locked. A last resort. |
| `public final boolean is Alive()` | Returns a `boolean` indicating whether the thread is active. Having an active thread means it has been started and has not been stopped. |
| `public void setPriority (int)` | Sets the thread's priority. Throws `IllegalArgument Exception` if the priority is not within the range `MIN_PRIORITY, MAX_PRIORITY`. |
| `public int getPriority()` | Returns the thread's priority. |
| `public void setName (String)` | Sets the thread's name. |
| `public String getName()` | Returns this thread's name. |
| `public ThreadGroup get ThreadGroup()` | Returns the thread group to which this thread belongs. |
| `public static int activeCount()` | Returns the current number of active active Count() threads in this thread's group. |
| `public static enumerate (Thread[])` | Copies, into the specified array, references to every active thread in thread's group. Returns the number of threads put into the array. |
| `public void join(long)` | Waits for this thread to die. A timeout in milliseconds can be specified. A timeout of 0 (zero) milliseconds means to wait forever. Throws InterruptedException if another thread has interrupted this one. |
| `public void join (long, int)` | Waits for the thread to die, with more precise time. Again, practically useless because no current VMs support nanosecond accuracy. Throws `InterruptedException` if another thread has interrupted this thread. |

*Continued*

## Table 14-4 *(continued)*

| Method | Description |
|---|---|
| `public void join()` | Waits forever for this thread to die. Throws `InterruptedException` if another thread has interrupted this thread. |
| `public static void dumpStack()` | Prints a stack trace for the current thread. A debugging procedure. |
| `public void setDaemon (boolean)` | Marks this thread as a daemon thread or a user thread. When there are only daemon threads left running in the system, Java exits. Throws `Illegal ThreadState Exception` if the thread is active. |
| `public boolean isDaemon()` | Returns the daemon flag of the thread. |
| `public void checkAccess()` | Modifies this thread. Throws `SecurityException` if the current thread is not allowed to access this thread group. |
| `public String toString()` | Returns a string representation of the Thread, including the thread's name, priority, and thread group. |

## Table 14-5
## java.lang.Thread Variables

| Variable | Description |
|---|---|
| `int MIN_PRIORITY` | The minimum priority that a thread can have. |
| `int NORM_PRIORITY` | The default priority that is assigned to a thread. |
| `int MAX_PRIORITY` | The maximum priority that a thread can have. |

While a thread is sleeping, it is said to enter a `Not Runnable` state. All the other threads are free to continue, but a sleeping thread is inactive until the amount of time specified has passed. Although this applet specifies a random amount of time, we can also specify exactly how long a thread should sleep:

```
Thread.sleep(2000); // sleep 2,000 milliseconds (2 seconds)
```

Because threads execute extremely fast, the sleep parameter is expressed in milliseconds. To help make sense of this parameter, just remember that 1,000 milliseconds equal 1 second.

You might have noticed that we didn't send the Kicker object the sleep() method. Instead, we called the Thread class method directly. The current thread is known because we're in its run() method, so we don't have to send it the sleep() method directly. The preceding line of code applies the sleep() method to the current thread, which happens to be kicker. In a more complicated program, we'd prefer to invoke the sleep() method of the thread we want to take a nap to avoid confusion, instead of taking direct advantage of the Thread classes' sleep() method, as seen here. However, in this simple example, the result is the same and fairly clear regardless of how we forced the thread to sleep. We could just as easily have called kicker.sleep( (int) (Math.random()*500));.

Because invoking sleep() may result in an exception being thrown, as most methods that operate on threads have the potential of doing, we must wrap a try-catch clause around this statement. You'll see, however, that nothing is done if an error is thrown.

What can we do? Nothing, really, except perhaps break out of the loop and terminate the life of the thread:

```
try {
    Thread.sleep( (int) (Math.random()*500));
}
catch (InterruptedException e) {
    break;
}
```

However, we just let the loop continue. If an error occurs while sleeping, we really don't want to terminate the entire animation. So, perhaps it will repaint the next image a little faster than expected. But it's not worth terminating the entire thread simply because our sleep() request wasn't fulfilled.

In this case, the result of a random sleep parameter is quite effective. The images used in the animation (see Figure 14-2) seem to blink on and off, with a little stutter between each blink, just like a neon sign.

When the browser in which this applet is viewed loads another page, the applet's stop() method is called. It's here that we bring the life of our thread to an abrupt end:

```
kicker.interrupt(); // kill thread
kicker=null; // mark for garbage collection
```

The interrupt() method causes anything executing in the run() method to stop, even if blocked. The exception can be caught or the code checked to see if it was interrupted by calling isInterrrupted(). The run() method then uses this signal to exit from the method cleanly, allowing the thread to die. When it's dead, we mark the thread as null, allowing the garbage collector to reclaim the memory allocated for it.

Homepage 1.gif

Homepage 2.gif

**Figure 14-2:** Using threads, the BlinkItem applet alternates between these two images to give the appearance of a neon sign.

When the page is revisited, the applet's own `start()` method kicks off another thread, and the entire process is repeated. Alternatively, we could have suspended the thread when the applet's `stop()` method was called and resumed it when the page was revisited.

## Don't Kill That Thread by Mistake!

You can get the currently executing process using the following statement:

```
Thread.currentThread();
```

You might be tempted to send `stop()` to the currently executing thread, assuming it's yours. Don't do it! If you blindly assume the current thread is yours, you might kill the main thread your applet is running under, or perhaps even the garbage-collector thread. If you want to be able to distinguish your thread from others, use the constructor that allows you to supply a name for your thread:

```
kicker = new Thread(this, "BlinkThread");
```

You can then use the `getName()` method to ensure that the thread you're dealing with is, in fact, yours.

However, in this case, there is no good reason to keep the thread alive when the page itself is left. We can't guarantee that the user will return, and it's just as easy to start a new one every time the page is visited. Threads are easy to create and set running.

## Using the Thread() constructor

The following code illustrates how to create a threaded class by implementing the Runnable interface. Notice that the run() method is overridden, a must for all threads created in this way:

```java
class MyThread implements Runnable {
  String name;
  MyThread() { // standard constructor
    name = null;
  }

  MyThread(String str) { // constructor with name
    name = str;
  }

  public void run() {
    if (name == null)
      System.out.println("A new thread was created");
    else
      System.out.println("A new thread named " +
    name + " was created");
  }

  public static void main (String args[]) {
    MyThread t = new MyThread();
    if(t != null) {
      System.out.println("new myThread() succeed");
    }
    else {
      System.out.println("new myThread() failed");
    }
  }
}
```

## Creating threaded objects

In addition to implementing the Runnable interface, we can use threads by extending the Thread class. In this way, we can create our own objects that use threads:

```java
class AnyClass extends Thread {
  ...
}
```

As you can see, all we have to do is extend the `Thread` class. Because the `java.lang` package is automatically available to all of our programs, we don't have to import it explicitly. Take a look at a class that extends `Thread`:

```
class EZThread extends Thread {
  public EZThread(String str) {
    super(str);  // pass up to Thread constructor
  }
  public void run() {
    for (int i = 0; i < 5; i++) {
      System.out.println(i + " " + getName());
      try {
        sleep((int)(Math.random() * 500));
      }
      catch (InterruptedException e) {
        i = 6; // to exit the loop
      }
    }
    System.out.println(getName() + " HAS EXPIRED!");
  }
}
```

The first thing this class does is implement a constructor that takes a string parameter and passes it along to the constructor of its superclass. The `Thread` class constructor that takes a string is invoked, returning a `Thread` object with this name. By naming threads, we can keep track of which ones are currently running.

Aside from this, we've implemented a `run()` method. Whenever an `EZThread` object is created, its `start()` method must be invoked before it can execute. Because we don't bother to define a `start()` method in this class, the superclass `start()` method is actually used (that is, the Thread class `start()` method is invoked). This method, in turn, invokes the `EZThread` `run()` method.

This `run()` method is quite simple: It executes a loop five times, outputting the loop iteration (i) on the same line as the name of the thread. To test this class, we can use the following:

```
class EZTest {
  public static void main (String args[]) {
    new EZThread("Hickory").start();
    new EZThread("Dickory").start();
    new EZThread("Dock").start();
  }
}
```

As you can see, this test is quite simple. We merely instantiate three new threads and start each of them. We don't even need to hold onto the `Thread` objects that are created. We create the threads, start them, and sit back as they execute. The output is shown in Figure 14-3. Note that it's not sequential; it doesn't follow any exact order. The threads are running independently of one another — each one executes whenever it has the chance. The order is determined on the Java thread scheduler and the underlying system architecture. However, you'll see in "Bringing It All Together," later in this chapter, how you can synchronize threads to execute in a nice, orderly fashion.

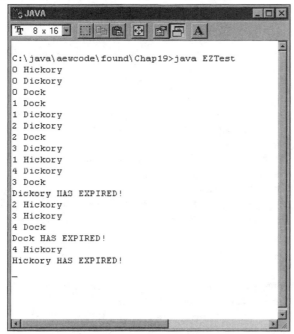

**Figure 14-3:** Because threads don't run in a predetermined order, the three in this program don't generate output sequentially.

## Using threads

Clearly, creating and using threads is easy in Java. In fact, it's recommended that you use threads whenever you have a specific sequence of events that can be executed independently of others that prevent control from returning to the user for a significant period of time. In this way, you can divvy up your program into a number of threads, each executing independently, and potential bottlenecks can be significantly reduced or eliminated entirely. Exactly what constitutes a significant period is up to the application, but if you see menus and parts of the screen not repainting quickly, then that is probably a good sign that a thread could be used.

Keep in mind that each time you create a Java thread, an underlying system thread is actually created. That is, the operating system of your computer — together with the Java runtime system — is responsible for handling the flow of execution of each thread you create. The more threads you create, the more the system is taxed. If you go mad, creating threads for everything you can think of, eventually you'll bring the system to its knees. It's best to think about the sequence of events you want to wrap inside a thread, rather than assume that everything needs to be threaded.

In fact, the Java runtime system already has threads running with which yours must share a slice of the CPU pie. For example, there's the Java garbage-collector thread. If the garbage collection mechanism weren't running in a thread, it would have to interrupt your program each time it tried to reclaim objects no longer in use. However, because this system is operating in a thread, it goes about its business without greatly affecting the performance of your program.

In addition, there's a thread always running that is responsible for gathering user input from the keyboard and the mouse. So there are already two threads running before you add your own to the mix. A third thread is then created when your application starts running. For an applet, the thread creates an instance of your applet class and calls the start and stop methods, while for a standalone application, this thread creates an instance of your class and calls the main() method.

We're not telling you to be stingy with threads; they are fast and easy to create, and when used properly, they can greatly enhance the performance of your programs. However, you must consider which operations lend themselves to threads. We recommend that whenever you have a sequence of steps that can operate independently from the rest of your program (such as the animation of a graphic), you place it into a thread.

## Runnable or thread?

When creating threads, you may wonder: should I implement the Runnable interface or extend the Thread class? The answer, of course, depends on what the class you're creating requires. If it must extend another class, you have no choice but to implement the Runnable interface because your classes can only inherit from one superclass. We recommend that you use the Runnable interface whenever you need to override only run() and no other thread methods. Classes shouldn't be subclassed unless you are modifying or enhancing their fundamental behavior, so there's no reason to subclass Thread if you need to implement only the run() method.

## Stopping threads

Although the Thread class defines a number of different methods for controlling thread execution, it does not mean that you should actually use them. One of the most dangerous methods to call is stop(). This literally halts a thread in its track and stops it from executing any further. If a thread has locked up a resource such as a file and then it is forced to stop, that resource is not freed for others to use. It is extremely easy to create a deadlock situation. (Deadlocking is covered shortly.)

The correct way to stop a thread is to use a condition flag and interrupt the thread by calling interrupt(). This tells the thread to stop whatever it is doing (for example, you saw the sleep() method earlier in the chapter) but doesn't force it to die. You can then check inside your run() whenever you get this by calling isInterrupted() and exiting run() appropriately—after freeing all resources that you've used.

```
run() {
  boolean finished = false;
  while(!finished) {
    try {
      // do something here....
    } catch(Exception e) {
      if(Thread.interrupted())
        finished = true;
    }
  }
}
```

Note that we need to catch Exception. A lot of your code doesn't explicitly throw InterruptedException, but the general exception condition can be used to catch interruptions. Because of the general nature of the catch clause, we always check to see if the thread was actually interrupted, rather than some other error condition, before exiting the loop.

## Under the Covers

As you know, Java threads are implemented by the Thread class, which is part of the java.lang package. Because java.lang is automatically included in your programs, you don't need to import this class to add thread support to your own programs.

This class provides you with a system-independent mechanism for dealing with threads. But under the covers, the actual implementation of threads is dependent on whatever operating system architecture Java is running on. As a result, your threaded programs are really taking advantage of the thread support of the OS on which they are executed. Luckily, you're isolated from the intricacies of individual platforms, thanks to the Thread class.

When creating a thread, you can give it a priority. The higher its priority, the more clout it carries with the runtime system. The Java runtime system uses a scheduler that is responsible for running all existing threads within all executing Java programs. This scheduler uses a fixed-priority scheduling algorithm that, in essence, ensures that the highest-priority threads in each program get the processor—the highest-priority thread is allowed to execute before any others.

In a case where a single program has more than one thread of the same priority waiting to execute, the scheduler chooses them in a round-robin fashion, choosing a thread not previously executed when the next choice must be made. All threads of the same priority receive equal treatment. Threads of lesser priority are given a chance to execute after those of higher priority have been killed or have entered a nonrunnable state. (See the "Not Runnable" section earlier in this chapter.)

Finally, sometimes your code will not respond to an interrupted exception if it is locked up doing something else — reading a file or network connection, for example. The easiest way to then force a break in these situations is to close the underlying item (such as the file or socket) from outside the code and let everything percolate through from there.

# Multithreaded Programs

Whenever you have multiple threads running simultaneously (or almost at the same time, as is the case with single-CPU systems), they may need to access the same piece of data at the same time. In fact, unless your program is running on a true multiprocessor system that supports parallel processing, your threads will never access a specific piece of data at exactly the same time. They will, however, be able to access the same piece of data at roughly the same time, with perhaps only milliseconds or less between each access.

The problem is that when threads share data, none of them can be certain that the data hasn't been changed by another thread before they got to it.

Think in terms of a basket full of eggs. If you're the only person at your Easter egg decorating party, you can be pretty sure that, when you reach into the basket, you'll get an egg (at least until there are no more eggs, or the cops break up your little party).

However, suppose you invite the local chapter of the Hell's Angels over to decorate eggs with you. Whenever you reach into the basket, you now run the risk of brushing up against a hairy forearm or two. Worse still, you might be expecting an egg, only to find that Alphonse got the last one. In this case, Alphonse is busy throwing his egg at Sebastian while you get hot under the pinstriped collar. And who's going to yell at a Hell's Angel?

Aside from the likelihood of encountering hirsute appendages, the same thing can happen when a number of threads operate on the same data. Unless their access to the data is synchronized, there's no way of guaranteeing that the data hasn't been changed by another thread.

## Synchronization

Up until this point, we've only looked at threads that operated where all the data and methods required for execution were inside the body of the thread. We have not considered threads that access data outside themselves.

A sticky situation can occur when multiple threads need to access the same piece of information. For example, suppose you wrote a simple `Counter` class that provided methods for incrementing and returning the `counter` variable. Using the class within a single thread is just fine, but what happens when multiple threads attempt to use this class?

Because each thread has the potential for accessing these methods at exactly (or nearly) the same time, the counter may become inconsistent. Suppose, for example, that one thread was incrementing the value of the counter at the same time another was retrieving it. Should the returned value reflect the incremented value? Suppose a dozen threads all tried to update the value at the same time and only one attempted to retrieve it. What value should be returned in that case?

In effect, the data becomes unreliable, yet it's almost impossible to track down precisely what's going on because everything seems to be jogging along smoothly. Then, every once in a while, seemingly inexplicably, the data gets clobbered. You might expect to retrieve a number such as 12 but find that only 2 is returned because of a synchronization error.

The way to avoid this distress is to use the `synchronized` keyword, as shown in the following code. In this way, you can guarantee that only one thread is accessing a method at a time. Every other thread has to wait its turn until the object is free:

```
synchronized void myMethod( ) {
    // all code in here is now synchronized!
}
```

The synchronized keyword can be applied to any block of code, not just methods:

```
synchronized (anyObject) {
    // the object and this block of code are synchronized
}
```

Depending on the situation, synchronized blocks of code may be better than synchronizing whole methods. If there is only one small part that is critical out of a large method, then it is better to protect only the block. Another variation would be if that small part is only executed some of the times that the method is called — for example, it is within an `if-else` statement. This prevents the rest of the method from suffering the performance penalty associated with synchronization.

The `synchronized` keyword makes use of *monitors*. A monitor acts like a bouncer at the door of an exclusive nightclub, allowing only one person in and out at any given time (not a very fun club, from the sound of it, but a club nonetheless). Whenever an object enters a synchronized method, the bouncer (monitor) marks it as locked and prevents any other threads from accessing it until the current thread is finished. Using the proper terminology, any time you apply the `synchronized` keyword to a method or to a block of code, you are marking a critical section.

Using `synchronized` to mark critical sections of code enables you to share data among threads without worrying that it will be clobbered. The `hit()` method in class `PingPong`, shown in Listing 14-3 in the "Bringing It All Together" section later in this chapter, is an example of a synchronized method.

Whenever a thread enters `hit()`, all others are locked out until it has finished. The others wait, blocked, until `hit()` becomes unlocked. In this way, we never have to worry about synchronization errors again.

**Tip**    Java has a reserved keyword, called `volatile`, that enables you to specify variables as being, you guessed it, volatile. A variable that is volatile is read from memory every time it is used and then stored after each use. This means that each time you access a variable, it's guaranteed not to have come from a register and not to have been stored in a previous memory location. The reason for needing this is that sometimes, multiple threads accessing the same variable may end up with two different values. If one is kept in a register that is then swapped out without being written back to the main memory when the thread context changes, you may end up working with the old value from memory.

## Deadlock

An interesting condition occurs when two or more threads are waiting for each other to unlock a synchronized block of code, where each thread relies on another to do the unlocking. This deadlock situation can occur if you're not careful in writing your synchronized methods. If the method being called attempts to access the synchronized method that invoked it and must wait for that method to become free before it can become free itself, the two methods will end up waiting on each other for eternity!

There are a few things you can do to ensure that your synchronized programs don't end up in deadlock. For one, try to execute locked code in as short an amount of time as possible. The longer you hold the lock, the more likely it is that another thread will come along and require that object.

Also, be careful when you're actually invoking synchronized methods from within another synchronized method. Whenever a synchronized method invokes another synchronized method, there is a potential for deadlock. The best way to avoid deadlock is to clearly define the task each thread has, and consider which data is to be used and when. Although you may not anticipate all potential scenarios, you'll be in better shape than if you simply attempt to wrap a thread around everything. By ensuring that every thread in your program has a specific purpose, you eliminate the threads that aren't required and reduce the chance of deadlock.

# Bringing It All Together

The following code listings bring many of the aspects you've just read about to life. Together, Listings 14-3, 14-4, and 14-5 illustrate a very simple example of a synchronized, threaded program that implements `wait()` and `notify()`. The program, `Ping Pong`, has a very simple algorithm:

```
If it is my turn,
     note whose turn it is next,
     then PING,
     and then notify anyone waiting.
otherwise,
     wait to be notified.
```

The first class is named `PingPong` and consists of a single synchronized method named `hit()`, whose only parameter is the name of the "player" who goes next. Any thread with a reference to an instance of class `PingPong` can synchronize itself with other threads holding that same reference. To illustrate this concept, the `Player` class (Listing 14-4) was written to instantiate a `PingPong` thread, and the `Game` class (Listing 14-5) was written to create several players and run them all at once.

Because each of these is a public class, they can't be stored in the same .java file. (Remember, only one public class to a file!) As a result, each resides in its own file. When compiled and executed, the output looks something like the following:

```
PING! (alice)
PING! (bob)
PING! (alice)
PING! (bob)
PING! (alice)
PING! (bob)
etc...
```

Because these threads are synchronized with each other, they run nice and orderly, each in turn, and quite unlike our `EZThread` example earlier where it was every thread for itself. Thanks to `PingPong`'s use of synchronization, only one thread at a time can enter hit(), so each waits for the other to finish before taking its turn. Contrast this with unsynchronized methods, where multiple threads can access the code at the same time.

The Ping Pong program is part of the JavaWorld "Synchronizing Threads in Java" article available at `http://www.JavaWorld.com`. Refer to this article (or one of the other two articles on threads) for a step-by-step breakdown of this program and detailed information regarding Java threads.

**Listing 14-3: PingPong.java modified from the original by Chuck McManis**

```java
// The "Player" class
public class PingPong {

  // state variable identifying whose turn it is.
  private String whoseTurn = null;

  public synchronized boolean hit(String opponent) {

    String x = Thread.currentThread().getName();

    if (whoseTurn == null) {
      whoseTurn = x;
      return true;
    }

    if (whoseTurn.compareTo("DONE") == 0)
     return false;

    if (opponent.compareTo("DONE") == 0) {
      whoseTurn = opponent;
      notifyAll();
      return false;
    }

    if (x.compareTo(whoseTurn) == 0) {
      System.out.println("PING! ("+x+")");
      whoseTurn = opponent;
      notifyAll();
    }
    else {
      try {
        long t1 = System.currentTimeMillis();
        wait(2500);
        if ((System.currentTimeMillis() - t1) > 2500) {
         System.out.println("****** TIMEOUT! "+ x +
                            " is waiting for " + whoseTurn +
                            " to play.");
        }
      }
      catch (InterruptedException e) {
      }
    }
      return true; // keep playing.
  }
}
```

### Listing 14-4: **Player.java by Chuck McManis**

```java
// The "Player" class
public class Player implements Runnable {
  PingPong myTable;         // Table where they play
  String myOpponent;

  public Player(String opponent, PingPong table) {
    myTable  = table;
    myOpponent = opponent;
  }

  public void run() {
   while (myTable.hit(myOpponent))
     ;
   }
}
```

### Listing 14-5: **Game.java by Chuck McManis**

```java
// The "Game" class
public class Game {
  public static void main(String args[]) {
    PingPong table = new PingPong();
    Thread alice = new Thread(new Player("bob", table));
    Thread bob   = new Thread(new Player("alice", table));

    alice.setName("alice");
    bob.setName("bob");
    alice.start();    // alice starts playing
    bob.start();       // bob starts playing
    try {
      // Wait 5 seconds
     Thread.currentThread().sleep(5000);
    }
    catch (InterruptedException e) {
    }

    // cause the players to quit their threads.
    table.hit("DONE");
    try {
      Thread.currentThread().sleep(100);
    }
    catch (InterruptedException e) {
    }
  }
}
```

# Threads and Performance

In the move from JDK 1.1 to JDK 1.2 (a.k.a. Java 2), the resource allocation and over-heads of synchronization and threading have been greatly improved. What was once a factor of 20 slower to call a synchronized method over a normal method is generally now around only a factor of 7 to 10 slower. In high-speed applications like network servers and animation, this is a great boost. However, it also indicates that you should use synchronization and threading only where it is really needed.

The move from JDK1.2 to JDK 1.3 has again improved performance - particularly with the introduction of the Hotspot JIT compiler included with the standard JVM. However, the increase is not as dramatic as the change between 1.1 and 1.2.

# Summary

A thread, also known as an execution context or lightweight process, is a single sequential flow of control. Think of it as a way to divide your programs into chunks, each capable of executing independent of others. When used properly, threads help eliminate bottlenecks and improve overall programming performance. Threads are quick and easy to add to your programs, but with such power comes the responsi-bility of clearly defining which tasks deserve their own threads.

✦ You can use threads by implementing the `Runnable` interface or by extending the `Thread` class.

✦ Threads have three key aspects: body, state, and priority.

✦ A thread can be specified as a daemon thread, which serves other threads, and may also be assigned to a thread group when you need to manage more than one at a time.

✦ The body of a thread is its `run()` method, which is where all the action takes place and can be thought of as the heart of a thread.

✦ Be careful to include in the body of a thread (its `run()` method) only those tasks that may operate independently from the rest of your program.

✦ Be aware that multithreaded programs can deadlock your program when they use synchronized methods; be careful when you use monitors in your methods.

✦     ✦     ✦

# Networking

The Java language comes from Sun Microsystems. Also from Sun, we get the motto *The network is the computer*. From this line of reasoning, you could assume that Java would have quite a bit of networking capabilities — and it does.

Java was built from the ground up with networking in mind, giving us the ability to write network-savvy programs relatively easily from day one. Today, Java's networking capabilities continue to grow by leaps and bounds as new features are layered on top of an already substantial foundation and research projects focused on Java networking make their way from JavaSoft's labs to our personal computers.

In this chapter, we'll explore the various elements that give Java a leg up over traditional programming languages when it comes to developing network-aware programs. In doing so, we'll dive into the "core" classes that together form Java's solid networking infrastructure.

## Stacking Data with Addresses and Ports

The technology of the Internet is based on the TCP/IP stack. This *stack* — a piece of software that connects your applications to the Internet — can work with a number of protocols that wrap and unwrap data and has some special addressing tricks that make the Internet work. Any number of computers can be connected; it works perfectly regardless of whether you are connecting two computers across the room from each other, or millions of computers scattered all over the world.

## What's in an address?

The most fundamental thing you need to know when sending data over the Internet is where the data should go. Like dialing a phone or addressing an envelope, you need to know some magic incantation that will direct your message. There is a computer out there that deserves to receive the data you want to send — all you have to do is make sure your data gets to the right program inside the right computer. do this, there are just three things you need to know:

✦ The IP address of the target computer

✦ The protocol that will be used to package the data

✦ The port number specifying a specific application to receive the data

That's it. Using these three pieces of information, you can send data to any program on any computer in the world. For example, if you want your Web browser to send a request to the Web server program at IDG Books Worldwide, you need to know that the IP address is 38.170.216.15, the protocol is TCP, and the port number is 80.

## The IP address

The Internet Protocol (IP) address is simply a 32-bit number. Every computer on the Internet is assigned one of these numbers. If you use a dial-up connection, your Internet provider has a whole bunch of these numbers and, when you make a connection, it assigns one to your computer for the duration of your connection. Computers that are always connected to the Internet, such as Web servers, are assigned numbers that they keep. That's how we can find them; we send out the URL (www.idgbooks.com, for example) and get the IP number back. We discuss URLs further in the "URL Operations" section later in this chapter.

The IP address is a 32-bit number. That means there are 4,294,967,694 of them. There need to be a lot of them because every computer on the Internet has to have one. They are not normally written as one big number, but rather, as four little numbers — one representing the numeric value of each of the four bytes of the complete number. An IP address written in this way, which is sometimes called the *dot* or *dotted-quad format*, looks like this:

```
206.80.51.140
```

The actual numeric value is 3,461,362,572, but we never write it that way.

## The protocol

The IP stack uses two protocols: Transmission Control Protocol (TCP) and User Datagram Protocol (UDP). (Actually, the stack uses other special-purpose protocols as well, but you don't need to know more about them to send data across the Internet.) The TCP protocol is the most robust of the two and is what makes the Internet work so well. This is not to minimize the value of UDP — there are some places where it really comes in handy. The real name of the stack should probably be TCP/UDP/IP, but that begins to get a bit unwieldy.

The reason the protocol can be considered part of the address is that a process that is expecting a message in one protocol will never receive a message that is sent in a different protocol. That is, if you write a program that receives messages in TCP protocol, a UDP message will never be delivered to it.

## The port number

Once an Internet message arrives at a computer, it works its way up through the stack until it locates the destination program (if it's running). Passing through this stack on the way to your application, the operating system looks at the port number and protocol (TCP or UDP) of the message. With this information, it is able to determine which of the programs waiting for messages should be awarded this particular message. The application is handed the message, usually through a socket connection, and the communication is complete.

Protocols can share port numbers without conflict. For example, if you write an application that receives TCP messages on port 2012, there can be another process, running simultaneously, that receives UDP messages on port 2012.

As you can see, the port number is a crucial part of the addressing scheme. If a port number is incorrect, messages will become scrambled among the applications. You need to make sure when choosing your own port number that you don't pick one that is already used for something. Generally, if you pick a number above 1,024, you should be safe (unless you just happen to run into someone else who is experimenting). The port number is an unsigned 16-bit number, so it can provide 65,536 individual ports.

### But Where's the dot com?

At the lowest level, IP addresses are all that are used to establish communications between two devices. The name, such as `www.idgbooks.com`, is just a construction that was invented to make remembering addresses easy.

When you type in an address in the text form, the underlying code will attempt to change that into an IP address before establishing the communications. There are many ways of doing this; the most common, and the basis of the entire Internet, is called Domain Naming System (DNS). DNS provides many services, of which domain name to IP address resolution is just one part.

There are a number of alternate services that also provide name resolution. The NIS/NIS+ services for UNIX machines and WINS services in the Microsoft environment also perform these same functions. A typical computer will attempt to use every available service to resolve a name. This is all provided at the operating-system level, well below even the Java code, so there is nothing special you need to do to make this happen.

There are certain preassigned port numbers used throughout the Internet. These are called *well-known ports*. They handle e-mail, file transfers, the World Wide Web, and all of the other services available on the Internet. Table 15-1 lists some examples.

| | Table 15-1 A Few Commonly Used Port Numbers | |
|---|---|---|
| **Port Number** | **Keyword** | **Description** |
| 5 | ECHO | Message returned to sender. |
| 9 | DISCARD | Message received and ignored. |
| 17 | QUOTE | Returns the quote of the day . |
| 20 | FTP-DATA | File Transfer Protocol port for data transfer. |
| 21 | FTP | File Transfer Protocol port for control messages. |
| 23 | TELNET | Remote terminal login. |
| 25 | SMTP | Simple Mail Transfer Protocol (e-mail). |
| 80 | HTTP | The Web server. |
| 53 | DOMAIN | Domain Name Server. |
| 101 | HOSTNAME | The InterNIC host name server. |
| 143 | NMB | NetBios Name lookup. |

# From network to internetwork

All Internet communication is made possible by the TCP/IP stack. This stack is the software that resides inside every computer connected to the Internet. It operates like a two-way bucket brigade passing the message from one hand to another until it reaches the destination. At the top of the stack are the user's application programs. At the bottom is the physical communications link. Messages flow up and down in the stack, all the while being appropriately packaged, unpackaged, and addressed along the way.

This software is called a stack because it is made of pieces that conceptually sit one on top of the other like the layers of a cake. Think of a network as a huge silver platter with a bunch of computers sitting on it like cakes, and think of the Internet as the connections among the platters. Some platters only hold one cake, and some hold hundreds. The icing on the top of each cake is the programmer's interface — the stuff that you write.

A message from an application program will proceed from the icing down through all the layers to the platter. The message will then move to the bottom of another cake—on another platter if need be—and then up through the layers of the other cake to the icing at the top and the application that is waiting for it. There are times when a message rising up through the layers will go only part of the way, be read-dressed, and then be sent back down to the platter to be moved on to another cake. This is the action of an Internet router, which can send a message from any platter to any other platter. This type of communication forms a wide area network (WAN).

# The TCP/IP Stack

The TCP/IP stack is a collection of protocols that fit together in a layered architecture. At each layer, it depends on the services provided only by the layer immediately below. Each layer higher presents a more abstract view of the network and a greater range of capabilities. In the simplest terms, the conversion between levels is in the form of wrapping the package for delivery and unwrapping it upon receipt. There can also be some other juggling for sizing, data verification, and other requirements of that layer.

The structure of a pair of TCP/IP stacks is diagrammed in Figure 15-1. An application is at one end of the stack (the top), while the network hardware and its drivers are at the other end (the bottom). For communications to occur, data passes from the application down through each layer of the stack and right out the bottom, where it is transmitted over some kind of data link. After being transmitted across the link, the data arrives at the bottom layer of another stack and works its way up until it arrives at some other application.

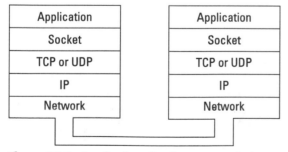

**Figure 15-1:** A pair of applications connected through a pair of TCP/IP stacks.

## Sockets

Strictly speaking, the socket layer is not a part of the traditional TCP/IP stack, but sockets are so useful that everyone who programs Internet communications uses them. It is possible to talk directly from an application to the TCP/UDP layer of the stack without using sockets, and things were done this way for several years, but sockets make life so much easier. Besides, there are sockets built into the Java API, so why go elsewhere when everything you need is at your fingertips? If you would like to hear a programmer rant on for a while, find one who programmed Internet communications before the days of sockets.

In Java, all you need to do is create an object from the `java.net.Socket` class and start reading and writing over the Internet. However, just like making a phone call or sending a letter, you need to know the address of the recipient or know how to get it.

## TCP or UDP

These two protocols differ in the way they carry out the action of communicating. The TCP protocol establishes a two-way connection between a pair of computers, while the UDP protocol is a one-way message sender. The common analogy is that TCP is like making a phone call and carrying on a two-way conversation, while UDP is like mailing a letter.

The basic actions of the two protocols are very similar. They both pack data in headers and footers before sending it, and they both unpack it upon receipt. The difference comes in the relationship between sender and receiver. With TCP, the receiver converses with the sender as necessary to verify the valid transmission of the data (which could have been divided into several packets). With UDP, the sender never expects to hear a response, and the receiver doesn't bother to send one.

## IP

This layer adds a new header to data being sent. Any human-readable names and addresses are encapsulated into binary blocks that are sent over the Internet. The IP address, the 32-bit binary number, is included in the header and is used to guide the data on its way. Upon receipt of data at this level, the binary headers are stripped off and what remains is passed up to the appropriate protocol on the level above.

## Network

This is where the rubber hits the road (or the hits hit the highway). The network is the connection to a dial-up modem, fiber link, LAN, cable modem, or whatever. What actually happens here varies from one type of network to another, but the end result is that a binary stream is sent over some physical link to another computer. It then becomes the problem of the stack on the target computer to figure out what to do with it.

# Sockets

At the lowest level of all network-related code in Java are the socket classes. Because you are so close to the raw networking at this level, you need to write quite a bit of code to get even minimal functionality. Everything from URLs to Enterprise Java Beans requires a socket. Its all just a matter of how much abstraction you place over the top.

The socket connection classes that get used vary depending on which type of socket you are creating (TCP or UDP) and whether you want to be a client application or a server application. Typically, during your coding for a customised application, you will need to write both.

## Finding an address

Before you start writing any networking code, you need to know who is doing the connecting and to what machine(s); that is, you can't just create a socket and have it magically know how to connect to the right server. If you are writing the client code, to establish a network connection, you need to know the address of and port number on the server that you want to use. Typically, these are supplied in raw form either by coding it into your application, or through some configuration option (for example, the Location text field in your Web browser). Once you have this raw string form, you need to turn it into something usable by your application code.

The Internet makes finding addresses quite simple, really. You supply the name, and the address will come right back for you. The class InetAddress will do this. Here is a simple program showing how it works:

```
import java.net.*;
public class GetAddresses {
  public static void main(String[] argv) {
    InetAddress ia;
      try {
        ia = InetAddress.getLocalHost();
        System.out.println("Local host: " + ia);
        ia = InetAddress.getByName(null);
        System.out.println("Null host: " + ia);
        ia = InetAddress.getByName("www.idgbooks.com");
        System.out.println("IDG host: " + ia);
      }
      catch(UnknownHostException e) {
        System.out.println(e);
      }
  }
}
```

This program retrieves three addresses: two of them are local and one is from the Internet. The output looks like this:

```
Local host: default/206.66.1.79
Null host: localhost/127.0.0.1
IDG host: www.idgbooks.com/38.170.216.15
```

This program was run from a computer with a dial-up connection, and the address 206.66.1.79 is the one that was assigned to the connection by the Internet service provider. That is the address returned from getLocalHost().

The second address, 127.0.0.1, is kind of special. This address is on every computer and is designed to not go anywhere. Whenever an application sends a message down the TCP/IP stack to this address, the message will simply reverse itself and return right back up the stack. You might find it handy if you have a couple of local applications that need to talk to one another, or if you want to test a client server connection by using a single computer.

The third address was retrieved from over the Internet. It is the address of the computer hosting the main Web page for IDG Books Worldwide. Now you know how we found the address of IDG Books Worldwide in the "What's in an Address?" section earlier in this chapter.

## Setting up a simple socket server

If you are a server, you want to pass out information to anyone who asks for it. However, you only want to tell those that ask for it, and with many different clients, the server may have to deal with many different simultaneous requests. To build a server, you need to have a good understanding of threads, which was discussed in Chapter 14. We must deal with each client on a case-by-case basis at the server side, which requires placing each connection with a client into a separate thread.

A server is there to serve. That is, it doesn't know who is going to connect to it until after that program has made the attempt. It must just sit there and wait until a client initiates a new connection. To do this, you need to use a ServerSocket. As its name suggests, it is a special-purpose class that is only used on the server and never in a client. If you used it in a client, that client would become another server.

To create a server socket, you need to tell it which port number to connect to. Note that by definition, the server socket connects to a port on the local machine, so you don't need to give it the name of a host to connect to.

This program sets itself up as a server and waits for a client connection to occur. Whenever a connection is made, the server spawns a new copy of itself (that is, it starts a new thread), and this copy is used to field requests and return responses. Any number of these threads can run at any one time, and they each remain active until the corresponding client — the program that initiated the connection — either requests a disconnect or drops its own connection:

```
int port = 9999;  // this comes from somewhere....
ServerSocket s = new ServerSocket(port);
```

Now, we need to let the server hang around until someone tries to connect. To do this, we call the `accept()` method. When this method returns, we know that a client has successfully begun the connection to our server. The `accept()` method returns another sort of socket — `Socket`. This is a generic network connection. On the server side, there is no other way of obtaining a connection from a client except through `accept()`.

This simple server doesn't do much. It simply receives character strings from the client and displays them. (See Listing 15-1.)

## Network Security Issues

If people with malicious intent want to gain access to your machine, they are going to need to send the data somewhere so they can use it. Of course, the way to do this is through some form of network connection.

When running applets, they could come from any source, some of which you probably wouldn't trust. Therefore, network connections are extremely restricted within applets. You can only make connections back to the server the applet came from, and you can't create any server code in the applet (no `ServerSockets`). You can control this through the security settings on your machine with the Java.net.SocketPermission.

The following permissions may be granted:

✦ accept: Allow incoming connections from other machines

✦ connec: Allow outgoing connections to other machines

✦ listen: Look for new connection requests on this machine

✦ resolve: Allows domain name to IP address resolution. This is implied if any other permission is granted.

For all of these types, you can specify which machine(s) you will allow and also which port numbers. The definition is sufficiently flexible enough to allow you to restrict connections by a range or single port number.

If you need to know more about how to set security permissions, please consult Chapter 25, "Deploying Applets and Applications."

## Listing 15-1: **A simple Socket server illustration**

```java
import java.net.*;
import java.io.*;
public class Server implements Runnable {
  private Socket socket;
  private int ID;

  public static void main(String[] arg) {
    int port = 9999;
    int count = 0;
    try {
      ServerSocket s = new ServerSocket(port);
      System.out.println("Waiting on port " + port);
      while(true) {
        Socket socket = s.accept();
        System.out.println("Connect! ID=" + ++count);
        Server server = new Server(socket,count);
        Thread thread = new Thread(server);
        thread.start();
      }
    }
    catch (Exception e) {
      System.err.println("Server error");
      System.err.println(e);
    }
  }

  Server(Socket socket,int ID) {
    this.socket = socket;
    this.ID = ID;
  }

  public void run() {
    try {
      InputStream is = socket.getInputStream();
      InputStreamReader isr = new InputStreamReader(is);
      BufferedReader br = new BufferedReader(isr);
      while(true) {
        String str = br.readLine();
        if(str.trim().equals("quit"))
          break;

        System.out.println("ID " + ID + ": " + str);
      }
    }
    catch (Exception e) {
      System.err.println(e);
    }
    finally {
```

```
        System.out.println("Disconnect! ID=" + ID);
        try {
          socket.close();
        }
        catch(IOException e) {
          System.out.println(e);
        }
      }
    }
  }
```

This socket server program waits on port number 9,999 for a connection request. It does this by creating a new ServerSocket object and then going into an infinite loop calling the accept() method. Whenever accept() returns, it is with a Socket object representing a connection that has just been made; that is, a new client has connected.

Whenever a new connection is made, a new thread is created to handle communications. This thread is assigned the newly connected Socket, and it is assigned a unique number. The loop then continues by calling accept(), again waiting for another thread. This architecture enables Java to handle as many sockets as the underlying operating system will allow.

Once the thread comes into existence, the run() method is called. The thread will remain alive until run() returns. Normally, to terminate a socket connection, either the server or the client will send a message to the other telling it to kill the connection. At this point, both forcibly kill the link by calling the close() method on the socket that they have been using. Calling close on the stream returned from the socket will do nothing, so you need to make sure that you actually kill the socket.

The run() method establishes input from the socket by calling getInputStream(). This is a raw input stream that you can interpret any way you like, but for the example here, we are assuming that the only input will be character strings. To handle them, an InputStreamReader is attached to the raw input stream and, in turn, a BufferedReader is attached to it. This allows us to use the readLine() method in the BufferedReader to interpret the incoming stream of bytes as character strings. In a real server, you might use this stream to pass command messages and data back and forth. Because you have just a raw stream, you may pass either text or binary data along it. As long as both ends are talking the same lingo, you won't have a problem.

The reading is done in a continuous loop until the word *quit* is received to break the connection. Note that only the one connection is broken (by making a call to the close() method of the socket); this has no effect on any other active connections, nor on the ServerSocket being used to establish connections.

**Note**    You may be wondering why we set up a separate thread for each client socket connection. Inside the `run()` method, you will notice that we have an infinite loop. That is, data is continually read. Once a line has been read, the code loops back and immediately waits for the next line to be sent. For a socket to work correctly, each connection needs to process the incoming data. If the code just fetched the socket and then immediately started reading data from it, without first starting a thread, you end up trapped inside the infinite loop. Your code couldn't return to accept more connections until after the first client had terminatedthe connection.

## A simple socket client

Now that we have a server ready to go, we need a client to send messages to it. This very simple client reads lines of text from the keyboard and sends it to the server:

```java
import java.io.*;
import java.net.*;
public class Client {
   public static void main(String[] args ) {
     int port = 9999;
     String inString;
     InputStreamReader isr = new InputStreamReader(System.in);
     BufferedReader br = new BufferedReader(isr);
     try {
       InetAddress address = InetAddress.getByName(null);
       Socket socket = new Socket(address,port);
       OutputStream os = socket.getOutputStream();
       OutputStreamWriter osw = new OutputStreamWriter(os);
       PrintWriter pw = new PrintWriter(osw);
       while((inString = br.readLine()) != null) {
         pw.println(inString);
         pw.flush();
         if(inString.trim().equals("quit"))
           System.exit(0);
       }
     }
     catch (IOException e) {
       System.err.println(e);
     }
   }
}
```

As you can see, the client side is much simpler than the server. It only has one computer to talk to, whereas the server has many. A `BufferedReader` is created to read lines of text from the keyboard. A socket is created with the same port number as the server. The number 9,999 was chosen arbitrarily. The other end of the socket could be anywhere on the Internet, but for this example, a call is made to `Inet Address.getByName(null)` to get the address of the local host. (We're connecting to the server on the local machine.) Once the socket is created, the `getOutput Stream()` method is called to get the writeable stream. This stream, along with an `OutputStreamWriter`, is then used to construct a `PrintWriter` that will be used to send strings through the socket connection.

**Tip**  One interesting point to note is that there is a call to the `flush()` method on the output stream. Sockets buffer data and won't send it until you tell it to. That is, if you never call `flush()` on the stream, that message(s) will not be sent to the socket on the other end. If you are writing code and find that the server (or client) is not receiving your messages, check for this first because it is the most common cause.

The loop reads one string after the other and sends it to the server. After each string is sent, it is tested to see if it's the termination command. If the string is 'quit', the server will have recognized it upon receipt and closed the other end of the socket. This application exits, causing the socket to close on this end.

These two simple programs — the server and the client — demonstrate the power of the Internet. Two simple programs like this can be anywhere in the world and, as long as the Internet address of the server is known to the client, they can hook up and communicate.

# URL Operations

If you are going to work with the Internet and the World Wide Web, you need to create and manipulate URLs. URL stands for Uniform Resource Locator. It provides all the information about the server, port number, which network protocol to use, and the actual resource to fetch, all conveniently wrapped up in a character representation. You're already familiar with them; that's what is typed in the Location text field of your favorite Web browser.

Java has a handy little class for representing URLs and taking care of most of the handling aspects. The class `java.net.URL` is a wrapper for the standard URL string and has some methods that you can use to find out about the string and to fiddle with it. It can even make the connection and fetch the resource for you. These methods are listed in Table 15-2.

Let's dissect a real URL so that you know what each of these terms refers to:

```
http://www.company.com:80/directory/file.html#intro
```

Starting at the lefthand side, the part up to the first semicolon is known as the protocol. This tells the system which networking protocol to use when talking to the server. From www to the next semicolon is the host, or the name of the server that you want to talk to. You could also use the numerical version of the IP address if you wanted. Next, the number 80 is the port number on which to talk to the server. This is optional in the string. If it is not specified, the default port for the protocol is used. (The URL class knows all about how to work this out.) From the slash following the port number until the pound (#) character is the file, or resource, part of the URL. Once you have contacted the server, you tell it that you want the file part. Finally, the last part following the pound character is the reference. This is used to reference something inside the named file. As such, that is not passed to the server when requesting the file.

## Table 15-2
## java.net.URL Methods

| Method | Description |
| --- | --- |
| Equals(Object) | Determines whether two URL objects represent the same resource in the same way. |
| getContent() | Makes a connection and reads addressed contents. |
| getFile() | Returns the file name portion of the URL. |
| getHost() | Returns the host name portion of the URL. |
| getPort() | Returns the port number from the URL. |
| getProtocol() | Returns the name of the protocol of the URL. |
| getRef() | Returns the anchor reference portion of the URL. |
| openConnection() | Establishes a connection and returns the URLConnection object for it. |
| openStream() | Establishes a connection and returns a stream for reading it. |
| sameFile(URL) | Determines whether two URL objects address the same resource (ignoring references). |
| setURLStreamHandler Factory() | Specifies the factory to be used to create any streams to establish connections. |
| toExternalForm() | Returns the URL in the string form used by Web browsers. |

Occasionally, you might also come across the question mark (?) character in the string in the file section. This is used by URLs to mark a query part. Typically, this is used to create dynamic pages or when you fill in a Web form. In the standard Java implementation of the URL, you cannot access this part of the information and you need to deal with it yourself (if you need to at all).

As you can see, the URL class supplies you with just about everything you need to read files and other resource data across an Internet. There are several ways to get an object of this class. You can use a constructor to create one, or you can call a method to return one to you. The constructors listed in Table 15-3 construct URL objects from String objects and from other URLs.

These are not the only ways you can get a URL object. If you are programming an applet, you can call the method getCodeBase() to get the URL of the directory containing the applet's class file, or you can call the method getDocumentBase() to get the URL of the directory containing the HTML file that invoked the applet. And, while this technique is not necessarily involved directly with networking, you can also get a URL object by calling the getResource() method of either Class or ClassLoader.

There is one other way. The method openConnection(), listed in Table 15-2, returns a URLConnection object for the URL, and a URLConnection object has a method named getURL() that returns a URLConnection. See the "Sockets" section earlier in this chapter for more information about the connections.

## The URL Family

URLs are the best-known class of a series of identifier types for resources. (Even to the experienced programmer, the rest of the family is not well known.) As you have seen, URL stands for Uniform Resource Locator. There are three others in the family:

✦ Uniform Resource Identifier (URI): The parent type of URLs and URNs. These identify a particular resource and allow you to name a resource and perform many different operations on them.

✦ Uniform Resource Name (URN): An identifier of a resource just by name and category. Unlike a URN, this identifier does not specify the server to find the resource. Instead, much of the searching is done under the covers. You could think of it as a bit like a glorified search query, although this is selling it far short of its real capabilities. For example, you can define this book by the following URN: urn:isbn: 0-7645-8030-2. Requesting this URN would then fetch all references it could find to the book *anywhere* it could get to.

✦ Uniform Resource Characteristic (URC):This defines metadata about the resource. For example, it could refer to the digital signature used to sign a resource, the publisher, date, and author of the book named in a URN, or any similar sort of characteristic.

URLs define an exact location to find a particular resource. For example, it says to find the resource on server xyz at the named directory location. If it does not exist there, you get the infamous 404 error. Therefore, URNs and URCs are a much more robust way of representing documents and resources that should be around for long periods of time (such as books in a library or photos).

Java 2 does not define the full capabilities of dealing with all of these items. The author does extensive work in this field and you can download a full library with all of these capabilities from http://www.vlc.com.au/liburi/ if this subject is of interest to you.

|  | Table 15-3 |
|---|---|
|  | **Class java.net.URL Constructors** |

| Constructor | Description |
|---|---|
| URL(String,String, int,String) | The first `String` is the protocol, such as `http`. The second `String` is the host, such as `www.idgbooks.com`. The `int` is the port number. The final `String` is the name of the file, such as index.html. |
| URL(String,String, String) | The first `String` is the protocol, such as `http`. The second `String` is the host, such as `www.idgbooks.com`. The final String is the name of the file, such as index.html. |
| URL(URL,String) | The `URL` argument is the basis on which to build the new one. The `String` is an incomplete form used to modify the settings found in the original URL. |
| URL(String) | The URL is built from a single `String`. |
| URL(String, String, int , String, URLStreamHandler) | The same arguments as the first row but allows the ability to provide a custom stream handler. |
| URL(URL, String, URLStreamhandler) | The same as the third version but allows the ability to provide a custom stream handler. |

## Basic URL manipulations

Just to show that it really works, here is a simple program that accepts your input string and uses it to construct a URL object from scratch:

```
import java.net.*;
public class ShowURL {
  public static void main(String[] arg) {
    try {
      URL url = new URL(arg[0]);
      System.out.println("The input was: " +
                          url.toExternalForm());

      System.out.println("Host: " + url.getHost());
      System.out.println("Port: " + url.getPort());
```

```
      System.out.println("Protocol: " + url.getProtocol());
      System.out.println("File: " + url.getFile());
      System.out.println("Ref: " + url.getRef());

      // The following methods are valid for JDK 1.3 only
      System.out.println("Authority: " + url.getAuthority());
      System.out.println("User info: " + url.getUserInfo());
      System.out.println("Query: " + url.getQuery());
    }
    catch(MalformedURLException e) {
      System.out.println(e);
    }
  }
}
```

**Caution**  JDK 1.2 and earlier did not correctly parse the URL string. Many parts that should have been separately treated were not used. For example, the user info part was incorrectly treated as part of the host name to contact. If you created a fully specified URL, it was possible for the system to crash when it should not have. To solve this, a number of new methods were added to the URL class. These have been commented in the previous example.

It is necessary to catch the MalformedURLException that could be thrown from the constructor of the URL object. If the exception is not thrown, it doesn't mean that the URL is valid — it only means that the input string is syntactically correct. This program allows you to enter the name of a URL and prints out its various parts. For example, typing this line:

```
java ShowURL http://justin:vlc@www.xyz.com:80/foo.cgi?who=justin#middle
```

results in this output:

```
The input was:
  http://justin:vlc@www.xyz.com:80/foo.cgi?who=justin#middle

Host: www.xyz.com
Port: -1
Protocol: http
File: /foo.cgi?who=justin
Ref: middle
Authority" justin:vlc@www.xyz.com
User info: justin:vlc
Query: who=justin
```

## URL Security Issues

URL connections are influenced by exactly the same security considerations as raw sockets. Various URL operations allow you to send out information as well as receive it. For this reason, a separate java.net.NetPermission has been created.

The permissions allow you to control the following:

✦ setDefaultAuthenticator: Control which class may provide authentication information when a Web server or ftp server asks for a password.

✦ requestPasswordAuthentication: If any authenticator has been set, this second check is for whether the system should call the authenticator. Like socket permissions, this can be described on a per-host basis, allowing some to request passwords and others not to.

✦ specifyStreamHandler: A factory can be set that allows you to provide customized stream handlers to override the default versions. If allowed, this means a malicious provider could use an HTTP connection to steal information from your machine.

For more information about how to set security permissions, please consult Chapter 25.

## The great Web-page snatch

Reading a Web page from across an Internet connection is almost as easy as calling it by name. Here is an example that will list the entire text of any Web page on the Internet:

```java
import java.net.*;
import java.io.*;
public class Snatch {
  public static void main(String[] arg) {
    int character;
    BufferedInputStream bin;
    try {
      URL url = new URL(arg[0]);
      bin = (BufferedInputStream)url.getContent();
      while((character = bin.read()) > 0)
        System.out.print((char)character);
      System.out.println();
    }
    catch(MalformedURLException mue) {
      System.out.println(mue);
    }
    catch(IOException ioe) {
      System.out.println(ioe);
    }
  }
}
```

All you need to do is type the URL string of a Web page, and the entire thing will be listed on the screen. Making a call to getContent() is the same as making a call to openConnection() to get a URLConnection object, and then calling its getConnect() method. The getContent() method returns an Object object that must be cast to the correct type before it can be used. This is described more in the "URLConnection Operations" section later in this chapter.

You have to catch the MalFormedURLException, which is thrown on a syntax error in the construction of the URL object. Also, you need to catch the IOException that could be thrown from the getContent() method or from reading from the BufferedInputStream object.

## Encoding the URL string

Certain characters have special meanings and, if you want to include them, you need to insert them in such a way that they will not have an unwanted effect. Say, for example, you want to include spaces, colons, slashes, or some other character that is used in the structure of a URL. To do this, take the URL string you would like to send and pass it through the encode() method of java.net.URLEncoder. Anything that might cause a problem is encoded so that it won't. Because this originated as a Multimedia Internet Mail Extension (MIME) process, it is known as MIME encoding.

This simple program accepts a string as a command-line argument and then displays the MIME encoded form of it.

The following command line:

```
java Encode "In character math 'a'+1 == 'b'"
```

resulted in this output:

```
In+character+math+%27a%27%2B1+%3D%3D+%27b%27
```

The encoding scheme converts all spaces to Plus (+) characters. The characters A–Z and a–z, as well as 0–9, are left unchanged. All other characters are converted to a three-character sequence beginning with a percent (%) sign and ending with a two-digit hexadecimal representation of the ASCII value of the character (which also happens to be the Unicode value).

## URLConnection operations

It is possible to use a URL object to create a URLConnection object. URLConnection represents the actual, established connection to the server. In fact, you can create several URLConnection objects from a single URL and maintain more than one simultaneous connection, although this is almost never necessary. The URLConnection constructor is protected, so to create a URLConnection, you need to make a call to openConnection() of a URL object. The reason for the constructor being protected is that the real work of talking the appropriate protocol is done through derived versions of this class, which you shouldn't instantiate directly.

Several default settings are established when a URLConnection object is created. Static methods in the class allow the defaults to be modified. In addition, you can use a number of methods to query and modify the current settings for a URLConnection object. Most of the fields listed in Table 15-4 are protected, which means they can only be accessed through the methods.

| Table 15-4 The Configuration Fields of the URLConnection | |
|---|---|
| **Field** | **Description** |
| allowUserInteraction | Set this boolean field to true if there is some sort of human reaction involved with the resource (such as a data entry form on a Web page). The default setting is false. |
| connected | This boolean becomes true when a connection is established. |
| doInput | This boolean is true if the URLConnection can be used to read the resource. |
| doOutput | This boolean is true if the URLConnection can be used to write to the resource. |
| fileNameMap | The public static FileNameMap class can be used to convert the name of a file into a MIME type (for example, mypic.gif ⇨ image/gif). |
| ifModifiedSince | This long holds a date. A request to retrieve a remote resource will use the one in local cache instead if the remote version is older than the date. |
| url | This field is a reference to the URL from which this URLConnection was constructed. |
| useCaches | Setting this boolean to false forces the URLConnection to never use a cache. It will always get a new copy of the resource. |

Table 15-5 is a list of the methods available in the URLConnection class. Several of them can be used to set the values of the internal fields. The defaults were designed to handle the most common situations, so unless you are doing something special, just leave them as they are. A number of them can be used to deal with the data.

Table 15-5
## java.net.URLConnection Methods

| Method | Description |
|---|---|
| connect() | Opens a communications link. |
| getAllowUserInteraction() | Returns the setting of the allowUserInteraction flag. |
| getContent() | Retrieves the object addressed by the URL. The actual type of object returned depends on the type of resource addressed by the URL. |
| getContentEncoding() | Returns the value of the content-encoding header field. Could be null. |
| getContentLength() | Returns the content length. Returns -1 if it is not known. |
| getContentType | Returns the value of the content-type header field. Could be null. |
| getDate() | Returns the value of the date header field as a long. Could be zero. |
| getDefaultAllowUser Interaction() | Returns the default setting of allowUser Interaction. |
| getDefaultRequestProperty (String) | Returns the default value of a request property. |
| getDefaultUseCaches() | Returns the default setting of the useCaches flag. |
| getDoInput() | Returns the current value of the doInput flag. |
| getDoOutput() | Returns the value of the doOutput flag. |
| getExpiration() | Returns the expiration date of the URL as a long. Could be zero. The date is normally set by the server application (for example, cache use by time). |
| getHeaderField(String) | Returns the value of the header field specified by its name. |
| getHeaderField(int) | Returns the header number (counting from the top). |
| getHeaderFieldDate (String,long) | The header field named as the String is taken to be a date and its long value is returned. If it is not found, the supplied default is returned. |
| getHeaderFieldInt (String,int) | The header field named as the String is taken to be an integer and its value is returned. If it is not found, the supplied default is returned. |

*Continued*

## Table 15-5 *(continued)*

| Method | Description |
| --- | --- |
| getHeaderFieldKey(int) | Returns the key value specified by the number. Could be null. |
| getIfModifiedSince() | Returns the value of the date ifModifiedSince. |
| getInputStream() | Returns an InputStream that can be used to read the resource. |
| getLastModified() | Returns, as a long, the date found in the last-modified header field. Could be zero. |
| getOutputStream() | Returns an OutputStream that can be used to write to the location addressed by the URL. |
| getRequestPoperty(String) | Returns the string value of the named property. |
| getURL() | Returns the URL used to establish this connection. |
| getUseCaches() | Returns the value of the useCaches flag. |
| guessContentTypeFromName (String) | Looks at the name passed to it and returns a string identifying the type of resources. For example, a name ending with .html would be assumed to be a Web page. |
| guessContentTypeFromStream (InputStream) | Reads the InputStream passed to it and attempts to determine the type of resource by reading from it and analyzing what it finds. |
| setAllowUserInteraction (boolean) | Sets the value of the allowUserInteraction flag. |
| setContentHandlerFactory (ContentHandlerFactory) | Specifies the ContentHandlerFactory. To be used by all URLConnection objects. |
| setDefaultRequestProperty (String,String) | Uses the first String as the key and the second as the general-request property. These properties are then used in the creation of every URL Connection. |
| setDefaultUsesCaches (boolean) | Sets the value of defaultUsesCaches. |
| setDoInput(boolean) | Sets the value of doInput. |
| setDoOutput(boolean) | Sets the value of doOutput. |

| Method | Description |
|---|---|
| setIfModifiedSince(long) | Sets the value of ifModifiedSince. |
| setRequestProperty (String, String) | Uses the first String as the key and the second as the value and sets the general-request property. These properties are then used only for this URL Connection. |
| setUsesCaches(boolean) | Sets the value of usesCaches. |

## The incoming headers

This is a simple program that, when given a URL string, opens a connection to the URL and displays all the header information:

```java
import java.net.*;
import java.io.*;
public class WhatIsIt {
  public static void main(String[] arg) {
    int i = 1;
    BufferedInputStream bin;
    try {
      URL url = new URL(arg[0]);
      URLConnection con = url.openConnection();
      String header = con.getHeaderField(i);
      String key = con.getHeaderFieldKey(i);
      while(header != null) {
        System.out.println("H" + i + ": " +
                            key + "=" + header);
        i++;
        header = con.getHeaderField(i);
        key = con.getHeaderFieldKey(i);
      }
    }
    catch(MalformedURLException mue) {
      System.out.println(mue);
    }
    catch(IOException ioe) {
      System.out.println(ioe);
    }
  }
}
```

This example uses the URL object to establish a connection and then retrieves all the headers from it. This command supplies the URL for the home page of an ISP:

```
java WhatIsIt http://www.xyz.net
```

The output is the complete list of headers and the values at the time the query was made:

```
H1: Date=Thu, 26 Feb 1998 20:28:05 GMT
H2: Server=Apache/1.1.3
H3: Content-type=text/html
H4: Content-length=1659
H5: Last-modified=Thu, 26 Feb 1998 04:24:18 GMT
H6: Connection=Keep-Alive
H7: Keep-Alive=timeout=15, max=5
```

The methods used, getHeaderField() and getHeaderKey(), retrieve the names of the fields and their values according to their positions in the file. Different locations on the Internet will supply different levels of detail—the number and content of the headers will vary—but you should always be able to determine content type.

# RMI Operations

The idea behind RMI (Remote Method Invocation) is very simple. A program running on a computer somewhere on the Internet can get access to objects and invoke their methods. These objects may be resident in a program running somewhere else on the Internet. To make this happen, several actions need to be done, and all of them are built in to the java.rmi package.

The best way to learn about RMI is to go through a step-by-step explanation of what it takes to set things up for an RMI invocation.

## RMI Security Issues

RMI, being a networking API, is subject to the same network security problems and restrictions as sockets. Therefore, if you wish to connect to a server with RMI, you need to enable the appropriate socket permissions.

Note that the registry application (which you will be introduced to shortly) is just as much restricted by security concerns as your applets. If you run into exceptions when starting the registry, check to see that you have the appropriate network permissions set.

If you need to know more about how to set security permissions, please consult Chapter 25.

# Select a package

Create a directory that has the name of the package you would like to use. This directory can be inside other directories as long as the CLASSPATH variable is set correctly and the package names are included in the source files. This example uses the package name rmitest, which means that the CLASSPATH list of names includes the name of the directory immediately above the directory named rmitest.

# Create a general interface

For one program to invoke the method of another, they have to agree on the name and arguments of the method. Java has a built-in way of handling this. If an interface is defined and they both use it, then the name and arguments are bound to match. So, the first thing to do is define the interface. For our example, the interface is a very simple one with a single method:

```
package rmitest;
public interface StringTag extends java.rmi.Remote {
  public String appendX(String instring)
    throws java.rmi.RemoteException;
}
```

This interface defines the single method appendX(). It takes a String object as an argument and supplies a String as its return value. For our example, all the method is going to do is append XXX onto the end of any string it receives.

The arguments and return values must be serializable. To do this, they must implement the Serializable interface. Most of the Java API implements this interface, but if you are going to write any classes to pass as remote arguments, you need to write them so that they can be written to a stream. (Serialization is covered in Chapter 13.)

Every method that provides an RMI method in this interface must throw Remote Exception. This is RMI's way of providing a catch-all exception for anything that goes wrong in the lower levels, such as network problems, nonserializable objects, and so on.

# Providing an implementation

You need to write a class that implements the interface. For this example, it is called StringTagImpl:

```
package rmitest;
import java.rmi.*;
import java.rmi.server.UnicastRemoteObject;
public class StringTagImpl extends UnicastRemoteObject
```

```
     implements StringTag {

     public StringTagImpl() throws RemoteException {
       super();
     }

     public String appendX(String s) throws RemoteException {
       return(s + "XXX");
     }

     public static void main(String[] arg) {
       System.setSecurityManager(new RMISecurityManager());
       try {
         StringTagImpl sm = new StringTagImpl();
         Naming.rebind("StringTag",sm);
         System.out.println("StringTag bound in registry");
       }
       catch(Exception e) {
         System.out.println("StringTagImpl: " + e);
       }
     }
   }
```

This is the server side of the RMI call—this is the class that holds the method that will actually be called. Not only does it implement the interface described in the previous section, but it also extends the UnicastRemoteObject class, thus making it capable of receiving remote method calls.

There is always a default constructor. This one doesn't do anything, but it is included here to point out that if you need to have a constructor, you have to define it as throwing a RemoteException. The exception is actually thrown from the constructor of the superclass.

The body of the method is defined. This example is very simple—it merely creates a return string by combining the one passed in with the three characters XXX.

This program is to be executed on the server, so it must have a main() method. The RMISecurityManager() method must be defined so it will be in place to control access requested from remote locations. Without the security manager in place, no RMI is possible. The fact that you can design and install your own security manager gives you a great deal of control over security.

This object has to register itself with the Naming registry. When a remote request arrives at this computer, there is a search in the registry for the name. If a match is found, the appropriate method is called.

## The stubs and the skeletons

Once the previous classes are defined, they can be compiled into class files with the Java compiler, like this:

```
javac StringTag.java
javac StringTagImpl.java
```

But there is one more step. The caller of the method will need a stub, and the method being called will need a skeleton. These are both class files, and you get both of them with this single command:

```
rmic rmitest.StringTagImpl
```

The output takes the form of these two files:

```
StringTagImpl_Skel.class
StringTagImpl_Stub.class
```

Then when the client calls the method, it actual calls the stub. The stub gathers up the necessary information and transmits it over the Internet to the machine that holds the server — the actual method. On the server side, there is a search in the registry for the name and, if found, the data that came over the Internet is turned over to the skeleton. The job of the skeleton is to unwrap the data and make the actual method call. When the method returns, the skeleton wraps up the answer and transmits it back to the stub. The stub then unwraps the returned data and passes the result to the original caller of the method.

This process of stubs and skeletons wrapping and unwrapping data is called marshalling and unmarshalling.

## Starting the registry

Before any calls can be made, the host system needs to have a registry. The registry is the program that resolves the name requests that come in across the Internet. It is the one that holds the information that is passed in the Naming calls.

To start the registry on Window 95 or NT, enter:

```
start registry
```

To start the registry on a UNIX system, enter:

```
registry &
```

The registry software is included as part of the JDK download. It is not a standard piece of software that you would expect to find on all machines. To run it, you must make sure that your PATH settings are properly set up first.

## Starting the server

If a stub is not already on a local machine, it will be downloaded from the remote machine. To make this possible, when the server is started, you have to specify the code base so that the stub can be found. The code base is defined this way on the command line that starts the server running:

```
java -Djava.rmi.server.codebase=file:/q/rmitest/ rmitest/StringTagImpl
```

## The applet that makes the call

The remote call can be made from an applet or an application. For this example, we have an applet that calls the method:

```
package rmitest;
import java.awt.*;
import java.rmi.*;
public class StringTagApplet extends java.applet.Applet {
  String tagged;

  public void init() {
    try {
      String rmi_str = "//" + getCodeBase().getHost() +
                       "/StringTag";
      StringTag st = (StringTag)Naming.lookup(rmi_str);
      tagged = st.appendX("The string ");
    }
    catch(Exception e) {
      System.out.println(e);
      e.printStackTrace();
    }
  }

  public void paint(Graphics g) {
    g.drawString(tagged,25,30);
  }
}
```

This applet uses the Naming.lookup() method to get a reference to the local stub for the remote class. Once the stub has been retrieved, the methods can all be called just as if the stub were a local object. In our example, there is only one method, and it is called to make modifications to the character string.

## The HTML

To run an applet, you need a browser and the HTML that controls it. Here is the HTML from this example:

```
<HTML>
<title>String appending</title>
<center><h1>Append X and Y</h1></title>
The result of appending to the strings is:
<p>
<applet codebase=".." code="rmitest.StringTagApplet"
    width=500 height=120>
</applet>
</HTML>
```

This HTML executes the applet. The setting of the codebase string depends on where the class files are located on your system. Note that the applet calls `getCodeBase()` to get a URL object representing the directory holding the class files.

Entering the command:

```
appletviewer StringTag.html
```

pops up a window that displays the string that was modified by a remote procedure call.

# Activation

One annoying feature that you will quickly notice is that to run an RMI server, you need to be logged in to the machine. There is all this command-line stuff that needs to be run every time that you want a server. Without a lot of extra work (and native code) making the RMI code automatically start when the machine is booted, it is almost impossible if you have a Microsoft Windows machine (although much simpler on a UNIX box).

To avoid some of these problems, Java 2 introduces a concept called *activation*. This makes use of the standard registry for RMI, but now adds the capability for a new registry system to dynamically create the remote objects only when requested. The idea behind this is that you can register the objects with the "system" and then forget about it. Once the setup is done, the startup code exits and you can run this in a stand-alone environment. This new "system" object is the rmid application. When you start the `rmiregistry`, you will also need to start `rmid`—in the identical fashion.

On the client side there is no difference in the code. What you use for normal RMI will also work for activatable objects. The server side is a different story.

We start with our basic server object from before. Now, because activation is not the same as the server code, we need to import a different package—`java.rmi.activation`. Of course, the original `UnicastRemoteObject` was part of the RMI server package `java.rmi.server`, so we will need to make the changes for that too. The object we need to extend is activatable, which comes with its own set of requirements:

```
package rmitest;
import java.rmi.*;
import java.rmi.activatable.*;
import java.net.MalformedURLException;
public class ActivatableStringTagImpl extends Activatable
  implements StringTag {

  public StringTagImplActivatable(ActivationID id,
                                  MarshalledObject data)
    throws RemoteException {
    super(id, data);
  }

  public String appendX(String s) throws RemoteException {
    return(s + "XXX");
  }

  public static void main(String[] arg) {
    System.setSecurityManager(new RMISecurityManager());

    String cwd = System.getProperty("user.dir");
    cwd = cwd.substring(3);
    cwd = cwd.replace('\\', '/');
    String location = "file:///" = cwd + '/';

    MarshalledObject data = null;
    try {
      ActivationDesc desc =
        new ActivationDesc("rmitest.ActivatableStringTagImpl",
                                        location,
                                        data);

      Remote obj = Activatable.register(desc);
      Naming.rebind("StringTag", obj);
    }
    catch(RemoteException re) {
      System.out.println("Remote setup: " + re);
    }
    catch(ActivationException ae) {
      System.out.println("Activatable setup: " + ae);
    }
    catch(MalformedURLException mue) {
      System.out.println("Bad URL: " + mue);
    }
  }
}
```

It doesn't take much to see that there is quite a difference between this and the earlier version. Now, instead of creating an instance of the object remotely, we create a description of the object and register the description. Whenever a client requests an object reference from the registry, it checks to see if it already has one. If it does, it passes back all the information; otherwise, it uses all of the information in the description to create a new instance and then pass the information back.

In the earlier example, passing setup information to the remote object was pretty easy because we could include whatever we wanted for parameters. Activation ties your hands up a lot more. We can use the `MarshalledObject` instance to pass any information that we like through to the object; it just has to be serializable first.

Activation gives you a lot more control over what happens in the surrounding environment as well. We can set up specific options for the JVM, create different security profiles on the fly, and many other really neat tricks. Tinkering with these can take quite a lot of effort, so we won't cover them here and instead refer you on to a much more advanced book on Java networking if you intend to seriously pursue it.

# Summary

Java takes the flexibility of the Internet and makes it easy. You should now understand how to add networking support to your own applications. Important points to remember abut this chapter include the following:

✦ The most fundamental thing you need to know when sending data over the Internet is where the data should go. To do this, there are just three things you need to know: the IP address of the target computer; the protocol that will be used to package the data; and the port number specifying a specific application to receive the data.

✦ Sockets have been around many years now, and they really simplified things, but with the Java socket classes, it has even become simpler. Beyond that, if you are working with URL addressing, the URL classes, which rest on top of the sockets, make that kind of work easier than it has ever been.

✦ The RMI system is quite unique, and it has some very interesting implications. Local applications will no longer need regular upgrades because critical methods actually reside on other machines. A programmer can write code to access database information without caring which machine holds the actual data; in fact, the data can be moved at will without affecting any of the programs or system configurations.

✦    ✦    ✦

# JDBC: Java API for Database Connectivity

**T**his chapter covers the Java Database Connectivity
Application Programming Interface (JDBC API), defined by
JavaSoft, Inc. as part of the core Java API. JDBC allows any applet
or application written in Java to access remote databases and
retrieve or update information stored in such databases. After an
introduction to JDBC, the chapter discusses how to connect to
databases and perform queries and updates. The subsequent
section is a reference that lists the contents of the whole API, and
finally, we discuss more advanced issues such as stored procedures, transactions, and three-tier partitioning. Where appropriate, specific features of the JDBC 2.0 specification is highlighted.
Although most drivers still implement the original JDBC specification (version 1.2), more and more drivers will be implementing
all or part of the JDBC 2.0 specification also put out by JavaSoft
as part of the Java 2 Enterprise Edition (J2EE).

**Cross-Reference**   For further information about JDBC, IDG Books Worldwide
also publishes *JDBC, Java Database Connectivity*, by
Bernard Van Haecke (ISBN 0-7645-3144-1). It contains
a comprehensive tutorial, numerous examples, and a complete reference for the JDBC API.

## Introduction to JDBC

JDBC, the Java Database Connectivity API, is one of the key
players in making Java an appropriate language and platform
for building world-class applications. In this introduction, you
learn the fundamentals of JDBC:

  ✦ Universal database connectivity

  ✦ Traditional client/server architectures

✦ SQL

✦ Database drivers

✦ The JDBC API

## Universal database connectivity from Java

The Java Database Connectivity API allows Java applets, servlets, and standalone applications to access data stored in relational database management systems (DBMS) in a universal way. The industry standard for accessing data is Structured Query Language (SQL), which permits maximum interoperability. Of course, SQL is the language used with JDBC. You build the connectivity itself using a single, standard API no matter what the DBMS: the JDBC API.

Relational databases are the most common kind of DBMS today and they impose absolute separation between physical and logical data. By accessing data through the logical model associated with it, you avoid the limitations of supplying information about physical storage locations. Relational databases let you define relationship and integrity rules among data sets organized in tables.

Using one query language (SQL) and one API (JDBC) lets you provide universal database connectivity from Java. Furthermore, with the introduction of J2EE, the JDBC API acts as a core piece providing interoperability among a number of different APIs such as Java Naming and Directory Interface (JNDI), Java Transaction Service (JTS), and JavaBeans. The database is no longer only a source of application data, but also an effective means of providing persistence services to Java objects.

Last but not least, JDBC will work independently of the network environment. It is well suited for the intranet as well as for the Internet.

## Basic characteristics of JDBC

To understand JDBC, you need to get acquainted with its most important characteristics. If you already have some knowledge of Open Database Connectivity (ODBC) under Microsoft Windows, you will probably see that JDBC and ODBC are similar in many ways.

✦ Call-level SQL interface: JDBC is a *call-level* SQL interface for Java used at the client side. It is totally independent of the various database management systems. It is a low-level application programming interface that allows Java programs to issue SQL statements and retrieve their results. It also provides methods for managing errors and warning messages. Figure16-1 shows where JDBC is usually used.

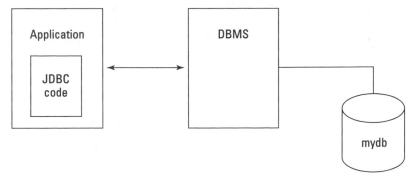

**Figure 16-1:** JDBC is used at the client side.

✦ SQL conformance: JDBC does not set any restrictions on the type of queries that can be sent to an underlying DBMS driver. An application may use as much SQL functionality as desired. The underlying drivers are authorized to claim JDBC compliance if they fully support ANSI SQL92 Entry Level, which is widely supported today and guarantees a wide level of portability. JDBC 2.0 adds support of the SQL3 standard, which adds interesting object-oriented capabilities as well as some new supported data types.

✦ Convenient implementation: JDBC can be implemented on top of common SQL-level APIs, in particular, on top of ODBC.

**Note** JDBC is usually implemented using native or nonnative drivers instead of being used on top of ODBC.

✦ Consistent API: JDBC provides a Java interface that stays consistent with the rest of Java. There are no conflicts due to opposed philosophies.

✦ KISS (Keep it simple, stupid!) paradigm: The JDBC mechanisms are simple to understand and use, although there are little restrictions on specific database functionalities.

✦ Strong, static typing: JDBC uses strong, static typing wherever possible. This allows for more error checking to be performed at compile time.

✦ One functionality, one method: JDBC, unlike many other complex DBMS SQL-level APIs, is simple enough for a beginner to use, yet powerful enough for an experienced programmer.

## JDBC components

A typical architecture involving JDBC to connect to databases usually involves four essential components: the application itself, the JDBC driver manager, specific drivers for the databases, and finally, the database management systems.

## Application

The user application invokes JDBC methods to send SQL statements to the database and retrieve results. It performs the following tasks:

✦ Requests a connection with a data source

✦ Sends SQL statements to the data source

✦ Defines storage areas and data types for the result sets

✦ Requests results

✦ Processes errors

✦ Controls transactions — requests commit or rollback operations

✦ Closes the connection

## Driver Manager

The primary role of the JDBC driver manager is to load specific drivers on behalf of the user application. It may also perform the following tasks:

✦ Locates a driver for a particular database

✦ Processes JDBC initialization calls

✦ Provides entry points to JDBC functions for each specific driver

✦ Performs parameter and sequence validation for JDBC calls

## Driver

The driver processes JDBC method invocations, sends SQL statements to a specific data source, and returns results back to the application. When necessary, the driver translates and/or optimizes requests so that the request conforms to the syntax supported by the specific DBMS. It is also the driver that controls which features of JDBC are available to the application. Most drivers are JDBC 1.2 compliant. More and more drivers implement the JDBC 2.0 specification. (The latest version as of the time this book was written was JDBC 2.2.) It is normal for a database vendor to have various JDBC drivers, each corresponding to a different version of JDBC. It is the application programmer's responsibility to use the correct JDBC version to comply with the features used in the application. For example, prior to JDBC 2.0, the concept of *batch updates* was not supported. If your application is going to use batch updates, then you must have a JDBC driver that supports this feature; otherwise, the program will not compile because the specific APIs that make batch updates possible were not implemented in JDBC drivers prior to 2.0. The driver handles these tasks:

✦ Establishes a connection to a data source

✦ Sends requests to the data source

✦ Performs translations when requested by the user application

✦ Returns results to the user application

✦ Formats errors in standard JDBC error codes

✦ Manages cursors if necessary

✦ Initiates transactions if it is explicitly required

## Data Source

The data source consists of the data the user application wants to access and its parameters (in other words, the type of DBMS and network layer, if any, used to access the DBMS).

The JDBC API defines the possible interactions between the user application and the driver manager; the JDBC Driver API defines interactions among the driver manager and all JDBC drivers. Figure 16-2 shows the relationship among the four JDBC components.

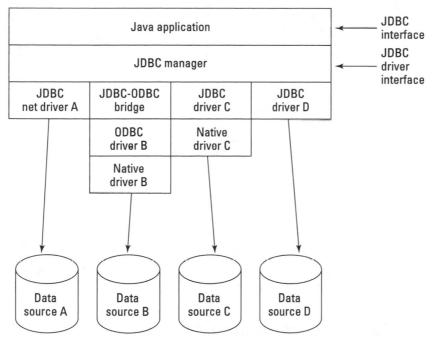

**Figure 16-2:** The complete JDBC architecture

## Ready for client/server

The first generation of client/server architectures is *two-tiered*. It contains two active components: the client, which requests or sends data, and the server, which can be a DBMS. This type of system processes database queries and updates separately from those associated with user-interface logic and presentation. In this respect, such a system differs from old-fashioned, mainframe-style user applications that handled gigabyte-long sequential files. Figure 16-3 depicts a typical client/server architecture.

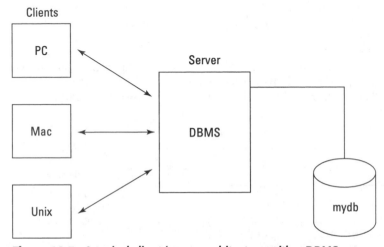

**Figure 16-3:** A typical client/server architecture with a DBMS

The two components usually run on different platforms, and in the Internet context, there may be numerous instances of client applications running at the same time. In the middle, the network serves as a transport mechanism for SQL messages containing database queries and rows of data resulting from these queries. This is illustrated in Figure16-4.

JDBC conforms to the traditional client/server architecture. As we will see later, however, alternatives to the two-tiered client/server have emerged: three-tiered and multi-tiered. These approaches are basically an extension of the two-tiered client/server, so JDBC also has a place in such advanced architectures.

## Data definition and manipulation using SQL

In contrast to the complete programming languages used to build complex applications, SQL is commonly used *within* a host language (which in turn offers the specific features for building complete applications). Nevertheless, SQL is an industry standard for database access. It enables data definition, manipulation, and management, as well as access protection and transaction control.

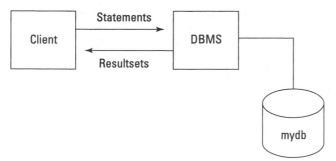

**Figure 16-4:** SQL messages and resultsets

SQL originated from the concept of relational databases; it handles many database objects for RDBMS purposes, including tables, indexes, keys, rows, and columns. First standardized by the American National Standards Institute (ANSI) in 1986, SQL was designed to be independent of any programming language or DBMS.

The ANSI 1989 standard defines three programmatic interfaces to SQL:

✦ Modules: These procedures may be defined within separate compiled modules and then called from a traditional programming language.

✦ Embedded SQL: This specification defines embedded statements for a few traditional programming languages. It allows static SQL statements to be embedded within complete programs.

✦ Direct invocation: Here, access is *implementation-defined*. It can be different for every platform.

Although embedded SQL was quite popular a few years ago, it is not the best answer to the problem of querying databases in client/server environments. It is static in all senses of the term, and this limitation makes it unsuitable for newer software architectures.

The newer ANSI specification, SQL-92, addresses the needs of modern environments. It contains many new features, including support for dynamic SQL—as well as support for *scrollable cursors,* an advanced technique for accessing result sets. Although dynamic SQL is not as efficient as static SQL, it does allow SQL statements to be prepared, to include parameters, and to be generated at runtime. (If you are using prepared statements, system performance may actually improve.) Dynamic SQL allows the database to prepare an access plan before execution, and to reuse the access plan each time the statement is called. JDBC 2.0 supports SQL3 (the latest SQL standard). Some of the features of SQL3 support are the ability to interact with binary large object (BLOB) and character large object (CLOB) data types more efficiently. Other features include distinct and structured types (discussed later), array data types, object persistence, and references.

The SQL language may be used for various purposes, including these:

✦ Querying a database, as interactive language used by humans

✦ Querying a database within a program

✦ Defining data organization

✦ Administering data

✦ Accessing multiple data servers

✦ Managing transactions

The SQL language supports a set of verbs used to define, store, manipulate, and retrieve data. These keywords include CREATE TABLE ..., SELECT ..., INSERT ..., DELETE ..., UPDATE..., and so on.

The following examples illustrate the most common actions you can perform with SQL:

✦ Creating a table:

```
CREATE TABLE employees
(
    id          int PRIMARY KEY,
    name        char(25) NOT NULL,
    address     char(25) NOT NULL,
    city        char(25) NOT NULL,
    zip         char(25) NOT NULL,
    dept        int,
    phone       char(12),
    salary      int
)
```

✦ Removing a table:

```
DROP TABLE employees
```

✦ Supplying new data:

```
INSERT INTO employees VALUES
(
    1,
    "John Doe",
    "10725 Java Drive",
    "Mountain View",
```

```
    "CA 94040",
    1,
    "415-960-1300",
    60000
)
```

✦ Removing rows of data:

```
DELETE FROM employees
WHERE dept = 0
```

✦ Retrieving data:

```
SELECT * FROM employees
WHERE dept = 1
ORDER BY salary DESC, name
```

✦ Modifying data:

```
UPDATE employees SET salary = 70000
WHERE name = "John Doe"
```

✦ Creating an index:

```
CREATE INDEX employees_idx
ON employees (name)
```

✦ Creating a stored procedure (SQL Server Transact-SQL):

```
CREATE PROCEDURE getMaxSalary (@themax int OUT)
AS SELECT @themax = MAX(salary)
    FROM employees
```

**Tip**    SQL is a rich language. Various options and parameters are available for these key-words. You can (for example) nest statements for database queries, join tables, and define transactions.

## JDBC drivers

As mentioned before, JDBC is independent of the various database management systems. Almost all of them use proprietary (non- or poorly documented) protocols to communicate with clients, so JDBC uses database drivers specific to these database engines.

Database vendors and third parties offer three types of JDBC drivers: native database drivers, bridge drivers, and DBMS-independent, all-Java net drivers.

## Native Database Drivers

These drivers process JDBC calls and send SQL statements to the data source. They may be *native-API/partly-Java* or *native-protocol/all-Java*. A native-API partly-Java driver forwards the calls to a locally installed library, usually developed in C and provided by the database vendor. It may be a DLL or a UNIX shared library, for example. Figure 16-5 shows the Java and non-Java sides of such a driver.

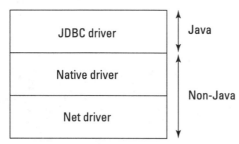

**Figure 16-5:** A native-API partly Java driver

A native-protocol, all-Java driver implements in Java all the layers necessary to communicate with the database. These drivers are obviously fully portable, because they do not use local libraries or other native code. This type of driver is illustrated in Figure 16-6.

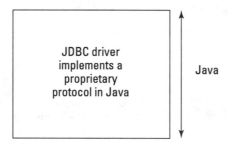

**Figure 16-6:** A native-protocol all-Java driver

## Bridge Drivers

A *bridge driver* acts as a bridge between JDBC and another call-level interface (CLI). For example, the JDBC-ODBC bridge is a bridge driver. It processes JDBC calls, and in its turn calls ODBC functions that send SQL statements to the ODBC data source. A bridge driver typically has very poor performance compared to other driver types. The obvious reason is the multiple layers that it has to go through. Figure 16-7 shows the Java and non-Java sides of such a driver.

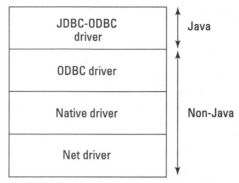

**Figure 16-7:** A JDBC-ODBC bridge driver

## DBMS-Independent, all-Java Net Drivers

These drivers use a DBMS-independent, published network protocol. They are obviously very portable because they are 100 percent Java. When dealing with Java applets, this type of driver is desirable because applets have security restrictions and cannot access DLL or shared libraries on the local machine. Figure 16-8 depicts such a driver.

**Figure 16-8:** A net driver

# Overview of the API

The two major components of JDBC are the JDBC API and the JDBC driver API. The JDBC API is a programming interface for database application developers; the JDBC Driver API is a lower-level programming interface for developers of specific drivers. We will focus on the JDBC API since that will be the primary concern of application developers. Figure 16-9 clearly indicates the role of both APIs.

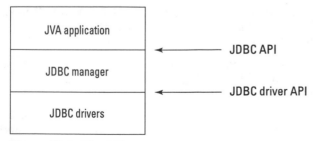

**Figure 16-9:** The APIs

Database application developers use these interfaces and classes:

✦ `java.sql.Array`: Provides a mapping to the new SQL3 data type `ARRAY`. This is part of JDBC 2.0.

✦ `java.sql.Blob`: Provides a mapping to the SQL data type BLOB. BLOB is a built-in type that stores a Binary Large Object as a column value in a row of a database table. The driver implements BLOB using a SQL locator (BLOB), which means that a Blob object contains a logical pointer to the SQL BLOB data rather than the data itself. A Blob object is valid for the duration of the transaction in which it was created. This is part of JDBC 2.0.

✦ `java.sql.CallableStatement`: Provides the same role, but in the context of database stored procedures.

✦ `java.sql.Clob`: Provides a mapping to the SQL data type CLOB. This is part of JDBC 2.0.

✦ `java.sql.Connection`: Represents a particular connection on which further actions is performed.

✦ `java.sql.DatabaseMetaData`: Provides information about the database as a whole including tables, rows, data types, columns, etc.

✦ `java.sql.PreparedStatement`: Provides the same role, but in the context of precompiled SQL.

✦ `java.sql.Ref`: Provides a reference to a SQL structured type value in the database. This is part of JDBC 2.0.

✦ `java.sql.ResultSet`: Allows access to the resulting rows of a statement.

✦ `java.sql.ResultSetMetaData`: Gives information such as the column type and column properties of the resultset.

✦ `Java.sql.SQLData`: Allows custom mapping of SQL user-defined types. This is part of JDBC 2.0.

✦ `java.sql.Statement`: Sends SQL statements to the database

✦ `java.sql.Struct`: Contains a value for each attribute of the SQL structured type that it represents. This is part of JDBC 2.0. The standard mapping for a SQL structured type.

✦ `java.sql.Date`: Identifies a millisecond value as a SQL DATE. A milliseconds value represents the number of milliseconds that have passed since January 1, 1970 00:00:00.000 GMT.

✦ `java.sql.DriverManager`: Provides methods to load drivers and to support the creation of database connections using methods expressed in the `java.sql.Driver` interface.

✦ `java.sq.DriverPropertyInfo`: Allows an application programmer to find out specific information and features of the underlying driver. This is handy because some drivers do not fully implement the specification, so a check is needed to make sure a specific feature is supported.

✦ `java.sql.Time`: A thin wrapper around `java.util.Date` that allows JDBC to identify this as a SQL TIME value. The `Time` class adds formatting and parsing operations to support the JDBC escape syntax for time values.

✦ `java.sql.Timestamp`: This class is a thin wrapper around `java.util.Date` that allows JDBC to identify this as a SQL `TIMESTAMP` value. It adds the ability to hold the SQL `TIMESTAMP` nanos value and provides formatting and parsing operations to support the JDBC escape syntax for timestamp values.

✦ `java.sql.Types`: Defines constants that are used to identify generic SQL types, called JDBC types. The actual type constant values are equivalent to those in XOPEN.

✦ `java.sql.CallableStatement`: Provides the same role, but in the context of database stored procedures.

## Typical uses

You can use JDBC to connect Java to databases, send SQL statements from a Java client, and then retrieve the results, if any, from the database. This is true for standalone Java applications, as well as for Java applets running in Web browsers (if a 100 percent Java JDBC driver is used) and Java servlets running at the side of Web servers.

However, you need to consider a few points when running JDBC in a client applet. As long as an applet is unsigned, it is considered *untrusted*. Some differences exist, however, between untrusted applets on the Internet (or on an intranet) and traditional standalone applications:

✦ Untrusted applets cannot access local files or open arbitrary network connections to remote hosts. In contrast, an application can access the local file system in accordance with the permissions that were granted to the user.

✦ Untrusted applets cannot rely on specific facilities provided by the underlying operating system — such as a local registry — to locate a database. Applications often rely on such facilities. For example, ODBC uses an .ini file or the registry, and most proprietary APIs use specific property and configuration files.

✦ Response times of untrusted applets may be arbitrary when sporadic traffic peaks arise on the Internet; connections may be interrupted in the middle of a transaction because of network failure.

✦ Estimating the maximum number of simultaneous users of an untrusted applet is difficult in the Internet scenario.

Despite these differences, JDBC is still a good option for letting applets communicate with a database located on the Web server side. An alternative method would be to have an applet communicate with a servlet via HTTP and then have the servlet (behind the firewall) make the JDBC calls. This deployment model eliminates the need for the applet to directly support the JDBC calls, which enhances performance and reduces the size of the applet. There are many situations in which you might want to use JDBC. To give you some examples, JDBC and 100 percent Java JDBC drivers are easier to use than HTML solutions in the following cases:

✦ Lookups of online catalogs, using multiple search criteria that return complex types such as text, images, compound documents, sounds, binary files, and so on.

✦ Any transactional Web application. JDBC allows you to group statements in one atomic transaction. This is mandatory when (for example) debit and credit have to happen at the same time on different tables.

✦ Replacement of any traditional database client software for a larger audience, on an intranet, an extranet, or the Internet using off-the-shelf Web browsers.

✦ Building decision-support tools that often rely on existing relationships among data entities, without any prior knowledge of these relationships.

✦ Simple, webtop-oriented administration tools for database administrators (DBAs) and database owners (DBOs).

# Connecting to a Remote Database

Java and your database can talk to each other, and they may as well start doing so. In this section, you will learn how to load a database driver, how to locate the database management system, and how to establish a connection to it.

A connection must be established to enable access to a database. Such a connection is a Java object, containing methods and data members that access the database and also hold and manage connection state. Various connection parameters are necessary to locate important elements of the database system—the database itself, specific drivers and protocols, user accounts and passwords in the DBMS, and so on. (You'll learn the format to use for such parameters later in this chapter.)

The first general step is to establish a connection. The last step will, of course, be to terminate (or *close*) the connection. Opening and closing the connection will create and release user resources within the driver manager, the driver, and the database management system.

## Choosing an appropriate driver

Databases talk with clients by using various—but incompatible—protocols. As a result, for every specific database connection you establish, you have to provide an appropriate driver to JDBC to let it manage the connection. Methods that load a driver and handle driver properties are provided within the `DriverManager` and `Driver` objects. To tell JDBC which drivers are available, you provide the needed information through a `jdbc.drivers` system property. You can do so from the `java` interpreter command line or by means of a property file.

The following code shows how to use the command line for standalone programs and applets:

```
% java -Djdbc.drivers=foobar MyProgram
% java -Djdbc.drivers=foobar sun.applet.AppletViewer
   MyApplet.html
```

The following code shows how to use a file, which you might want to do when you use Applet Viewer or the HotJava Web browser, for example:

```
# on unix, this is ~/.hotjava/properties
jdbc.drivers=vendor1.driver1
```

As explained later in the chapter, you can also specify the drivers programmatically.

**Note** The exact driver name is set by the driver manufacturer. Refer to your driver's documentation for more details about its package name and class name.

**Tip** Although the database URL specifies a specific database and protocol to be used, it may sometimes be useful to let the JDBC choose among two or more drivers — especially when you're using multiple databases. If you want to do so, just specify a list of drivers in the `jdbc.drivers` property, separating the driver class names with colons:

```
'vendor1.dbdrv:vendor2.sql.foodriver:vendor3.db.connectdrv'
```

JDBC will then try to use each of the drivers listed in `jdbc.drivers` until it finds one that can successfully connect to the given URL. Drivers that contain untrusted code are skipped. The driver will register itself with the driver manager to allow connections to be established.

In case the `jdbc.drivers` system property is unavailable, you might want to use a programmatic technique to force a particular driver to be loaded. For example, the following line of Java code loads a JDBC-ODBC Bridge driver:

```
Class.forName("sun.jdbc.odbc.JdbcOdbcDriver");
```

Another method is to use the following statements:

```
java.sql.Driver myDriver = new sun.jdbc.odbc.JdbcOdbcDriver();
java.sql.DriverManager.registerDriver(myDriver);
```

These statements explicitly instantiate the `JdbcOdbcDriver` class and register it with the driver manager.

## Locating the database

JDBC uses a particular syntax for naming a database. The JDBC designers wanted to adopt a syntax widely used in the Internet context: the URL syntax. The URL for JDBC data sources has this form:

```
jdbc:<subprotocol>:<subname>
```

In this syntax, `jdbc` indicates that the protocol is JDBC, the subprotocol field is the name of the JDBC driver to be used, and the subname is a parameter string that depends on the subprotocol. This mechanism is depicted in Figure 16-10.

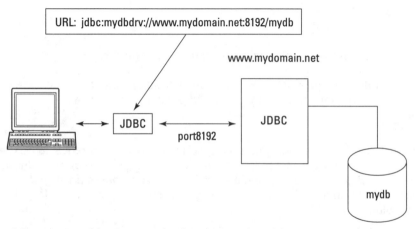

**Figure 16-10:** The JDBC mechanism for naming a data source

These two examples show you how you can use database URLs:

```
jdbc:odbc:sampledb;UID=javauser;PWD=hotjava
```

In this example, a JDBC-ODBC bridge is used, and the ODBC data source name (DSN) is `sampledb`. The database user name is `javauser`, and the password is `hotjava`.

```
jdbc:mydbdrv://www.mydomain.net:8192/mydb
```

In this case, the subprotocol is called `mydbdrv`, the database engine is running on the `www.mydomain.net` host (the subname field), the TCP/IP port used is 8192, and `mydb` is the name of the database to be accessed. The meaning of these parameters is somewhat arbitrary: for example, if the subprotocol (the driver) always uses the same port number, you don't have to provide it in the URL. You could also interpret `mydb`, which is a "subsubname," as anything else as well.

The ODBC subprotocol URL should always conform to this syntax:

```
jdbc:odbc:<dsn>[;<attribute-name>=<attribute-value>]*
```

As you can see, the JDBC URL syntax is flexible enough to allow specific drivers to interpret their own syntax. You should always consult the documentation for the specific JDBC driver you want to use to see what the exact syntax for its usage is. Unfortunately, different database vendors use different syntax for specifying the URL to load their driver. This is also a great source of frustration for new JDBC programmers because they can't test the rest of their programs (which contains JDBC calls) until the appropriate driver is properly loaded and initialized.

## Creating a connection

This URL string is used to create connections to the database. For this purpose, the `get Connection()` method on the driver manager is used to request a Connection object:

```
...
Connection connection;
String url = "jdbc:odbc:datasource";
Class.forName("sun.jdbc.odbc.JdbcOdbcDriver");
Connection = DriverManager.getConnection(url, "javauser",
"hotjava");
...
```

This example shows how to pass the URL string to the driver manager and specific parameters to the driver itself. Here is some further explanation of the code:

✦ The protocol is JDBC.

✦ The driver is a JDBC-ODBC bridge.

✦ The ODBC DSN is datasource.

✦ A username is provided: javauser.

✦ A password is provided: hotjava.

The driver manager will try to find a registered JDBC driver that is allowed to reach the data source specified in the URL. Note that there are other methods that allow you to make a connection to the database. They have the same name, but they accept different parameters:

```
Connection getConnection(String url);
Connection getConnection(String url, String user, String
    password);
Connection getConnection(String url, java.util.Properties info);
```

A connection will not last forever, so there is a method to terminate it: `close()`. This method releases driver and database resources of the connection. Listing 16-1 illustrates how to open and close a connection to a database using a JDBC-ODBC bridge.

---

Listing 16-1: **Opening and Closing a Connection**

```java
// opening and closing a connection

import java.sql.*;

class SimpleExample
{
    public static void main(String args[])
    {
        String url = "jdbc:odbc:mysource";

        try {
            Class.forName("sun.jdbc.odbc.JdbcOdbcDriver");
            Connection connection =
                DriverManager.getConnection(url,
                "javauser", "hotjava");

            // ...
            connection.close();
        } catch (Exception ex) {
            System.out.println("A problem occurred during the
                establishment of the connection: " + ex);
        }
    }
}
```

---

In case of problems during the creation of the Connection object, the `getConnection()` method throws a `java.sql.SQLException`. You should catch such exceptions and write appropriate code to handle them, at least to warn the user that there was a problem. The exception will usually include error messages directly from the database. This will allow you to consult the database documentation to deal with database-specific issues. If the problem is related to loading the driver or other Java-related issues, then the message will be a Java exception with no messages from the database. This distinction in error messages will further help you isolate and resolve connectivity issues.

# Performing Database Queries and Updates

You are now ready to surf in your database management system and perform queries and updates from Java. This section teaches you these techniques through comprehensive examples. Queries generally refer to read-only operations on the database. Operations that insert new data, change existing data or delete data are collectively referred to as "Updates."

# Database queries and updates

You use the Connection object to send SQL statements to the database engine. You can use different methods for doing this depending on the kind of operation needed. In this chapter, we will focus on sending normal SQL statements. Unlike prepared statements or calls to stored procedures, which is discussed later, normal SQL statements are usually built, sent, and executed only once. This is the case, for example, within an interactive query tool where the user is allowed to build his or her own queries on the fly. Normal statements include both statements to query data from the database and statements to update the data.

Immediately after creating the connection, you have to create a SQL statement. This is not to say that you can't build a SQL query string before opening the connection. You are free to do so. A JDBC statement is an object associated with a connection, and it is used later to execute the SQL statement string within this connection environment on the DBMS.

This is the method used to create a statement object:

```
Statement createStatement();
```

You obtain the statement object by invoking this method on the connection instance, as shown in the following example:

```
...
Connection connection = DriverManager.getConnection(url,
    "javauser", "hotjava");

Statement statement = connection.createStatement();

myConnection.close();
...
```

The SQL statement will finally be sent to the DBMS, where it is parsed, optimized, and then executed. But we have not build the statement text yet. Indeed, the SQL string is passed to the database at the time the call for execution of the statement is issued. Figure 16-11 illustrates this mechanism.

This SQL string may be converted into the DBMS native SQL grammar by the driver. It is possible to see the converted string without sending it to the database. You will normally not use this facility, but in some cases, you might want to know what the native translation of a query is prior to sending it.

This method requires the Connection object because it is DBMS-dependent. Indeed, a connection is associated to one and only one DBMS through its driver:

```
String nativeSQL(String sql);
```

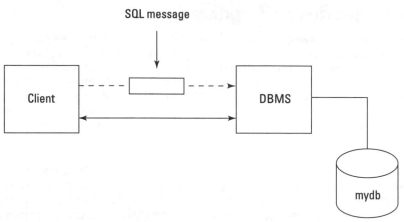

**Figure 16-11:** Sending a SQL statement

The string passed as an argument is the "user" SQL statement; `nativeSQL()` returns the native form of this statement.

Opening a connection and creating a statement is necessary before executing a query. This is required in all your JDBC-based applications.

SQL statements that return an integer, such as `DELETE`, `UPDATE`, and `INSERT`, do not need additional processing. The method to send them returns the integer, which usually is interpreted as a counter. Other SQL statements do not return rows of data or a counter.

This is not the case with queries that return normal rows of data; the resultset is composed of zero, one, or multiple rows coming from the database. Consequently, the next step is to scan this resultset, row by row, until all the rows of data have been fetched. You perform this operation within a loop. We will see later how to analyze the data that composes rows.

You create the `ResultSet` object when you send the statement to the DBMS. You do so by executing the `Statement` object. Closing the resultset releases all data associated with it.

You can use different methods to send a SQL statement to the database. They vary depending on the type of statement and the type of data they return. They apply to the newly created `Statement` object:

```
ResultSet executeQuery(String sql);
```

If the query returns normal rows of data, then you should use the `executeQuery()` method. In this case, the query is typically a static SQL `SELECT` statement. The SQL text is simply passed as a `String` argument.

**Note**    The text does not have to be translated to the native form, which you could otherwise do by using `nativeSQL()`.

This method returns a `ResultSet` object, which is discussed in the next section of this chapter.

```
int executeUpdate(String sql);
```

In case the SQL statement returns nothing (returning nothing is different than returning 0 rows) or an integer value, as is the case with SQL INSERT, UPDATE, or DELETE clauses, you should use the `executeUpdate()` method. The call returns the integer value or 0 for statements that return nothing.

```
boolean execute(String sql);
```

When a SQL statement returns more than one result, you have to use `execute()` to request execution of the statement, as shown in Listing 16-2.

---

**Listing 16-2: Querying the Database**

```java
// querying the database

import java.sql.*;

class SimpleExample
{
    public static void main(String args[])
{
    String url = "jdbc:odbc:mysource";
    try {
        Class.forName("sun.jdbc.odbc.JdbcOdbcDriver");
        Connection connection =
            DriverManager.getConnection(url,
            "javauser", "hotjava");

        String sql = "SELECT * FROM employees";
        System.out.println("native form: " +
            connection.nativeSQL(sql));

        Statement statement = connection.createStatement();

        ResultSet rs = statement.executeQuery(sql);
        connection.close();
        } catch (Exception ex) {
            System.out.println("A problem occurred: " + ex);
        }
    }
}
```

---

# Retrieving the results

Result sets are composed of rows of data. You use the `resultSet.next()` method in a loop to access and retrieve all these rows, row by row. Figure 16-12 illustrates the mechanism used to scan the rows contained in the resultset.

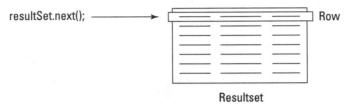

**Figure 16-12:** The next() method used to scan a resultset

Note that a resultset is initially positioned before its first row. You need to call the method first to access the first row. After the first call, the first row becomes the current row, and it is ready to be processed. Successive calls to `next()` will make the subsequent rows current, row by row. The method returns `false` when there are no more rows available in the resultset.

## Getting the Number and Label of Columns

A row is usually composed of table data that may be organized in columns of different types. You may want to obtain the properties of the resultset's rows—their number, type, and so on—at runtime. You can use the metadata methods on resultsets to obtain column and type information for your dataset. Only the column number and column labels are in the following examples.

The `getMetaData()` method returns a `ResultSetMetaData` object, which you can use to call `getColumnCount()`:

```
int getMetaData().getColumnCount();
```

The return type is `integer`. It is the number of columns contained in the rows composing this resultset.

```
String getMetaData().getColumnLabel(int i);
```

The parameter is the column index, where a value of 1 indicates the first column. The method obviously returns the label for the column at this index. Needless to say, the index range is 1 to `getColumnCount()`.

## Accessing Columns

Columns must be fetched until there are no more to be fetched. You can do so in a loop using the column indexes or column names that you obtained with the ResultSetMetaData object. This is illustrated in Figure 16-13.

The rows' contents are accessible via getXXX() methods that allow extraction of values from the columns of rows contained in the resultset.

You can access columns in two ways: by column index or by column name. Accessing a column by name is more convenient, but certainly less efficient. Certain SQL statements return tables without column names or with multiple identical column names. It is absolutely necessary to use column numbers in these cases. Figure 16-14 shows how to access the columns of a resultset.

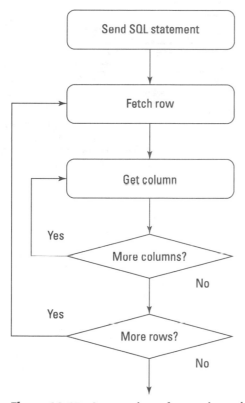

**Figure 16-13:** An overview of accessing columns

**Note** It may be more efficient to store the `ResultSetMetaData` object once instead of calling the `getMetaData()` method to create it each time you need to access a property. The driver may provide caching, but it is a good idea not to use features such as caching unless they're really necessary. Because JDBC allows you to access a wide variety of data sources, it's a good idea not to rely on any inherent driver behavior if you expect your applications to be portable.

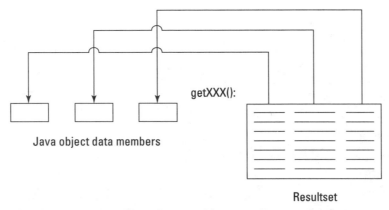

**Figure 16-14:** Accessing columns with getXXX()

All the columns within a row must be read in left-to-right order, and each column must be read only once. This rule may not be true with some DBMSs, but observing it ensures maximum portability.

### Accessing columns by column indexes

These are the `getXXX()` methods available to fetch columns in a row:

```
Array getArray(int columnIndex);
Blob getBlob(int columnIndex);
Clob getClob(int columnIndex);
String getString(int columnIndex);
boolean getBoolean(int columnIndex);
byte getByte(int columnIndex);
short getShort(int columnIndex);
int getInt(int columnIndex);
long getLong(int columnIndex);
float getFloat(int columnIndex);
double getDouble(int columnIndex);
Ref getRef(int columnIndex);
java.math.BigDecimal getBigDecimal(int columnIndex, int scale);
byte[] getBytes(int columnIndex);
java.sql.Date getDate(int columnIndex);
java.sql.Time getTime(int columnIndex);
```

```
java.sql.Timestamp getTimestamp(int columnIndex);
java.io.InputStream getAsciiStream(int columnIndex);
java.io.InputStream getUnicodeStream(int columnIndex);
java.io.InputStream getBinaryStream(int columnIndex);
Object getObject(int columnIndex);
```

All these methods return the column value of the current row. Column indexes are integers.

The following code snippet shows how to execute a SQL statement and retrieve the results using column indexes. The rows are always read from left to right; columns are read only once.

```
...
java.sql.Statement statement = connection.createStatement();

ResultSet rs = statement.executeQuery("SELECT name, title,
salary FROM employees");

while (rs.next()) {
    // print the columns of the row that was retrieved
    String name = rs.getString(1);
    String title = rs.getString(2);
    long salary = rs.getLong(3);

    System.out.println("Employee " + name + " is " + title + "
        and earns $" + salary);
}
...
```

### Accessing columns by column names

Column names may be more convenient to use as a means of access; the following getXXX() methods support column names:

```
Array getArray(String columnName);
Blob getBlob(String columnName);
Clob getClob(String columnName);
String getString(String columnName);
boolean getBoolean(String columnName);
byte getByte(String columnName);
short getShort(String columnName);
int getInt(String columnName);
long getLong(String columnName);
float getFloat(String columnName);
double getDouble(String columnName);
java.math.BigDecimal getBigDecimal(String columnName, int scale);
byte[] getBytes(String columnName);
java.sql.Date getDate(String columnName);
```

```
java.sql.Time getTime(String columnName);
java.sql.Timestamp getTimestamp(String columnName);
java.io.InputStream getAsciiStream(String columnName);
java.io.InputStream getUnicodeStream(String columnName);
java.io.InputStream getBinaryStream(String columnName);
Object getObject(String columnName);
```

The parameter you use should match exactly the column name of the row that you want to access.

The following code shows the same example as before, this time using column names:

```
...
java.sql.Statement statement = connection.createStatement();

ResultSet rs = statement.executeQuery("SELECT name, title,
salary FROM employees");

while (rs.next()) {
    // print the columns of the row that was retrieved
    String name = rs.getString("name");
    String title = rs.getString("title");
    long salary = rs.getLong("salary");

    System.out.println("Employee " + name + " is " + title + " and
        earns $" + salary);
}
...
```

## Addressing performance issues

Database connection is usually a key part of an application and, therefore, optimized performance is often desired. After all, without data, the program is not going to have much to do. JDBC 1.x has not been a star performer in the performance category. Based on our discussion so far, you may have noticed one source of performance deterioration. Each SELECT, INSERT, UPDATE or DELETE statement is sent to the database separately. Establishing a database connection and the send/receive process that follows the initial connection are very expensive operations. It would be much faster if in a single connection, we could send multiple commands to the database. Also, the way JDBC retrieves rows from a SELECT statement one by one is not very efficient. It would be faster if rows were retrieved in batches. Again, the goal is to minimize the number of send/receive operations between the application and the database server, and at the same time, maximize the amount of data that is transported in each cycle.

To give you a perspective on the problem, consider a case where a driver fetches 20 rows at a time. That certainly would address our main issue in performance (where each row was retrieved one by one). The main challenge is what happens if, after your application fetches 20 rows, another application makes an update to one of those rows. While the update is reflected in the database, your application is not going to go back to the database until you scroll through all 20 rows.

JDBC 2.0 introduced a new feature by which you can specify the number of rows that you want to fetch. You can call the setFetchSize() method on either the Statement or a ResultSet object. If you specify the fetch size to be zero, then the driver behaves like a JDBC 1.x driver. Here is how this can be used:

```
Statement stmt = conn.createStatement();
stmt.setFetchSize(40);
ResultSet rset = stmt.executeQuery("SELECT * FROM CUSTOMERS");
rset = stmt.executeQuery("SELECT * FROM PAYROLL");
rset.setFetchSize(1);
```

By setting the fetch size for a statement, any result sets created by that statement will conform to the new size. A specific ResultSet object can override the value when the setFetchSize() method is called on the ResultSet object itself.

The same way that we can control the size of the batch of rows retrieved as a result of a SELECT, we need a way to "bundle" multiple INSERT/UPDATE/DELETE statements together to achieve better performance. JDBC 2.0 introduces the concept of batch updating. Basically, instead of using executeUpdate(), you need to use addBatch(). Once all the statements are added, you call the method executeBatch() to send all the statements to the database for execution. Here is an example:

```
conn.setAutoCommit(false);
Statement stmt = conn.createStatement();
stmt.addBatch("UPDATE CUSTINFO SET STATUS = 3 WHERE CUSTOMERNUM
= 3876");
stmt.addBatch("DELETE FROM ORDERS WHERE CUSTOMERNUM = 87878");
stmt.addBatch("INSERT INTO INVENTORY VALUES (87, 'Sofa')");
int[] results = stmt.executeBatch();
```

Note that we disabled auto commit mode before attempting the updates in batch mode. This is often desirable because we want to either complete all the statements in the batch or none of them.

## Putting the JDBC to work

Listing 16-3 illustrates the previous techniques we learned for sending and executing database queries as well as for retrieving the results. It is an Interactive SQL program written using JDBC; it allows SQL statements to be sent interactively using the keyboard. The program parses the keyboard input and sends the statements to the database if the input is not a keyword such as go or exit. The results are then displayed on the screen. Note how we handled statements that return multiple resultsets and/or update counts.

## Listing 16-3: **The Interactive SQL Application**

```java
import java.sql.*;
import java.io.*;
import java.util.*;

public class isql {

    static DataInputStream kbd = new
DataInputStream(System.in);

    static String url = "jdbc:odbc:netbank";
    static String driver = "sun.jdbc.odbc.JdbcOdbcDriver";
    static String login = "dba";
    static String passwd = "javabank";

    static Connection curConn = null;

    public static void main(String argv[]) throws IOException
    {
        String temp = "";

        System.out.println("Simple Java Isql.\n");
        System.out.print("Enter the url or [ENTER] for " + url +
            " : ");
        System.out.flush();
        temp = kbd.readLine();
        if (!temp.equals("")) url = temp;
        System.out.print("Enter the login or [ENTER] for " +
            login + " : ");
        System.out.flush();
        temp = kbd.readLine();
        if (!temp.equals("")) login = temp;
        System.out.print("Enter the passwd or [ENTER] for default
            : ");
        System.out.flush();
        temp = kbd.readLine();
        if (!temp.equals("")) passwd = temp;

        isql session = new isql();
    }

    public isql() throws IOException
    {
        try {
            Class.forName(driver);
            curConn = DriverManager.getConnection(url, login,
                passwd);
```

```
                    checkForWarnings(curConn.getWarnings ());
            }
        catch(java.lang.Exception ex) {
            System.out.println("url      : " + url);
            System.out.println("login    : " + login);
            System.out.println("passwd   : " + passwd);
            ex.printStackTrace();
            return;
        }
        processQueries();
        finalize();
    }

    protected void finalize()
    {
        try {
            curConn.close();
        }
        catch (SQLException ex) { }
    }

    private void processQueries() throws IOException
    {
        int i = 1;
        String temp = "";
        String query = "";
        String results = "";

        System.out.println("Type 'quit' on a blank line to
exit,
            or 'go' to execute the query.");
        do {
            System.out.print(i + "> ");
            System.out.flush();
            temp = kbd.readLine();
            if (temp.equals("quit"))
                break;
            if (temp.equals("go")) {
                executeThisQuery(query);
                i = 1;
                query = "";
            }
            else {
                query = query + " " + temp;
                i++;
            }
        } while (true);
    }
```

*Continued*

**Listing 16-3** *(continued)*

```java
private void executeThisQuery(String sqlText)
{
    boolean resultSetIsAvailable;
    boolean moreResultsAvailable;
    int i = 0;
    int res=0;
    try {
        Statement curStmt = curConn.createStatement();
        resultSetIsAvailable = curStmt.execute(sqlText);
        ResultSet rs = null;
        for (moreResultsAvailable = true;
            moreResultsAvailable; )
        {
            checkForWarnings(curConn.getWarnings());
            if (resultSetIsAvailable)
            {
                if ((rs = curStmt.getResultSet()) != null)
                {
                    // we have a resultset
                    checkForWarnings(curStmt.getWarnings());
                    ResultSetMetaData rsmd =
                        rs.getMetaData();
                    int numCols = rsmd.getColumnCount();

                    // display column headers
                    for (i = 1; i <= numCols; i++)
                    {
                        if (i > 1) System.out.print(", ");
                        System.out.print
                            (rsmd.getColumnLabel(i));
                    }
                    System.out.println("");

                    // step through the rows
                    while (rs.next())
                    {
                        // process the columns
                        for (i = 1; i <= numCols; i++)
                        {
                            if (i > 1)
                                System.out.print(", ");
                            System.out.print
                                (rs.getString(i));
                        }
                        System.out.println("");
                    }
                }
```

```
                }
                else
                {
                    if ((res = curStmt.getUpdateCount()) != -1)
                    {
                        // we have an updatecount
                        System.out.println(res + " row(s)
                            affected.");
                    }
                    // else no more results
                    else
                    {
                        moreResultsAvailable = false;
                    }
                }
                if (moreResultsAvailable)
                {
                    resultSetIsAvailable =
                        curStmt.getMoreResults();
                }
            }
            if (rs != null) rs.close();
            curStmt.close();
        }
        catch (SQLException ex) {

            // Unexpected SQL exception.
            ex.printStackTrace ();
        }
        catch (java.lang.Exception ex) {

            // Got some other type of exception.  Dump it.
            ex.printStackTrace ();
        }
    }

    private static void checkForWarnings (SQLWarning warn)
            throws SQLException
    {
        while (warn != null) {
            System.out.println(warn);
            warn = warn.getNextWarning();
        }
    }
}
```

# The JDBC API

This is a reference to the JDBC interfaces and classes. All these interfaces and classes are available in the `java.sql` package, which has been part of the JDK since JDK 1.1: they are the "application" side API of JDBC. The "driver" side API is not covered here because it is only useful for writers of JDBC drivers. Note that the `java.sql.DatabaseMetaData` interface is not covered here.

## Interface Array

```
JDBC 2.0
public interface Array
```

Methods:

```
public String getBaseTypeName()
                    throws SQLException
public int getBaseType()
                    throws SQLException
public Object getArray()
                    throws SQLException
public Object getArray(Map map)
                    throws SQLException
public Object getArray(long index, int count)
                    throws SQLException
public Object getArray(long index,int count, Map map)
                    throws SQLException
public ResultSet getResultSet()
                    throws SQLException
public ResultSet getResultSet(Map map)
                    throws SQLException
public ResultSet getResultSet(long index, int count)
                    throws SQLException
public ResultSet getResultSet(long index, int count, Map map)
                    throws SQLException
```

## Interface Blob

```
JDBC 2.0
public interface Blob
```

Methods:

```
public long length()
                    throws SQLException
public byte[] getBytes(long pos, int length)
                    throws SQLException
public InputStream getBinaryStream()
                        throws SQLException
```

```
public long position(byte[] pattern, long start)
            throws SQLException
public long position(Blob pattern, long start)
            throws SQLException
```

## Interface java.sql.CallableStatement

```
public interface CallableStatement
extends PreparedStatement
```

**Methods:**

```
public Array getArray(int i)
    throws SQLException
public abstract BigDecimal getBigDecimal(int parameterIndex,
int scale)
    throws SQLException
public Blob getBlob(int i)
    throws SQLException
public abstract boolean getBoolean(int parameterIndex)
throws SQLException
public abstract byte getByte(int parameterIndex)
  throws SQLException
public abstract byte[] getBytes(int parameterIndex)
  throws SQLException
public Clob getClob(int i)
    throws SQLException
public abstract Date getDate(int parameterIndex)
  throws SQLException
public Date getDate(int parameterIndex,
                    Calendar cal)
    throws SQLException
public abstract double getDouble(int parameterIndex)
  throws SQLException
public abstract float getFloat(int parameterIndex)
  throws SQLException
public abstract int getInt(int parameterIndex)
  throws SQLException
public abstract long getLong(int parameterIndex)
  throws SQLException
public abstract Object getObject(int parameterIndex)
  throws SQLException
public Object getObject(int i, Map map)
    throws SQLException
public Ref getRef(int i)
    throws SQLException
public abstract short getShort(int parameterIndex)
  throws SQLException
public abstract String getString(int parameterIndex)
    throws SQLException
public abstract Time getTime(int parameterIndex)
```

```
        throws SQLException
public Time getTime(int parameterIndex, Calendar cal)
    throws SQLException
public abstract Timestamp getTimestamp(int parameterIndex)
    throws SQLException
public Timestamp getTimestamp(int parameterIndex,Calendar cal)
    throws SQLException
public abstract void registerOutParameter(int parameterIndex,
int sqlType)
    throws SQLException
public abstract void registerOutParameter(int parameterIndex,
int sqlType, int scale)
    throws SQLException
public abstract boolean wasNull()
    throws SQLException
```

# Interface java.sql.Clob

```
JDBC 2.0
```

```
public interface Clob
```

**Methods:**

```
public long length()
        throws SQLException
public String getSubString(long pos,  int length)
        throws SQLException
public Reader getCharacterStream()
        throws SQLException
public InputStream getAsciiStream()
        throws SQLException
public long position(String searchstr, long start)
            throws SQLException
public long position(Clob searchstr, long start)
            throws SQLException
```

# Interface java.sql.Connection

```
public interface Connection
extends Object
```

**Variables:**

```
public final static int TRANSACTION_NONE
public final static int TRANSACTION_READ_COMMITTED
public final static int TRANSACTION_READ_UNCOMMITTED
public final static int TRANSACTION_REPEATABLE_READ
public final static int TRANSACTION_SERIALIZABLE
```

Methods:

```
public abstract void clearWarnings() throws SQLException
public abstract void close() throws SQLException
public abstract void commit() throws SQLException
public abstract Statement createStatement()throws SQLException
public Statement createStatement(int resultSetType, int
      resultSetConcurrency)
   throws SQLException
public boolean getAutoCommit() throws SQLException
public abstract String getCatalog() throws SQLException
public abstract DatabaseMetaData getMetaData() throws
   SQLException
public abstract int getTransactionIsolation()  throws
   SQLException
public Map getTypeMap() throws SQLException
public abstract SQLWarning getWarnings() throws SQLException
public abstract boolean isClosed() throws SQLException
public abstract boolean isReadOnly() throws SQLException
public abstract String nativeSQL(String sql) throws SQLException
public abstract CallableStatement prepareCall(String sql) throws
   SQLException
public CallableStatement prepareCall(String sql, int
      resultSetType, int resultSetConcurrency)
         throws SQLException
public abstract PreparedStatement prepareStatement(String sql)
   throws SQLException
public PreparedStatement prepareStatement(String sql, int
      resultSetType, int resultSetConcurrency)
   throws SQLException
public abstract void rollback() throws SQLException
public abstract void setAutoCommit(boolean autoCommit) throws
   SQLException
public abstract void setCatalog(String catalog) throws
   SQLException
public abstract void setReadOnly(boolean readOnly) throws
   SQLException
public abstract void setTransactionIsolation(int level) throws
   SQLException
public void setTypeMap(Map map) throws SQLException
```

## Interface DatabaseMetaData

```
public interface DatabaseMetaData
```

Variables:

```
public static final int procedureResultUnknown
public static final int procedureNoResult
public static final int procedureReturnsResult
```

```
public static final int procedureColumnUnknown
public static final int procedureColumnIn
public static final int procedureColumnInOut
public static final int procedureColumnOut
public static final int procedureColumnReturn
public static final int procedureColumnResult
public static final int procedureNoNulls
public static final int procedureNullable
public static final int procedureNullableUnknown
public static final int columnNoNulls
public static final int columnNullable
public static final int columnNullableUnknown
public static final int bestRowTemporary
public static final int bestRowTransaction
public static final int bestRowSession
public static final int bestRowUnknown
public static final int bestRowNotPseudo
public static final int bestRowPseudo
public static final int versionColumnUnknown
public static final int versionColumnNotPseudo
public static final int versionColumnPseudo
public static final int importedKeyCascade
public static final int importedKeyRestrict
public static final int importedKeySetNull
public static final int importedKeyNoAction
public static final int importedKeySetDefault
public static final int importedKeyInitiallyDeferred
public static final int importedKeyInitiallyImmediate
public static final int importedKeyNotDeferrable
public static final int typeNoNulls
public static final int typeNullable
public static final int typeNullableUnknown
public static final int typePredNone
public static final int typePredChar
public static final int typePredBasic
public static final int typeSearchable
public static final short tableIndexStatistic
public static final short tableIndexClustered
public static final short tableIndexHashed
public static final short tableIndexOther
```

**Methods:**

```
public boolean allProceduresAreCallable()
                              throws SQLException
public boolean allTablesAreSelectable()
                              throws SQLException
public String getURL()
              throws SQLException
public String getUserName()
                  throws SQLException
public boolean isReadOnly()
                  throws SQLException
```

```
public boolean nullsAreSortedHigh()
                        throws SQLException
public boolean nullsAreSortedLow()
                        throws SQLException
public boolean nullsAreSortedAtStart()
                            throws SQLException
public boolean nullsAreSortedAtEnd()
                        throws SQLException
public String getDatabaseProductName()
                        throws SQLException
public String getDatabaseProductVersion()
                            throws SQLException
public String getDriverName()
                throws SQLException
public String getDriverVersion()
                    throws SQLException
public int getDriverMajorVersion()
public int getDriverMinorVersion()
public boolean usesLocalFiles()
                        throws SQLException
public boolean usesLocalFilePerTable()
                        throws SQLException
public boolean supportsMixedCaseIdentifiers()
                            throws SQLException
public boolean storesUpperCaseIdentifiers()
                            throws SQLException
public boolean storesLowerCaseIdentifiers()
                            throws SQLException
public boolean storesMixedCaseIdentifiers()
                            throws SQLException
public boolean supportsMixedCaseQuotedIdentifiers()
                                throws SQLException
public boolean storesUpperCaseQuotedIdentifiers()
                                throws SQLException
public boolean storesLowerCaseQuotedIdentifiers()
                                throws SQLException
public boolean storesMixedCaseQuotedIdentifiers()
                                throws SQLException
public String getIdentifierQuoteString()
                            throws SQLException
public String getSQLKeywords()
                    throws SQLException
public String getNumericFunctions()
                        throws SQLException
public String getStringFunctions()
                        throws SQLException
public String getSystemFunctions()
                        throws SQLException
public String getTimeDateFunctions()
                        throws SQLException
public String getSearchStringEscape()
                        throws SQLException
```

```
public String getExtraNameCharacters()
                              throws SQLException
public boolean supportsAlterTableWithAddColumn()
                                       throws SQLException
public boolean supportsAlterTableWithDropColumn()
                                        throws SQLException
public boolean supportsColumnAliasing()
                              throws SQLException
public boolean nullPlusNonNullIsNull()
                            throws SQLException
public boolean supportsConvert()
                    throws SQLException
public boolean supportsConvert(int fromType,  int toType)
                    throws SQLException
public boolean supportsTableCorrelationNames()
                                      throws SQLException
public boolean supportsDifferentTableCorrelationNames()
                                             throws SQLException
public boolean supportsExpressionsInOrderBy()
                                   throws SQLException
public boolean supportsOrderByUnrelated()
                                throws SQLException
public boolean supportsGroupBy()
                    throws SQLException
public boolean supportsGroupByUnrelated()
                              throws SQLException
public boolean supportsGroupByBeyondSelect()
                                  throws SQLException
public boolean supportsLikeEscapeClause()
                                throws SQLException
public boolean supportsMultipleResultSets()
                                 throws SQLException
public boolean supportsMultipleTransactions()
                                   throws SQLException
public boolean supportsNonNullableColumns()
                                 throws SQLException
public boolean supportsMinimumSQLGrammar()
                                 throws SQLException
public boolean supportsCoreSQLGrammar()
                              throws SQLException
public boolean supportsExtendedSQLGrammar()
                                 throws SQLException
public boolean supportsANSI92EntryLevelSQL()
                                   throws SQLException
public boolean supportsANSI92IntermediateSQL()
                                     throws SQLException
public boolean supportsANSI92FullSQL()
                            throws SQLException
public boolean supportsIntegrityEnhancementFacility()
                                           throws SQLException
public boolean supportsOuterJoins()
                         throws SQLException
```

```
public boolean supportsFullOuterJoins()
                                throws SQLException
public boolean supportsLimitedOuterJoins()
                                    throws SQLException
public String getSchemaTerm()
                    throws SQLException
public String getProcedureTerm()
                        throws SQLException
public String getCatalogTerm()
                    throws SQLException
public boolean isCatalogAtStart()
                        throws SQLException
public String getCatalogSeparator()
                            throws SQLException
public boolean supportsSchemasInDataManipulation()
                                        throws SQLException
public boolean supportsSchemasInProcedureCalls()
                                    throws SQLException
public boolean supportsSchemasInTableDefinitions()
                                        throws SQLException
public boolean supportsSchemasInIndexDefinitions()
                                        throws SQLException
public boolean supportsSchemasInPrivilegeDefinitions()
                                            throws SQLException
public boolean supportsCatalogsInDataManipulation()
                                        throws SQLException
public boolean supportsCatalogsInProcedureCalls()
                                        throws SQLException
public boolean supportsCatalogsInTableDefinitions()
                                        throws SQLException
public boolean supportsCatalogsInIndexDefinitions()
                                        throws SQLException
public boolean supportsCatalogsInPrivilegeDefinitions()
                                            throws SQLException
public boolean supportsPositionedDelete()
                                throws SQLException
public boolean supportsPositionedUpdate()
                                throws SQLException
public boolean supportsSelectForUpdate()
                                throws SQLException
public boolean supportsStoredProcedures()
                                throws SQLException
public boolean supportsSubqueriesInComparisons()
                                    throws SQLException
public boolean supportsSubqueriesInExists()
                                    throws SQLException
public boolean supportsSubqueriesInIns()
                                    throws SQLException
public boolean supportsSubqueriesInQuantifieds()
                                        throws SQLException
public boolean supportsCorrelatedSubqueries()
                                throws SQLException
```

```
public boolean supportsUnion()
                    throws SQLException
public boolean supportsUnionAll()
                    throws SQLException
public boolean supportsOpenCursorsAcrossCommit()
                              throws SQLException
public boolean supportsOpenCursorsAcrossRollback()
                                throws SQLException
public boolean supportsOpenStatementsAcrossCommit()
                                throws SQLException
public boolean supportsOpenStatementsAcrossRollback()
                                    throws SQLException
public int getMaxBinaryLiteralLength()
                        throws SQLException
public int getMaxCharLiteralLength()
                        throws SQLException
public int getMaxColumnNameLength()
                        throws SQLException
public int getMaxColumnsInGroupBy()
                        throws SQLException
public int getMaxColumnsInIndex()
                    throws SQLException
public int getMaxColumnsInOrderBy()
                        throws SQLException
public int getMaxColumnsInSelect()
                        throws SQLException
public int getMaxColumnsInTable()
                        throws SQLException
public int getMaxConnections()
                    throws SQLException
public int getMaxCursorNameLength()
                        throws SQLException
public int getMaxIndexLength()
                    throws SQLException
public int getMaxSchemaNameLength()
                        throws SQLException
public int getMaxProcedureNameLength()
                            throws SQLException
public int getMaxCatalogNameLength()
                          throws SQLException
public int getMaxRowSize()
                throws SQLException
public boolean doesMaxRowSizeIncludeBlobs()
                                throws SQLException
public int getMaxStatementLength()
                        throws SQLException
public int getMaxStatements()
                    throws SQLException
public int getMaxTableNameLength()
                        throws SQLException
public int getMaxTablesInSelect()
                        throws SQLException
```

```
public int getMaxUserNameLength()
                            throws SQLException
public int getDefaultTransactionIsolation()
                                    throws SQLException
public boolean supportsTransactions()
                            throws SQLException
public boolean supportsTransactionIsolationLevel(int level)
                                        throws SQLException
public boolean
supportsDataDefinitionAndDataManipulationTransactions()

throws SQLException
public boolean supportsDataManipulationTransactionsOnly()
                                                throws
SQLException
public boolean dataDefinitionCausesTransactionCommit()
                                                throws
SQLException
public boolean dataDefinitionIgnoredInTransactions()
                                            throws SQLException
public ResultSet getProcedures(String catalog,
                            String schemaPattern,
                            String procedureNamePattern)
                        throws SQLException
public ResultSet getProcedureColumns(String catalog,
                            String schemaPattern,
                            String
procedureNamePattern,
                                String columnNamePattern)
                            throws SQLException
public ResultSet getTables(String catalog,
                        String schemaPattern,
                        String tableNamePattern,
                        String[] types)
                    throws SQLException
public ResultSet getSchemas()
                        throws SQLException
public ResultSet getCatalogs()
                        throws SQLException
public ResultSet getTableTypes()
                        throws SQLException
public ResultSet getColumns(String catalog,
                        String schemaPattern,
                        String tableNamePattern,
                        String columnNamePattern)
                    throws SQLException
public ResultSet getColumnPrivileges(String catalog,
                            String schema,
                            String table,
                            String columnNamePattern)
                        throws SQLException
```

```
public ResultSet getTablePrivileges(String catalog,
                                    String schemaPattern,
                                    String tableNamePattern)
                       throws SQLException
public ResultSet getBestRowIdentifier(String catalog,
                                      String schema,
                                      String table,
                                      int scope,
                                      boolean nullable)
                       throws SQLException
public ResultSet getVersionColumns(String catalog,
                                   String schema,
                                   String table)
                       throws SQLException
public ResultSet getPrimaryKeys(String catalog,
                                String schema,
                                String table)
                       throws SQLException
public ResultSet getImportedKeys(String catalog,
                                 String schema,
                                 String table)
                       throws SQLException
public ResultSet getExportedKeys(String catalog,
                                 String schema,
                                 String table)
                       throws SQLException
public ResultSet getCrossReference(String primaryCatalog,
                                   String primarySchema,
                                   String primaryTable,
                                   String foreignCatalog,
                                   String foreignSchema,
                                   String foreignTable)
                       throws SQLException
public ResultSet getTypeInfo()
                    throws SQLException
public ResultSet getIndexInfo(String catalog,
                              String schema,
                              String table,
                              boolean unique,
                              boolean approximate)
                       throws SQLException
public boolean supportsResultSetType(int type)
                       throws SQLException
public boolean supportsResultSetConcurrency(int type,
                                            int concurrency)
                            throws SQLException
public boolean ownUpdatesAreVisible(int type)
                       throws SQLException
public boolean ownDeletesAreVisible(int type)
                       throws SQLException
public boolean ownInsertsAreVisible(int type)
                       throws SQLException
```

```
public boolean othersUpdatesAreVisible(int type)
                              throws SQLException
public boolean othersDeletesAreVisible(int type)
                              throws SQLException
public boolean othersInsertsAreVisible(int type)
                              throws SQLException
public boolean updatesAreDetected(int type)
                        throws SQLException
public boolean deletesAreDetected(int type)
                        throws SQLException
public boolean insertsAreDetected(int type)
                        throws SQLException
public boolean supportsBatchUpdates()
                              throws SQLException
public ResultSet getUDTs(String catalog,
                     String schemaPattern,
                     String typeNamePattern,
                     int[] types)
               throws SQLException
public Connection getConnection()
                        throws SQLException
```

## Interface java.sql.Driver

```
public interface Driver
```

Methods:

```
public abstract boolean acceptsURL(String url)  throws
   SQLException
public abstract Connection connect(String url, Properties info)
   throws SQLException
public abstract int getMajorVersion()
public abstract int getMinorVersion()
public abstract DriverPropertyInfo[] getPropertyInfo(String
url,
   Properties info) throws SQLException
public abstract boolean jdbcCompliant()
```

## Interface java.sql.PreparedStatement

```
public interface PreparedStatement
extends Statement
```

Methods:

```
public void addBatch() throws SQLException
public abstract void clearParameters() throws SQLException
```

```
public abstract boolean execute() throws SQLException
public abstract ResultSet executeQuery() throws SQLException
public abstract int executeUpdate() throws SQLException
public ResultSetMetaData getMetaData() throws SQLException
public void setArray(int i, Array x) throws SQLException
public abstract void setAsciiStream(int parameterIndex,
    InputStream x, int length) throws SQLException
public abstract void setBigDecimal(int parameterIndex, BigDecimal
    x) throws SQLException
public abstract void setBinaryStream(int parameterIndex,
    InputStream x, int length) throws SQLException
public void setBlob(int i,Blob x) throws SQLException
public abstract void setBoolean(int parameterIndex, boolean x)
    throws SQLException
public abstract void setByte(int parameterIndex, byte x) throws
    SQLException
public abstract void setBytes(int parameterIndex, byte x[])
    throws SQLException
public void setCharacterStream(int parameterIndex,
                               Reader reader,
                               int length)
                    throws SQLException
public void setClob(int i, Clob x) throws SQLException
public abstract void setDate(int parameterIndex, Date x)
        throws SQLException
public void setDate(int parameterIndex, Date x, Calendar cal)
            throws SQLException
public abstract void setDouble(int parameterIndex, double x)
    throws SQLException
public abstract void setFloat(int parameterIndex, float x) throws
    SQLException
public abstract void setInt(int parameterIndex, int x) throws
    SQLException
public abstract void setLong(int parameterIndex, long x) throws
    SQLException
public abstract void setNull(int parameterIndex, int sqlType)
    throws SQLException
public abstract void setObject(int parameterIndex, Object x,
        int targetSqlType, int scale) throws SQLException
public abstract void setObject(int parameterIndex, Object x,
        int targetSqlType) throws SQLException
public abstract void setObject(int parameterIndex, Object x)
    throws SQLException
public void setRef(int i, Ref x) throws SQLException
public abstract void setShort(int parameterIndex, short x)
    throws SQLException
public abstract void setString(int parameterIndex, String x)
    throws SQLException
public abstract void setTime(int parameterIndex, Time x)
    throws SQLException
```

```
     public void setTime(int parameterIndex, Time x,
                    Calendar cal)
            throws SQLException
public abstract void setTimestamp(int parameterIndex,
     Timestamp x)
         throws SQLException
public void setTimestamp(int parameterIndex, Timestamp x,
              Calendar cal)
                throws SQLException
public abstract void setUnicodeStream(int parameterIndex,
    InputStream x, int length) throws SQLException
```

## Interface java.sql.Ref

```
JDBC 2.0

public interface Ref

public String getBaseTypeName()
                        throws SQLException
```

## Interface java.sql.ResultSet

```
public interface ResultSet
```

Variables:

```
public static final int FETCH_FORWARD
public static final int FETCH_REVERSE
public static final int FETCH_UNKNOWN
public static final int TYPE_FORWARD_ONLY
public static final int TYPE_SCROLL_INSENSITIVE
public static final int TYPE_SCROLL_SENSITIVE
public static final int CONCUR_READ_ONLY
public static final int CONCUR_UPDATABLE
```

Methods:

```
public boolean absolute(int row) throws SQLException
public void afterLast() throws SQLException
public void beforeFirst() throws SQLException
public void cancelRowUpdates() throws SQLException
public abstract void clearWarnings() throws SQLException
public abstract void close() throws SQLException
public void deleteRow()  throws SQLException
public abstract int findColumn(String columnName) throws
    SQLException
public boolean first() throws SQLException
```

```
public Array getArray(int i)  throws SQLException
public Array getArray(String colName) throws SQLException
public abstract InputStream getAsciiStream(int columnIndex)
   throws SQLException
public abstract InputStream getAsciiStream(String columnName)
   throws SQLException
public abstract BigDecimal getBigDecimal(int columnIndex, int
   scale) throws SQLException
public abstract BigDecimal getBigDecimal(String columnName, int
   scale) throws SQLException
public abstract InputStream getBinaryStream(int columnIndex)
   throws SQLException
public abstract InputStream getBinaryStream(String columnName)
   throws SQLException
public Blob getBlob(int i)  throws SQLException
public Blob getBlob(String colName) throws SQLException
public abstract boolean getBoolean(int columnIndex) throws
   SQLException
public abstract boolean getBoolean(String columnName) throws
   SQLException
public abstract byte getByte(int columnIndex) throws
SQLException
public abstract byte getByte(String columnName) throws
   SQLException
public abstract byte[] getBytes(int columnIndex) throws
   SQLException
public abstract byte[] getBytes(String columnName) throws
   SQLException
public Reader getCharacterStream(int columnIndex)
                         throws SQLException
public Reader getCharacterStream(String columnName)
                         throws SQLException
public Clob getClob(int i)  throws SQLException
public Clob getClob(String colName) throws SQLException
public int getConcurrency() throws SQLException
public abstract String getCursorName() throws SQLException
public abstract Date getDate(int columnIndex) throws SQLException
public abstract Date getDate(String columnName)  throws
   SQLException
public Date getDate(int columnIndex, Calendar cal)
            throws SQLException
public Date getDate(String columnName, Calendar cal)
            throws SQLException
public abstract double getDouble(int columnIndex) throws
   SQLException
public abstract double getDouble(String columnName) throws
   SQLException
public int getFetchDirection() throws SQLException
public int getFetchSize() throws SQLException
public abstract float getFloat(int columnIndex) throws
   SQLException
```

```
public abstract float getFloat(String columnName) throws
   SQLException
public abstract int getInt(int columnIndex) throws SQLException
public abstract int getInt(String columnName) throws SQLException
public abstract long getLong(int columnIndex) throws SQLException
public abstract long getLong(String columnName) throws
   SQLException
public ResultSetMetaData getMetaData()
                               throws SQLException
public Object getObject(int columnIndex)
            throws SQLException
public Object getObject(int i, Map map)
            throws SQLException
public Object getObject(String columnName)
            throws SQLException
public Object getObject(String colName, Map map)
            throws SQLException
public Ref getRef(int i)  throws SQLException
public Ref getRef(String colName) throws SQLException
public int getRow() throws SQLException
public abstract short getShort(int columnIndex) throws
   SQLException
public abstract short getShort(String columnName) throws
   SQLException
public Statement getStatement() throws SQLException
public abstract String getString(int columnIndex) throws
   SQLException
public abstract String getString(String columnName) throws
   SQLException
public abstract Time getTime(int columnIndex) throws
SQLException
public abstract Time getTime(String columnName)  throws
   SQLException
public Time getTime(int columnIndex, Calendar cal)
           throws SQLException
public Time getTime(String columnName, Calendar cal)
           throws SQLException
public abstract Timestamp getTimestamp(int columnIndex) throws
   SQLException
public abstract Timestamp getTimestamp(String columnName)
throws SQLException
public Timestamp getTimestamp(int columnIndex,
                        Calendar cal)
                     throws SQLException
public Timestamp getTimestamp(String columnName,
                        Calendar cal)
                     throws SQLException
public int getType() throws SQLException
public SQLWarning getWarnings() throws SQLException
public void insertRow() throws SQLException
public boolean isAfterLast() throws SQLException
```

```
public boolean isBeforeFirst() throws SQLException
public boolean isFirst() throws SQLException
public boolean isLast() throws SQLException
public boolean last() throws SQLException
public void moveToCurrentRow() throws SQLException
public void moveToInsertRow() throws SQLException
public boolean next() throws SQLException
public boolean previous() throws SQLException
public void refreshRow() throws SQLException
public boolean relative(int rows) throws SQLException
public boolean rowDeleted() throws SQLException
public boolean rowInserted() throws SQLException
public boolean rowUpdated() throws SQLException
public void setFetchDirection(int direction)
                        throws SQLException
public void setFetchSize(int rows)
                   throws SQLException
public void updateAsciiStream(int columnIndex,
                              InputStream x,
                              int length)
                        throws SQLException
public void updateAsciiStream(String columnName,
                              InputStream x,
                              int length)
                        throws SQLException
public void updateBigDecimal(int columnIndex,
                             BigDecimal x)
                        throws SQLException
public void updateBigDecimal(String columnName,
                             BigDecimal x)
                        throws SQLException
public void updateBinaryStream(int columnIndex,
                               InputStream x,
                               int length)
                        throws SQLException
public void updateBinaryStream(String columnName,
                               InputStream x,
                               int length)
                        throws SQLException
public void updateBoolean(int columnIndex,
                          boolean x)
                   throws SQLException
public void updateBoolean(String columnName,
                          boolean x)
                   throws SQLException
public void updateByte(int columnIndex,
                       byte x)
                throws SQLException
public void updateByte(String columnName,
                       byte x)
                throws SQLException
public void updateBytes(int columnIndex,
```

```
                             byte[] x)
                    throws SQLException
public void updateBytes(String columnName,
                             byte[] x)
                    throws SQLException
public void updateCharacterStream(int columnIndex,
                                      Reader x,
                                      int length)
                        throws SQLException
public void updateCharacterStream(String columnName,
                                      Reader reader,
                                      int length)
                        throws SQLException
public void updateDate(int columnIndex,
                         Date x)
                    throws SQLException
public void updateDate(String columnName,
                         Date x)
                    throws SQLException
public void updateDouble(int columnIndex,
                           double x)
                    throws SQLException
public void updateDouble(String columnName,
                           double x)
                    throws SQLException
public void updateFloat(int columnIndex,
                          float x)
                    throws SQLException
public void updateFloat(String columnName,
                          float x)
                    throws SQLException
public void updateInt(int columnIndex,
                        int x)
                    throws SQLException
public void updateInt(String columnName,
                        int x)
                    throws SQLException
public void updateLong(int columnIndex,  long x)
                    throws SQLException
public void updateLong(String columnName, long x)
                    throws SQLException
public void updateNull(int columnIndex) throws SQLException
public void updateNull(String columnName) throws SQLException
public void updateObject(int columnIndex, Object x)
                    throws SQLException
public void updateObject(int columnIndex, Object x, int scale)
                    throws SQLException
public void updateObject(String columnName, Object x)
                    throws SQLException
public void updateObject(String columnName, Object x,
                           int scale)
                    throws SQLException
```

```
public void updateRow() throws SQLException
public void updateShort(int columnIndex, short x)
                throws SQLException
public void updateShort(String columnName, short x)
                throws SQLException
public void updateString(int columnIndex, String x)
                throws SQLException
public void updateString(String columnName,  String x)
                throws SQLException
public void updateTime(int columnIndex, Time x)
                throws SQLException
public void updateTime(String columnName, Time x)
                throws SQLException
public void updateTimestamp(int columnIndex, Timestamp x)
                    throws SQLException
public void updateTimestamp(String columnName, Timestamp x)
                    throws SQLException
public boolean wasNull() throws SQLException
```

# Interface java.sql.ResultSetMetaData

```
public interface ResultSetMetaData
```

Variables:

```
public final static int columnNoNulls
public final static int columnNullable
public final static int columnNullableUnknown
```

Methods:

```
public abstract String getCatalogName(int column) throws
    SQLException
public String getColumnClassName(int column)
                        throws SQLException
public abstract int getColumnCount() throws SQLException
public abstract int getColumnDisplaySize(int column) throws
    SQLException
public abstract String getColumnLabel(int column) throws
    SQLException
public abstract String getColumnName(int column) throws
    SQLException
public abstract int getColumnType(int column) throws
SQLException
public abstract String getColumnTypeName(int column) throws
    SQLException
public abstract int getPrecision(int column)  throws
SQLException
public abstract int getScale(int column)  throws SQLException
```

```
public abstract String getSchemaName(int column) throws
    SQLException
public abstract String getTableName(int column) throws
    SQLException
public abstract boolean isAutoIncrement(int column) throws
    SQLException
public abstract boolean isCaseSensitive(int column) throws
    SQLException
public abstract boolean isCurrency(int column) throws
    SQLException
public abstract boolean isDefinitelyWritable(int column) throws
    SQLException
public abstract int isNullable(int column)  throws SQLException
public abstract boolean isReadOnly(int column) throws
    SQLException
public abstract boolean isSearchable(int column) throws
    SQLExccption
public abstract boolean isSigned(int column)  throws
SQLException
public abstract boolean isWritable(int column) throws
    SQLException
```

## Interface java.sql.SQLData

```
public interface SQLData
```

**Methods:**

```
public String getSQLTypeName() throws SQLException
public void readSQL(SQLInput stream,  String typeName)  throws
SQLException
public void writeSQL(SQLOutput stream)  throws SQLException
```

## Interface java.sql.SQLInput

```
JDBC 2.0
```

**Methods:**

```
public Array readArray() throws SQLException
public String readString() throws SQLException
public boolean readBoolean() throws SQLException
public byte readByte() throws SQLException
public short readShort() throws SQLException
public int readInt() throws SQLException
public long readLong() throws SQLException
public float readFloat() throws SQLException
public double readDouble() throws SQLException
```

```
public BigDecimal readBigDecimal() throws SQLException
public byte[] readBytes() throws SQLException
public Date readDate() throws SQLException
public Time readTime() throws SQLException
public Timestamp readTimestamp() throws SQLException
public Reader readCharacterStream() throws SQLException
public InputStream readAsciiStream() throws SQLException
public InputStream readBinaryStream() throws SQLException
public Object readObject() throws SQLException
public Ref readRef() throws SQLException
public Blob readBlob() throws SQLException
public Clob readClob() throws SQLException
public boolean wasNull() throws SQLException
```

## Interface java.sql.SQLOutput

```
JDBC 2.0
```

Methods:

```
public void writeString(String x)  throws SQLException
public void writeBoolean(boolean x)  throws SQLException
public void writeByte(byte x)  throws SQLException
public void writeShort(short x) throws SQLException
public void writeInt(int x) throws SQLException
public void writeLong(long x) throws SQLException
public void writeFloat(float x throws SQLException
public void writeDouble(double x) throws SQLException
public void writeBigDecimal(BigDecimal x) throws SQLException
public void writeBytes(byte[] x)  throws SQLException
public void writeDate(Date x) throws SQLException
public void writeTime(Time x) throws SQLException
public void writeTimestamp(Timestamp x) throws SQLException
public void writeCharacterStream(Reader x) throws SQLException
public void writeAsciiStream(InputStream x)
        throws SQLException
public void writeBinaryStream(InputStream x)
                    throws SQLException
public void writeObject(SQLData x)  throws SQLException
public void writeRef(Ref x) throws SQLException
public void writeBlob(Blob x)  throws SQLException
public void writeClob(Clob x) throws SQLException
public void writeStruct(Struct x) throws SQLException
public void writeArray(Array x) throws SQLException
```

## Interface java.sql.Statement

```
public interface Statement
```

**Methods:**

```
public void addBatch(String sql) throws SQLException
public abstract void cancel() throws SQLException
public void clearBatch() throws SQLException
public abstract void clearWarnings() throws SQLException
public abstract void close() throws SQLException
public abstract boolean execute(String sql)  throws SQLException
public int[] executeBatch() throws SQLException
public abstract ResultSet executeQuery(String sql) throws
    SQLException
public abstract int executeUpdate(String sql) throws
SQLException
public Connection getConnection() throws SQLException
public int getFetchDirection() throws SQLException
public int getFetchSize() throws SQLException
public int gctMaxFieldSize() throws SQLException
public int getMaxRows() throws SQLException
public boolean getMoreResults() throws SQLException
public int getQueryTimeout() throws SQLException
public abstract ResultSet getResultSet() throws SQLException
public int getResultSetConcurrency() throws SQLException
public int getResultSetType() throws SQLException
public abstract int getUpdateCount() throws SQLException
public abstract SQLWarning getWarnings() throws SQLException
public abstract void setCursorName(String name) throws
    SQLException
public abstract void setEscapeProcessing(boolean enable) throws
SQLException
public void setFetchDirection(int direction)
                        throws SQLException
public void setFetchSize(int rows)
                    throws SQLException
public abstract void setMaxFieldSize(int max) throws SQLException
public abstract void setMaxRows(int max) throws SQLException
public abstract void setQueryTimeout(int seconds) throws
    SQLException
```

# Class java.sql.Struct

JDBC 2.0

```
public interface Struct
```

**Methods:**

```
public String getSQLTypeName() throws SQLException
public Object[] getAttributes() throws SQLException
public Object[] getAttributes(Map map)  throws SQLException
```

## Class java.sql.Date

```
java.lang.Object
    |
    +----java.util.Date
            |
            +----java.sql.Date

public class Date
extends Date
```

Constructors:

```
public Date(long date)
```

Methods:

```
public void setTime(long date)
public String toString()
public static Date valueOf(String s)
```

## Class java.sql.DriverManager

```
java.lang.Object
    |
    +----java.sql.DriverManager

public class DriverManager
extends Object
```

Methods:

```
public static void deregisterDriver(Driver driver) throws
SQLException
public static synchronized Connection getConnection(String url,
    Properties info) throws SQLException
public static synchronized Connection getConnection(String
    url, String user, String password) throws SQLException
public static synchronized Connection getConnection(String
    url) throws SQLException
public static Driver getDriver(String url) throws SQLException
public static Enumeration getDrivers()
public static int getLoginTimeout()
public static PrintWriter getLogWriter()
public static void println(Stringmessage)
public static synchronized void registerDriver(Driverdriver)
    throws SQLException
public static void setLoginTimeout(int seconds)
public static void setLogWriter(PrintWriter out)
```

## Class java.sql.DriverPropertyInfo

```
java.lang.Object
     |
     +----java.sql.DriverPropertyInfo

public class DriverPropertyInfo
extends Object
```

Variables:

```
public String choices[]
public String description
public String name
public boolean required
public String value
```

Constructors:

```
public DriverPropertyInfo(String name, String value)
```

## Class java.sql.Time

```
java.lang.Object
     |
     +----java.util.Date
             |
             +----java.sql.Time

public class Time
extends Date
```

Constructors:

```
public Time(int hour, int minute, int second)
public Time(long time)
```

Methods:

```
public String toString()
public static Time valueOf(String s)
public void setTime(long time)
```

## Class java.sql.Timestamp

```
java.lang.Object
     |
```

```
    +----java.util.Date
            |
            +----java.sql.Timestamp

public class Timestamp
extends Date
```

Constructors:

```
public Timestamp(long time)
```

Methods:

```
public boolean after(Timestamp ts)
public boolean before(Timestamp ts)
public boolean equals(Object ts)
public boolean equals(Timestamp ts)
public int getNanos()
public void setNanos(int n)
public String toString()
public static Timestamp valueOf(String s)
```

## Class java.sql.Types

```
java.lang.Object
   |
   +----java.sql.Types

public class Types
extends Object
```

Variables:

```
public static final int ARRAY
public static final int BLOB
public static final int CLOB
public static final int REF
public final static int BIGINT = -5
public final static int BINARY = -2
public final static int BIT = -7
public final static int CHAR = 1
public final static int DATE = 91
public final static int DECIMAL = 3
public static final int DISTINCT
public final static int DOUBLE = 8
public final static int FLOAT = 6
public final static int INTEGER = 4
public static final int JAVA_OBJECT
public final static int LONGVARCHAR = -4
public final static int LONGVARBINARY = -1
```

```
public final static int NULL = 0
public final static int NUMERIC = 2
public final static int OTHER
public final static int REAL = 7
public final static int SMALLINT = 5
public static final int STRUCT
public final static int TIME = 92
public final static int TIMESTAMP = 93
public final static int TINYINT = -6
public final static int VARBINARY = -3
public final static int VARCHAR = 12
```

# Class java.sql.DataTruncation

JDBC 2.0

```
java.lang.Object
  |
  +--java.lang.Throwable
        |
        +--java.lang.Exception
              |
              +--java.sql.SQLException
                    |
                    +--java.sql.BatchUpdateException
```

```
public class BatchUpdateException
extends SQLException
```

**Constructors:**

```
public BatchUpdateException(String reason,
                            String SQLState,
                            int vendorCode,
                            int[] updateCounts)
```

```
public BatchUpdateException(String reason,
                            String SQLState,
                            int[] updateCounts)
```

```
public BatchUpdateException(String reason,
                            int[] updateCounts)
```

```
public BatchUpdateException(int[] updateCounts)
```

```
public BatchUpdateException()
```

**Methods:**

```
public int[] getUpdateCounts()
```

## Class java.sql.DataTruncation

```
java.lang.Object
    |
    +----java.lang.Throwable
              |
              +----java.lang.Exception
                        |
                        +----java.sql.SQLException
                                  |
                                  +----java.sql.SQLWarning
                                            |
                                            +----java.sql.DataTruncation
```

```
public class DataTruncation
extends SQLWarning
```

### Constructors:

```
public DataTruncation(int index, boolean parameter, boolean
read,
    int dataSize, int transferSize)
```

### Methods:

```
public int getDataSize()
public int getIndex()
public boolean getParameter()
public boolean getRead()
public int getTransferSize()
```

## Class java.sql.SQLException

```
java.lang.Object
    |
    +----java.lang.Throwable
              |
              +----java.lang.Exception
                        |
                        +----java.sql.SQLException
```

```
public class SQLException
extends Exception
```

### Constructors:

```
public SQLException(String reason, String SQLState, int
    vendorCode)
public SQLException(String reason, String SQLState)
public SQLException(String reason)
public SQLException()
```

Methods:

```
public int getErrorCode()
public SQLException getNextException()
public String getSQLState()
public synchronized void setNextException(SQLException ex)
```

## Class java.sql.SQLWarning

```
java.lang.Object
    |
    +----java.lang.Throwable
            |
            +----java.lang.Exception
                    |
                    +----java.sql.SQLException
                            |
                            +----java.sql.SQLWarning
```

```
public class SQLWarning
extends SQLException
```

Constructors:

```
public SQLWarning(String reason, String SQLstate, int
vendorCode)
public SQLWarning(String reason, String SQLstate)
public SQLWarning(String reason)
public SQLWarning()
```

Methods:

```
public SQLWarning getNextWarning()
public void setNextWarning(SQLWarning w)
```

# Advanced Techniques

JDBC also has some nice features that allow developers to program enterprise-class applets and applications. This section focuses on prepared statements, stored procedures, database transactions, and three-tiered software design.

## Database prepared statements

A *prepared statement* is a SQL statement sent to the database prior to its execution. Unlike stored procedures, prepared statements do not remain in the database after the resources associated with them are freed. They may be called a number of times with different parameter values. Figure 16-15 and Figure 16-16 illustrate some differences between the execution of simple SQL statements and the execution of prepared statements.

In the first case, the SQL text is sent to the database along with specific values and literals. Figure16-15 illustrates an `INSERT` statement:

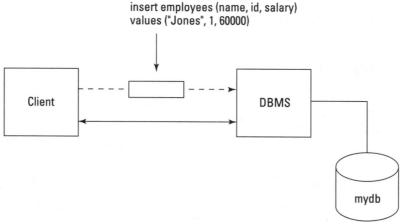

**Figure 16-15:** Sending a static statement

When executing a prepared statement, the SQL statement is already at the database side. It has been sent there using a specific mechanism. Only parameter values are passed; the call may be issued many times with different parameter values. Depending on the DBMS, the SQL statement may or may not have been optimized and precompiled at the database side, shown in Figure 16-16:

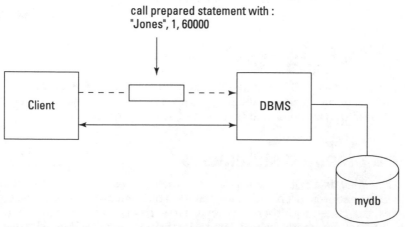

**Figure 16-16:** Sending parameters to a prepared statement

To summarize this, you must follow these steps to use prepared statements with JDBC:

1. Prepare the SQL statement.

2. Set IN parameters.

3. Execute the statement.

4. Get the results, if any.

5. If necessary, set new IN parameter values and reexecute this statement:

```
PreparedStatement prepareStatement(String sql);
```

This method is used to get a PreparedStatement object that will later be executed. Parameters are symbolized by question mark (?) characters.

## Passing IN Parameters

When you use callable statements, IN parameters must be set individually. The following methods are available for this purpose:

```
void setNull(int parameterIndex, int sqlType);
void setBoolean(int parameterIndex, boolean x);
void setByte(int parameterIndex, byte x);
void setShort(int parameterIndex, short x);
void setInt(int parameterIndex, int x);
void setLong(int parameterIndex, long x);
void setFloat(int parameterIndex, float x);
void setDouble(int parameterIndex, double x);
void setBigDecimal(int parameterIndex, java.math.BigDecimal x);
void setString(int parameterIndex, String x);
void setBytes(int parameterIndex, byte x[]);
void setDate(int parameterIndex, java.sql.Date x);
void setTime(int parameterIndex, java.sql.Time x);
void setTimestamp(int parameterIndex, java.sql.Timestamp x);
void setAsciiStream(int parameterIndex, java.io.InputStream x,
    int length);
void setUnicodeStream(int parameterIndex, java.io.InputStream x,
    int length);
void setBinaryStream(int parameterIndex, java.io.InputStream x,
    int length);
void setObject(int parameterIndex, Object x);
void setObject(int parameterIndex, Object x, int
targetSqlType);
void setObject(int parameterIndex, Object x, int targetSqlType,
    int scale);
void clearParameters();
```

The `setObject()` and `clearParameters()` methods have the same meaning as they do for callable statements.

## Executing the Query and Retrieving Results

Once all IN parameters have been set, you execute a prepared statement as you do a normal one. A prepared statement may return a count value as well as a resultset. The following code shows all of these steps put together:

```
...
Connection connection = DriverManager.getConnection(url,
    "javauser", "hotjava");

PreparedStatement stmt = connection.prepareStatement
    (    "UPDATE employees SET salary = ? WHERE name = ?");

stmt.setInt(1, 100000);
stmt.setString(2, "Jones");

int res = stmt.executeUpdate();

stmt.close();
connection.close();
..
```

One of the common complaints about JDBC 1.x was the inability to move backward within the result set. You could only move forward and one row at a time. JDBC 2.x fixes that shortcoming by offering full scrolling capability. When you create a statement, you can specify the resultSetType and the resultSetConcurrency. The resultSetType refers to one of the following:

✦ `TYPE_FORWARD_ONLY`: The type for a ResultSet object whose cursor may move only forward

✦ `TYPE_SCROLL-INSENSITIVE`: The type for a ResultSet object that is scrollable but generally not sensitive to changes made by others

✦ `TYPE_SCROLL_SENSITIVE`: The type for a ResultSet object that is scrollable and generally sensitive to changes made by others

The other argument is resultSetConcurrency. This refers to the ability to modify the data returned by a result set. Possible values are the following:

✦ `CONCUR_READ_ONLY`: The concurrency mode for a ResultSet object that may *not* be updated

✦ `CONSUR_UPDATABLE`: The concurrency mode for a ResultSet object that may be updated

Methods such as `insertRow()` and `deleteRow()` can be used to modify a ResultSet object. A series of `updateXXX()` methods are provided that modify the data in the result set's current row. There is a one-to-one correspondence between the `updateXXX()` methods and the `readXXX()` methods used to retrieve the data. Support for concurrency modes depends on the JDBC driver you are using. You can use the `supportsResultSetConcurrency()` method in the DatabaseMetaData class to verify that appropriate support is provided.

When dealing with scrollable result sets, you can move up and down the list of rows retrieved from the database. The following is a list of common methods used for scrolling:

- ✦ `Absolute (int row)`: Positions the cursor at the specified row. If a negative value is specified, then the cursor is positioned at an offset relative to the end of the result set instead of the beginning.

- ✦ `AfterLast()`: Positions the cursor past the end of the result set (after the last row).

- ✦ `BeforeFirst()`: Positions the cursor at the beginning of the result set (before the first row). This is the same location that the cursor is initially in when a result set is created.

- ✦ `First()`: Positions the cursor at the first row.

- ✦ `Last()`: Positions the cursor at the last row.

- ✦ `Next()`: Moves the cursor forward one row. This is the only method available for cursor navigation with JDBC 1.x-style result sets.

- ✦ `Previous()`: Moves the cursor to the previous row in the result set.

- ✦ `Relative(int rows)`: Moves the cursor either forward or backward the specified number of rows. If the value specified is possible, the cursor is moved forward by that amount. Otherwise, it moves backward the indicated number of rows.

JDBC 2.x also addresses the issue of another application making updates to the database while a result set is open within our own application. That's where `TYPE_SCROLL_SENSITIVE` comes into play. By specifying the resultSetType to this value, you indicate that the result set should be sensitive to changes made by other applications or processes to the underlying data in the database. That is, the result set should display what is currently stored in the database, including changes made to the data after the result set was opened.

Once again, you should use the `DatabaseMetData` class to check specific capabilities of your database system and the JDBC driver that you are using.

## Stored procedures

A *stored procedure* is a SQL statement sent once to the database. The DBMS will precompile it and store it in the database. Stored procedures are often used to store and perform some processing on the data that would be irrelevant if done within the clients. Database vendors claim it is the place to put the core business logic (as far as relational data is concerned). Figure 16-17 illustrates this statement:

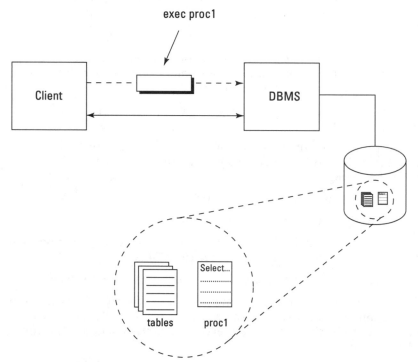

**Figure 16-17:** Invoking a stored procedure

Statements that invoke stored procedures should use the JDBC Callable Statement class. You must call a dedicated method to prepare the callable statement. You then use the usual methods to execute the statement:

```
CallableStatement prepareCall(String sql);
    where the argument is of the form:
    "{? =call stored_procedure_name ?, ?, ....}"
```

This is the method used to prepare a callable statement. It returns a Callable Statement object. You will discover the reason we need something more elaborate than a simple Statement object soon.

Stored procedures may, of course, return multiple result types, because they may be composed of SQL statements that return diverse result types. You use the usual methods to retrieve these results. If results such as resultsets are returned by a procedure, they must be retrieved first before accessing other kinds of return values from the procedure. Indeed, stored procedures may also have parameters.

Stored procedures may be called with parameters. They provide maximum flexibility by allowing values to be passed from and to the user's application. Such parameters are of two types: IN and/or OUT. IN parameters are used to pass data to the stored procedure, and OUT parameters are values returned by the procedure code. Special JDBC methods let you set and access these parameters. Once the statement has been executed, you can explore all its OUT parameters one by one, in left-to-right order. If your stored procedure returns a resultset, you would simply add a loop to fetch the resultset *before* accessing the OUT parameters.

## Setting IN Parameters

IN parameters receive a value from the user's application. They are set via setXXX() methods that take two arguments: the parameter index, beginning at 1, and the value to set. The following methods are used to set values corresponding to their parameter's specific type:

```
void setNull(int parameterIndex, int sqlType);
void setBoolean(int parameterIndex, boolean x);
void setByte(int parameterIndex, byte x);
void setShort(int parameterIndex, short x);
void setInt(int parameterIndex, int x);
void setLong(int parameterIndex, long x);
void setFloat(int parameterIndex, float x);
void setDouble(int parameterIndex, double x);
void set BigDecimal(int parameterIndex, java.math.BigDecimal x);
void setString(int parameterIndex, String x);
void setBytes(int parameterIndex, byte x[]);
void setDate(int parameterIndex, java.sql.Date x);
void setTime(int parameterIndex, java.sql.Time x);
void setTimestamp(int parameterIndex, java.sql.Timestamp x);
void setAsciiStream(int parameterIndex, java.io.InputStream x,
    int length);
void setUnicodeStream(int parameterIndex, java.io.InputStream x,
    int length);
void setBinaryStream(int parameterIndex, java.io.InputStream x,
    int length);
void setObject(int parameterIndex, Object x);
void setObject(int parameterIndex, Object x, int targetSqlType);
void setObject(int parameterIndex, Object x, int targetSqlType,
    int scale);
void clearParameters();
```

The `setObject(...)` methods belong to advanced JDBC features. They allow given Java objects to be stored in the database. However, they are converted to the database target SQL datatype before they are actually sent to the database. Note that it is possible to pass database-specific abstract datatypes by using a driver-specific Java type and using a `targetSqlType` of `java.sql.types.OTHER` with the `setObject(int parameterIndex, Object x, int targetSqlType)` and the `setObject(int parameterIndex, Object x, int targetSqlType, int scale)` methods.

## Setting OUT Parameters

OUT parameters must be registered prior to executing the callable statement. This is the way to specify their type. You can use the following methods to register these OUT parameters:

```
void registerOutParameter(int parameterIndex, int sqlType);
```

The first argument is the parameter index, beginning at 1. The `type` argument must be defined in `java.sql.Types`.

```
void registerOutParameter(int parameterIndex, int sqlType, int scale);
```

This method is used to register OUT parameters of type SQL `Numeric` or `Decimal`. The `scale` argument represents the desired number of digits to the right of the decimal point.

## Accessing Parameters

You must access parameters in left-to-right order with the appropriate method that matches their type. The following methods are provided for this purpose:

```
boolean wasNull();
String getString(int parameterIndex);
boolean getBoolean(int parameterIndex);
byte getByte(int parameterIndex);
short getShort(int parameterIndex);
int getInt(int parameterIndex);
long getLong(int parameterIndex);
float getFloat(int parameterIndex);
double getDouble(int parameterIndex);
java.math.BigDecimal getBigDecimal(int parameterIndex, int
    scale);
byte[] getBytes(int parameterIndex);
java.sql.Date getDate(int parameterIndex);
java.sql.Time getTime(int parameterIndex);
java.sql.Timestamp getTimestamp(int parameterIndex);
Object getObject(int parameterIndex);
```

If an OUT parameter has a null value, `wasNull()` returns `true`. Note that you must call the corresponding `getXXX()` method *before* calling `wasNull()`.

The following code snippet illustrates how to prepare a callable statement, set IN parameters, register OUT parameters, execute the statement, and access the OUT parameters:

```
...
Connection connection = DriverManager.getConnection(url,
    "javauser", "hotjava");

CallableStatement stmt = connection.prepareCall(
    "{call my_stored_procedure ?, ?}");

stmt.setString(1, "Hotjava");
stmt.registerOutParameter(2, java.sql.types.VARCHAR);

int res = myStmt.executeUpdate();

String outParam = stmt.getString(2);

stmt.close();
connection.close();
...
```

With JDBC 2.0 and the new Java-aware database management systems, you can change the way you interact with stored procedures. Within your database, you can define new data types (user- defined data types, or UDT) that correspond to Java classes. You can then create tables with columns that allow you to store instances of the class associated with that column's UDT. The objects are read and written using the readObject() and writeObject() methods, but the underlying persistence is handled by the database.

JDBC supports database transaction management. Transactions provide a way to group SQL statements so that they are treated as a whole: Either all statements in the group are executed or no statements are executed. All statements within a transaction are treated as a work unit. Transactions are, thus, useful to guarantee data consistency, among other things.

## Database transactions

JDBC supports database transaction management. Transactions provide a way to group SQL statements so that they are treated as a whole: Either all statements in the group are executed or no statements are executed. All statements within a transaction are treated as a work unit. Transactions are thus useful to guarantee data consistency, among other things.

Completing a transaction is referred to as *committing the transaction*, while aborting it is referred to as *rolling back the transaction*. A rollback undoes the whole transaction. Therefore, a transaction's boundaries are the beginning of its block and the commit or rollback. Once a commit has been issued, the transaction cannot be rolled back. Note that some DBMSs support nested transactions as well as intermediate markers within a transaction to indicate the point to which the transaction can be rolled back.

## Transaction Modes

Two transaction modes are usually supported by commercial DBMSs: unchained mode and ANSI-compatible chained mode. You should check your documentation to find out which one is the default.

✦ The unchained mode requires explicit statements to identify the beginning of a transaction block and its end, which will always be a commit or rollback statement. The transaction block may be composed of any SQL statements.

✦ The chained mode does not require explicit statements to delimit the transaction statements, because it implicitly begins a transaction before any SQL statement that retrieves or modifies data. The transaction must still be explicitly ended with a transaction commit or rollback.

Be aware that stored procedures that use the unchained transaction mode may be incompatible with other chained-mode transactions.

## Transaction Isolation Levels

ANSI defines three standard levels of transaction isolation. Transaction isolation makes sense when concurrent transactions execute simultaneously. The ANSI specification defines restrictions on the kind of actions permitted in this context of concurrent transactions to prevent *dirty reads, nonrepeatable reads,* and *phantoms.*

✦ Level 1, No dirty reads: Dirty reads occur when a transaction updates a row and then a second transaction reads that row before the first transaction commits. If the first transaction then rolls back the change, the information read by the second transaction becomes invalid.

✦ Level 2, No nonrepeatable reads: Nonrepeatable reads occur when a transaction reads a row and then another transaction updates the same row. If the second transaction commits, subsequent reads by the first transaction get different values than the original read.

✦ Level 3, No phantoms: Phantoms occur when a transaction reads a set of rows that satisfy a search condition and then another transaction updates, inserts, or deletes one or more rows that satisfy the first transaction's search condition. In this situation, if the first transaction performs subsequent reads with the same search condition, it obtains a different set of rows.

Note that the higher levels include restrictions imposed by all the lower levels. In practice, you achieve compatibility with all the transaction isolation levels by using locking techniques. You should check your database documentation for information on these techniques and see how they can affect performances in a multiuser environment. As a general rule, remember that the higher the transaction isolation level, the longer the locks are held.

## Managing Transactions with JDBC

JDBC always opens connections in *auto-commit mode*. This means that each statement is executed as a separate transaction without the need for supplying commit or rollback commands. In this default mode, it is not possible to perform rollbacks.

JDBC provides methods to turn off auto-commit mode, to set the transaction isolation level and to commit or roll back transactions. JDBC transactions begin as soon as the auto-commit mode is disabled. In this case, an implicit transaction is associated with the connection, and it is completed or aborted with commit and rollback methods. The commit or rollback will then start a new implicit transaction. Note that the commit and rollback makes JDBC close all PreparedStatements, CallableStatements, and ResultSets opened during the transaction. Simple Statements objects stay open. This is the default behavior, and it may be disabled.

These are the JDBC methods to manage transactions:

```
void setTransactionIsolation(int isolationlevel);
int getTransactionIsolation();
void setAutoCommit(boolean autocommit);
boolean getAutoCommit();
void commit();
void rollback();
void setAutoClose(boolean autoClose);
boolean getAutoClose();
```

Table 16-1 lists the possible JDBC transaction isolation levels for setTransactionIsolation().

### Table 16-1
### JDBC Transaction Isolation Levels for setTransactionIsolation()

| Transaction Isolation Level | Description |
| --- | --- |
| TRANSACTION_READ_UNCOMMITTED | Dirty reads are done |
| TRANSACTION_READ_COMMITTED | Only reads on the current row are repeatable |
| TRANSACTION_REPEATABLE_READ | Reads on all rows of a result are repeatable |
| TRANSACTION_SERIALIZABLE | Reads on all rows of a transaction are repeatable |
| TRANSACTION_NONE | Transactions are not supported |

Note that this method cannot be called while in the middle of a transaction:

```
int setTransactionIsolation();
```

It returns the current transaction isolation levels. Note that a value of 0 means that transactions are not supported.

```
Void setAutoCommit(boolean autocommit);
```

setAutoCommit(false) will implicitly begin a new transaction. You have to use either commit() or rollback() to terminate the transaction.

```
boolean getAutoCommit();
```

This method returns the current auto-commit state. False means that user transactions are in use.

```
void commit();
```

This method completes the transaction. All changes made since the previous transaction termination (committed or rolled back) are made permanent. All transaction locks are released.

```
void rollback();
```

All changes made since the previous transaction termination (committed or rolled back) are dropped. This method "undoes" the current transaction statements. All transaction locks are released.

```
void setAutoClose(boolean autoClose);
```

When the connection is in auto-close mode, all its PreparedStatements, Callable Statements, and ResultSets are closed when the transaction is committed or rolled back. This is the default behavior, but you can disable it by passing false as the parameter. Note that some databases allow these objects to remain open across commits, whereas other databases close them.

```
boolean getAutoClose();
```

This method returns the current auto-close state for this connection.

## Three-tiered design

Although the two-tiered architecture is widespread today, another design is becoming more common. To avoid embedding the application's logic at both the database side and the client side, a third software tier may be inserted, as shown in Figure 16-18:

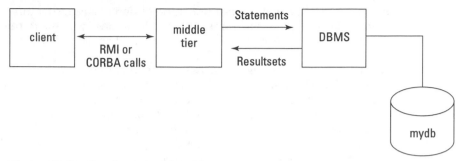

**Figure 16-18:** The three-tiered architecture

In three-tiered architectures, most of the business logic is located in the middle tier. One of the reasons for doing this is simple: it is easier to implement light changes in the logic whenever the business activity or business rules change because only the middle tier must be adapted.

A complete study of three-tiered architectures involving a database management system is beyond the scope of this chapter. However, we can mention the primary directions in which this architecture is headed:

The middle tier will show a number of functionalities to the clients using a well-defined API. These functionalities may be defined after the business services that the client has to access to perform its role. Methods such as getAverageSalary(), getListOfEmployees(), setNewEmployee(), and getEmployeesByDepartment() are examples of such business-oriented services. These methods will return business objects — Java objects defining an Employee, a SetOfEmployees, a Department, a Company, a Product, a ProductCatalog, a PriceList, and so on. Clients will then simply invoke these methods to send or retrieve these business objects, or to perform some processing irrelevant to them, but encapsulated in a business service. Speaking of processing that is irrelevant to clients, consider the following business service: ProductCatalog.sendToCustomerByEmail(). It can easily be written once and then be reused everywhere!

The middleware of choice for such an architecture is a simple, lightweight remote method invocation protocol such as RMI or CORBA on top of IIOP. These protocols are extremely simple to use from Java, but that's a whole other story!

## The JDBC optional package

The java.sql package is part of the standard Java API that we have discussed in this chapter. The JDBC API includes another set of APIs that are not part of standard Java. This part of JDBC is referred to as the standard extension API, or the

*"JDBC Optional Package."* Not all drivers support the optional package features, but the ones that do, make a set of new features and functionalities available to the application developer. This section provides an overview of some of these features.

One of the first steps in using JDBC is to create a connection to the database. As you have learned, this is done by first specifying an address in a URL-like format and then making use of the available methods. The URL may contain items like table names, usernames, and passwords. The problem with this approach is that if one of these parameters changes, the program needs to be modified and recompiled. There is no isolation between the program and the details of database connectivity. JDBC's `DataSource` interface provides this isolation if needed. A `DataSource`, usually made accessible through JNDI, contains the information and logic needed to connect to a particular database. The application uses a `DataSource` to acquire a connection to the database but it does not have to know all the details of that connection. Here is how a connection through a `DataSource` may work:

```
Context ctx = new InitialContext();
DataSource ds = (DataSource)ctx.lookup("jdbc/Inventory");
Connection conn = ds.getConnection("username", "password");
```

Since JNDI is used to dynamically get the connection, the physical server hosting the database or the port number can change without modifying the application. JNDI will always provide the correct information to the application.

Another feature of the JDBC Optional Package is connection pooling. Obtaining a database connection is a relatively slow operation and applications usually frequently need to obtain and release connections. A middleware application, for example, has to make frequent database connections on behalf of the users. The number of concurrent connections is less than the total number of users because at any given time, not everyone is going to access the database. This is where connection pooling is useful. Connection pooling involves the creation of a group, or *"pool"* of open database connections, and connection requests are then satisfied by returning a connection from the pool instead of creating a new one for each request. When a connection is released by application, it's returned to the pool instead of being closed and can be used again later. This approach eliminates the overhead involved in creating a new connection for each request and allows applications to run more quickly. While JDBC 1.x included no connection-pooling API, the Optional Package does. Remember, it's up to the vendors to implement the interfaces specified for connection pooling, so check the documentation that comes with your JDBC driver.

Another feature of the JDBC 2.0 optional package is the `Rowset` interface. A `Rowset` is similar to a `ResultSet` with some differences. Unlike a ResultSet, a Rowset is serializable, which means it can be sent across the network from one machine to another. Another feature of Rowsets is that they are self-contained. They will connect to the database just long enough to get the data they need, and subsequent connections are made as needed to update the database. Finally, Rowsets support bound properties. Just like bound properties in JavaBeans, a Rowset can notify listeners when one or more of the items it contains changes.

The other major part of the Optional Package is support for distributed transactions. Large applications access data that's spread across multiple databases. Therefore, it is necessary to commit changes to multiple databases at the same time. This is accomplished using a distributed transaction, which is usually handled by a transaction manager. The optional package includes interfaces that allow a transaction manager to use database connections in a two-phase commit.

## The Future of Java Database Connectivity – Java Blend

Java Blend provides mappings between Java classes and relational tables. Developers can choose a mapping optimized for the expected kinds of queries, which better represent the underlying design of the database. Java Blend includes a mapping tool, which performs the mapping, and uses schema information such as foreign keys to determine a default mapping that can be enhanced by the user. Java Blend includes the following abilities:

✦ Handles one-to-one, one-to-many, and many-to-many relationships. Foreign keys in the database are mapped to references in Java.

✦ Automatically infers inheritance relationships among tables, or creates them for Java subclasses.

✦ Maps one class to multiple tables, or multiple classes to one table, through various partitioning algorithms.

✦ Easily ports between DBMS products. Because the Java Blend programmer's interface is specifically designed to conform to the ODMG (Object Data Management Group)standard for Object/Relational mappings and object databases, it is easy to port to various DBMS products. (See www.odmg.org for more information on ODMG standards).

✦ Uses any DBMS for which JDBC or ODBC-compliant drivers have been defined. Java Blend implements ODMG on top of JDBC, bridging these higher-level and lower-level standards.

For more information on Java Blend, refer to Sun's Java Web site at http://java.sun.com.

# Summary

This chapter covered the Java Database Connectivity API, part of the core Java API. We have introduced JDBC and explained how to connect to databases and perform queries and updates. Important points to remember when you use the JDBC include these:

✦ The Java Database Connectivity API is the universal way to connect to a database from Java, and it is a key enabler for real client/server capabilities using Java.

✦ We learned how to connect to relational databases using specific JDBC drivers and JDBC URLs to locate these databases.

✦ Database queries and updates require diverse approaches to the retrieval of resultsets, using column indexes and column names.

✦ The JDBC API reference section listed the API briefly.

✦ Advanced techniques such as prepared statements, stored procedures, and database transaction management can help you build more robust database client applications.

✦ The three-tiered design can easily be implemented by using JDBC behind your servers.

✦     ✦     ✦

# Looking out the Windshield: User Interaction

# Abstract Windowing Toolkit (AWT) Overview

**U**ntil now, the programs we've created have lacked a true graphical user interface (GUI). However, to create really compelling and useful software programs with Java, you're likely to need to implement one. After all, what good is a program without buttons, scroll bars, text fields, menus, check boxes, windows, and other GUI goodies?

To be fair, you can do quite a bit without a GUI (as Perl, DOS and Linux programmers are quick to point out). However, whether you're creating Web applets or standalone applications, chances are good that you'll need a GUI component at some point, even if it's only a simple button. In addition, you must understand how to handle the events generated by your user interfaces.

This chapter provides a high-level introduction to Java's low-level user interface and event-handling classes, known formally as the Abstract Windowing Toolkit or the Abstract Window Toolkit (AWT). The AWT is quite large and complex, as you'll see. As a result, we've broken the discussion of it into several chapters. In this chapter, you learn about the AWT in a general sense: how it's organized, what it can do, and the basic concepts you need to understand to use it. In the chapters that follow, we put the pedal to the metal and make good use of the things you learn here.

**Note**    Depending on who you talk to, the "W" in AWT stands for either "windowing" or "window." Both are correct; documentation on Sun's own Java Web site (http://java.sun.com/) flip-flops between the two. We tend to favor "windowing," as it is term that lends itself to a broader description, whereas "window" sounds as if it's limited to creating only window objects (which certainly is not the case with the AWT).

# AWT versus JFC and Swing

You'll notice that we refer to AWT as a collection of *fundamental* Java user interface (UI) classes; they're not the only game in town when it comes to creating user interfaces for your Java programs, not by a long shot. AWT has been the foundation for Java user interface programming and event handling since it was originally introduced with Java 1.0. After its initial debut, however, the AWT classes proved to be overly cumbersome when it came to creating sophisticated Java applications.

Although quite adequate for relatively simple programs such as you're creating now, the AWT struggled early in its life because it is based on a *heavyweight*, or *peer-based*, windowing system. Peers act as the glue between the AWT classes that you use and the underlying operating system: For every graphical AWT object that you create (such as windows, buttons, check boxes, menus, and so forth), a corresponding peer object is created by the operating system. As a result, the GUI that you create with AWT will look and feel like a native application because it really does use native windowing elements of the underlying system.

In other words, AWT applications will look slightly different on varying platforms because they will take on the look and feel of the platform on which they are running. This, in fact, was a major selling point of Java in the early years. Developers were lured to Java in large part because it gave them the ability to write and maintain one body of source code that could execute on every Java-enabled computer system, sporting a "native" look and feel that the user was already familiar with.

Unfortunately, Java failed to completely satisfy the promise of cross-platform applications until Java 2 was released primarily because of problems related to the AWT. Specifically, peers take a toll on performance and cross-platform usability. Because a native peer object is created for every AWT windowing object that you instantiate, a great deal of Java's internal overhead goes into managing these objects. To make matters worse, there are slight variations in how such items actually look and act across operating systems. A popup menu on a Macintosh, for example, doesn't look or act precisely like a popup menu on Windows or Linux. They may be close, but they're not exactly the same. A lot of little differences can quickly add up to big problems, especially when it comes to creating an appealing and truly usable interface.

In addition, Java 1.0 was based on a relatively simple event handling mechanism wasn't suited for sophisticated or complex applications. Consequently, developers often spend a great deal of time testing their AWT programs across a variety of systems in order to ensure that they look and act as they should when deployed to the public. Often, platform-specific tweaks must be made to a program's AWT code so that it performs as expected across all major platforms (this frustrating process led many early developers to deride Java as a "Write Once, Debug Everywhere" technology, not "Write Once, Run Anywhere" that Sun had originally positioned it as).

To solve the problems associated with heavyweight, peer-based windowing, Sun later introduced a higher level suite of GUI facilities known as the Java Foundation Classes (JFC) and Swing components that were layered on top of AWT. Starting with Java 1.1, JFC and Swing emerged as optional packages that made creating user interfaces easier and more reliable. Instead of relying on peers for every windowing object, JFC and Swing instead take a lightweight approach in which only a window is created from a peer. Everything else that appears in the window (buttons, scroll bars, check boxes, menus, etc.) is painted directly onto the window's canvas using Java-only techniques; heavyweight peers need not apply!

At about the same time, Java's original *hierarchical* event mechanism was complimented with a much more sophisticated *delegation* event model. Beginning with Java 1.1 the AWT was overhauled to support both event models, as explained later in this chapter. By revamping Java's event-handling mechanism, while also introducing a lightweight suite of graphical user interface facilities, Sun managed to get its original vision of Java as a cross-platform application development environment back on track.

Today, JFC and Swing classes are built into Java 1.3; they are no longer separate packages, meaning you can guarantee that every user who has Java 1.3 also has JFC and Swing. Similarly, the new event model has been part of the AWT since Java 1.1, so it's also guaranteed to be available whenever you run application runs in a Java 1.1 environment or higher.

Indeed, the AWT and Swing are considered to be *part* of the larger suite of JFC APIs. JFC represents an all encompassing suite of user interface classes, and includes:

✦ JFC and Swing components, offering a lightweight alternative to peers.

✦ Plugable look and feel capabilities that developers can employ to give their users the ability to dynamically change the look and feel of an application while it is running.

✦ Accessibility classes that let applications interact with screen readers, screen magnifiers, and speech recognition devices.

✦ Java 2D API, which support robust two-dimensional graphics capabilities including enhanced paint styles, definable shapes, and rendering control.

✦ Drag-and-drop support, both for pure Java applications and also with native applications.

The AWT, in particular, offers developers:

✦ User interface components (windows, buttons, scroll bars, menus, and so on).

✦ Graphics and imaging facilities (including drawing, shape, color, and font classes).

✦ Layout managers that let you place components in windows in flexible manner independent of window size and screen resolution.

✦ Two different event-handling models: hierarchical and delegation (although we'll use the most current, more powerful delegation event model in this book).

✦ Data transfer capabilities that support cut, copy, and paste via the "clipboard" mechanism of the native platform.

In the chapters that follow you'll learn how to use the most essential JFC classes offered by Java 1.3, although JFC is so vast that we'd need at least another two Bible-sized books to cover it all! Instead, we focus on the fundamentals, giving you everything you need to know to create rich graphical user interfaces and event handling mechanisms for your Java programs. We'll begin by taking a look as several of the fundamental classes that make up the AWT, as you'll use them in just about every GUI or event-driven program that you create.

## Optional Packages and Java Web Start

JFC, Swing and AWT classes that are built into Java 1.3 are focused exclusively on two-dimensional graphics and imaging, or simply "2D". An optional package called *Java 3D*, however, is available should you require three-dimensional (3D) graphics capabilities. Optional packages (previously known as "standard extensions") are packages of classes that Sun offers to extend the base capabilities of the Java platform. A number of optional packages have already been released by Sun, offering diverse capabilities such as 3D graphics, integrated email, advanced imaging, rich media creation and playback, cryptography, help systems, and more. To get your hands on these and other freely available optional packages visit http://java.sun.com/products/OV_stdExt.html , and http://java.sun.com/products/javawebstart/ to learn how you can use Java Web Start technology to create a 1-click Web installation process for your applications.

# Introducing the Abstract Windowing Toolkit

The Java AWT is actually a generic user interface toolkit, a collection of classes that lets you create platform-independent user interfaces. Just as Java programs are platform-independent, capable of running on any computer that has the Java run-time system installed, so too are the user interfaces created with the AWT.

You'll note that we didn't use the term *graphical* user interface to describe the AWT. This is because most people associate only a specific set of elements with a GUI, namely those parts of that a program that present windows and their contents (such as scroll bars, menus, and buttons).

Although the term *Windowing Toolkit* might lead you to believe that's all the AWT does, it really goes above and beyond the typical GUI to encompass all aspects of a user interface — not just GUI elements. An image that you draw on the screen, for example, is considered part of the user interface). Whatever users *see* and, many believe, whatever they *hear*, is part and parcel of a user interface.

The AWT actually includes methods that enable your program to access and play audio clips. Because we've used these in earlier chapters, we'll stay focused on the portions of the AWT's main `java.awt` package that provide a visual user interface and handle events.

A UI that you create using the AWT looks and acts appropriately for any platform on which it runs. With Java, you don't have to worry about writing code for a specific platform. And thanks to the AWT, you don't have to bother learning specific UI routines, either.

The AWT doesn't attempt to support every UI feature of every platform. Its aim is more modest: to provide the minimum necessary to develop a complete interface that is functional and consistent across all platforms. Even so, the AWT encompasses dozens of classes. Windows, dialog boxes, menus, buttons, scroll bars, text fields, check boxes, and drawing and painting canvases are but a few of the GUI components the AWT offers. In addition, it provides an event mechanism that allows your UI to respond to user input, such as mouse clicks and key presses.

The AWT is designed to be extensible, allowing developers to subclass existing AWT classes and create their own, special-purpose GUI elements (animated 3D scroll bars, anyone?). Thanks to platform-independence, the result is a brand-spanking new GUI widget that looks smashing on every user's computer.

This assumes, of course, that whatever special-purpose GUI element you create is, in fact, smashing. If it is dull and lifeless, it will look dull and lifeless on all platforms. But with Java, at least you have to write dull, lifeless GUI widgets only once, rather than having to write a special version for each platform on which your dull, lifeless program runs.

Cross-
Reference

Java 1.3 introduces a number of enhancements to the AWT, including support for multiple monitors (giving applications the ability to display on multiple screens), a "Robot" class (`java.awt.Robot`) designed for automated testing of your GUI code, faster screen painting, two new classes in the `java.awt.print` package (`JobAttributes` and `PageAttributes`) that give developers fine-grained control over print jobs and paper settings, and more. For details visit the Java 1.3 AWT enhancements page at `http://java.sun.com/j2se/1.3/docs/guide/awt/enhancements.html`, and `http://java.sun.com/j2se/1.3/docs/` to get your hands on Sun's full suite of Java 1.3 documentation.

## Fundamental organization

The AWT is quite complex and so large that it is organized into a main package (`java.awt`) and eleven supporting packages listed in Table 17-1. Although you won't use all of these packages when you are just beginning to learn Java (and possibly never, as several offer very specific and highly focused facilities that you may not need in your programs), they're there if you need them; these packages are part of every Java 2 version 1.3 implementation. We'll begin by exploring the fundamental organization of the `java.awt`, as it's the primary AWT package around which all others revolve.

### Table 17-1
### AWT Packages

| Package | Description |
| --- | --- |
| java.awt | Main AWT package used to create graphical user interfaces. |
| java.awt.color | Used to create color space classes. |
| java.awt.datatransfer | Used to transfer data between and within applications. |
| java.awt.dnd | Used to implement a "drag-and-drop" information transfer mechanism. |
| java.awt.event | Used to handle events generated by the AWT components. |
| java.awt.font | Used to create and manipulate fonts. |
| java.awt.geom | Used to implement two-dimensional (2D) graphics. |
| java.awt.im | Used to support text editing components through various "input methods" such as foreign language keyboards, handwriting, and even speech recognition devices. |

| Package | Description |
|---|---|
| java.awt.im.spi | Used to support the input method package described above. |
| java.awt.image | Used to create and manipulate images. |
| java.awt.image.renderable | Used to create rendering-independent images. |
| java.awt.print | Used to add basic printing capabilities to Java programs. |

## The java.awt package

The main java.awt package contains most of the classes and interfaces for creating graphical user interfaces. In this package, all the classes for creating windows, menus, buttons, check boxes, and other essential GUI elements are found. See Tables 17-2 and 17-3 for a listing of the interfaces and several essential classes defined in java.awt (keep in mind that Table 17-3 contains only a *very* small sampling of java.awt classes, as the package is immense; visit the Java 1.3 documentation area described earlier for a comprehensive overview of this API)

### Table 17-2
### Package java.awt Interfaces

| Interfaces | Description |
|---|---|
| ActiveEvent | Supports events that dispatch themselves. |
| Adjustable | Supports objects that have an adjustable numeric value. |
| Composite | Used to compose a draw primitive with underlying graphics area. |
| CompositeContext | Encapsulates an optimized environment compositing operations. |
| ItemSelectable | Supports objects that contain selectable items. |
| LayoutManager | Supports objects that know how to lay out containers. |
| LayoutManager2 | Supports constraint-based layout managers. |
| MenuContainer | Superclass of every menu-related container. |
| Paint | Supports color patterns for Graphics2D operations. |
| PaintContext | Supports color patterns in device space for Graphics2D fill or stroke operations. |
| PrintGraphics | Ancestor of classes that define a graphics context for a printed page. |

*Continued*

## Table 17-2 *(continued)*

| Interfaces | Description |
| --- | --- |
| Shape | Supports objects that represent some form of geometric shape. |
| Stroke | Allows Graphics2D objects to obtain a decorated outline, or stylistic representation of the outline, of a specified Shape. |
| Transparency | Supports common transparency modes for implementing classes. |

## Table 17-3
## Essential java.awt Classes

| Classes | Description |
| --- | --- |
| AWTEvent | Granddaddy of all AWT event classes. |
| Button | Labeled button component. |
| Canvas | Generic canvas component (must be subclassed to produce some functionality). |
| Checkbox | Graphical user interface element that has an on/off (true or false) state. |
| CheckboxGroup | Set of check boxes that allow for multiple selections. |
| CheckboxMenuItem | Check box that represents a choice in a menu. |
| Choice | Pop-up menu of choices, where current choice is displayed as the menu title. |
| Color | Color class that encapsulate colors in a variety of color spaces. |
| Component | Generic component from which special purpose components are derived (Button, Checkbox, Choice, Container, and so on). |
| Container | Generic container component that can contain other components (such as a Window, Panel, or Applet) |
| Dialog | Dialog box (a window that takes input from the user). |
| Dimension | Encapsulates width and height values. |
| Event | Encapsulates events from the graphical user interface. |
| FlowLayout | Default layout manager used to position components added to a container. |
| Font | Collection of glyphs (typographic font). |

| Classes | Description |
|---|---|
| Frame | Top-level window having a title and border. |
| Graphics | Abstract base class for all graphic contexts for various devices. |
| Graphics2D | Extended Graphics class for sophisticated control over geometry, coordinate transformations, color management, and text layout. |
| Image | Abstract superclass class to all graphical image classes. |
| JobAttributes | Encapsulates attributes that control a print job. |
| Label | Single line of read-only text. |
| List | Scrolling list of text items. |
| Menu | Menu that is a component of a MenuBar. |
| MenuBar | Menu bar bound to a Frame. |
| MenuItem | Item in a Menu object. |
| PageAttributes | Attributes that control output of a printed page. |
| Panel | The most generic form of container. |
| Point | An x,y coordinate. |
| Polygon | List of x and y coordinates. |
| PopupMenu | Menu that can dynamically pop up at a specified location in a component. |
| PrintJob | Abstract class that initiates and executes a print job. |
| Rectangle | Rectangle defined by x, y, width, and height. |
| Robot | Native input event generator used for automated GUI testing. |
| Scrollbar | Scroll bar component. |
| ScrollPane | A container that provides scrolling support for its child component. |
| SystemColor | Provides symbolic names for the colors of UI features, such as buttons, captions, control highlights and shadows, and so on. |
| TextArea | Multi-line area used to display text. |
| TextComponent | Component that allows the editing of some text. |
| TexturePaint | Image painting object that fills a Shape with a texture image. |
| TextField | Component that allows the editing of a single line of text. |
| Window | Top-level window having no borders or menu bar. |

The basic `java.awt` class hierarchy is shown in Figure 17-1.

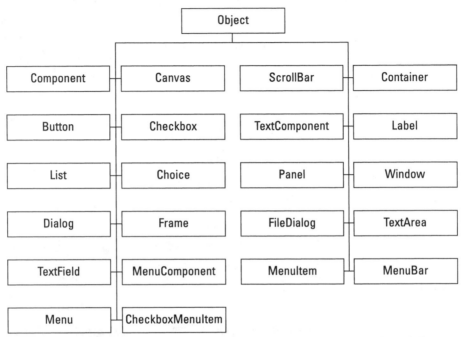

**Figure 17-1:** The java.awt class hierarchy is comprised of a large number of classes that together form the AWT.

As you can see, the `java.awt` package contains a number of classes that together form the AWT. There are four main aspects to the class hierarchy:

✦ Primitive graphics

✦ Colors

✦ Fonts

✦ Standard GUI elements ("widgets")

Let's take a closer look at each.

## Primitive Graphics

The main `java.awt` package includes `Graphics`, a class that defines a primitive set of drawing methods that enable you to draw and fill lines, rectangles, ovals, polygons, and arcs. These can be drawn and filled by using a preset range of colors or by using ones you define yourself. (See Figure 17-2.) In addition, the `java.awt` package provides methods for clearing, clipping, and copying the drawing area, giving you the ability to manipulate images and graphics after they are placed on the screen.

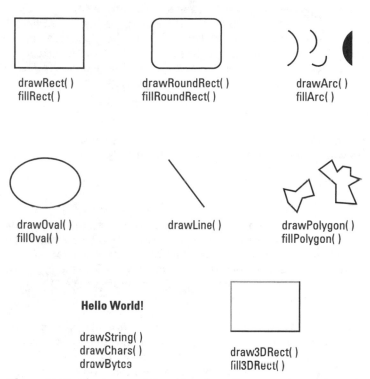

**Figure 17-2:** The java.awt.Graphics class allows you to create and draw primitive graphics.

The AWT contains an abstract class called Image and a subpackage of classes (java.awt.image), both for dealing with bitmap images. Initially, you won't work with these classes directly because the Graphics class implements all the methods you'll need to use bitmap images.

In addition to using the image methods provided in the Graphics class, you can always create a subclass of Image for your own purposes. The Image class contains abstract methods that you must implement for a specific platform. For example, you might create a subclass of Image to create a class that allows you to use BMP (BitMaP) format images.

At times, the only way to tell if we're talking about the Image class (java.awt.Image) or the image package (java.awt.image) is by the capitalization of the word Image for a class. Class names begin, by convention, with a capital letter. Packages, however, are typically all lowercase.

## sRGB vs. RGB

The Standard Default Color Space for the Internet, better known as sRGB, is a proposed enhancement to the traditional Red Green Blue (RGB) color space that has dominated computer graphics in the recent past. Proposed by Hewlett-Packard and Microsoft in 1996, sRGB is gaining traction in the world of Internet graphics because it is a modern color space that is also backwards compatible with previous color space models. For details, read the sRGB proposal online at http://www.w3.org/pub/WWW/Graphics/Color/sRGB.html

Currently, the AWT supports GIF (.gif ) and JPEG (.jpg) image formats. You can easily retrieve and draw graphics of both formats, either directly from the local hard disk or over the network.

### Colors

The main `java.awt` package contains a `Color` class that is used to create color objects that are represented, by default, in the sRGB (Standard Red, Green, and Blue) color space. Alternately, developers can call upon classes in the `java.awt.color` package to create colors that correspond to another color space, such as traditional RGB (Red Green Blue), HSV (Hue Saturation Value), CMYK (Cyan Magenta Yellow blacK) and many others.

As you'll learn in the next chapter, you can set the color of the `Graphics` object to change the color in which primitive graphics are drawn. In other words, by changing colors in the Graphics object you can alter the actual color of your ovals, rectangles, lines, ovals, and other primitive graphics. In addition, you can change a component's foreground and background colors if the default colors don't suit your tastes.

### Fonts

Many graphics systems treat fonts as graphics, and the AWT is no different. After all, fonts are the graphical representation of characters. If characters, strings, numbers, and letters were never displayed on the screen, there would be no need for fonts. However, as soon as you output them to the screen, they technically become graphics.

With the `Font` class (`java.awt.Font`), you can output text using any typeface you want; for example, Times New Roman, Courier, Helvetica, and Zapf Dingbats. You can also choose from styles such as regular, bold, italic, and underlined, and point sizes such as 8pt, 12pt, 36pt, and 72pt. Figure 17-3 shows an example of text output in a number of faces, styles, and point sizes.

Although you can tell Java to use any font you like, be warned that not all users have the same fonts on their computers as you do. Although you may be able to see a specific font when the applet is running on your computer, others may see a substitute that doesn't look anything like what you want! Play it safe and be conservative in your font choices as describe in the next chapter.

**Figure 17-3:** The java.awt.Font class enables you to draw text on the screen in a variety of faces (fonts), sizes, and styles.

## Standard GUI Elements

When most people think of the AWT, they think of it in terms of a graphical user interface toolkit. Indeed, the AWT is often considered a GUI toolkit simply because of the name. After all, what do you think of when you hear the word *windowing*? You think of all the widgets that usually come along for the ride: menus, scroll bars, buttons, text fields, check boxes, and Bill Gates

All such widgets, including windows and dialog boxes themselves, descend from the Component class as illustrated by Figure 17-4. To keep our terminology clear and simple, we refer to anything that ultimately falls under the Container class (panels, applets, windows, dialog boxes, file dialog boxes, and frames) as containers. You can put other components and containers in them.

As for the buttons, scroll bars, text fields, and other user interface elements, we'll refer to them all as widgets. If the term *widgets* gets under your skin, feel free to substitute your favorite term every time we say it (perhaps doohickey, dealybobber, or thingamajig?).

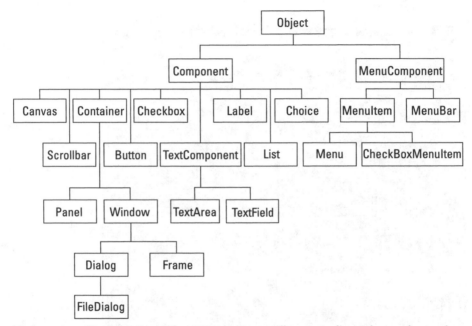

**Figure 17-4:** The majority of the AWT classes you'll use are direct descendants of the java.awt.Component class.

It's not that we mean to belittle these essential creatures, but the term *element* is a bit too stuffy and serious to use when referring to buttons, scroll bars, and their ilk. And we don't want to refer to them as components because we use that term when talking about anything that falls under the Component class.

Some folks might like the term *control*, which most of these user interface items are, but we prefer to group them all under a more general term, since some of them (labels and canvases, specifically) don't actually control anything. More importantly, we just can't let go of the word *widget* when it comes to classifying these things. Whenever we see one, the words *widget . . . Widget . . . WIDGET*!! insidiously enters our minds, refusing to go away. Sadly, we are compelled to pass this compulsion on to you.

When referring to both containers and widgets, we'll use the term *component*. With this in mind, we now have a simple and effective jargon for AWT elements:

✦ Containers: Any component that can *contain* another component. Panels, applets, windows, dialog boxes, file dialog boxes, and frames are all examples of containers (panels are the most simplistic of all containers, while applets are arguably the most sophisticated).

✦ Widgets: Buttons, scroll bars, text fields, choices, and similar interface elements; need we say more?

✦ Components: Every descendant of the `Component` class.

As you'll soon see, using the AWT to build a GUI is quite easy. You just create a container, if you even need one (more on that later), and slap on widgets to your heart's desire. Of course, they'll do you no good whatsoever, but they sure look cool.

What's this? Worthless widgets? Delinquent doohickeys? Trivial thingamajigs? Yes, indeed. They may look pretty, but don't be deceived: It's all fluff. Clicking them will get you nowhere — until, of course, you respond to the events they generate.

# Handling Events

Events enable your program to interact with a user. (See the "About Events" sidebar.) Whenever a user interacts with an element of your program's user interface through the keyboard, the mouse, a button, or a menu item, the element generates an event. To react to an event, it's necessary to create some code that executes whenever the event occurs — this is called *trapping the event*. By trapping events, your program can respond to the user's input in a meaningful way.

In the early days of programming, event trapping was considered by many to be cruel and inhumane. Reports of helpless events trapped for days on end in event handlers flooded newsgroups, sparking public outcry. Feeding the flames of this controversy, some hackers reported coming across events that had actually gnawed off portions of their data structure to get free.

Today, we know that event trapping is completely safe and harmless, causing no damage or trauma to the event whatsoever. Many times, the event is simply released after being gently probed for information by the handler — set free to crawl up the hierarchy, where others might trap and inspect it as well. If the event actually reaches the top of the hierarchy, it's released into the wild since the system has no use for it. In cases where the event must be terminated for the good of the program, however, it's done quickly and in a humane manner; the event doesn't feel a thing.

## About Events

An *event* refers to any unpredictable change of state in a program's environment. Two kinds of events occur in a typical environment: physical events and simulated events. A *physical* event corresponds to a change of state in the system's physical environment, such as a user's mouse movement. A *simulated* event corresponds to a change of state in a simulated environment, such as a graphical user interface. For example, window systems, such as Windows 95 and Motif, generate a simulated event whenever a user interacts with a visual control, such as a push button or a menu item.

Semantic events are an important subclass of simulated events. A *semantic* event conveys a specific meaning to the application program and is often defined independently of a particular type of widget. For example, in the Java environment, several different types of widgets, including buttons, menu items, and check boxes, can generate a type of semantic event known as an action event. An *action* event means "Perform the action associated with this component."

Every system provides a standard mechanism for detecting, queuing, and responding to events. This mechanism, known as an *event model,* typically divides event-handling duties between the operating system and the application. The operating system handles event detection and queuing because these tasks are generic. The application program handles the task of responding to events in specific ways, as dictated by the application.

Java provides two system-independent mechanisms, or models for handling events, known as the *hierarchical* model and the *delegation* model. The hierarchical model, so-called because it assigns event-handling duties to a program's widget-container hierarchy, came first (with Java 1.0) and is today considered obsolete. However, at this point, only standalone Java interpreters fully support its replacement, the delegation model, which lets a program delegate event-handling chores to any properly qualified object. If you want to create an applet that can run on older Web browser, you must use the hierarchical model, at least until more browsers fully support the delegation model. Because you may have occasion to use either model, you will learn how to use both in this chapter.

**Tip**    Use the original hierarchical event model when creating applets that must run under Netscape Navigator or Internet Explorer version 3, or earlier, and the new delegation event model if you are certain that your users will be running version 4 or later.

From a practical perspective, the main difference between the two models lies in how a program traps events. In the hierarchical model, a program traps events by overriding certain default methods defined by the AWT's `Component` class. For example, if you want to trap a button click, you override the button's `action()` method or the `action()` method of its container. With the delegation model, on the other hand, you trap events by registering event handlers, called *listeners*, with the components in which the events occur. For example, if you want to trap a button click, you register an action listener with the button. In either case, you need to have a basic understanding of how the model operates to use the model successfully. So let's explore each model in turn.

# The hierarchical model

The hierarchical model is an object-oriented model: it treats events as objects and as if they occur in objects, specifically UI components, such as buttons or panels. From your perspective as a Java developer, the most important feature of the hierarchical model is that it provides a means for you to trap and respond to events as they occur in your program's UI. The way you do this is by overriding default AWT event-handling methods, replacing them with your own. Which methods you override depends on the type of events you want to trap and where they occur in your program's UI. To know which methods to override, you need to know the basics of the hierarchical model event-handling mechanism.

The mechanism works as follows. Whenever an event occurs, the Java interpreter calls the `handleEvent()` method of the UI component in which the event occurs, passing it an instance of the `java.awt.Event` class. The method processes the event, using information about the event provided by the fields of the `Event` object, which includes the event's type (`ID`), the object in which it occurred (`target`), the time it occurred, and other data specific to that type of event, such as the position of the mouse in the case of mouse events. (See Table 17-4.)

### Table 17-4
### java.awt.Event Instance Variables

| Variable | Description |
| --- | --- |
| `int ID` | Unique event identifier (refer to Table 17-5). |
| `Object target` | Specfic "target" of an event (`CheckBox`, `Button`, `ScrollBar`, `Text Field` objects, and so on). Use the `instanceof` keyword to find determine the class type of a target. |
| `long when` | Time-stamp (when the event was generated). |
| `int x, int y` | Coordinates (*x,y*) where the event occurred. |
| `int key` | Keyboard key that was pressed (keyboard events). |
| `Object arg` | Arbitrary argument associated with an event (such as the name of the button selected). |
| `int modifiers` | State of the modifier keys when an event was generated. |

The `Event` class simplifies the job of `handleEvent()` by defining constants for every type of event recognized by the hierarchical model. (See Table 17-5.)

The AWT supports the hierarchical model by defining a default `handleEvent()` method in the `Component` class, the ancestral class for all AWT UI components. Every AWT widget either inherits or overrides this default method. Aha! Finally, we've discovered the secret of handling events in the hierarchical method. Just override the `handleEvent()` method of components in which events of interest occur. Actually, the situation is a bit more complicated than that.

## Table 17-5
## Component-Generated Events

| Component | Event ID | Description |
|-----------|----------|-------------|
| Button | ACTION_EVENT | User clicked the button. |
| CheckBox | ACTION_EVENT | User clicked the check box. |
| Choice | ACTION_EVENT | User selected an item. |
| Component | GOT_FOCUS | Component received input focus. |
| Component | LOST_FOCUS | Component lost input focus. |
| Component | KEY_ACTION | User pressed a function key. |
| Component | KEY_ACTION_RELEASE | User released a function key. |
| Component | KEY_PRESS | User pressed a key. |
| Component | KEY_RELEASE | User released a key. |
| Component | MOUSE_ENTER | Mouse entered the component. |
| Component | MOUSE_EXIT | Mouse exited the component. |
| Component | MOUSE_DOWN | User pressed a mouse button. |
| Component | MOUSE_UP | User released a mouse button. |
| Component | MOUSE_MOVE | User moved the mouse. |
| Component | MOUSE_DRAG | User dragged the mouse. |
| List | ACTION_EVENT | User double-clicked a list item. |
| List | LIST_SELECT | User selected a list item. |
| List | LIST_DESELECT | User deselected a list item. |
| MenuItem | ACTION_EVENT | User selected a menu item. |
| ScrollBar | SCROLL_LINE_UP | User requested scroll line up. |
| ScrollBar | SCROLL_LINE_DOWN | User requested scroll line down. |
| ScrollBar | SCROLL_PAGE_UP | User requested scroll page up. |
| ScrollBar | SCROLL_PAGE_DOWN | User requested scroll page down. |

| Component | Event ID | Description |
|-----------|----------|-------------|
| ScrollBar | SCROLL_ABSOLUTE | User requested an absolute change. |
| TextField | ACTION_EVENT | User pressed Enter or Return. |
| Window | WINDOW_DESTROY | Window was destroyed. |
| Window | WINDOW_ICONIFY | Window was iconified. |
| Window | WINDOW_DEICONIFY | Window was deiconified. |
| Window | WINDOW_MOVED | Window was moved. |

For one thing, the AWT's default handleEvent() method acts as an event-handling switch, diverting certain common types of events, specifically keyboard, mouse, and action events, to more specific event-handling methods. For these types of events, it makes more sense to override the more specific default methods. (See Table 17-6.) Moreover, if the event is not an action or mouse event, or the more specific method does not handle the event, the default handleEvent() method kicks the event upstairs to the handleEvent() method of its containing object, where the whole process is repeated on a higher level in your UI's hierarchy (hence, the name hierarchical model). What this means is that it is possible for you to handle all events at a high level in the hierarchy. In fact, in the case of applets, you can handle all events at the highest level, namely, the applet itself. That's because unless your applet spawns secondary windows, it is the top-level container in its UI hierarchy.

### Table 17-6
### Essential Event-Handling Methods

| Event ID | Method | Description |
|----------|--------|-------------|
| ACTION_EVENT | action(Event, Object) | Event indicating menu item, button, check box, or the contents of a choice, text, or list control has been interacted with. |
| KEY_PRESS | keyDown(Event, int) | Key-press keyboard event. |
| KEY_RELEASE | keyUp(Event, int) | Key-release keyboard event. |
| KEY_ACTION | keyDown(Event, int) | Non-ASCII (i.e. function) key pressed. |
| KEY_ACTION_RELEASE | keyUp(Event, int) | Non-ASCII key released. |

*Continued*

| Table 17-6 (continued) | | |
|---|---|---|
| **Event ID** | **Method** | **Description** |
| MOUSE_DOWN | mouseDown(Event, int, int) | Mouse-down event. |
| MOUSE_UP | mouseUp(Event, int, int) | Mouse-up event. |
| MOUSE_MOVE | mouseMove(Event, int, int) | Mouse-move event. |
| MOUSE_ENTER | mouseEnter(Event, int, int) | Mouse-enter event. |
| MOUSE_EXIT | mouseExit(Event, int, int) | Mouse-exit event. |
| MOUSE_DRAG | mouseDrag(Event, int, int) | Mouse-drag (down+move) event. |

When developers use the hierarchical model, they generally elect to handle events at the highest possible level in the UI hierarchy, specifically at the applet level in the case of applets. Here's the reason why: To trap events at a lower level in the hierarchy, you must override the default event-handling methods of the lower-level components. This, in turn, entails creating a new class derived from the appropriate AWT component class, for example, the Button class. If you elect to handle events at a low level, you end up having to create a bunch of new classes, often for no reason other than to customize event handling. In contrast, if you handle events at a higher level, you cut down significantly on the number of new classes you need to create. In the case of applets, you need to create only one new class, namely, a derivative of the AWT's Applet class. This is hardly a burden because as you've seen, developing an applet entails subclassing Applet anyway.

With this in mind, let's take a look at handling a common type of event.

## Handling Action Events

The AWT provides a set of widgets that let a user control various aspects of a Java program. This set includes the widgets defined by the AWT's Button, CheckBox, Choice, List, MenuItem, and TextField classes. The following chapters explore these widgets in detail. For the moment, it's enough for you to know that when a user interacts with any of them—for example, when a user clicks a button or double-clicks a list item—the widget posts an ACTION_EVENT event. You can trap and handle the event by overriding the action() method of the target widget or its container.

As Table 17-6 reveals, when an action event occurs, the handleEvent() method of the relevant component passes two parameters to the action() method: an Event instance and an Object parameter:

```
public boolean action(Event evt, Object what) {
  ...
}
```

The Event instance provides all the information you really need to identify an event. However, as a convenience, handleEvent() passes additional information in the Object parameter that simplifies identifying the event's target, such as the target's label in the case of buttons and menu items. The Object parameter is particularly useful when you assign action-handling chores to an Applet action() method. In this case, the action() method typically must identify the target of an action event to respond appropriately. The Object parameter makes this easy in the case of buttons and menu items. Simply query the Object parameter to find out the button or menu item's label like so:

```
public boolean action(Event evt, Object what)
{
  if (evt.target instanceof Button) { // Button event?
    String buttonName = (String)what; // get button name

      ... // process based on which button it is

    return true; // kill event after handling it
  }

  if (evt.target instanceof Choice) { // Choice event?
    // Get the selected Choice menu item:
    int item = Integer.getInteger((String)what).intValue();

      ... // process based on which item it is

    return true; // kill event after handling it
  }

  return false; // not handled; let it crawl up hierarchy
}
```

Notice that the preceding example returns true when it handles an event. Returning true prevents handleEvent() from passing the event on up the UI hierarchy.

**Tip**  The action() method has been deprecated as of Java 1.1, meaning you shouldn't use it unless your program must run on Java 1.0 systems. If that's not the case, you should instead register your components as an ActionListener for components that fire action events (see "The delegation model" below for details on how to handle events for Java 1.1 and higher). To get detailed information about deprecated (outdated) methods or classes in your programs, simply compile your program with the deprecation switch (javac HelloWorld.java -deprecation).

## Handling Non-action Events

AWT widgets produce other types of events besides action events. If the events are any of the types specified in Table 17-6, you can process them by overriding the corresponding default handler. If you want to trap events for which there is no specific handler—for example, scroll bar or window events—you'll have to override the handleEvent() method of the widget (or its container).

As you have already seen, whenever an event occurs, the Java runtime environment invokes the handleEvent() method of the component in which it occurs, passing it an Event instance. Because the default handleEvent() method automatically passes the event up the widget hierarchy, you can override this method at any convenient point in the hierarchy. The first thing your customized method should do is test the ID field of the Event instance to determine the type of event being processed. If the event is of interest to you, go ahead and process it. Otherwise, invoke the AWT's default handleEvent() method as illustrated below:

```
public boolean handleEvent(Event e)
{
  if (e.id == Event.WINDOW_DESTROY) {

      ...// do window exit cleanup

  return true; // kill event
  }

  return super.handleEvent(e); // let crawl up hierarchy
}
```

Note that a common mistake is to forget to invoke the default AWT handleEvent() method for events not handled by a custom handleEvent() method. This can short-circuit the handling of other events. For example, suppose that your program includes a custom action() method as well as a custom handleEvent() method. If the custom handleEvent() method does not invoke the default handleEvent() method, your custom action() method is not invoked either. As a result, your program ignores all action events, which is probably not what you want to happen.

## The delegation model

Like the hierarchical model, the delegation model is object-oriented: events are objects and occur in objects (widgets, for example). Some significant differences show up, however. For one, unlike the hierarchical model, which defines only one event class, the delegation model defines an entire suite of events (see Table 17-7) derived from a common ancestor, the AWTEvent class.

The AWTEvent class defines the general characteristics of events. The specific classes extend this common definition to include the characteristics of specific types of events, such as mouse events, action events, and so on. Representing events by a class hierarchy instead of a single class is not only more object-oriented, but it also makes it possible for developers to extend the event hierarchy (by defining new subclasses of AWTEvent).

The delegation model differs from the hierarchical model in another important way. The hierarchical model predetermines which object handles events. By contrast, the delegation model lets a program delegate event handling to any object it chooses (hence the name *delegation event model*) as long as that object implements an interface of type EventListener.

An object that implements the EventListener interface, which is defined in the java.util package, is called a *listener*. The jave.awt.event package defines specific listener interfaces for all the event classes defined by the AWT (See Table 17-7.) Each listener interface declares methods for handling a particular class of events. Any object that implements a listener interface can be a listener for the corresponding class of events.

A program delegates event handling to a listener by registering the listener at runtime with a component. A program can register as many listeners with a component as it likes, including multiple listeners for a particular class of events. A program can also remove listeners at any time. Each AWT component provides methods for registering listeners for each of the classes of events that can occur in it. By convention, these methods are named addEVENTListener(), where **EVENT** is the name of the class of event handled by the listener; for example, addActionListener(). Each component also provides methods for removing listeners. By convention, these methods are named removeEVENTListener(), where **EVENT** is the corresponding event class, for example, removeActionListener().

Whenever an event occurs in a component, the component dispatches the event to all the listeners registered for that class of event. If more than one listener is registered for a particular class of events, the component calls the listeners (although not necessarily in the order in which the program registered them). The program dispatches an event by calling a method specifically defined for that event in the corresponding interface.

For example, the MouseListener interface defines mouseClicked(), mouse Entered(), mouseExited(), mousePressed(), and mouseReleased() methods for mouse clicked, entered, exited, pressed, and released events, respectively. Whenever one of the events occurs in a component, the component calls the corresponding method of any previously registered mouse listeners. If the event is a mouse click, for instance, the component calls the mouseClicked() method.

Note that the delegation model does not guarantee that a component will dispatch events to listeners in a particular order. Moreover, when passing an event to multiple listeners, a component makes a fresh copy of the event for each listener. Thus, one listener cannot communicate with another by altering an event's instance variables. The moral is, if you want to set up a chain of event listeners, register only the root of the chain with the component, and make each handler responsible for invoking the next handler in the chain.

Table 17-7
**Delegation Model Event Hierarchy**

| *Class* | *Listener* | *Description* |
|---|---|---|
| ActionEvent | ActionListener | Generated when a user selects a menu item, button, or check box; selects a choice or list element; or presses Enter in a text field. |
| AdjustmentEvent | AdjustmentListener | Generated when the size of an adjustable object, such as a scroll bar, changes. |
| ComponentEvent | ComponentListener | Generated when the layout of a component changes (for internal use only). |
| ContainerEvent | ContainerListener | Generated when a container object changes. |
| FocusEvent | FocusListener | Generated when a widget gains or loses keyboard input focus. |
| InputEvent | n/a | For internal use. |
| ItemEvent | ItemListener | Produced when the user selects a check box or a list or choice item. |
| KeyEvent | KeyListener | Produced by a key-down or key-up event. |
| MouseEvent | MouseListener, | Produced by a mouse event. |
| PaintEvent | n/a | *For internal use by Java.* |
| TextEvent | TextListener | Generated when the contents of a text widget change. |
| WindowEvent | WindowListener | Generated when a window opens or closes or changes its state in some other way. |

## Creating Listeners

Because event handling depends on the application, the delegation model does not define event listeners for you. This is a task you have to perform yourself. The way you define a listener for a specific class of events is by creating a class that implements the corresponding interface. For example, to handle a button click, create a class that implements the methods declared by the ActionListener interface, and then register it with the button as illustrated below:

```
public class MyApplet extends Applet
{
```

```
// "Do" button handler (implemented as inner class):
class DoButtonListener implements ActionListener
{
  public void actionPerformed(Event e) {
      ... // perform "Do" button action
  }
}

class MyApplet extends Applet
{
  // Construct applet:
  public MyApplet {

    // Create "Do" button and register listener:
    Button doButton = new Button("Do");

    // Register button listener:
    doButton.addActionListener(new DoButtonListener());

    // Add button to layout:
    add("Center", doButton);
  }
}
```

## Dedicated versus Nondedicated Listeners

The delegation model gives you a great deal of flexibility in implementing listener interfaces. At one extreme, you can define nondedicated event listeners for each event type and each event source in your program (as we did in the preceding example). At the other extreme, you can define dedicated event listeners that handle multiple event types for multiple source objects as well as performing other functions. For example, in the preceding example, we could have defined MyApplet as a listener for all action events that occur within it, effectively mimicking the hierarchical event model.

Although you are free to design listeners in any way you want, the dedicated listener approach makes sense in most applications. One good reason to do so is because dedicated listeners isolate event handling to small, easily identifiable chunks of code, making it easier to understand and modify your program. Also, dedicated listeners eliminate the need to identify the source of an event, greatly simplifying your code.

"But," you protest, "using dedicated event handlers will mean a proliferation of classes — at least one class for every action widget in my applet or application — and this will make my program tedious to create and to read." In fact, it seems at first sight rather silly to clutter up a program with a lot of one-shot classes, each of which will never spawn more than one instance. Java 1.1 and higher, however, supports two facilities that greatly mitigate this objection: event adapters and anonymous classes.

## Event Adapters

The `java.awt.event` package defines a set of adapter classes specifically intended to simplify creation of dedicated listeners. Each mouse adapter class implements an interface for a corresponding listener interface. For example, the `MouseAdapter` class implements each of the methods declared by the `MouseListener` interface. Close inspection of these classes reveals that event adapter methods do nothing, so what's the big deal? The point is that when you derive a dedicated listener from an adapter class, you only have to implement the methods for the specific events that you want to handle. In contrast, if you derive your listener class from a listener interface, you have to implement all the methods declared by the interface, regardless of whether you are interested in all the events they handle.

Event adapters can greatly simplify listener creation. For example, suppose you want to create a listener to handle mouse-down and mouse-up events on a `Canvas` instance. Deriving your listener from the `MouseAdapter` class requires you to define only two methods, versus five methods if you derive your listener from the `MouseListener` interface.

## Anonymous Classes

An anonymous class is a class that has no name and only one instance. Java 1.1 extended the syntax of the `new` expression to let us define and instantiate an anonymous class in the same expression. The syntax consists of the `new` keyword, followed by the constructor of the parent class, followed by the class body of the anonymous class:

```
Object obj = new Object() {
  public String toString() {
    return "I am an instance of a class with no name";
  }
}
```

Anonymous classes are instances of inner classes, a new type of class defined by Java 1.1. Unlike outer classes, which can appear only at the package level, inner classes can appear anywhere an expression can appear — even in the argument list of a function call. Anonymous inner classes allow you to code very tersely. In particular, they let you define, instantiate, and pass an object to a function in a single statement. This greatly facilitates creating dedicated event handlers, as the following example demonstrates:

```
public class MyApplet extends Applet
{
  // Construct applet:
  public MyApplet {

    // Create "Do" button and register listener:
    Button doButton = new Button("Do");
```

```
    // Define, instantiate and register button listener:
    doButton.addActionListener(new ActionListener() {
      public void actionPerformed(Event e) {

        ... // perform "Do" button action

      }
    });

    // Add button to layout:
    add("Center", doButton);
  }
}
```

Note that in this example, the anonymous listener appears to derive from an interface (`ActionListener`). In fact, Java derives the anonymous class from the `Object` class with the specified listener interface. The anonymous class body implements the specified listener interface.

# The Coordinate System

In all graphics systems, including Java, a coordinate system allows programmers to explicitly place items on the screen for users to see. In the case of Java, only a two-dimensional coordinate system is available by default, as the base classes supplied with Java are concerned only with two-dimensional graphics that are drawn on a 2D plane described in terms of $x$ and $y$ axes (Java 3D is an optional package that supports 3D graphics; see the "Optional Packages and Java Web Start" sidebar earlier in this chapter for details).

In the case of two-dimensional graphics systems such as the one employed by Java, the coordinate system is expressed in terms of two axes (an "up and down" axis, usually referred to as the $x$ axis, and "side to side" axis commonly known as the $y$ axis). Hence, the name two-dimensional graphics system (an axis exists for each dimension). To identify a point on such a coordinate system requires a pair of numeric values, one for each axis.

**Note**   Java's coordinate system (and most other coordinate systems based on a two-dimensional graphics systems) is a form of the Cartesian coordinate system that you may recall from high school math classes. Instead of plotting points on a piece of grid paper, however, you plot them on a screen using pixels!

## The *x,y* coordinates

As with most graphics systems, Java's coordinate system begins in the upper-left corner, at the *x,y* coordinate of 0,0 (commonly known as the *origin* of the graphics coordinate system). The *x* axis runs from left to right, and the *y* axis runs from top to bottom. As you run away from the origin 0,0 the numbers increase, extending into infinity (coordinates are a measure of pixels and the coordinate plane in Java is conceptually infinite in size). This coordinate system is illustrated in Figure 17-5.

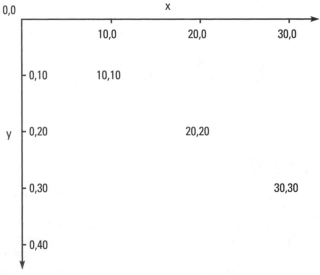

**Figure 17-5:** Java's graphics coordinate system, showing the horizontal *x* axis and the vertical *y* axis

When you are drawing and painting in an applet, however, the coordinate system isn't what you might expect. The browser window has its own coordinate system, which your applet can't draw to. Your applet's coordinate system begins wherever the applet is placed on the screen, and you're allowed to draw only inside it (or create a window and draw inside that; more on windows in later chapters). When you draw or paint in an applet, you're doing so in the coordinate system relative to that applet, not in the one relative to the browser. (See Figure 17-6.)

## Integer values

Keeping the Java coordinate system in mind, you can precisely place graphic elements directly on your applet using either two or four integer values:

✦ **X**: The *x* coordinate

✦ **Y**: The *y* coordinate

✦ **WIDTH**: The *width* of the item (optional in many methods)

✦ **HEIGHT**: The *height* of the item (optional in many methods)

For example, when you painted a image on the screen in the first part of this book you supplied only the *x* and *y* coordinates to specify where on the applet to place the upper-left corner of that image. The *width* and *height* parameters for the image were automatically calculated for you.

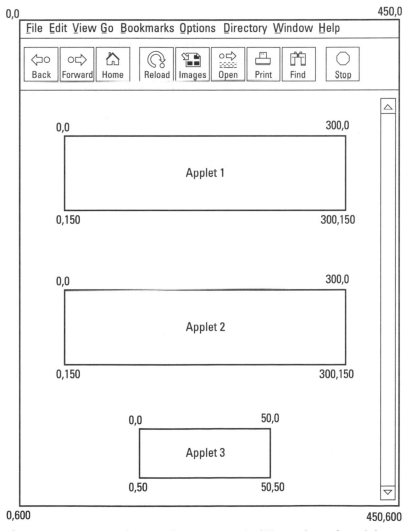

**Figure 17-6:** Your applet coordinate system is different from that of the browser in which it is executed.

Suppose, for example, that you wanted to draw an image on the screen with *x* and *y* coordinates of 25 and 18, respectively:

```
drawImage (myImage, 25, 18, this); // drawImage at 25, 18
```

When the image was drawn to the screen, you'd see the upper-left corner of the image appear at exactly 25 pixels on the x axis (the horizontal axis), 18 on the y axis (the vertical axis). The rest of the image would be drawn to the right and down, taking up as many pixels on the screen as the image measured in width and height. In this example, assume that the image is 45 pixels wide and 20 pixels high. When drawn on the screen, you'd see something similar to Figure 17-7.

Another `drawImage()` method exists that takes both *x* and *y* and *width* and *height* parameters. (This method is described in following chapters.) If the image isn't exactly the same width and height as the specifications you supply, it is scaled to fit. Using this method, you can stretch or shrink images at will.

Many other methods also take *width* and *height* parameters. Such is the case with `drawOval()`, which draws an oval of the size you choose. In the following line of code we draw an oval whose upper left-hand corner is positioned at 5,5 on the coordinate system, which extends 100 pixels to the right (*width*) and 150 pixels down (*height*):

```
drawOval(5, 5, 100, 150);
```

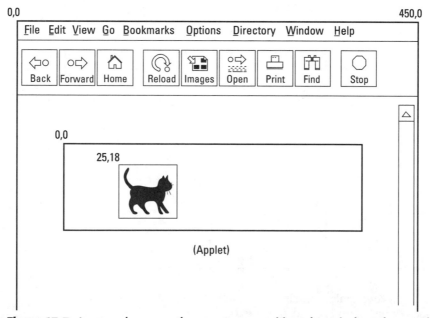

**Figure 17-7:** Images drawn on the screen are positioned precisely at the *x* and *y* coordinates supplied.

## The Bounding Box

Text, images, and graphical images are contained in what is known as a bounding box. The upper-left corner of the bounding box is placed at the exact *x,y* coordinates you provide. This is important to realize, because you may rip your hair out trying to figure out why the image you positioned on the screen is appearing several pixels off the mark.

Images don't have to begin at the upper-left corner of their bounding box. For example, when you use graphics software to create GIF and JPEG images, you can control the size of the bounding box (often called a canvas in graphics programs, but not to be confused with the `Canvas` class in Java). You might assume that the image begins at the upper-left corner, but it may not, as shown in Figure 17-8. If it doesn't, you may have a problem positioning it precisely where you want.

**Figure 17-8:** An image doesn't necessarily begin in the upper-left corner of its bounding box.

To see just how big the bounding box for an image is, open the image in a graphics package. Alternately, you can open the image in Netscape Navigator (which displays the dimensions of images on the browser menu bar). If there is excessive space around the image, just crop it.

Tip

Netscape Navigator is a handy tool for quickly determining the dimensions of an image. Simply open a GIF or JPEG image directly in Navigator and you'll see its height and width (measured in pixels) displayed in the title bar of the browser.

## The Dimension Class

Because we use *width* and *height* parameters so often, the AWT provides a `Dimension` class that we can use to hold such values. In the following snippet of code we place the return value of a call to an AWT object's `getSize()` method directly into a `Dimension` variable called `mySize`, out of which we then extract the integer height and width values and assign them to integer variables of the same name.

You should note that Dimension's getHeight() and getWidth() methods actually return a double precision floating point number (a double, in Java jargon), which requires an explicit cast into an int (in other words, Java won't cast a double to an int automatically so you must be explicit do the cast yourself):

```
Dimension mySize = new anyAWTComponent.getSize();
int width = (int) mySize.getWidth();
int height = (int) mySize.getHeight();
```

This can be particularly helpful if you need to know the size of your applet. Simply call getsize() or this.getZize() in the init() method of your applet, and place the results in a Dimension object method (note that if you're writing a Java 1.0 applet you must call size() because getSize() wasn't introduced until Java 1.1). You can then retrieve the size of your applet through the Dimension object's width and height instance variables as needed later on. Alternately, you can invoke getHeight() and getWidth() directly within your applet as they'll return the information you're looking for (in which case you might opt to instead stuff the resulting data into a Dimension object for storage and later retrieval).

Applications, meanwhile, can simply invoke getHeight() and getWidth() on the frame (or window) for which you wish to get the height or width. Both of these methods are actually defined in the java.awt.Component class, which is why they can be called on a Dimension, Frame, Window, Applet, Panel, or any other AWT component (all AWT components inherit this method from Component). Similarly, getSize() is also defined in the Component class (although Dimension provides its own implementation of this method in order to parallel the one defined in Component).

# Putting It All Together

As you may have noticed in Figure 17-4, an applet is actually a subclass of Panel, which is itself a subclass of Container. And Container, of course, is a descendant of Component. As a result of this inheritance tree, every applet already knows a great deal about handling user interaction, and also supports drawing and painting directly on it.

In fact, you've been taking advantage of this all along. You didn't have to create a container in which to draw your images, because applets inherit indirectly from the Container class. You just began slapping your text and image right on the applet, without bothering with such details.

However, as you get deeper into the AWT in the next chapter, you need to know how everything fits together. In particular, you need to see how the graphics coordinate system and the event-handling mechanism are affected as you create a real UI for your programs (see the previous discussions on these topics for details).

Without much effort, you can begin adding widgets to your applets. With a little more effort, you can handle the events that the applets generate when the user interacts with them. Again, because your applets are already containers, you can start slapping on the various UI elements you want without concerning yourself with the details.

Eventually, however, this may become impractical. In many cases, you'll want to create a nice, clean way to group the various widgets your program supports. You may also want a user to be able to resize the applet without screwing up the placement of your various graphics and widgets.

## Containers

To deal with both the grouping and resizing issue, you can create a container for each distinct group of UI elements. Containers are components that we can draw to, paint on, and add widgets to. Windows, dialog boxes, and even applets are descendants of the `Container` class (which in turn is a descendant of `Component`).

Suppose, for example, that you are developing a painting applet that supports a number of brushes and palettes. You might create two new windows and make them much like floating palettes in today's most popular graphics programs. (See Figure 17-9.)

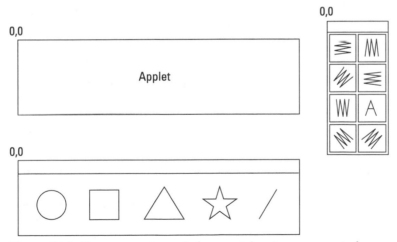

**Figure 17-9:** You can create a window container to group controls. Each container (such as these windows) has its own coordinate system.

Alternately, you could instantiate a `Panel` object (the simplest of all containers, which you will learn to use in later chapters) for each container and add them both to the applet. If you did this, you would be nesting containers. In either case, each container has its own coordinate system. As a result, you need to be aware of the containers your program uses, and take care to draw and paint according to their respective coordinate systems.

For example, an *x,y* coordinate of 250,300 might be valid for your applet but be completely out of the range of the other containers. However, because you can declare a `paint()` or `paintComponents()` method for each container that you create, you don't have to worry about managing the drawing and painting for every container through a single method.

## Layout managers

Whenever you add a widget to a container, it gets placed on the screen according to placement rules imposed by whatever layout manager is associated with that container. As you will learn in later chapters, you don't place widgets on the screen using explicit *x,y* coordinates. Instead, you simply create them and add them using an `add()` method. Where they actually appear is based entirely on the layout manager being used by that container.

At first this may seem strange, but in reality, it's quite necessary. Because all Java programs are supposed to be platform-independent, allowing widgets to be placed at explicit screen locations would create a real problem. The coordinate system for your computer and for the computers of other potential users around the world aren't going to be the same. What looks just beautiful on your screen might be a jumbled mess on another.

And what if the user resizes the container? If you want your program to respond to resize directives, as real applications do, you'd have to rearrange your widgets accordingly. Because you would need to know details about the system on which the container has been resized to do a decent job, the whole idea of using explicit *x,y* coordinates for placement becomes an utter nightmare to implement.

Rather than making you deal with such details, Java provides a layout mechanism that you can rely on instead (which is, by default, a `FlowLayout` object). Your widgets are drawn in the order that you add them, according to the layout manager associated with the container to which they are added. When the container is resized, the layout manager rearranges and redraws each widget you've added to it, so you don't have to. As you will learn in the Chapter 20, you can choose from a number of different layout managers, each of which lays out widgets differently.

# Summary

The Java AWT is actually a generic user interface (UI) toolkit, a collection of classes that enables you to create platform-independent user interfaces. It is part of the larger suite of Java Foundation Classes (JFC), and a kissing cousin to Swing. Whereas AWT components are peer-based, JFC and Swing are lightweight alternatives for windowing. Nonetheless, AWT provides a fundamental windowing and event infrastructure that JFC and Swing are built upon. Just as Java programs are platform independent, capable of running on any computer that has the Java run-time system installed, so too are the user interfaces created with the AWT.

✦ Whenever a user interacts with an element of your program's user interface, such as the keyboard, mouse, a button, or a menu item, the element generates an event. To react to an event, you must create some code that executes whenever the event occurs — this is called trapping the event.

✦ Even though we've discussed a good deal of the AWT, we really didn't do much actual programming. This should tip you off to how large the AWT is, since we've covered a considerable amount of material without getting into the nuts and bolts of it.

✦ As with most 2D graphics systems, Java's coordinate system begins in the upper-left corner, at $x,y$ coordinates 0,0 (also known as the coordinate system origin). The x axis runs from left to right, and the y axis runs from top to bottom, increasing from zero to infinity in both directions.

✦ You have learned about the fundamental organization of the AWT and how it encompasses primitive graphics, text, fonts, color, bitmap images, GUI components and two event models (hierarchical, and delegation). This gives you a better understanding of how each part of the AWT works and how you can make use of it in your own programs and in the chapters that follow.

✦     ✦     ✦

# Basics of Color, Fonts, and Images

**W**ith your basic understanding from the previous chapter of how to get a GUI in front of the user, now you need to make some useful customized improvements to make your application something special. In this chapter, you'll learn how to use AWT to draw custom primitives and images to your blank window. Following that, you'll learn how to print both whole windows and make custom output to really give your application a professional touch.

## Introducing Java 2D

In the beginning there was Java. It was very simple: all you needed to do was place buttons and check boxes on the screen. Capabilities were also provided to allow simple drawing routines. These basic primitives included lines, circles, and filled areas. However, this was not enough.

Most early Java developers either had a UNIX or Windows background and were used to having highly capable rendering systems. They were very quickly frustrated by the lack of variable line thickness and types, semitransparent rendering, and image manipulation routines. After all, when the underlying windowing system supported it on every platform that Java was deployed on, why couldn't Java also supply those capabilities?

With the start of the Java 2 work, Sun set about to correct these major deficiencies and thus, Java 2D was born. Java 2D is designed to bring to Java programmers all the capabilities that they normally would expect of any decent application.

Previously, they were lucky to be able to build a PaintBrush style application with the given functionality. With Java 2D, the aim was to be able to build something more akin to Adobe Photoshop. In this, they were largely successful, and this is what we will begin to introduce to you in this chapter.

## What does Java 2D do?

When you boil a windowing system like Win32 or the Mac user interface down to its most basic components, you have a set of routines for managing the display hardware (video card and screen) and routines that draw lines, circles, and text on the screen.

Take a look at the border around one of the windows on your screen. Those are not magical areas that your video card provides. At some level, the operating system must draw a rectangle, fill it with some color, text, and maybe an icon. A button is similar — typically a gray filled rectangle with black text in the center. A window is nothing but a series of rectangles drawn on the screen with appropriate highlighting and text to make them look sexy. These same routines are what you use to make your own custom component. The only difference is that the windowing system provides a collection of prepackaged routines that do many standard user interface components for you. If you want something different, say a round button, you need to create this yourself.

The first task of Java 2D is to provide an interface to these basic capabilities. The simple stuff, which you'll be introduced to in this chapter, involves drawing primitives like lines and circles onscreen. The more complex areas include image manipulation routines to change the color types, warp images (morphing), and other sophisticated tricks.

At the other end, everyone has different displays. A gamer has a 3D accelerator card with a couple of gigabytes of RAM on it, capable of photorealistically rendering the entire world thirty times a second. Your parents probably have a $500 machine full of cheap components, and the entire machine probably costs less than the video card of the gamer's machine. Obviously, the capabilities are not the same. A well-written application needs to be able to detect these differences and adapt appropriately.

The second task of Java 2D is to present environmental information about the display hardware in which the application finds itself. This includes information like the number of colors available, the number of display devices (monitors), screen size, and other input capabilities like tablets, scanners, and so on. These are presented in the typical Java philosophy of platform-independence so that one application can run on many different types of windowing systems without requiring special code for each.

## Keeping in context

Java represents the platform-independent graphics capabilities through a number of different classes.

The main class that you will deal with is the `Graphics` class. This provides a context-free way of telling the application to draw something or to query for some capabilities like font information. For any given application, many instances of this class are floating around. Hidden away in this class is all the information needed to draw to one particular element. For instance, each image that you load will have its own graphics information and, therefore, a separate `Graphics` classinstance.

Other classes include `GraphicsContext`, which has information about your display system. This is used less often, as it is mainly for setup purposes. For example, a 3D graphics window with Java 3D or a video player with Java Media Framework (http://java.sun.com/products/java-media/jmf/) would need access to this class to find out about specific hardware capabilities. Once the display has been established, the class is rarely used. Similarly, `GraphicsEnvironment` provides information about the screen. For example, it would know about how many monitors you have attached to your computer and what sort of display input devices you might have (mice, tablets, and so on).

# Handling Color

Before we look at how to render information, we need to quickly examine Java color handling. Drawing anything onscreen requires you to set a color value — regardless of whether it is basic black/white or something more complex. We also happen to use color to illustrate interesting points when dealing with primitive rendering later in the chapter.

## Color representation

Java represents color information with the `java.awt.Color` class. Regardless of where you need color information in the standard APIs, this will be the class you always use.

Color is represented using the Red-Green-Blue (RGB) model and includes transparency (alpha) information as well. Each component may be represented as either byte or floating-point values. A value of 0 in either case is no intensity and a value of 255 or 1.0 is full intensity. For the alpha value, a value of 0 means the object is completely transparent, while a value of 1.0 or 255 means the object is completely opaque (visible).

## Foreground/background color

Although color is explained in more detail later in the chapter, we also need to introduce a little bit about it here too. To the first-time user, Java color handling can be a bit strange.

Like most graphics system, when you draw, you can assign a color value for both the foreground and background colors. Both the component and graphics context have color setting methods. You might be wondering what color gets set when.

A foreground color is the color that objects will appear in when you draw them. Draw a square and the outline of the square will appear in this color. With the `Graphics` class, you set color using the `setColor()` method.

If you call the `setForeground()` method of a component, this defines the color that borders the component and that other items should be drawn in. For example, a button would use this color to draw the edges and the text.

To set the background color of the component, you would call the `setBackground()` method. In the button, this would be the gray color that fills the button area. When drawing lines and text on the component through the Graphics class methods, this color has no effect; that is, it does *not* automatically clear an area under the text/line in this color when drawn. If you need to do that, then you must first draw a filled area of the appropriate color and then change color to draw the text/line.

# Creating Graphics

To draw graphics on the screen, you need to do the following:

1. Obtain graphics context information represented by the `Graphics` class.

2. Make calls on `Graphics` to render specific information.

Despite the apparent simplicity of these two steps, there is a little more to know. For example, you can't just go creating new instances of a `Graphics` class and expect it to automatically draw something. You should do this only in certain times and places in your code.

## Fetching a graphics context

When you want to draw something — either to screen or to image, you can do this only at certain times. During this time, you will be given access to an instance of `Graphics` with which to make the drawing.

> **Note**    It is important that you use only the instance of `Graphics` given at the time and do not save it for later use. Java will periodically change the instance between calls to the method. If you use the wrong instance, all sorts of little — or big — errors will be generated by your code. Only use what Java provides you.

Java will let you draw information to the window in three defined places. These are outlined in the following sections.

## Repainting a Component

In the previous chapter, you saw the Component and Canvas classes. These form the two bases of your custom application. Component provides the base area for making a custom component — for example, a color picker or round button. Canvas provides a drawing area for building paint-style applications. They both share a common method (well, Canvas extends Component, so they should!) called paint().

The paint() method takes a single parameter, an instance of Graphics. Your custom component, which extends one of these classes, must implement this method. When this method is called, that is the Java runtime telling you that now is a good time to draw anything onscreen that you need.

You can't predict when paint() is to be called, and it should never be called directly by your code. If it is, this might be suddenly interrupted by the Java runtime deciding that it also wants to call your paint method. This can lead to some rather interesting, and probably unwanted, onscreen effects.

> **Note**  Another method called update() also takes a Graphics instance. This is normally called just before paint(). A typical Java tactic is to override the update() method and have it directly call paint(). This is because the default implementation of update() clears the background of the component in its default color first and then calls paint(). If you see odd things like your component being turned blank after a paint call or flashing as it is being displayed, then try this.

## Forced Painting

No matter how much you try to let the system tell you everything, sometimes you need to force your own painting. Should this be the case, then you can make use of the getGraphics() method.

You can call getGraphics() at any time and get a Graphics instance returned. With this, you can then draw whatever you need onto your component. As a word of caution, you should not call this method if you are already inside paint() or update(), as you already have a graphics context to play with.

## Images

Early in Java's development, images could be loaded only from external files. For programmers wanting to create fancy graphics applications, this was a major pain. Without a Graphics instance, you could not draw anything onto an offscreen image. After much complaining by developers, Sun relented and added the ability to draw directly to an image. So now, there is a getGraphics() call within java.awt.Image.

After fetching the Graphics instance from an image, you can use it to draw to that image, and that image only. If you have two images to draw to, you need to make separate calls to each image instance for their particular Graphics instance.

## Drawing primitives

Strolling through the documentation for Graphics, you will see that you can do an awful lot of things. A full explanation of all the capabilities is outside the scope of this book: we'll just go through the most commonly used areas. The rest is left as an exercise for the reader.

**Note** In the following examples, all of the code segments will use the variable name g. This represents an instance of Graphics that you would be using to draw to the primitive. You may obtain an instance of the Graphics class through any of the means outlined previously in the chapter.

### Rectangles

Java provides three different types of rectangles, each of which may be filled or left empty when drawn on the screen. Examples of each of these are shown in Figure 18-1. To draw any one of these, we must supply, at a minimum, four arguments: the two coordinates of the upper-left corner, and the rectangle's width and height. For the most basic of rectangles, that's all we need:

```
g.drawRect(15, 20, 150, 150);
g.fillRect(15, 20, 150, 150);
```

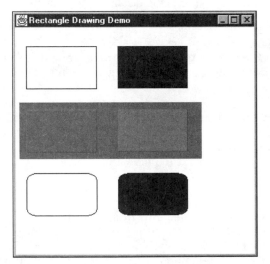

**Figure 18-1:** The three different types of rectangles provided by Java's graphic routines. From top to bottom: Standard rectangle, 3D shadow rectangle, Rounded rectangle.

**Cross-Reference** The RectangleDemo class can be found on the book's Web site with the rest of the code from Chapter 18. It is better that you run and look at this code because the highlights with the 3D shadow effects are much nicer than the black and white you see in the book.

The first version draws a plain rectangle, beginning at the x,y position of 15,20. As it turns out, this rectangle is actually a perfect square, since it's as wide (150) as it is high (150):

```
g.draw3DRect(15, 185, 150, 150, true);
g.fill3DRect(15, 185, 150, 150, true);
```

The second version draws a rectangle that has a 3D look to it — much like the borders of buttons typical of a Windows user interface. To generate the 3D shadow effects, the drawing routines automatically work out which shades of color are needed. Another parameter has been added that defines whether the rectangle should look raised or lowered compared to the surrounding area. Passing a value of true makes it look like the rectangle is raised above the surrounding area. As you can see from Figure 18-1, there's nothing particularly special about these rectangles; they look exactly as you'd expect them to look.

```
g.drawRoundRect(30, 200, 150, 150, 50, 10);
g.fillRoundRect(30, 200, 150, 150. 30, 30)
```

The final version of the rectangle produces a rounded version.

Instead of square corners, these ones have a rounded look to them, much like many buttons on the Macintosh user interface. Notice that they also take two extra parameters:

✦ arcWidth: The horizontal diameter of the arc at the four corners (integer value)

✦ arcHeight: The vertical diameter of the arc at the four corners (integer value)

These parameters determine just how sharp or rounded the corners of rounded rectangles are. The first determines how sharp the angle is on the horizontal, and the second determines how sharp the angle is on the vertical. The larger the last two parameters become, the more rounded the rectangle. Increasingly, large numbers begin to make a rectangle look more like a circle, until eventually, it looks exactly like one.

It is preferable to draw a circle using the oval methods, described in the next section. However, to draw a circle using the rounded rectangle methods, simply provide the height and the width of the rectangle for these two additional parameters:

```
g.drawRoundRect(20,185,150,150,150,150); // draws a circle
```

## Ovals

Ovals are just as easy to use as the plain rectangle you just learned about. In fact, when you draw an oval, you actually define a rectangle in which the oval will appear. You can draw in outline or filled ovals:

```
g.drawOval(10,10,50,100); // draw an oval
g.fillOval(150,10,130,20); // fill an oval

g.drawOval(10,150,100,100); // draw circle (same height width)
g.fillOval(150,150,30,30); // fill circle (same height width)
```

Figure 18-2 shows several ovals, the result of calling the preceding methods. As you can see, ovals can be a variety of shapes. They can look long and elliptical, or as round as a circle. In fact, to create a circle, you should use the oval methods, by creating an oval that is exactly as wide as it is high. You can see this in the last two lines of code.

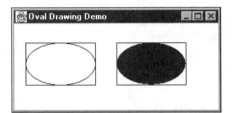

**Figure 18-2:** A demonstration of the different ways of drawing an oval. A rectangle surrounds each oval to show the extents that are provided by the code during the method calls.

## Polygons

In addition to basic lines, rectangles, and ovals, you can also create polygons. These are much more complex than the simple graphics we have been discussing thus far. Polygons (affectionately known as "polys" to many programmers) can have any number of sides, each of which is specified as a pair of x,y coordinates. In fact, you can think of a polygon as a digital game of connect-the-dots.

Simply supply all the dots as x,y coordinates. When drawn, a line travels from dot-to-dot, connecting them in the order in which they were provided. You can option-ally fill a polygon, as you can other graphics primitives. Figure 18-3 shows a plain and a filled polygon.

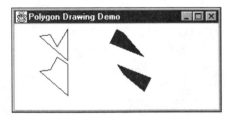

**Figure 18-3:** A number of different polygons drawn using the Java graphics methods. The top polygons use the addPoint() method, while the bottom polygons use arrays of points.

To create a polygon, use either the `drawPolygon()` or `fillPolygon()` method. These draw an outline or filled object in the same way the previous methods have. When invoking these methods, we can either provide an array of x and y coordinates to specify the dots to be connected, or we can supply a `Polygon` object. Let's first take a look at how to create a polygon and then we will fill it and draw with it.

To create a polygon, we simply instantiate a `Polygon` object:

```
Polygon myPoly = new Polygon(); // create new, empty poly
```

This creates an empty polygon, which we can then fill with x,y coordinates (dots, or points) using the `addPoint()` method:

```
myPoly.addPoint(40,40);
myPoly.addPoint(55,38);
myPoly.addPoint(65,55);
myPoly.addPoint(80,30);
myPoly.addPoint(80,75);
myPoly.addPoint(40,40);
```

Here we've added a number of points to our `Polygon` object. When we're done, we can give this polygon to the `drawPolygon()` or `fillPolygon()` methods:

```
g.drawPolygon(myPoly); // draw it
g.fillPolygon(myPoly); // fill it
```

Although this may be the easiest way to deal with polygons, it's not the only way. We could instantiate a `Polygon` object and supply an array of x coordinates, an array of y coordinates, and an integer number that specifies the total number of coordinates we'll be using. Instead of creating a `Polygon` object and then adding a point at a time, this allows us to create a polygon with all its points right off the bat:

```
int xCoords[] = {40,55,65,80,80,40}; // create x values
int yCoords[] = {40,38,55,30,75,40}; // create y values

// create poly from arrays
Polygon myPoly = new Polygon(xCoords,yCoords,xCoords.length);
```

We can now pass this new polygon to the `fillPolygon()` or `drawPolygon()` method.

However, we don't necessarily have to create a Polygon object first. By supplying an array of x and y coordinates, in addition to the total number of points to connect, we can draw or fill the polygon directly:

```
g.drawPolygon(xCoords,yCoords,xCoords.length);
g.fillPolygon(xCoords,yCoords,xCoords.length);
```

Rather than instantiate a Polygon object, we can directly provide all the essential information to these `drawPolygon()` and `fillPolygon()` methods. This is useful if we want to draw or fill a polygon on the fly but have no need to hang onto the object for later reference.

You can supply any number of points for your polygon. They can be incredibly complex or simple, depending on how you like them.

In the previous examples, the last point added was the same as the first point, effectively closing the polygon. You can also have polygons that are "open," meaning the last point does not connect to the first point. Since we've specified the last x,y coordinate in these examples to be the same as the first x,y coordinate, the result is a closed polygon. However, if the first and last set of x,y coordinates are not the same, an open polygon is created.

## Arcs

Finally, we come to the primitive graphic that may, at first, seem the most difficult to understand: the arc.

```
drawArc(int x, int y, int width, int height, int startAngle,
int arcAngle)
```

The first four coordinates of the arc are nothing new. They define the rectangle we used for the oval graphics described moments ago. Again, we provide an upper-left coordinate, and the height and width. The last two coordinates, however, can be quite confusing if you've never dealt with arcs before:

- ✦ x: The standard x coordinate
- ✦ y: The standard y coordinate
- ✦ width: The width of the arc's bounding box (rectangle)
- ✦ height: The height of the arc's bounding box (rectangle)
- ✦ startAngle: The angle to begin drawing the arc
- ✦ arcAngle: The angle of the arc (relative to startAngle)

The first of these two new parameters, `startAngle`, is the beginning angle of the arc. This value can run from 0 to 360 degrees. Contrary to intuition, these angles increase counterclockwise. Zero is at 3:00, while 90 degrees is at 12:00, 180 degrees is at 9:00, and 270 degrees is at 6:00. It may help to draw this clock on a piece of paper. The value that you choose for the start angle determines, of course, where that arc's going to start. To get a better feel for the degrees you can choose for your start angle, see Figure 18-4.

It's the last parameter, arcAngle, however, that determines where the arc ends, by indicating how far the arc is going to travel.

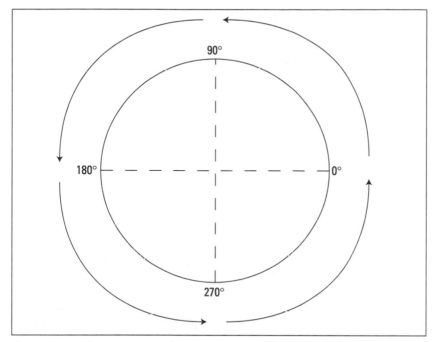

**Figure 18-4:** The arc startAngle parameter specifies an angle between 0 and 360 degrees. Zero starts at the 3:00 position and turns counterclockwise to 360 degrees.

Don't be confused by this ending argument. The arcAngle argument is not actually a specific angle, in the way that startAngle is. It's a magnitude — simply a value that tells you how far, in degrees, the arc is going to continue in your rectangle (here, a perfect square). For instance, if you wanted an arc that begins at 12:00 (90 degrees) and runs to 3:00 (–90 degrees), you would specify the following:

```
g.drawArc(10,10,100,100,90,-90); // run clockwise
```

Since positive arcAngle values result in an arc sweeping counterclockwise, we used a negative value (-90 degrees) to effectively say "run clockwise for 90 degrees."

However, if you wanted an arc that began at 12:00 and ran to 9:00, you would use the following:

```
g.drawArc(10,150,100,100,90,90); // run counterclockwise
```

As you can see, values that are positive take an arc counterclockwise and values that are negative take them clockwise.

Arcs, just like their rectangular, polygonal, and oval brethren, can be filled or left empty. Some examples can be seen in Figure 18-5.

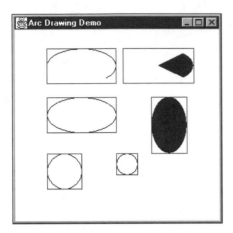

**Figure 18-5:** Examples of the types of figures you can draw with arcs. The faint outlines indicate the bounding box supplied to the drawArc() method.

# Handling Fonts

In addition to drawing primitive shapes onscreen, you can also draw text. In many ways, drawing text is just as important as being able to draw a square. Buttons and mouse-over handling use text in status bars or tooltips to describe their actions to the user.

Simple font handling can be just creating a font that you want to use and then drawing the text with drawString() or drawChars() from the Graphics class. For more complex applications, you need to know a lot of information about the font as well. For example, you want to place the text so that the top aligns with an image, so you need to know how high in pixels the text is so that it is correctly located.

## Creating fonts

To use fonts within a drawing, we need to create an instance of a Font object. This describes the visual aspects of the font. You will be familiar with most of the information here from your standard word processor. A new instance needs the name of the font (for example, Times New Roman), the style (for example, bold or italic), and the point size of the font.

```
Font myFont = new Font("Serif", Font.BOLD, 12);
```

Here we've created a Font object using a serif font face, bold style (via Font.BOLD, which accesses the BOLD static integer variable of the Font class), and 72 point size. We chose Serif since every system is likely to have at least one serif font. If you specify Serif, Java will substitute the system's default serif face, usually Times New Roman. If you choose a specific font face that isn't installed on a particular machine, Java will substitute a default font (Courier, for example).

Note

Serif fonts have feet at the base line. The font in this book is a serif font. Typically, most people find serif fonts easier to read—that's why you see them in most books. Sans serif fonts eliminate the feet. (*Sans* is a French word that means without). The Arial and Helvetica typefaces are prime examples of sans serif fonts. With monospace fonts, every character is the same width. The Courier typeface is a good example of a monospace font.

Even though you can choose any font face you want, we recommend that you use only a narrow set—those likely to be available on the systems on which your applets will be running. For example, you really don't want to have hard-coded a Microsoft-specific font like Wingdings into an application that could run on any platform. If you stick to the following, you'll be in good shape:

✦ Serif: The default serif font, typically Times New Roman

✦ Monospaced: The default monospaced font, typically Courier

✦ SansSerif: The default sans serif font, typically Helvetica

## Finding installed fonts

If you need much more variety than the available fonts, such as for a paint program, alternatives are available. The typical need for this is to display all fonts that have been installed on that machine. Doing this allows you to create a machine-and-operating-system-independent way of giving the user choice over the fonts they use.

You obtain a listing of the available fonts from the `GraphicsEnvironment` class. To obtain this list, the first step is to get an instance of `GraphicsEnvironment`. This class contains a static method that you can call:

```
GraphicsEnvironment env =
    GraphicsEnvironment.getLocalGraphicsEnvironment();
```

With this instance, you can then call one of two methods:

✦ `getAvailableFontFamilyNames()`—Returns an array of strings that represent the names of all the fonts installed on the system. Really useful if you want to have a font dialog box or something similar to put in front of the user if he or she doesn't need all fonts immediately.

✦ `getAllFonts()`—Returns an array of `Font` instances that represent all of the fonts available in a standard style and point size. Because the style and point size are fixed, it does not provide much flexibility for the user. (There are ways around this.) Also, because it must create instances of all the fonts, it is much slower than the other method.

You need to be careful when calling these methods. They force the JVM to examine the system for every available font. If your system has a lot of fonts installed, this could take some seconds to return. This time delay presents some problems from the user-interface perspective if the list is used in a dialog box because it may take several seconds for that component to appear onscreen.

## Using fontmetrics

Most of the time when dealing with drawing text, you will want more information about the rendered text than what drawString() presents you. For example, if you need to justify text in the center or to the right, you need to know how long the rendered text is so that you can specify the correct x,y position to drawString(). The FontMetrics class gives you a way of finding out all this information.

Font metric information is provided for many different elements of the text, as described in Figure 18-6. The two most common methods that you will use will be getAscent() and stringWidth(). These provide you with enough information to place text precisely on the screen for most applications.

 **Caution**    When determining the width of a string, you should always call stringWidth() or getStringBounds(). Do not try to sum up the individual spaces surrounding a series of letters. The reason for this is that as a string, the rendering system may end up providing something different than the raw characters. Some scripted fonts like Arabic will change spacings around characters as one letter is joined to the next, causing the overall length to change.

Adequately describing all the ways of using metric information about fonts could quite easily fill a whole chapter by itself. As a shortened version, the following example shows you how to accurately position two lines of text of different font sizes, one below the other. You can see the output in Figure 18-6.

We start by creating the fonts and obtaining the appropriate FontMetrics instances:

```
Font small_font = new Font("Serif", Font.BOLD, 14);
Font large_font = new Font("Courier",
                           Font.ITALIC | Font.BOLD, 24);

FontMetrics small_fm = getFontMetrics(small_font);
FontMetrics large_fm = getFontMetrics(large_font);
```

The getFontMetrics() method call comes directly from the parent component in which we are rendering. You cannot create a direct instance of the FontMetrics class because it is declared abstract, so you need to request the information through the parent component. Typically, this setup information is done in the constructor or initialization phase for the component. It is fairly expensive to create these classes, so it's a good idea not to fetch them every single time paint() is called.

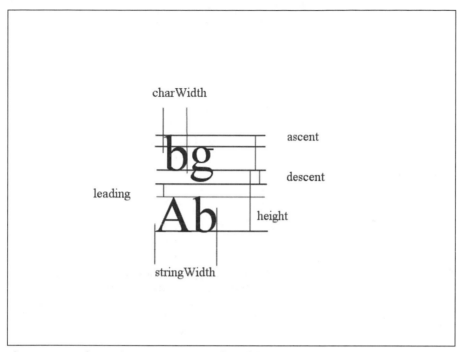

**Figure 18-6:** The main measurements describing font metric information. All of these can be obtained through the FontMetrics class and used to accurately render text information on screen.

Once you have been called to paint, you need to work out the height of the font, add a little offset to bring it away from the edge of the component, and then call the drawString() method with the appropriate position. Make sure that you pay attention to the x,y positions that are used in drawString(). These are for the baseline of the characters, not the upper-left corner. This means you always need to find at least the height information of the font before drawing it:

```
g.setFont(small_font);
int sm_height = small_fm.getHeight() + 5;
g.drawString("Why, what a small font you have!",
             10, sm_height);
```

Drawing the second font is a case of adding the height of the new font to the baseline of the previous line. The getHeight() method returns the height needed between the baseline of this line and the baseline of the line above—when using the same font. It automatically includes a standard gap between the lines (the leading). Now, the important point to remember here is that the height is based on the line above being the same height. As you can see from Figure 18-7, with a small font above and a large one below, the gap is based on the large font so you get quite a big gap between the two.

```
int lg_height = large_fm.getHeight();

int y_pos = sm_height + lg_height;

g.setFont(large_font);
g.drawString("A much larger one", 10, y_pos);
```

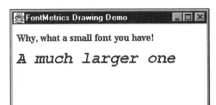

**Figure 18-7:** A demo program illustrating the use of two lines of text separated by the FontMetrics information.

If we want this to look a little better, then we need to do more of it ourselves. Figure 18-8 shows how we have fixed this up by using a combination of the font metric information to get the right proportioned effect. The new code looks like this:

```
int descent = small_fm.getDescent();
int lg_ascent = large_fm.getAscent();

int y_pos = sm_height + descent + lg_ascent;

g.setFont(large_font);
g.drawString("A much larger one", 10, y_pos);
```

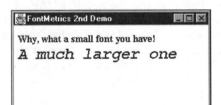

**Figure 18-8:** A more proportioned-looking demo that has the spacing set using a combination of font metric information.

# Handling Images

Sometimes you don't want to do everything yourself. It can be terribly tedious writing a pile of code to draw the icons on your buttons. Besides, you might not be a very good artist. It is much easier to use a collection of standard images that someone else has drawn up. What you need to do is then load that image and draw it on the screen.

Reading through the documentation for Java, you might wonder just exactly what images are. After all, there is the drawImage() method as part of the Graphics class and there is also a java.awt.image package that doesn't contain any code at all for drawing images. The confusion comes about due to some historical reasons.

In the early versions of Java, there was the `java.awt.Image` class. You could load an instance of this class in many ways, which we'll explain shortly. The problem with this was they were very fixed. There was almost nothing you could do with them. For instance, there was no way you could create a new blank image and then draw lines and circles on that image. You could only do this to screen. To make matters worse, when loading a large image into memory, the representation was extremely huge. There was no real capability for progressively loading images. To fix this, Java 2 introduced the `BufferedImage` class that existed as part of the new `java.awt.image` package. The new image representation included a lot of other neat tricks like drawing to images, dynamically producing scaled versions, etc. For backwards compatibility, the old ways had to remain, but they are much less used these days.

## Standard images

All images are part of the `java.awt.Image` class as their representation within the Java environment. Even the `BufferedImage` class extends `Image`. Everything you learn over the next few sections can be applied to both versions of images.

### Loading Images

There are several different ways to load images within the Java environment. Loading images requires the use of the Java AWT. For the purposes of learning how to load images, we will only cover two of these: using a String file name, and using a URL class instance. Table 18-1 covers all of the available methods for loading an image. Return values are not included because all methods return an instance of Image.

### Table 18-1
### The AWT Class Methods for Loading Images

| Method | Description |
|---|---|
| `createImage(byte[] data)` | Interprets the raw bytes as an image format and attempts to create an image from it. The bytes can be in any of the acceptable formats such as GIF, JPG, or PNG. |
| `createImage(byte[] data, int offsett, int length)` | Interprets the raw bytes in the array at the given length and number (length) of bytes and attempts to create an image from it. |
| `createImage(ImageProducer p)` | Provides the bytes to the createImage demand as they become available. |
| `createImage(String file)` | Reads the named file (may be relative or absolute path) and interprets the bytes as an image format. |

*Continued*

| Table 18-1 *(continued)* | |
|---|---|
| **Method** | **Description** |
| `createImage(URL url)` | Opens the URL and reads the bytes as an image format. |
| `getImage(String file)` | Reads the named file and creates an image from the contents. If the file has already been loaded, then use the cached data instead. |
| `getImage(URL url)` | Opens the URL and reads the bytes as an image format. If the file has already been loaded, then use the cached data instead. |

**Note**   The java.awt.Toolkit class is used to bind the platform-independent java.awt classes with their java.awt.Peer class counterparts. Many of the methods in the java.awt.Toolkit class should not be called directly because they interact directly with the platform's operating system.

Loading an image assumes that you know where to find one in the first place. So let's assume that we have an image named test.jpg. Loading it requires the following simple two lines:

```
Toolkit tk = Toolkit.getDefaultToolkit();
Image img = tk.createImage("test.jpg");
```

Here, the assumption is that test.jpg is in the same directory as the applet or application that is loading it. You could provide a fully qualified path name if you want (for example, the information returned from a `FileOpen` dialog box you saw in the previous chapter). It is usually best to declare your Image variable at the class scope level rather than within the method as shown in the previous code. This saves the image from being loaded every time the method is called. It is a good idea to put this code inside an initialization method. Putting it in the constructor is not a good idea because it slows down the startup process way down.

If you want to access the file from somewhere other than the local disk, the previous method is not much use. To access it from a Web server or other remote location, you need to make use of the `java.net.URL` class. For example, say we have an image located at

```
http://www.javabible.com/examples/ch18/remote_image.jpg
```

The previous loader code would now change to:

```
try{
  URL url =
    new URL("http://www.javabible.com/" +
```

```
                "examples/ch18/remote_image.jpg");
    Image img = tk.createImage(url);
}
catch(MalformedURLException mue){
    System.out.println("Created a bad URL!!!");
}
```

**Cross-Reference** You can find more information about how to create and manage instances of the `java.net.URL` class in Chapter 15, "Networking."

In each case, you will get an image instance returned. If the code fails to create an instance of the image, then you get `null` returned.

## Drawing Images

With the image loaded, now you need to do something with it—draw it to the screen. Like the other drawing primitives, rendering an image uses the `Graphics` class. To do this, you need the `drawImage()` method. There are a number of different options for drawing an image (see Table 18-2), but we will only cover a couple of the available options.

### Table 18-2
### Methods Available in the Graphics Class to Draw an Image

| Method | Description |
| --- | --- |
| `drawImage(Image img, int x, int y, ImageObserver obs)` | Draws an image at location x,y in the coordinate system of the `Graphics` context. Transparent pixels in the source image do not overwrite the existing pixels in the destination. The simplest option when drawing an image. |
| `drawImage(Image img, int x, int y, Color bgcolor, ImageObserver obs)` | Draws an image at location x,y. If transparent parts are in the source image, then use the given background color in their place. |
| `drawImage(Image img, int x, int y, int w, int h, ImageObserver obs)` | Draws an image at location x, y and scales it to fit within the given width and height (in pixels). Transparent pixels in the source image do not overwrite the existing pixels in the destination. |
| `drawImage(Image img, int x, int y, int w, int h, Color bgcolor, ImageObserver obs)` | Draws an image at location x, y and scales it to fit within the given width and height (in pixels). Transparent pixels in the source image are replaced by the background color, obliterating the destination pixels at those points. |

*Continued*

| | Table 18-2 *(continued)* |
|---|---|
| **Method** | **Description** |
| `drawImage(Image img, int dx1, int dy1, int dx2, int dy2, int sx1, int sy1, int sx2, int sy2, ImageObserver obs)` | Draws the portion of the source image defined by sx1, sy1 and sx2, sy2 into the region in the destination region defined by dx1, dy1 and dx2, dy2. The source image region is scaled as necessary to fit into the destination region and transparent pixels do not affect the destination image. |
| `drawImage(Image img, int dx1, int dy1, int dx2, int dy2, int sx1, int sy1, int sx2, int sy2, Color bgcolor, ImageObserver obs)` | Draws the portion of the source image defined by sx1, sy1 and sx2, sy2 into the region in the destination region defined by dx1, dy1 and dx2, dy2. The source image region is scales as necessary to fit into the destination region and transparent pixels are changed to the given background color when rendered. |

The most used method is the simplest of these — taking just the source image and the x, y location to render it to. The rendering system will then draw the picture in its natural width and height on the target component:

```
public void paint(Graphics g) {
   g.drawImage(img, 0, 0, null);
}
```

You might be wondering what the ImageObserver reference is all about in all of the `drawImage()` calls. The observer provides a way for you to get feedback about how the image-loading process is going. Normally you don't need this, so the parameter can be set to `null` like in the example code.

## Drawing on an Image

Another option that you might like to have in your application is the ability to draw to an offscreen image. This is typically done when you want to draw everything first before putting it on the screen (a process known as *double buffering*).

To draw on an image, you first need to either load an existing one or create a blank image. Once you have the image, you can request a graphics context directly from the image. Drawing on an image is no different than drawing on the screen. All of the methods to draw primitives are contained in the Graphics class. For an image you call the `getGraphics()` method to return the instance for that image to you. Once you have an instance, you can use that to draw to that image.

**Note**     You can create new blank images by using the `BufferedImage` class and calling one of the constructors. For example

```
Image img =
    new BufferedImage(200, 200,
                      BufferedImage.TYPE_INT_RGB);
```

will create a blank image for you that is 200 pixels square and uses just three color components (no transparency).

Remember that each Graphics instance only ever refers to one image. You cannot have a single instance of the Graphics class and expect to be able to draw to multiple image instances.

Once you have an instance of Graphics for the image, you can perform all the same operations as what you used to draw to the screen. You can draw lines, circles, filled areas, and even draw other images on top of this image.

**Caution**     If you create a new image that has transparency (TYPE_INT_ARGB) and then draw another image over that, which contains transparent sections, the transparency is lost. That is, when you draw the destination image to the screen, the transparent bits will be white (or whatever background color the image is). This is because the default pixel color is opaque.

## More efficient images

The techniques that you used in the previous sections will be adequate for most simple applications. However, once you start building commercial quality or reasonably complex apps, you will start to notice several shortfalls in efficiency. Some of these you may have already noticed just by looking at the documentation.

### BufferedImages

In the previous section, the sidebar noted how to create a new blank image. Instead of using `Image`, it used a `BufferedImage`. This is the first step to more efficient image management. Examining the documentation will reveal that you can't directly instantiate an instance of `Image`. `BufferedImage` is the only class that will allow you to do this. There are other good reasons, too.

`BufferedImage`s work slightly differently than normal images. Instead of attempting to load all of the data at once, a `BufferedImage` reads in the bytes and then loads things on demand. Much more control is also associated with it. There are the basic image bytes, and then you have a color model as well as the raw pixels.

Using the standard loading process, you don't really know which sort of image instance you are getting back. There is no way to really overcome this, so you need to make use of BufferedImage anywhere that you can inside your code. These images take a lot of memory by default.

**Note**   Sun's implementation of the image-loading routines has been the subject of intense criticism for years by many people, including these authors. Unfortunately, on their test cases, it is impossible to note what is happening, so Sun refuses to acknowledge the problems. This has continued right through to the current JDK 1.3.

The problem boils down to the memory used and speed of loading. In each image, Sun's standard loaders keep four copies of the image around in the 4-bytes-per-pixel format. That is, if you have a 10x10 pixel image, there will be 10x10x4x4 bytes of memory taken up. This isn't normally an issue when all you are doing is loading a few icons. But build a serious program that uses large images (e.g., 4000x4000 pixels), and it becomes ridiculous. In our testing, we were loosing as much as 180MB to a single image instance where native code applications were only using 67MB.

If image handling will be an issue for you, then access a set of image-loading classes that replace the standard issue versions at

    http://www.vlc.com.au/imageloader/

These will load many more formats (GIF, JPG, PNG, TGA, TIFF, XPM) at twice the speed and using a quarter of the memory of the standard Sun implementations. Some minor changes to your code will be needed, but image handling will no longer be an issue.

The `flush()` method of images is a useful memory saver. The effect of this is to clear out any internal extra bits of memory that an image may have used. Typically, this will cut the amount of memory used in half! There are a few catches to this, too. If you flush the image and then ask for the width or height (`getWidth()`, `getHeight()`), then that memory is reloaded again. This annoying trait is impossible to overcome. Just make sure that you request the width and height only once and store those in a variable somewhere.

## Using the Toolkit.getImage() method

If you read between the fine print of the `createImage()` method used earlier, you noticed the following statement in the Javadoc:

> "The returned Image is a new object that will not be shared with any other caller of this method or its getImage variant."

This means that if you request the same file twice through the `createImage()` method, it will read the entire file's content twice and create two separate instances of the image. Naturally, this is a waste if you are using the same image in a number of different places. You really just want to use a single instance everywhere.

Two approaches can be used. First, create your own image cache that checks to see if the requested image has already been loaded. Second, use the getImage() methods. These will cache any loaded images and return an existing instance if one has already been loaded. You can call getImage() in the same places that you call createImage(). The method outlines were described in Table 18-1. You'll notice that a few less options are available, however.

While the getImage() method sounds like a great way to save memory, some small problems are associated with it. The implementation permanently stores a reference to the image. In long running applications, this extra memory hanging around is bad. Consider an application that creates a number of icons and then occasionally displays larger images onscreen. These images get shown only once. As you go along, you are chewing up more memory without ever releasing the memory used by the early images that are no longer used. For nontrivial applications, it is better to implement your own image caching.

## Offline Loading with MediaTracker

In the previous code examples involving the image rendering, you may have noticed some interesting artifacts. When the application first runs, it comes up with a blank area. The image doesn't show until you resize the window a bit or cover it with another and uncover it again. In particular, you will have noticed this on the example that uses the URL to a Web server.

The reason for this odd behavior is due to timing. When the image first loads, it takes some time to open the stream, read the bytes, and then turn them into pixels. What you see onscreen is the fact that the image has not yet completed loading. Internally, the graphics system decides that it can draw half an image; therefore, it doesn't draw anything at all. You end up with the white background color. Fortunately, there is a way around this problem by using the MediaTracker class.

MediaTracker is designed to load classes asynchronously to the normal program execution. It also provides a number of built-in functions to deal with errors during the load. Originally, it was supposed to handle all forms of media, but Sun never got around to defining anything other than image handling, so it remains to this day.

Cross-Reference

The code for this example can be found in the file MediaTrackerLoader.java and can be found with the rest of the examples for this chapter. It uses the Java Bible Web site for the remote image location to demonstrate the slow load time effects. To make sure the code runs correctly, make sure you are connected to the Internet at the time or make your own modifications to the code.

To use the MediaTracker, you need to create an image and then tell the tracker that you are interested in following the results. We start by creating an image in the normal fashion:

```
Toolkit tk = Toolkit.getDefaultToolkit();

try {
```

```
URL url = new URL(IMAGE_LOCATION);

img = tk.createImage(url);
```

Next we need to create an instance of the media tracker and register our image with it:

```
mt = new MediaTracker(this);
mt.addImage(img, 0);
mt.waitForAll();
}
catch(MalformedURLException mue) {
  System.out.println("Created a bad URL!!!");
}
catch (InterruptedException ie) {
  // ignore it
}
```

The last line before the exception handling tells the tracker to wait until all of the registered images have been loaded. In the line prior to that, we register an image and give it an ID. The ID can be any number you like, so we chose zero because we really have only one image to load. (Yes, media tracker will work with multiple images at once.)

**Note**   The media tracker code shown here is usually put inside a run() method of a thread. This allows the image to load away from the main application execution.

At the end of this code segment, you may or may not have an image. For example, if the URL was bad or the image file was corrupt, it would have continued along normally. You need to check for errors.

```
if(mt.isErrorAny()) {
  System.err.println("error loading image " +
                     img.toString());
  return;
}
```

If an error occurred, there is no point continuing further, so we print out an error message and exit from the method.

Assuming that we got a correctly loaded image, we can now continue on our merry way with the image. We might want to paint it to the screen. Just so that you can see what is going on, the Frame was deliberately set larger in size than the image. When the image is loaded correctly, the frame is resized to the same size as the image and then repainted.

```
if(img != null) {
  img_height = img.getHeight(this);
```

```
    img_width = img.getWidth(this);

    // Set size will also force a repaint so we don't need
    // to call repaint() explicitly.
    this.setSize(img_width, img_height);
}
```

# Printing

With all of these sexy graphics being drawn on the screen, now you might want to take a picture of it for posterity. Of course if you print it out, you can hang it on the wall and show off to all your friends.

The aim of the printing APIs in Java is to make them look as much like drawing to screen as possible. As you will see shortly, Sun has managed a pretty good job of this. The only difference between printing and drawing on screen is the setup process.

## Printing classes

When drawing items on the screen, all of the interface is done through the Graphics class. For printing, we still use an instance of Graphics, this time a little different. A new class called `PrintGraphics` extends `Graphics` and has been created to deal with the extra printing specific issues.

Actually, there's not that much extra — only one method:

```
public PrintJob getPrintJob()
```

The `PrintJob` class provides the interface to the printing process. Once you have initiated a print process, the Java printing process will give you this class. From this, you can determine all the information needed to create a printed page.

The other important point to keep in mind is that the aim of `PrintJob` is to make printing a hard copy as easy as drawing on the screen. Indeed, `PrintJob` assumes that you want to print exactly what is on the screen. If that is the case, `PrintJob` makes the job easy because it lets you use the same Java code that you use to display output on the screen for the printer, effectively redirecting output from the screen device to a printer. (Nifty, huh?) On the other hand, if you want to print a document that doesn't fit entirely inside a window on the computer screen (a long document, such as word processor file, a large drawing, or some other large and complex body of material that doesn't fit into the dimensions of a computer screen), you have to work a bit harder to get the job done with `PrintJob`.

## Starting the printing process

When you need to print, you request what's known as a print job from the AWT using the Toolkit's getPrintJob() method. This method constructs and returns a platform-specific PrintJob class that you can then use to print your data. This seemingly roundabout way of doing things shields you from having to deal with the peculiarities of printing on a particular platform.

The first step is to get a PrintJob instance for the platform on which your application is running, which you do by invoking the getPrintJob() method of the Toolkit for the current platform. The getPrintJob() method has two different methods of calling, as outlined in Table 18-3.

| Table 18-3<br>**The AWT Methods to Start Printing** | |
|---|---|
| *Method* | *Description* |
| getPrintJob(Frame frame, String jobtitle, Properties props) | Creates a new print job for the given parent frame. Uses platform-specific properties to control what should be printed. The frame cannot be null. |
| getPrintJob(Frame frame, String jobtitle, JobAttributes ja, PageAttributes pa) | Creates a new print job using the given list of job and page attributes. Allows printing when there is no GUI, such as a server. |

**Note** The second of these getPrintJob() methods has been added with JDK 1.3. Previously, there was no platform-independent way to find out information such as page orientation or scale. Programmers had to write platform-specific code or not print because of this.

The getPrintJob() method returns a PrintJob object that is the result of initiating a print operation on the underlying operating system. This process starts the platform-specific printing process such as asking the user which printer to use, determining specific properties, etc (Table 18-4). If the user cancelled the print job, it returns null. There is no messing around with putting dialog boxes onscreen, calculating the different page types and orientation, etc. One simple call and you have all the information you need to print a page.

Once you have a PrintJob instance, you need to fetch the Graphics instance with which you will be drawing. You can do this with the getGraphics() method of PrintJob. Once you have this instance, you can draw just like you were drawing to the screen.

## Table 18-4
## The Methods of the PrintJob Class

| Method | Description |
|---|---|
| `Graphics getGraphics()` | Returns a `Graphics` instance that allows you to draw to a printed page. |
| `Dimension getPageDimension()` | Returns the dimensions of the output page in pixels. |
| `int getPageResolution()` | Returns the resolution of the page in pixels per inch. |
| `boolean lastPageFirst()` | Returns `true` if the last page is printed first. |
| `void end()` | Instructs the printing system that the printing has finished. |

When you have finished drawing the page, you need to tell the printing system that it is OK to send it all to the printer. By calling `end()` in `PrintJob`, you signal that everything is complete and to print it all now.

# Controlling the printing

If you tried printing just with the basic graphics information, things will probably turn out a little weird. Most likely, you will find all the objects squashed up in the upper left corner. This is due to the page resolution being very different than on the screen. If you are printing a long document, it will probably span multiple pages, but you only have one coming out of the printer.

What other information might be useful to the programmer? How about printing the last page first or landscape versus portrait printing? These are all important as far as the software is concerned so that it acts correctly.

## Page Size

Apart from portrait or landscape mode, the most important knowledge is exactly how big the page is. While the screen is limited in size, a page may be huge (for example, A0 on a plotter), and everything needs to be scaled accordingly. If you are printing text on an A4 page and the user changes to A3, you should now be able to print twice as much.

To find out the page size, you call the `getPageResolution()` method. This returns an instance of `Dimension` that gives you width and height information in pixels. You don't need to worry about converting to real page sizes in centimeters or whether to use portrait or landscape. The page orientation is given to you just in the dimensions. If the page is wider than long, you are using landscape; otherwise, you are using portrait.

Sometimes, you might need to print information true to scale. One inch on the page corresponds to one foot. By calling the `getPageResolution()` method, you can determine what one inch is in pixels and draw everything to the correct scale.

## Multiple Pages

Scanning through the `PrintJob` methods in Table 18-4, you might be wondering how you deal with multiple pages. If you draw off the end of the dimensions of the page, does it automatically go to the next page?

Each time you call the `getGraphics()` method, it returns a new instance to use. Each instance corresponds to a single page. Simply by calling the `getGraphics()` method for each page you need, you can produce multiple-page documents. For double-sided pages, you still must call the method once for each page.

## Extra Information

Another area of information that might be useful is the supplementary information provided by the JobAttributes and PageAttributes classes. Normal printing usually does not require the extra information provided in these, but they may be useful for performing more advanced operations. Most of the information supplied will probably seem useless to you. It seems that it is aimed at people implementing printing systems in the underlying JVM.

`JobAttributes` provides information about the entire print job as a whole: for example, if you want to know whether you are printing to a file or printer and most importantly, whether to print all pages or just a range of them.

`PageAttributes` contain information about the properties of the page. You might want to know whether color printing is available or should be done in black and white only. (You might want to provide your own dithering rather than the default supplied by the printer.) Other information supplied is what size page you are printing to and the orientation of the paper (portrait or landscape).

**Note**    Java provides complete independent print handling in the `java.awt.print` package. The attributes classes that you have seen form part of this. The idea is to provide a server-based application the ability to send output to a printer without needing to present a dialog box on the screen.

Why would you want to do this? One example is a user wanting to implement a remote printing service through the Internet Printing Protocol. This is a protocol that provides printing services through an HTTP connection. Using a combination of servlets and the printing APIs, you could implement your own simple remote printing system.

# Summary

Color, drawing, and images all form the core of being able to provide a customized application. Unless you are producing a set of form type reports, you are almost guaranteed to need these capabilities in every application or applet you write. Even if it is something simple like setting the background color of a text field, there will be some need for these basic tasks.

The highlights of this chapter were the following:

✦ Learning how to use and set color values

✦ Drawing simple primitives to the screen such as lines, circles, and filled areas

✦ Drawing text to the screen while controlling attributes like font information

✦ Loading and drawing images to the screen from external files

✦ Being able to provide simple printing capabilities for your application

✦   ✦   ✦

# Containers and Basic Concepts

**B**y now you must be wondering just how we build a complete user interface like you see in your everyday applications. You've seen an overview of how the AWT works and the event mechanisms in Chapter 17. In Chapter 18, you learned how to create your own graphics. Now you're only missing the normal things like buttons to press and lists to choose from. Of course, a major part of any modern application is the use of menus, so we'll cover those too.

## Opening the Window

Unless you are writing command-line-based applications, you are almost certainly going to need to know how to create and manage windows for your user interface. Windows are the top level of the GUI. They provide decorations like the title bar and the buttons to open, close, and minimize the windows. Also, a major feature of all GUI applications is the dialog box. Whether it be the humble About box, a request for username and password, or a complex piece of information for entering the geographic information about a point, all these tasks require the ability to effectively manage dialog boxes.

### Windows to the world

We start this process by looking at windows. In Java terminology, the normal thing that goes on the screen—complete with the title bar and other decorations—is termed a `Frame`. Frames provide all of the normal services that you would expect of an application. If you need to get more heavily customized, say drawing your own borders, then you need to use a `Window`. `Dialogs` are a specialized form of window that provide a more limited set of controls as well as other restrictions.

We'll get into some more detail about these components shortly. Just so you know what the differences look like, Figure 19-1 contains a snapshot of the basic window types without any fancy contents. The frame contains all of the usual controls for close, minimize, and maximize, as well as the system menu. The dialog box provides the same borders but has only a single button to close it. Finally, a `Window` doesn't have any borders or decorations at all. Notice that all you see is the outline of a white area over the desktop, which represents the window's bounds.

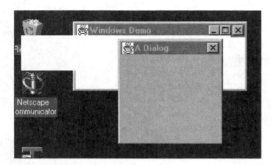

**Figure 19-1:** These are the basic, unadorned types of windows available in Java (taken on a Win32 machine). We've had to overlay them so that you can see what a Window looks like.

## Frames

Frames are the most commonly used of the windows. Every application with a GUI is going to need at least one `Frame` object. Frames are handy because you can create menus for them with minimal effort and listen for all the important changes like window resizes and minimize/maximize requests.

To create a frame, you can just construct an instance of the class like this:

```
Frame myFrame = new Frame();
```

Of course, this is pretty boring because all you get is an empty window. If you provide a string in the constructor, that is used as the text in the title bar. Of course, you can always change the text at a later date with the `setTitle()` method of `Frame`.

```
myFrame.setTitle("A new title!");
```

**Tip**    When you create any window, it doesn't appear on the screen. By default, it is hidden. To show a window or dialog box, you need to call the `show()` method. If you want to hide it again later, you need to call the `hide()` method.

**Note**    There are more ways of constructing frames than this. These other techniques involve the use of the `GraphicsConfiguration` class, which is beyond the scope of this book.

### Changing the icon

If you would like to set the image that the icon should use, then you can call the `setIconImage()` method. On Win32 computers, this causes the icon in the top left corner of the window to change. For UNIX machines, depending on the window manager you use, this usually sets the icon for when the window has been iconified.

To change the icon, you need to load an image using the techniques you learned in the previous chapter. Typically, this will be around 32 × 32 pixels and using a GIF image for transparency. Once you know that the image has completed loading, you can call this method.

### Resizing the control

Frames allow you some control over whether they can be resized. By calling the `setResizable()` method with a `true` or `false` value, you can control whether you will allow the user to resize the window.

To change the size of the window from within your code, you can call the `setSize()` method with the width and height values in pixels. Even if you have told the window that it is not resizable, it is ignored by this method. That is, the resize control only works to stop the user from changing the size, not the coder!

Another handy method to know about is `pack()`. This provides a way to tell the window to place all of its components into the smallest size possible. Internally, the window goes through all of the bits that have been added to it, queries them for their preferred size, calculates the minimum size needed, and sets the window to that. This method is very handy for dealing with a window that may be different sizes on different operating systems (or just users with different sized fonts), and it always ensures that you will get something decent looking.

## Listening for Control Events

Windows must be able to respond when the user tries to close them. If you played with any of the demo code in the previous chapter, you noticed that clicking on the Close button or selecting the Close option from the system menu did absolutely nothing. The only way to kill the application was to use Ctrl+C on the command line.

The reason for this odd behavior is that Java windows aren't capable of closing themselves. You need to provide this information. You need to grab the events from the window, looking for when it is told to close, and then make it close yourself.

### Window events

Information about the state of the window can be received through the `Window Listener` interface, which can be found in the `java.awt.event` package. You can add a listener using the `addWindowListener()` method of the parent class `Window`.

Cruising through the API documentation shows that you can get events for almost everything that can happen to a window. For us, the most important method is windowClosing(). This is called whenever a user requests that the window be closed. Inside this method, we can then write our own code.

### Closing a window in response to a user

A typical way of dealing with the user closing the window is to exit the application. Even when you don't want to exit, you still need to listen for the event because you'll need to write a small amount of code to hide the window from visibility anyway. As an example, we'll create the ClosingWindowDemo.

As previously mentioned, we need to use the WindowListener interface. Since we only have a simple application and we already extended the Frame object, we need to implement the listener. The class declaration looks like this:

```
import java.awt.*;
import java.awt.event.*;
public class ClosingWindowDemo extends Frame
    implements WindowListener
```

Next, we need to make sure that we register our listener with the frame. We do this in the constructor, which is the most common way of doing it:

```
public ClosingWindowDemo() {
    super("ClosingWindow Demo");
    addWindowListener(this);
}
```

Now we've established that we will get these events. Because we've implemented the listener, we need to provide definitions for all the methods. We'll leave all those out here (you can see them in the code on the accompanying Web site to this book) and look at only one in particular: windowClosing(). As the documentation says, this gets called whenever the user has requested the window to be closed. Inside this method, you must do whatever should be done to make the application behave correctly. For example, if we just wanted to hide the window (not exit the application), we would write the following:

```
public void windowClosing(WindowEvent e) {
  hide();
}
```

To make the application exit (as in the case of the demo), we need to force the application to exit by calling System.exit():

```
public void windowClosing(WindowEvent e) {
  System.exit(0);
}
```

**Tip** To exit the application when you've written a GUI, you must always call System.exit(). If you merely closed the windows and disposed of them, you would find that at the command line, the application would still be running. This is because a bunch of threads are happening internally. The JVM will not exit until those threads finish—i.e., never. The only way to force the application to exit is with the system call.

### Customized Windows

If the normal frame contains too much decoration for you, then you might want to think about creating your own custom window by extending the Window class. Windows contain absolutely nothing. As you saw in the earlier demo, it becomes just a white square on the screen. There are no title bars, menus, or even window borders. You must do all of this yourself.

Despite the apparent agony and huge amounts of code that you must write to do this, raw windows are quite useful. By far the most common use for these is to provide startup splash screens. Almost every commercial application has one of these. Notice how they don't have the traditional borders and title area.

The technique to create your own custom window is fairly straightforward. With the blank area to work with, you use the same drawing routines that you learned about in the previous chapter. Override the paint() method and then draw everything that you need to with the provided Graphics instance.

## Dialog Boxes

When you need to query the user for some information or provide warnings, you need to use a dialog box. These specialized windows cannot exist on their own. They must always have a parent Frame or another dialog box. (You can't have a Window as parent.)

Dialog boxes have access to the same information as windows and frames. If you want to know when the user has requested the dialog box to close, you can register a WindowListener for it, just like the bigger windows. Also, you have the same pack() capability too. The major difference between dialog boxes and the window classes are that you lose the maximize/minimize buttons and you can make the dialog box *modal* (prevent the user from using any other window until this one has been closed). The rest is the same.

**Tip** One common behavior—using the Esc key to cancel the dialog box—takes a little more work to do. You need to register for a Key event and look for the Esc key being pressed. When you get this, you can then call the hide() method of the dialog box.

## Modal Dialog Boxes

The use of dialog boxes creates some interesting behavioral differences. A modal dialog box does not allow the user to use any other window within the application until that dialog box has been closed. For example, an error message dialog box will be modal because you want the user to know that something really bad has happened.

Obviously, you also need to be a careful with the use of modal dialog boxes. They can block the user from doing something useful at the wrong time. Also, it is possible that one modal dialog box may be interrupted by another from somewhere else in the application (for example, a network processing error). You can end up with some nasty conflicts about modality that cause the entire application to lock with no way out of it — particularly on UNIX machines.

If the dialog box is set to modal, then when you call the `show()` method of the dialog box, your code will not run any further until the dialog box has closed. (The `show()` method becomes blocking.) If the dialog box is not modal, the `show()` method puts the dialog box onscreen and your code continues to process.

**Caution**    If you call `show()` inside the constructor of a modal dialog box, you end up with some real problems with the application locking up. The different behaviors have surprised many a programmer, so pay attention to what is happening.

## The FileDialog Class

Java provides a number of standard dialog boxes that match the underlying system. In the previous chapter, you saw the use of the printing dialog boxes. In that case, you weren't allowed to directly control the dialog box: it was always part of the request to get a new print job. Under the AWT, you are allowed to use only one standard dialog box. (Swing, as you will see in later chapters, has many more.)

The `FileDialog` class provides an interface to the standard Open and Save dialog boxes. Depending on the constructor arguments, you end up with one or the other. The advantage of using this over creating your own is that a lot of the standard functionality is already provided for you. For example, using filters, changing directories, and checking that the file already exists (the Save dialog box) is performed without you needing to write one line of code.

File dialog boxes are modal, and this cannot be changed. You need to make sure all the information is set before you call `show()`, and you'll know that after the method returns, you can fetch the user-selected information immediately.

### Creating a File dialog box

Save dialog boxes are used when you want to fetch a file name and location from the user to save a file to. The dialog box will test, before closing, that the file name is not already existing and warn the user about it.

To create a new Save dialog box, you need the following code:

```
FileDialog fd = new FileDialog(parentFrame,
                               "Save something as",
                               FileDialog.SAVE);
```

The first argument is the parent frame for the dialog box. The middle argument is a string that you want to use for a title. The last argument is the mode — save or load. If you don't provide this, the default is to create a load dialog box. An example file load dialog box is shown in Figure 19-2.

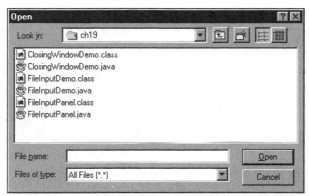

**Figure 19-2:** A sample FileDialog in load mode on the Win32 platform

### Getting and setting file and directory information

By default, creating a new file dialog box will set the directory to the user's home directory (the value specified by the system property $user.home). After creating the instance, and once the user moves around in the directory structure, the next time that same instance is shown, it will stay in the last selected directory.

Obviously, the most important reason for using a file dialog box is to get file and directory information. These arrive separately. The directory information is obtained through the getDirectory() method. This will normally return the directory name as a string. However, if you get the value of null back, that means that no directory information was set, i.e., the user clicked the Cancel button. In your code, if you get this value, then that says to exit the method now because the user didn't want to open/save the file.

Assuming that the directory information is okay, you will possibly also want the file name that was entered. You can obtain this through the getFile() method that returns a string representation of the file name.

Setting file and directory information just uses better versions of these methods. The setFile() method sets the name of the file in the dialog box, while the setDirectory() method will change the dialog box to the nominated directory.

**Note** With the standard AWT file dialog box, there is no capability to customize the look and behavior. For example, if you wanted a dialog box that would only select a directory name without a file name, that cannot be done. In either mode, if no file name has been selected/entered, the dialog box will not allow you to close it, i.e., you cannot just select a directory and expect the dialog box to behave correctly.

### Custom Dialog Boxes

Creating your own custom dialog box requires that you extend the Dialog class. As for windows and frames, you can create an instance and then fill it with a collection of buttons, labels, text fields, and so on. Title and size information are set using the same methods too.

**Note** Like windows and frames, you don't have to literally extend the class. It is possible to create an instance of the class and then call the methods on it from outside to set the panels, listeners, etc. However, due to the complexity of even the most simple dialog box, you will rarely see this done in code.

# Containing the World

Windows, frames, and dialog boxes are just part of a much larger group of user interface elements known as containers. These classes allow you to place other components inside them. For example, you might want to create a common panel that is used across multiple dialog boxes. Instead of creating the same components over and over and writing the same code over and over, you can build a customized container and create new instances of that as often as you need that particular functionality.

Four classes form the basic of all user interface elements that you'll deal with, except for menus:These classes are Component, Container, Canvas, and Panel. We'll deal with each of them in turn, starting from the most general first.

## Components

Some items on the screen cannot contain anything else. An example is the text label. Just a single string is printed onscreen; there is no need to be able to add another component (say another label) to it. However, there is still quite a lot of common functionality between these classes and those that contain a collection of other items. The base class is called a Component.

Components provide all of the raw handlers for putting something onto the screen. Whether it is a custom component where you do all the drawing or it is an interface to a component provided by the native toolkit, all the functionality is provided in this class. At this level, we also deal with the raw interaction with both mouse and keyboard. In the more recent versions, capabilities for dealing with alternate input methods have also been added specifically to make Java applications easier to use for handicapped people.

## Dealing with Screen Updates

In the previous chapter, we dealt a lot with drawing lines and circles to screen. All of the examples were written so that the code was called in the paint() method. paint() is not just for frames, it works for any component. Simply by overriding this method, you can quickly create a customized component. Every time the screen needs updating, this method is called. Using the supplied Graphics instance, you can draw your own output.

You may have noticed that there is another method called update() that also gets passed an instance of Graphics. This method is called just before paint(). You can also do drawing here, but it really isn't advisable. By default, this method clears the component and then calls paint(). If you see a white flash in your drawing when it repaints, this is why. It's unclear why this method was included because the first action that every custom component does is override the method and get it to directly call paint():

```
public void update(Graphics g) {
   paint(g);
}
```

If you look at the demo code in the previous chapter, you'll see that it does this.

## Listening for Events

Like everything else in the AWT, there are a whole swag of different events that you can access as a component. Every component has access to keyboard, mouse, focus, and information about the component's state.

Each of these types of events has an associated listener and a set of event classes for which you can register. Table 19-1 outlines these values. A couple are missing that the average programmer will rarely use. These deal with changes in component hierarchy (adding and removing nested components and containers).

Table 19-1
**The Listeners You Can Register with a Component**

| Listener | Description |
|---|---|
| ComponentListener | Deals with the state of the component. For example, when you add a component to a container and make it visible, you will get one of these events. |
| FocusListener | Deals with when the component gains or loses focus. |
| InputMethodListener | Deals with text entry information — in particular, nonkeyboard entry systems like voice dictation. Not generally used unless you are implementing another text component. |
| KeyListener | Handles all of the key input. When the component has focus, each keystroke will be delivered through this interface. Handy for providing keyboard shortcuts. |
| MouseListener | Deals with the mouse interacting with the window. Provides click, move, and enter/exit information. |
| MouseMotionListener | Deals with movement information not associated with standard mouse events. Useful for dealing with drag-and-drop events. |

These listeners can be registered using the standard `addXXXListener()` methods provided by the component class.

## Cursor Handling

A standard feature of modern GUIs is the changing of the mouse cursor to indicate state; for example, turning the cursor into a watch or an hourglass while the application is doing something that takes a while.

Changing the cursor requires the use of the `Cursor` class. A number of standard cursor shape types are defined as constants here. Using these, you can construct the correct cursor type. For example, to create a waiting cursor, you can use either of these options:

```
Cursor c1 = Cursor.getPredefinedCursor(Cursor.WAIT_CURSOR);
Cursor c2 = new Cursor(Cursor.WAIT_CURSOR);
```

Once you have an instance of a `Cursor` object, you can set the cursor for this component using the `setCursor()` method. Note that this sets it only for this component; however, it does work in a nested fashion. If you want to set the cursor to the wait cursor for the whole window, then call `setCursor()` on the `Frame`.

To clear the cursor, you can provide `null` as the argument to `setCursor()`. This allows the component to use whatever the cursor is of its parent container. If this is not the default, then you can grab the default cursor by calling `Cursor.getDefaultCursor()`.

 **Tip** To create a customized cursor, you can load a normal image and then call `Toolkit.createCustomCursor()`. This returns you a `Cursor` object that you can use just like the predefined types.

## Graphical Information

Information about the component's state, such as location and size, is also handy to know when creating custom components.

### Location

The location information provides you the position, in pixels, of the component. If the component is nested inside other containers, this is the location relative to the parent container. If it is a window or dialog box, this is the physical location on the screen. Location is always the top left corner.

The `getLocation()` method returns a `Point` instance that contains the x and y position of the component. To change the location, call `setLocation()` with either an x,y value as `int`s or using an instance of `Point`.

### Size

Size information is represented by the `Dimension` class. This is the width and height of the component (relative to the location, of course).

To find out the size of the component, call `getSize()`, which will return you a `Dimension` instance. You set the size through `setSize()` and it is passed either x,y as `int`s or using an instance of `Dimension`.

If you want to combine size and location information, you can always use the `get/setBounds()` methods. These provide both pieces of information. When fetching the bounds, you are returned an instance of the `Rectangle` object.

### Interactive state

Finally, you want to know whether a component is able to receive events. A typical example is dimmed menu items and toolbar buttons. This disabling of a component is more than just changing the rendering color. It also means that events should not be generated for the component unnecessarily. For example, a component should not receive mouse or keyboard events if it has been disabled.

To check the enabled state of a component, call the `isEnabled()` method. This returns you a `boolean` value indicating the state. To change the state, you can call `setEnabled()`, again with a `boolean` value to set it enabled (`true`) or disabled (`false`).

### Drag and Drop

Components also support drag and drop. Doing a full explanation of implementing drag and drop (DnD) features is a complex task that would take a chapter in its own right, which we don't have the time for.

In the `Component` class, you will see a number of methods that deal with objects like `DropTarget`. To properly implement DnD requires that you implement mouse listeners for the drag events and also use the capabilities provided in the `java.awt.dnd` package.

**Caution**    Drag and drop with Java has been a love/hate affair. There have been many problems with it over the years, but it is slowly getting better. Within a Java application, DnD works well. Almost everything works as you expect it to. (There were a couple of nasty bugs when trying to change the cursor in the middle of drag/drops, but the general behavior was fine.) Interacting with the outside world is a little more tricky. It is possible to do, but it takes a reasonable amount of work to figure out. In the end, you have to code platform-specific solutions to work correctly with the information that is supplied to you. (It is not specified at all in the Java APIs.) Unfortunately, this breaks the write-once, run-anywhere mantra.

## Containers

In the previous section, the term *container* was mentioned several times. Containers are a special type of component that can hold other components as children. Although it is possible for you to create a custom component that you can add components to, it is not a recommended solution—there's just too much fiddling around to do. The `Container` class provides everything you need already.

`Container` extends the `Component` class, so you get all of these features plus some more:

✦ Manages a collection of children components

✦ Provides facilities for automatically laying out components according to rules provided by a layout manager.

✦ Provides depth management of overlaying components

Layout managers are covered in the next chapter in detail. As a basic summary, they provide a set of rules to organize a group of components onscreen. For example, you can make them all form a grid pattern or make them stay attached to the sides. Each type of class derived from `Container` has a default layout manager already set. They aren't all the same, so check the next chapter for more information.

## Canvas

If you need to present a drawing area to the user, you'll probably use the `Canvas` class. This provides a blank rectangle where the code can grab events (provided by the `Component` base class methods as you saw earlier) but does not provide layout capabilities.

Canvases do not provide any extra capabilities over a standard component. Back in the dim, dark days of JDK1.0, this was the only way that you could create custom components. You couldn't derive classes from `Component` directly, so the only way was to use a canvas. In the latest revisions that is no longer an issue, so the canvas has fallen out of use for almost everything except for providing drawing areas for paintbrush-type applications. Even then, it is debatable whether it is actually better to subclass components and provide a customized component for your own use.

## Panels

A `Panel` is the most frequently used container class. This provides a blank area in which you can place other components. Being the simplest of the containers, it is also the most lightweight. It doesn't provide too much extra overhead, and you can nest panels within panels, etc.

When you build a lot of applications, you will see that panels are used most often to create a customized collection of components that need to be used in a number of different places. A class will extend `Panel` and provide a number of convenience methods to get and set pieces of information. For example, you might create a file name input panel that contains a text field and a browse button that shows the File dialog box.

**Cross-Reference**
There is an example of creating a reusable panel on the accompanying Web site to this book. This provides the basic file name input panel described in the previous paragraph. The class name is called `FileInputPanel` and can be found with the other code for Chapter 19. The demonstration window is `FileInputDemo`.

# Simple Components

With windows and container classes now under your belt, you no doubt want to start filling them with things. Text, labels, buttons, and menus all go into making a good user interface.

In this section, we are going to be looking at the simple components of labels, buttons, and various ways to select items. Menus are covered in a separate section, while text input handling is covered in the next chapter.

# Labels

Of the provided components, the label is the simplest. In its AWT form, all you can provide is a single line of text. There is no capability to change the font, create multiple lines, or even include an image. Labels are typically used with other components to give them meaning.

Labels may be left, right, or center justified. By default, they are left justified. To create a new label that is right justified, you write the following:

```
Label l1 = new Label("A label title", Label.RIGHT);
```

If you want to use the default left justification, then you can leave out the second argument altogether.

# Buttons

Buttons are the next most simple component. No doubt you are very familiar with what buttons do, so we'll skip the explanation. Like labels, they can only contain a single line of text and no images.

## Listening for Button Clicks

The most important reason for having a button is to know when the user has clicked on it. To find this out in your code, you register an `ActionListener` listener with the button that you have created. This listener notifies you when the button has been clicked.

There is only one method that you need to implement for the action listener: `action Performed()`. The argument to this is an `ActionEvent` that contains all of the information that you need to know about which button was pushed.

## Action Commands

If you want to provide a little more information with the button when it is clicked, there is always the option of associating an action command with it. This is just a simple `String`, but it allows a lot of extra information to be passed through. For example, you might have three buttons all saying "Browse" on a window, but you really need to know exactly what each one is supposed to be browsing.

By registering a string with the button using the `setActionCommand()` method, you can provide this extra information. You can extract this information from the button at any time using `getActionCommand()`; however, it is most useful when processing a button push and using the `getActionCommand()` method of `ActionEvent`.

# Check boxes and Radio Buttons

Java supports two kinds of check boxes: exclusive and nonexclusive. Outside of the Java world, these are usually known by two different names: radio buttons and check boxes, respectively. The difference between the two is whether you collect a series of check boxes into a group or not.

## Check Boxes

A check box allows you to select a single yes/no answer. Like all AWT components, the look of this depends on the platform. On Win32, you normally have a square box with a tick in it, and Unix/Motif uses a small square button-like area. Both of these have a label associated with them.

To create a new check box, you have a choice of three constructors: the option combinations of providing a label and setting the initial state. If you want to create a check box with the label "Select me" and it is already in the selected state, this is what would be written:

```
Checkbox cb = new Checkbox("Select me", true);
```

Create a few of these and arrange them into a grid, and you get Figure 19-3.

To set the state of a check box, you can call the setState() method with a boolean value. If the value is true, then the check box is set to a selected state, and if false, it is set to an unselected state. If you want to check what the state is, you can call the getState() method.

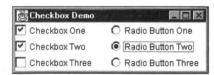

**Figure 19-3:** Several check boxes on the left and a group of radio buttons on the right

## Radio Buttons

A radio button is a check box that forms part of a mutually exclusive group. By definition, you can never have just one radio button. If you did, that would just be a check box because it's not part of a group.

Java distinguishes between radio buttons and check boxes by the constructors you use for the Checkbox class. If you provide an instance of the CheckboxGroup class as one of the parameters, that makes the check box become a radio button. All of the check boxes that use the same CheckboxGroup instance will form a group of mutually exclusive buttons.

To change an already created check box into a radio button or to change the group of buttons to which it belongs, you can use the setCheckboxGroup() method. The check box will form part of the group that you provide it. If you provide it with null, then it turns the radio button back into a check box.

### Receiving Selection Events

In many applications, selecting a check box will cause other parts of the user interface to change in response. For example, selecting a check box may enable a section of the user interface that is normally not selected. While it is easy to ask for the state using the getState() method, it is not easy to know when to call it unless you have the GUI tell you that the state has been changed.

To receive notification of when a user has selected a check box, you register an ItemListener. This interface has a single method: itemStateChanged(). This gets called when the registered item (the check box) has changed state. If you have a radio button group, each time the user selects one of the radio buttons, you'll get one event, which is the button being selected. You don't have a deselected event for the old button. You will see this in action in the CheckboxDemo code that is on the companion Web site.

Once you have received the event, you can use the getItemSelectable() method to return you the check box that was changed. (Checkbox implements the Item Selectable interface.) From there, you can process the state and whatever else you need to do (such as enable that piece of user interface).

## Choice Menus

Choice menus provide a list of items from which you can select one item at a time but provide it in menu format. Another name that you might be more familiar with is drop-down lists.

Items on the menu are just text strings. Each string represents something that you would want to select, and one item will always be selected (usually the first one added). To construct a choice menu, you first create an instance of the Choice class and then use the addItem() method for each option that you want to add:

```
Choice choice = new Choice();
choice.addItem("First option");
choice.addItem("Second option");
```

Choice menus use the same ItemListener interface as check boxes to notify you of a selection. The difference is that the selectable item that is returned is always the Choice instance. This is not particularly useful because you already know that; what you really want to know is which of the items was selected. You need to call the getSelectedItem() method to get the option that was selected.

Even though the name suggests that these are menus, there is no commonality between these and standard menu items that we cover in the next section. You can't create an instance of menu items and then add them to a `Choice` menu. They also provide different ways of providing user feedback.

# Lists

The final component that we are going to introduce is the list. Lists are just like their name suggests: a collection of strings from which you can choose. The difference between these and choice menus is that many options are presented onscreen at once and you can choose more than one.

To create a new list, you specify the number of visible rows and, optionally, the selection criteria. (More on that shortly.) To create a list with five visible items, you would write:

```
List list = new List(5);
list.add("First item");
list.add("Second item");
list.add("Third item");
list.add("Fourth item");
list.add("Fifth item");
list.add("Sixth item");
```

Note that we've added six items to a list that we've said would have five visible items. The key word here is *visible*. You can add many more, or less, and the list will automatically adjust. If you add more than the number of visible items, then a scroll bar will be added and the list will expand to accommodate the extras. The onscreen size stays the same, but internally, there is more space.

The `List` class defined here is different than the `List` class that you saw in Chapter 12. This class belongs in the `java.awt` package, while the other belongs in `java.util`. Because of their natural similarity (one represents data, the other displays it), you will regularly find both classes being used within the one class of your code. The compiler will most certainly complain about this, so you must make sure you fully qualify the class names each time you declare a variable of the `List` type.

## Controlling Selection Criteria

Unlike choice menus, a list can allow you to select more than one object at a time. Using the multiple mode option, you can tell the list to allow the user to select more than one item.

For the AWT, multiple mode allows you to select any items from the list using the conventions of the local platform — for example, Win32 users use Shift+left mouse to multiple-select items. The items selected do not need to be in a contiguous block.

If the `multipleMode` parameter of either the constructor or the `setMultipleMode()` method is `true`, then the users can select many options at once. Setting the value to `false` will allow them to select only one item at a time. To check on the current state, you can call the `getMultipleMode()` method and check the `boolean` value returned.

### Selection Events

Lists provide two different sets of events. Like choice menus and check boxes, you have the item selection events. This is generated whenever someone selects an item in the list. Also provided is an `ActionEvent` for when the user double clicks on an item.

A standard feature of GUI lists is that when you double-click on an item in a list, it will "do something." The most common behavior that you see would be opening the file that you've selected. To allow the same behavior within Java applications, you can register an `ActionListener` with the list. When the user double-clicks on an item in the list, you will be notified.

 Run the ListDemo code from the companion Web site to see how the various listeners work. A small list display will be shown and you can click on items and press the Fetch button to see the selected contents.

# Menus

Chances are if you create a `Frame`, you'll also want to create a menu bar and some menus to go with it. Menus provide access to all those important features like accessing Help, closing the application, and using the About dialog box.

Java menus have four parts:

- ✦ Menu bar: The thing that sits at the top of a frame and contains pull-down menus
- ✦ Menu item: Each label that can be clicked on a menu
- ✦ Pull-down menu: A collection of menu items that can be put into a menu bar
- ✦ Pop-up menu: The context-sensitive menu that normally appears when you right-click on an object on the screen.

Together, you can mix and match these items so that you can get common functionality. For example, you might want some context-sensitive items that also appear in a pull- down menu. Java allows you to do this.

# Menu Items

Menu items represent the individual items that you select. For the AWT, this is limited to just text strings. Menu items can be used in both pull-down and pop-up menus. This allows you to have common code to create the items and then share it around for whoever needs it within the application.

**Caution**
Although menu items can be used in both pull-down and pop-up menus, you cannot share a single instance between them. If you want the same item to appear in both menus, then you need to create two instances and register the same event listener with them.

## Standard Menu Items

All menu items use the `MenuItem` class. To create a new instance, you pass the constructor a label and an optional shortcut item (covered shortly). The label is what appears on the screen.

```
MenuItem mi = new MenuItem("Exit");
```

This creates an item with the text *Exit* on it.

Like with all other components, menu items can be enabled and disabled using the `setEnabled()` method. A disabled menu will have dimmed text on it and you won't be able to select it.

## Selection Events

The only way to find out when someone has selected a menu item is through the event listener mechanism. Menu items use the `ActionListener` class to send click events. The functionality is the same as the buttons you saw earlier. When a user clicks on a menu, the `ActionEvent` is generated with the details. You only get these events once an item has actually been selected; there are no events for having the mouse/keyboard just pass over the item.

Like buttons, you can also associate an action command string with the menu item. You can get and set the string with the `getActionCommand()` and `setAct-ionCommand()` methods, respectively. A major benefit of this is that you can now share a single instance of the `ActionListener` among numerous components on the screen and have them all use a single piece of code. In a typical application, you will see a Save menu item, a button on the toolbar, and probably a context-sensitive menu all at once. Instead of writing the same piece of save code three times, you can just set the same action command and action listener with all three and write the save action only one.

## Keyboard Shortcuts

A standard feature of many menu items is the keyboard shortcut. This allows the user to access the menu's function without taking the hands off the keyboard to use the mouse.

Shortcuts use different keys to trigger on different operating systems; Windows users normally use the Ctrl key, while UNIX users normally use the Alt key. In keeping with the platform-independent model of Java, the MenuShortcut class represents the shortcut keys without the user having to specify what the trigger key is. The underlying AWT implementation takes care of the rest of those details for you.

 In Java, menu shortcuts are not the same as menu accelerators. A shortcut gets used when the menu has not been opened. Accelerators are the little mnemonic keys that allow you to flick between menu items quickly once the menu has already been opened. (Normally indicated by an underline under the appropriate letter.) Java does not provide a way of specifying menu shortcuts.

Here is how you create a shortcut:

```
MenuShortcut msc = new MenuShortcut('E', false);
```

The first parameter is the character used for the shortcut. This can be any normal legal character, although using the Enter key probably isn't such a good idea. If you want to use function keys, then have a look at the java.awt.event.KeyEvent class. There is a list of all the key codes there defined as standard abstractions.

The second parameter specifies whether the user needs to press the Shift key as well. For example, Using *s* for save is not the same as Shift+S. Note that this effectively says the shortcut key is the uppercase *S* rather than the lowercase *s*. In Java, there is no difference. All characters are translated to the lowercase equivalent regardless of how you specify them in the constructor. Using the shift modifier should usually be reserved for the function keys and ancillary keys like Ins and Home.

So, to summarize all of this, if you want to create a shortcut to Shift+F6, this is the code you would write.

```
MenuShortcut msc = new MenuShortcut(KeyEvent.VK_F6, true);
```

## Check box Menu Items

Some menu items don't provide any action, but instead act like a toggle. These combine the check box functionality with the menu functionality. Normally, you can tell these menu items because they have a tick beside them.

CheckboxMenuItem is derived from MenuItem. That means you should get all of the standard functionality you normally get with this class — at least that is what you would expect. The reality is somewhat different. For a start, there are no menu shortcuts available. If you set one, it is ignored. Also, the normal action listeners don't work either. Instead, you use the ItemListener class that normal check boxes use to listen for state changes.

You create check box menu items the same way as you create a normal menu item. Provide a string and an optional initial state.

```
CheckboxMenuItem cbmi =
    new CheckboxMenutItem("Select me", false);
```

## The Menu bar

The menu bar is the area at the top of a frame that contains menus. By itself, it doesn't do much except provide an area to place pull-down menus.

A new menu bar is created without any arguments. It is then registered with the frame using the setMenuBar() method.

```
Frame frame = new Frame("Menubar test");
MenuBar menubar = new MenuBar();
frame.setMenuBar(menubar);
```

Some windowing systems like to highlight the Help menu as a separate entity from the rest of the pull-down menus. If your application does have a Help menu, you can register it using the setHelpMenu() method. You can have only one Help menu registered at a time in a given menu bar.

## Pull-down menus

Pull-down menus belong in a menu bar. A single complete menu is represented by the Menu class. This is a container for holding a number of menu items and any submenus of this menu.

All menus have a label associated with them, which is the text you see onscreen. Optionally, you can also specify if the menu is capable of being removed from its parent menu bar. Tear-off menus are a feature of some windowing systems that allow the menu to be separated from the window it is in and displayed as a small window—rather handy if you are using the functionality very regularly because it becomes like a toolbox. The field to set this is only advisory. That is, if the underlying windowing system does not support the functionality, it won't be shown in the application.

After creating a menu, you add it to the menu bar using the add() method of the MenuBar class. This will append this menu to the currently set menus:

```
MenuBar menubar = new MenuBar();
Menu file_menu = new Menu("File");
Menu edit_menu = new Menu("Edit");
Menu help_menu = new Menu("Help");

menubar.add(file_menu);
menubar.add(edit_menu);
menubar.setHelpMenu(help_menu);
```

## Adding Menu Items

With the collection of menu items that you've created from the earlier sections, you need to add these to a menu so that they can be seen.

Using the `addMenuItem()` method of the `Menu` class, you can build up a menu. The method places the menu items in the order in which you add them. Should you wish to remove an item, you call `remove()` method with either the index of the item removed (starting from index 0 for the first item) or with a reference to the item. To insert an item, the `insertMenuItem()` method can be called.

An alternate way to add items to the menu is to not use `MenuItems` at all. You can create new items on the menu just by calling `add()` and providing a string. This adds a new menu item to the end of the list with the given label. Of course, this isn't much good unless you have some way of being notified that the user has clicked on an item. Since you can only add an `ActionListener` to a `MenuItem` instance, you will need to call the `getItem()` method to return an instance of `MenuItem` to use.

For many applications, you want to divide the items in a menu into a number of logical groups. This is done by inserting a separator between a pair of menu items. Visibly, this looks like a line or dashed characters between two menu items. In Java, there is no separate class to represent such a break. Instead, you call the `add Separator()` method between calls to `add()` when you want to use a separator.

## Creating Submenus

Sometimes you would like to create submenus within a method to hold a collection of related actions. To do so requires no extra capabilities than what you have already seen.

First, create a menu that collects together the required functionality:

```
Menu show_menu = new Menu("Show");
MenuItem nav_mi = new MenuItem("Navigation Toolbar");
MenuItem location_mi = new MenuItem("Location Toolbar");
MenuItem std_mi = new MenuItem("Standard Toolbar");
MenuItem status_mi = new MenuItem("Status Bar");

show_menu.add(nav_mi);
show_menu.add(location_mi);
show_menu.add(std_mi);
show_menu.add(status_mi);
```

Now this menu needs to be added to a parent menu (this is the submenu of a View menu):

```
Menu view_menu = new Menu("View");
MenuItem fullscreen_mi = new MenuItem("Full Screen");
MenuItem source_mi = new MenuItem("Page Source");

view_menu.add(show_menu);
```

```
view_menu.addSeparator();
view_menu.add(fullscreen_mi);
view_menu.add(source_mi);

menubar.add(view_menu);
```

The result here is that you have a menu bar with a top-level menu of View, which contains the Show submenu, a separator followed by the two menu items.

## Pop-up menus

Context-sensitive menus are represented by the PopupMenu class. Unlike pull-down menus, pop-up menus can be used anywhere on the screen. To associate one with any component, just call the add() method of the component with the instance of PopupMenu that you want to show.

PopupMenu is derived from Menu, meaning that everything you can do with normal pull-down menus you can do with pop-ups. The only restriction is that no tear-off capability is available (not that useful for a pop-up anyway because you have nothing to tear it from). Taking the example from the previous section on submenus, you could create a pop-up menu to do the same thing with:

```
PopupMenu popup = new PopupMenu("View");
...
popup.add(show_menu);
popup.addSeparator();
popup.add(fullscreen_mi);
popup.add(source_mi);

Button button = new Button();
button.add(popup);
```

Okay, using a button and placing a pop-up menu on it might seem a bit odd, but it just illustrates that you can add pop-up menus to any component — it doesn't have to be just a panel or canvas.

So now that you have a pop-up menu registered, how do you use it? Just because you have it registered with a component does not mean that it will automatically show it for you. You still need to do this yourself.

The standard way of dealing with pop-up menus is to use a MouseListener and look for button presses. If the button is the correct one, then show the pop-up:

```
public class MyCanvas extends Canvas
  implements MouseListener {

  private PopupMenu edit_popup;

  public MyCanvas() {
    ...
```

```
        addMouseListener(this);

        edit_popup = new PopupMenu("Edit");

        add(edit_popup);
    }

    ...

    public void mousePressed(MouseEvent evt) {
      if(e.isPopupTrigger())
        edit_popup.show();
    }
  }
```

Notice here that we use a method called isPopupTrigger() from the MouseEvent class. This method tells you whether the mouse button clicked is the one that is normally used for pop-up menus on the platform. Each platform has different numbers of mouse buttons and triggers (mouse plus keypress), so this convenience method does all the hard work for you.

## Summary

Well, that just about covers everything to do with constructing elements of a user interface. We've covered quite a lot very quickly. These are all the major elements of a standard user interface that you'll come across. Only one more element is available — text input — and that is covered in depth in the next chapter.

These are the areas that have been covered in this chapter:

✦ The use of windows and dialog boxes, including some of the standard dialog boxes available.

✦ The basic hierarchy of how components and onscreen areas are constructed.

✦ The simple components of buttons, check boxes, and various forms of listing things.

✦ The process of adding both pull-down and pop-up menus to components and windows.

✦    ✦    ✦

# Layout Managers and More Components

The subjects that are covered in the chapter have been introduced in the earlier chapters. We expect that you have at least some understanding of layout managers and their components, and now you want to know a lot more detail about how to use them. Well, you've come to the right place! Sit back and sharpen those keyboards because now we're going to get technical.

## What Is a Layout Manager?

In the previous chapters, we have effectively turned a blind eye to how we place parts of the user interface on the screen. When adding new pieces like a button or panel, we've just called the add() method and hoped for the best. If you've tried to do anything more complex than the examples in this book, you will have quickly noticed how things don't always look the way you've wanted them to.

Getting all of your components correctly positioned onscreen is the job of the layout manager. Every container has a layout manager associated with it. Only the smaller components like buttons do not have a manager. This means that even when you don't explicitly set a manager, one is provided for you anyway. You will see what the defaults are shortly.

Layout managers are important for all GUI work. It doesn't matter whether you are using the AWT, the lightweight Swing toolkit covered in the next few chapters, or your own custom components. All these components need to be managed on the screen somehow, and the layout managers do this for you.

**Note**     Layout managers are a common concept in almost every GUI toolkit. Even if you come from a Visual Basic or Delphi background, similar principles apply to placing components, widgets, controls, etc. in a window. The only difference is in the types of layout facilities provided. If Java does not provide one that you are used to (a typical complaint is the lack of the XmForm layout manager from Motif), then you can always write your own.

## Types of managers

Different managers lay out components according to their own set of rules. Some will place everything in a grid-like pattern, while others will just slide components around until they all fit nicely. Which one you use depends on how you want the screen to look.

Java supports five basic managers:

   ✦ FlowLayout

   ✦ BorderLayout

   ✦ CardLayout

   ✦ GridLayout

   ✦ GridBagLayout

Each of these are constructed differently and use different ways to control their components. When you want to change the layout manager, you construct an instance of the appropriate type and call the `setLayout()` method of the desired component, such as this example that creates a 2×2 grid for child components:

```
setLayout(new GridLayout(2, 2));
```

The normal behavior is to set the layout as one of the first actions in a new GUI component class. This ensures that everything is set correctly before you start building the user interface.

**Caution**     If you change layout managers after all the components have been added, you should remove the components and re-add them with the new manager. This ensures that they are correctly placed with respect to the new rules. You cannot guarantee what a layout manager will do with old components from an old manager. It is quite likely they will not even appear onscreen.

In addition to the five simple managers just listed, the Swing toolkit also provides a number of fixed-purpose managers as well. These more complex classes are typically used in areas like laying out the parts of a scrollable window or elements in a combo box.

## The default managers

As previously mentioned, the basic container classes already have a default layout manager assigned. You can use these without change if you want.

Frames, windows, and dialog boxes use the BorderLayout manager. This allows components to be placed around the edges and one in the center. Menu bars are not considered to be part of the Frame or Window layout management scheme. They have their own handlers for placement.

Panels and Applets (the Applet class is derived from Panel) have a flow layout as the default manager. This just places objects one after the other until they fit.

A number of container classes like ScrollPane have no layout manager by default. Make sure that you check the documentation of the class before beginning.

## Custom layout managers

All layout managers are extended from the LayoutManager interface. This provides a basic set of capabilities for registering/unregistering components and requesting that the manager perform layout duties.

On top of the basic layout manager, another interface called LayoutManager2 is designed for constraint-based component management. Managers that implement this interface typically use a set of rules about component relationships that accompany each individual component. For example, always place component X on the left side of the screen.

If you are feeling restricted by the wide choice that the standard library provides, you also have the option of creating your own custom layout manager. By implementing one of the two interfaces described earlier in this chapter, you may provide custom screen handling and component placement. One of the more standard variants is a fixed position/size layout manager (definitely not recommended, though!).

# Layout Managers in Detail

Now we can get down to business describing each of the managers and how they work. The following sections will examine the five basic implementations provided with the AWT.

You can find code for each of the screen shot examples on the companion Web site. We don't provide the full code for a number of the examples in the text because a lot of extra UI handling is not important to the functionality being demonstrated.

## The FlowLayout manager

The simplest of the layout managers, FlowLayout, provides a basic alignment capability. All components that are added are stacked one after the other, left to right, according to the options of left, right, or center. If the components take up more than one line, they are automatically wrapped onto the next until all are drawn on the screen. Each component takes up only the minimum amount that it needs.

For the purposes of this demonstration, the flow layout demonstration code has three buttons. Clicking on one will cause the alignment to change for the button within the layout manager. We can control the alignment using the setAlignment() method.

To create the demo, we set up the components in the constructor as follows:

```
private FlowLayout layout;

private Button left_b, center_b, right_b;

....

setSize(300, 100);

// Set the layout to the default FlowLayout
layout = new FlowLayout(FlowLayout.RIGHT);

setLayout(layout);

left_b = new Button("Left");
center_b = new Button("Center");
right_b = new Button("Right");

add(left_b);
add(center_b);
add(right_b);
```

To be different, the initial layout is set to be right justified. (The default is center justified.) Once we detect a button press, we set the new alignment and request the container to lay out the components again according to the new rules:

```
layout.setAlignment(FlowLayout.LEFT);
doLayout();
```

As you can see, with some fairly trivial work, you end up with a small user interface that looks like Figure 20-1.

**Figure 20-1:** The flow layout demo with the buttons aligned to the left of the parent component (the Frame)

# The BorderLayout manager

Apart from the GridBagLayout that you'll see later on, BorderLayout is probably the most frequently used layout manager. This manager arranges components around the edges of the parent container. The components become "stuck" to the edges of the parent and move with it as it resizes (Figure 20-2).

Components located around the edges always take the smallest size that they need. Naturally, if components are located around the edges, there is also a hole in the center. With the edge components staying constant in size, the center section grows and shrinks with the size of the parent. Take a look at the BorderLayoutDemo code that is included with the chapter. Resize the window and see how the center component changes in response.

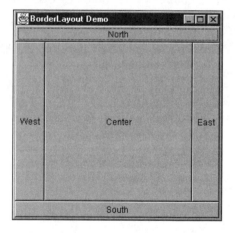

**Figure 20-2:** BorderLayout arranges components around the edges and fits the center component to the rest of the available space.

In the FlowLayout examples, you called the add() method of the container with just the component that was to be added. For BorderLayouts, you need to include more information—which border to locate the component on. A series of defined constants are in the class for these values (NORTH, SOUTH, EAST, WEST, and CENTER). The demo code uses the following construction:

```
layout = new BorderLayout();
setLayout(layout);

north_b = new Button("North");
south_b = new Button("South");
```

```
east_b = new Button("East");
west_b = new Button("West");
center_b = new Button("Center");

add(north_b, BorderLayout.NORTH);
add(south_b, BorderLayout.SOUTH);
add(east_b, BorderLayout.EAST);
add(west_b, BorderLayout.WEST);
add(center_b, BorderLayout.CENTER);
```

**Note**    If you add a component and do not specify on which border to add it, then it goes into the center by default.

## The GridLayout manager

When building user interfaces like dialog boxes, you often want a grid of objects that should look evenly distributed — a row of radio buttons, for example. A GridLayout manager makes sure that all the components occupy exactly the same amount of space.

Grids are specified by the number of rows and columns that should be occupied. As you start to add components, the manager starts with the first row and fills it up completely before moving to the next. The GridLayoutDemo application shows this effect quite nicely as you press a button and a new component is added each time (Figures 20-3, 20-4, and 20-5). An interesting effect of this manager is that if you add more components than the number of cells that you originally specified (rows * columns), then the extras are added to the end of each row. That is, new columns are created rather than new rows to accommodate the extras. Following the wrapping rule, if you add one extra, the number of columns increments by one and the first component of each row moves up to the row above.

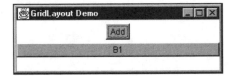

**Figure 20-3:** The effects of adding more components to a GridLayout: A single component.

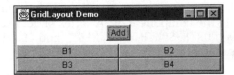

**Figure 20-4:** The effects of adding more components to a GridLayout: The 2x2 grid as specified when constructed.

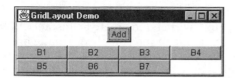

**Figure 20-5:** The effects of adding more components to a GridLayout: More components mean more columns added.

# The GridBagLayout manager

If fixed grids with one component per cell are not necessarily what you want, but you still want a grid-style structure, then the GridBagLayout manager is probably what you need to use. This offers much more control over what you see onscreen. It also happens to be the most powerful of the standard layout managers. Consequently, it is the most complicated to use, too.

GridBagLayout is more flexible than GridLayout, although it shares the concept of positioning items according to a grid. Furthermore, unlike GridLayout, GridBagLayout has a GridBagConstraints object associated with it.

GridBagConstraints specifies how the component is positioned over one or more cells, known as the display area. To use the GridBagLayout, you must customize one or more of the components' GridBagConstraints. You do this by setting the variables of a GridBagConstraints object with the values you want.

In another interesting twist compared to other managers, you don't just call set Layout() with the manager and forget all about it after that. Due to the complexity of the code, you must also add the component directly to the layout manager as well as the parent containers — something no other layout manager requires of you.

Let's look at a typical piece of code:

```
GridBagConstraints gbc = new GridBagConstraints();
GridBagLayout gbl = new GridBagLayout();

setLayout(gbl);

Button button = new Button("Button 1");
gbc.fill = GridBagConstraints.BOTH;
gbc.weightx = 1.0;
gbc.weighty = 0.5;
gbc.gridwidth = 2.0;
gbc.gridheight = 1.5;
gbc.gridx = 2;
gbc.gridy = 1;

gbl.setConstraints(button, gbc);
add(button);
```

What we have here is a fairly complete definition of the fields with which you can play. (Table 20-1 provides a complete list.) First, we need to create an instance of the layout manager as well as the constraints class. Due to the complexity of the options, we need more than just a single NORTH, SOUTH, and CENTER type option that you pass to the add() method like all the other managers. The constraints class contains all of the information needed to properly position and weight the component within the grid. GridLayout allows only fixed-sized cells, while GridBagLayout allows variable-sized cells; we need to specify both the cell size and how to fill it.

After setting the layout manager and creating our button (it could be any other component), we start to fill in the list of constraints. Note that these are all publicly accessible fields. There are no methods to call on this class. After setting a heap of properties, we then tell the layout manager about the constraints information and the component it belongs to using the setConstraints() method. Finally, we add the component to the parent container.

The use of constraints can lead to some quite complex arrangements of components. Sometimes the use of a single GridBagLayout can implement exactly the same look as a collection of nested panels with simpler layout managers. A little more work to start with can make your user interface much faster and simpler to maintain. An example of a moderately complex use of this layout manager is included at JavaBible.com and is shown in Figure 20-6.

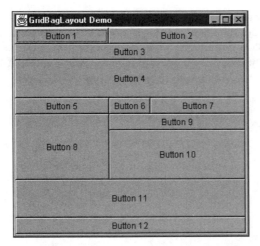

**Figure 20-6:** An example of using the Grid BagLayout manager to produce a moderately complex look

## Table 20-1
## The Fields of the GridBagConstraints Class

| Field Name | Description |
|---|---|
| anchor | When the component hasn't filled up all of the allocated area, this tells where to place the component in that cell (top, bottom, left, right, and so on). |
| fill | When the component hasn't filled up all of the allocated space with it's preferred size, then this instructs the layout manager whether to resize it and how to do it. |
| gridheight | The number of cells in the column that the component should take up. |
| gridwidth | The number of cells in the row that the component should take up. |
| gridx | The horizontal position in the grid that the component should occupy. This is the left edge because the component may span multiple cells (see gridwidth). |
| gridy | The vertical position in the grid that the component should occupy. This is the top edge because the component may span multiple cells (see gridheight). |
| insets | The amount of space between the outside of the layed out area and the other components. |
| ipadx | Internal padding space for the width of the component. |
| ipady | Internal padding space for the height of the component. |
| weightx | A weighting of how much extra space in the horizontal area a component should occupy. This is for when a total component area is larger than the minimum required and shows how toredistribute the extra. |
| weighty | A weighting of how much extra space in the vertical area a component should occupy. This is for when a total component area is larger than the minimum required and shows how to redistribute the extra. |

A neat trick, and something that you will see in the example code on the CD, is that you can reuse the GridBagConstraints instance for multiple components. When you call setConstraints(), the layout manager makes a copy of what you passed it. This allows you to keep using the same constraints object and change only the fields that need to change for each component. As you will see in the GridBag ConstraintsDemo class, only one or two lines change between adding each component, rather than completely respecifying all the information for each component.

## The CardLayout manager

The final layout manager that we will look at is `CardLayout`. This provides a method of page flipping multiple components in front of the user. The simplest example of this would be a tabbed pane-type setup (although the Swing `JTabbed Pane` does something different). It allows you to prepare a number of alternate components and only show one at a time.

The typical process for creating a collection of cards is to first create all of the components to register with the layout manager. Later, you create the control components. (Usually a card layout is swapped in response to the user clicking somewhere else onscreen.) Because card layouts work with the parent container, we normally need to keep a reference to that lying around as well. For example:

```
private CardLayout layout_manager;
private Panel card_panel;

public CardLayoutDemo() {

    ...

    layout_manager = new CardLayout();
    card_panel = new Panel(layout_manager);

    Label l1 = new Label("First card", Label.CENTER);
    card_panel.add(l1, FIRST_PAGE);

    ...

    add(card_panel, BorderLayout.CENTER);
}
```

There are two options when you want to use a card layout to flip. First you might just want to page flip—keep going page after page in a sequential order. The other option is to change to arbitrary components.

If you want to just flip through sequential components, there is nothing special you need to do to use this layout manager. Just create the component and then `add()` it to the parent container without any constraints. (Use the single argument version of `add()`.)To swap between pages, you can then use the `next()`, `previous()`, or `first()` and `last()` method calls. For arguments, you pass in the parent container. Using the previous example, we might do this in response to a button click:

```
public void actionPerformed(ActionEvent evt) {
    layout_manager.next(card_panel);
}
```

This will keep swapping the cards over to the next one. It also provides an endless loop so that if you get to the last card, next will be the first card again.

For the times when you want to arbitrarily select a card, you need to provide only a little more information. Actually, the first code snippet shows you how. You need to associate a label with each card. Then, to show that card, you just nominate the label. Associating a label is done using the normal add() method call and making the second argument the label for that card (where the label must be a String). In the first code snippet, you will see that we've provided them as constants because the information is used in a number of places.

To show a labelled card, we use the show() method. This takes two arguments — the parent container, like next() and other methods, and the label string of the card to show:

```
layout_manager.show(card_panel, FIRST_PAGE);
```

If you want to make this more complex, you can then combine it with other elements like the action command of a Button or MenuItem to provide the label as well. This is how we do it for the CardLayoutDemo program shown in Figure 20-7.

**Figure 20-7:** The CardLayoutDemo code showing the middle page.

# Text Components

Despite the prevalence of point-and-click interfaces, text is still needed frequently. Just to log in to your computer, you probably need to enter a name and password — two text entry areas. These components still form a vital basis of most applications.

The text-handling model in the AWT provides average capabilities. It allows you to have some moderate control over what is presented, but not enough to provide a word processor. If you need that sort of capability, you need to go to the Swing components that are presented in the following chapters.

# Text components

The AWT provides two components for editing text: `TextArea` and `TextField`. These contain a lot of common functionality, so there is a base class for the two called `Text Component`. What sort of functionality is common? Well, all components that have text need to have methods to set and retrieve the current text, define whether it is editable, and manage the position of the insertion marker (caret/cursor).

## Setting/Reading the Text

Naturally, the first thing you want to do with text is to set something that people can read. If the user has typed something in, you might also want to read it so that the program can deal with it internally.

The `setText()` method sets the text to the new string. Any text that is already in the component is replaced by this new text. To clear the component, the argument can either be a zero-length string "" or `null` can be provided.

To retrieve the text in the field, call the `getText()` method. If the text is empty, then you get a zero-length string returned. Even if the text component contains multilined text (the `TextArea`), you get the entire lot back as a single very long `String`.

## Controlling Editing

Text components are useful to have in both the enabled and disabled form. Yes, despite not being able to edit text, a noneditable text component is of value. Think of all those endless clickwrap license agreements on Web pages and software install routines. These are all noneditable text components. Usually you can tell the difference just from the look of the components, as Figure 20-8 illustrates.

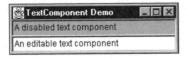

**Figure 20-8:** The changed looked for disabled (top) and enabled (bottom) text fields

Why would you use a noneditable text field instead of a label? Usually it is because you want to present some information and indicate that under certain circumstances, it would be possible to edit the text. For example, a form where you need to select one of two options, where one option allows the addition of extra data.

To change the editable state of the component, you use the `setEditable()` method. This takes a `boolean` parameter — `true` to make it editable, `false` to make it noneditable. By default, all text components are editable.

**Note** You will notice from the demo code that noneditable components still display a cursor and allow selection of text. This is one benefit of a text component over a label. Text components still allow text to be selected for cut-and-paste operations, whereas a label will not.

## Dealing with Text Changes

Sometimes you want to know when the text has changed as the user is typing. This might allow you to implement an autocompletion mechanism or check for valid characters as the user types.

At the basic level, you can register a `TextListener`. Within the `TextComponent`, there is not much you can do. You get an event (`TextEvent`) that specifies that text has changed. There is no other extended capability provided from there. For simple tasks it is useful, but for the more complex tasks, you need to look at the specialized capabilities provided by the subclasses of `TextComponent`.

## Selecting Text

A common task is to select and change text using the normal cut-and-paste methods. The text component provides a standard way of doing this through the selection methods. These provide a programmable way of selecting and manipulating text, but they do not interface with the native clipboard capabilities. That is provided elsewhere.

Let's start with a text field that contains 30 characters. We want to set the selection to be characters 10–15 and then fetch the text associated with it:

```
TextField tf = new TextField();
tf.setText("This is some test text to use");
```

Selecting text is defined by the start position and end position. In any text component, the start position (first character) is zero. To select the text, we then set a start and end position using the numbers just mentioned:

```
tf.setSelectionStart(14);
tf.setSelectionEnd(19);
```

Now you can immediately read the selected text back from the component with `getSelectedText()`. Using the following line of code

```
System.out.println("Selected text is \"" +
                   tf_3.getSelectedText() + "\"");
```

you would get the output:

```
Selected text is "est t"
```

## Text field

A TextField is a single line item of editable text. You cannot enter multiple lines (ending in <CR> and/or <LF> characters), but the line of text can be potentially infinite in length.

### Creating New Instances

There are four ways to create a TextField: you can provide a length in characters, a string to be shown, both, or none. In the earlier code snippets, we didn't provide any arguments. This creates a default component of 20 characters long with no text set. When you set the number of columns, this is the number of visible columns onscreen. There is no way to restrict the user from entering more characters.

To change the visible length of the field, you can use the setColumns() method. The number provided is the number of characters to display on the screen. The real size of the component in pixels is automatically computed from the system fonts set. All you need to know is how many characters should appear onscreen.

### Controlling the Visible Output

Sometimes you want to control what is being shown on the screen. The most common example is a password entry field. In this, you still keep the real text but want to substitute another character for that which is typed, an asterisk ('*'), for example.

Using the setEchoChar() method, you can set the character that is to be displayed for the keypresses. Simply specify the character like this:

```
tf.setEchoChar('*');
```

You can query the current echo character using the getEchoChar() method. If you just want to know if one is set, then call echoCharIsSet(), which will return a boolean indicating yes or no. If, for some reason, you need to clear the current echo character, to return normal text display, you can call the method with the value of 0:

```
tf.setEchoChar(0);
```

This will reset the text field to be a normal field that shows all the characters as they are typed.

## Text area

The TextArea component is a bigger version of the TextField—it allows multiple lines of text to be shown at once. As part of this, it will automatically increase in size and provide scroll bars if necessary for larger amounts of text.

## Creating New Instances

Like the `TextField`, there are a variety of ways of constructing new instances. With the multiline capability comes the ability to specify the number of rows as well as the number of columns to be shown. Add to this the option of whether to show text or not, and you have the same sort of constructors as the single-line sibling. However, because we may want to provide a large amount of text onscreen, we also get to add scroll bars.

Scroll bars are controlled by one of four flags that can be passed to the constructor. These are outlined in Table 20-2. The idea is that you can force the area to have scroll bars even when there is no text to be shown. Typically, this is used as an indicator to the users that they are expected to have large amounts of text to insert.

| Table 20-2 The Constants Controlling Scroll Bar Visibility | |
|---|---|
| **Constant Name** | **Description** |
| `SCROLLBARS_BOTH` | Always show both scroll bars regardless of whether they are needed or not. |
| `SCROLLBARS_HORIZONTAL_ONLY` | Show only the horizontal scroll bar. If text is wider than the visible area, the scroll bar will automatically enlarge with the area used. |
| `SCROLLBARS_VERTICAL_ONLY` | Show only the vertical scroll bar. This means that if text is wider than the area, it is automatically wrapped rather than adding a new width to the window. |
| `SCROLLBARS_NONE` | Don't show any scroll bars so the text area is fixed in size. |

## Manipulating Text

Because text areas show a lot more text than just a one-line field, a few more methods are needed to allow some flexibility. From the TextField, you loose the capability to set the echo character, but you gain a couple of methods for inserting and replacing text.

The base TextComponent defines methods for manipulating selected text, but for an area, we need some more control. Most commonly we want to insert new text in the middle of the existing characters. This is done by calling the `insert()` method and providing the `String` and start position in characters:

```
TextArea ta = new TextArea(5, 15);
ta.setText("This is a really long string ....

ta.insert("This is inserted text", 50);
```

In this example, the text area is 5 rows by 15 columns wide. The insert position is character 50. That is, we start from the first character on the first line and count 50 characters from there and then insert the text. We don't know which line or column we're at, just an offset from the beginning of the text. Naturally, with large amounts of text as you might get in a page, this can be a bit cumbersome to deal with. However, since most of the methods for text components deal with character position, if you need to add text where the cursor is, then the work involved is not too difficult.

**Note**    In TextAreas, you can't change the font from what the system defines. This makes it very difficult to create a WYSIWIG text editor. If you need these capabilities, then you should look to the Swing text components or to third-party component libraries.

Replacing text is similar to inserting new text. This time you provide a string and the start and end positions of the text that should be replaced. The positions refer to the original text rather than the new text. In this way, if the replacement text is longer or shorter than the target length, the displayed text changes to accommodate it (growing or shrinking, respectively).

## Summary

In this chapter, we looked at two distinct parts of the AWT — controlling the onscreen layout of components and dealing with text. Layout managers are needed regardless of which GUI toolkit you use. You'll use them with the AWT widgets, but you will notice in the following chapters on the Swing lightweight toolkit that these same managers will keep showing up.

The highlights of this chapter were the following:

✦ We learned about layout mangers.

✦ We used and described the five major layout manager implementations.

✦ We added the capability to add and edit text in the user interface.

✦    ✦    ✦

# Swing Basics: Components and Containers

**S**wing is huge. This is true of both the size of the Swing libraries and the importance of Swing to the Java programming language. In this chapter, you'll begin to see how to create a *look* using Swing. We'll start to cover the *feel* in the next chapter when we cover the event model and look at examples using menus and buttons.

We'll start by creating a Swing version of a frame, called a JFrame. As you might expect, there are many similarities between this class and the Frame class you learned about in Chapter 17, "Abstract Windowing Toolkit." You'll begin to see the differences, however, when you try to set the layout of and add components (such as buttons and labels) to a JFrame. You don't have to completely understand content panes, root panes, layer panes, and glass panes to understand and use Swing containers. On the other hand, it will help your design if you have some picture of this underlying structure.

The Swing version of buttons and labels are also different than the Button and Label classes you encountered in the AWT. First, they are lightweight components. That is, there is no corresponding entity on your native OS with which they communicate. They live completely within the JFrame on which they appear. Second, they can display more than their AWT counterparts. You will be able to easily display HTML text and icons. In fact, Sun provides with a variety of Swing, "look and feel" buttons at the Swing button repository at http://developer.java.sun.com/developer/techDocs/ hi/repository. Third, you'll find it easy to set a default button or add a ToolTip to a button. Swing makes it easier for you to provide an interface with features that your users have come to expect.

# Introducing Swing

Many people have a lot invested in the AWT. We'll begin our introduction to Swing with a look at why you should consider putting in the effort to make the change. Then we'll take a quick look at the Swing component hierarchy. At that point, an overview of the JComponent class will be in order. Most Swing components derive from JComponent, so much of the information on core Swing functionality is contained in the JComponent class.

## From AWT to Swing

So you've just spent a lot of time wading through the last four chapters to figure out what the AWT is all about (or you knew the material from previous incarnations of Java), and now we're telling you to move to Swing — this time with the AWT was not wasted; Swing does not replace all of the AWT. For example, the Swing class JFrame extends the AWT class Frame. Also, the Swing classes still use AWT classes for functionality such as color and font. Even in those cases where a Swing class has replaced an AWT class, there is still plenty of good news:

✦ Most of what you learned will translate. For example, the Button you learned about in AWT is replaced by the JButton in Swing; the List is now the JList. Although not everything you learned in the AWT has been replaced by a Jsomething, you will find it easy to port your AWT applications to Swing.

✦ The functionality you wish you had in the AWT has been provided in the Swing libraries (desktops, sliders, trees, ToolTips, tabs, and so on). Even features you never knew you were missing are now there. For example, you'll see that a JButton does more than a Button ever did. Some of the changes are in appearance and some are in functionality.

✦ The event handling and performance continues to improve. You'll see that most of the Swing components are no longer tied to peer components on your native system. If you create a JLabel that lives entirely within a JFrame, there is no reason to tell the underlying operating system about the JLabel.

 **Tip**  Don't attempt to write a Swing application without the JavaDocs by your side. Download them for free from http://java.sun.com/docs or use them online; just make sure you can refer to them while you program. Actually, this is a good indication of how large the Swing libraries are. The Swing documents occupy over 30MB while the documents for the entire API (including Swing) comes in at around 90MB. You will get a better feel for the hierarchy this way and be able to quickly navigate to explore the fields and methods inherited by the class you are using. Being able to see all the way up the inheritance tree will help you realize that "this class can do that." You'll also find it helpful to see the various signatures available for a given method.

In the following subsections, we'll look a little more closely at some of the features that the Sun engineers included in Swing.

## Written in 100 Percent Pure Java

There is a concept of lightweight versus heavyweight components that comes up when you are comparing Swing to the AWT. AWT components such as Frames and Buttons are tied to components on the native operating system. These are thought of as *heavyweight* because of this overhead. The AWT classes are peers (which you may think of as being proxies or wrappers) for windows and components in the underlying operating system. The idea is that a user interacts with a Button or other AWT component. It communicates with the Windows, Mac, or other operating system button currently running on your machine.

This dependency on the underlying system means that your GUI could appear to have different bugs on different systems, or even on different VMs running on the same system. The Java AWT principal was that the various widgets should look and feel the same on each platform. This means that the step of translating from the Java side to the native OS side had to be possible on the various platforms. This is part of the reason why early Java applications had this primitive look and feel — in a way; it was the worst of all worlds.

What if you could eliminate this dependence on the underlying OS? You would still need to create native windows at some level. One of the keys to Swing is that once you have this top-level container, everything that's going to go inside could be written in Java. In a way, you are in this protected little world of a Swing JFrame, so you could just communicate with it. Now when you put a button (now called a JButton) inside of a JFrame, the underlying OS doesn't need to know anything about that button. The button is written entirely in Java and has no associated peer.

In fact, this was Sun's solution. These new components are referred to as *lightweight* and all subclass the Swing class JComponent that extends the AWT class Container that, in turn, extends the AWT class Component. You can choose to create a lightweight component instead of a heavyweight component as long as a heavyweight component already exists that will eventually contain your new lightweight component.

Except for a few top-level components, most of the Swing components are 100 percent pure Java. Now Sun can enhance and improve the GUI and not worry about what the various native platforms support. You'll see that you can create transparent components that might have nonrectangular shapes (using the Polygon class, for example). Functionality can be added to many components without duplicating code across these components.

This separation from the various native systems also localizes their mistakes. A bug in a Swing component is probably a bug on all platforms, and something that works on one platform should work on all of them. The good news is that you should only need to fix an issue once and not on all platforms. You will, however, notice the use of a lot of qualifier words such as *probably* and *should*. Parts of Swing are built on top of the AWT, so some of the bugs could be platform-dependent. If you suspect the problem is in the Swing component, check out the Java source code for that class file.

## Allows Changes to the Look and Feel

Inside of this silver lining was a cloud for Sun that they addressed with a cool new feature. If components were no longer tied to the native OS, then how could you write an application that looks like a Windows application on a Windows machine, like a Mac application on a Mac, and so on? Sun had to be responsible for providing the various looks and feels of these different platforms. They have added classes for managing the look and feel of an application and provided support for pluggable look and feel (PLaF).

What's been abstracted out of the model is that which is not essentially part of the component. For instance, it may be important that you be able to select a given item using the mouse. On some platforms, this might be done with a single mouse click and on others, it might be done with a double-click. This difference is only important to users of the respective platforms who have certain expectations of the UI. These features should be collected in a single location separate from the description of the components. The programmer shouldn't have to worry about whether a user will be using one or two mouse clicks to select the component. In fact, Swing supports the dynamic substitution of a look and feel.

A related feature is the fact that Swing provides a single API that you use to programmatically control the components (for example, change the text label, scroll a list to a certain item, and so on), even though the actual component that the end user interacts with may look or act quite different from the one you used to test your program. This is where we get the feature of being able to substitute new look and feels (LaFs) without having to change the code.

## Follows JavaBeans' Design Principles

There are many integrated development environments (IDEs) that allow you to use visual tools to design your Swing-based application. You can often select buttons, sliders, text boxes, and other Swing components and place them on the frame. You can then often set the properties and actions of these components using a property sheet. It's as if these components are being treated like JavaBeans. The names of properties and methods inside of these Swing components use the JavaBeans' naming conventions, so they can be accessed by the IDE.

The advantage is that you can have an attractive Swing interface up and working quite quickly. A disadvantage is that part of the code has been generated by the IDE and may be difficult to modify or unacceptable to begin with: for example, a major manufacturer's Java 2 IDE-generated code that used the Java 1.02 event model. Whether or not you use such tools is your call; their quality should improve with time, although maintainability issues will remain. The point is that the design of Swing facilitates such capabilities.

# The Swing component hierarchy

Four Swing classes derive directly from their corresponding AWT classes. The JDialog, JFrame, JWindow, and JApplet extend, respectively, the Dialog, Frame, Window, and Applet classes. Creating one of these four adds the functionality needed by Swing, but, for example, a JFrame *is a* Frame, which is a heavyweight component. Looking at the inheritance hierarchy of javax.swing.JFrame, you'll see that it inherits from the java.awt classes Frame, then Window, then Container, then Component, and finally, from java.lang.Object. We'll take a closer look at JFrame later in this chapter.

Except for these four top-level Swing component classes, all of the other Swing components extend the JComponent class. This is what allows these elements to be lightweight. A JButton does not extend java.awt.Button. It extends the javax. swing classes AbstractButton, then JComponent. If a JButton is a JComponent, then you might wonder why we need this intermediate AbstractButton class. The reason is that there are many components that basically are just buttons. For example, when you use a menu, you click on a menu item to make a selection. A JMenu Item is another subclass of AbstractButton.

Understanding JComponent will help you understand much of the Swing class library. As we've said, unlike the AWT classes, a component that extends JComponent does not have a corresponding native component. This means that a lightweight component must be completely contained in a top-level Swing component. It may be contained in other lightweight components along the way, but there must be a JDialog, JFrame, or JWindow class as the root container.

# The JComponent base class

We'll begin our exploration of Swing components with a look at the base class JComponent. JComponent extends directly from (or subclasses) java.awt. Container, which extends java.awt.Component. This may be puzzling. Why doesn't JComponent extend Component? The answer, of course, is in the extra functionality provided by the Container class. Every subclass of JComponent can contain other components. You could, for example, create a button that acts like a rocker switch by using two buttons internally. It wouldn't make sense to have a container that wasn't a component. This explains why there is no JContainer class. Any behavior specific to such a class would be found in JComponent.

You don't just create an instance of a JComponent, you create an instance of a subclass of JComponent or you write a customized subclass yourself. JComponent encapsulates all of the behavior we expect in a lightweight component. It contains methods for managing listeners, dealing with events, responding to mouse and keyboard actions, creating and displaying ToolTips, and handling focus. There are methods that handle the appearance of the component. Painting and repainting are defined here along with methods for setting size, alignment, and even transparency. You can use methods in JComponent to specify a border or a given look and feel. We'll see many of these features in the examples in the next few chapters.

# Basic Swing Components

For the remainder of the chapter, we'll look at three basic Swing components: JFrame, JButton, and JLabel. In the process, we'll also include simple examples of JToolTips and ImageIcons and take time to understand the underlying structure of Swing containers. Creating a fairly complex-looking interface won't be hard once you get the idea of how to set up a frame (what we would call a window) with buttons and labels. At this point, the buttons won't do anything. We will discuss the Swing event model in Chapter 22.

## The class javax.swing.JFrame

To get at some of the differences between a Frame and a JFrame, let's create a simple application that displays a JFrame:

```
import javax.swing.*;

public class FrameExample1
{
  public JFrame aFrame; //declare a JFrame

  public FrameExample1()
  {
    aFrame = new JFrame("FrameExample1");
    aFrame.setSize(200,150);
    aFrame.setVisible(true);
  }
  public static void main(  String[] args)
  {
    new FrameExample1();
  }
}
```

This doesn't look very different than creating a Frame. Compile and run the code and you will get a fairly boring looking application, as shown in Figure 21-1.

Already there are differences between this JFrame and the AWT's Frame class. We'll explore a few of those and discuss some of what makes up a JFrame.

### Closing JFrames

Let's take the previous example for a test drive. There's not a lot we can do. Go ahead and use your mouse to resize the window and you'll see that it behaves as it should. You can choose to maximize or minimize the window. You can even choose to close the window. Oops, there's your first indication that we're not in Kansas anymore. When you click on the close window box of a Frame, the default behavior is for it to do nothing. When you click on the close window box of a JFrame, the JFrame is closed but the JVM continues.

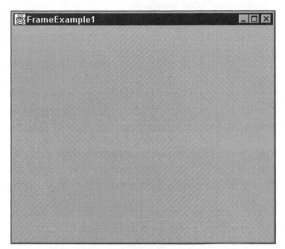

**Figure 21-1:** A simple JFrame

In fact, you can select the default close behavior of a JFrame to be one of the following: do nothing, hide, dispose, or exit. Those of you who have been programming in Java since 1.0 appreciate how much easier this task became with the new event model and inner classes. With Swing, it's even easier.

You choose the default close behavior by using JFrame's method setDefault CloseOperation( *intArgument* ). The first three choices, DO_NOTHING_ON_ CLOSE, HIDE_ON_CLOSE, and DISPOSE_ON_CLOSE, are constants in the Window Constants interface. The default behavior that you observed in the previous example was HIDE_ON_CLOSE. If we had wanted the JFrame to feel like a default Frame, we could have added the following line

```
aFrame.setDefaultCloseOperation( WindowsConstants.DO_NOTHING_ON_CLOSE );
```

to the constructor.

**Note** The fourth choice is the constant EXIT_ON_CLOSE found in the JFrame class. It causes the behavior to be similar to the System.exit(0) call that you made to quit an application by clicking on the close box of a Frame. This choice is new with version 1.3.

## Layout Managers (Take 1)

There's not much good in having a frame unless it's going to contain something. You know from your experience with the AWT that you'll need to use a LayoutManager of some sort. Your first guess might be the following:

```
import javax.swing.*;
import java.awt.*;
```

```
public class FrameExample2
{
  public JFrame aFrame;

  public FrameExample2()
  {
    aFrame = new JFrame("FrameExample2");
    aFrame.setSize(200,150);
    aFrame.setVisible(true);
    aFrame.setDefaultCloseOperation(JFrame.EXIT_ON CLOSE);
    aFrame.setLayout(new BorderLayout()); //wrong -doesn't work
  }
  public static void main(  String[] args)
  {
    new FrameExample2();
  }
}
```

If you were using a `Frame` instead of a `JFrame`, this would be the correct way to set the layout (although the `setDefaultCloseOperation` wouldn't work). If you compile this code, you'll find that it compiles without an error. If you run it, you get the following exception:

```
Exception in thread "main" java.lang.Error: Do not use
javax.swing.JFrame.setLayout() use
javax.swing.JFrame.getContentPane().setLayout() instead at...
```

Something interesting is going on here. `JFrame` extends `Frame`, so `setLayout()` must have been overwritten to deliberately have this behavior. This means that the next thing (topic) we have to understand are content panes.

**Tip**    Beginning Java programmers often hate compiler errors and exceptions and don't take the time to carefully read the messages. They aren't always as helpful or instructive as this one was, but they often lead you towards a solution. Another thing to note is that it is easy for beginning Java programmers to become overwhelmed by a long list of errors. You may want to start out by fixing the errors one at a time. Often fixing one error will eliminate many of the error messages you are getting.

## Working with Content Panes

There is no such class as `ContentPane` or `JContentPane`. If you look at a `JFrame`, then the part that is visible but isn't part of the border, menu bar, or title bar, is the content pane. It is the middle rectangle into which the content of the `JFrame` goes. When you call the method `getContentPane()`, what is returned is an instance of `Container`. You will add children to this object and not directly to the `JFrame`. You will assign a `LayoutManager` to the content pane and not to the `JFrame`. The `Container` is the class you saw in the discussion of the AWT. It has methods for layout management, for adding and removing components, as well as for displaying components.

As the rewritten code shows, you add components such as JButtons and JLabels to the content pane after using it to set the layout:

```
public JFrame aFrame;

  public FrameExample3()
  {
    aFrame = new JFrame("FrameExample3");
    aFrame.setSize(200,150);
    // now setLayout and add components to the content pane
    aFrame.getContentPane().setLayout( new BorderLayout() );
    aFrame.getContentPane().add( new JLabel(
      "See next section"));
    aFrame.getContentPane().add( new JButton(
      "Or the one after that"),BorderLayout.SOUTH);
    aFrame.setVisible(true);
  }
  public static void main(  String[] args)
  {
    new FrameExample3();
  }
}
```

Figure 21-2 illustrates what you see on your screen.

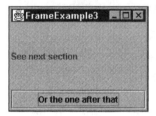

**Figure 21-2:** A JFrame with a JLabel and a JButton

Content panes aren't the only subpart of a JFrame, and other classes besides JFrame contain these subparts. The top level Swing containers have the subparts of root panes, content panes, layer panes, glass panes, and menu bars. We'll look briefly at this hierarchy in the next subsection when we look at Swing containers.

## Swing containers

We noted before that all Swing components derive from the AWT class Component. Actually, we saw that they derive from Container, which is a subclass of Component. This meant that all Swing components could be containers, but let's look at those components that should actually be thought of as containers. The heavyweight containers are JApplet, JDialog, JFrame, and JWindow. The lightweight containers that extend JComponent are JPanel and JInternalFrame.

JComponent has a method paintChildren() that paints the component's children. Layers help Swing paint components so that they appear above the components they should. You know that the x coordinate tells you how far left or right you are on a component (beginning at 0 on the left side and increasing as you move to the right). Similarly, the y coordinate tells you how far up or down you are on a component (beginning at 0 at the top and increasing as you move down the component). Layers refer to a third coordinate system that you can imagine as giving you the depth on the screen. You will also hear the term z-order, referring to the depth of a component. If you imagine your screen consisting of six layers, you will get Swing's concept of layers.

## Layering

For some of the Swing components, you have control over where the items appear. You can use a layout manager to have a button appear in a particular location. For other items, you have no control at all. You just set the text of a ToolTip. You don't say where you want it to appear. It would do you no good if a ToolTip appeared behind the component it was describing. Swing's layer model specifies six layers in which different components are displayed. From back to front, the layers are as follows.

✦ Frame Content layer: This layer holds the menu bar and the content pane.

✦ Default layer: This layer is where components involved in a layered user interface would go. This is where you put your panels, buttons, labels, text field, and so on.

✦ Palette layer: This layer holds floating toolbars and palettes that need to appear above components in the default layer.

✦ Modal layer: This layer holds elements such as dialogs boxes. Some of these need to be dismissed before the program can continue. This means that you need to avoid having them hidden by persistent components. Therefore, they are placed in a layer above those elements.

✦ Popup layer: This layer holds items that temporarily pop up. This includes ToolTips, drop-down lists, and menus. As in the modal layer, you can see that this has to appear above the modal layer, as dialog boxes could have ToolTips and other popups.

✦ Drag layer: When you drag a component, it moves to this layer so that it drags above all other components. When you release the component, it returns to its previous layer.

We're not quite done yet, as we still need to look at where these layers exist and what manages them.

## The Root Pane Container

You can think of the JRootPane as managing all of the content of a JFrame. This includes the content pane, the menu bar and other layers, called JLayeredPanes, and a front pane called the glass pane. All of Swing's top-level containers have a `JRootPane`, as does the `JInternalFrame`.

In (No these are actual Java classes. They should be the way I had them and struck through) other words, `JApplet`, `JDialog`, `JFrame`, `JInternalFrame`, and `JWindow` implement the interface `RootPaneContainer` and each contain a component called the root pane. When we set a default button, you will see an example of having to use the root pane. For the most part, you use the root pane indirectly. For example, when we were setting the layout and adding components to a `JFrame`, we used the method `getContentPane()` to get the content pane. The `getContentPane()` method is declared in the `RootPaneContainer` interface.

The default root pane consists of four parts: the glass pane, the layered pane, the content pane, and the Menu bar. You've seen that the content pane and menu bar are located in one of the frame content layers in the layered pane. The piece you haven't yet looked at is the glass pane.

The glass pane is suggestively named. You can imagine looking through it at everything else inside the container. Think of a glass pane as an invisible `JPanel`. To use it, you need to make the glass pane visible. What good is the glass pane? Well, it sits in front of every other component. You can use it for items that you want to appear on top. You can do your football analyst imitation and circle and diagram the components that are on lower layers. Actually, this UI annotation is useful if you are creating demos for your software. A more common and useful application of the glass pane is to intercept mouse events.

In the AWT, when frames were simple, there was only one place an added component could go. In Swing, you can see why you can't just add a component to a `JFrame` but instead need to add it to the content pane. Although you could specify a layer, you should let Swing take care of the depth placement.

In the next two sections, we will look at labels and buttons.

## Displaying Text with javax.swing.JLabel

The `JLabel` is the Swing replacement for the AWT `Label` component. Although `JLabel` is a no-frills component, you have more options with `JLabel` than you did with a `Label`. A `JLabel` can display text or images or a combination of text and an image, in any combination of both vertical (top, center, bottom) and horizontal (left, center, right) alignments. Here's how you could instantiate and position a `JLabel`:

```
JLabel lblJustText = new JLabel("This is short.");
lblJustText.setVerticalAlignment(JLabel.TOP);
lblJustText.setHorizontalAlignment(JLabel.RIGHT);
```

## HTML-Formatted Text

Although a JLabel can display only a single line of standard text, if you use a recent version of Swing, you can display multiple lines using HTML-formatted text. This example will show the difference between the HTML- and non-HTML-formatted text:

```java
import javax.swing.*;
import java.awt.*;

public class LabelEx1
{
  public JFrame aFrame;

  public LabelEx1()
  {
    aFrame = new JFrame("LabelEx1");
    aFrame.setSize(200,150);
    aFrame.setDefaultCloseOperation( JFrame.EXIT_ON_CLOSE);
    aFrame.getContentPane().setLayout( new GridLayout());

    //the first JLabel will be displayed on a single line
    aFrame.getContentPane().add( new JLabel( "I've been"
      + " thinking about how to introduce an example that"
      + " might show what happens to very long text in a"
      + " JLabel. I'm sure that such an example will occur"
      + " to me soon."));

    //the second JLabel uses HTML to display on multiple lines
    aFrame.getContentPane().add( new JLabel( "<html>"
      + "<H1>Finally!</H1>"
      + "<font color=blue>Multi-line</font><BR>"
      + "<b>and</b>"
      + " <font color=red>HTML</font> Text.</html>"));
    aFrame.setVisible(true);
  }
  public static void main(  String[] args)
  {
    new LabelEx1();
  }
}
```

Compile this code and run it, and you will see something similar to Figure 21-3.

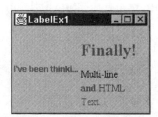

**Figure 21-3:** JLabels with standard text and HTML text

Play with the screen size. (You'll have to drag the corner of the JFrame and let go.) Notice that as the width is increased and decreased, more or less of the first JLabel's text is displayed. An ellipsis appears at the end to indicate that there isn't enough room to display all of the text. The text never continues on the next line.

The HTML text is behaving the way it does in a browser. If the width is adjusted, then the text continues on the next line. Some notes on the source: the HTML code must begin with <html>. Make sure you use lowercase for the opening tag. After that, the tags are not case sensitive. The closing </html> tag is optional but should be included.

## Icons in a JLabel

A JLabel can contain text or HTML-formatted text together with an icon. You can use Swing to create an icon by creating a class that implements the Icon interface. More commonly, you will have an image file that you would like to use as an icon. In this example, we're using a JPEG image of an arrow that has been saved as "LabelEx.jpg."

A JLabel could consist of this image, text, or this image together with text. You create the icon from the file called *filename* using the ImageIcon constructor:

```
Icon icon = new ImageIcon("filename");
```

Now you choose what your JLabel will contain by choosing the appropriate JLabel constructor. Other than the default constructor, you could choose a constructor with the following:

✦ A single argument. Either an Icon or a String

✦ Two arguments: Either an Icon or a String together with an int that specifies the horizontal alignment as being one of the SwingConstants LEFT, RIGHT, CENTER, LEADING, or TRAILING

✦ Three arguments: The first is a String, the second an Icon, and the third specifies horizontal alignment as in the previous bullet.

In the following example, the JLabel has both text and an ImageIcon that has been created from the file LabelEx2:

```
import javax.swing.*;
import java.awt.*;

public class LabelEx2
{
  public JFrame aFrame;

  public LabelEx2()
  {
    aFrame = new JFrame("LabelEx2");
```

```
      aFrame.setSize(200,150);
      aFrame.setDefaultCloseOperation(JFrame.EXIT_ON_CLOSE);
      Icon icon = new ImageIcon("LabelEx.jpg"); //create icon
      aFrame.getContentPane().add( new JLabel(
        "c'mon follow me",  icon , SwingConstants.CENTER));
      aFrame.setVisible(true);
    }
    public static void main(  String[] args)
    {
      new LabelEx2();
    }
  }
```

Figure 21-4 shows the final result.

**Figure 21-4:** A JLabel with an icon and text

# Swing's button

Now that you've seen how to display text and icons, you can move on to the Swing implementations of the various things(elements) that you click, namely, buttons. At the top of the button hierarchy is the AbstractButton base class. The three child classes of AbstractButton are JButton, JMenuItem, and JToggleButton. We'll look at JButtons in this section. The JMenuItem and its descendents are covered in Chapter 22. The JToggleButton is the parent of the JCheckBox and Jradio Button — that's right, check boxes and radio buttons have been separated in Swing. We'll look at them in Chapter 22 as well.

## The Abstract Button Base Class

As the name suggests, AbstractButton is an abstract class and can't be instantiated. The purpose of such a class is to consolidate the common behavior for the subclasses such as what happens when a button is pushed, what text appears as a label, and which ActionEvent is triggered when a button is pushed. When we look at JButton and the other button classes, you'll see the power of abstracting this common button behavior.

Many of the features have to do with the appearance of the button; others add listeners to the button (as did `java.awt.Button`'s `addActionListener()` method). The `doClick()` method clicks the button from your code with the same result as if you clicked the button with a mouse at that point. There are other methods for dealing with mouse events. `JButton`s can also accommodate mnemonics. The abstract button also has methods for changing its appearance when the mouse "rolls over" the region.

## The Class javax.swing.JButton

The `JButton` replaced the `Button`. If you check out the API, you may be surprised at how small the `JButton` class is. Remember that an `AbstractButton` can't be instantiated. This means that the first additional functionality is found in the constructors. You can use the default constructor to create a button with no text label and no icon. You can pass in a `String` as a single argument to the constructor to create a button with the given `String` as the text that's displayed on the button. You could also pass in an `Icon` as we did in the `JLabel` examples to get a button with the given `Icon` appearing on it. Finally, you could create a button with both text and an icon using the constructor `JButton( String text, Icon icon )`. This example shows all but the default (and not very informative) button:

```
import javax.swing.*;
import java.awt.*;

public class ButtonEx1
{
   public JFrame aFrame;

   public ButtonEx1()
   {
     aFrame = new JFrame("ButtonEx1");
     aFrame.setSize(400,350);
     aFrame.setDefaultCloseOperation(JFrame.EXIT_ON_CLOSE);
     Icon icon1 = new ImageIcon("LabelEx.jpg");
     Icon icon2 = new ImageIcon("ButtonEx.jpg");
     aFrame.getContentPane().setLayout(new FlowLayout());
     aFrame.getContentPane().add( new JButton( icon2));
     aFrame.getContentPane().add( new JButton("Don't Move"));
     aFrame.getContentPane().add(
       new JButton("forward", icon1 ));
     aFrame.setVisible(true);
   }
   public static void main( String[] args)
   {
     new ButtonEx1();
   }
}
```

Figure 21-5 shows what you get when you compile and run the code.

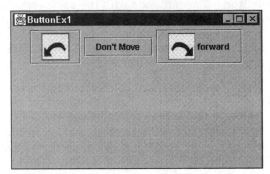

**Figure 21-5:** JButtons with text and icons

The buttons don't do anything. You can click on them and their appearance changes. You can tab through them or Shift+Tab the other way through them. We'll attach actions to buttons when we look at button events in Chapter 22.

### Default buttons

Often you would like a button to act as the default button. A JButton can tell you (by responding to the isDefaultButton() method) whether it is the default button. It can also tell you (using isDefaultCapable()) or be told (using setDefault Capable()) whether it could be the default button. On the other hand, a button can't set itself to be the default button. This could lead to conflicts if two buttons wanted to each be the default button. You will use the setDefaultButton() method of JRootPane.

With just a few changes to the previous example, we can create a default button that acts as the user expects:

```
import javax.swing.*;
import java.awt.*;

public class ButtonEx2
{
  public JFrame aFrame;

  public ButtonEx2()
  {
    aFrame = new JFrame("ButtonEx2");
    aFrame.setSize(400,350);
    aFrame.setDefaultCloseOperation(JFrame.EXIT_ON_CLOSE);
    Icon icon1 = new ImageIcon("LabelEx.jpg");
    Icon icon2 = new ImageIcon("ButtonEx.jpg");
```

```
      JButton button = new JButton("Don't Move");
      aFrame.getContentPane().setLayout(new FlowLayout());
      aFrame.getContentPane().add( new JButton(  icon2));
      aFrame.getContentPane().add( button);
      aFrame.getContentPane().add(
        new JButton("forward",  icon1 ));
      aFrame.getRootPane().setDefaultButton(button);
      aFrame.setVisible(true);
    }
    public static void main(  String[] args)
    {
      new ButtonEx2();
    }
  }
```

You'll notice by looking at Figure 21-6 that the middle button is outlined. If you are running this example and type the "Enter" button, the default button is selected.

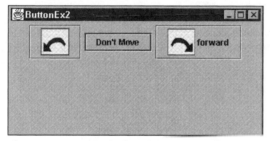

**Figure 21-6:** A Default JButton

### ToolTips

In this example, it's pretty clear what the back arrow icon means. You have used programs where the meaning of certain icons wasn't clear at all. In this case, it was useful to have ToolTips or bubbles or pop-up balloons that gave you a brief description of the purpose of the button. As is true about so many classes in the Swing library, you don't generally deal with the JToolTip class itself. To create a ToolTip in the modified example, just use the setToolTipText() method that each component inherits from the JComponent class. Here's the code:

```
  import javax.swing.*;
  import java.awt.*;

  public class ButtonEx3
  {
    public JFrame aFrame;

    public ButtonEx3()
```

```
    {
      aFrame = new JFrame("ButtonEx3");
      aFrame.setSize(400,350);
      aFrame.setDefaultCloseOperation(JFrame.EXIT_ON_CLOSE);
      JButton button1 = new JButton(new
        ImageIcon("ButtonEx.jpg"));
      JButton button2 = new JButton(new
        ImageIcon("LabelEx.jpg"));
      button1.setToolTipText("Go to previous page");
      button2.setToolTipText("Go to the next page");
      aFrame.getContentPane().setLayout(new FlowLayout());
      aFrame.getContentPane().add( button1 );
      aFrame.getContentPane().add( button2 );
      aFrame.setVisible(true);
    }
    public static void main(  String[] args)
    {
      new ButtonEx3();
    }
  }
```

We've created the buttons using the constructor that takes the icon as an argument. Each button then sets its ToolTip text and is added to the content pane. Figure 21-7 shows a tool tip in action.

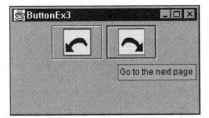

**Figure 21-7:** A JButton with a ToolTip

Check out the Swing APIs to see what else you can do with JButtons. For example, you can change the icon that's displayed on a button depending on whether or not the mouse is over the button. The button could have a special look if it's been pressed or if it's been armed (when the user presses the mouse button but doesn't release it). We'll return to buttons in Chapter 22, when we look at the event model.

# Summary

We've started to make the transition to using the Swing libraries. You've gotten a feel for some of what is different and just how much there is to learn. You've also seen that much of the material has a familiar feel to it. In particular, you've learned the following:

✦ Except for top-level components, Swing components are not tied to system resources. This means that they are more flexible and extensible than the heavyweight AWT components.

✦ Programmers can take advantage of the fact that Swing components are 100 percent pure Java. This also helps in tracking down bugs.

✦ Because most Swing components are lightweight, their look and feel can be "plugged in" even at runtime. Their appearance can also accommodate transparency, nonrectangular shapes, including other components that their AWT equivalents couldn't.

✦ Swing containers consist of multiple layers including root panes and content panes that are used to properly display the components so that items overlap correctly without the programmer having to worry about it.

✦ Swing components are either top-level components that extend their AWT counterparts (JFrame, JDialog, JWindow, or JApplet) or they are subclasses of the JComponent class.

✦ The JComponent class extends the AWT classes Component and Container. It provides much of the Swing behavior needed by Swing components such as buttons and labels.

✦ You can display text, HTML text, and icons in JLabels and JButtons. You can create the icons using Swing or from existing images.

✦ Use the content pane to set the layout of and to add components to a top-level component. Use the root pane to set default buttons.

✦    ✦    ✦

# Basic Swing Components and the Events They Generate

**P**eople who use the software you create will have expectations of how your program should look and feel. Maybe they expect your application to have a menu bar with a File menu as the first item. Maybe they expect a toolbar with icons to help them select the tasks they want to perform. In this chapter, we present some of the Swing components that will help make your application have a familiar feel to it. You'll see menu bars, menus, and menu items. We'll also look at toolbars and pop-up menus. In Chapter 23, we will look at the rest of the new Swing widgets not covered in this chapter and the previous one.

In Chapter 21, we introduced JButtons, but they didn't do anything. We can't really talk about the feel of components without introducing the Swing event model. You can still use listeners and adapters and the Observer-Observable pattern that you learned about for the AWT model. Swing does, however, add some very nice functionality to event handling that you will want to take advantage of. We'll cover the Action interface, PropertyChangeListeners, and options when dealing with focus management. Finally, you should understand that Swing events take place on a single event dispatch thread. You'll find yourself in situations where you'll need to create Timer objects or use the methods invokeLater() or invokeAndWait() to accomplish certain tasks while maintaining responsiveness of your GUI.

As noted in the introduction to Chapter 21, Swing is huge. Once you feel comfortable with these examples, you should explore the Swing APIs to see what else you can do. Once you are coding, you will use the JavaDocs and the Swing tutorials from Sun to quickly add what you need. These are freely downloadable at `http://java.sun.com/docs`.

In Chapter 21, you began to explore basic Swing classes such as containers and those which provided for buttons, labels, and ToolTips. The component classes introduced in this chapter are, in some sense, optional. You can find a way to provide their functionality in other ways. So even if your program doesn't need a menu bar, you should consider whether adding one might make your program easier to use.

# Swing Menus

Without thinking about it, several times a day you click (or use a shortcut) on the File menu and move your cursor down until Save As is highlighted, and then you click that. This simple action means that you have selected a menu item within a menu that is part of a menu bar that is attached to a frame. Let's look into how you can provide the same functionality for your audience using Swing. In these examples, we will create menus that look and feel right—they just don't do anything.

## Menu bars and menus

We'll start at the end of this process and work backwards. First, we'll create a `JFrame` and hang a `JMenuBar` on it. Remember that this will be part of the `Root Pane` but not part of the `ContentPane`. We'll then add `JMenus` to the `JMenuBar` and finally, we'll add `JMenuItems` to the `JMenus`.

### Adding a JMenuBar to a JFrame

Let's start by creating the `JFrame` and a `JMenuBar`. The following code provides the basic structure for our examples in this section:

```
import javax.swing.*;

public class MenuExample1
{
  public JFrame aFrame;
  public JMenuBar aMenuBar;

  public MenuExample1()
  {
    aFrame = new JFrame();    //create the JFrame...
    aMenuBar = new JMenuBar();  //create the JMenuBar
```

```
      aFrame.setJMenuBar(aMenuBar); //add it to the JFrame
      aFrame.setSize(200,150);
      aFrame.setVisible(true);
      aFrame.setDefaultCloseOperation(JFrame.EXIT_ON_CLOSE);
    }
  public static void main( String[] args)
  {
    new MenuExample1();
  }
}
```

When you run the example, you'll notice that the effect is subtle. You've created a JFrame, set its size, and made it visible. You then create a JMenuBar and attach it to the JFrame. Unfortunately, there are no menus in the JMenuBar, so it is barely visible. Test your powers of observation by compiling and running the example with the line

```
   aFrame.setJMenuBar(aMenuBar )
```

commented out and not commented out. Or pretend that you did and keep reading.

### Adding JMenus to the JMenuBar

The next step is to add some menus to the menu bar. Again, the code to do this is pretty straightforward. You initialize the menus and then use the add() method in the JMenuBar class:

```
import javax.swing.*;

public class MenuExample2
{
  public JFrame aFrame;
  public JMenuBar aMenuBar;
  public JMenu fileMenu, editMenu, viewMenu, windowMenu,
  helpMenu;

  public MenuExample2()
  {
    aFrame = new JFrame("Menu Example2");
    aMenuBar = new JMenuBar();

    fileMenu = new JMenu("File"); // create the menus
    editMenu = new JMenu("Edit");
    viewMenu = new JMenu("View");
    windowMenu = new JMenu("Window");
    helpMenu = new JMenu("Help");

    aMenuBar.add(fileMenu);
    aMenuBar.add(editMenu);   //add the menus to the menu bar
```

```
      aMenuBar.add(viewMenu);
      aMenuBar.add(windowMenu);
      aMenuBar.add(helpMenu);

      aFrame.setJMenuBar( aMenuBar);
      aFrame.setSize( 200,150);
      aFrame.setVisible( true);
      aFrame.setDefaultCloseOperation( JFrame.EXIT_ON_CLOSE);

   }
   public static void main( String[] args)
   {
      new MenuExample2();
   }
}
```

Figure 22-1 shows what we have so far.

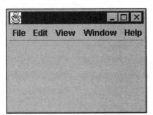

**Figure 22-1:** A JMenubar with JMenus

## Adding JMenuItems to the JMenuBar

Our next step is to add items to the menus. We'll simplify the previous example so that our only menu is the File menu. Let's add the items New and Open followed by a break and then Save, and Save As. Notice that the pattern is the same as in the previous code. Define the items and add them to the component that contains them in the order in which we want them to appear. We have JMenuItems contained in JMenus contained in a JMenuBar. The one additional element is the separator we want to put between Open and Save. The class JMenu has a method addSeparator() that adds the separator at the current position.

Here is the code for this example:

```
import javax.swing.*;

public class MenuExample3
{
   public JFrame aFrame;
   public JMenuBar aMenuBar;
   public JMenu fileMenu, viewMenu;
   public JMenuItem newMenuItem, openMenuItem, saveMenuItem,
saveAsMenuItem;
```

```
    public MenuExample3()
    {
      aFrame = new JFrame("Menu Example3");
      aMenuBar = new JMenuBar();
      fileMenu = new JMenu("File");
      viewMenu = new JMenu("View");
      newMenuItem = new JMenuItem("New"); //create the menu items
      openMenuItem = new JMenuItem("Open");
      saveMenuItem = new JMenuItem("Save");
      saveAsMenuItem = new JMenuItem("Save As");

      aMenuBar.add( fileMenu );
      aMenuBar.add(viewMenu);
      fileMenu.add(newMenuItem);  //add the menu items to the
      fileMenu.add(openMenuItem); // file menu
      fileMenu.addSeparator();
      fileMenu.add(saveMenuItem);
      fileMenu.add(saveAsMenuItem);


      aFrame.setJMenuBar(aMenuBar);
      aFrame.setSize(200,150);
      aFrame.setVisible(true);
      aFrame.setDefaultCloseOperation(JFrame.EXIT_ON_CLOSE);
    }
    public static void main( String[] args)
    {
      new MenuExample3();
    }
}
```

Figure 22-2 shows what it looks like onscreen.

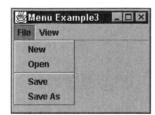

**Figure 22-2:** A JMenu with JMenuItems

You can nest a menu inside of another menu to create submenus. With very few changes, we can create a Save submenu within the File menu to display the choices:

```
import javax.swing.*;

public class MenuExample4
```

```
{
  public JFrame aFrame;
  public JMenuBar aMenuBar;
  public JMenu fileMenu, saveMenu;
  public JMenuItem newMenuItem, openMenuItem, saveMenuItem,
saveAsMenuItem;

  public MenuExample4()
  {
    aFrame = new JFrame("Menu Example3");
    aMenuBar = new JMenuBar();
    fileMenu = new JMenu("File");
    saveMenu = new JMenu("Save"); //create the submenu
    newMenuItem = new JMenuItem("New");
    openMenuItem = new JMenuItem("Open");
    saveMenuItem = new JMenuItem("Save");
    saveAsMenuItem = new JMenuItem("Save As");

    aMenuBar.add( fileMenu );
    fileMenu.add(newMenuItem);
    fileMenu.add(openMenuItem);
    fileMenu.addSeparator();
    fileMenu.add(saveMenu); //add the submenu
    saveMenu.add(saveMenuItem); //add items to the submenu
    saveMenu.add(saveAsMenuItem);

    aFrame.setJMenuBar(aMenuBar);
    aFrame.setSize(200,150);
    aFrame.setVisible(true);
    aFrame.setDefaultCloseOperation( JFrame.EXIT_ON_CLOSE);
  }
  public static void main( String[] args)
  {
    new MenuExample4();
  }
}
```

Figure 22-3 shows the submenu example.

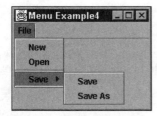

**Figure 22-3:** A JMenu with a submenu

# Mnemonics and accelerators for menus

In the previous section, we created menus. This means that people don't have to memorize tons of key sequences to use your software. On the other hand, people using your software are never satisfied. They will want keyboard shortcuts for menu items that they use frequently. They don't want to take their hands off of the keyboard and navigate through the menus to find a feature that they use all the time. Also, certain keyboard shortcuts are part of their vocabulary.

The two basic types of keyboard shortcuts are *accelerators* and *mnemonics*.

When you want to save or print a document, you probably don't go to the File menu and choose the appropriate selection. You probably hold down the Ctrl key and press S to save and P to print. This is called an accelerator. In each application, a given accelerator can be attached only to a single option.

To select and navigate through menus using your keyboard instead of your mouse, you will use mnemonics. This is when you press a hot key (for example, Alt in Windows) followed by some letter that usually appears in the item you wish to select. For example, the key sequence Alt+F often brings up the File menu. This is suggested to the user by displaying the File menu as *File*. The mnemonics used within menus need to be unique only within that menu — the File and View menus could each have items that are selected by the key sequence Alt+Q. There is no ambiguity because only the choice from the active menu could be called. The component that is able to respond to keyboard inputs and mouse clicks is said to have focus. We'll return to the subject of focus later in this chapter.

Here we revise MenuExample3 to include accelerators and mnemonics. You set the mnemonic for a JMenuItem in the constructor. For example, you can select the *N* in *New* to be the mnemonic with the code:

```
newMenuItem = new JMenuItem("New", 'N');
```

With a JMenu, you don't have the same option. Once you've constructed a JMenu, you can call the setMnemonic() method:

```
fileMenu = new JMenu("File");
fileMenu.setMnemonic('F');
```

To define the accelerators, you need to first import the java.awt.event.KeyEvent class and then use the setAccelerator() method. The revised code is as follows:

```
import javax.swing.*;
import java.awt.event.*; //needed for the accelerator

public class MenuExample5
```

```
{
  public JFrame aFrame;
  public JMenuBar aMenuBar;
  public JMenu fileMenu, viewMenu;
  public JMenuItem newMenuItem, openMenuItem, saveMenuItem,
saveAsMenuItem;

  public MenuExample5()
  {
    aFrame = new JFrame("Menu Example3");
    aMenuBar = new JMenuBar();
    fileMenu = new JMenu("File");
    fileMenu.setMnemonic('F'); //setting mnemonic for a menu
    viewMenu = new JMenu("View");
    viewMenu.setMnemonic('V');
    newMenuItem = new JMenuItem("New", 'N'); //setting mnemonic
        // for a menu item in the constructor
        // below we set the Accelerator for the same menu item
    newMenuItem.setAccelerator(KeyStroke.getKeyStroke(
        KeyEvent.VK_N, InputEvent.CTRL_MASK, false));
    openMenuItem = new JMenuItem( "Open",'O' );
    saveMenuItem = new JMenuItem( "Save",'S' );
    saveMenuItem.setAccelerator(KeyStroke.getKeyStroke(
        KeyEvent.VK_S, InputEvent.CTRL_MASK, false));
    saveAsMenuItem = new JMenuItem( "Save As");

    aMenuBar.add( fileMenu );
    aMenuBar.add(viewMenu);
    fileMenu.add(newMenuItem);
    fileMenu.add(openMenuItem);
    fileMenu.addSeparator();
    fileMenu.add(saveMenuItem);
    fileMenu.add(saveAsMenuItem);


    aFrame.setJMenuBar(aMenuBar);
    aFrame.setSize(200,150);
    aFrame.setVisible(true);
    aFrame.setDefaultCloseOperation(JFrame.EXIT_ON_CLOSE);
  }
  public static void main( String[] args)
  {
    new MenuExample5();
  }
}
```

Figure 22-4 shows a more familiar-looking File menu for this revised program.

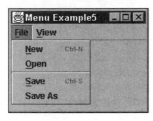

**Figure 22-4:** A JMenu with Accelerators and Mnemonics

## Pop-up menus and triggers

When you click on the word *File* in the JMenuBar, a JMenu appears below it. In a sense, it is a pop-up menu — it just pops up in a predefined location that we have associated with a menu attached to a menu bar. What is happening is that some panel (in this case, a JPanel) appears in a location directly below the word *File*. It has a layout that correctly organizes the menu items (two words is fine, thanks) into a vertical list. The menu items behave like buttons (in fact, they are buttons).

The items themselves could be submenus. When you click on them, the submenu appears off to the side. It, too, is a sort of pop-up menu created with a panel on which the submenu items are arranged vertically. We could customize this process so that we could bring up a menu anywhere with a trigger that is platform specific (for example, a right mouse click).

We'll adapt MenuExample3 by changing the File menu to a pop-up menu and by eliminating the View menu. The changes are surprisingly straightforward. We can eliminate the code for the View menu and for the menu bar itself. Instead of a JMenu, we create a JPopupMenu. We've changed the name of this menu to filePopup from fileMenu. Other than the name change, the code for adding items to the menu is exactly the same. The biggest change is that we need a way of knowing when and where to display the pop-up menu.

The AWT event handling you learned is still very useful.Use a MouseListener to listen for and handle mouse clicks. In fact, we'll use the MouseAdapter so that you only have to override the one MouseEvent that you care about. In the following code, we'll use an inner class PopupMenuListener that extends MouseAdapter. It listens for the mouse buttons to be released. If it's the right mouse button, the JPopupMenu is displayed (see Figure 22-5):

```
import javax.swing.*;
import java.awt.event.*;

public class MenuExample6
{
```

```java
public JFrame aFrame;
public JPopupMenu filePopup;
public JMenuItem newMenuItem, openMenuItem, saveMenuItem,
  saveAsMenuItem;

public MenuExample6()
{
  aFrame = new JFrame("Menu Example6");
  filePopup = new JPopupMenu(); // JPopupMenu not JMenu
  newMenuItem = new JMenuItem("New");
  openMenuItem = new JMenuItem( "Open" );
  saveMenuItem = new JMenuItem( "Save" );
  saveAsMenuItem = new JMenuItem( "Save As");

  filePopup.add(newMenuItem);
  filePopup.add(openMenuItem);
  filePopup.addSeparator();
  filePopup.add(saveMenuItem);
  filePopup.add(saveAsMenuItem);
  //use an inner class to listen for the popupMenu trigger
  aFrame.addMouseListener( new PopupMenuListener());
  aFrame.setSize(400,350);
  aFrame.setVisible(true);
  aFrame.setDefaultCloseOperation(JFrame.EXIT_ON_CLOSE);}
public static void main( String[] args)
{
  new MenuExample6();
}
class PopupMenuListener extends MouseAdapter
{  // the inner class listens for mouseReleased and checks
   // if it was the right mouse button (for Windows behavior)
  public void mouseReleased(MouseEvent e)
  {
    if (e.isPopupTrigger())
    {
      filePopup.show(e.getComponent(), e.getX(), e.getY());
    }
  }
}
}
```

Because the action of the `PopUpMenuListener` was so straightforward, we could have used an anonymous inner class instead. Eliminate the code for the `PopUpMenuListener` and change the code where we registered the listener as follows:

```java
//use an inner class to listen for the popupMenu trigger
//this time it is an anonymous inner class
aFrame.addMouseListener( new MouseAdapter()
{
  public void mouseReleased(MouseEvent e)
  {
    if (e.isPopupTrigger())
```

```
        {
```

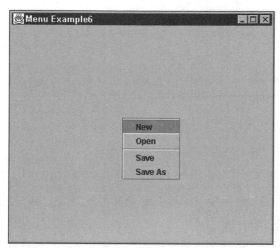

**Figure 22-5:** A JPopupMenu

```
        filePopup.show(e.getComponent(), e.getX(), e.getY());
      }
    }
  });
```

Note two distinctions between heavyweight and lightweight components relative to pop-up menus. First, as long as the pop-up appears entirely within the JFrame, it is a lightweight component; otherwise, it is heavyweight. If possible, for the reasons given in Chapter 21, you may want to make sure that the pop-up stays within the JFrame. Second, there are warnings throughout the Swing documentation against mixing heavyweight and lightweight components. One of the reasons becomes clear when you use pop-up menus. Remember from Chapter 21 that there are various layers associated with the JFrame so that Swing components display at the proper height. If in the middle of the JFrame, you have an AWT Button, the pop-up menu won't display on top of it unless you force the JPopupMenu to be a heavyweight component.

## JToolBars

If you look in the Swing hierarchy, you'll notice that a JMenu is a subclass of a JMenuItem, which in turn extends the abstract classes AbstractButton and JComponent. You've seen that we create submenus by treating a menu as a menuItem to be added to another menu. On the other hand, the JPopup menu cannot be a menuItem, so it inherits directly from JComponent. Similarly, the JToolbar directly extends JComponent and is used to create toolbars to allow users to make selections based on icon buttons.

The following code looks a lot like the menu examples in the previous sections. You may want to refer back to Chapter 21 for details on creating buttons that display icons:

```
import javax.swing.*;
import java.awt.*;
import java.awt.event.*;

public class MenuExample7
{
  public JFrame aFrame;
  public JToolBar aToolbar;
  public JButton firstButton, secondButton, thirdButton;

  public MenuExample7()
  {
    aFrame = new JFrame("Menu Example7");
    aToolbar = new JToolBar(); // JToolbar instead of JMenu
    firstButton = new JButton(new ImageIcon("ButtonEx1.jpg"));
    secondButton = new JButton(new ImageIcon("ButtonEx2.jpg"));
    thirdButton = new JButton(new ImageIcon("ButtonEx3.jpg"));

    aToolbar.add(firstButton);
    aToolbar.add(secondButton);
    aToolbar.add(thirdButton);
    aFrame.getContentPane().setLayout(new BorderLayout());
    aFrame.setSize(400,350);
    aFrame.getContentPane().add(aToolbar, BorderLayout.NORTH);
    aFrame.setVisible(true);
    aFrame.setDefaultCloseOperation(JFrame.EXIT_ON_CLOSE);
  }
  public static void main( String[] args)
  {
    new MenuExample7();
  }
}
```

You'll see the toolbar at the top of the frame. (See Figure 22-6.)

**Figure 22-6:** A simple example
of a JToolBar

Because we've used a `BorderLayout`, you can drag the toolbar to any of the four sides of the enclosing `JFrame`. As you drag it to the right or left edge, notice that the orientation changes to vertical. You can even drag it right off of the frame to get a floating palette. (See Figure 22-7.) Notice that when you do that, it now appears in its own frame with a minimize and close button. (The maximize button isn't active.)

**Figure 22-7:** The JToolBar as a Floating Palette

The minimize button acts like you might expect. The close button returns the `JToolBar` to its preferred spot at the top of the `JFrame`. When you check out the `JToolBar`, you'll see methods that allow you to set the orientation of the toolbar to vertical or horizontal. You'll also see that you have the ability to set or discover whether the toolbar is floatable. There are other methods for controlling the look and behavior of the toolbar including margins, borders, and separators.

# Swing Events

Now we have a small collection of event-generating components. We can select menu items with a mouse or a keyboard and play with toolbars, pop-up menus, and buttons. So far, we haven't seen how these generate any behavior. In this section, we'll look at how the delegation model you learned with the AWT works with Swing components. We'll also look at some of the new event-handling functionality that is available in Swing.

## A button and menu event example

In our first example, we'll summarize what we've seen so far. We will use buttons on a toolbar and menus to control the background color of a panel that occupies the center portion of a border layout. The toolbar is at the bottom of the `JFrame` in Figure 22-8 so that you can see more of the components at once.

The code is long, but not particularly difficult. To help you keep track of what we're doing, here's a summary of what the code contains:

✦ Declarations of all used components (`JFrame`, `JPanel`, `JMenubar`, `JToolbar`, `JMenus`, `JMenuItems`, and `Jbuttons`), as well as the `ActionListeners` and an array of `Colors` and an `int` that holds the index of the current color.

✦ Initialization of these elements

✦ Connections of all components and the appropriate listeners

✦ Mnemonics and accelerators for each of the menu items

✦ Tooltips for the buttons

✦ A `setBackgroundColor` method that is used to set the `JPanel`'s background color

✦ The inner classes that are action listeners for the buttons and menu items

✦ A `main` method that kicks the whole thing off

Most of the code in Listing 22-1 should be familiar. Commentary follows the listing.

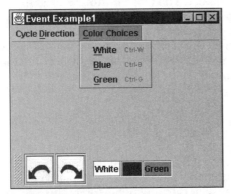

**Figure 22-8:** Using JMenus and JToolBars to generate events

---

## Listing 22-1: **Swing Event Demo**

```
import javax.swing.*;
import java.awt.*;
import java.awt.event.*;

public class EventExample1
{
  //declarations of all used components
  public JFrame aFrame;
  public JPanel aPanel;
  public JMenuBar aMenuBar;
  public JMenu cycleMenu, chooseMenu;
  public JMenuItem forwardMenuItem, backwardMenuItem,
    whiteMenuItem, blueMenuItem,greenMenuItem;
  public JToolBar aToolbar;
  public JButton forwardButton, backwardButton, whiteButton,
```

```
     blueButton, greenButton;
public ActionListener forwardListener, backwardListener,
   whiteListener, blueListener, greenListener;
public Color[] colorChoice = {Color.white, Color.blue,
   Color.green};
public int currentColor;

public EventExample1()
{
// creating the JFrame, JPanel, JToolBar, and JMenuBar
   aFrame = new JFrame("Event Example1");
   aPanel = new JPanel();
   aToolbar = new JToolBar(); // JToolbar instead of JMenu
   aMenuBar = new JMenuBar();

// creating the menus and menu items
   cycleMenu = new JMenu("Cycle Direction");
   chooseMenu = new JMenu("Color Choices");
   forwardMenuItem = new JMenuItem("Next Color");
   backwardMenuItem = new JMenuItem("Previous Color");
   whiteMenuItem = new JMenuItem("White");
   blueMenuItem = new JMenuItem("Blue");
   greenMenuItem = new JMenuItem("Green");

// creating the buttons for the toolbar
   forwardButton = new JButton( new
      ImageIcon("ButtonEx3.jpg"));
   backwardButton = new JButton(new
      ImageIcon("ButtonEx1.jpg"));
   whiteButton = new JButton("White");
   whiteButton.setBackground(Color.white);
   blueButton = new JButton("Blue");
   blueButton.setBackground(Color.blue);
   greenButton = new JButton("Green");
   greenButton.setBackground(Color.green);

// creating the action listeners
   forwardListener = new ForwardListener();
   backwardListener = new BackwardListener();
   whiteListener = new WhiteListener();
   blueListener = new BlueListener();
   greenListener = new GreenListener();

// connecting menu items to the action listeners
   forwardMenuItem.addActionListener(forwardListener);
   backwardMenuItem.addActionListener(backwardListener);
   whiteMenuItem.addActionListener(whiteListener);
   blueMenuItem.addActionListener(blueListener);
```

*Continued*

**Listing 22-1** *(continued)*

```
greenMenuItem.addActionListener(greenListener);

  // connecting buttons to the action listeners
    forwardButton.addActionListener(forwardListener);
    backwardButton.addActionListener(backwardListener);
    whiteButton.addActionListener(whiteListener);
    blueButton.addActionListener(blueListener);
    greenButton.addActionListener(greenListener);

  //creating Mnemonics for MenuItems
    cycleMenu.setMnemonic('D');
    chooseMenu.setMnemonic('C');
    forwardMenuItem.setMnemonic('N');
    backwardMenuItem.setMnemonic('P');
    whiteMenuItem.setMnemonic('W');
    blueMenuItem.setMnemonic('B');
    greenMenuItem.setMnemonic('G');

  // creating Accelerators for MenuItems
    forwardMenuItem.setAccelerator(KeyStroke.getKeyStroke(
      KeyEvent.VK_N, InputEvent.CTRL_MASK, false));
    backwardMenuItem.setAccelerator(KeyStroke.getKeyStroke(
      KeyEvent.VK_P, InputEvent.CTRL_MASK, false));
    whiteMenuItem.setAccelerator(KeyStroke.getKeyStroke(
      KeyEvent.VK_W, InputEvent.CTRL_MASK, false));
    blueMenuItem.setAccelerator(KeyStroke.getKeyStroke(
      KeyEvent.VK_B, InputEvent.CTRL_MASK, false));
    greenMenuItem.setAccelerator(KeyStroke.getKeyStroke(
      KeyEvent.VK_G, InputEvent.CTRL_MASK, false));

  // setting tooltips for buttons
    forwardButton.setToolTipText("Next color");
    backwardButton.setToolTipText("Previous color");
    whiteButton.setToolTipText("Change background to white");
    blueButton.setToolTipText("Change background to blue");
    greenButton.setToolTipText("Change background to green");

  // adding components to the menu bars, toolbar, and menus
    aToolbar.add(backwardButton);
    aToolbar.add(forwardButton);
    aToolbar.addSeparator();
    aToolbar.add(whiteButton);
    aToolbar.add(blueButton);
    aToolbar.add(greenButton);
    aMenuBar.add(cycleMenu);
    cycleMenu.add(forwardMenuItem);
    cycleMenu.add(backwardMenuItem);
    aMenuBar.add(chooseMenu);
```

```
      chooseMenu.add(whiteMenuItem);
      chooseMenu.add(blueMenuItem);
      chooseMenu.add(greenMenuItem);

  // setting the layout and default button and adding the
  // JMenubar, JToolbar, and JPanel. Also setting default
  // close operation to EXIT_ON_CLOSE
      aFrame.getContentPane().setLayout(new BorderLayout());
      aFrame.setSize(400,350);
      aFrame.setJMenuBar(aMenuBar);
      aFrame.getContentPane().add(aToolbar, BorderLayout.NORTH);
      aFrame.getContentPane().add(aPanel, BorderLayout.CENTER);
      aFrame.getRootPane().setDefaultButton(forwardButton);
      aFrame.setVisible(true);
      aFrame.setDefaultCloseOperation(3);
  } //end of constructor

  // method that sets the background color
  public void setBackgroundColor(int i)
  {
    currentColor = i;
    aPanel.setBackground(colorChoice[i]);
  }

//
  {
    public void actionPerformed(ActionEvent e)
    {
      setBackgroundColor(0);
    }
  }
  public class BlueListener implements ActionListener
  {
    public void actionPerformed(ActionEvent e)
    {
      setBackgroundColor(1);
    }
  }
  public class GreenListener implements ActionListener
  {
    public void actionPerformed(ActionEvent e)
    {
      setBackgroundColor(2);
    }
  }
  public class ForwardListener implements ActionListener
  {
    public void actionPerformed(ActionEvent e)
    {
```

*Continued*

> **Listing 22-1** *(continued)*
>
> ```
>         setBackgroundColor(++currentColor%3);
>     }
>   }
>   public class BackwardListener implements ActionListener
>   {
>     public void actionPerformed(ActionEvent e)
>     {
>       setBackgroundColor((--currentColor+3)%3);
>     }
>   }
>
> // main creates the EventExample1
>   public static void main(String[] args)
>   {
>     new EventExample1();
>   }
> }
> ```

## The Containers

The first section of the constructor begins by creating a JFrame called aFrame, a JPanel called aPanel, a JToolBar called aToolbar, and a JMenuBar called aMenuBar. The last section of the constructor sets the layout of aFrame to be a BorderLayout. The JPanel is added to the CENTER, the JToolBar is added to the NORTH, and the JMenuBar is added to the JFrame in its usual place. In addition, the default button is set to be the button that cycles forward through the colors. You can see this in Figure 22-8, as this button has a heavy border.

## The ActionListeners

What makes this program different from our previous Swing examples is that it actually performs actions. When you press buttons or select menu items or use keyboard shortcuts, you can see the result of your action as a change in the color of the JPanel. This is accomplished using action listeners. To implement the interface ActionListener, you just have to implement the method

```
public void actionPerformed(ActionEvent e);
```

In this case, each action listener calls the setBackgroundColor() method. This method uses the array of Colors

```
colorChoice = {Color.white, Color.blue, Color.green};
```

This shortcut allows us to quickly implement the event that we're trying to illustrate. This level of coupling should be avoided in your own code. In other words, the listener responsible for turning the `JPanel` green should not know that it needs to pass the constant 2 to the method `setBackgroundColor()`. To cycle through the `Colors`, we use another cheat that you should avoid and store the `colorChoice` array index of the current state of the `JPanel` in a variable called `currentColor`.

The `GreenListener` will listen for the `greenButton` to be pressed and for the `greenMenuItem` to be selected. It will respond to either action by calling

```
setBackgroundColor(2)
```

This will set the `JPanel`'s background color to green and set the value of `current Color` to 2. The other color listeners act similarly.

The `ForwardListener` listens for the `forwardButton` to be pressed or for the `forwardMenuItem` to be selected. It responds to either action by incrementing the value of the `currentColor` and using the remainder operator to force it to cycle among the numbers 0, 1, and 2. The new value is passed on to the `setBackground Color()` method. The `BackwardListener` acts similarly. The main difference is that the arithmetic is slightly different because of quirks in the remainder operator.

## The Toolbar and its Buttons

For this example, we have five buttons. Two of them are created with `ImageIcons` and three are just buttons with text. They've been placed on the toolbar and the `forwardButton` has been set as the default. To get a feel for buttons, use the Tab key to tab through the button order. Stop when you see that, for example, the `greenButton` has been highlighted. Pressing your Enter key will select the `forward Button` and pressing the Spacebar will select the `greenButton`. Like before, you can drag the toolbar to a different location in the `JFrame` or completely off of the `JFrame` as a floating palette.

The buttons are tied to the action listeners just as they were using the AWT. You are using the Observer-observable pattern. Because the buttons can generate an `Action Event`, you can add `ActionListeners` to them using code such as

```
greenButton.addActionListener(greenListener);
```

We'll actually register the `greenListener` with more than one event generator. You could also have one event generator notify more than one listener of the changes. For kicks, we've given each button a ToolTip to help prompt the user.

## The Menu Bar, Keyboard Shortcuts, and Events

In this following example, we had two menus: one to cycle through the colors and the other to directly select a color. Play around with the menus a bit and you'll notice that if one menu is open, you can use the arrow keys to navigate within and between menus. To open a menu, you can use your mouse or take advantage of the mnemonics we've added. Notice that the *D* is underlined in the menu with the name *Cycle Direction*. On a Windows machine, pressing Alt+D will pull down the `cycle Menu`. At this point, you could take advantage of the mnemonics to use Alt+N to select Next or Alt+P to select Previous. When the `cycleMenu` isn't active (or not in focus), the Alt+N will not have this effect.

The `JMenuItems` have also each been assigned accelerators. You can have accelerators without mnemonics and mnemonics without accelerators. In this example, each menu item just happens to have both. On a Windows machine, Ctrl+N will automatically cycle to the next color without opening the `cycleMenu`. Notice that the `cycleMenu` has a mnemonic and not an accelerator. In general, menus can not have accelerators.

Although we discussed mnemonics and accelerators before, let's stop and see what's so different about this approach. In the past when you wanted to use the keyboard to control events, you created a keyboard listener. The problem with this was that you had to create stubs for all of the keys that you were ignoring. In a sense, this meant that you had to account for every possible keystroke whether you cared about it or not. Even if you used a keyboard adapter, these events were accounted for by extending the keyboard adapter and overriding the methods you cared about. With Swing, you are registering only the key sequences that you care about.

## More Swing-specific event-handling functionality

### PropertyChangeListeners

Let's extend the example from the previous section. Right now, the `JPanel` changes colors while the toolbar stays gray. There's nothing wrong with this, but what if we wanted the toolbar to change colors along with the `Jpanel`? We could do this by changing the `setBackgroundColor` method to the following:

```
public void setBackgroundColor(int i)
  {
    currentColor = i;
    aPanel.setBackground(colorChoice[i]);
    aToolbar.setBackground(colorChoice [i]);
  }
```

In this case, this is the cleanest, simplest way to make this change. However, it doesn't illustrate our point, so we'll look at a slightly more complicated example of how to achieve this behavior.

The idea of a `PropertyChangeListener` is that you can listen for changes in some so-called *bound* property of some Swing component. For example, we could register a `PropertyChangeListener` with the `JPanel` that listens for when the background color changes. When it changes, the listener changes the color of toolbar's background.

You need to make the following changes to your source code:

✦ In the `import` section, add: `import java.beans.*;` This idea comes out of the JavaBeans technology, so the `PropertyChangeListener` is part of the `beans` package.

✦ Create an inner class with the following code:

```
public class ToolBarChanger implements PropertyChangeListener
  {
    public void propertyChange( PropertyChangeEvent e)
    {
      if (e.getPropertyName().equals("background"))
      {
        aToolbar.setBackground(aPanel.getBackground());
      }
    }
  }
```

✦ Register the `PropertyChangeListener` with the following code:

```
aPanel.addPropertyChangeListener(new ToolBarChanger());
```

So now, when you change the background color of the `JPanel` using a menu item, button, or keystroke, the `JPanel` notifies its `PropertyChangeListener` that something has changed. `JPanel` has lots of properties that could change, but if it was the background color that changed, then the `JToolBar` will change its background color accordingly.

## The Action Interface

The previous two examples used classes that implemented the `ActionListener` by providing the body for the method

```
public void actionPerformed(ActionEvent e)
```

Swing provides an `Action` interface that extends the `ActionListener`. In our example, selecting the `forwardMenuItem` and the `forwardButton` resulted in the same action. Implementing this interface allows us to create an object that specifies the action we want. When this action object is added to a `JToolBar` you get a button that is associated with the action. When this action object is added to a `JMenu`, you get a menu item associated with the action. Notice that you are just specifying the action you want performed; the correct widget is created for you depending on the context. The downside is that the object will therefore need to know how it might be displayed in these different contexts.

The `javax.swing.Action` interface includes some constants that enable you to set the value of the text that will appear in a menu item or tooltip, the icon that will appear, and a few other properties. It also declares the `getValue()` and `setValue()` methods to access these properties as well as methods to add and remove a `PropertyChangeListener` and to set and get whether the action is enabled.

The `AbstractAction` class implements `Action`. It provides stubs for the methods and has three constructors. Like before, you extend `AbstractAction` by overriding the `actionPerformed()` method. You can pass in the text that appears on a `JMenuItem` by calling the constructor `AbstractAction(String aString)`, or you can pass in the text and icon by calling the constructor `AbstractAction(String aString, Icon anIcon)`. Call these from within your constructor for your subclass of `AbstractAction` using the `super` keyword.

In Listing 22-2, we revise the previous example so that we are creating `Abstract Action`s that are `ForwardAction`s or `BackwardAction`s. Notice that we add the same instance of these actions (`forwardAction` and `backwardAction`) to the `JToolBar` and to the `JMenu`:

### Listing 22-2: **Abstract Action Demo**

```java
import javax.swing.*;
import java.awt.*;
import java.awt.event.*;
import java.beans.*;

public class EventExample3
{
  //declarations of all used components
  public JFrame aFrame;
  public JPanel aPanel;
  public JMenuBar aMenuBar;
  public JMenu cycleMenu;
  public JToolBar aToolbar;
  public AbstractAction forwardAction, backwardAction;
  public Color[] colorChoice = {Color.white, Color.blue,
Color.green};
  public int currentColor;

  public EventExample3()
  {
    // creating the components
    aFrame = new JFrame("Event Example3");
    aPanel = new JPanel();
    aToolbar = new JToolBar();
    aMenuBar = new JMenuBar();
    cycleMenu = new JMenu("Cycle Direction");
```

```java
    // creating the abstract actions
    forwardAction = new ForwardAction();
    backwardAction = new BackwardAction();

    // adding components to the menu bars, toolbar, and menus
    aToolbar.add(backwardAction);
    aToolbar.add(forwardAction);
    aMenuBar.add(cycleMenu);
    cycleMenu.add( forwardAction);
    cycleMenu.add(backwardAction);

    // setting the layout and adding the
    // JMenubar, JToolbar, and JPanel. Also setting default
    // close operation to EXIT_ON_CLOSE
    aFrame.getContentPane().setLayout(new BorderLayout());
    aFrame.setSize(400,350);
    aFrame.setJMenuBar(aMenuBar);
    aFrame.getContentPane().add(aToolbar, BorderLayout.NORTH);
    aFrame.getContentPane().add(aPanel, BorderLayout.CENTER);
    aFrame.setVisible(true);
    aFrame.setDefaultCloseOperation(3);
} //end of constructor

// method that sets the background color
public void setBackgroundColor(int i)
{
  currentColor = i;
  aPanel.setBackground(colorChoice[i]);
}

// the inner classes that change the color of the JPanel
public class ForwardAction extends AbstractAction
{
  ForwardAction()
  {
    super("Next", new ImageIcon("ButtonEx3.jpg"));
  }


  public void actionPerformed(ActionEvent e)
  {
    setBackgroundColor( ++currentColor%3);
  }
}
public class BackwardAction extends AbstractAction
{
  BackwardAction()
  {
```

*Continued*

**Listing 22-2** *(continued)*

```
      super("Previous", new ImageIcon("ButtonEx1.jpg"));
   }
   public void actionPerformed(ActionEvent e)
   {
      setBackgroundColor((--currentColor+3)%3);
   }
}

// main creates the EventExample3
public static void main( String[] args)
{
   new EventExample3();
}
}
```

In Figure 22-9, you can see that the result of adding forwardAction to the JTool Bar and to the JMenu is slightly different. This supports good design. Because we have added the same object in each case, we have localized where we need to make changes.

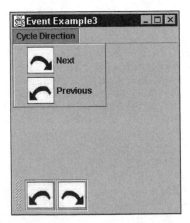

**Figure 22-9:** Creating Menu Items and Buttons from Actions

## Focus Management in Swing

In the button and menu example that began this part of the chapter, you were able to select menu items and buttons using the keyboard. With the exception of keyboard accelerators, how the application responded to your keyboard input depended on the state of the program. What elements are actively listening for your input? Just like with the AWT, when a component can receive keyboard input, it has *focus*.

As a first example, one of the buttons on the `JToolBar` had the focus. You were able to select it by pressing the Spacebar. You could cycle through the focus order using your Tab key or you could cycle backwards through the focus order using Shift+Tab. This is not the same as a default button that can be selected using the Enter key. Remember that you needed to set the default button using the RootPane and not through the button itself.

Another example is the mnemonics associated with menu items. Two menu items on different menus could have the same mnemonic associated with each of them. This is because only the menu that is in focus can respond to this keyboard input.

In addition to the AWT methods for handling focus, Swing provides a class `FocusManager` along with some functionality in the `JComponent` class. We'll illustrate some of Swing's focus capabilities with two versions of the same example. In this example, we change the cycle order of the buttons in our button and menu example by adding the following code:

```
forwardButton.setNextFocusableComponent(backwardButton);
backwardButton.setNextFocusableComponent(forwardButton);
whiteButton.setNextFocusableComponent(blueButton);
blueButton.setNextFocusableComponent(greenButton);
greenButton.setNextFocusableComponent(whiteButton);
```

Now the Tab key will toggle between the forward and backward buttons. If you have selected one of the color buttons, the Tab key will cycle you through the colors.

You can accomplish similar behavior by putting the different button groups inside of their own components (such as a `JPanel`). Instead of adding the previous code to our button and menu example, we'll change the section where we add the buttons to the toolbar using this code:

```
// adding components to the menu bars, toolbar, and menus
  FocusPanel cyclePanel = new FocusPanel();
  aToolbar.add(cyclePanel);
  cyclePanel.add(backwardButton);
  cyclePanel.add(forwardButton);
  FocusPanel choicePanel = new FocusPanel();
  aToolbar.add(choicePanel);
  choicePanel.add(whiteButton);
  choicePanel.add(blueButton);
  choicePanel.add(greenButton);
  aMenuBar.add(cycleMenu);
  . . .
```

We have created two `FocusPanel`s and added the two cycle buttons to the `cyclePanel` and the three color buttons to the `choicePanel`. Now, if we have selected a button on either `FocusPanel`, Tab and Shift+Tab will cycle through the buttons only on that `FocusPanel`. So what is a `FocusPanel`? To create the behavior of cycling through components in a specific `JComponent`, we have to override the

JComponent method isFocusCycleRoot() so that it returns true. For this example, we created an inner class FocusPanel that overrode this method as follows:

```
public class FocusPanel extends JPanel
  {
    public boolean isFocusCycleRoot()
    {
      return true;
    }
  }
```

What happens if you skip this step and just create choicePanel and cyclePanel as JPanels? In this case, you haven't changed the initial tab order and, even though they are in separate JPanels, pressing Tab while the forwardButton has the focus will cause the whiteButton to grab the focus. This example gives you an idea of how to work with focus in Swing. To create applications with specific focus needs in Swing, check the APIs for JComponent and FocusManager.

## Thread Issues in Swing

All developers know that working with threads can lead to all sorts of problems. The problems are often hard to anticipate, track down, or fix. We will start our discussion with an example that doesn't work and then address the Swing issues in threading. The reason for proceeding in this way is that we are starting with a very common error that seems as if it should work. It leads us to understand how threading works in Swing.

### A flawed example

Let's start with a pared down version of our current example. We've eliminated all the menus and all but one button. This button is similar to the forward button except that it keeps moving through the colors. This code is used to show what is going wrong; it doesn't behave like you might think it should (see Listing 22-3).

### Listing 22-3: **Faulty Thread Example**

```
import javax.swing.*;
import java.awt.*;
import java.awt.event.*;

public class ThreadExample1
{
  //declarations of all used components
  public JFrame aFrame;
  public JPanel aPanel;
  public JToolBar aToolbar;
  public JButton cycleButton;
  public ActionListener cycleListener;
  public Color[] colorChoice = {Color.white, Color.blue,
    Color.green};
```

```java
public int currentColor;

public ThreadExample1()
{
  aFrame = new JFrame("Thread Example1");
  aPanel = new JPanel();
  aToolbar = new JToolBar();
  cycleButton = new JButton("Cycle Colors");
  cycleButton.addActionListener(new CycleListener());
  aToolbar.add(cycleButton);
  aFrame.getContentPane().setLayout(new BorderLayout());
  aFrame.setSize(400,350);
  aFrame.getContentPane().add(aToolbar, BorderLayout.NORTH);
  aFrame.getContentPane().add(aPanel, BorderLayout.CENTER);
  aFrame.setVisible(true);
  aFrame.setDefaultCloseOperation(JFrame.EXIT_ON_CLOSE);}

public void setBackgroundColor(int i)
{
  currentColor = i;
  aPanel.setBackground(colorChoice[i]);
  System.out.println("The Background is " + colorChoice[i]);
}

public class CycleListener implements ActionListener
{
  public void actionPerformed(ActionEvent e)
  {
    while(true)                                   //*
    {                                             //*
    setBackgroundColor( ++currentColor%3);
    }                                             //*
  }
}

public static void main( String[] args)
{
  new ThreadExample1();
}
}
```

The big change is in the inner class CycleListener. The while means that the setBackgroundColor() will continue to increment the color index and the background color will cycle through. In the setBackgroundColor() method, notice a println call that prints the current background color to the console. This may seem odd until you compile and run this program and press the cycleButton.

The JPanel's background color doesn't change. Hey, wait a minute! Nothing is happening. You know from the stream of output on the console panel that, in fact, setBackgroundColor() is being called and is updating the JPanel's background color. Why can't we see the changes? Go ahead and click the close box on the JFrame to quit the program. Again, nothing happens. We are getting no information to or from our UI. You actually have to quit the application by destroying your session.

You can convince yourself that the code is basically sound and that the problem is with the threading by commenting out the three lines marked //*. Now the cycleButton works the same as the forwardButton used to.

### Using the Timer class

The problem with the previous example is that the Swing events run on a single thread. The cycleButton started a process that never released control back to the GUI. This tied up the event dispatch thread. The GUI was no longer responsive to any user input nor was it able to call repaint() because the thread was busy. Another thread would be handy in this case.

One solution is to use a Timer. We'll create a Timer and specify the Action Listener that it notifies and the time in milliseconds that it delays between calls. The Timer will still execute in the event dispatch thread, but it releases control after each execution of what should be a short method. The cycleButton then notifies the CycleListener when it's been clicked. The CycleListener has a timer that is started or stopped by clicking the cycleButton. If the timer is running, it notifies the CycleRunner every twenty milliseconds. The CycleRunner, in turn, increments the background color of the JPanel. Here's the code for the two inner classes: CycleListener has been changed and CycleRunner is the new name for the inner class that contains the call to setBackgroundColor():

```
public class CycleListener implements ActionListener
  {
    boolean isRunning = false;
    Timer timer = new Timer(20, new CycleRunner());
    public void actionPerformed(ActionEvent e)
    {
      if (isRunning) timer.stop();
        else timer.start();
        isRunning = !isRunning;
    }
  }
public class CycleRunner implements ActionListener
  {
    public void actionPerformed(ActionEvent e)
    {
      setBackgroundColor( ++currentColor%3);
    }
  }
```

Now when you click the cycleButton, you will see the JPanel's background colors cycle through white, blue, and green. Click it again and the cycling stops. The Timer has allowed the GUI to receive and respond to user input.

### Other Options

Swing also provides the methods invokeLater() and invokeAndWait(). You pass a Runnable object to the invokeLater() method and it will call the run() method of the object on the event dispatch thread. The Runnable object might contain a thread or a Timer. The point of using invokeLater() is that you aren't really concerned when the called method completes and you want the event dispatch to continue along its merry way.

You also could pass a Runnable object to invokeAndWait(). In this case, you are suspending the event dispatch thread until the run() method in this called object returns. This could bring up all sorts of problems, so you need to catch an InterruptedException and an InvocationTargetException.

Notice that the main difference between these two methods is when you continue with your other pending operations. A similarity is that neither executes before all pending AWT events are cleared. You should have a very good reason for using the invokeAndWait() method. In many ways, it is just asking for trouble.

# Summary

You can now create more interesting-looking applications that contain more of the standard GUI controls that your users will be looking for. You've also begun to explore how to provide these widgets with functionality. Specifically, you have seen the following:

✦ JMenus, JMenuBars, and JMenuItems are all JComponents. In fact, the add() method that allows you to place (sub)menus and menu items inside of menus is inherited from the Container class. JMenuItems inherit from the abstract class AbstractButton, and JMenu extends JMenuItem. Creating a pop-up menu is similar to creating a menu, although you do need to use a trigger to make the pop-up menu appear.

✦ Swing supports keyboard shortcuts. You use the Keystroke class to create accelerators. You can also create mnemonics either using one of the constructors for JMenuItem or using the method setMnemonic() from the Abstract Button class.

✦ Now that buttons support icons, it is very easy to create toolbars. You can change the tab order for buttons using the setNextFocusableComponent() method. You can also set a default button and create logical groups of buttons so that tabbing stays within the designated group. If your toolbar is used in a BorderLayout, you can change its position and orientation with calls or by dragging it. You can even drag it out of the enclosing frame.

✦ With Swing, you can still use the `Listeners` and `Adapters` that you learned about and loved with the AWT. You can also use a listener from the JavaBeans technology to listen for when a property (such as background color of a `JFrame`) has changed. This `PropertyChangeListener` allows one component to change in response to changes in another.

✦ The Swing GUI events all run on the event dispatch thread. If you need more control, you can use `Timers` or choose from the `invokeLater()` and the `invokeAndWait()` methods.

✦     ✦     ✦

# New Widgets in the Swing Library

In Chapter 21, we began looking at how Swing components were designed. We looked at the difference between light-weight and heavyweight components and saw that, except for a few top-level containers, the Swing components all inherited from `JComponent`. There were Swing versions of the AWT components, but they behave a little differently. In Chapter 22, we looked at how events are generated and handled in Swing.

In this chapter, we'll look at the new widgets that have been introduced in Swing. Some of the components are just Swing versions of the AWT components. For the most part, we won't include those in this chapter. For example, we will talk about the `JScrollPane` class in the context of an example of another component. Some classes are brand new. For example, there was no progress bar or slider in the AWT. Also, certain AWT classes have been changed in ways that are significant enough that the Swing versions shouldn't be seen as just a port of the AWT version. For example, Swing now has both a check box and a radio button, whereas AWT just had the check box that was treated differently based on the context.

Flip through this chapter and find screen shots of the widget you're looking for. The nearby code example and explanation will introduce you to that particular component. As in the past two chapters, we urge you to keep the APIs close to you while developing Swing applications. There are just too many details that you're going to need to double check and functionality that you'll discover while looking through the methods.

# Buttons

Many components behave like buttons and, therefore, extend Swing's Abstract Button class. We've looked at the JButton in Chapter 21 and the JMenuItem and JMenu buttons (thanks) in Chapter 22. Now we'll look at the two toggle buttons and their menu versions. Menus and toolbars are the two basic mechanisms for organizing buttons in a panel that makes it easier for users to quickly find what they need. Keep in mind that because these elements inherit from AbstractButton, they can display icons and inherit from JComponent. This means they can contain other components and take advantage of the features of JComponent, Container, and Component.

## JToggleButtons

As mentioned before, Swing has both check boxes and radio buttons. In the AWT, these were both implemented by CheckBox and acted differently based on whether they were in a button group or not. Similarities do exist, however, between the classes JCheckBox and JRadioButton. These similarities have been encapsulated in the Swing class JToggleButton.

A JToggleButton behaves differently than a JButton. When you select a JButton using the mouse or keyboard and then release it, the button pops back out. A JToggleButton stays selected until you click on it again. On most word processors, there are four buttons for specifying the text positioning (left, center, right, and justify). These are JToggleButtons. When you select left, it stays depressed until you make a different selection. This is just a set of radio buttons. You also probably have three buttons that allow you to select the text style (bold, italic, underline). These are also JToggleButtons. The bold button stays depressed until you select it again. If, while the bold button is depressed, you select the italic button, you get text that is bold and italicized. These are basically check boxes. On the other hand, if you click on the print button, it calls a different action and then it is released. This is just an ordinary button.

## JCheckBoxes

The JCheckBox will feel like an old friend to your users. They click it to select and deselect the box that appears next to text and/or an icon describing the particular selection. The basic way to create and use a JCheckBox is to use code like the following:

```
JCheckBox aCheckBox = new JCheckBox( descriptiveText, isSelected);
```

Here the descriptiveText is just a String that appears next to the actual check box that identifies it for the user. The boolean isSelected indicates whether the check box is initially selected or not. You could also have done this using the following two lines:

```
JCheckBox aCheckBox = new (JCheckBox (descriptiveText));
aCheckBox.setSelected(true);
```

Other constructors allow you to specify an icon as well. In fact, using methods you inherit from AbstractButton, you can customize the look to include your own icons that indicate whether the button has been selected. If you don't choose to specialize, you will get an empty box or a checked box to indicate whether the button is selected. The buttons can also be assigned mnemonics, as you saw in Chapter 22.

We'll continue with the example we introduced in Chapter 22. The code in Listing 23-1 shows how you could use JCheckBoxes to control a JPanel's background color. We create a toolbar and three check boxes that we add to the toolbar. The check boxes are each initially deselected. You need to decide how to handle events that are generated by clicking on the check box. Both an item event and an action event are generated. In most cases, you'll want to perform an action based on the current state of the check box. The easiest way to accomplish this is with an ItemListener.

Notice in Listing 23-1 that we're only responding to the check box being clicked, so we could have used either type of listener.

## Listing 23-1: **CheckBox Example**

```
import javax.swing.*;
import java.awt.*;
import java.awt.event.*;

public class CheckBoxEx
{
  //declarations of all used components
  public JFrame aFrame;
  public JPanel aPanel;
  public JToolBar aToolbar;
  public JCheckBox redCheckBox, greenCheckBox, blueCheckBox;
  public float colorRed, colorGreen, colorBlue;

  public CheckBoxEx()
  {
  // constructing and connecting all components
    aFrame = new JFrame("CheckBoxEx");
    aPanel = new JPanel();
    aToolbar = new JToolBar(); // JToolbar instead of JMenu
    redCheckBox = new JCheckBox("Red", false);
    greenCheckBox = new JCheckBox("Green", false);
    blueCheckBox = new JCheckBox("Blue", false);
    aToolbar.add(redCheckBox);
    aToolbar.add(greenCheckBox);
    aToolbar.add(blueCheckBox);

    // add the ItemListeners as anonymous inner classes
```

*Continued*

**Listing 23-1** *(continued)*

```
   redCheckBox.addItemListener( new ItemListener()
     {
       public void itemStateChanged(ItemEvent itemEvent)
       {
         colorRed = (float)(colorRed + 1)%2;
         setBackgroundColor();
       }
     });
   greenCheckBox.addItemListener( new ItemListener()
     {
       public void itemStateChanged(ItemEvent itemEvent)
       {
         colorGreen = (float)(colorGreen + 1)%2;
         setBackgroundColor();
       }
     });
   blueCheckBox.addItemListener( new ItemListener()
     {
       public void itemStateChanged(ItemEvent itemEvent)
       {
         colorBlue = (float)(colorBlue + 1)%2;
         setBackgroundColor();
       }
     });

   // putting the big pieces together
   aFrame.setSize(400,350);
   aFrame.getContentPane().add(aToolbar, BorderLayout.NORTH);
   aFrame.getContentPane().add(aPanel, BorderLayout.CENTER);
   aFrame.setVisible(true);
   aFrame.setDefaultCloseOperation(JFrame.EXIT_ON_CLOSE);
 } //end of constructor

 // method that sets the background color
 public void setBackgroundColor()
 {
   aPanel.setBackground( new Color(colorRed, colorGreen,
     colorBlue));
 }
 // main creates the CheckBoxEx
 public static void main( String[] args)
 {
   new CheckBoxEx();
 }
}
```

The check boxes allow you to mix and match colors. You can select red and blue to get magenta. You can select all three to get white or none of the boxes to get black.

Figure 23-1 shows this application. In the next section, you'll see how to force a single choice using radio buttons.

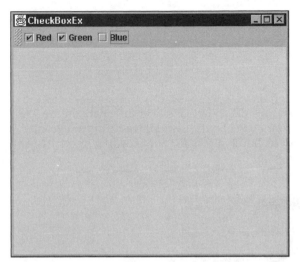

**Figure 23-1:** Using a JCheckBox

## JRadioButtons and ButtonGroups

Sometimes people have to choose exactly one item from a set of choices. If the breakfast special includes your choice of juice, then you can have tomato, grapefruit, or orange. You can't have a little tomato and a little orange or some other nonstandard offering. The computer interface that users associate with this situation are radio buttons.

The class JRadioButton is also a subclass of JToggleButton. You will use it similarly to how you used JCheckBoxes. You will create a JRadioButton with some initial configuration and add it to some container. (We'll use the JToolBar again in this example). Unlike the JCheckBox, a JRadioButton will also belong to a Button Group and the events generated should be handled differently.

The difference between JCheckBoxes and JRadioButtons is largely based on user expectation. You can change the code in the last example so that every reference to a check box is replaced with a radio button. For example,

```
        ...
    public JToolBar aToolbar;
      public JRadioButton redRadioButton, greenRadioButton,
        blueRadioButton;
        ...
        redRadioButton = new JRadioButton("Red", false);
        greenRadioButton = new JRadioButton("Green", false);
```

```
blueRadioButton = new JRadioButton("Blue", false);

aToolbar.add(redRadioButton);
aToolbar.add(greenRadioButton);
aToolbar.add(blueRadioButton);

// add the ItemListeners as anonymous inner classes
redRadioButton.addItemListener( new ItemListener()
 ...
```

You'll end up with an application that responds exactly the same way as the previous example — the buttons just look different. This is unfortunate. In the AWT, you only got radio buttons when your check boxes were part of a button group. The new way in Swing is more flexible, but it allows for a misleading or confusing GUI. Figure 23-2 shows the new program.

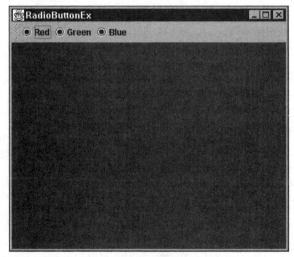

**Figure 23-2:** Using JRadioButtons

A button group in and of itself is not the answer. If you declare and initialize a button group by adding the following lines, the application will still behave unexpectedly:

```
   ...
ButtonGroup aButtonGroup = new ButtonGroup();
   ...
// add components to button group
aButtonGroup.add(redRadioButton);
aButtonGroup.add(greenRadioButton);
aButtonGroup.add(blueRadioButton);
```

To understand what's going wrong, you need to understand the events fired. When you click on a radio button that is not the currently selected one, one action event is fired and two item events are fired: one for the item being selected and one for the previously selected item that is being deselected. When you click on a radio button that is currently selected, you get one action event and one item event. This means that, in our current setup, it is easy to get out of sync with the buttons and that we can still get the screen to appear magenta even though the radio buttons will indicate only one color choice at a time.

The reason for this is (deliberately) sloppy coding to make this point. We never tested whether an item was selected or not in the JCheckBox example. We took advantage of what we know check boxes do. In this case, we need to set up our event handler to take advantage of the expected behavior of radio buttons. We will use an action listener. Only one button should be active at a time, so we will enforce this with our model. In this example, we'll take advantage of the fact that JRadioB utton **extends** AbstractButton and therefore has getters and setters for ActionCommand**s.**

If you've played with radio buttons in button groups, you've encountered the situation where once a JRadioButton has been selected in a ButtonGroup, there's no way to go back to the situation where none are selected. You can still create a radio button that you add to the button group but not to the container. When you set this radio button to true, it appears to reset the other elements of the button group. Another solution is to add a JToggleButton to the button group. This will effectively act as a reset button.

Finally, you should arrange buttons from the same group so that it is immediately clear to the user which button belongs to which group. You can easily imagine a situation where you have more than one button group on the screen. Listing 23-2 shows the logical structure the GUI organization should imply.

## Listing 23-2: **Radio Button Example**

```
import javax.swing.*;
import java.awt.*;
import java.awt.event.*;

public class RadioButtonEx
{
  //declarations of all used components
  public JFrame aFrame;
  public JPanel aPanel;
  public JToolBar aToolbar;
  public JRadioButton redRadioButton, greenRadioButton,
blueRadioButton;
  public ButtonGroup aButtonGroup;
  public RadioButtonListener aListener;
  public Color[] colors = {Color.red, Color.green, Color.blue};
```

*Continued*

**Listing 23-2** *(continued)*

```java
public RadioButtonEx()
{
// constructing and connecting all components
  aFrame = new JFrame("RadioButtonEx");
  aPanel = new JPanel();
  redRadioButton = new JRadioButton("Red", false);
  greenRadioButton = new JRadioButton("Green", false);
  blueRadioButton = new JRadioButton("Blue", false);
// add components to containers
  aToolbar = new JToolBar();
  aToolbar.add(redRadioButton);
  aToolbar.add(greenRadioButton);
  aToolbar.add(blueRadioButton);
// add components to button group
  aButtonGroup = new ButtonGroup();
  aButtonGroup.add(redRadioButton);
  aButtonGroup.add(greenRadioButton);
  aButtonGroup.add(blueRadioButton);
// set the Action Commands
  redRadioButton.setActionCommand("0");
  greenRadioButton.setActionCommand("1");
  blueRadioButton.setActionCommand("2");
// create ActionListener
  aListener = new RadioButtonListener();
  redRadioButton.addActionListener(aListener);
  greenRadioButton.addActionListener(aListener);
  blueRadioButton.addActionListener(aListener);
  // putting the big pieces   together
  aFrame.setSize(400,350);
  aFrame.getContentPane().add(aToolbar, BorderLayout.NORTH);
  aFrame.getContentPane().add(aPanel, BorderLayout.CENTER);
  aFrame.setVisible(true);
  aFrame.setDefaultCloseOperation(JFrame.EXIT_ON_CLOSE);
} //end of constructor

class RadioButtonListener implements ActionListener
{
  public void actionPerformed( ActionEvent e)
  {
    aPanel.setBackground( colors[new
Integer(e.getActionCommand()).intValue()]);
  }
}
// main creates the CheckBoxEx
public static void main( String[] args)
{
  new RadioButtonEx();
}
}
```

Now let's add a JToggleButton that acts as a reset button to the button group. It will remove any indication that any of the other buttons are selected. In our case, it is easy to adapt the code to accommodate this button. In the appropriate places, you could add these lines:

```
public JToggleButton aToggleButton;
aToggleButton = new JToggleButton("Reset", false);
    aToolbar.add(aToggleButton);
aButtonGroup.add(aToggleButton);
aToggleButton.setActionCommand("3");
aToggleButton.addActionListener(aListener);
```

Figure 23-3 shows this setup.

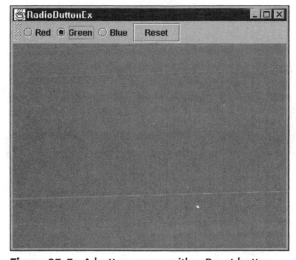

**Figure 23-3:** A button group with a Reset button

A final comment is that you should arrange buttons from the same group in such a way that it is immediately clear to the user which button belongs to which group. You can easily imagine a situation where you have more than one button group on the screen. The GUI organization should imply the logical structure.

## JRadioButtonMenuItems and JCheckBoxMenuItems

Java makes it easy for you to place radio buttons and check boxes as elements in a menu. First of all, there really are classes called JRadioButtonMenuItem and JCheckBoxMenuItem. Second, they behave exactly as you might expect. They are basically classes that encapsulate the behavior of JRadioButtons and JCheckBoxes but are added to JMenus and not to JToolBars.

For example, we can easily adapt the `JCheckBox` example by making the following changes:

```
    ...
public JMenuBar aMenubar;
public JMenu aMenu;
public JCheckBoxMenuItem redCheckBox, greenCheckBox,
   blueCheckBox;
public float colorRed, colorGreen, colorBlue;
    ...
  aMenubar = new JMenuBar();
  aMenu = new JMenu("Set Color");
  redCheckBox = new JCheckBoxMenuItem("Red", false);
  greenCheckBox = new JCheckBoxMenuItem("Green", false);
  blueCheckBox = new JCheckBoxMenuItem("Blue", false);
  aMenu.add(redCheckBox);
  aMenu.add(greenCheckBox);
  aMenu.add(blueCheckBox);

    ...
  aFrame.setSize(400,350);
  aFrame.setJMenuBar(aMenubar);
  aMenubar.add(aMenu);
    ...
```

Everything else is the same. With these minor changes, we have moved the check boxes from a button group to items on a menu. Figure 23-4 shows the effects of these changes.

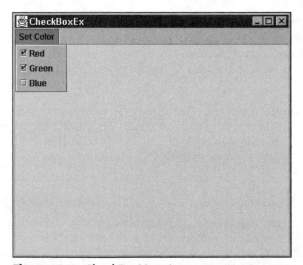

**Figure 23-4:** CheckBoxMenuItems on a menu

# Other Devices for Making Choices

So far, our two main options for making choices have been buttons and menus. We've seen that there is a great deal of flexibility in what you accomplish with these two mechanisms. There are some techniques that you would end up implementing again and again. Swing provides you with some custom-made widgets for meeting some of these needs. In this section, we'll take a brief look at some of the classes available to you.

## JOptionPane

The JOptionPane provides the user with the familiar dialog boxes that they have to deal with or dismiss. They come in four basic styles depending on which method you use to invoke them. Each style comes in two types depending on whether you are using a heavyweight component or a lightweight component to display them. The methods that are of the form show [style]Dialog() specify the heavyweight component, while the showInternal [style]Dialog() methods specify the lightweight components. We'll look at each style in turn.

### Message Dialog Boxes

Message dialog boxes are specified using the method showMessageDialog() or show InternalMessageDialog(). You use these to present users with a message that they are forced to dismiss. The following code that brings up a message dialog box:

```
import javax.swing.*;
import java.awt.*;
import java.awt.event.*;

public class OptionPaneEx1
{
  //declarations of all used components
  public JFrame aFrame;
  public JButton aButton;
  public JOptionPane anOptionPane;

  public OptionPaneEx1()
  {
  // constructing and connecting all components

    // creating the JFrame, JPanel, JToolBar, and JMenuBar
    aFrame = new JFrame("OptionPaneEx1");
    aButton = new JButton("Display Option Pane");
    aButton.addActionListener(new OptionListener());
    anOptionPane = new JOptionPane();

    // setting the layout and default button and adding the
```

```
   // JMenubar, JToolbar, and JPanel.

   aFrame.setSize(400,350);
   aFrame.getContentPane().add(aButton);
   aFrame.setVisible(true);
   aFrame.setDefaultCloseOperation(JFrame.EXIT_ON_CLOSE);
} //end of constructor

public class OptionListener implements ActionListener
{
   public void actionPerformed(ActionEvent e)
   {
      anOptionPane.showMessageDialog(aFrame, "This is a
         Warning", "Warning Box", JOptionPane.WARNING_MESSAGE);
   }
}

// main creates the OptionPaneEx1
public static void main( String[] args)
{
   new OptionPaneEx1();
}
}
```

When the button is pressed, the message dialog box shown in Figure 23-5 appears.

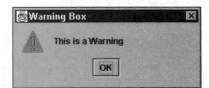

**Figure 23-5:** A Message dialog
box JOptionPane

The meat is in the line:

```
showMessageDialog(aFrame, "This is a Warning", "Warning Box",
JOptionPane.WARNING_MESSAGE);
```

This brings up a message dialog box with the text specified by the second argument. You can also include icons in the message dialog box. There are built-in icons for the standard types WARNING_MESSAGE, ERROR_MESSAGE, INFO_MESSAGES, PLAIN_MESSAGE, and QUESTION_MESSAGE. You can override these icons by specifying your own icon. There are other signatures for this method that allow you to specify more or less. The choices are the same for the showInternalMessageDialog() method.

## Confirm Dialog Boxes

Sometimes you want to give users a limited set of choices. You might want them to be able to respond yes or no or maybe even have the option to cancel. A confirm dialog box lets you ask users if they're sure that they know what they're doing. You bring one up using either the method `showConfirmDialog()` or `showInternal ConfirmDialog()`. We can just change the body of the `actionPerformed()` method of the `OptionListener` in the last example to:

```
anOptionPane.showConfirmDialog(aFrame,
   "You're about to do something really stupid. Are you sure?",
   "Reality Check", JOptionPane.YES_NO_OPTION);
```

The main difference is that the user gets to choose a response. Figure 23-6 shows the result.

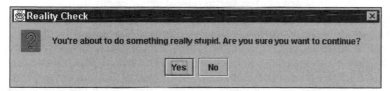

**Figure 23-6:** A Confirm dialog box JOptionPane

Your main choices are to specify whether the options are Yes or No, Yes, No, or Cancel, or OK versus Cancel. You can also have a confirm dialog box where your only choice is OK, but that is more of a message dialog box. The constants that specify these choices are again found in the `JOptionPane` class and are `YES_NO_OPTION`, `YES_NO_CANCEL_OPTION`, `OK_CANCEL_OPTION`, and `DEFAULT_OPTION`.

As you might guess, if the user is able to choose among or between responses, you should figure out what the response is. The method `showConfirmDialog()` returns an `int` that corresponds to `OK_OPTION`, `YES_OPTION` (which are both 0), `NO_OPTION`, `CANCEL_OPTION`, and the `CLOSED_OPTION`.

## Option Dialog Boxes

You can further customize the confirm dialog boxes to display choices with text or icons that you specify on the buttons. Use the methods `showOptionDialog()` or `showInternalOptionDialog()` and create your own responses. Again, we just change the body of the `actionPerformed()` method of the `OptionListener` to the following:

```
String[] choices = {"pretty sure", "not sure"};
anOptionPane.showOptionDialog(aFrame,
   "You're about to do something really stupid. Are you sure?",
```

```
"Reality Check", JOptionPane.YES_NO_OPTION,
JOptionPane.QUESTION_MESSAGE, null, choices,choices[1]);
```

Figure 23-7 shows an option dialog box.

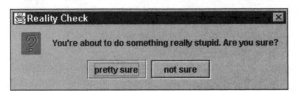

**Figure 23-7:** An Option dialog box JOptionPane

Note that there is only one version of this method and that the arguments are the following (in order): a `Component` that is the parent component for the option dialog box, an `Object` that is the message (text and/or icon) being displayed, a `String` that appears as the title of the option dialog box, an `int` that gives the option types that were covered for the confirm dialog box, an `int` that gives the message types that were covered for the message dialog box, an `Icon` that could appear in place of the icon specified by the message type, an `Object[]` array that includes the messages to appear on the buttons, and an `Object` that specifies which button is the default button.

## Input Dialog Boxes

It's hard to say whether input dialog boxes or option dialog boxes are more flexible. With input dialog boxes, the option type is `OK_CANCEL_OPTION`. Although you can specify the message type, its default value is `QUESTION_MESSAGE` and the title of the input dialog box has the default value `Input` but can be changed. Here's an example of how you might use an input dialog box. Again, this is just the `actionPerformed()` method's body:

```
String[] choices = {"choice 1", "second pick","third place",
  "hardly worth mentioning", "last"};
anOptionPane.showInputDialog(aFrame,
  "What is your choice?","Input", JOptionPane.QUESTION_MESSAGE,
  null, choices,choices[2]);
```

Figure 23-8 shows that we get a dialog box with a drop-down list comprised of the choices we specified. Notice that the last argument determines the default item. We'll look at how such lists work when we consider `JLists` and `JComboBoxes` in the next two subsections.

When the user clicks OK, the return value is returned; if he or she clicks Cancel, then `null` is returned. You can also implement an input dialog box so that the user has to input text. In this case, the entered `String` is returned when OK is clicked.

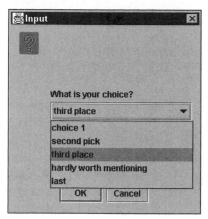

**Figure 23-8:** An Input dialog box
JOptionPane

## JList

We just looked at the showInputDialog() method of JOptionPane to build a list
of choices. You can add the list part of that component by itself to any container.
Let's look at an example where we construct a JList and listen for the element
selected:

```
import javax.swing.*;
import javax.swing.event.*;
import java.awt.*;

public class ListEx
{
  //declarations of all used components
  public JFrame aFrame;
  public JLabel aLabel;
  public JList aList;

  public ListEx()
  {
    aFrame = new JFrame("ListEx");
    aLabel = new JLabel("Selection:");
    String[] choices = {"first", "next", "another", "last"};
    aList = new JList(choices);
    aList.addListSelectionListener( new ChoiceListener());

    aFrame.setSize(400,350);
    aFrame.getContentPane().add(aLabel,BorderLayout.SOUTH);
    aFrame.getContentPane().add(aList, BorderLayout.CENTER);
    aFrame.setVisible(true);
```

```
      aFrame.setDefaultCloseOperation(JFrame.EXIT_ON_CLOSE);
    } //end of constructor

    public class ChoiceListener implements ListSelectionListener
    {
      public void valueChanged( ListSelectionEvent e)
      {
        aLabel.setText("Selection: " +
          aList.getSelectedValue().toString());
      }
    }

    // main creates the ListEx
    public static void main( String[] args)
    {
      new ListEx();
    }
  }
```

Notice that we don't use an `ActionListener` but instead use a `ListSelection
Listener`. This is an interface with the method `valueChanged()`. It is invoked only
when a different item is selected from the `JList`. You could have constructed your
list from a vector of objects and if your list had been large enough, you might have
wanted to put it inside of a scroll pane. The class `JList` includes a lot of methods
designed to customize the scrolling behavior and to otherwise set the look of
your list.

Our simple example (shown in Figure 23-9) does not have a very compelling UI.
Notice that, by default, `JList` supports the selection of more than one object, but
this application only prints out the `String` associated with the object closest to the
beginning of the list. You can set your `JList` to accept only a single selection or a
single range of selected items. The APIs make it clear how to set these various looks
and behaviors.

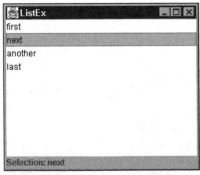

**Figure 23-9:** A simple JList with a
JLabel

# JComboBox

In the next chapter, we'll look at how Swing is built on top of Model-View-Controller, but this is a good place to introduce the idea. Both JComboBox and JList let the user interact with lists. In a way, they provide the user with a different view and different controls for the same underlying model. Compare this code for a JComboBox with the example we just saw for a JList.

```java
import javax.swing.*;
import javax.swing.event.*;
import java.awt.*;
import java.awt.event.*;

public class ComboBoxEx
{
  //declarations of all used components
  public JFrame aFrame;
  public JComboBox aComboBox;
  public JLabel aLabel;

  public ComboBoxEx()
  {
    aFrame = new JFrame("ComboBoxEx");
    String[] choices = {"first", "next", "another", "last"};
    aLabel = new JLabel("Selection:");
    aComboBox = new JComboBox(choices);
    aComboBox.addItemListener( new ChoiceListener());
    aComboBox.setEditable(true);
    aFrame.setSize(400,350);
    aFrame.getContentPane().add(aComboBox, BorderLayout.NORTH);
    aFrame.getContentPane().add(aLabel, BorderLayout.SOUTH);
    aFrame.setVisible(true);
    aFrame.setDefaultCloseOperation(JFrame.EXIT_ON_CLOSE);
  } //end of constructor

  public class ChoiceListener implements ItemListener
  {
    public void itemStateChanged( ItemEvent e)
    {
      aLabel.setText("Selection: " +
      aComboBox.getSelectedItem().toString());
    }
  }

  // main creates the ComboBoxEx
  public static void main( String[] args)
  {
    new ComboBoxEx();
  }
}
```

There aren't very many differences between setting up the JComboBox or the array of Strings. One difference is that we can set a JComboBox so that the user can type in input not on the list by using the setEditable() method. Another difference is that our JComboBox uses an ItemListener, while the JList used a ListSelection Listener. To display the currently selected item, we used the getSelectedItem() method of JComboBox and the getSelectedValue() method of JList. Such differences aren't difficult to figure out from the APIs that you should have access to.

A final difference is that we added the JList to the CENTER of the layout, while we added the JComboBox to NORTH. This was only because we didn't like the look and behavior when the JComboBox was added to the CENTER. You may want to make this change, recompile, and see how it compares to Figure 23-10.

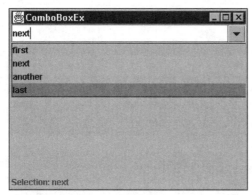

**Figure 23-10:** An editable JComboBox with a JLabel

# JFileChooser

If you will be dealing with File I/O, you will need to present the user with some way of indicating the file that needs to be opened or the location where a file needs to be saved. Like with so much of this part of the Swing library, the user will come to this widget with some expectations.

The good news is that it is very straightforward to set up a JFileChooser. Take a look at the third menu example from Chapter 22. Let's say that we wanted the Open JMenuItem in the File JMenu to bring up an open dialog box. You just need to add a few short lines. First, you have to declare and initialize the file chooser:

```
public JFileChooser aFileChooser = new JFileChooser();
```

Next, you tie the JMenu item to an action listener that will handle the file chooser:

```
openMenuItem.addActionListener(new OpenListener());
```

Finally, you provide the body of the `actionPerformed()` method of the action listener to ask the file chooser to bring up an open dialog box. The `null` as the argument indicates that the dialog box window does not have a parent container:

```
aFileChooser.showOpenDialog(null);
 These simple lines of code will bring up Figure 23-11 when the
Open menu item is selected.
```

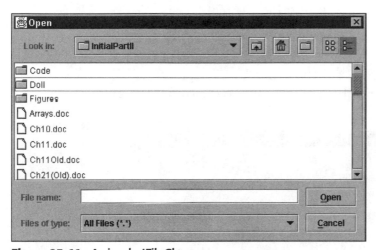

**Figure 23-11:** A simple JFileChooser

You can navigate and select a file. You can change the view of the files and create a new directory. When the time comes, however, this application won't open the file that is specified. The `JFileChooser` class has many methods and properties. You can open up a Save dialog box instead, as well as filter your selections. Check the APIs for the specific functionality that meets your needs.

## JColorChooser

A class you will probably use even less frequently than the `JFileChooser` is the `JColorChooser`. It provides three mechanisms for selecting colors that you can tie to elements in your application: one that allows you to click on the color, one that lets you specify hue, saturation, and brightness, and the third that lets you specify red, green, and blue. The following may be the shortest program in this book:

```
import javax.swing.*;
import java.awt.*;

public class ColorChooserEx
{
```

```
  public JColorChooser aColorChooser;

  public ColorChooserEx()
  {
    aColorChooser = new JColorChooser();
    aColorChooser.showDialog(null, "Color Chooser Example",
      Color.red);
  }

  public static void main( String[] args)
  {
    new ColorChooserEx();
  }
}
```

One of the views of the JColorChooser is shown in Figure 23-12.

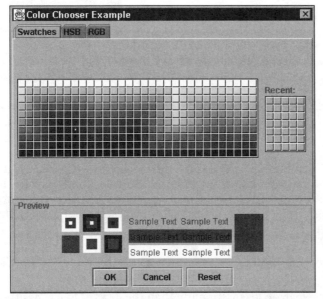

**Figure 23-12:** A JColorChooser

The JColorChooser is declared and defined and then appears as a dialog box.
Like with our JFileChooser example, no parent has been assigned. The text that
appears in the JColorChooser's menu bar is specified as is the initial color. Like
our JFileChooser example, this JColorChooser doesn't really effect anything. It
does, however, exhibit the full functionality of a color chooser (unlike the example
we've been following for the past two chapters).

If the OK button is clicked, the selected color is returned; otherwise, null is returned. We'll use this to adapt our running example to use the color chooser to select the panel's background color:

```java
import javax.swing.*;
import java.awt.*;
import java.awt.event.*;

public class ColorChooserEx2
{
  //declarations of all used components
  public JFrame aFrame;
  public JPanel aPanel;
  public JButton aButton;
  public JColorChooser aColorChooser;

  public ColorChooserEx2()
  {
  // constructing and connecting all components

    // creating the JFrame, JPanel, JToolBar, and JMenuBar
    aFrame = new JFrame("ColorChooserEx2");
    aPanel = new JPanel();
    aButton = new JButton("Choose Color");
    aButton.addActionListener(new ColorListener());
    aColorChooser = new JColorChooser();

    // setting the layout and default button and adding the
    // JMenubar, JToolbar, and JPanel. Also setting default
    // close operation to EXIT_ON_CLOSE
    aFrame.getContentPane().setLayout(new BorderLayout());
    aFrame.setSize(400,350);
    aFrame.getContentPane().add(aButton, BorderLayout.NORTH);
    aFrame.getContentPane().add(aPanel, BorderLayout.CENTER);
    aFrame.setVisible(true);
    aFrame.setDefaultCloseOperation(JFrame.EXIT_ON_CLOSE);
  } //end of constructor

  public class ColorListener implements ActionListener
  {
    public void actionPerformed(ActionEvent e)
    {
      aPanel.setBackground(
        aColorChooser.showDialog(aFrame,
          "Color Chooser Example", aPanel.getBackground()));
    }
  }
}
```

```
    // main creates the ColorChooserEx2
    public static void main( String[] args)
    {
      new ColorChooserEx2();
    }
  }
```

Here the JButton uses the implementation of ActionListener called Color Listener. This, in turn, uses the JColorChooser to select the color of the panel. A user can use any of the color-choosing widgets to select the new color. If a user presses OK, then the background color is set to the new color. We could have tested whether what was returned was null. The user probably expects that clicking Cancel will allow the original color to remain. However, our current version sets the background color to gray if the user clicks Cancel.

## JSlider

The JColorChooser used sliders and tabbed panes. We'll cover tabbed panes later in this chapter, but let's take a look at the JSlider in Figure 23-13.

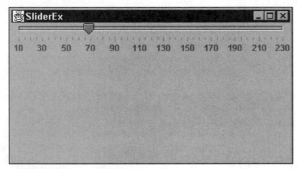

**Figure 23-13:** A JSlider

When you create a slider, you can use constructors that allow you to specify the orientation of the slider as well as its minimum and maximum values. You can also set the initial value of the slider. You can generate labels automatically from these minimum and maximum values or, because the slider is highly customizable, you can create your own labels as well.

In Figure 23-13 you can see that below the slider are major and minor ticks. You set the interval for these using the methods setMinorTickSpacing() and setMajor TickSpacing(). By now, you're familiar enough with Swing to know that you will have set the spacing but not made them visible. You need to explicitly call the set PaintTicks() method and pass it the boolean value true. Finally, if you would like to label the major ticks, you should pass `true` to the `setPaintLabels` method. Putting this together, we get the following code:

```
import javax.swing.*;

public class SliderEx
{
  //declarations of all used components
  public JFrame aFrame;
  public JSlider aSlider;

  public SliderEx()
  {
    aFrame = new JFrame("SliderEx");
    aSlider = new JSlider(10,230,68);
    aSlider.setMajorTickSpacing(20);
    aSlider.setMinorTickSpacing(5);
    aSlider.setPaintTicks(true);
    aSlider.setPaintLabels(true);

    aFrame.setSize(400,350);
    aFrame.getContentPane().add(aSlider);
    aFrame.setVisible(true);
    aFrame.setDefaultCloseOperation(JFrame.EXIT_ON_CLOSE);
  } //end of constructor

  // main creates the SliderEx
  public static void main( String[] args)
  {
    new SliderEx();
  }
}
```

You no doubt noticed that this slider doesn't do anything. You need to register a `ChangeListener` to listen for when the slider has been slid. A problem, however, is that while the slider is sliding, it is generating a lot of events. For the most part, you only care about where the slider ends up. If this is the case, then you should check that `aSlider.getValueIsAdjusting()` returns `false`. This means that `aSlider` is stationary and the value can be updated using the command `aSlider.getValue()`.

# Containers

In some of the examples of other Swing components we have seen split panes, scroll panes, and tabbed panes. In this section we will briefly look at the two components new to Swing: the split pane and the tabbed pane. We will also look at components that support a desktop look and feel. For an example that uses `JScrollPane`, see the `JTextArea` example in the next section.

## JSplitPane

Sometimes you want to split a frame into two pieces. Your basic choices are whether to split it horizontally or vertically. Once you have split it, you need to be able to refer to each piece so that you can add components to them. With a horizontal split, there is a top and a bottom subcomponent that can be assigned with the setTop Component() and setBottomComponent() methods. You can set the initial position of the divider and specify the smallest each subcomponent can be. The following code sets up a trivial split pane with a vertical divider with a white panel on the left side and a black panel on the right side. The divider is set to be about a third of the width from the left side:

```java
import javax.swing.*;
import java.awt.*;

public class SplitPaneEx
{
  //declarations of all used components
  public JFrame aFrame;
  public JPanel whitePanel, blackPanel;
  public JSplitPane aSplitPane;

  public SplitPaneEx()
  {
    aFrame = new JFrame("SplitPaneEx");
    whitePanel = new JPanel();
    blackPanel = new JPanel();
    whitePanel.setBackground(Color.white);
    blackPanel.setBackground(Color.black);
    aSplitPane = new JSplitPane(JSplitPane.HORIZONTAL_SPLIT,
      true, whitePanel, blackPanel);
    aSplitPane.setDividerLocation(150);
    aFrame.setSize(400,350);
    aFrame.getContentPane().add(aSplitPane);
    aFrame.setVisible(true);
    aFrame.setDefaultCloseOperation(JFrame.EXIT_ON_CLOSE);
  } //end of constructor

  // main creates the SplitPaneEx
  public static void main( String[] args)
  {
    new SplitPaneEx();
  }
}
```

Perhaps it's not clear that a HORIZONTAL_SPLIT refers to a vertical divider, but to split the frame into a right and left side (a horizontal split), we need such a divider. The next argument in the split pane's constructor allows us to specify the behavior when a user drags the divider back and forth. If true, then the divider moves along with the two sides as the user moves back and forth. If false, then when the user releases the mouse button, the JSplitPane will update. In the next line, we've set the divider's initial position in terms of pixels. Figure 23-14 shows the `JSplitPane` from the previous codes.

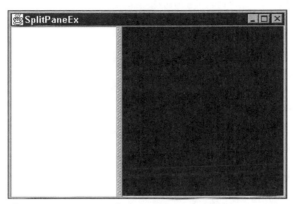

**Figure 23-14:** A JSplitPane

## JTabbedPane

The `JTabbedPane` allows the user to click on a tab and bring the attached pane to the top immediately. It's like a much more convenient card layout. Like so many Swing components, the `JTabbedPane` is easily configured. Besides, the default constructor is one that allows you to specify whether the tabs are on the `TOP`, `BOTTOM`, `LEFT`, or `RIGHT`. Once you have created a `JTabbedPane`, you add components as tabs using the `addTab` methods. These allow you to specify the text that goes in the tab along with the component. Other signatures give you the ability to add an `Icon` and a `ToolTip`. The following code shows a simple setup for a tabbed pane:

```
import javax.swing.*;
import java.awt.*;

public class TabbedPaneEx
{
  //declarations of all used components
  public JFrame aFrame;
  public JPanel panel1, panel2, panel3, panel4;
  public JLabel aLabel;
  public JTabbedPane aTabbedPane;

  public TabbedPaneEx()
  {
    aFrame = new JFrame("TabbedPaneEx");
    aTabbedPane = new JTabbedPane(JTabbedPane.BOTTOM);
    aLabel = new JLabel("Top Panel");
    panel1 = new JPanel();
    panel1.add(aLabel);
    panel2 = new JPanel();
```

```
        panel3 = new JPanel();
        panel4 = new JPanel();
        aTabbedPane.addTab("Choose Me", panel1);
        aTabbedPane.addTab("No Me", panel2);
        aTabbedPane.addTab("Hey, wait", panel3);
        aTabbedPane.addTab("I never get picked",panel4);

        aFrame.setSize(400,350);
        aFrame.getContentPane().add(aTabbedPane);
        aFrame.setVisible(true);
        aFrame.setDefaultCloseOperation(JFrame.EXIT_ON_CLOSE);
    } //end of constructor

    // main creates the TabbedPaneEx
    public static void main( String[] args)
    {
        new TabbedPaneEx();
    }
}
```

This application brings up a JTabbedPane with four tabs along the bottom. The panel on top contains a JLabel with the text *Top Panel*. Figure 23-15 shows what you see on the screen.

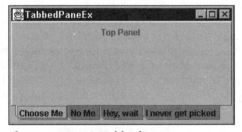

**Figure 23-15:** A JTabbedPane

## JDesktopPane and JInternalFrame

You can get the feel of lightweight frames that exist within a desktop by using the JDesktopPane together with JInternalFrames. As an example, you may be used to having more than one document opened by your word processor where the documents can be resized and moved around anywhere within the application's frame. The following code creates a desktop pane and adds two internal frames to it:

```
import javax.swing.*;
import java.awt.*;

public class DesktopPaneEx
{
```

```
    //declarations of all used components
    public JFrame aFrame;
    public JInternalFrame frame1, frame2;
    public JDesktopPane aDesktopPane;

    public DesktopPaneEx()
    {
      aFrame = new JFrame("DesktopPaneEx");
      aDesktopPane = new JDesktopPane();
      aFrame.setContentPane(aDesktopPane);
      frame1 = new JInternalFrame("One", true, true, true);
      frame2 = new JInternalFrame("Two",true, true,true);
      frame1.setSize(150,130);
      frame1.setVisible(true);
      frame2.setBounds(180,150,140,120);
      frame2.setVisible(true);
      aDesktopPane.add(frame1);
      aDesktopPane.add(frame2);
      aFrame.setSize(400,350);
      aDesktopPane = new JDesktopPane();
      aFrame.setVisible(true);
      aFrame.setDefaultCloseOperation(JFrame.EXIT_ON_CLOSE);
    } //end of constructor

    // main creates the DesktopPaneEx
    public static void main( String[] args)
    {
      new DesktopPaneEx();
    }
  }
```

After creating the JDesktopPane, you have to set it to be the containing JFrame's content pane. Then you create your JInternalFrames, set their position, set them to be visible, and then add them to the desktop pane. For kicks, you can comment out the lines where you set their size or set them to be visible and see what happens. This JInternalFrame constructor allows you to specify the title of the internal frame and then set whether you can resize, close, and maximize the frame. Figure 23-16 shows what the desktop pane looks like before you start messing with the internal frames.

# Text

So far we've only looked at working with text that was fixed ahead of time. In JLabels and in the radio buttons and check boxes, the choices were set. We would like to provide a way for users to be able to enter text into appropriate containers. In this section, we'll look at Swing's components for handling text input.

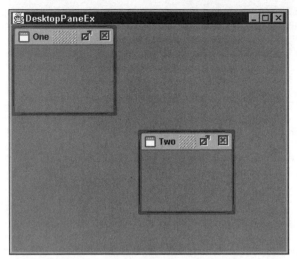

**Figure 23-16:** A JDesktopPane with two JInternalFrames

The Swing text components all inherit from the `JTextComponent`. This class contains the basic functionality that allows you to highlight portions of the text, scroll through text, and use a caret for moving through a document. You can set the color and handle events and set generic properties for text components using `JText Component`. We'll see some of these effects when dealing with the subclasses `JEditorPane`, `JTextArea`, and `JTextField`.

## JTextField and JPasswordField

The most basic text component is the `JTextField`. You can create a `JTextField` by specifying the `String` that will appear as the initial text for the text field and/or the width of that text field. Here is the code for an example that takes the `String` entered into the text field and places it into a `JLabel`. The action listener responds when the user presses the Enter key at the end of the text input:

```
import javax.swing.*;
import java.awt.event.*;
import java.awt.*;

public class TextFieldEx
{
  //declarations of all used components
  public JFrame aFrame;
  public JLabel aLabel;
  public JTextField aTextField;

  public TextFieldEx()
  {
    aFrame = new JFrame("TextFieldEx");
    aLabel = new JLabel("Output");
```

```
        aTextField = new JTextField("Input", 40);
        aTextField.addActionListener( new InputListener());

        aFrame.setSize(400,350);
        aFrame.getContentPane().add(aTextField,BorderLayout.NORTH);
        aFrame.getContentPane().add(aLabel, BorderLayout.CENTER);
        aFrame.setVisible(true);
        aFrame.setDefaultCloseOperation(JFrame.EXIT_ON_CLOSE);
    } //end of constructor

    public class InputListener implements ActionListener
    {
        public void actionPerformed( ActionEvent e)
        {
            aLabel.setText(aTextField.getText());
        }
    }

    // main creates the TextFieldEx
    public static void main( String[] args)
    {
        new TextFieldEx();
    }
}
```

Figure 23-17 shows the resulting screen.

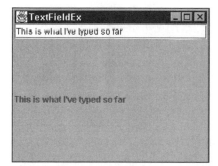

**Figure 23-17:** A JTextField and a JLabel

Let's change this example so that we are inputting a password. In this case, our input will be masked. Basically, the changes you need to make are to change the word `TextField` to `PasswordField` wherever it occurs (even in the middle of a word). The more subtle change is what you need to do with the `actionPerformed()` method. To get the text entered into a `JPasswordField`, you use the method `get Password()` instead of `getText()`. The text is returned as a character array instead of as a `String`. This is for security reasons. You can reset the primitive character elements as soon as you read them. If you reset a `String`, the original `String` still exists (without a handle to it) until it is garbage collected.

Not being security-minded in this example, we have constructed a String from the character array and passed that to the JLabel. The rewritten actionPerformed() method is the following:

```
public void actionPerformed( ActionEvent e)
{
  String s = new String( aPasswordField.getPassword());
  aLabel.setText(s);
}
```

Figure 23-18 shows the masked password in the JPasswordField and the unmasked password in the JLabel. You can change the character used for masking with the setEchoChar(*yourCharacterHere*) call.

**Figure 23-18:** A JPasswordField and a JLabel

## JTextArea

Of course, every now and then you'd like your text area to be more than one line long. For simply formatted text, that is where you use JTextArea. In the following example, we've created a JTextArea into which the user can type text. We don't want to leave it up to the user to keep text in the window we provide, so we'll enable automatic line wrapping. We'd also like the line wrapping not to break a word in the middle. We accomplish these two tasks with the following simple calls:

```
aTextArea.setLineWrap(true);
aTextArea.setWrapStyleWord(true);
```

If the user has a lot to say, we'd like a scroll bar to kick in to allow us to scroll through his or her thoughtful prose. This is surprisingly straightforward. We just create a scroll pane and pass the text area in as an argument to the constructor. Then instead of adding the text area to the frame's content pane, we add the scroll pane:

```java
import javax.swing.*;

public class TextAreaEx
{
  public JFrame aFrame;
  public JTextArea aTextArea;
  public JScrollPane aScrollPane;

  public TextAreaEx()
  {
    aFrame = new JFrame("TextAreaEx");
    aTextArea = new JTextArea();
    aScrollPane = new JScrollPane(aTextArea);
    aTextArea.setLineWrap(true);
    aTextArea.setWrapStyleWord(true);
    aFrame.setSize(300,200);
    aFrame.getContentPane().add(aScrollPane);
    aFrame.setVisible(true);
    aFrame.setDefaultCloseOperation(JFrame.EXIT_ON_CLOSE);
  } //end of constructor

  // main creates the TextAreaEx
  public static void main( String[] args)
  {
    new TextAreaEx();
  }
}
```

As you can see in Figure 23-19, the text wraps correctly and the scroll bar is working as well. Given its flexibility, this component is surprisingly easy to use. It took half a dozen lines to provide this functionality.

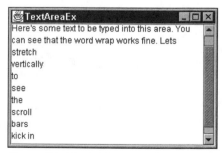

**Figure 23-19:** A JTextArea that uses a JScrollPane

## JEditorPane and JTextPane

The JEditorPane and the JTextPane are components designed for displaying more complicated text. If you are going to work frequently with these components, you will need to understand the class javax.swing.text.EditorKit. This class and its subclasses contain the details on how to display content that is plain text, HTML, or Rich Text Format (rtf). The examples in this section will merely hint at your possible options.

In addition to the default constructor, you can create a JEditorPane by specifying the MIME type as text/plain, text/html, or text/rtf along with a String containing the text you wish to display. You can also construct a JEditorPane from a URL that you provide as a String or as a URL. In this example, you'll see two JEditorPanes, one with the HTML code specified and the other loaded from a URL:

```
import javax.swing.*;
import java.awt.*;
import java.io.*;

public class EditorPaneEx
{
  public JFrame aFrame;
  public JEditorPane anEditorPane1, anEditorPane2;
  public JScrollPane aScrollPane;

  public EditorPaneEx()
  {
    aFrame = new JFrame("EditorPaneEx");
    anEditorPane1 = new JEditorPane("text/html",
      "<P> <B> Help</B> me </P>");
    try{anEditorPane2 = new JEditorPane(new File( "readme.html"
      ).toURL());}
    catch(IOException e){System.out.println("not found");}
    aScrollPane = new JScrollPane(anEditorPane2);
    aFrame.setSize(400,350);

aFrame.getContentPane().add(anEditorPane1,BorderLayout.NORTH);
    aFrame.getContentPane().add(aScrollPane);
    aFrame.setVisible(true);
    aFrame.setDefaultCloseOperation(JFrame.EXIT_ON_CLOSE);
  } //end of constructor

  // main creates the EditorPaneEx
  public static void main( String[] args)
  {
    new EditorPaneEx();
  }
}
```

It even looks as if the bottom JEditorPane has hyperlinks. (See Figure 23-20.)

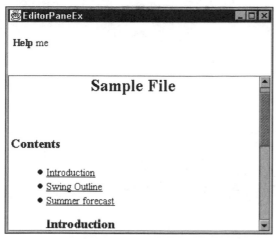

**Figure 23-20:** Two JEditorPanes

You'll see the HTML-formatted text, but you'll notice that if you click on the hyper-links, they don't take you anywhere. The `JEditorPane` class contains methods to add or remove a hyperlink listener and the ability to fire a hyperlink update. The `HyperlinkListener` interface implements the `EventListener` interface and adds the signature for the method `public void hyperlinkUpdate( HyperlinkEvent h )`. The class `HyperlinkEvent` constructs a hyperlink event from an `Object` that is the source of the event, a `HyperlinkEvent.EventType` that specifies the type of the event as one of `ACTIVATED`, `ENTERED`, or `EXITED`, a URL, and possibly a `String` describing the hyperlink event.

The `JTextPane` is designed to support someone wanting to work with plain text. It is not just a `JTextArea` because it has strong support for formatting text. You can easily change the size of some text, or the color or alignment of other text. You realize these capabilities by using the classes `AttributeSet`, `StyledDocument`, `Styled EditorKit`, and `Document` in the `javax.swing.text` package.

We can see in our first example that, as in most Swing components, there is a Model-View-Controller pattern working. We will create a `JTextPane` that has a `StyledDocument` associated with it. We add a `Style` to this document that sets the font size to 36 points. The `JTextPane` then uses the method `setLogicalStyle()` to invoke this style. This is not a very flexible example, but this code helps us see the various components:

```
import javax.swing.*;
import javax.swing.text.*;
import java.awt.*;

public class TextPaneEx
```

```
{
  //declarations of all used components
  public JFrame aFrame;
  public JTextPane aTextPane;
  public Style aStyle;

  public TextPaneEx()
  {
    aFrame = new JFrame("TextPaneEx");
    StyledDocument document = new DefaultStyledDocument();
    aTextPane = new JTextPane(document);
    aFrame.setContentPane(aTextPane);
    aStyle = document.addStyle("Big", null);
    StyleConstants.setFontSize(aStyle, 36);
    aTextPane.setLogicalStyle(aStyle);

    aFrame.setSize(400,350);
    aFrame.setVisible(true);
    aFrame.setDefaultCloseOperation(JFrame.EXIT_ON_CLOSE);
  } //end of constructor

  // main creates the TextPaneEx
  public static void main( String[] args)
  {
    new TextPaneEx();
  }
}
```

We end up with a `JTextPane` in which the text is quite large. (See Figure 23-21.)

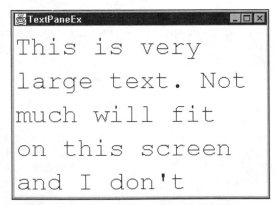

**Figure 23-21:** A JTextPane with large font

In the previous example, we used `Style` to change the look of the document. In our next example, we'll use a `SimpleAttributeSet` and set the attributes of the text we wish to change. You can skip pretty far down in the following code to see what we're doing in the JTextPane. Much of the initial code is dedicated to setting up three radio buttons on a toolbar.

For the JTextPane, we define the attribute sets Big, Bold, and Plain and use radio buttons to toggle among them. The RadioButtonListener checks to see which button is selected and sets the CharacterAttributes accordingly. Notice that the JTextPane requests focus as part of the actionPerformed() method. This is because when the user clicks on a radio button, the focus has moved to the radio button. The user would have to click back on the JTextPane to continue typing into it. You can check this out by commenting out the line aTextPane.requestFocus().

If you compile and run this code, you'll find that you get a lot for free when you use a JTextPane. For example, you can select some text and click on a radio button to change the selected text, or you can just click on a radio button and the text you type afterwards will be in the new style. If you select text and click a radio button, then you will notice that the cursor stays in place at the end of the selected text. You could also click a different radio button and change the previously selected text again. Listing 23-3 shows how easy it is to include this functionality.

## Listing 23-3: **A JTextPane Example**

```
import javax.swing.*;
import javax.swing.text.*;
import java.awt.event.*;
import java.awt.*;

public class TextPaneEx2
{
    //declarations of all used components
    public JFrame aFrame;
    public JTextPane aTextPane;
    public Style aStyle;
    public SimpleAttributeSet Big, Bold, Plain;
    public JRadioButton bigButton, boldButton, nothingButton;
    public StyledDocument document;
    public JToolBar aToolbar;
    public ButtonGroup aButtonGroup;
    public ActionListener aListener;

    public TextPaneEx2()
    {
    aFrame = new JFrame("TextPaneEx2");
//button management - same as radio button example
    bigButton = new JRadioButton("Big", false);
    boldButton = new JRadioButton("Bold", false);
    nothingButton = new JRadioButton("No Formatting", true);
    aToolbar = new JToolBar();
    aToolbar.add(bigButton);
    aToolbar.add(boldButton);
```

*Continued*

**Listing 23-3** *(continued)*

```java
    aToolbar.add(nothingButton);
    aButtonGroup = new ButtonGroup();
    aButtonGroup.add(boldButton);
    aButtonGroup.add(bigButton);
    aButtonGroup.add(nothingButton);
    aListener = new RadioButtonListener();
    boldButton.addActionListener(aListener);
    bigButton.addActionListener(aListener);
    nothingButton.addActionListener(aListener);
// setting up the text pane and defining attributes
    document = new DefaultStyledDocument();
    aTextPane = new JTextPane(document);
    Big = new SimpleAttributeSet();
    StyleConstants.setFontSize(Big, 36);
    Bold = new SimpleAttributeSet();
    StyleConstants.setBold(Bold, true);
    Plain = new SimpleAttributeSet();
    StyleConstants.setBold(Plain, false);
    StyleConstants.setFontSize(Plain, 12);
    aFrame.getContentPane().add(aToolbar, BorderLayout.NORTH);
    aFrame.getContentPane().add(aTextPane, BorderLayout.CENTER);
    aFrame.setSize(400,350);
    aFrame.setVisible(true);
    aFrame.setDefaultCloseOperation(3);
    } //end of constructor

    public class RadioButtonListener implements ActionListener
    {
      public void actionPerformed(ActionEvent e)
      {
        if (boldButton.isSelected())
        {
          aTextPane.setCharacterAttributes(Bold, true);
        }
        else
        {
          if (bigButton.isSelected())
          {
            aTextPane.setCharacterAttributes(Big, true);
          }
          else
          {
            aTextPane.setCharacterAttributes(Plain, true);
          }
        }
        aTextPane.requestFocus();
      }
    }
}
```

```
// main creates the TextPaneEx2
public static void main( String[] args)
{
  new TextPaneEx2();
}
}
```

With the JTextPane and its helper classes, it is easy to design your options so that you are changing the format of the whole document, a paragraph, or just specific characters. Figure 23-22 shows what you might come up with playing with this program.

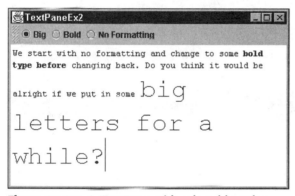

**Figure 23-22:** A JTextPane with selectable styles

You can see that we've just scratched the surface in these examples. JEditorPanes and JTextPanes have a lot of functionality and flexibility. They also are built to take advantage of the output of other Swing components.

# Display

For our last three Swing components, perhaps the heading *miscellaneous* would be more appropriate. On the other hand, these items all distinguish themselves by using visuals to help convey information to the user. The JProgressBar gives the user a clear idea of how much of the task remains, the JTable cleanly displays tabular data, and the JTree provides the user with a flexible view of hierarchical data.

# JProgressBar

Swing provides you with several mechanisms for indicating progress. One of the more user-friendly is the progress bar. A JProgressBar gives the user a visual indication of how much of the task has been completed. In our example, you can use a button to start or stop the process. As we saw in the last chapter, the process has to run on a separate thread (which we create with a Timer) or you won't be able to see the updates.

In our simple example (Listing 23-4), we have created a JButton that we've tied to an implementation of ActionListener called ButtonListener. The Button Listener creates a Timer that pauses for 20 milliseconds and is tied to the ExampleRunner class. The ButtonListener responds to button clicks by stopping and starting the timer. The ExampleRunner calls the currentValue() method to update the current value of the process and then passes this value on to the JProgressBar so that it can update its display. We have told the JProgressBar that its minimum value is 0 and its maximum value is 250 so that it can figure out how far along in the process we are. It also displays, by default, a percentage that indicates how far along we are because of the call setStringPainted(true);:

### Listing 23-4: **A Progress Bar Example**

```
import javax.swing.*;
import java.awt.*;
import java.awt.event.*;

public class ProgressBarEx
{
  //declarations of all used components
  public JFrame aFrame;
  public JButton aButton;
  public JProgressBar aProgressBar;
  public int amount =0;

  public ProgressBarEx()
  {
    aFrame = new JFrame("SliderEx");
    aProgressBar = new JProgressBar(0,250);
    aProgressBar.setValue(0);
    aProgressBar.setStringPainted(true);
    aButton = new JButton("Start/Stop");
    aButton.addActionListener(new ButtonListener());

    aFrame.setSize(400,350);
    aFrame.getContentPane().add(aProgressBar,
```

```
        BorderLayout.SOUTH);
    aFrame.getContentPane().add(aButton, BorderLayout.NORTH);
    aFrame.setVisible(true);
    aFrame.setDefaultCloseOperation(JFrame.EXIT_ON_CLOSE);
  } //end of constructor
  public int currentValue()
  {
    int i = (int)(Math.random() * 10);
    while(i >0 && amount <250)
    {
      amount++;
      i--;
    }
    return amount;
  }

  public class ButtonListener implements ActionListener
  {
    boolean isRunning = false;
    Timer timer = new Timer(20, new ExampleRunner());
    public void actionPerformed(ActionEvent e)
    {
      if (isRunning) timer.stop();
        else timer.start();
        isRunning = !isRunning;
    }
  }
  public class ExampleRunner implements ActionListener
  {
    public void actionPerformed(ActionEvent e)
    {
      aProgressBar.setValue(currentValue());
    }
  }

  // main creates the ProgressBarEx
  public static void main( String[] args)
  {
    new ProgressBarEx();
  }
}
```

A JProgressBar could get its input from many sources. You could use a progress bar to indicate the current state of a system that you need visual information about (as in a sound mixing board). Our simple application of the progress bar is shown in Figure 23-23.

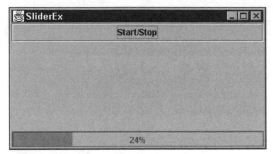

**Figure 23-23:** A JProgressBar

# JTable

The JTable class is a very complicated class for dealing with tabular data. There is, in fact, a collection of classes in the package javax.swing.table designed to help JTable manage its tables. You can access, edit, and display a wide range of Objects stored in a table using the various methods provided in the JTable class and the helpers. You'll find that JTable uses several models to appropriately handle the data.

As an introduction to JTables, our example is fairly simplistic. A little girl's favorite baseball players are displayed in a table (yes, she always lists Robby twice) built from a double String array. The headings for each column are entered in another String array. The JTable is then constructed using one of its seven constructors. The table is added to a scroll pane but, as shown in Figure 23-24, it behaves differently from other components in this scroll pane.

| First Name | Last Name | Position |
| --- | --- | --- |
| Robby | Alomar Junior | 2nd Base |
| Roberto | Alomar | 2nd Base |
| Omar | Vizquel | Short Stop |
| Manny | Ramirez | Right Field |
| Sandy | Alomar | Catcher |
| Einar | Diaz | Catcher |
| Kenny | Lofton | Center Field |

**Figure 23-24:** A JTable

Notice that as we scroll down the page, the cell data scrolls while the column headings stay in place. You can see from the following code that this example is surprisingly easy to generate:

```
import javax.swing.*;
import java.awt.*;

public class TableEx
```

```
    {
      public JFrame aFrame;
      public JTable aTable;
      public JScrollPane aScrollPane;
      public String[][] tableData= {
          {"Robby", "Alomar Junior", "2nd Base"},
          {"Roberto", "Alomar","2nd Base"},
          {"Omar", "Vizquel", "Short Stop"},
          {"Manny", "Ramirez", "Right Field"},
          {"Sandy", "Alomar", "Catcher"},
          {"Einar", "Diaz", "Catcher"},
          {"Kenny", "Lofton", "Center Field"},
          {"Jim", "Thome", "1st Base"},
          {"Travis", "Fryman", "3rd Base"}};
      public String[] columnHeadings= {"First Name", "Last Name",
          "Position"};

      public TableEx()
      {
       aFrame = new JFrame("TableEx of Maggie's Favorite Players");
       aTable = new JTable(tableData, columnHeadings);
       aScrollPane = new JScrollPane(aTable);
       aFrame.getContentPane().add(aScrollPane);
       aFrame.setSize(400,150);
       aFrame.setVisible(true);
       aFrame.setDefaultCloseOperation(JFrame.EXIT_ON_CLOSE);
      } //end of constructor

      // main creates the TableEx
      public static void main( String[] args)
      {
         new TableEx();
      }
    }
```

Because the JTable will accept Objects as cell entries, you can create JTables
that are made up of the Swing components you've seen in this chapter. At this
point, you may wonder why you don't just use a GridLayout and add the components to the layout. You'll find that for tabular data, the JTable has a great deal of
functionality that you would just have to reinvent. The JTable does not just display
the data, but it also provides ways for you to access and change the data.

## JTree

The best way to display hierarchical data is with a JTree. With the help of classes
in the javax.swing.tree package (notably the DefaultMutableTreeNode class),
you can easily construct fairly complex trees. You can also choose to allow your
tree to be editable and take care of adding and removing nodes at runtime. In our
example, we'll just insert some nodes into a tree using the add() and insert()

methods of the `DefaultMutableTreeNode`. By clicking, the user will be able to expand and collapse the tree.

Notice that this tree has been placed inside a scroll pane. In this case, it isn't necessary, but in general, it's a good idea. The line

```
aTree.putClientProperty("JTree.lineStyle", "Angled");
```

creates the lines that help you see the relationships among the various levels. You can easily spot which nodes are children and which are siblings. When you have even more levels, this is a more important feature.

`JTree` is a pretty complicated class. You can create trees from an array of `Objects`, a `Vector`, or from a `Hashtable`. There are also `TreeModels` that you use to manage your data. We've created an object using `DefaultMutableTreeNode` objects so we can manipulate the objects using the `DefaultTreeModel`. The following code just scratches the surface of what you can accomplish using a `Jtree`:

```java
import javax.swing.*;
import javax.swing.tree.*;
import java.awt.*;

public class TreeEx
{
   //declarations of all used components
   public JFrame aFrame;
   public JTree aTree;
   public JScrollPane aScrollPane;
   public DefaultMutableTreeNode root, parent, child;

   public TreeEx()
   {
     aFrame = new JFrame("TreeEx");
     root = new DefaultMutableTreeNode("javax");
     aTree = new JTree(root);
     parent = root;
     child = new DefaultMutableTreeNode("swing");
     parent.add(child);
     parent = child;
     parent.add(new DefaultMutableTreeNode("JButton"));
     parent.add(new DefaultMutableTreeNode("JFrame"));
     parent.add(new DefaultMutableTreeNode("JLabel"));
     child =new DefaultMutableTreeNode("event");
     parent.insert(child,1);
     child.add(new DefaultMutableTreeNode("ChangeListener"));
     child =new DefaultMutableTreeNode("tree");
     parent.add(child);
     child.add(new DefaultMutableTreeNode(
       "DefaultMutableTreeNode"));
     aTree.putClientProperty("JTree.lineStyle", "Angled");
```

```
   aScrollPane = new JScrollPane(aTree);
   aFrame.getContentPane().add(aScrollPane);
   aFrame.setSize(400,350);
   aFrame.setVisible(true);
   aFrame.setDefaultCloseOperation(JFrame.EXIT_ON_CLOSE);
} //end of constructor

// main creates the TreeEx
public static void main( String[] args)
{
   new TreeEx();
}
}
```

Remember from Chapter 21 that you can specify a look and feel so that your hierarchy looks like those used on your native system. For the previous code, we haven't specified a look and feel. This means that the appearance will be the standard Java look and feel. (See Figure 23-25.)

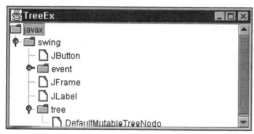

**Figure 23-25:** A JTree

# Summary

This chapter was a whirlwind tour of the various Swing components. You can flip back through these pages when you're searching for the appropriate widget for your UI. Although many of these may seem fancier than what you need, they do provide the user with the interface gadgets that they've come to expect. In short, we've seen the following:

✦ JToggleButtons are basically buttons that stay pressed until the user clicks on them again. Special kinds include JCheckBoxes that indicate their state by presenting a box that is either selected or it isn't. JRadioButtons are also JToggleButtons. That means that they actually become deselected if they are clicked a second time — their interface makes it appear as if they are still selected. The way to ensure that a JRadioButton behaves properly is to put it in a ButtonGroup.

✦ JOptionPanes include simple alert boxes to provide the users with the option of accepting or rejecting an action and to provide a list of options from which users can select. All of this is done by calling different methods from the JOptionPane class.

✦ Users are able to make more visually sophisticated choices using JSliders to set levels fairly easily and with built-in JColorChoosers and JFile Choosers. You can also allow them to select from a list using either a JCombo Box or a JList or to use an editable JComboBox to type in their own choice. The JProgressBar gives your users a quick visual cue of the state of a given process.

✦ The components that support text input range from the single line simply formatted JTextField to the multiline, multiformat, multifile typed JEditor Pane. In between is the ability to mask simple text input using the JPassword Field or to input many lines of singly formatted text using JTextArea, or to input text that supports different formatting for different paragraphs and characters using JTextPane.

✦ The JTree supports the display, editing, and accessing of data stored hierarchically. The JTable provides the same support for tabular data. Each comes with their own package of support classes.

✦ ✦ ✦

# Swing Odds and Ends

In the last three chapters, we have looked at Swing components. We have created instances of most of them and let them generate events. We've taken them out for a spin and gotten a feel for how we could take better advantage of their functionality. You've been advised to check out the APIs for details on the method calls for which you're looking. For the most part, what's left is odds and ends.

In this chapter, you'll add to your arsenal of ways to display these components. You'll use a border factory to produce borders that organize your page and clarify the interface. You can create borders with or without titles, in solid colors, or from icons, at the same level or raised, lowered, or etched. You can combine these effects to create custom borders.

You'll also look at some of the new layout managers that Swing provides. The `BoxLayout` is used in conjunction with the `Box` class to lay out components either horizontally or vertically with a great deal of flexibility. The `OverlayLayout` allows you to specify the position of components so that one can appear above another. You'll see how easy it is to change the look and feel to match different platforms, or a look that you've imagined, or to support assistive technologies. Finally, you'll see that once you've stripped away the various looks and feels, behind the Swing components are powerful models that make the whole structure work.

## Borders

In Swing, any `JComponent` can set its border using the `setBorder()` method. Don't think that the only reason for using borders is to give your GUI a polished look. Borders help organize the choices that your user has and provides a visual cue that reinforces logical groupings. We'll start by looking at the various borders available to you in the `javax.swing.border` package and how to construct them using the `BorderFactory` class. We'll then consider various borders that contain titles as well as borders that are made up of more than one border style.

## BorderFactory and the javax.swing.border package

In a way, creating a `Border` may remind you of the process of creating various `JOptionPanes`. The `javax.swing.border` package consists of the `Border` interface, the `AbstractBorder` class and its subclasses `BevelBorder`, `Compound Border`, `EmptyBorder`, `EtchedBorder`, `LineBorder`, `MatteBorder`, `SoftBevel Border`, and `TitleBorder`. Like with the `JOptionPane`, you don't tend to create these borders by calling one of their constructors. For the most part, you will use methods in the `BorderFactory` class to create the type of border you want. (You can't create a `SoftBevelBorder` using `BorderFactory`.)

`BorderFactory` is a pretty unusual class in that it consists only of `static` methods. This means that to create a border, you will make a call like the following:

```
BorderFactory.create[border type]Border([possible argument list]);
```

For example, to create a green line border for a component called `aPanel`, you could either type:

```
Border aBorder = BorderFactory.createLineBorder(Color.green);
aPanel.setBorder(aBorder);
```

or you could combine these two lines and avoid naming the `Border`:

```
aPanel.setBorder(BorderFactory.createLineBorder(Color.green));
```

The variety of methods in `BorderFactory` allows you to set the appropriate parameters for each type of border. As an example, let's look at creating a `BevelBorder`. You can use the methods `createLoweredBevelBorder()` or `createRaised BevelBorder()`, each of which takes no arguments and creates a lowered or raised `BevelBorder`. You could also use the method `createBevelBorder()` and specify whether the type is raised or lowered using the constants `LOWERED` or `RAISED` from the `BevelBorder` class. In other words, the following two lines are equivalent:

```
BorderFactory.createLoweredBevelBorder();
BorderFactory.createBevelBorder(BevelBorder.LOWERED);
```

The `createBevelBorder()` method has two other signatures. One allows you to specify the colors used as highlight and shadow for the `BevelBorder`. The other allows you to be even more specific and specify colors for the inner and outer highlights as well as for the inner and outer shadows.

We'll look at `TitledBorder`s and `CompoundBorder`s in a minute. Here's a summary of the parameters that you can set for the remaining predefined border types:

✦ `EmptyBorder`: Either nothing or `int`s that specify the insets for the top, left, bottom, and right sides.

✦ `EtchedBorder`: Either nothing or the colors for the highlight and shadow of the border.

✦ `LineBorder`: Either the color of the line or the line color together with an `int` that specifies its thickness in pixels.

✦ `MatteBorder`: Extends the `EmptyBorder` class and fills the empty border with a tiling of an icon or with a solid color. So either the four insets are specified, or the dimensions are taken from the `Icon` used to tile the border. (This second option is available only by directly calling a `MatteBorder` constructor.) In addition to the insets, the methods in `BorderFactory` either specify the `Color` or the `Icon`.

✦ `SoftBevelBorder`: Extends the `BevelBorder` class and has the same constructors and properties. Unlike BevelBorder, you cannot construct a `SoftBevelBorder` from `BorderFactory`.

Here's an example that shows many of these border elements added to `JLabel`s that display the code used to create them. Except for the `SoftBevelBorder`, these are each created from the `BorderFactory` methods. (See Listing 24-1.)

### Listing 24-1: **A Variety of Borders Example**

```
import javax.swing.*;
import javax.swing.border.*;
import java.awt.*;

public class BorderEx
{
  //declarations of all used components
  public JFrame aFrame;
  public JLabel[] aLabel = new JLabel[8];
  public AbstractBorder[] aBorder = new AbstractBorder[8];

  public BorderEx()
  {
    aFrame = new JFrame("BorderEx");
    aLabel[0] = new JLabel("createLineBorder(Color.black)");
    aLabel[0].setBorder(
      BorderFactory.createLineBorder(Color.black));
```

*Continued*

Listing 24-1 *(continued)*

```
    aLabel[1] = new JLabel("createLineBorder(Color.black,6)");
    aLabel[1].setBorder(
      BorderFactory.createLineBorder(Color.black, 6));
    aLabel[2] = new JLabel("createRaisedBevelBorder()");
    aLabel[2].setBorder(
      BorderFactory.createRaisedBevelBorder());
    aLabel[3] = new JLabel(
      "new SoftBevelBorder(BevelBorder.RAISED)");
    aLabel[3].setBorder(
      new SoftBevelBorder(BevelBorder.RAISED));
    aLabel[4] = new JLabel("createLoweredBevelBorder()");
    aLabel[4].setBorder(
      BorderFactory.createLoweredBevelBorder());
    aLabel[5] = new JLabel(
      "createEtchedBorder(Color.white, Color.black)");
    aLabel[5].setBorder(
      BorderFactory.createEtchedBorder(
        Color.white, Color.black));
    aLabel[6] = new JLabel("createEtchedBorder()");
    aLabel[6].setBorder(BorderFactory.createEtchedBorder());
    aLabel[7] = new JLabel(
      "createMatteBorder(4,8,12,16,Color.black)");
    aLabel[7].setBorder(
      BorderFactory.createMatteBorder(4,8,12,16,Color.black));

    aFrame.setSize(550,300);
    aFrame.getContentPane().setLayout(new GridLayout(4,2,5,5));
    for (int i = 0; i<8; i++)
    {
      aFrame.getContentPane().add(aLabel[i]);
    }
    aFrame.setVisible(true);
    aFrame.setDefaultCloseOperation(JFrame.EXIT_ON_CLOSE);
  } //end of constructor

  // main creates the BorderEx
  public static void main( String[] args)
  {
    new BorderEx();
  }
}
```

Figure 24-1 pretty much tells the story.

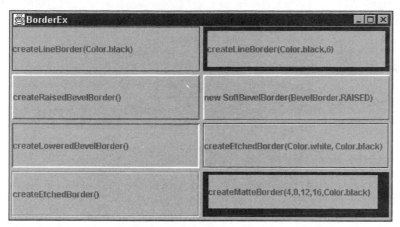

**Figure 24-1:** A bunch of borders

# TitledBorders

In Chapter 23, you saw examples of radio buttons that were functionally linked into button groups. We mentioned that your UI should imply these logical groupings. For example, Figure 24-2 presents an interface for ordering breakfast where the options are not immediately clear.

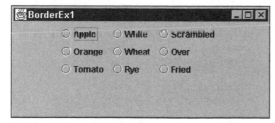

**Figure 24-2:** A confusing collection of radio buttons

Sure, you probably understood that the buttons in each column formed button groups. But consider how adding borders and a little text helps clarify the programmer's intent, as shown in Figure 24-3.

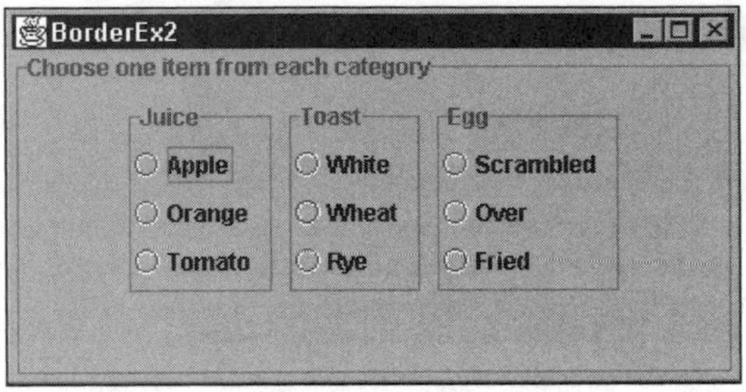

**Figure 24-3:** Using TitledBorders for clarification

Each button group is actually on a JPanel, so it is easy to create borders with titles for these panels using the method createTitledBorder() from the class Border Factory. For example, the eggPanel's border is created using the following code:

```
eggPanel.setBorder(BorderFactory.createTitledBorder("Egg"));
```

As we mentioned, the setBorder() method is in the JComponent class. This means that a JFrame can't be assigned a border. To create the border that you see around the juicePanel, toastPanel, and eggPanel, you have to create a JPanel and add it to the JFrame's component. We've created a JPanel called dummyPanel that gets its own titled border and is the container for the other three JPanels. Specifically, this part of the code is as follows:

```
//...
eggPanel.setBorder(BorderFactory.createTitledBorder("Egg"));
dummyPanel.setBorder(
  BorderFactory.createTitledBorder(
    "Choose one item from each category"));
aFrame.setSize(400,350);
aFrame.getContentPane().add(dummyPanel);
dummyPanel.add(juicePanel);
dummyPanel.add(toastPanel);
dummyPanel.add(eggPanel);
```

As you might expect, you have quite a bit of flexibility in the look of TitledBorder. You can select any border style as the border to which you are adding a title. For example, change the setBorder() call for the dummyPanel to:

```
dummyPanel.setBorder(BorderFactory.createTitledBorder(
    BorderFactory.createRaisedBevelBorder(),
    "Choose one item from each category"));
```

If you also similarly change the other borders to lowered BevelBorders, you've created the look shown in Figure 24-4.

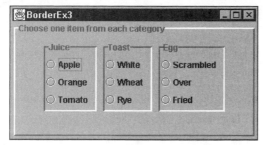

**Figure 24-4:** Changing the border style in a TitledBorder

You can also specify the position and justification of the text used in the title using constants defined in the class TitledBorder. Finally, you can also specify the font and the font color for the border.

## CompoundBorders

In the previous example, you get more of a feeling of depth for the panels containing the radio button groups because the panel containing these panels looks raised. As you play with borders, you'll find combinations that you really like. You don't want to have to add an additional JPanel inside of a JComponent just to get that special effect. The solution is to use CompoundBorders. BorderFactory has two createCompoundBorder() methods. One takes no arguments and the other allows you to specify the outer border and the inner border. Because the CompoundBorder is itself a border, you can build up fairly complex borders in this way.

Here's a simple example that builds a CompoundBorder from two other CompoundBorders:

```
import javax.swing.*;
import java.awt.*;

public class BorderEx4
{
  public JFrame aFrame;
  public JPanel dummyPanel;

  public BorderEx4()
  {
  // constructing and connecting all components
    aFrame = new JFrame("BorderEx4");
    dummyPanel = new JPanel();

    //borders
```

```
    dummyPanel.setBorder(BorderFactory.createCompoundBorder(
       BorderFactory.createCompoundBorder(
          BorderFactory.createLineBorder(Color.darkGray, 4),
          BorderFactory.createRaisedBevelBorder()),
       BorderFactory.createCompoundBorder(
          BorderFactory.createEmptyBorder(4,4,4,4),
          BorderFactory.createLoweredBevelBorder())));

    // putting the big pieces  together
    aFrame.setSize(400,350);
    aFrame.getContentPane().add(dummyPanel);
    aFrame.setVisible(true);
    aFrame.setDefaultCloseOperation(JFrame.EXIT_ON_CLOSE);
    } //end of constructor

    // main creates the BorderEx4
    public static void main( String[] args)
    {
       new BorderEx4();
    }
}
```

The result looks like Figure 24-5.

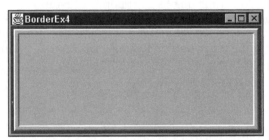

**Figure 24-5:** Combining borders using
CompoundBorder

The downside of all of these options is that you'll end up spending hours fiddling around trying to get the interface to look just right. You may even decide that there aren't enough choices and you want to create your own border class. Your time could probably be better spent, but you'll probably have to find that out for yourself!

# Swing Layout Managers

You may have noticed that even in the Swing chapters, we have been using the AWT layout managers. You've frequently seen BorderLayout in the previous three chapters. In the previous section on borders, we used both FlowLayout and

GridLayout. In Chapter 23, it may have occurred to you that the JTabbedPane could be used in place of the CardLayout to allow the user to access a hidden panel without cycling through all of the panels between where they are and where they want to be. We also didn't see the GridBagLayout because we didn't encounter any layouts with any complex requirements.

Swing introduces four layout managers: BoxLayout, OverlayLayout, ScrollPanel Layout, and ViewportLayout. ScrollPaneLayout is a helper class for the JScroll Pane and you wouldn't tend to use it directly. The ScrollPaneLayout is designed for laying out the scroll bars, corner components, headers for the columns and rows (which don't scroll), and the JViewport itself. Similarly, the ViewPort is the helper class for the JViewport and won't be called directly.

## BoxLayout

On first view, the BoxLayout is a tricked-out version of FlowLayout. It is the layout manager associated with the Box class in the same way that ScrollPanelLayout is the layout manager associated with JScrollPane. The Box class is one of three swing classes that directly extend java.awt.Container. One of the other classes is the abstract class JComponent. You use a Box together with BoxLayout to lay out components either vertically or horizontally. Although horizontal layout can be accomplished with the FlowLayout, the BoxLayout allows for a greater degree of control. Likewise, you can use GridLayout to lay out components vertically or horizontally by specifying GridLayout(0,1) or GridLayout(1,0), respectively, but you still don't get the control you can insist on with BoxLayout.

When you create a new Box, the argument of the constructor is one of the ints BoxLayout.X_AXIS or BoxLayout.Y_AXIS that specify whether the components of the Box will be layed out horizontally or vertically. You can insert a fixed amount of space between components by creating struts using the createHorizontalStrut() or createVerticalStrut() method from Box (depending on the orientation of the Box). You can insert a variable amount of space to nicely distribute components using glue. In this case, you use the createHorizontalGlue() or createVertical Glue() method from Box. This layout manager may feel familiar to those who have used TeX to produce documents.

We can return to the radio button breakfast-order example and provide each of the four panels with a BoxLayout. Notice that if you create a BoxLayout for a component other than a Box, the constructor is BoxLayout( *componentName*, *orientation*). This means that you've told the component who its layout manager is and the layout manager who its component is. Also note is that we've specified an alignment as well as the orientation for the three panels that contain button groups:

```
public class BoxEx
{
  //...
  public JFrame aFrame;
  public JPanel juicePanel, toastPanel, eggPanel, dummyPanel;
```

```
public BoxLayout juiceLayout, toastLayout, eggLayout,
   dummyLayout;

public BoxEx()
{
// constructing and connecting all components
  aFrame = new JFrame("BoxEx2");
  juicePanel = new JPanel();
  toastPanel = new JPanel();
  eggPanel = new JPanel();
  dummyPanel = new JPanel();
  juiceLayout = new BoxLayout(juicePanel, BoxLayout.X_AXIS);
  toastLayout = new BoxLayout(toastPanel, BoxLayout.Y_AXIS);
  eggLayout = new BoxLayout(eggPanel, BoxLayout.X_AXIS);
  dummyLayout = new BoxLayout(dummyPanel, BoxLayout.Y_AXIS);
  juicePanel.setLayout(juiceLayout);
  juicePanel.setAlignmentX(1.0f);
  toastPanel.setLayout(toastLayout);
  toastPanel.setAlignmentX(0.0f);
  eggPanel.setLayout(eggLayout);
  eggPanel.setAlignmentX(1.0f);
  dummyPanel.setLayout(dummyLayout);
  // ...
```

The argument to the `setAlignmentX()` and `setAlignmentY()` methods is a `float` between `0.0` and `1.0`. The resulting image on the screen (see Figure 24-6) is not particularly attractive, but it does illustrate some of the functionality of the `BoxLayout`.

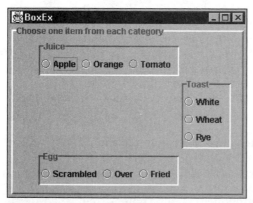

**Figure 24-6:** The BoxLayout

## OverlayLayout

If you don't have a good reason for using `OverlayLayout`, then don't use it. As you might expect, this is the layout manager that you use when you want components to be able to overlap either partly or completely. You could use it in the same way as a `GlassPane` to keep users from using components you wish to restrict. You can use the `OverlayLayout` to get great GUIs (see Figure 24-7), or you can use it to get something as ugly as this.

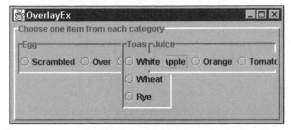

**Figure 24-7:** An ugly application of OverlayLayout

The code that generated this is similar to our previous example. The `dummyPanel` has an `OverlayLayout` and the actual position of the other components has been set so that they overlap. Notice again that this layout manager is passed the name of the component to which it is assigned:

```
public OverlayLayout dummyLayout;

   public OverlayEx()
   {
   // ...
     dummyLayout = new OverlayLayout(dummyPanel);
     juicePanel.setLayout(juiceLayout);
     juicePanel.setAlignmentX(0.0f);
     juicePanel.setAlignmentY(0.0f);
     toastPanel.setLayout(toastLayout);
     toastPanel.setAlignmentX(0.5f);
     toastPanel.setAlignmentY(0.0f);
     eggPanel.setLayout(eggLayout);
     eggPanel.setAlignmentX(1.0f);
     eggPanel.setAlignmentY(0.0f);
     dummyPanel.setLayout(dummyLayout);
     // ...
```

# Pluggable Look and Feel

In Chapter 21, we introduced some of the fundamental Swing ideas. One of the keys was that within a top-level container such as `JFrame` or `JApplet`, you should only add other Swing components. The reason is that these components are light-weight — they aren't just a proxy for a native component. The AWT components are heavyweight and are each associated with a native component. So an AWT button had to be tested on all platforms, whereas a `JButton` was a component written entirely in Java to work in a Java world.

This good news for you means more work for Sun's engineers. They are no longer relying on the native operating system, so they are responsible for making sure that the look and feel of components is correct for the target platforms. Again, this is good news for you because with the flip of a switch (or more accurately, the call of a method), you can change the look and feel from Metal (the Java cross-platform default) to Windows, Motif, or Mac. Of course, as soon as you have this ability, you'll want more. Java allows you to customize the various looks and feels or to set up your own. We'll look at how this helps people who use assistive technologies to access your software.

## Setting look and feel

There are basically two situations when you will want to set the look and feel for an application:

✦ You have a look and feel that you really like, such as a custom color set, and you want each user to view the application in that specific way.

✦ You want each user to experience your application as if it were written for the platform he or she is using. You want your application to feel like a Windows program for Windows users and a Mac program for Mac without having to change your code. In fact, when it comes to these two look and feels, you are only supposed to use them on the appropriate platform. You aren't supposed to use the Mac look and feel on a Windows machine or the Windows look and feel on a Mac.

The workhorse for the examples in this section is the UIManager class. Let's add a JPanel to our breakfast-ordering application that displays the current look and feel. We need to add only the following three lines in the appropriate places:

```
public JLabel aLabel;
aLabel = new JLabel(UIManager.getLookAndFeel().toString());
aFrame.getContentPane().add(aLabel, BorderLayout.NORTH);
```

The String displayed in the JLabel gets the information on the current look and feel from the UIManager. (See Figure 24-8.)

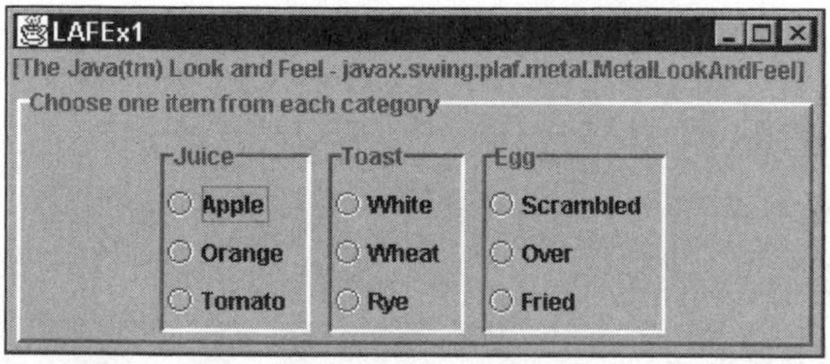

**Figure 24-8:** The Metal Look and Feel

If, instead, you want to set the look and feel to match your system, use the UI Manager to set it to the system look and feel that the UIManager also accesses. Different versions of the UIManager's setLookAndFeel() method take either a Look AndFeel object or a String specifying the class name of the look and feel. The first version throws an UnsupportedLookAndFeelException, while the second throws a ClassNotFoundException, an InstantiationException, and an IllegalAccess Exception. We can easily adapt our last example by adding the following try-catch block to main:

```
try
{
  UIManager.setLookAndFeel(
    UIManager.getSystemLookAndFeelClassName());
}
catch(Exception e){}//not really catching the exceptions
// create the base class...
```

On a laptop, you'll get the following screen, which indicates that the UIManager's getSystemLookAndFeelClassName() method was able to determine that you're running Windows and that the UIManager's setLookAndFeel() method was able to set this application's look and feel accordingly. (See Figure 24-9.)

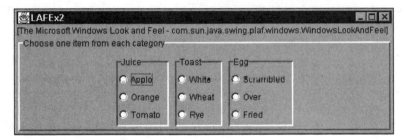

**Figure 24-9:** The Windows look and feel

Without much work, you can specify another look and feel. The following changes to the code in main specify the Motif look and feel:

```
try
{
  UIManager.setLookAndFeel(
    "com.sun.java.swing.plaf.motif.MotifLookAndFeel");
}
catch(Exception e){}
```

The result is a window that looks like Figure 24-10.

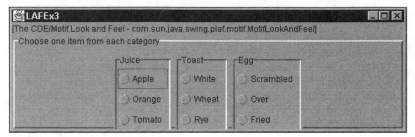

**Figure 24-10:** The Motif look and feel

What about the Mac look and feel? Well, it's not supported except on the Mac in the same way that the Windows look and feel is supported only on a Windows machine. This doesn't mean that you can't easily hack your code so that it appears that the Mac (or Windows) look and feel is `isSupportedLookAndFeel()`. Java support for the Macintosh look and feel under the new MacOS X is only supported on that platform. Java applications actually look like native applications. If you like this look and feel, you should go out and buy the latest Mac.

For any supported look and feel, savvy users can try to specify the look and feel themselves if they run your program from the command line. For example, the name of the Metal look-and-feel example is LAFEx1. You can use a call similar to the `try` block in the Motif example to specify the Motif look and feel. Without recompiling, a user can change the look and feel to Motif from the command line by typing:

```
java -Dswing.defaultlaf=com.sun.java.swing.plaf.motif.MotifLookAndFeel LAFEx1
```

Be careful that your only spaces are between `java` and `-D` and between `MotifLookAndFeel` and `LAFEx1`, or whatever your application is named. Also, don't think that you can be slick and call the Mac look and feel this way. The command

```
java -Dswing.defaultlaf=com.sun.java.swing.plaf.mac.MacLookAndFeel LAFEx1
```

results in a message that indicates there is a `"can't load Error"`.

If you change the look and feel after parts of it are up and running, you need to tell the currently displayed components to update themselves. You do this by calling the method `SwingUtilities.updateComponentTreeUI()` and passing it a handle to the component at the top of the tree (for example, the containing `JFrame`). You can also direct specific components to `updateUI()`.

## Customizing look and feel

Although you can create your own look and feel from scratch, you are more likely to want to customize an existing one. Swing makes it easy for you to customize the Metal look and feel by extending the class `DefaultMetalTheme` from the `javax.swing.plaf.metal` package. In it, you'll find methods that you can override that return `ColorUIResource`s such as `getPrimary[#]()` and `getSecondary[#]()`, where `[#]` is either 1, 2, or 3. You can also override methods that return `FontUI Resource`s such as `getControlTextFont()`, `getMenuTextFont()`, `getSubText Font()`, `getSystemTextFont()`, `getUserTextFont()`, and `getWindowTitle Font()`. The method `getName()` returns a `String`.

Let's change some of the color scheme in the Metal look and feel breakfast-ordering example. We'll create a class called `MyOwnTheme` that extends `DefaultMetalTheme`. Import the package `javax.swing.plaf.metal.*`. Here's the code for this class:

```
class MyOwnTheme extends DefaultMetalTheme
{
  public ColorUIResource getSecondary3()
  {
    return new ColorUIResource(Color.black);
  }
  public ColorUIResource getPrimary1()
  {
    return new ColorUIResource(Color.white);
  }
  public ColorUIResource getSecondary1()
  {
    return new ColorUIResource(Color.white);
  }
}
```

We just override three `ColorUIResource`s so that the color scheme will be different. Within the calling class `LAFEx4`, the body of `main` becomes the following:

```
public static void main( String[] args)
  {
    MetalLookAndFeel.setCurrentTheme(new MyOwnTheme());
    new LAFEx4();
  }
```

We just use the `static` method `setCurrentTheme()` of the `MetalLookAndFeel` class to apply these color changes before creating the UI. Figure 24-11 shows that the background color is now black and some of the text and the edges of the radio buttons are now white.

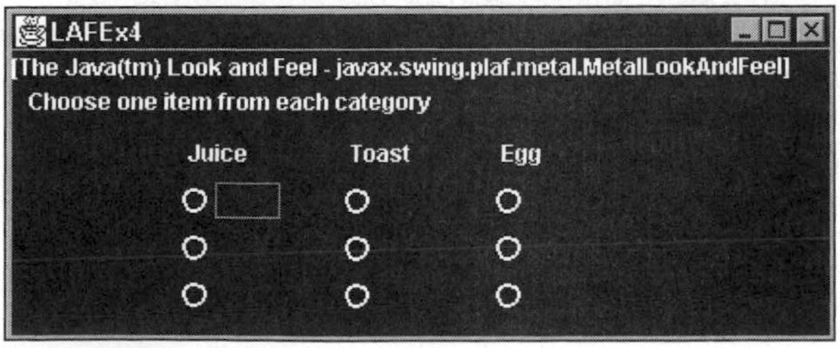

**Figure 24-11:** Changing themes

You can make further and more specific changes by overriding the methods from the DefaultMetalTheme's parent class MetalTheme in your version of the MyOwn Theme extension to DefaultMetalTheme. By changing the value that is returned by the appropriate get method, you have changed the effective value of the corresponding property.

Another way to change a specific property is with the UIManager's put method. Suppose you wanted to change the appearance of your original Metal view of the breakfast-order form by changing the background color of the radio buttons from gray to white. You can put the color white into the UIManager's lookup by changing the body of the main method as follows:

```
public static void main( String[] args)
{
  UIManager.put("RadioButton.background", Color.white);
  new LAFEx5();
}
```

As you can see, the call is fairly simple. A typo here can compile and run without a warning—no changes end up being made. The line that contains the single put() will change the background of all of the radio buttons. Here's what it looks like:

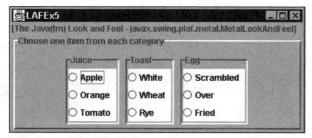

**Figure 24-12:** The result of a UIManager.put()

## Accessibility

Take a look at the package javax.accessibility. There are seven interfaces, three abstract classes, two concrete classes that consist only of constants, and two classes. These are the hooks that developers creating assistive technologies should write to. Unless you are writing such applications, your main concern is providing support for these technologies in your programs.

When you use Swing components, much of the work is done for you. All Swing components implement the javax.accessibility.Accessible interface. This interface contains the signature for a single abstract method getAccessibleContext() that returns an object of type AccessibleContext.

The abstract class `AccessibleContext` contains methods that begin with the words `getAccessible` and allow you to find the values of the accessible `Action`, `ChildrenCount`, `Component`, `Description`, `IndexInParent`, `Name`, `Parent`, `Role`, `Selection`, `StateSet`, `Text`, and `Value`.

Your job is to support this functionality. If you take the time to `setToolTipText()` for your components or at least to `setAccessibleDescription()`, assistive technologies can use this text to help users with particular needs. The `setAccessible Description()` method should be used whenever you want to provide a brief description for a component that doesn't have a name, a label, or a ToolTip associated with it. Name your components and choose names that can be read out loud and be easily understood.

You'll find yourself supporting assistive technologies without really thinking about it. In our breakfast example, the juice radio buttons were in their own panel as were the toast and egg radio buttons. Providing that panel with an accessible description gives a person in need of assistive technologies the same cues that you are providing to other users. You are evaluating the ease of use of your interface using a whole new set of standards. Keyboard shortcuts can be accessed using the keyboard or perhaps voice. We provided toolbars and menu bars for the same `Action` to make our application more flexible and easy to use. Providing more options also means that various assistive technologies can take advantage of them.

# Model-View-Controller

This chapter has focused on improving the various looks and feels of your applications. In fact, while we've been discussing Swing, we've ignored some of what's going on under the hood. Behind most of the Swing components is a corresponding model. Think of the component as the user's interface to the underlying model. Actually, this is not just a convenient metaphor; at the heart of the Swing architecture is Model-View-Controller.

Think of an old school video game such as Tetris or Pac-Man (or, if you'd prefer, keep a device such as an ATM in mind). At any given time, the game has a state that is kept by the model. The user plays the game using the Controller. The input could come from the keyboard, a joystick, or from a mouse. The input changes the state of the game, but the model doesn't really care which device the user is playing with. Similarly, the output is displayed on a screen, but changing the look of the game window doesn't affect the underlying model. You could create a Tetris game where the shapes float up instead of fall down without changing the underlying logic of the game. In short, the model, the view, and the controller have been decoupled.

The model contains the state — in a way, it is the idea underlying what you are dealing with. You might be able to think of lots of gadgets that interact with a list. But a list is an entity that underlies these various representations. A list knows whether it is empty or not. It knows how to access, add, and remove elements. None of this knowledge has anything to do with how a user will see the results of these changes or how they will make these changes.

A view displays some part of the model in some way — display in a broader sense than just a frame on a screen. The display might be an audio description of the model, text output to the console, or a visually attractive UI. You may register more than one view with a given model so that when the data held by the model changes, all of the views are changed at once. The view may also reflect the state of some of the controllers by showing the position of a slider or the state of a button.

The controller takes input from the user and communicates this to the model and the view. In turn, it may receive messages from these objects that change the messages it can now send. In the Tetris example, you could set up the controller so that one key moves the falling piece to the left, another moves the falling piece to the right, a third rotates the piece, and a fourth accelerates the drop. The action could be communicated to the model, and the model passes the new state to be displayed to the view. The action could be communicated to the view and the model at the same time.

Consider a different sort of controller for Tetris. Say you have four buttons on the screen as part of the game board. A player uses the mouse to click on one of the buttons to perform one of the four actions described in the previous paragraph. Your view and your controller are now linked together in a fundamental way. They still communicate with the model, but not to the same degree that they communicate with each other. By definition, your UI is always the sum of the view and the controller. In this case, the two pieces are interconnected. This description fits most of Swing's components.

The components in Swing, for the most part, consist of a view and a controller that together have an underlying model. As an example, let's start with a model of a list. The story begins with the `javax.swing` interface `ListModel`. The interface consists of four method signatures `getSize()`, `getElementAt()`, `addListDataListener()`, and `removeDataListener()`. The `AbstractListModel()` implements this interface and is extended by the concrete class `DefaultListModel()`, which adds in methods for adding and removing elements from the list. At this point, you have a workable model of a list and can tie it to a view and a controller.

Chapter 23 introduced the `JList`, a component that allows users to make selections from a list. A `JList` doesn't implement a `ListModel` or extend one. It uses one. The `JList` is the view and controller for a `ListModel`. In fact, you can use the `getModel()` method to return the corresponding `ListModel`. Similarly, the `JComboBox` has a `getModel()` method that returns a `ComboBoxModel`, which is the model that sits under the `JComboBox` view and controller. In general, look at the type returned by a given component's `getModel()` method to find the model that underlies the given component.

# Summary

This chapter finished off our look at Swing. In previous chapters, we have concentrated on the various components and the events they generate. In this chapter, we looked at customizing the appearance of our applications. We also considered what was going on behind the piece that we could see. In short, we learned the following:

✦ A nice way to organize the look of an application is by putting borders around various groups of components. You have lots of choices that included `Titled Borders`, `EtchedBorders`, and raised and lowered `BevelBorders`. Don't create these borders by calling their constructor; use the static methods in the `BorderFactory` class.

✦ You can still use the layout managers from the AWT, but Swing also provides you with more. Some are just helper classes, but the `BoxLayout` is like a souped up `FlowLayout` that can organize components vertically or horizontally, and the `OverlayLayout` allows you to stack components over each other in the z- direction.

✦ You can create an application that looks pretty much the same on all platforms or that looks pretty much like a native application using Swing's pluggable look and feel. The `UIManager` class keeps track of many of the properties you'll need to `get` and `set`. You can also override the methods in the `DefaultMetal Theme` to easily vary the look and feel of applications you're designing for a single cross-platform look.

✦ The Swing components support the `Accessible` interface. You just need to make sure that you have provided some basic support for assistive technologies that others are providing. Make sure your components have names, labels, ToolTips, or accessible descriptions. Add keyboard shortcuts or accelerators for common actions.

✦ Swing components often encapsulate both the view and the controller in the Model-View-Controller architecture. Underneath many of them is a model that handles the state of what's being managed and viewed. Think of the controller as getting input from the user to the model and the view. The view communicates the state of some part of the model back to the user and perhaps a visual interface for the state of the controls.

✦ ✦ ✦

# Parking it: Deploying Applets and Applications

# Deploying Applets and Applications

◆ ◆ ◆ ◆

**In This Chapter**

Learn how to
package and deploy
both applications
and applets

Understand the
Java security model
and change it

Learn what a Java
ARchive (JAR)
file is

Learn how to create,
manipulate, and
customize JAR
files within your
application code

Create executable
Java applications

◆ ◆ ◆ ◆

**B**y now, you should be able to write a nontrivial Java applet or application. In the previous chapter, we looked at debugging and testing your newly created application. Now that we're 100 percent confident that it works as advertised, we need to package the whole lot up and ship it off to the clients. Making sure that they install and run it in the manner that you intended is the focus of this chapter.

**Note**  Throughout this chapter, we'll refer to both applets and applications as interchangable entities. Any nontrivial applet can be treated as an application regardless of its initial environment. Some applets contain over 200,000 lines of code, which certainly puts them well into the application-sized arena!

Deploying an applet or application means making your applet available to everyone (rather than just on your own test area of the Web server) or installing the application on a client machine. Typically, there is a big difference between your development environment and how you run the application, compared to how the real users will use the same code. For example, your development code would exist in a series of directories on the local drive. On the other hand, the deployed version might consist of a single signed JAR file with all of the code, configuration files, and images in one file. You need to do quite a bit of work to go from your development environment to the deployed one.

Let's look at the typical development cycle of an application:

1. Your boss requests that you write an application.

2. You do some analysis and design.

**3.** You write the code.

**4.** You test the code.

**5.** You wrap up the code into a deployed version.

**6.** You do more testing.

**7.** You deploy the code (in other words, you send it to the client, publish it on the Web server, and so on).

You don't really play with the code in its final form until the last three steps. In between, the way you develop the code will mean that you may miss some of the aspects of the security model that could profoundly affect the code. In particular, the area most likely to affect you when least expected is the security model.

# Understanding Java Security

Unlike many other technologies touted to provide glorified Web pages, Java security was one of the prime considerations right from the start. Over the years, due to the hype associated with this feature, it has come under very close scrutiny from experts around the world. This has served to make it even more secure — as soon as loopholes were found and confirmed, fixes were made available.

## What is controlled?

When first writing a Java applet, you probably don't know exactly what is likely to run into security stops. It is only with experience that you are likely to know what is going to cause problems. Therefore, within this book, we've attempted to highlight most of the common areas that will cause you problems.

For a typical program, you count on networking and file I/O to cause you security problems. However, a number of other areas can cause you problems too. In Chapter 14, we've already discussed the security restrictions of threads. Here is the standard list of additional trouble areas you should keep an eye on:

✦ AWT internals: Allows you to poke around within the event queue and other subversive acts on the user interface.

✦ File access: Enables you to set permissions to read, write, delete, and create files on the user's computer, and general directory traversal and so forth, too – so, without security a hostile applet could even search your computer for interesting files.

✦ Network access: Allows applets to make connections to servers other than where they came from. Standard applets may create network connections to the server they came from and nowhere else. If you want to do more, such as create a server in the applet or connect to other machines, you need to set this property.

✦ Property access: Enables you to read and write standard system properties such as $user.home and $java.class.path.

✦ The runtime environment: Covers quite a large range of Java runtime associated elements such as starting an external application, setting new security managers, setting various factory classes, and exiting the Java Virtual Machine.

✦ The security environment: Covers the main gate to controlling security information such as changing the policy, adding and removing digital certificates, and using signature information.

✦ Classes: If all else fails, consider manipulating classes, which covers the rest of the startup and running process—for example, allowing serialization or manipulating the serialized stream.

## Permissions

Security control is realized through the `Permission` class from `java.security`. It actually takes two forms—a specification of which permissions are to be granted and the runtime representation of those through the class instances.

**Note**     How can you tell whether something has a permission associated with it? The simplest way is to go to the `java.security.Permission` class in the Javadoc. From there, you can follow the collection of derived classes. At the top of the Javadoc for each class, you will find a table that describes each value and what it allows you to do. Alternatively, on the index page of the Java documentation set, there is a link to the security section. Either look for a document titled "Permissions in the Java 2 SDK" or go to the file `$jre.docs.home/guide/security/permissions.html`.

Permissions are granted in a policy file. (We'll cover the syntax of the policy file in the following section.) There are many ways of specifying a policy file. For example, you can use the default system version, found in `$jre.home/lib/security`, and you can provide a custom version on the command line of the application. The policy file defines the list of permissions that you will grant to any given application. The policy file is very fine-grained, allowing complete control dictated by the source URL and/or the signer.

**Note**     You cannot assign a policy file for applets because this would allow you to override the user's security settings. If you wish to do things that are not normally permitted within an applet, you need to create a signed JAR file and request the appropriate permission within the code.

Permissions are only ever granted. Unless you explicitly grant a permission, it will be denied to all requestors. If you have the standard default policy file that the Java environment provides when you installed it, that means applets are very heavily constrained.

# Reading a policy file

Before you can use permissions in your code, you first need to look at how the permissions are specified in the policy file. This way, you can understand what other permissions have been granted and make the necessary modifications.

First you need an example policy file. You can find Java's default policy file in $java.home/lib/security/java.policy. The first few lines of the file look like this:

```
grant codeBase "file:${java.home}/lib/ext/*" {
  permission java.security.AllPermission;
};
```

Starting from the first line, here's what the code means:

✦ grant starts a new section of permissions that we are about to give.

✦ codeBase says that we are granting them based on the location where the classes can be found. This is a standard URL, so it could refer to a Web site or, as in this case, a particular directory on disk. Relative URLs are not permitted. The other option is the keyword signedBy and the name of the digital signature that is acceptable. You can use both of the keywords together, or one or the other.

✦ The opening brace ({) suggests that the list of permissions is about to be granted.

✦ Each following line starting with the word permission is a definition of a new item that we are about to grant. This is followed by the permission name that is being granted. This is the fully qualified name of the Java class that is to be used.

✦ After a white space gap, quoted is the name of the particular property within that permission that is being granted if needed. In this case, because we are granting the core Java APIs full rights to do everything, no further qualification is needed.

✦ Finally, if additional arguments are needed, then a comma and a quoted list of the arguments are provided. The line of that permission is terminated by a semicolon (;).

✦ To end the grant of the permissions for that code base or signer, you put in a close brace (}) and another semicolon (;).

As you can see from the default policy file, you can have multiple grant statements in one file. This allows you to independently control many different lots of code.

To save you the hassle of having to hand-modify this file all the time, Sun provides the following three tools for manipulating policy files and security information:

✦ keytool: A tool for managing digital signatures. Allows you to add and remove digital signature information on your machine.

✦ `jarsigner`: A tool for turning a regular JAR file (covered shortly) into a digitally signed file. Makes sure that the right certificates and policy information are set up inside your archives.

✦ `policytool`: A tool to manage the standard policy file and create new, customized policy files for a local machine. Allows you to add and remove permissions and who grants are made to.

## Specifying a custom policy

If you have an application with specific needs, you can provide custom policy information on the command line. For example, say you download a Java application from the Internet and you have no idea about the provider's credentials. To stop it from running amok on your machine, you might want to give it a set of very restricted permissions.

You provide a custom policy by specifying a value for the `java.security.policy` property on the command line, such as:

```
java -Djava.security.policy=\
    file:///users/justin/policys/unknown_application.policy
```

Note that because this is a security-related issue, you cannot set the name of this policy within the application code like you can with many other properties. Also, because we are dealing specifically with applications, applets cannot have any policy file defined for them by the application's author. This is provided only by the user and configured using tools like the Java Plugin's manager.

## Requesting permissions

The problem with deploying applets on a wide distribution medium like the Internet is that you just don't know what sort of settings your users will have. Some might allow certain freedom, while others have them locked down tight. What you need to do is write your code so that it can deal with these problems and not have it die unexpectedly.

There are several ways of doing this. The first and most simplistic way is to wrap any code that may cause problems in a `try-catch` block and catch `Security Exception`. If your code does violate a security point, this is what will be thrown and it allows you to do something else.

A more correct option is to use the capabilities of the `java.security` package. Inside this package, you will find a lot of classes for requesting permissions as well as performing privileged acts. In general, these all revolve around the `Access Controller` class.

A typical approach to applets is to check which permissions have been granted right at the startup of your application. The idea is to check and then load a different version of the code depending on what is available. If you want to just check if a permission has been granted, you have to create an instance of the particular permission and then call the checkPermission() method. If this exits quietly, everything is okay. The following code checks to see if you can write a temporary file:

```
try {
  FilePermission perm =
    new FilePermission("/temp/testFile", "write");
  AccessController.checkPermission(perm);
}
catch(AccessControllerException ace) {
  // do something here
}
```

By placing a whole heap of these into a single block, you can determine up front when the applet loads what your application is capable of. This is a lot cleaner than catching security exceptions inline and then having a lot of if/else statements dealing with the problems.

However, if you need to have inlined security checks, you can use the do Privileged() method instead. Providing an instance of PrivilegedAction as the parameter, this will automatically check and catch any potential problem code. Typically, the code will use an anonymous inner class to do this, but ordinary classes also work, as shown in this example (ignoring IOExceptions):

```
writeFile(String filename) {
  AccessController.doPrivileged(
    new PrivilegedAction() {
      public Object run() {
        FileOutputStream fos = new FileOutputStream(filename);

        // write a heap of stuff like...
        fos.write(0x01b);

        fos.close();
        return null;
      }
    }
  );
}
```

Now, when you attempt to write to the file, the previous code will check and catch any security problems that you'll run into. Notice that the run() method returns an Object instance. We had to return null in this case because there was nothing worthwhile. If you want to use that value, the value is passed back through the return value of `doPrivileged()`. We didn't use it here, but the Java documentation contains plenty of examples of how to use it.

# Introducing the Java Plugin

Now that you are familiar with how the security model works, we actually need to give you something so that you can play with it. After the browser wars finally died down, we ended up with two major browsers, both of which were barely capable of displaying Java 1.1 code, let alone Java 2 code. This led to the development of the Java Plugin by Sun to encourage the use of Java 2 on the Internet. The idea of this plugin is to provide a flexible architecture that allows your browser to run any Java code and keep it up to date with the latest standards.

Unfortunately, what this all means is that to use Java 2, your prospective clients must have the Java Plugin installed. Over the Internet, this severely limits your potential audience, but on a closed, controlled intranet, this is much less of a problem.

## Installing the Java Plugin

As a maintainer of the Java 3D FAQ, you would be surprised at just how many questions we get regarding how to install the Java Plugin. No matter how simple we make the instructions, people still don't seem to be able to get it right. This wasn't helped by some bugs in the early Java 2 implementations.

You can find the Java Plugin in one of two places — included with the standard JDK development environment or as a separate download from `http://java.sun.com/products/plugin/`.

As part of the JDK install, the Java Plugin will be automatically configured for whatever browser you use. Once you have installed the Java Plugin, you need to configure it for your particular settings. Figures 25-1 to 25-3 illustrate the various options available for your normal use.

Figure 25-1 illustrates the basic options available. These options allow you to:

✦ Disable the plugin.

✦ Use a console for outputting debug information (this is where `System.out` and `System.err` get written to).

✦ Cache any JAR files used in memory for better performance.

✦ Include specific command-line parameters as desired. Why would you want command-line parameters in an applet? Unlike standard VMs included with browsers, this allows you to specify all the normal Java runtime options like memory size, garbage collection rules, and extra classpath information.

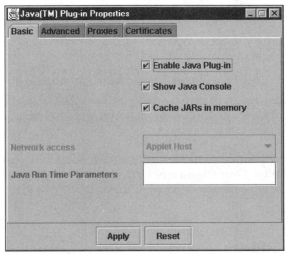

**Figure 25-1:** Configuration of basic options

Figure 25-2 shows the advanced options for controlling which JVM you want to use and how you want to use it.

At the top is a selection of available JVMs. Note that you can use both the standard JDK or the runtime environment for Java 2. If you wanted to select between different versions of the JDK, these would be available here too.

**Note** In Java 2 v1.2, the Java Runtime Environment (JRE) is separate from the standard application environment (JDK). With the arrival of Java 2 v1.3, the JRE is no longer a separate option. The application and runtime environment are the same.

To use a different VM than the standard JDK options (for example, IBM's Jikes compiler and runtime), select the Other option. Then, in the text box below, type in the path to the alternative VM.

The debug settings are quite interesting. Java 2 delivers the start of a VM-independent mechanism for allowing debuggers to hook into the runtime environment called JVMPI. If you enable debugging, this opens the port for listening to a debugger that can work with your runtime environment regardless of whether the code is running within a browser or an applet.

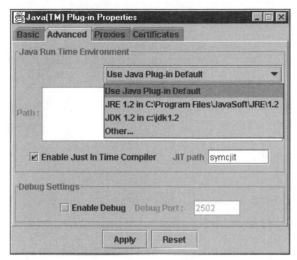

**Figure 25-2:** Advanced options for controlling the JVM in use

Figure 25-3 shows the proxy settings. You are probably already quite familiar with proxy settings that normal Web browsers use. This is no different. The check box at the top of the panel nominates whether to use the browser settings or a completely different set.

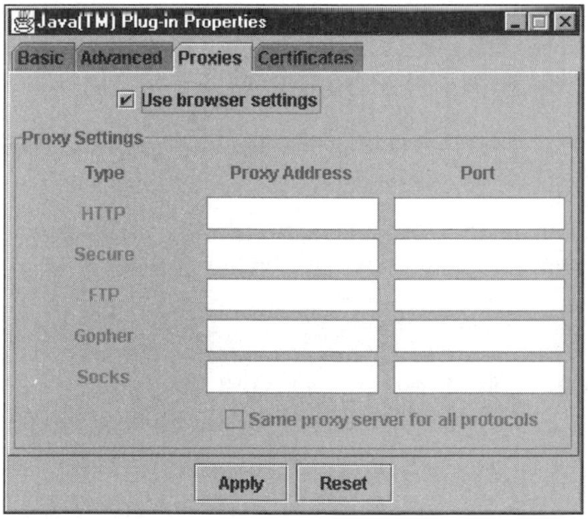

**Figure 25-3:** Proxy configuration options for dealing with firewalls

## Using the Java plugin

You've got your applet code compiled, the enclosing HTML is written, and the Java Plugin is installed. However, when you try to run the applet, you'll notice a series of `ClassNotFoundException`s. Why? Well, it's a pretty safe bet that your HTML file looks something like this:

```
<HTML>
<HEAD>
  ....

<BODY>

  ...

<APPLET CODE="MyApplet.class" ARCHIVE="myarchive.jar">
<PARAM NAME="answer" VALUE="42">
</APPLET>

...
</HTML>
```

When you fire up your applet, the browser is clued in to look for the <APPLET> tag in the code. When it sees this tag, it fires up the internal VM and runs the code there. Because the internal VM is no doubt only Java 1.1 compliant, many of the classes that you've used, such as the Swing classes, will not be found. What you need to do is trick the Web browser into using the Java Plugin.

**Tip**    To trick the browser, you need to change the HTML code so that the Web browser believes it is running a normal plugin like Shockwave instead of the Java interpreter. You can do this by using an <OBJECT> tag instead.

**Note**    In the HTML 4.0 spec, the <APPLET> tag is not defined. The only way to embed Java code is to use the <OBJECT> tag.

If you have written a lot of code using the applet tags, there is the HTML converter for you. This automatically converts the old code into the new version that will run correctly.

You can download the converter from `http://java.sun.com/products/plugin/1.3/converter.html`. This will generate your correct HTML. The previous code should now look like this if you are using Netscape Communicator/Navigator:

```
<HTML>
<HEAD>
  ....

<BODY>
```

```
...

<EMBED type="application/x-java-applet CODE="MyApplet.class"
ARCHIVE="myarchive.jar">
<PARAM NAME="answer" VALUE="42">
</EMBED>


...
</HTML>
```

Unfortunately, for most users, Internet Explorer and Netscape Communicator do things very differently. Showing the code here to get both working would look really ugly, so instead, we'll send you off to the Converter page for the HTML specification at:

`http://java.sun.com/products/plugin/1.3/docs/tags.html`

# Working with Java Archives

When you come to deliver your Java applet to a client, having to deal with all of those class files can become quite tricky. All sorts of things can go wrong; you might forget to include a file, or worse, the user might accidentally delete one. Java Archive (JAR) files were created to solve this problem.

You've probably come across JAR files before. Some applets deliver their content this way. The core classes that come with the JDK are also packaged like this. Finally, almost any third-party library that you've used is probably delivered as a JAR file, too. They are very common and handy to use.

## What is a Java archive?

In short, a JAR file is just a form of a standard zip file with a particular internal structure. That is, by changing the .jar extension to .zip, you could use one of the popular extraction tools like PKZIP or WinZip to look at the contents.

A JAR file may contain anything. Typically, it contains your class files and maybe images if you use them. If you wanted, you could also have another JAR file to contain the images or other data separately. Inside the JAR file, it looks just like your standard directory setup. Everything has a location and directory. If you have a class that belongs in a package, you will find a directory inside the JAR file corresponding to that package, just as you would on your hard disk.

Apart from the normal classes and other files, a JAR file also contains a special directory called META-INF. In this directory, you'll find all of the administrative information about the contents of your JAR file. As you will see later in the chapter, this is very handy if you want to customize the behavior of your standard JAR file.

Because JAR files tend to be the method of shipping bulk Java code around the Internet, a security mechanism is also incorporated. Using a combination of a digital signature and the information in the META-INF directory, you can sign your JAR file and let others be sure of its authenticity. Signatures can then be used to check whether the file has been tampered with or even to explicitly set security privileges only for that archive.

Because they can be signed, JAR files make a great mechanism for distributing almost any sort of information. As you will see later, you can sign individual items in the file and even use different signatures. It doesn't really matter what the archive contains, it provides a nice, relatively secure way of distributing information and content.

# Using JAR Files

Before you learn how to create your own JAR file, first you need to know how to use someone else's archive file in your application or applet.

The use of JAR files does not require anything special inside the code you write. You simply need to make sure that the Java environment is aware of the JAR file and that it needs to search it when loading classes and other information.

## In an application

In the application environment, you always tell the Java VM where to find things using the CLASSPATH environment variable. Naturally, using a JAR file is just an extension of that practice. Say you have the CLASSPATH set up as follows:

```
c:\java\classes;c:\mydir\java
```

and now you want to add the archive MyLibrary.jar that contains your new code library and you've copied it to the directory c:\java\archvies. Adding a JAR file is just a simple matter of pointing the class path at that new JAR file like this:

```
c:\java\classes;c:\mydir\java;c:\java\archives\MyLibrary.jar
```

Now your application will find any of the classes contained in the archive.

How does this work? Remember that the JAR file contains directories, just like your hard disk. The VM takes those directories like real packages and searches them for the desired class. For example, if you have a class mypackage.MyClass, then the VM will search inside the JAR file for the directory mypackage and try to locate the class MyClass. It does all this without you knowing it.

The one minor drawback of all of this is that now you need to explicitly name all of the JAR files that you use in the CLASSPATH. So if the directory c:\java\archives contains two JAR files lib1.jar and lib2.jar, then you need to make the CLASSPATH point to both of them like this:

```
c:\java\classes;c:\mydir\java;c:\java\archives\lib1.jar;c:\java\
archives\lib2.jar
```

If you don't, the VM will not find your classes. You can't just point the CLASSPATH at c:\java\archives and expect the VM to find the right archive files.

**Note**      JAR files are subject to the same ordering as the directories in your CLASSPATH. If a directory and a JAR file contain the same class and the directory appears in the CLASSPATH before the archive, it will use the definition in the directory. It is good practice to always put the JAR files before the directories.

## In an applet

Using JAR files in an applet follows similar rules to using them in an application. Applets define their environment using information embedded in the HTML tags that you saw back in Chapter 4, "HelloWorld Application and Applet."

To include JAR files, you need to name them in the <APPLET> tag with the archives attribute. This attribute contains the list of archive names to use. The VM that runs the applet then attempts to find those archives either on the local machine or on the server that gave you the applet in the first place. For example:

```
<APPLET CODE=MyApplet.class archive="jars/mylib.jar">
  <PARAM name=foo value="bar">
</APPLET>
```

would launch the applet called MyApplet and look for the classes in the JAR file called mylib.jar. The "archive" directory is taken as relative to the code base of the applet, which, in this case, is the same as the directory that the HTML page is in.

If you want to name more than one JAR file, then you may create a list of them and separate each entry with a comma. If the classes from the previous example were located in two different archives, for example, applet.jar and network.jar, the HTML would now look like this:

```
<APPLET CODE=MyApplet.class archive="applet.jar, network.jar">
  <PARAM name=foo value="bar">
</APPLET>
```

On the client side, the Web browser also uses the `CLASSPATH` environment variable to hold information about local archives, in the same way an application uses them. If you have a bunch of local standard libraries that you like to use when browsing the Web, then you may use the `CLASSPATH` to set this as well as whatever the applet provides.

# Managing JAR Files

To make your life easier, the JDK comes with a standard tool for creating and managing JAR files. This tool is called "jar." (Note the lowercase name and that it is not the same as a JAR file.)

For UNIX users, the arguments for jar are almost identical to those of the tar command.

## Creating a new JAR file

To create a new JAR file, change to the top directory that contains your code. For example, if you have some code in c:\mycode\java that also contains some packaged code in the subdirectory mypackage, you would do the following:

```
c:\>cd mycode\java
c:\mycode\java>jar cf mylib.jar *
```

This will then take *all* of the files in this directory and all subdirectories and add them to the JAR file by the name of mylib.jar.

Let's take a closer look at the previous command line. We start with the JAR tool "jar." Next we tell it to create a new archive file with the c argument. We now need to tell it what the name of the file is so we give it the argument 'f' and then the name of the file — including the extension .jar. Finally, the last argument(s) are the names of the files and/or directories to include in the JAR file. The jar tool automatically recurses subdirectories of the directories named on the command line, whether wild-carded or not.

If you don't specify the f argument and the file name, jar will attempt to write the output file to the standard output — in other words, your screen. This is great on a UNIX system where you might want to pipe the output to some other application, but not terribly helpful on a Windows box.

Now you have your basic JAR file. You can place this file in your `CLASSPATH`, in an applet, or whatever else you may need it for.

# Extracting information

Sometimes you might want to find out the contents of someone else's JAR file or even grab some of the contents for a separate use. You can use JAR for this too.

Extracting, and any other form of JAR manipulation, is just a matter of changing the first argument group. Table 25-1 takes you through the list of different arguments and a summary of what they provide.

| Table 25-1 |
| --- |
| **The Arguments of the Jar Application** |

| Argument | Description |
| --- | --- |
| c | Creates a new archive. This overwrites the file if the file already exists. |
| t | Lists the contents only of the named archive. It does not add or remove files from the archive. |
| x | Extracts files from the named archive. If you name a file(s), then these are extracted only; otherwise, the entire contents of the archive are placed in the current directory. |
| u | Updates the contents of the archive with the given files. These files may overwrite the existing files or be added to the archive. |
| v | Makes the tool user verbose output. Lists everything that is currently going into or out of the archive. This is printed to standard output. This is very similar to the 't' argument, so it is pointless using the two together. |
| 0 | Stores all files being added without compression in the archive. |
| m | Adds the manifest file to the archive. The name of the manifest file always appears just after the name of the archive, if given. |

You may be wondering why there is an argument that allows storage only for jar. This is because there are some known problems with some items inside JAR files that can't handle compression. In particular, there is a known bug that will not allow you to read an image from a JAR file with the current versions of Java.

To extract the contents of a jar file, you could use the following command:

```
jar xvf mylib.jar
```

This would result in all of the files in mylib.jar being extracted into the current directory and the output would list everything as it happens.

# Introducing java.util.jar

When writing large applications, it is handy to be able to directly manipulate the contents of a JAR file. One such handy tool would be to create a GUI version of the jar tool. Java provides these capabilities for everyone through the classes in the `java.util.jar` package. Most of what you would use this package for is more advanced than this book, so we'll just stick to a light description of each of the classes and what they do. (See Table 25-2.)

| Table 25-2 Classes provided by the java.util.jar package | |
|---|---|
| **Class** | **Description** |
| JarFile | This is the representation of a complete JAR file. It contains all of the information that you need to know about such as accessing individual items and the information relating to each item. It also allows access to the top-level manifest information. |
| JarEntry | This class represents everything there is to know about a particular item in the archive. It allows you access to any digital certificates and extra attribute information. Most of the interesting functionality is in the `ZipEntry` class that this extends. You may get individual comment information on files, set the type of compression, check for errors in the file, and perform a whole host of other operations. |
| Manifest | This is the representation of the manifest that controls the archive. There is only one instance of the Manifest per JAR file. With this class, you can extract attribute information about the archive as a whole and for individual entries in the file. Using the class, you can programmatically construct a complete new manifest on the fly. |
| Attributes | A manifest attribute is a description of a particular capability that an entry in the JAR file might have. Most of these attributes will be covered shortly when we look at how to control the JAR behavior. In summary, they describe information like the actual signature, which other JAR files should be referenced, and which class could be used to start an application running. |
| JarInputStream/ JarOutputStream | One of the most important aspects of dealing with a JAR file programmatically is the ability to read it in and write it back out again from within the application. The input stream allows you to take any arbitrary input stream and then read entries from that stream. The output stream allows the reverse, where you can send a JAR file, complete with manifest, to any stream that you want. |

# Controlling JAR Behaviors

One of the more common needs when dealing with JAR files is to control their behavior somehow. These modifications are always done through the manifest file mentioned a few times already.

The manifest file is just a standard ASCII text file that contains entries, one per line. By convention, the manifest file name ends with the .mf extension, but it is not required. To add the manifest to the file, you don't need to do anything special, other than making sure you use the m argument and corresponding file in the jar command line.

Digital signatures may also be added to the archive. By convention, these end with .sf as an extension. They contain the signature in one of the formats supported by Java (typically MD5 and PGP).

 **Note**   All line lengths in a manifest file must be less than 72 characters. If your line goes past this, you will need to end the line with a slash (\) character and continue again on the next line.

## Versioning

When you start distributing libraries wrapped as JAR files, keeping track of the version of the current installed library and minimum requirements can become quite a nightmare on large deployments. While the manifest file does not help to make this any easier, it does allow for version control of the signature information by including two entries: one for the required version and one for the current version. At a minimum, all manifest files must contain the current version:

```
Manifest-version: 1.0
Required-version: 1.0
```

If the version of the manifest file is greater than the required version, any of the new capabilities introduced by the new version may be used if the application/VM supports it. For example, some of the header information might have changed, or new items might be added for the particular application.

## Digital signing

If you want to digitally sign a file (or set of files) in the archive, then you will need to provide a couple of items. First, there is the digital certificate information itself. As indicated earlier, this file ends in .sf and is an ASCII text file. Each file defines one particular signer and lists all of the classes that are signed by that person/company.

A drawback of this is that you can't name a group of files: you need to itemize every single class in the package.

A signature file looks like this:

```
Signature-version: 1.0
Name: mypackage/MyClass.class
Digest-Algorithms: MD5
MD5-Digest: (base64 representation of MD5 digest)
```

**Note**    The length of the signature file name should not exceed eight characters, not including the extension, and consist only of alphanumeric characters or a dash (-) character.

Next, you need to provide the actual signature itself. This is held in a binary file that has the same file name as the signature definition file, but with a different extension indicating the type of signature. For example, you would need the following files to completely sign the class `mypackage.MyClass` with a PGP key.

```
mymanifest.mf
jtc-sig.sf
jtc-sig.pgp
```

Finally, to provide the glue for everything, you need to add entries to the manifest file to name who the signers are. In the manifest file, you must again mention every class that is signed. The difference now is that the manifest file contains all entries from all signature files, rather than just the entries for a particular signer.

## Self executable archive files

In the Microsoft Windows environment, it is fairly typical to place items on the desktop and click on them to start them. An extension added to the manifest specification allows you to place a JAR file on the desktop and nominate the class that is to be executed when it is activated by a click.

Say we have a class called `MyApplication.class` that contains a `main()` method as well as a number of other classes inside the archive. By adding the following entry to your manifest file, it will allow the archive to be "executed":

```
Main-Class: MyApplication
```

Note a couple of points here: the name used is the class name, fully qualified like you would use it on a Java command-line call. The class can belong to any package as long as it contains a `main()` method.

## Nominating other archives

When executing a JAR file from the command line or with a self-executing archive as in the previous section, one thing that you need to specify is the list of other JAR archives that you need in order to run. An archive on the desktop doesn't have the luxury of having a complete environment set up that you might have if you were launching it from a shell script or a command line. To overcome this, you can nominate the archives that you want loaded as well using the `Class-Path:` manifest entry.

The `Class-Path` entry is just like your `CLASSPATH` environment variable. You can name relative URLs or absolute URLs to the archives that you want loaded. The only difference is that each archive is separated by spaces rather than semicolons. For example:

```
Class-Path: mylib1.jar mylib2.jar
```

**Caution**

If you are referring to archives kept on the local drive, you should always use relative references. If the user moves your archive to a location other than the one you installed it in, it will break the application. Relative information is always the safest option.

When nominating relative locations, these are always relative to wherever the current archive was loaded from. For example, if the archive came from a Web server, the VM would attempt to fetch the other named archives from there, too. However, if you saved the archive to the local drive, the next time you try to run it, the VM will look in that directory locally instead of the Web server.

# Summary

This chapter introduced you to the extremely useful JAR file. While we have barely skimmed the surface with the amount of customization that you can perform, we have looked through all of the basic tools needed to get you up and running with them. We have covered the following areas:

✦ Adding JAR files to your environment so they may be used in applets or applications.

✦ Creating and managing JAR files using command-line tools.

✦ Using the `java.util.jar` package and seeing what it allows you to do within an application.

✦ Customizing the behavior of JAR files.

✦ ✦ ✦

# Installing and Configuring the Java Software Development Kit (SDK)

**T**o develop applets and applications in Java, you must first install Sun's Java Software Development Kit (SDK) on your computer. The SDK includes the standard Java runtime environment plus all the tools you need to begin creating your very own Java programs, including a Java compiler, interpreter, and testing tools. This chapter explains how to get, install, and configure the most recent release of the SDK for Solaris, Windows 95, 98, 2000 and NT 4.0 computer systems. (At the time of this writing a beta Linux version was also available, although Macintosh users should visit Apple's Java development site at http:// developer.apple.com/java/ since Sun doesn't support Mac systems) In addition, this appendix briefly looks at each of the tools in the SDK.

**Note**    Before downloading and installing the SDK as described in this appendix, you should first ensure that you have at least 100MB of free space available on your desktop computer and a minimum of 32MB of RAM.

# SDK versus JDK

Java 2 comes in two distinct flavors: the Java Runtime Environment (JRE) and the Java Software Development Kit (SDK, formerly known as the Java Development Kit, or JDK). The JRE is intended for the average end user, and it is simply the core run-time engine (Virtual Machine) and Java Plug-in that together allow your computer to execute Java applications and applets. The SDK, on the other hand, is for programmers. The SDK is a full-blown software development environment that includes the entire JRE as well as several software development tools and sample Java programs.

The only tool lacking in the SDK is a text editor, which you'll need to type in your Java source code. Every major computer operating system comes with a text editor, however, so there's no need to fret. Windows users, for example, can use the Notepad program that comes with that operating system for free, while Macintosh users can fire up their trusty SimpleText editor when it comes time to write code. Alternately, you can use a standard word processor (such as Microsoft Word) as long as you take care to save your Java source code files in pure ASCII text format as explained in the following appendix.

**Note**    The SDK is a freely available development environment, making it an ideal starter package for those new to Java. As you become more experienced with Java, however, you'll likely outgrow the bare-boned tools provided with the SDK. Fortunately, several fully integrated development environments (IDEs) are commercially available that you can turn to when the SDK and text editor approach become too limiting for your needs. Products such as Symantec's Visual Café (http://www.symantec.com/), for example, are better suited for professional software development projects, while Sun's SDK and a standard text editor are just fine when you're just starting out with Java.

You can download the SDK from Sun's Java Web site—the official Java support site—at http://java.sun.com/. Clicking on the "Products and APIs" link on the left hand side of the page will take you to the most current SDK version for the Solaris, Linux, and Windows machines, as well as older versions of the JDK for these systems and Apple Macintosh computers. (At the time this book was written, only JDK 1.1.8 was available for the Mac!) Sun's Java division (a Sun-owned company focused entirely on Java development) regularly releases new versions of Java implementations and development tools at this site. Links to third-party ports, such as those for Macintosh and Linux, are also available through Sun's Java support site.

**Note**    Macintosh users should visit Apple's Java development site at http://developer. apple.com/java/ to get their hands on a Mac-savvy development environment.

You'll notice that we use the term *JDK* when referring to older versions of the SDK. This isn't an oversight; it's a result of the new naming scheme introduced by Sun when it shipped the Java 2 platform in late 1998. Prior to Java 2, Sun's development environments went by the name Java Development Kit (JDK), meaning the Java

1.0.x and 1.1.x family of development tools were called Java JDKs (that is, JDK 1.0, JDK 1.1). However, when the Java 2 platform was announced, the name *Software Development Kit (SDK)* was given to the latest and greatest batch of development tools, causing a fair amount of confusion for those programmers who had become accustomed to the term JDK.

For the most part, the terms *JDK* and *SDK* are interchangeable; both refer to a software package that combines Sun's Java runtime environment along with a suite of Java development tools. To be entirely accurate, however, the term *JDK* describes only versions 1.0.x and 1.1.x development environments, while *SDK* refers to version 1.2.x and later. In this book, we use the most current version of Sun's development environment, SDK 1.3, to compile and test our Java programs (whenever we refer to the SDK we're talking about version 1.3 unless otherwise stated).

**Tip**    One of the most important Web sites Java developers should get into the habit of visiting is the Java Developer Connection (JDC), located at `http://java.sun.com/jdc/`. JDC is a free service offering online training, bug databases, product discounts, feature articles, tools, and more. JDC also features online discussion forums with industry luminaries and Sun's Java team members.

# Java 2 Standard Edition 1.3 Packages

In this book we use Java 2 Standard Edition (J2SE) version 1.3, the latest and greatest version of Java available at the time this publication went to print. J2S3 1.3 is busting at the seams with pre-made classes ready for you to use in your own Java programs. Table A-1 lists these classes' organized packages (descriptions provided by Sun's API specification at `http://java.sun.com/j2se/1.3/docs/api/`).

| Table A-1 | |
|---|---|
| **Premade Classes** | |
| **Packages** | **Description** |
| `java.applet` | Provides the classes necessary to create an applet and the classes an applet uses to communicate with its applet context. |
| `java.awt` | Contains all of the classes for creating user interfaces and for painting graphics and images. |
| `java.awt.color` | Provides classes for color spaces. |
| `java.awt.datatransfer` | Provides interfaces and classes for transferring data between and within applications. |

*Continued*

## Table A-1 *(continued)*

| Classes | Description |
| --- | --- |
| java.awt.dnd | Drag and Drop is a direct manipulation gesture found in many Graphical User Interface systems that provides a mechanism to transfer information between two entities logically associated with presentation elements in the GUI. |
| java.awt.event | Provides interfaces and classes for dealing with different types of events fired by AWT components. |
| java.awt.font | Provides classes and interface relating to fonts. |
| java.awt.geom | Provides the Java 2D classes for defining and performing operations on objects related to two-dimensional geometry. |
| java.awt.im | Provides classes and interfaces for the input method framework. |
| java.awt.im.spi | Provides interfaces that enable the development of input methods that can be used with any Java runtime environment. |
| java.awt.image | Provides classes for creating and modifying images. |
| java.awt.image.renderable | Provides classes and interfaces for producing rendering-independent images. |
| java.awt.print | Provides classes and interfaces for a general printing API. |
| java.beans | Contains classes related to Java Beans development. |
| java.beans.beancontext | Provides classes and interfaces relating to bean context. |
| java.io | Provides for system input and output through data streams, serialization, and the file system. |
| java.lang | Provides classes that are fundamental to the design of the Java programming language. |
| java.lang.ref | Provides reference-object classes, which support a limited degree of interaction with the garbage collector. |
| java.lang.reflect | Provides classes and interfaces for obtaining reflective information about classes and objects. |

| Classes | Description |
| --- | --- |
| java.math | Provides classes for performing arbitrary-precision integer arithmetic (BigInteger) and arbitrary-precision decimal arithmetic (BigDecimal). |
| java.net | Provides the classes for implementing networking applications. |
| java.rmi | Provides the RMI package. |
| java.rmi.activation | Provides support for RMI Object Activation. |
| java.rmi.dgc | Provides classes and interface for RMI distributed garbage-collection (DGC). |
| java.rmi.registry | Provides a class and two interfaces for the RMI registry. |
| java.rmi.server | Provides classes and interfaces for supporting the server side of RMI. |
| java.security | Provides the classes and interfaces for the security framework. |
| java.security.acl | The classes and interfaces in this package have been superseded by classes in the java.security package. |
| java.security.cert | Provides classes and interfaces for parsing and managing certificates. |
| java.security.interfaces | Provides interfaces for generating RSA (Rivest, Shamir, and Adleman AsymmetricCipher algorithm) keys as defined in the RSA Laboratory Technical Note PKCS#1, and DSA (Digital Signature Algorithm) keys as defined in NIST's FIPS-186. |
| java.security.spec | Provides classes and interfaces for key specifications and algorithm parameter specifications. |
| java.sql | Provides the API for accessing and processing data in a data source using the JavaTM programming language. |
| java.text | Provides classes and interfaces for handling text, dates, numbers, and messages in a manner independent of natural languages. |
| java.util | Contains the collections framework, legacy collection classes, event model, date and time facilities, internationalization, and miscellaneous utility classes (a string tokenizer, a random-number generator, and a bit array). |

*Continued*

| | Table A-1 *(continued)* |
|---|---|
| **Classes** | **Description** |
| `java.util.jar` | Provides classes for reading and writing the JAR (Java ARchive) file format, which is based on the standard ZIP file format with an optional manifest file. |
| `java.util.zip` | Provides classes for reading and writing the standard ZIP and GZIP file formats. |
| `javax.accessibility` | Defines a contract between user-interface components and an assistive technology that provides access to those components. |
| `javax.naming` | Provides the classes and interfaces for accessing naming services. |
| `javax.naming.directory` | Extends the javax.naming package to provide functionality for accessing directory services. |
| `javax.naming.event` | Provides support for event notification when accessing naming and directory services. |
| `javax.naming.ldap` | Provides support for LDAPv3 extended operations and controls. |
| `javax.naming.spi` | Provides the means for dynamically plugging in support for accessing naming and directory services through the javax.naming and related packages. |
| `javax.rmi` | Contains user APIs for RMI-IIOP. |
| `javax.rmi.CORBA` | Contains portability APIs for RMI-IIOP. |
| `javax.sound.midi` | Provides interfaces and classes for I/O, sequencing, and synthesis of MIDI (Musical Instrument Digital Interface) data. |
| `javax.sound.midi.spi` | Supplies interfaces for service providers to implement when offering new MIDI devices, MIDI file readers and writers, or sound bank readers. |
| `javax.sound.sampled` | Provides interfaces and classes for capture, processing, and playback of sampled audio data. |
| `javax.sound.sampled.spi` | Supplies abstract classes for service providers to subclass when offering new audio devices, sound file readers and writers, or audio format converters. |
| `javax.swing` | Provides a set of "lightweight" (all-Java language) components that, to the maximum degree possible, work the same on all platforms. |

| Classes | Description |
|---|---|
| javax.swing.border | Provides classes and interface for drawing specialized borders around a Swing component. |
| javax.swing.colorchooser | Contains classes and interfaces used by the JColorChooser component. |
| javax.swing.event | Provides for events fired by Swing components. |
| javax.swing.filechooser | Contains classes and interfaces used by the JFileChooser component. |
| javax.swing.plaf | Provides one interface and many abstract classes that Swing uses to provide its pluggable look-and-feel capabilities. |
| javax.swing.plaf.basic | Provides user interface objects built according to the Basic look-and-feel. |
| javax.swing.plaf.metal | Provides user interface objects built according to the ``metal'' look-and-feel. |
| javax.swing.plaf.multi | The multiplexing look and feel allows users to combine auxiliary look and feels with the default look and feel. |
| javax.swing.table | Provides classes and interfaces for dealing with javax.swing.JTable. |
| javax.swing.text | Provides classes and interfaces that deal with editable and noneditable text components. |
| javax.swing.text.html | Provides the class HTMLEditorKit and supporting classes for creating HTML text editors. |
| javax.swing.text.html.parser | Provides the default HTML parser, along with support classes. |
| javax.swing.text.rtf | Provides a class (RTFEditorKit) for creating Rich-Text-Format text editors. |
| javax.swing.tree | Provides classes and interfaces for dealing with javax.swing.JTree. |
| javax.swing.undo | Provides support for undo/redo capabilities in an application such as a text editor. |
| javax.transaction | Contains three exceptions thrown by the ORB machinery during unmarshalling. |

*Continued*

## Table A-1  *(continued)*

| Classes | Description |
| --- | --- |
| org.omg.CORBA | Provides the mapping of the OMG CORBA APIs to the JavaTM programming language, including the class ORB, which is implemented so that a programmer can use it as a fully-functional Object Request Broker (ORB). |
| org.omg.CORBA_2_3 | The CORBA_2_3 package defines additions to existing CORBA interfaces in the Java 2 Standard Edition. These changes occurred in recent revisions to the CORBA API defined by the OMG. The new methods were added to interfaces derived from the corresponding interfaces in the CORBA package. This provides backward compatibility and avoids breaking the JCK tests. |
| org.omg.CORBA_2_3.portable | Provides methods for the input and output of value types, and contains other updates to the org/omg/CORBA/portable package. |
| org.omg.CORBA.DynAnyPackage | Provides the exceptions used with the DynAny interface (InvalidValue, Invalid, InvalidSeq, and TypeMismatch). |
| org.omg.CORBA.ORBPackage | Provides the exception InvalidName, which is thrown by the method ORB.resolve_initial_ references and the exception InconsistentType Code, which is thrown by the Dynamic Any creation methods in the ORB class. |
| org.omg.CORBA.portable | Provides a portability layer, that is, a set of ORB APIs that makes it possible for code generated by one vendor to run on another vendor's ORB. |
| org.omg.CORBA. TypeCodePackage | Provides the user-defined exceptions BadKind and Bounds, which are thrown by methods in the class TypeCode. |
| org.omg.CosNaming | Provides the naming service for Java IDL. |
| org.omg.CosNaming. NamingContextPackage | Provides the exceptions used in the package org.omg.CosNaming (AlreadyBound, CannotProceed, InvalidName, NotEmpty, and NotFound) and also the Helper and Holder classes for those exceptions. |
| org.omg.SendingContext | Provides support for the marshalling of value types. |
| org.omg.stub.java.rmi | Contains RMI-IIOP Stubs for the Remote types that occur in the java.rmi package. |

# Getting the SDK for Windows

Although the following discussion leads you through the acquisition of Sun's Java SDK for Windows, the steps are quite similar for Solaris and Linux platforms. Sun's JRE, SDK, and original JDK installers are available free of charge from the company's Java Web site, as well as comprehensive documentation for each. You can access these downloads by selecting the Products and APIs link from the home page (http://java.sun.com/) or directly through the site's products page (http://java.sun.com/products/). Associated documentation is available on the same page as each installer, although you can also go to Sun's master documentation page (http://java.sun.com/docs/) for fast and easy access to a wide variety of Java documentation.

Sun's SDK is available for Windows 95, 98, 2000 and NT 4.0 systems running Intel 486/DX or faster processors. Although the SDK will operate properly on Windows systems equipped with as little as 32MB of RAM, for best performance, you should have at least 48MB of RAM installed. In addition, you should ensure that you have at least 100MB of free hard disk space available before attempting to download and install the SDK.

Sun's SDK is also available for those running the Solaris operating system on top of either Sun SPARC or Intel hardware. (An Intel 486/DX or faster is required for Intel-based systems.) In both cases, only versions 2.5.1, 2.6, and 7 (also known as 2.7) of Solaris are supported. Such systems require a minimum of 32MB of RAM, although 48MB of RAM or more is recommended. At the time of this writing a beta version of Java SDK 1.3 was available for Linux users as well.

You should have at least 100MB of free hard disk space available before attempting to download and install the SDK on any platform. You can get away with as little as 65MB of free disc space, although we'd suggest 100 to give yourself some breathing space.

When you reach Sun's Java products page, you should locate and download the installer for the most current production release of the SDK. (We'll use the Java 2 SDK Standard Edition version 1.3.0 for Windows throughout the remainder of this book.) At the time of this writing, the current production version is Java 2 SDK 1.3, although a newer version may be available when you visit the site, so you should look for an installer named "Java 2 SDK, Standard Edition, v1.3.1" or later. The SDK is currently considered a member of Sun's Java Development family, meaning you might have to click on a link called Java Development Kit (JDK) Software to find the SDK installer (or you can jump directly to version 1.3 at http://java.sun.com/j2se/1.3/)

Once you've located the SDK installer for your particular platform, download it to your desktop computer. For most of the instructions that follow, we'll assume that you're using Microsoft Windows, although you can adapt these instructions for your own platform if you're not using Windows. In any case, you'll be given the option of downloading the installer directly from Sun's Web site, or from a variety of "mirror" Web sites. In addition, you'll be able to download the installer using either the File Transfer Protocol (FTP) or the HyperText Transfer Protocol (HTTP).

**Tip**

The Java 2 SDK is also available as a *source release*, meaning you can get your hands on the complete programming source code used to create this version of Java. There's no need to download the full source release version, however, unless you're interested in the hard-core plumbing of Java. For most people, the standard SDK release is more than enough because it includes the source code for the core Java class libraries as well as a number of sample Java programs to get you going. If you do decide to download the SDK source release, be sure to read about the Community Source license under which it is distributed (http://www.sun.com/software/communitysource/java2/).

Generally speaking, FTP is faster and more efficient than HTTP when downloading large files (hence, the name *File Transfer Protocol*,) whereas HTTP was designed specifically for lightweight Web page delivery. However, network security systems (such as firewalls) sometimes block FTP downloads, leaving HTTP as the only option. If you're unable to download the SDK installer via FTP, try the HTTP option.

Be warned, however, that the complete Java 2 SDK Standard Edition installer is approximately 30MB in size! This may take a great deal of time to download depending on the speed of your Internet connection, so you should seriously consider downloading the SDK as a series of smaller, individual pieces if you do happen to connect to the Internet with a modem. These individual SDK installer files can be reassembled into a complete installer, as described in the following section.

**Caution**

The Java 2 SDK Standard Edition version 1.3 is approximately 30MB in size, meaning it could take a very long time to download if you're using a dial-up modem connection. If this is the case, consider downloading the SDK installer as a number of smaller, individual pieces that can later be reassembled onto your hard disk as explained here. Although we illustrate how to do this using Windows operating system, the concepts are similar for Solaris and Linux platforms.

## More than a mouthful

Although Java 2 has a great many advantages over past versions of Java, it comes at a price. Yes, Java is free, but you still have to take the time to download it from the Web. And with Java 2, downloading is no trivial matter: the Java 2 SDK Standard Edition version 1.3 is huge!

If you're like most Web surfers, chances are pretty good that you connect to the network using a dial-up modem. Downloading 30MB over a dial-up modem connection isn't difficult—it's unmitigated pain and suffering. If you use a modem to connect to the Web, you're better off downloading the SDK in smaller chunks rather than one giant bite. Doing so will save you a great deal of frustration, and possibly your sanity.

When you reach the Java 2 SDK for Microsoft Windows download page, scroll to the bottom. Here you'll find an option to download 23 individual floppy disk-sized files (approximately 1.4MB each) instead of the entire 30-MB installer. Select this option, and proceed to download each of the installer pieces. As illustrated in Figure A-1, each of these SDK installer pieces can be downloaded either directly from Sun's Web site or from various mirror Web sites. In addition, you can choose to download each piece of the installer using either the FTP or HTTP. (See the previous section for details.)

The SDK for the Windows installer download Web page contains buttons that correspond to each of the installer pieces, which are named j2sdk1_3_0-win-a.exe, j2sdk1_3_0-win-b.exe, j2sdk1_3_0-win-c.exe, and so forth, through j2sdk1_3_0-win-w.exe. Click on a button and begin downloading a particular piece of the installer. A moment or two after clicking on a button, the standard Windows Save dialog box will appear (see Figure A-2), allowing you to specify where on your computer to place the downloaded file. Be sure that you place each of the files into the same folder on your hard disk, as they all need to be together to be assembled into a single SDK installer. (See "The DOS Prompt Tango.")

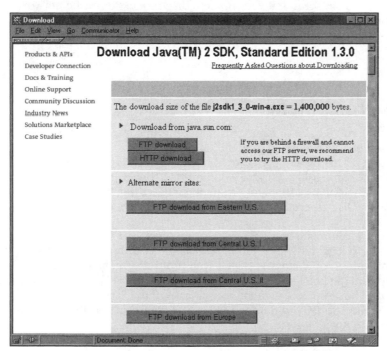

**Figure A-1:** SDK installer files can be downloaded directly from Sun or from mirror Web sites using FTP or HTTP.

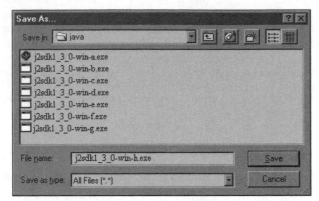

**Figure A-2:** Be sure to save each of the 23 SDK installer pieces into the same folder on your hard disk so they can later be combined into a single installer file.

The advantage of downloading a number of smaller files is pretty clear. You don't have to start over from scratch if your modem disconnects from the network during the download, or if one or more of the files becomes damaged in transit. Simply reconnect and resume downloading those files that didn't make it. It's simple and painless. There is one catch, however: you have to use DOS to combine each of these files into a single installer.

## The DOS prompt tango

The catch is that you'll have to manage 23 different files instead of just one. Once all pieces have been downloaded to your computer, you must then merge them into one giant installer. This means you have to be very careful to download each of the 23 pieces into the same folder on your computer so they're all together in one place when you're ready to merge them into a single installer file. It also means that you have to use DOS (Disk Operating System) to merge the files together.

**Note**

MS-DOS is a command-line operating environment that predates the graphical Windows operating system. Windows actually runs on top of DOS, although the graphical nature of Windows shields you from the gory details. Thanks to Windows, you can point and click, as opposed to typing DOS commands. You have to use DOS, however, to merge the many pieces of the SDK into a single installer file. You'll also use DOS to run the various SDK tools, such as the Java compiler, launcher, and Applet Viewer.

Specifically, you'll use MS-DOS to merge the various SDK files into a single installer program. You'll also use MS-DOS to execute the various development tools that come with the SDK, as described later in this chapter. To use MS-DOS, you need only access the MS-DOS Prompt program that comes with Windows.

The MS-DOS Prompt is an application located under the Start‡Programs menu of your Windows operating system. Selecting the MS-DOS Prompt will open a window similar to the one in Figure A-3.

Inside this window is a prompt (the command line) that lists the current folder path. By default, the MS-DOS Prompt program opens into the Windows folder located on the root level of your boot hard disk, so the following command-line prompt is the first thing you'll see (where C:\ is assumed to be the letter designation for your boot hard disk):

```
C:\WINDOWS>
```

At this prompt, you can type DOS commands, such as DIR (Directory), or CD (Change Directory). DOS commands are terse, cryptic, and unforgiving. If you don't type in exactly the right command, you'll receive a "Bad command or file name" error message and nothing more. Fortunately, you don't have to know too much about MS-DOS to merge your freshly downloaded Java 2 SDK files into a single installer application.

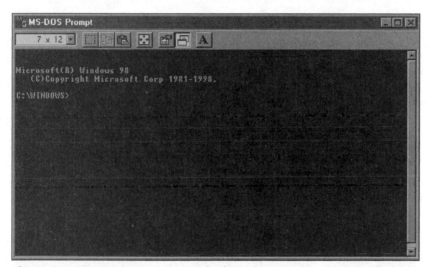

**Figure A-3:** MS-DOS runs as a standard Windows program, inside of which you can type DOS commands.

Perhaps the most important MS-DOS command that you must master is the Change Directory (CD) command, since you have to actually move into the directory (folder) that contains the SDK files. You'll also have to become comfortable changing directories to get the most out of SDK tools such as the Java compiler described later in his chapter.

Because moving from folder to folder within MS-DOS can be a hassle, you should first drag the folder containing your installer files into the root level of your boot disk (typically the C drive). You should also rename the folder containing your installer files to something very simple, and without spaces (DOS hates spaces in directory names!), such as java.

Suppose, for example, that you downloaded the 23 SDK files into a folder called Java 2 SDK that resides on your desktop. Before you even bother firing up the MS-DOS Prompt, rename the folder to java and then drag it onto the root level of your C drive. This would result in a very simple path (c:\java) leading to your installer files.

The trick, now, is to move the MS-DOS prompt out of the default Windows directory and into the java folder containing the 23 SDK files. Fortunately, it only takes a few simple CD commands to change directories:

1. Type in **CD ..** (don't forget to include the two periods after CD!) and then press the Enter key on your keyboard. This will move you up on one directory level, taking you out of the Windows directory and into the root level of C drive.

2. Type **CD java** to move into the java directory containing your files.

If you've followed these instructions to the letter, your MS-DOS window will contain the following lines when complete:

```
C:\WINDOWS> CD ..
C:\ CD java
C:\java>
```

In this example, you've moved "up" one directory level (CD ..), and then back down into the java folder (CD java). Alternately, you can provide a full, explicit path to the directory that you want to move into, as follows (substitute the actual letter of your hard drive if it isn't C as shown here):

```
C:\WINDOWS> CD C:\java
```

Once you are inside the java folder containing the SDK installer files, as indicated by the C:\java> command-line prompt, you're ready for the big event. It's now time to merge those 23 Java 2 SDK files into a single installer application. To do this, you must now issue a DOS COPY command that will copy the contents of each individual file into a single, unified file. First, however, you need to know the exact name of each of the 23 files.

By default, the Java 2 SDK version 1.3 file names are j2sdk1_3_0-win-a.exe, j2sdk1_3_0-win-b.exe, j2sdk1_3_0-win-b.exe, and so on. These are pretty long names to deal with, and you'll likely make a mistake at least once when typing all 23 file names at the command line. To make your job at the command line a little easier, take a moment to rename each of them before going any further. Simply strip off the j2sdk1_3_0-win- portion of the file name (switch to the Windows Explorer interface to do so, and then rename the file as you would any other file or document). Be sure to leave the letter intact to identify which file is which. You'll then have 23 files named alphabetically (a.exe, b.exe, c.exe, d.exe, and so on), which are much easier to type at the command line than the original file names. (See Figure A-4.)

Assuming that you've renamed your files alphabetically, the COPY command is now a cinch to type at the command line (where C:\java> is the DOS prompt):

```
C:\java> COPY /b a.exe + b.exe + c.exe + d.exe + e.exe + f.exe
+ g.exe + h.exe + i.exe + j.exe + k.exe + l.exe + m.exe + n.exe
+ o.exe + p.exe + q.exe + r.exe + s.exe + t.exe + u.exe + v.exe
+ w.exe INSTALLER.exe
```

The previous COPY command essentially tells DOS to copy each of the 23 files that follow into a single application named INSTALLER.exe (or any other name that you want to give the installer program). If each of the files is present, and none were damaged during the download, you'll have a fresh new Java 2 SDK Installer weighing in at approximately 30MB located inside the same directory. To be sure everything went correctly, check the size of the file (using DOS or your Windows Explorer interface). If it's not in the ballpark, you may have omitted one of the necessary pieces during the COPY process.

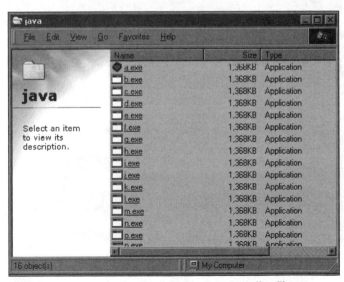

**Figure A-4:** Rename each of the 23 SDK installer files alphabetically to spare yourself time, effort, and potential typing errors in the merging process.

Alternately, you can copy this COPY command into a batch file that resides in the same folder as the SDK files, and simply double-click on the batch file to execute the command and create the installer. A batch file is nothing more than a text file that has a .bat file extension, such as combine.bat, which means you can create batch files from scratch using a standard text editor (such as Notepad).

Whether you issue the copy command at the MS-DOS prompt or through a batch file, the end result is a stand-alone installer application created by merging together each of the individual 23 SDK files. (See Figure A-5.)

Double-click on this installer program, as you would any other Windows application, and you'll see the Java 2 SDK installation splash screen appear as seen in see Figure A-6. This begins the SDK installation.

**Tip**    If you have problems merging the files into a single installer file, or you suspect that one of the files may be damaged, consult Sun's Java 2 SDK installation help page (available through the SDK download page or directly at http://java. sun.com/j2se/1.3/install-windows.html). To learn more about the MS-DOS commands that you can use with Java once you've installed the SDK, visit http://www.mantiscorp.com/autoforward/javados.html.

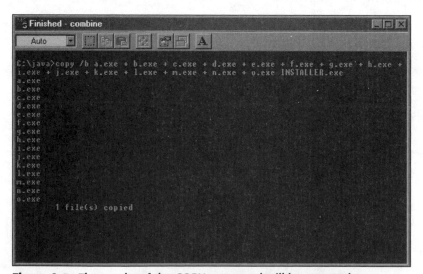

**Figure A-5:** The results of the COPY command will be reported to you through the MS-DOS command prompt. In this example, only a portion of the 23 SDK files have been combined (a through o) since all 23 can't be displayed in a single DOS window, although you should combine *all* of them (a through w).

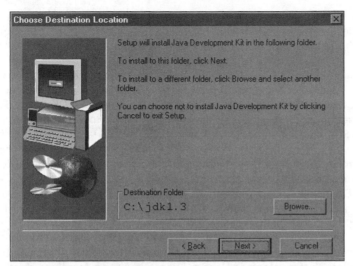

**Figure A-6:** After creating the installer program, you're only a mouse-click away from installing the Java 2 SDK on your Windows computer.

# Installing the SDK

After downloading the SDK from the Web, you'll first have to decompress the archive it comes in before you can actually use it. Fortunately, both the Solaris and Windows versions of the SDK are self-extracting installers, making them relatively easy to use. Simply run the installer as you would any other application as described in the next section. After running the installer, you can delete it if you'd like to free up the 30MB of hard disk space it consumes.

**Note**    These steps assume that you're attempting to install Java 2 Standard Edition version 1.3; if you're using a different version, be sure to adjust your commands to accommodate any differences in file and directory names.

## Windows

You expand the Windows self-extracting archive by double-clicking the SDK installer program to start the extraction process and begin the installation.

Upon running the SDK installer for Windows, the various compressed packages that comprise the product are unpacked (extracted, or decompressed). In a moment or two, you'll be presented with the Java SDK installer dialog box shown earlier in Figure A-6. At this point, you're asked to specify the folder into which the Java runtime environment and the various SDK tools should be installed on your computer.

By default, the folder is named jdk1.3 and is located on the root level of your hard disk (c:/jdk1.3). Unless you have good reason not to use this default location, accept it and continue with the installation by clicking Next in the installation dialog box.

**Note**

The default folder name jdk1.3 is a remnant of the days when the SDK was actually named *JDK*, and reflects the fact that you've installed version 1.3 of the development environment. The name *JDK* was formally changed to *SDK* when Sun Microsystems introduced the Java 2 platform in late 1998. However, the current version of the SDK installer still uses the original JDK folder name, which can be confusing if you're not aware of the name change. You'll also notice that a good deal of Sun's online documentation still refers to the JDK when, in fact, the SDK is actually being discussed. In time, the name *JDK* will give way entirely to SDK. Because the SDK installer places the various files that make up the Java development environment into a folder called jdk1.3 by default, however, we'll use that folder name in the examples that follow.

You will then be asked which of the Java components you'd like to install, which includes Program Files, Native Interface Header Files, Old Native Interface Header Files, Demos, and Java Sources. Each of these components is installed by default, although you can omit any one of these if necessary. You might, for example, choose to omit the Java Sources or Demo components if you're particularly tight on hard disk space, although doing so will prevent you from having access to some of the most valuable development examples that you can get your hands on!

After selecting those components that you wish to install, click the Next button again. The selected components will then be placed into the newly created Java folder on your desktop computer (named c:/jdk1.3 by default), which may take a few minutes. Following the installation of these components, another dialog box will appear asking if you'd like to install the JRE, as seen in Figure A-7. The JRE, which includes the Java Plug-in, comes as part of the SDK for Windows systems. (See Chapter 2.) Like with all other SDK installation options, you should accept the default installation location of the JRE (C:\Program Files\JavaSoft\JRE) unless you have good reason not to.

When installation of the JRE and SDK tools is complete, the installer will then ask if you'd like to view the README text file that comes with your new suite of goodies. Not only should you accept the opportunity to read this README file, but you should also take a moment to print this document when it is displayed. The README file will give you a basic overview of the SDK files that were installed on your system, and it also provides a bevy of useful links to related online content. The README document can be found in the Java folder created by the SDK installer (c:\jdk1.3 by default), where you'll find both text file and HTML formats of this file.

Upon completion of the SDK installation, you should set the PATH environment variable as described in the "Setting Up Your Java Environment" section that follows.

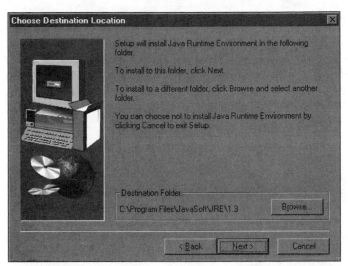

**Figure A-7:** Sun's standalone JRE is part of the Window's SDK installation.

**Note**

The JRE is actually placed in two different places on your Windows computer by the SDK installer. A JRE is placed in the default Java tools folder (C:\jdk1.3\jre) for development purposes, and a standalone version is placed in the Windows programs folder (C:\Program Files\JavaSoft\JRE). The former provides a Java runtime for the SDK, while the latter is as a standalone runtime for applets and applications that execute outside of the development environment. They are exactly the same JRE, actually, although documentation isn't provided with the one placed in your Java folder.

## Solaris

You expand the Solaris self-extracting archive from the command line. This is also a straightforward process, and one you're likely familiar with if you've dealt with self-extracting archives before:

1. Use this command to change the SDK archive file into an executable file:

   chmod a+x jdk1.3-solaris2-sparc.bin

2. Type this command to extract the SDK files:

   ./jdk1.3-solaris2-sparc.bin

You can expand the Solaris SDK archive anywhere on your Solaris machine.

Upon completion of the SDK installation, you should set the PATH environment variable as described in the "Setting Up Your Java Environment" section that follows.

## The Java Folder

Once the SDK archive has been expanded and executed, a Java folder similar to the one shown in Figure A-8 will reside on your computer. This folder is named jdk1.3 by default, and it is found on the root level of your boot drive (c:\jdk1.3 for Windows users, unless you choose a location other than the default provided during installation, in which case the Java folder resides wherever you've specified).

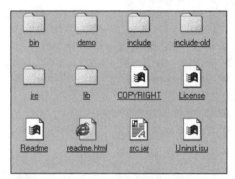

**Figure A-8:** Upon installing the SDK, a Java folder containing the JRE and various development tools resides on your computer.

This Java folder contains a number of subdirectories, tools, and files, which together make up the Java 2 SDK. The directory tree for this folder looks like this:

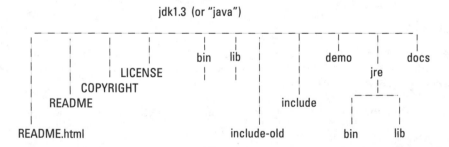

Every Java tool in the bin directory is actually an executable program that runs on the command line. (See Table A-2 for a summary of the most essential tools provided with the SDK, which are described more detail later.) Following is a brief description of the main subfolders found in the master Java folder. (These descriptions are based on the Windows installation; Solaris is nearly identical — see the README file found in your newly installed Java folder for more details.)

## c:\jdk1.3\ bin

This folder contains the binary executable files used by the SDK, such as the Java compiler (javac), the Java launcher (java), and the Applet Viewer test program (appletviewer) that you'll use to develop and test your very own Java programs. Table A-2 lists the most commonly used of these tools, all of which are run on the command line (such as the MS-DOS prompt). Because these tools are run on the command line, you'll need to set the PATH environment variable for your computer accordingly, as described in the "Setting Up Your Java Environment" section that follows. When configured properly, the PATH variable contains a complete path location leading to this folder, allowing the files it contains to be run on the command line.

## c:\jdk1.3\lib

This folder contains files used by the SDK tools, such as the tools.jar file (a Java Archive, or JAR, that contains noncore classes used by SDK tools and utilities) and dt.jar (a JAR used by JavaBeans development environment tools).

## c:\jdk1.3\jre

This folder contains the JRE used expressly by the SDK tools, which is exactly the same as the standalone JRE installed separately into the C:\Program Files\JavaSoft\ JRE folder by the Windows SDK installer. (The Solaris SDK installer doesn't include a standalone JRE.) This version of the Java runtime environment, however, is only for development purposes, so it does not include the same documentation that comes with the standalone JRE. Although Sun's standalone JRE can be redistributed free of charge with your own Java programs, the one in this directory is off limits and cannot be redistributed in any way.

Note

The c:\jdk1.3\jre folder contains its very own library folder (c:\jdk1.3\jre\lib), inside of which is a Java Archive (JAR) file named rt.jar. The rt.jar file contains what are known as the core *bootstrap* Java classes, which are the runtime classes that form the core Java API described in Part I of this book. The raw Java source code for these bootstrap classes is located in the src.jar file found in the root Java folder (c:\jdk1.3\), which you can take a look at if you're interested in the internal implementation of the Java core classes. You can decompress the src.jar archive using the SDK Java Archive tool (see Chapter 25, "Deploying Applets and Applications") or a standard ZIP compression utility such as WinZip (http://www.winzip.com/). To use a standard ZIP utility, you must first change the .jar file extension to .zip.

## c:\jdk1.3\demo

This folder contains a variety of demonstration Java programs, together with the source code used to create these programs. The folder c:\jdk1.3\demo\applets is loaded with Java applets, while the folder c:\jdk1.3\demo\jfc contains various Java Foundation Classes (JFC) examples such as Swing GUI applets and applications. (JFC and Swing are described in Part IV of this book.) Later in this appendix, you'll see how to run these demonstration programs for testing purposes. (See "Testing the SDK Installation.")

**Tip**

Although the source code for these demonstration applets is provided for both Windows and Solaris installations, you may find that viewing these files is a bit tricky in Windows. Because these source code files come from Sun, maker of the Solaris operating system, they're stored in a text format that uses a different carriage return (end-of-line marker) than that of Windows. As a result, if you open these source code files using a very simple text editor such as Notepad, they will appear scrambled—every line of code runs together as a result of Windows not recognizing the Solaris carriage return characters. To view the contents of these source code files, you should use a more sophisticated word processing program than Notepad (such as Microsoft Word). Just be sure to save any changes in a plain text file, since ASCII text is the only format the Java compiler understands.

### c:\jdk1.3\include and c:\jdk1.3\ include-old

The include folders found in the Java folder contain C/C++ header files used to support native-code programming using the Java Native Interface (JNI) and the Java Virtual Machine Debugger Interface (JMDI). These are advanced topics beyond the scope of this book. (See Sun's online documentation for details.)

| Table A-2 | |
| :-- | :-- |
| **Essential Java SDK Tools** | |
| **Tool** | **Description** |
| appletviewer | The Applet Viewer tool used to run and debug applets outside of a Web browser. |
| jar | The Java Archive (JAR) tool used to create and manage JAR files. |
| java | The Java application launcher tool (sometimes called the Java interpreter). |
| javac | The Java compiler tool, used to convert source code files into bytecode class files. |
| javadoc | The Java API documentation generator tool. |
| javah | The C header and stub file generator, used to write native methods in Java. |
| javap | The Java class file disassembler. |
| jdb | The Java debugger, a simple debugging tool. |
| extcheck | A JAR utility to detect JAR file conflicts. |

**Tip**

Table A-2 lists only a few of the most essential Java 1.3 SDK tools, but not all of them. Version 1.3 of the SDK is packed with tools, including Security Tools (keytool, jarsigner, policytool), Internationalization Tools (native2ascii), Remote Method Invocation (RMI) Tools (rmic, rmiregistry, rmid, serialver), Java IDL and RMI-IIOP Tools (tnameserv, idlj), and Java Plug-in Tools (unregbean). To learn more about the entire suite of Java 1.3 SDK tools visit http://java.sun.com/ j2se/1.3/docs/tooldocs/tools.html

# Setting Up Your Java Environment

After you've installed the SDK, you must ensure that the PATH environment variable is set properly. The correct settings for this variables hinges on *where* you install the SDK onto your computer, since this variable must point to the folder containing the SDK binary files (which is found at C:\jdk1.3\bin on Windows systems by default).

The PATH environment variable specifies where the operating system looks for executable files when you don't supply the full directory path leading to the file you'd like to execute. To run SDK tools such as the Java compiler (javac) from the command line, you must either have set the operating system's PATH environment variable in advance, or specify a brand new PATH environment variable each time the tool is executed. It is much more convenient to set the PATH environment variable in advance, however, and simply forget it once done rather than to go through the trouble of setting the variable each time you use an SDK tool. The following sections describe how to permanently set the PATH variable for Windows and Solaris systems.

## Windows 95, 98, and 2000

Windows 95, 98, and 2000 users set environment variables in the autoexec.bat file, which is typically found on the root level of the primary hard disk (such as C:\). Since some Windows users don't have an autoexec.bat file, you might have to create one manually using a text editor. (The autoexec.bat file is simply a text file with the .bat extension.) If this is the case, be sure that you name the file exactly, and be certain to place it on the root level of your hard disk. If you don't, Windows won't bother loading this file at startup, and the environment variables you specify here won't have a chance to become active.

To modify the setting of your PATH environment variable in the autoexec.bat file, add the following line to that file:

```
set PATH=%PATH%;C:\jdk1.3\bin
```

Like with the Solaris instructions, we're assuming that the SDK has been installed into a directory called jdk1.3. If this isn't the case, you'll have to substitute the actual directory name you placed the JDK anywhere the directory name jdk1.3 appears.

Once you've made these changes, you must either restart your computer or manually force the operating system to reread your autoexec.bat file by entering this command at the MS-DOS prompt (where C:\> is the command prompt located inside the same directory as the autoexec.bat file itself):

```
C:\> autoexec
```

If you opt to execute the autoexec batch file (.bat) at the command line as seen here, keep in mind that the PATH settings will only go into effect for *that particular* MS-DOS prompt window. If you close the MS-DOS prompt window after issuing this command, for example, these changes to the PATH environment variable will be lost. You'll have to either reboot your computer or reissue the previous command when the next MS-DOS prompt window is opened.

## Windows NT 4.0

Unlike Windows 95/98/2000 users, who access environment variables by way of editing the autoexec.bat file, Windows NT users have the luxury of using the System program in Control Panel. Simply open Control Panel, double-click the System program, and select the Environment tab. Next, locate the PATH environment variable (or create one if it doesn't already exist) and enter the following value:

```
set path=%path%;C:\jdk1.3\bin
```

You might notice that these two lines of text are exactly the same as those used for Windows 95/98/2000, and for good reason: They're all similar in how they deal with environment variables. The most significant difference lies in how you enter them. While Windows NT uses the System program, Windows 95/98/2000 users have to edit an autoexec.bat file. Either way, the environment variables are loaded at startup.

Once you've made these changes in the Windows NT System program, you can either click the Done button, at which point you must restart you computer for the changes to take effect, or you can force Windows NT to reload your environment variables on the spot by clicking the Apply button. (If you click Done, you must reboot before Windows NT will recognize your changes. Clicking Apply is a faster, more convenient way to accomplish the same task.)

## Solaris

Solaris users typically set environment variables in the startup file for the shell being used. Since most Solaris users do this through either a variation of the *sh* shell or the *csh* shell, we'll include a brief description of each here. In both cases, we'll assume that the SDK has been installed into a directory called jdk1.3. If this isn't the case, you'll have to substitute your actual Java folder name anywhere the folder named jdk1.3 appears in the instructions that follow.

To modify the setting of your PATH environment variable in your .cshrc file (for *csh* shell variants), insert the following line of text in that file:

```
set path=(/usr/local/jdk.1.3.1/bin $path)
```

Once you've made these changes, you should force the operating system to reread your .cshrc file by entering this command:

```
source ~/.cshrc
```

To modify the setting of your PATH environment variable in your .profile file (for *sh* shell variants), insert this line in that file:

```
PATH=($PATH:/usr/local/jdk1.3/bin) export PATH
```

Note that the same line can be used for the bash shell (the default shell in Linux), but the file needed is .bash_profile. Once you've made these changes, you should force the operating system to reread your .profile file by entering this command:

```
. ~/.profile
```

# Testing the SDK Installation

After you've installed the SDK and set your PATH environment variable, it's time to test your new Java installation. To do so, you'll work on the command line (See "The DOS Prompt Tango" section of this appendix to learn how to run the Windows MS-DOS Prompt.)

The first thing you should do is issue the Java launcher command (java) followed by the version option, which will, in turn, report back the current version of Java that you've installed:

```
> java -version
```

If you have properly installed the SDK, version information such as the following will appear on the command line:

```
java version "1.3.0"
Java(TM) 2 Runtime Environment, Standard Edition (build 1.3.0-C)
Java HotSpot(TM) Client VM (build 1.3.0-C, mixed mode)
```

This indicates that Java 1.3 has indeed been installed on your system. It further lists the specific type of Virtual Machine (VM) that you're running (HotSpot, which comes standard with Java 1.3) along with the exact build of the SDK you're running. If you don't receive information similar to this, but instead you see a message such as "Bad command or file name," try once again to set your PATH environment variable. (Such a message indicates that the library tools cannot be found.) If resetting the PATH variable doesn't do the trick, consult the installation troubleshooting section found later in this chapter.

Assuming that Java is properly installed, meaning that the Java -version command actually returns meaningful information, you're ready to move on to the next test. The next test is great fun, actually, because you have a chance to explore and play with the various demonstration programs that come with the SDK.

Simply change to one of the demo subfolders in your new java directory (which is named jdk1.3 by default, although you may have specified a different name at installation) and run the Applet Viewer program along with an associated HTML file.

For instance, to run the TicTacToe demonstration applet from a Windows installation, start by changing to that directory:

```
> cd C:\jdk1.3\demo\applets\TicTacToe
```

Note that SDK files on Sun Solaris installations have the same path as on Windows installations, although Windows uses backslashes (\) to separate directories, whereas Sun systems use forward slashes (/), and Solaris doesn't refer to an explicit drive letter such as C: used by Windows. To move to the same directory on a Sun Soloris system, for example, type this line:

```
> cd jdk1.3/demo/applets/TicTacToe
```

In either case, this command will place you inside the folder of the TicTacToe demonstration applet that comes with the SDK (jdk1.3\demo\applets\TicTacToe), making it the current directory. The SDK comes with a number of demonstration applets, of which TicTacToe is only one. To obtain a listing of the other demonstration applets that you can play with, simply issue the Change Directory command to move into the main jdk1.3\demo\applets\ folder and type **DIR** (short for directory), as the following Windows example illustrates:

```
> cd C:\jdk1.3\demo\applets\
> dir
```

Following is a listing similar to what you should see after issuing the previous MS-DOS commands:

```
 Volume in drive C has no label
 Volume Serial Number is 3541-A475
 Directory of C:\jdk1.3\demo\applets

ANIMATOR       <DIR>        07-06-00  11:02p  Animator
ARCTEST        <DIR>        07-06-00  11:02p  ArcTest
BARCHART       <DIR>        07-06-00  11:02p  BarChart
BLINK          <DIR>        07-06-00  11:02p  Blink
CARDTEST       <DIR>        07-06-00  11:02p  CardTest
CLOCK          <DIR>        07-06-00  11:02p  Clock
DITHER~1       <DIR>        07-06-00  11:02p  DitherTest
DRAWTEST       <DIR>        07-06-00  11:02p  DrawTest
FRACTAL        <DIR>        07-06-00  11:02p  Fractal
GRAPHL~1       <DIR>        07-06-00  11:02p  GraphLayout
GRAPHI~1       <DIR>        07-06-00  11:02p  GraphicsTest
IMAGEMAP       <DIR>        07-06-00  11:02p  ImageMap
JUMPIN~1       <DIR>        07-06-00  11:02p  JumpingBox
MOLECU~1       <DIR>        07-06-00  11:02p  MoleculeViewer
NERVOU~1       <DIR>        07-06-00  11:02p  NervousText
```

```
SIMPLE~1        <DIR>        07-06-00  11:02p  SimpleGraph
SORTDEMO        <DIR>        07-06-00  11:02p  SortDemo
SPREAD~1        <DIR>        07-06-00  11:02p  SpreadSheet
SYMBOL~1        <DIR>        07-06-00  11:02p  SymbolTest
TICTAC~1        <DIR>        07-06-00  11:02p  TicTacToe
WIREFR~1        <DIR>        07-06-00  11:02p  WireFrame
```

The names found on the far left of this listing are known as aliases, which are MS-DOS names that conform to the file naming limitations of DOS. Because DOS is limited to files having no more than eight characters in the name and three characters in the file extension (which constitutes the DOS 8.3 naming convention), you'll often see aliases that contain a tilde character (~) to indicate that the actual file or folder name exceeds these limitations. The alias TICTAC~1, for example, indicates that the real folder name TicTacToe exceeds the limit of eight characters in the name. (There is no extension in folder names.) Windows 95, 98, and NT, on the other hand, support long file names such as those found on the far right of the previous listing (TicTacToe, for example).

You can use either short or long file names when working on the MS-DOS command line, although you should keep in mind that spaces are a big problem in either case. When you create your own folders for use with Java, take great care to ensure that no spaces are included in the names of such folders. (Notice that no spaces are found in the demo applet folders provided with the SDK.) In situations where a folder or file name actually contains one or more spaces, you can encase the name in a pair of double quotes to refer to it on the command line, as the following examples illustrate:

```
> cd  "my applets"
> appletviewer  "my test file.html"
```

**Note**    All Java files are long file names as a result of naming conventions set by Sun. (Java source code files have the four character .java file extension, while compiled Java class files end in .class.) You'll also notice in your Java wanderings that most Java file names contain more than eight characters, further breaking with the old 8.3 file naming conventions of DOS.

Inside each applet demo directory, such as TicTacToe, there is an HTML file that contains the <APPLET> tag used to execute that demonstration applet. In this case, as with most of the demos included with the SDK, the HTML file is named example1.html. Once you're in the TicTacToe folder (jdk1.3\demo\applets\TicTacToe), run the Applet Viewer program (appletviewer) followed by the name of that HTML file:

```
> appletviewer example1.html
```

If everything was installed properly, you should now be playing a game of TicTacToe, as illustrated in Figure A-9, and can then proceed to explore the remaining applets as well as the JFC/Swing demos found the jdk1.3\demo\jfc folder. If not, see the "Installation Troubleshooting for Solaris" or "Installation Troubleshooting for Windows" sections found at the end of this appendix.

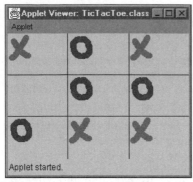

**Figure A-9:** Java TicTacToe, one of
the many demo applets supplied
with the JDK

Although many of the JFC/Swing demos are applets, meaning you'll execute them using
the Applet Viewer tool just as you did with the TicTacToe applet, several of these are
actually java applications. In this case, you cannot use Applet Viewer, but must instead
use the Java launcher tool (java). As you'll learn by reading this book, executable Java
classes contains a `main( )` method, which in turn can call upon any number of other
classes. (Both applets and applications can be created using a variety of classes, only
one of which is the entry point for execution.) This is the class that you must supply
on the command line to the Java launcher, as the following illustrates:

```
> java Metalworks
```

This example assumes that we've changed directories so that the current command
prompt is jdk1.3\demo\jfc\Metalworks, and that we've also read the README.txt
file located in that folder. Every JFC demo program comes with its own README text
file that describes how to run that applet or application, which is how we knew that
the class file named Metalworks was the main entry point into this particular application and should therefore be passed to the Java launcher, as we've done here.

**Note**    Java classes are passed to the Java launcher (java) without their associated file
extension, as seen here. (The full name of the Java class named Metalworks is
actually Metalworks.class, although only Metalworks is passed to the Java
launcher.) Both the Applet Viewer (appletviewer) and Java compiler (javac) tools,
however, require a file extension when you pass file names tothese programs.

# Using Java Tools

Using the Java development environment means you'll have to learn each of the SDK
tools outlined in Table A-2 earlier in this chapter. The three most commonly used tools
are the compiler (javac), the launcher (java), and Applet Viewer (appletviewer). With

these three tools and a source code editor such as Notepad, you'll be able to create and test your own Java applications and applets. During the course of reading this book you'll learn in detail how to use these tools. For now, consider this appendix a crash course to get you up and running immediately. (Full documentation for each tool is available through Sun's Web site at http://java.sun.com/j2se/1.3/docs/tooldocs/tools.html.)

Using a text editor, you'll type the commands that make up your Java program into a window (much as you might write a letter in a word processor), the results of which will be saved as a standard text file. Using the Java compiler tool, you will then compile your source code file into a bytecode class file. If the program you wrote is an application, you can execute this class file on the command line using the Java launcher. If it's an applet, however, you'll have to first weave it into an HTML Web page that can be read by Applet Viewer or a Java-savvy browser.

Not surprisingly, Java source code files contain the actual Java source code commands that you write using a text editor. These commands are saved in plain text files, meaning they're stored in ASCII text format. As long as you save your source files in ASCII text format with a .java extension, you'll be fine. The following are examples of valid Java source file names:

```
HelloWorld.java
MyProgram.java
CoolGame.java
```

If you omit the .java extension, or if the file is in any format other than ASCII text, the compiler will generate an error message. If you were to compile these hypothetical source code files, you would use the following Java compiler command lines:

```
> javac HelloWorld.java
> javac MyProgram.java
> javac CoolGame.java
```

Assuming that each of these files contains only one class definition, you would wind up with three unique class files: HelloWorld.class, MyProgram.class, and CoolGame.class. If each of these were a Java application, you could execute them on the command line using the Java launcher as follows. (Keep in mind that the class file extension is not used by the launcher, which will generate an error if you include it.):

```
> java HelloWorld
> java MyProgram
> java CoolGame
```

However, if these class files contained applet code instead of application code, each would first have to be woven into an HTML Web page, the name of which would be passed to the Applet Viewer program for execution. Although Web page file names do not have to correspond to the applet class file they contain, you could weave each into a file named after the class itself just to keep things simple, in which case, the three applets would be executed as follows:

```
> appletviewer HelloWorld.html
> appletviewer MyProgram.html
> appletviewer CoolGame.html
```

Table A-3 lists these and other popular Java tools with their proper usage syntax. To help make sense of these, we'll step through the process of writing a small application called HelloWorld. Although the details of HelloWorld (both application and applet versions of the program) are covered in Part I of this book, we'll use it here to illustrate the use of the Java tools.

Since the actual source code isn't important for the following examples (we'll go over code in detail in the book), assume that you have already entered the following source code in a text editor:

```
class HelloWorld {

  public static void main (String args[]) {
    System.out.println("Hello World!");
  }

}
```

You would save this code as ASCII text (just plain text) in a file named HelloWorld having the .java extension HelloWorld.java. Ignoring the issue of how your development environment directories should be structured (more on that later), assume that you have saved your HelloWorld.java file in an appropriate directory on your hard disk. Because the source code needs to be compiled before it can be executed, the next step is to do just that.

## Table A-3
## Java Tool Usage (bracketed items optional) **

**Applet Viewer:**
appletviewer [options] URL (See Table A-6 for details.)

**Launcher:** (See Table A-4 for details)
java [options] class [arguments]
java [options] -jar file.jar [arguments]
javaw [options] class [arguments]
javaw [options] -jar file.jar [arguments]
oldjava [options] class [arguments]
oldjavaw [options] class [arguments]

**Compiler:** (See Table A-4 for details.)
javac [options] [sourcefiles] [@files]

**Documentation Tool:**
javadoc [options] [packagenames] [sourcefiles] [@files]

**C Header and Stub File Generator:**
javah [options] fully-qualified-classname
javah_g [options] fully-qualified-classname

**Class File Disassembler:**
javap [options] class

**Debugger:**
jdb [options] [class] [arguments]

**JAR Checker:**
extcheck [-verbose] targetfile.jar

✦✦ **[options]** are command-line options, **[sourcefiles]** are one or more source code files to be compiled (such as HelloWorld.java), **[@files]** are one or more files that list Java source files (you may specify one or more @files that contain one file name per line, allowing source files to be batch processed), **[arguments]** are command line arguments passed to an application's main() method, class is the name of the bytecode class to be executed, and **file.jar** is the name of a JAR file.

# Compiling

You can run the Java compiler, javac, with a wide array of options. (See Table A-4.) This is the basic syntax of javac:

```
javac [options] sourcefile.java
```

We just want to compile the source file without any options, so we could simply execute the compiler with the name of our source code file. The following example shows how to compile a program without any options. (The angle bracket (>) indicates a command-line prompt.):

```
> javac HelloWorld.java
```

Any syntax errors or bugs caught by the compiler would be displayed on the command line immediately following this command, although you can assume there are none in this example. If all goes well, the compiler will convert the human-readable source code into machine-readable bytecode. The compiler creates a bytecode file for each class declared in the program. Assuming the HelloWorld.java source file declares only one class, `HelloWorld`, the compiler creates the following corresponding class file:

```
HelloWorld.class
```

This class file contains the bytecode generated by the compiler based on the `HelloWorld` class definition declared in your raw source code file (HelloWorld.java). If there were other classes declared in your program, the compiler would create a new bytecode class file for each. For instance, supposing your single HelloWorld.java source code file declared three different classes (HelloWorld, GoodbyeWorld, and SpinWorld), a bytecode file for each would have been created by the compiler (HelloWorld.class, GoodbyeWorld.class, and SpinWorld.class).

At this point, the source code of this simple HelloWorld application has been converted to bytecode, which can now be executed by the Java launcher. (See the next section.) In this example, you've simply used the compiler as is, without specifying any of the options it understands. For a description of each option, see Table A-4.

<table>
<tr><td colspan="2" align="center">Table A-4<br>**The Java Compiler (javac) Tool**</td></tr>
<tr><td>*Option*</td><td>*Description*</td></tr>
<tr><td>-classpath *classpath*</td><td>Sets the user class path, overriding the user class path in the CLASSPATH environment variable. If neither CLASSPATH nor -classpath is specified, the user class path consists of the current directory. See "Setting the Class Path" sidebar for more details. If the -sourcepath option is not specified, the user class path is searched for source files as well as class files.</td></tr>
<tr><td>-d *directory*</td><td>Sets the destination directory for class files. If a class is part of a package, javac puts the class file in a subdirectory reflecting the package name, creating directories as needed. For example, if you specify -d c:\myclasses and the class is called com.mypackage.MyClass, then the class file is called :\myclasses\com\mypackage\MyClass.class.</td></tr>
<tr><td></td><td>If -d is not specified, javac puts the class file in the same directory as the source file. Note that the directory specified by -d is not automatically added to your user class path.</td></tr>
<tr><td>-deprecation</td><td>Shows a description of each use or override of a deprecated member or class. Without -deprecation, javac shows the names of source files that use or override deprecated members or classes.</td></tr>
<tr><td>-encoding</td><td>Sets the source file encoding name, such as EUCJIS/SJIS. If -encoding is not specified, the platform default converter is used.</td></tr>
</table>

| Option | Description |
|---|---|
| -g | Generates all debugging information, including local variables. By default, only line number and source file information is generated. Note that -g:none tells javac not to generate debugging information. |
| -g:{keyword list} | Generates only some kinds of debugging information, specified by a comma-separated list of keywords. Keywords are: <br><br> **source**  (Source file debugging info) <br> **lines**   (Line number debugging info) <br> **vars**    (Local variable debugging info) . |
| -nowarn | Disables warning messages. |
| -O | **Note:** the -O option does nothing in the current implementation of javac and oldjavac. The following is based on previous versions: <br><br> Optimizes code for execution time. Using the -O option may slow down compilation, produce larger class files, and make the program difficult to debug. Prior to JDK 1.2, the -g and -O options of javac could not be used together. As of JDK 1.2, you can combine -g and -O, but you may get surprising results, such as missing variables or relocated or missing code. -O no longer automatically turns on -depend or turns off -g. Also, -O no longer enables inlining across classes. |
| -sourcepath sourcepath | Specifies the source code path to search for class or interface definitions. As with the user class path, source path entries are separated by semicolons (;) and can be directories, JAR archives, or ZIP archives. If packages are used, the local path name within the directory or archive must reflect the package name. Note that classes found through the class path are subject to automatic recompilation if their sources are found. |
| -verbose | Generates verbose output. This includes information about each class loaded and each source file compiled. |

## Setting the CLASSPATH

The CLASSPATH environment variable is one way that you can tell Java programs and SDK tools where to look for classes on the user's system, although Sun recommends using the classpath command-line option described later. If you must deal directly with the CLASSPATH variable you should first read Sun's material on the subject (for Windows) at http://java.sun.com/j2se/1.3/docs/tooldocs/win32/classpath.html.

# Cross-Compilation Options

By default, javac compiles classes against the bootstrap and extension classes that come with the SDK. It can, however, also handle cross-compiling so that classes are compiled against a bootstrap and extension classes of a different Java platform implementation. To do so you must use the -bootclasspath and -extdirs options as illustrated here:

```
C:> javac -target 1.1 -bootclasspath jdk1.1.8\lib\classes.zip \
           -extdirs "" OldCode.java
```

In this example we use the compile code that will run on a 1.1.8 VM. Following is a summary of options that can be supplied when cross-compiling.

## -target *version*

Generate class files that will work on VMs with the specified version. The default is to generate class files to be compatible with both 1.1 VMs and VMs of the Java 2 SDK. The versions supported by javac in the Java 2 SDK are:

## 1.1

Ensure that generated class files will be compatible with 1.1 and VMs in the Java 2 SDK. This is the default.

## 1.2

Generate class files that will run on VMs in the Java 2 SDK, v 1.2 and later, but will not run on 1.1 VMs.

## 1.3

Generate class files that will run on VMs in the Java 2 SDK, v 1.3 and later, but will not run on 1.1 or 1.2 VMs.

## -bootclasspath *bootclasspath*

Cross-compile against the specified set of boot classes. As with the user class path, boot class path entries are separated by semicolons (;) and can be directories, JAR archives, or ZIP archives.

## -extdirs *directories*

Cross-compile against the specified extension directories. Directories is a semicolon-separated list of directories. Each JAR archive in the specified directories is searched for class files.

# Executing applications with the Java launcher

Once the bytecode class for your application has been generated by the compiler, it can be executed. This is simple enough in the case of actual applications, since all you have to do is run the Java launcher (also known as the Java interpreter) and provide it with the name of the bytecode file:

```
> java HelloWorld
```

Notice that we didn't supply the .class extension for the HelloWorld bytecode file. Although the launcher requires the file to have such an extension, because every valid Java class has the .class file extension, we don't need to provide it. In fact, an error would be reported if we did. For instance, suppose we did this:

```
> java HelloWorld.class
```

In this case, the launcher would report the following error:

```
> Can't find class HelloWorld/class
```

Note that there are actually two ways to run your Java programs:

✦ The java command invokes the Java launcher with a console window.

✦ The javaw command invokes the launcher without a console window.

Tip

Don't forget that the compiler (javac), requires you to include the file name with its .java extension, while the launcher (java) wants only the base name of the bytecode file, without the .class extension. You can use the launcher with a number of options, many the same as those the compiler supports. These options are listed in Table A-5.

| Table A-5 | |
|-----------|---|
| **The Java Launcher (java) Tool** | |
| **_Options_** | **_Description_** |
| -classpath*classpath* | |
| -cp *classpath* | Specifies a list of directories, JAR archives, and ZIP archives to search for class files. Class path entries are separated by semicolons (;). Specifying -classpath or -cp overrides any setting of the CLASSPATH environment variable. Used with java or javaw, -classpath or -cp only specifies the class path for user classes. Used with oldjava or oldjavaw, -classpath or -cp specifies the class path for both user classes and bootstrap classes. If -classpath and -cp are not used and CLASSPATH is not set, the user class path consists of the current directory (.). |

*Continued*

| Options | Description |
|---------|-------------|
| **Table A-5** *(continued)* | |
| *Options* | *Description* |
| -D*property*=*value* | Sets a system property value. |
| -jar | Executes a program encapsulated in a JAR file. The first argument is the name of a JAR file instead of a startup class name. For this option to work, the manifest of the JAR file must contain a line of the form Main-Class: classname. Here, classname identifies the class having the `public static void main(String[] args)` method that serves as your application's starting point. See the Jar tool reference page and the Jar trail of the Java Tutorial for information about working with Jar files and Jar-file manifests. When you use this option, the JAR file is the source of all user classes, and other user class path settings are ignored. The oldjava and oldjavaw tools do not support the -jar option. |
| -verbose<br>-verbose:class | Displays information about each class loaded. |
| -verbose:gc | Reports on each garbage collection event. |
| -verbose:jni | Reports information about use of native methods and other Java Native Interface (JNI) activity. |
| -version | Displays version information, then exit. |
| -showversion | Displays version information and continue. |
| -?<br>-help | Displays usage information, then exit. |
| -X | Displays information about nonstandard options, then exit. |

# Executing applets with Applet Viewer

Java applications are full-blown applications that are executed outside a Java-savvy browser. Unlike applets, which run inside a browser environment, applications need only the runtime environment to execute. Applets, on the other hand, require the help of a browser in order to run.

Since firing up a browser each time you want to test an applet can be time-consuming—and even impossible at times because of memory constraints—you may prefer to use the Applet Viewer tool included with the SDK. This tool, shown running a demo applet in Figure A-10, executes your applets without the aid of a browser, greatly reducing the time and memory issues that come with launching a browser or keeping one running while developing your programs.

Keep in mind that applets are called into action through the `<APPLET>` tag in an HTML file, regardless of whether you use Applet Viewer or a Java-savvy Web browser to execute them. This means you'll need to write a small HTML file for each applet to run these little Java programs.

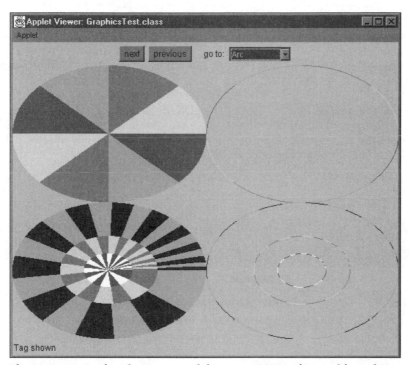

**Figure A-10:** Applet Viewer, one of the many SDK tools, provides a fast, effective way to test your Java applets.

While not difficult, the details of doing this are covered in this book, so we won't bother going through the steps here. Assume you've written an HTML file for your HelloWorld program. Furthermore, assume you've rewritten the application in the form of an applet (also detailed in Chapter 6) and have already compiled it.

**Note**    Although the `<APPLET>` tag is used to execute applets through a browser's built-in runtime environment, the `<OBJECT>` and `<EMBED>` tags are used to run applets with Sun's standalone JRE via the Java Plug-in. (See Chapter 25, "Deploying Applets and Applications" for details.)

Assuming you have your applet bytecode class file and HTML file already prepared, you can test it with the Applet Viewer tool by simply issuing a command such as the following (where HelloWorldTest.html is the name of the Web page in which the applet is woven):

```
> appletviewer HelloWorldTest.html
```

Applet Viewer opens the supplied HTML file, which can be named anything you wish, and then looks for the <APPLET> tag specifying your program and executes it. This process is quite speedy when compared with launching a Java-savvy Web browser, so we recommend using Applet Viewer during development instead of a browser.

If you followed the instructions in "Testing the SDK Installation" earlier in this chapter, you've actually used the Applet Viewer program already to execute the TicTacToe applet. The syntax is about as simple as you can get, as the following command line example illustrates, although you may wish to use the options described in Table A-6:

```
> appletviewer -debug HelloWorldTest.html
```

| Table A-6 The Applet Viewer (appletviewer) Tool | |
|---|---|
| **Option** | **Description** |
| -debug | Executes Applet Viewer inside the Java debugger (jdb), which lets you debug the applets embedded in the Web page. |
| -encoding *encoding name* | Specifies the input HTML file encoding name. |
| -J *javaoption* | Supplies the specified string as a single argument to the Java interpreter that actually runs the Applet Viewer tool. This argument should not contain spaces, and multiple argument words must each begin with the prefix -J (which is stripped off before being handed to the interpreter). This command is useful for setting the compiler's execution environment or memory use, for example. |

# Installation Troubleshooting for Windows 95, 98, 2000, and NT 4.0

The following troubleshooting information is taken from Sun's Java 1.3 SDK installation documentation, available online at http://java.sun.com/j2se/1.3/install-windows.html.

**Tip**    Visit Sun's Java Frequently Asked Questions (FAQ) page at `http://java.sun.com/products/jdk/faq.html` for more details related to installation troubleshooting.

If you see the following error message on Windows 2000

```
config.nt. The system file is not suitable for running MS-DOS
and Microsoft Windows Applications.
```

it indicates a problem with the %SystemRoot%\System32\COMMAND.COM file that has been seen on some installations of Windows 2000. If you encounter this error message when you try to launch the installer, consult the Microsoft web site at `http://support.microsoft.com/support/kb/articles/Q142/2/71.asp` for information about resolving the problem.

If you see the following error message

```
corrupt cabinet file
```

then the file you have downloaded is corrupt. (A cabinet file contains compressed application, data, resource, and DLL files.) Check its file size against the expected file size listed in these instructions. If they don't match, try downloading the bundle again.

If you have downloaded the small disk size pieces, you must first concatenate all of the pieces together into a large piece before you can install it.

If you see the following error message

```
net.socketException: errno = 10047
```

or

```
Unsupported version of Windows Socket API
```

check which TCP/IP drivers you have installed. Applet Viewer supports only the Microsoft TCP/IP drivers included with Windows 95. If you are using third-party drivers (e.g., Trumpet Winsock), you'll need to change over to the native Microsoft TCP/IP drivers if you want to load applets over the network.

If you see the following error message

```
System Error during Decompression
```

then you might not have enough space on the disk that contains your TEMP directory.

If you see the following error message

```
This program cannot be run in DOS mode.
```

then do the following:

1. Open the MS-DOS shell (Windows@->Start@->Programs@->MS-DOS Prompt)
2. Right-click on the title bar.
3. Select Properties.
4. Choose the Program tab.
5. Click the Advanced button.
6. Make sure the item "Prevent MS-DOS-based programs from detecting Windows" is cleared.
7. Click OK.
8. Click OK again.
9. Exit the MS-DOS shell.
10. Restart your computer.

If Applet Viewer does not load applets, try the following:

1. set HOMEDRIVE=c:
2. set HOMEPATH=\ and then Restart Applet Viewer (in the same Command Prompt window).

or

1. Set HOME=c:\ and then restart Applet Viewer (in the same Command Prompt window).

If none of these work, try the following:

```
java -verbose sun.applet.AppletViewer
```

This lists the classes that are being loaded. From this output, you can determine which class Applet Viewer is trying to load and where it's trying to load it from. Check to make sure that the class exists and is not corrupted in some way.

✦ **Applet Viewer locks up:** This happens with NT Workstation 4.0, update 3, where the DISPLAY is configured for true color. Applet Viewer (and perhaps other entities) will lock up by running and then freezing the system consuming 100 percent CPU. To test this, run the java -verbose sun.applet.AppletView and notice that it locks up when it tries to run the MTookit.class.

- **Winsock Issues:** The Java 2 SDK software no longer includes Microsoft Winsock 2.0. It is extremely likely that your system already has Winsock 2.0. Windows NT 4.0 and Windows 98 operating platforms come with Winsock 2.0. The Windows 95 operating platform comes with Winsock 1.1 or 1.2, but most Windows 95 systems have been upgraded to Winsock 2.0 by now. To check which version of Winsock you have, search for winsock.dll. Then choose Properties from the File menu and click the Version tab. Microsoft provides a free software bundle, the Microsoft Windows Sockets 2.0 Software Development Kit, that includes Winsock 2.0. Even if you don't need to upgrade your own system, you may want to obtain this kit so you can deploy network applications on Windows 95 systems. For more information, see the Java 2 Runtime Environment README.

✦ **Creating Source Files in Notepad:** In Windows Notepad, to save a file with the java extension, you have to type the new file name with the .java extension in the File name field and choose All Files in the Save as type pop-up menu. If you specify one but not the other, your file will be saved as filename.java.txt. Each subsequent time you save the file, you must choose All Files in the Save as type pop-up menu.

# Installation Troubleshooting for Solaris

The following troubleshooting information is taken from Sun's Beta Java 1.3 SDK installation documentation for Solaris, available online at http://java.sun.com/j2se/1.3/ (note that a Beta Linux installation is available at the same site, although the instructions below apply specifically to Solaris).

 **Tip**   Visit Sun's Java Frequently Asked Questions (FAQ) page at http://java.sun.com/products/jdk/faq.html for more details related to installation troubleshooting.

## Non-default Installation

If you get a message that reads

```
# An unexpected exception has been detected in
# native code outside the VM.
# Program counter= ...
#
# Problematic Thread: prio=... tid=... nid=...
#
```

first check that your PATH, CLASSPATH, JAVA_HOME and LD_LIBRARY_PATH variables, if set, point consistently to the correct Java installation.

If these variables are consistent, and you are running native code through JNI, check the JNI documentation at http://java.sun.com/j2se/1.3/docs/guide/jni

## Location of libjvm.so files

If you use the Invocation API to launch an application directly rather than using the Java application launcher, be sure to use the correct paths to invoke the Java HotSpot Client VM or Java HotSpot Server VM as desired. The path within the SDK to the Java HotSpot Client VM is:

```
jre/lib/sparc/client/libjvm.so (on SPARC)
jre/lib/i386/client/libjvm.so (on x86)
```

The path to the Java HotSpot Server VM is:

```
jre/lib/sparc/server/libjvm.so (on SPARC)
jre/lib/i386/server/libjvm.so (on x86)
```

The Exact VM and Classic VM are no longer part of the Java 2 platform, and legacy code that uses the Invocation API to launch an application based on old paths to the Exact or Classic VMs will not work.

## *libthread* panic or I/O exception

If you get an error message mentioning a libthread panic or an I/O exception, it is possible that the file descriptor limit has been reached.

The Java2D demo is an example of an application that requires a higher file descriptor limit than the default. The number of file descriptors can be increased in the C shell (*csh*) using this command:

```
limit descriptors 256
```

The number of file descriptors can be increased in the Bourne shell (*sh*) or the Korn shell (*ksh*), using this command:

```
ulimit -n 256
```

## Solaris patch installation

If you get a message such as the following, refer to the README.sparc or README.i386 for information on Solaris patches. You must install Solaris patches to run this version of the Java runtime environment.

```
http://java.sun.com/j2se/1.3/install-solaris-patches.html
```

If there is a libthread patch required for your version of Solaris software, it should always be installed after the other appropriate patches in the README.

**Note** It is essential that you install the appropriate Solaris patches for the JDK to function properly. For a list of recommended and required patches, see README.sparc or README.i386. If there is a libthread patch required for your version of Solaris software, it should always be installed after the other appropriate patches in the README.

## Out of memory

If you get a message that reads \*\*\*Out of memory, exiting\*\*\* , check to see that the application is linking with libthread.so before libjvm.so. In this event, messages will appear in the early phase of VM initialization

To avoid this problem, link libthread before libjvm or set LD_PRELOAD to include libthread.so. In *csh* type:

```
setenv LD_PRELOAD libthread.so
```

In *sh* or *ksh*, type:

```
LD_PRELOAD=libthread.so export LD_PRELOAD
```

**Note** For more information, see the ld.so.1(1) man page.

✦    ✦    ✦

# Using the JavaDOC Tool

In any professional programming environment, documenting your code is one of the most important aspects of the
job. You may leave the company, or someone else might have
to maintain your code. Without good documentation of what
you have written, that task can be a nightmare.

Realizing that this was a standard problem, Sun set out to
encourage good documentation practice by including a tool
that automatically generates documentation from your code.
This tool is called Javadoc.

## Commenting Your Code

The first step in generating documentation is to add comments
of the appropriate style to your code. Javadoc style comments
take advantage of Java's standard comment delimiters but add
a couple of extra tricks to make life easier for itself and for you.

### Overviews and package documentation

At the top of our documentation tree, you want to document
what the whole application does, how it is laid out, and which
packages are available. To do this, you need to provide raw
content to use.

To provide raw content, you need to write HTML files. These
files are processed according to Javadoc conventions looking
for internal tags. Only information between the <BODY> HTML
tags are actually used in the final output. Any information that
is outside this, for example <TITLE> tags in the header, are
ignored completely. You are free to use what you like in these
files, but common sense should prevail.

Overview information appears at the top level of the documentation. It is pulled into the first page that all users see. It should talk about what the application or library does and how it is to be used. This file may be named anything, but by convention, it is named overview.html and is placed in the root directory of all your code for that library.

Per package information is provided in a similar fashion. In each directory that contains your code, you should provide a file called package.html. This file will describe the contents of that package. Javadoc takes the first sentence after the opening <BODY> tag and uses that as a summary in the overview that it generates. Therefore, you should not use any HTML tags in that first sentence — particularly not header <H?> tags.

You can place quite a variety of documentation information here. For example, by using the @since javadoc tag inside your packages.html file, you can tell the reader which version of your code the package was introduced in. Because this tag can take any text, you could include dates, version numbers, or some witty comment if you wanted.

If backwards compatibility is an issue, yet you want to indicate that the package is going to disappear soon, you can use the @deprecated tag. In the accompanying message, you should indicate what the replacement code and classes would be to get similar functionality.

## Source documentation

To provide a comment within your source file, you need to wrap it in a slightly modified version of the block comment characters /* ... */. For Javadoc to recognize a comment for it, you need to add an extra asterisk (*) to the opening comment — that is, /** ... */. Next, the comment must directly precede the item it is documenting. Arbitrary javadoc comments in the middle of a file or method are ignored. So, to document your method, the following is valid:

```
/** My method comment */
public void myMethod() {
}
```

but the following will be ignored

```
/* My method comment */
public void myMethod() {
}

public void myMethod() {
   /** some comment */
}
```

In particular, if you are documenting a class, then the comment must be placed after the package and import statements but before the class definition.

## Class definition

To another programmer using your code, the documentation of what a particular class does is probably the most important piece of documentation. Even if the methods did not have one piece of documentation, a thorough overview of what the class does can usually get you through most needs. This information is available at the top of the class documentation.

The class documentation defines the most general information. Table B-1 describes the various tags that can be used at this level.

| | Table B-1 Class Documentation tags |
|---|---|
| **Tag** | **Description** |
| @author | Describes the author. Usually useful to include a link to the author's e-mail address or home page. |
| @version | Describes the version number. Can use anything here, so it might be a version number or something that describes a special build status or something similar. |
| @since | Describes when this class was introduced. Like the package-level comment, this could be anything, such as a date or version number. |
| {@link}, @see | Links to another document. The first version provides in-sentence linking, while the second has a separate section devoted to it in the documentation (titled "See Also"). You may reference a fully qualified class name, method, or even just a standard URL. Read the documentation for Javadocfor a better description of how to use it. |

## Method documentation

The method documentation provides the details of what a method does. Ideally, it should document all of the assumptions and preconditions, errors (depending on what you give it), what it will return, and the state it leaves the class in.

Table B-2 describes the types of tags that can be used on methods. The @see, @link and @since tags from the class documentation also apply here.

Table B-2
**Method Documentation Tags**

| Tag | Description |
|---|---|
| @param | Describes a parameter and what its range of values are. The first word following the tag is the name of the parameter *exactly* as it appears in the method declaration. Following this is a description of what it represents and a range of values. For example, it is good practice to say what happens if you pass a null in to a reference to a class. |
| @return | Describes the return value. It should give the range of values to be expected given the various circumstances. |
| @throws, @exception | Describes an exception that is thrown by the method. These are not just standard exceptions, but should also include any exceptions based on RuntimeException. |

## Linking in example code and images

Sometimes in your javadoc, you might want to include images, such as screen shots of your GUI components. Similarly, example code illustrating how to use the APIs or other relevant information might also be useful, and you want this to go along with the documentation.

In each package directory, you can create a subdirectory called doc-files to place all of this information in. Javadoc will then copy this entire directory and its contents into the output directory. Unlike the overview and package HTML documents, no processing is done on the files contained in this directory. To include these files inside the documentation output, you use the standard HTML anchor tags:

```
/**
 * This is an example summary.
 * <P>
 * Then you might want an expanded comment with a
 * <A HREF="doc-files/code_example.java">code example</A>. At
 * the same time, you might want to
 * <IMG SRC="doc-files/image.gif">Inline an image</A>
 *
 * @author <A HREF="mailto:justin@vlc.com.au">Justin Couch</A>
 * @see Javadoc arguments
 */
```

**Note** For an example of using the doc-files directory for including images and code, have a look at the HTML source for the class javax.swing.JScrollPane.

# Generating Documentation

Once you are reasonably familiar with what you need to put inside your comments, you can move on to generating the output files. Generation of documents is always performed with the javadoc application. Most of the features that you have been introduced to may be controlled using command-line arguments. In this section, we will look at how to customize and control the output to get exactly what you want.

## Default generation

The simplest use of javadoc comes when you use the command with no parameters. The basic command line looks like this:

```
javadoc [options] [packagenames] [sourcefiles]
```

Ignoring the options for the moment, we've provided some example javadoc code on the companion Web site to show you how all this works. By default, javadoc looks in the current working directory to locate the source files. Any packages and unpackaged files you name in the arguments will be sourced relative to the current directory.

As an example run, copy the classes for this appendix from the CD to a local directory on your hard disk. Bring up a command prompt and change to that directory. At the prompt, type

```
javadoc example another
```

and watch. Once this has completed, list the contents of the directory. You will now see that there is a pile of HTML files there. If you open index.html in your browser, you should now see that familiar documentation style for your own code. What you have just created is a set of Javadoc documentation for the two packages named example and another.

**Tip**    If you don't like the use of frames, you may load the overview-summary.html file instead. This contains just the package listing that you see on the righthand side.

Javadoc also allows you to document unpackaged files together with the packaged files. When typing in the command line, unpackaged classes must be placed after the package names like this:

```
javadoc example another SimpleClass
```

Now, when you reload index.html, you will see in the bottom lefthand frame a reference to the unpackaged class as well as all the other classes. When viewing javadoc, the normal use (assuming you are using the frames version) is to have the contents of the current package in the bottom left frame. The only way to view unpackaged files is to click on the All Classes link in the top left frame. There is no separate index page for these classes. This is rather unfortunate because in any serious application, there could well be a couple of hundred classes, making the listing rather difficult to deal with.

## Controlling the output

You have probably already noticed that the default output for javadoc is to place everything in the current directory. Because it also uses the current directory for the source files, you'll see that the source directories are now full of HTML files — one for each source file. This can make life in the code directories difficult to manage.

Typically, you want the output to be placed in another directory away from the source code. You can do this by using the -d option. The argument of -d is the directory, either relative or absolute, to where you want your documentation to go. For example, we might want the documentation in a the doc directory under the current working directory:

```
javadoc -d doc example another SimpleClass
```

Javadoc will barf if the directory does not exist, so make sure it does before you attempt to run it. Now, to display your documentation, you can grab index.html from the doc directory. (If you ran the previous examples, you might want to go through and clean up all the HTML files from that first.)

Depending on how complex your environment is (how many Java projects you have running in parallel), you may also want to control the classpath setting as well. Like the other Java tools, you can use the -classpath option to set the real classpath to be used. If you use this option, it can get quite tedious typing it in, so you're better off putting your javadoc command into a batch file of some form.

## Including nonpublic information

If you have looked through the example code and the generated documentation, you will have noticed a discrepancy. While the source contains public, protected, package-private, and private methods and variables, the documentation only contains information on the public and protected stuff. Depending on your needs, you can control exactly what level of information is generated using the following options:

| | |
|---|---|
| -public | Only generate information for public variables, classes, and methods. |
| -protected | Generate information for public and protected variables and methods. This is the default setting. |

| | |
|---|---|
| -package | Include information for package-private variables, classes, and methods. |
| -private | Document everything. |

Note that these arguments apply to the class files as well as methods and variables. If a class is package-private in scope, only the -package and -private options will generate documentation on them.

## Adding supplementary information

In an earlier section of this appendix, it was mentioned that you can provide per-package and summary information along with the normal source documentation.

When generating documentation, javadoc looks for a file called package.html in every package that you have named to document on the javadoc command line. If that file exists in the source directory, the information between the <BODY> tags is stripped out and added to the package overview. This happens by default with every package that is named.

On the other hand, the overview information is not included by default. To include an overview of all the documentation, you need to tell javadoc which file to use. This can be done using the -overview option like this:

```
javadoc -overview overview.html example another
```

The file named after the -overview option can be named anything you like Normally, it is placed in the root of all your packaged code, although it may be placed almost anywhere.

**Caution**  For some reason, javadoc does not seem to like using relative directory references for the overview argument. If you provide a directory, it must be fully qualified, or just the file name in the current directory.

## Custom titles, headers, footers, etc.

By default, javadoc does not provide any information to make your documentation look professional. If you look closely at the Web browser title for these pages, you'll see it says something like this:

```
Generated Documentation (Untitled)
```

For professional-looking documentation, you obviously want it looking a bit nicer than that. We can change two options:

| | |
|---|---|
| -doctitle | Controls the title of the documentation that appears on the individual pages. This is normally just some straight text. |

-windowtitle    Sets the value of the <TITLE> tag that appears in the javadoc output of each page. This may contain HTML tags.

Normal use would set these two values to be exactly the same string. For example, in a DOS environment:

```
c:\mycode>set TITLE= "Java 2 Bible Example Javadoc"
c:\mycode>javadoc -doctitle %TITLE% -windowtitle %TITLE%
example another
```

Note that the title string must be quoted to prevent javadoc from interpreting the words as command-line arguments.

Another option to control is the header and footer information that is to appear on the main pages. For example, you might want to include a version number or other information on the footer of each page. The options are -header, -footer, and -bottom. Each of these tags may include HTML formatting if you wish.

## Linking to other documentation

Finally, once you start generating documentation for large projects, you might have a number of separate lots of code. Ideally, you would like to link them all together so that classes in one set can access documentation from another. The most common example of that is linking your documentation to the core Java documentation.

You can link your documentation with any other set of documentation using the -link option. The argument of this option is a URL to the top-level directory of this other documentation. For example, if you wanted to link to the Javadoc documentation of the core classes on Sun's site, you would use the following command line:

```
javadoc -link http://java.sun.com/products/jdk/1.2/docs/api
example another
```

Because this link is to an HTTP server, you must be online when you do it. This is because javadoc attempts to download the file called package-list from this URL. The list file contains a list of all the packages that the site contains.

If you can't be online when generating the documentation, you could use the -linkoffline option instead. This takes the same URL argument as before but it also needs another that will point to the package-list file on the local file system. Say you have downloaded the file from Sun's site (or fetched a copy that came when installed Java):

```
javadoc -link http://java.sun.com/products/jdk/1.2/docs/api
file:///c|/jdk1.2/docs/api/ example another
```

**Note**  You are supposed to be able to have multiple -link options specified on the command line. Unfortunately, a bug in JDK 1.2 does not allow this. It should be fixed in later releases.

## Managing large commands

As you can see from the previous links, the command line can get awfully long. There are two ways of managing this — using batch files or using external files.

With external files, javadoc allows you to package up command-line parts in separate files and then include them in the javadoc command. Say we put the list of options in the file called args and the package list in the file called packages. We can now make direct reference to them like this:

```
javadoc @args @packages
```

Each file should look exactly like what you would type on the command line. You can't use the local shell variables or other niceties. There is no limit on how many files you can include, as long as the order of the information in the files corresponds to the correct command-line order.

The alternative is to make use of the local shell batch capabilities, which allows some degree of interactive programming. An example of this is provided on the companion Web site to this book, in the code directory for this appendix called docs.bat.

# Further Information

As you can see, javadoc is an extremely flexible tool. This appendix covered only a small part of the options available. To get a full listing, run javadoc with no arguments.

Apart from the standard document generation, Sun provides all of the source code to the javadoc. Introduced in JDK 1.2 is the ability to provide custom document generation, called doclets. For example, you might want to generate PostScript documentation rather than HTML. Using the doclets and Sun's source, you can create your own custom output.

To find out more information about javadoc, look at the API pages available at Sun and also with the downloadable documentation.

✦    ✦    ✦

# Surfing for Source Code

There is an old rule among programmers—never reinvent the wheel if at all possible. If you can take someone else's code and use it or tweak it to your purposes, that is much better than starting from scratch.

The Internet contains a huge variety of sources for creating and using Java applications. To give you some pointers, we've assembled a collection of the more popular sites that contain either code or resources like documentation, tutorials, and anything else useful.

## Source Code

The first section describes sites that offer you source code and libraries for you to use in your application. Most of these sites have been around since the beginning of Java. They provided an excellent resource to find trick bits of source code. These days they have become much more commercial and it is harder and harder to find decent collections of source code around the web.

### JARS

The Java Applet Rating Service (JARS) is a site that rates applets and applications developed by programmers. The ratings are based on usefulness and how cool the apps are—particularly at doing something new. All content in the site is based on programmer submissions. Commercial companies cannot submit their libraries or applications to the rating service.

Ratings are grouped into the top 5 percent, the top 25 percent, and so on, which describe how the reviewers feel that piece of code/library and so on relates to all of the submitted code they've seen. Searching through the site breaks code down into familiar areas like networking, GUI toolkits, etc.

The site can be found at

```
http://www.jars.com/
```

## Gamelan

Gamelan is one of the biggest developer resources on the Internet. Here you can find resources for almost every language imaginable. Like JARS, it's content is entirely driven by people submitting their code, except commercial listings are allowed. A quick trawl through the site will show up references to the standard Sun libraries and standard extensions as well as many other commercial libraries and applications.

Apart from Java code, Gamelan also offers references to documentation, tutorials, and books. Again, like the code, these are all submitted by you, the average programmer.

The Java portion of Gamelan can be accessed at

```
http://www.developer.com/directories/pages/dir.java.html
```

## alphaWorks

IBM is one of the largest commercial contributors of Java code to the Internet. At the IBM alphaWorks site, you can find libraries, usually with source code, to do almost anything you ever wanted. As a bonus, this code is usually very well written and extremely efficient.

The site can be found at:

```
http://www.alphaworks.ibm.com/
```

# Documentation and Tutorials

As you are well aware, this book does not cover in detail many of the more advanced parts of Java or many of the libraries that may be available. The following sites contain tutorials and lots of information about the Java APIs, libraries, and information to help you make the most of your Java code.

## Doug Lea

Doug Lea is one of the leading Java authorities outside of Sun. Author of many books and libraries, his site offers a wonderful resource into all the dark corners of Java programming. In particular, his tutorials and code illustrating the inner workings of the JVM and threading models are worth the visit alone. Doug's site is:

```
http://g.oswego.edu/dl/
```

## The Java Developer Connection

The Java Developer Connection (JDC) is Sun's developer site where they release early beta versions of Java release software. Here you can also find tutorials and unusual code examples. Another bonus is the access that it provides to Sun's bug database for Java (although the search and user interface is pretty terrible).

JDC requires a login, but it costs you nothing. The main site is

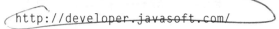

```
http://developer.javasoft.com/
```

but there are other sites with more specific information such as the Swing Connection for Swing information.

## Javaworld

Of the online magazines, *Javaworld*, is probably the most popular. Part of IDG's online Xworld site group (sister sites include Sunworld and Linuxworld, for example), this is a monthly magazine of reviews, code tips, and links to other resources. Here you can find probably the world's best collection of Java book references in almost any language you care to name.

The site is at:

```
http://www.javaworld.com/
```

# Groups

Sometimes, just being around other Java programmers can greatly increase your knowledge and help you out with any problems you have. The following groups are very active in this area.

## Java Lobby

The Java Lobby group is the main lobby group that represents programmers. The Java Lobby works as an industry representative that lobbies Sun and other big companies for changes to Java and related areas. It contains a wide selection of links to other lobby groups, sites for further information, and Java news.

The site is at:

```
http://www.javalobby.com/
```

## Java User Groups

Almost all major areas around the world now have a local Java User Group (JUG). These groups usually meet face to face once a month and contain all levels of Java programmers—from beginners to gurus. Meetings usually have presentations by both locals and companies, and they form a valuable networking tool for you personally.

## Usenet

Of course, no discussion of help sites would be complete without reference to the appropriate Java newsgroups. At last count, there were approximately 15 different groups dealing just with the Java programming language and APIs under

```
comp.lang.java.*
```

These groups are extremely high-volume with often over 1,000 messages per day. No doubt you will come across an answer to your question simply by looking through the archives or the relevant FAQs.

✦ ✦ ✦

# Extensions to the Core

**O**nce you start getting into Java programming seriously, you'll probably need to use or have code that uses some of the standard extensions to the Java core. What are these beasts, and how did they come about?

## What Are Java Extensions?

*Java extensions* are a standardized set of interfaces to some functionality that does not belong in the core API set but has been through Sun's standardization process. Over time, it is possible that standard extensions will migrate into the core APIs. An API must go through quite a process before it gets the official "Optional Package" moniker.

Note    Until late 1999, Optional Packages were known as Standard Extensions.

A typical use of a standard extension is to describe an action that can be platform specific, but still general enough for a write-once, run-anywhere policy. A good example of this is dealing with serial and parallel ports. Most large PC computers have these ports, but once you move to smaller packages like PalmPilots and Windows CE handhelds, a communications port might be quite different (for example, IrDA infrared). Standard extensions are developed to allow you to deal with these problems of moving code within a smaller set of hardware than what the generic core API allows you to deal with.

# The javax packages

Standard extensions are easy enough to spot. The core API set always starts with `java.` as the top-level name in the package. All standard extensions start with the top-level designator of `javax`.

Once a series of classes has taken on the javax extension, anyone is free to implement these APIs. However, to be official, they must still go through a testing process defined by Sun. This keeps the behavior within a tight set of bounds to the specification, while allowing many people to implement a set of common extensions that may be found on many computers.

If you've been paying attention throughout this book, you will notice that the Swing classes all start with javax. There's quite an interesting history because these are now one of the core API sets and no longer considered a standard extension. Originally, the Swing 1.0 packages were `com.sun.swing`. With the arrival of JDK 1.2 (this all happened in the beta periods before it became known as Java 2), it was decided to change the package to `java.swing`. This caused a real problem because the Swing classes were supposed to be used with JDK 1.1 and JDK 1.2. Suddenly, a whole bunch of noncore classes were being labeled as core — at least as far as JDK 1.1 was concerned. Causing great uproar within the Java community, Sun relented and changed the package name to `javax.swing` to recognize that Swing was an extension to JDK 1.1 but now has moved to core status for Java 2.

With the arrival of JDK 1.3, even more standard extensions are added. Now, the sound APIs, the naming and directory interface (JNDI), and the CORBA-capable version of RMI have been added.

# Creating new extensions

To understand how standard extensions end up on your computer, a little background in the process might help.

At the core of the process is Sun's realization that it cannot create an API for every single use that Java might have. Despite the marketing hype, other companies out there know more about Java and how it might work for a given set of situations than Sun. To encourage others to participate in the expansion of the Java religion, a set of guidelines for proposing new standards was developed, and this became the Standard Extensions process.

To create a standard extension, a group must form to solve a particular problem. This group must consist of more than one person or company to show that some form of industry requirement is needed for a standard. Over time, this group thrashes out a new standard, together with a couple of different implementations, test suites, and documentation. After acceptance, anyone implementing a set of APIs to perform that task is recommended to use the standard extensions and get it passed through the group's test suite.

# Using Optional Packages

Inside your code, using standard extensions is no different than using the core libraries or custom third-party libraries. Assuming you know what you want to use, you simply import the classes with an appropriate import statement and let the compiler look after the rest.

One of the main benefits of standard extensions is that they are supposed to act on your machine as though they were part of the core API set. That is, they should appear invisible in your standard environment until you need to use them. To do so, the Java runtime environment uses some special directory structures so that you don't need to continually have the CLASSPATH full of many different JAR files.

When installing standard extensions, they always get placed in the directory $java.home/jre/lib/ext. Anything located in this directory will then be treated as a standard extension and does not need the CLASSPATH pointing at it for the VM and the compiler to find it. Archives located in this directory will also be found by the Java Plugin too.

There is a well know bug in the Java Plugin with JDK 1.2 where the JDK does not look in the jre/lib/ext directory for JAR files. Instead, the JDK looks in jre/lib. This bug is expected to be fixed with the release of JDK 1.2.2. Interestingly, the standard java and javaw commands do find archives in the proper directory. If you have standard extensions that your applets use, you should make sure that you copy the classes to both jre/lib and jre/lib/ext until this bug has been fixed.

Apart from this minor setup requirement, there is nothing special about using standard extensions. Download, let the installer place the classes, and get to coding!

# Some Optional Packages

A large number of standard extensions are already defined. In this next section, we are going to look over a number of the more common ones that you may want to use in your applications and applets. The three that we cover allow you to talk to external devices, show 3D virtual worlds, and integrate greater multimedia capabilities.

You can find the full list of optional packages at http://java.sun.com/products/
OV_stdExt.html.

## Communications

Early in the life of Java, one of the features programmers coming from other languages missed the most was the high level of abstraction that Java had over the operating system and hardware. Suddenly they were stripped of the ability to read and write to external devices like joysticks, printers, scanners, and modems. Basically, anything that came through a serial port or parallel port was off limits — at least without writing your own custom native code. The JavaComm APIs were introduced to give this ability back to programmers.

JavaComm provides abstractions of serial and parallel ports for any piece of hardware. In either case, you have almost all of the control that you might expect with native interfaces all wrapped up in the convenient OO classes of Java. You can set baud rates, read and set control lines as well as the data, and so on. The one shortcoming at the time of writing is that JavaComm does not currently support USB or Firewire connections.

All of the code for the JavaComm interface is kept in the `javax.comm` package.

## Java 3D

With the 3D gaming environment driving the acceptance of accelerated 3D hardware in the consumer PC, the demand for a generic 3D API for Java was great. Before the arrival of Java3D, you could use one of many different commercial and noncommercial bindings for the existing 3D APIs like OpenGL and Direct3D. Each varied in detail as well as abstraction from the native C APIs that they used.

Java3D was designed to be a mid-level of abstraction in terms of 3D rendering. It didn't restrict itself to low-level triangle-only type rendering like OpenGL, but it also didn't have the purely modeling nature like VRML. Instead, it chose the middle ground and attempted to provide an all encompassing environment for dealing with user input and behavioral aspects.

3D modeling is not for the faint of heart, and Java3D makes no exception. The initial learning curve can be a bit steep, but well worth it once you see that first 3D world up and running. Java 3D is a pure rendering API. That is, for a cube to be shown on the screen, you need to describe every coordinate in code, set up the polygons, and then tell the system to draw it. To make life easier, it relies on external file formats like DXF and VRML to define the geometry, and it uses loader classes (usually written by a third party) to convert the file format to Java 3D primitive objects.

Java 3D packages are `javax.media.j3d` and `javax.vecmath`. The latter is a general-purpose package catering for vector math manipulation that can be used separately from Java 3D.

## Java Media Framework

One of the more important uses of Java is for multimedia applications. Unfortunately, in the core packages, support for images, movies, and sound is pretty poor — at least for creating a real multimedia experience. The Java Media Framework (JMF) seeks to establish a simple Java-oriented framework for integrating third-party handlers for these requirements. JMF caters for movies and images, while the JavaSound portion of JMF enables sound rendering. (JavaSound can be downloaded separately from the rest of JMF.)

JMF provides a framework with a couple of default players for AVI and MPEG files. From there, third-party suppliers, such as Apple, provide viewers for other file formats. Like Java 3D, it relies mainly on third-party packages to provide support for a wide range of file formats.

Like the other rendering APIs, such as Java 3D, JMF uses native peer components to ensure decent performance. The penalty for this is that Swing is almost useless when you do this due to the different repaint cycles. If you want to use Java3D, you really need to stick to the core AWT packages.

Classes for JMF can be found in the packages under javax.media. That means that Java 3D is also one component of JMF. In fact, there are quite a few different API areas that form part of JMF. The Java Advanced Imaging (JAI) API is also part of JMF and provides capabilities for looking at *very* large images (on the order of hundreds of megabytes in size).

## Java Advanced Imaging

If you want to create an application that displays and manipulates very large images, you will find that the standard image-loading techniques are not up to the task. The main problems are that the loading takes too long or that you quickly run out of memory—particularly when loading them over the network from a remote site.

JAI is used to deal with large-scale images in a manner compatible with the standard Java 2D mechanisms. Where it is of most use is creating GIS-type applications where you want to display images thousands of pixels across. In this case, memory consumption of a 10,000 x 10,000 pixel image gets astronomical. Using the tiling capabilities of JAI allows you to manage this aspect while still providing reasonable performance.

## JavaMail

Being the age of the Internet, e-mail is a very important part of life. The JavaMail API provides a common interface to most of the standard mail systems available. Typically, it focuses on SMTP mail but is useful for other applications as well.

Mail is just one of many different messaging protocols. The ability to send a simple or complex message using a predominantly text-based format is useful to many types of applications. The JavaMail APIs form the core with a number of other extensions of the enterprise version of Java 2.

## Java's Buggy Image Loading

In day-to-day use, we've found that JAI is almost useless dealing with images below 10,000 pixels across. The problems are based around Java's image- handling and loading techniques that contain major memory leaks.

Under normal usage, the memory consumed is four times greater than a native application; that is, normal images have 4 bytes per pixel in the image (32-bit color) and then multiply that by 4 to give you the amount of memory Java uses. There is a real hole between images of around 1,000 pixels up to 10,000 pixels. Java just consumes way too much memory to be useful as a client application. JAI tends to suffer from this problem too, as it just creates lots of smaller images from the source. We don't recommend it unless you count your raw image sizes in megabytes.

Sun is aware of these problems since JDK 1.1 has gone through numerous bug reports, all of which have been brushed aside as not being a problem and removed from the bug parade. It is still evident in JDK 1.3.

## JavaHelp

No real-world application is complete without a help system. JavaHelp is designed to provide both an integrated help system and a standalone help application. Apart from just a viewer, this help package also provides a search engine, context-sensitive help, and a normal Web browser in one kit.

JavaHelp uses the HTML rendering capabilities of Swing to display pages. That makes creating help really easy because all you really need is an HTML editor (or a text editor if that is your weapon of choice!). Being based on the Swing renderer, it also means that you can use XML for the pages as well. This takes a little more work, but it is very useful nonetheless.

## Java Cryptography Extension

Another core part of a good Internet-enabled application is the ability to work across an open network with a reasonable degree of security. The RSA and DES algorithms and SSL sockets are probably the most well known cryptographic icons known. The Java Cryptography Extension (JCE) is a set of APIs that allows you to create secure communication streams using these and other algorithms.

JCE is based around a stream approach so that you can encrypt/decrypt both files and socket connections. All of the well-known classes of encrypting information are supported at the API level. Not only will it support the standard algorithms, but you can also supply your own if the need arises.

## Servlets

Almost since the beginning of the web, having a webserver dynamically generate content has been a feature. In the very early days this was through a CGI (Common Gateway Interface) script that was normally written in UNIX shell scripts or C. Slowly this was replaced by PERL and other languages.

The problem that these all had was that each time the web server needed to use one of these scripts it would need to start a new process. On very heavily loaded servers, this would grind them to a halt due to the overheads of starting and stopping processes. The basic solution to the problem was to load the script into memory once and continue to run it. You will see this solution in Apache's mod_perl and Microsoft's IIS - ASP architecture. Java's solution to this is servlets.

A Java servlet is designed as a mechanism to present a server architecture that processes requests and sends back responses. Although typically seen as the HttpServlet inside a web server, they can exist outside of this environment too. Servlets are part of the J2EE core specification.

## Java Naming and Directory Interface

JNDI is another form Optional Package that has migrated into the core of the standard edition of Java with JDK 1.3. In the enterprise world, directory services are huge business for keeping track of people and equipment. These can be seen in Novell's Directory Service (NDS) and Microsoft's ActiveDirectory. LDAP is also extremely widely used.

All of these services provide the same basic capabilities — a hierarchical structuring and naming of resources and their attributes. They are a form of database, though not a real database like the traditional SQL system from Oracle and others. They have a specific purpose and structure. This makes building a simple API for them relatively easy and is the role of JDNI. It provides a common set of APIs for querying naming services (like the Domain Name System (DNS) that powers the internet) and directory services without you needing to know the implementation details. Like Servlets, JNDI is also part of the J2EE specification.

# Extending the Java 2 Platform

While the previous sections in this appendix have dealt with providing a standard set of extensions for most common tasks, creating applications usually requires a collection of these classes. In certain important markets like e-commerce, almost all applications will need the same set of optional packages.

At the JavaOne conference in June 1999, Sun announced a series of different versions of the Java 2 platform with the aim of providing a common set of APIs that are available for particular market segments. This lead to the creation of Java 2 Enterprise Edition (J2EE) and Java 2 Micro Edition. The standard JDK that we'd all been using was named Java 2 Personal Edition.

## Java 2 Enterprise Edition (J2EE)

J2EE is designed to cater to largescale enterprise sites where you have mainframes, lots of wide area networking, and big databases all collaborating. The main focus of enterprise applications in the short term is the Web based e-commerce and business-to-business e-commerce applications.

At the enterprise level, you need support for ensuring that everything works correctly. For this, you have the Java Transaction (JTA) API, the Java Messaging Service (JMS), as well as CORBA and RMI over IIOP to provide the bulk of the connectivity side. To pass the information out to the client, we use Enterprise Java Beans (EJBs), Servlets, and Java Servlet Pages (JSP).

## Java 2 Micro Edition (J2ME)

At the opposite end of the scale is the Micro Edition of Java. The focus this time is to throw as much of the core APIs out so that the application will run on very limited devices such as palmtops, pagers, and mobile phones.

To slim Java down to a restricted device like a mobile phone, you are left with minimal functionality. Gone are Swing, the AWT, maths, RMI, JDBC, and CORBA. Basically, all this leaves you with are the simple utility classes, the core language (java.lang), minor networking (most of java.net has gone), and a minimal replacement graphics capability for the loss of the AWT and Swing.

Despite these losses, it is surprising just how much you can still implement on a restricted API. Games and calendar-type programs are still easy to implement. Also, more involved applications like sketch programs with sketch recognition are also possible.

✦     ✦     ✦

# The Future of Java

**A**lthough Java is unquestionably one of the most significant software developments of our time, the question inevitably comes around to, "What next?" After all, we're dealing with the most explosive area ever: network computing in general, and the World Wide Web in particular. Innovations on the Web are being made by the bucketload, with previously unseen technology appearing on the ether every day. We're accustomed to new and exciting Web technology hurtling towards us at Mach 9. So what's in store for Java, and will it keep pace?

Although it's impossible to answer these questions with absolute confidence, it's a sure bet that Java is here to stay. In the short time since it's been available, Java has sparked a revolution on the World Wide Web as well as on computer desktops around the world, thanks to the relative ease with which you can use Java to build cross-platform, network-savvy programs.

But the buzz doesn't stop there. Java is well on its way to revolutionizing the entire consumer-electronics market as well — the very area for which it was originally developed, but which it failed to penetrate at the time. Today, however, it's clear that Java will soon invade home appliances and hand-held gizmos almost as fast as it invaded the Web and our personal computer systems. Gird thyself, friends.

Thanks to a flurry of Java technologies recently released by Sun Microsystems and their many partners, we can expect the Java invasion to continue at a blistering pace. From chips, and cards, to lightning-fast Just In Time (JIT) compilers, brand new APIs, fully distributed computing capabilities, and Java Network Computer — Java promises to grow by leaps and bounds in just about every way you can imagine.

The question really isn't "*Will Java survive?*" so much as it is "*How in the world can I keep up with Java?*" Fortunately, there's an easy way to do just that. As a Java Bible reader, we have a special place for you to visit when it comes to learning about the future of Java. Simply point your Web browser to the following Web site whenever you feel out of touch with the rapidly changing world of Java, and drink it all in:

```
http://www.javabible.com/
```

JavaBible.com is our way of saying "thanks" to you for reading this book. We hope that you've enjoyed the book, and look forward to hearing from you in our new online forum.

◆    ◆    ◆

# Index

*Continued*

*Continued*

*Continued*

# my2cents.idgbooks.com

## Register This Book — And Win!

Visit **http://my2cents.idgbooks.com** to register this book and we'll automatically enter you in our fantastic monthly prize giveaway. It's also your opportunity to give us feedback: let us know what you thought of this book and how you would like to see other topics covered.

## Discover IDG Books Online!

The IDG Books Online Web site is your online resource for tackling technology — at home and at the office. Frequently updated, the IDG Books Online Web site features exclusive software, insider information, online books, and live events!

### 10 Productive & Career-Enhancing Things You Can Do at www.idgbooks.com

- Nab source code for your own programming projects.

- Download software.

- Read Web exclusives: special articles and book excerpts by IDG Books Worldwide authors.

- Take advantage of resources to help you advance your career as a Novell or Microsoft professional.

- Buy IDG Books Worldwide titles or find a convenient bookstore that carries them.

- Register your book and win a prize.

- Chat live online with authors.

- Sign up for regular e-mail updates about our latest books.

- Suggest a book you'd like to read or write.

- Give us your 2¢ about our books and about our Web site.

You say you're not on the Web yet? It's easy to get started with IDG Books' *Discover the Internet,* available at local retailers everywhere.